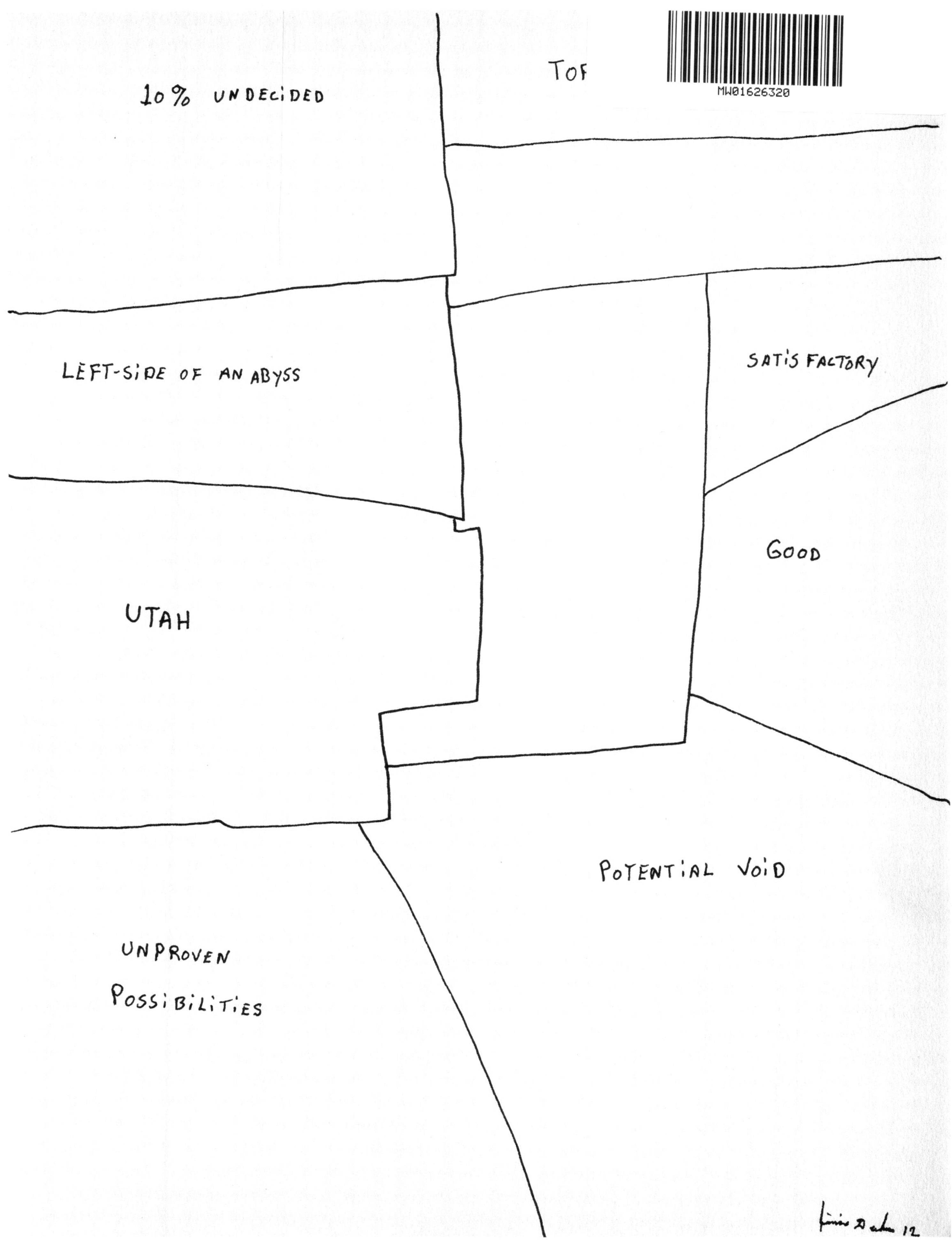

10% UNDECIDED
TOF
LEFT-SIDE OF AN ABYSS
SATIS FACTORY
GOOD
UTAH
POTENTIAL VOID
UNPROVEN
POSSIBILITIES

JIMMIE
DURHAM

JIMMIE DURHAM

ANNE ELLEGOOD

HAMMER MUSEUM
UNIVERSITY OF CALIFORNIA, LOS ANGELES

DELMONICO BOOKS • PRESTEL
MUNICH LONDON NEW YORK

AT THE CENTER OF THE WORLD

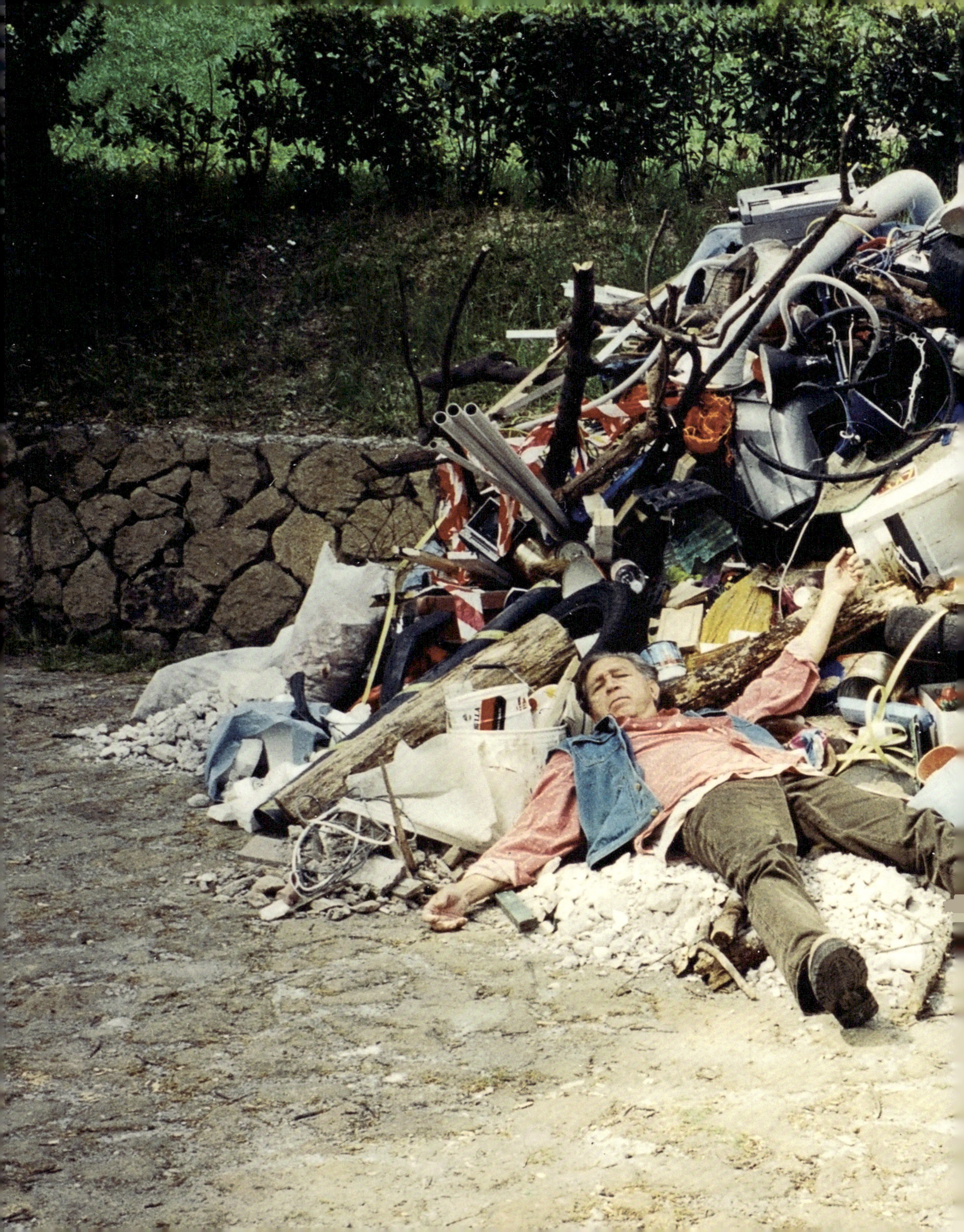

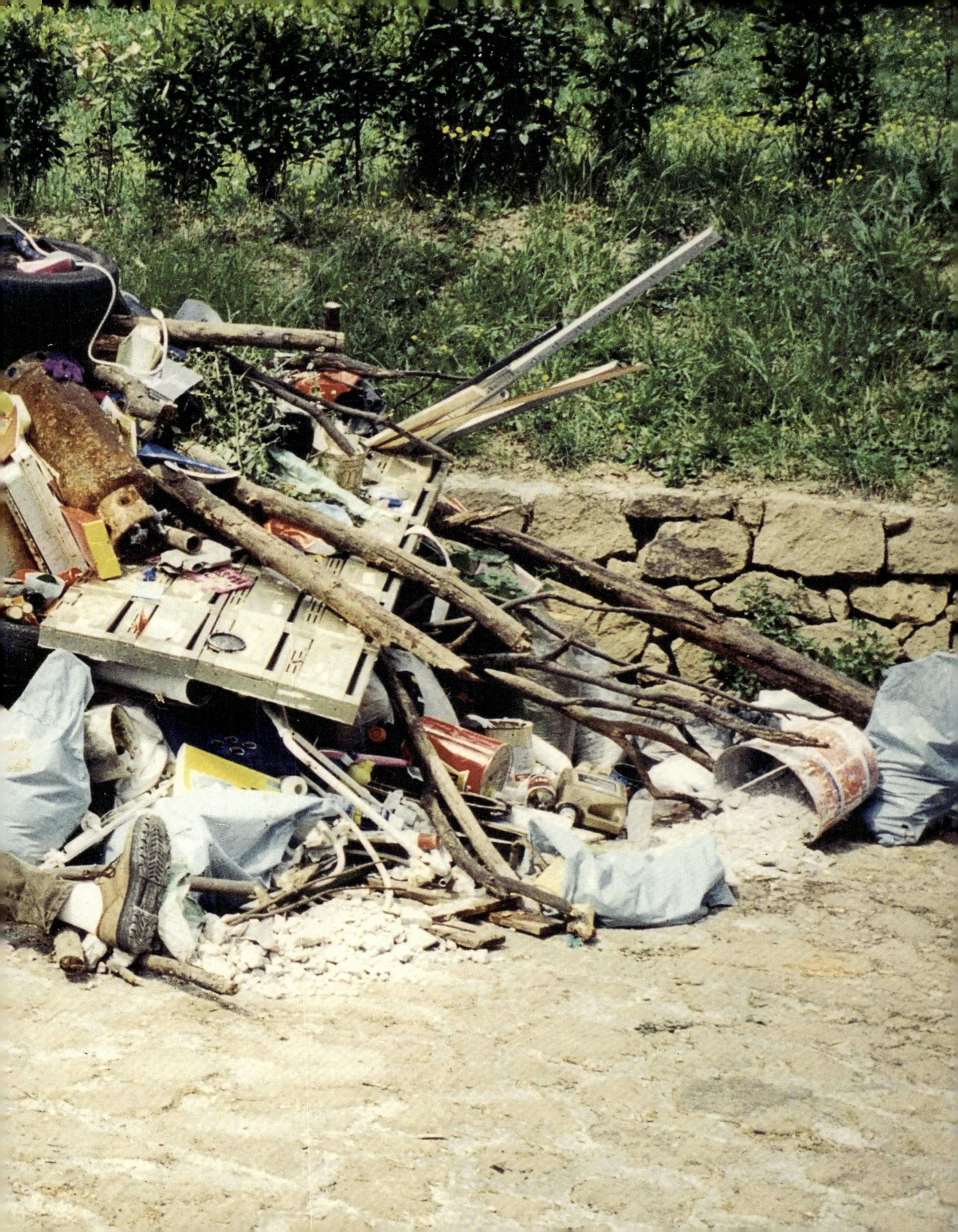

CONTENTS

POEMS

ESSAYS

FOREWORD

The Hammer Museum is thrilled to present *Jimmie Durham: At the Center of the World.* A visual artist, performer, writer, and activist of Cherokee descent, Durham is one of the most compelling, inventive, and complex artists working internationally today. For American audiences, however, he has been an elusive figure. After studying art in Geneva in the late 1960s and early 1970s, he returned to the United States following the uprising on the Pine Ridge Reservation in Wounded Knee, South Dakota, and became an organizer for the American Indian Movement, ultimately serving as director of the International Indian Treaty Council in New York from 1975 to 1979. When he left the movement, Durham turned his energies back to making art and became an active participant in the vibrant New York City downtown art scene in the 1980s. Having moved to the city during this same period to begin my own career in the arts, I, too, was immersed in the activities of this exhilarating moment. Although I did not know him personally, I recall seeing Durham's work and was struck by its potency and poetry. I also appreciated very much his work as an activist. We traveled in overlapping and concentric circles of people who were responding to the AIDS crisis, the Iran-Contra scandal, apartheid in South Africa, and other critical concerns, as well as fighting for equality, recognition, and support for artists who had largely been relegated to the margins. Durham participated—as both an artist and a curator—in many group shows that sought to bring visibility to artists of color or were organized around the most urgent political concerns of the day. His advocacy for other artists and the causes to which he is deeply committed also extended to his work as a writer. An accomplished poet and essayist, he coedited the newspaper *Art and Artists* in his capacity as the executive director of the Foundation for the Community of Artists and contributed insightful and memorable catalogue texts for exhibitions at the New Museum, Artists Space, and elsewhere.

In 1987 Durham chose to leave the United States with his partner, Brazilian artist and activist Maria Thereza Alves, moving first to Cuernavaca, Mexico, and then to Europe, where they have lived since 1994. While in Cuernavaca, he returned regularly to the States and continued to participate in the American contemporary art scene. During this period, his work was also being recognized internationally. Since moving to Europe more than twenty years ago, however, Durham has largely chosen not to exhibit his work in the United States. While the artist's reasons for this are numerous, his work is meaningfully, and indeed crucially, connected to important activities, movements, and genres of American artistic production. With recent efforts in our field to historicize the 1980s and 1990s in American art, it is imperative that Durham's practice be reinserted into exhibitions and the accompanying dialogue. His singular and vital voice on such topics as colonization, genocide, exile, statehood, and the politics of subjectivity is crucial to understanding the history of American art, while at the same time Durham is a role model of sorts for what it means to be an artist who is a "citizen of the world."

For many years, it has been senior curator Anne Ellegood's dream to organize a major exhibition of Durham's work, and we are truly honored to be staging his first retrospective in North America. Despite Durham's lack of exposure here during the past two decades, he is an artist who is held in high esteem by curators around the country, and also notably by many artists, and yet most have been unable to see the work in any depth. Thus, the anticipation for the exhibition is palpable, and we are grateful that its tour to the Walker Art Center, the Whitney Museum of American Art, and the Remai Modern in Saskatoon will allow the work to be experienced by a broad audience across the country and in Canada. The exhibition and catalogue will provide visitors a deeper understanding of, or perhaps a first-time encounter with, Durham's expansive practice, which encompasses sculpture, drawing, collage, printmaking, painting, photography, video, performance, and poetry. The Hammer has also expressed our commitment to Durham through a number of significant acquisitions, and we are delighted to now have eight works in our collections through acquisition and promised gifts, more than any other museum in the United States and internationally.

I am grateful to Anne for her vision, diligence, and patience in remaining committed to this project and bringing it to life. Many thanks are due to our great colleagues at the three other museums hosting the show: at the Walker, director Olga Viso, artistic director Fionn Meade, and curator Vincenzo de Bellis; at the Whitney, director Adam Weinberg, chief curator Scott Rothkopf, and curator Elisabeth Sussman; and at the Remai Modern, director Gregory Burke and director of programs and chief curator Sandra Guimarães. We felt these were the ideal venues for the exhibition's tour, and we are immensely heartened by their enthusiasm. My sincere appreciation goes to the generous funders of the exhibition, without whom this project would not have been possible. The lead corporate sponsor is Taubman, headed by William Taubman, and we are thrilled to be working together for the first time. William's wife, Ellen, has a deep understanding of American Indian art and is a long-standing admirer of Durham's work, so it is especially meaningful to have the Taubmans' commitment to the exhibition. The Henry Luce Foundation and The Andy Warhol Foundation for the Visual Arts both came through with major grants to make this exhibition possible. We are extremely thankful for their generous support and encouragement at every stage of this project. We thank our good friend Maggie Kayne, who has made an important gift to this exhibition, as well as the National Endowment for the Arts, a long-standing supporter of the Hammer's work. The support of The Ampersand Foundation/Jack Kirkland, Lonti Ebers, and Adam Lindemann has also been critical to realizing the exhibition. I thank kurimanzutto for its championing of the artist and sponsorship of this publication. We also profoundly appreciate the institutions and individuals—the majority of whom are outside the United States—who generously allowed us to borrow their artworks for this exhibition. Their names can be found on page 319. To all of the above, we express our deep gratitude.

ANN PHILBIN
DIRECTOR

INTRODUCTION: THE BEST WAY OUT IS ALWAYS THROUGH

I met Jimmie Durham a decade ago when I asked him if he would be interested in working with me to submit an exhibition proposal to the State Department for the US Pavilion at the Venice Biennale. I was, frankly, shocked when he took me up on my offer, knowing that he had been living outside the country since the 1980s. I suggested that we take up the subject of nationalism itself, and we developed provocative ideas to engage with the troubling fact that the pavilion's Palladian-style architecture so clearly references Thomas Jefferson's Virginia plantation Monticello, and thus the history of colonization, violence, and slavery in the United States. In the end, we never submitted the proposal. For various reasons—both personal and political—he felt unable to proceed. At that time, I didn't fully grasp the nuances that the cultural context of the United States carried for him, nor would I have presumed to be attuned to the enormously layered composition that made up his life and work up to that point, but I appreciated and respected the complexity and intensity of the situation for him.

Despite my disappointment, I knew I could not give up on my hope to work with this artist. I experienced a palpable sense that to know Jimmie Durham and to work with him would be much more than an aesthetic and intellectual act of discovery, investigation, and presentation. I understood profoundly, albeit subconsciously, that the process would also be intensely emotional, filled with affective embodied experiences of his work and deep contemplation of the many chapters of his life. I would somehow need to match—or at least attempt to reflect—the level of dogged commitment he has brought to his own politics and practice over many years. I stayed in touch with Durham and saw his work whenever and wherever possible. I wrote to him periodically, and would show up at his openings when I could. I would visit him and his partner, Maria Thereza Alves, in Berlin. Being a social animal and a gentleman, he would always welcome me into their home and his studio to spend time together. I began to propose the idea of working together on a retrospective of his work in the United States. Each time he would listen as I argued my case. Each time he would smile and nod, seemingly pleased by the invitation. And then he would politely decline. There were many times during the eight years we were in periodic discussions about this when I thought I should give up, but upon reflection, I would always come back to the simple conviction that this was an exhibition that needed to happen.

I believed that, despite Durham's decision to locate his practice largely outside of the United States, the history of American art has benefited greatly from this artist. And yet I felt increasingly concerned, even distressed, as I recognized that his role in this history was starting to be overlooked in the absence of consistent visibility of his work within America's borders. Though I respected his decision to distance himself from the United States and to reject most invitations to exhibit here, I knew unequivocally that it would be an egregious art historical oversight for his work to disappear from the critical and historical discourse of American art—and, for that matter, of art in the Americas. Such an omission would reinforce the marginalization and masking of practices that never did, and still do not, fit neatly into the mainstream, especially those critical of this very mainstream, not only in art but also most certainly in politics. During one of our visits and yet another failed attempt to convince him, he looked at me after declining my offer and said, "Ask me again." No doubt he knew I would. Three years ago, after visiting him in Berlin, I awoke on a Sunday morning and checked my e-mail and there was a note from Jimmie, which simply read, "Let's do it." I cried. Champagne was poured. And then the work really began.

One ongoing dilemma, which is a source of both endless fascination and persistent anxiety, has been that of negotiating my wish to evaluate Durham's practice within the history of American art—to see him and his work as inextricable from his background as an American and, indeed, as an American Indian—with the fact that he is a distinctly international artist. In fact, one of the primary reasons he left the country was to reject the limitations that the American context seemed to place upon him, with its proclivity to interpret his work almost exclusively in relationship to his identity. What became evident to me very quickly is that he is a both/and, not an either/or, artist. Thus, it was crucial that the project reflect this complexity rather than reduce the work to simple categories or clearly articulated summaries, that it argue for the value of reinserting him into the trajectory of American art even while calling into question the need for such an argument. As an artist working in numerous mediums—as well as being an essayist, poet, and activist—Durham cannot easily be defined. His practice seems to exist somewhere between these disciplines and always involves a combination of them. Moreover, his resistance to seeing them as distinct is in keeping with his steadfast suspicion of all forms of categorization and labeling.

I also grew to understand something Durham recognized from our earliest conversations: that a retrospective is a ridiculous thing indeed. It is a beautifully irrational process. During our initial conversations on the subject, he would argue that retrospectives are for the dead, reminding me that he is still alive and producing work. He was, understandably, more interested in his current work and moving forward than in looking back. In curatorial practice, there is often a false premise, an ingrained presumption, that to stage a retrospective is to tell a comprehensive story of an artist's life and production. Yet, the impossibility of this task is rarely acknowledged. To try to honor nearly fifty years of work is as unwieldy as it is exhilarating. If one can accept, or overlook, the deeply embedded problematics of the retrospective as a form, I would argue that it is a methodology of exhibition making that should be for the living. In my desire to work closely with him, I shared art critic Craig Owens's intention to write "not necessarily *about* critical and oppositional practices but *alongside* them" and filmmaker and writer Trinh T. Minh-ha's commitment to speak *nearby* rather than *about*.[1]

To tell *a* story (with the understanding that there are more to tell) over time and in dialogue with an artist as complex, brave, unstoppable, and difficult to encapsulate as Jimmie Durham has been as joyful as it has been enduringly, productively overwhelming. It is an experience of a lifetime, and the responsibility has been an incredible honor. I am continuously aware that for all I have researched and investigated about his work, and for all I have gained from the bottomless intellect and insatiable curiosity of the man himself, there is so much I do not know. I have learned from him in ways I have yet to comprehend. For me, his work represents what art does at its best: interrogate, complicate, implicate, remind, lament, satirize, and savor, giving us hope that intelligence today might outweigh the stupidity of yesterday. His work has contributed immeasurably to this task, and contemporary art—including but not limited to the history of American art—is all the better for it.

ACKNOWLEDGMENTS

In addition to my enormous gratitude to the artist himself, there are numerous others I would like to thank. When I joined the Hammer in 2009, director Ann Philbin asked me what exhibitions I most wanted to organize. I told her of my desire to curate a retrospective of Durham's work, but explained that I felt it was only a remote possibility. She immediately recognized the importance and potential impact of a retrospective in the United States. I told her that having the Hammer behind me, and specifically her support, gave me much more confidence. I believed that the museum's reputation as an "artists' museum"—with its vital role in the city as a gathering place for artists in the community and long-standing commitment to working closely with artists to realize projects that strongly cleave to their needs and aspirations—and its affiliation with a university made it the ideal venue and context for Durham's work. Indeed, when I broached the subject of a retrospective again with Durham, he recognized that Los Angeles, with its renowned art schools and vital art communities, would be a fitting location for his work. When Connie Butler came on board as chief curator in 2013, she similarly got fully behind the exhibition and made the institution's support of the project clear to the artist. I continue to believe that Durham's practice meaningfully aligns with the Hammer's mission to champion artists who help us see the world in new ways and its belief in the capacity of art to inspire change. I am grateful for the incredible leadership and fearlessness of both Annie and Connie, and for their unwavering encouragement and assistance with this exhibition.

Organizing a retrospective is a time-consuming and involved process, and this exhibition, its catalogue, and its accompanying programs required and benefited enormously from the Hammer's extraordinary staff. I am incredibly grateful to MacKenzie Stevens, curatorial assistant, who put her heart and mind into all aspects of this project, always at the ready to help in any way she could, and whose research skills were indispensible. I also want to acknowledge the hours of diligent work and invaluable support provided by our long-term research assistant Alexanndra Nicholls. My sincere thanks go to Melanie Crader, director of exhibition and publication management, for her dedication and great talent in overseeing many aspects of this publication and the tour. Courtney Smith, project manager, exhibitions and publications, has coordinated the innumerable details of this catalogue with great proficiency and patience, never dropping the ball on even the smallest aspect. I am also beholden to the entire curatorial team, including Cindy Burlingham, Ali Subotnick, and Aram Moshayedi, whose support and feedback along this journey are greatly appreciated. Peter Gould, assistant director of exhibition design and production, was a true partner in planning the layout of the galleries, designing the display cases and other exhibition furniture, and troubleshooting the many facets of the installation. Chief preparator Jason Pugh oversaw the installation itself with great dexterity and his characteristic calm demeanor, assisted by Luke Whitlatch and Michael Terzano; their expertise and hard work always give me enormous confidence. Special thanks to Jim Fetterley, museum and theater technical director, for his oversight of all the audio-visual needs for the exhibition. Director of registration and collections management Portland McCormick was fundamental to the complex choreography of crating and shipping, and senior associate registrar Kate Lally expertly managed the many details of all the loans with grace and good humor. I also want to thank Daniel Munoz, assistant director of security, and our security staff, along with our manager of visitor experience Annie Kee and the wonderful visitor experience representatives, for safeguarding the works of art and interfacing with the public on a daily basis. Our development team did an excellent job of raising the necessary funds to mount the exhibition, and my sincere appreciation goes to Catherine Massey, associate director of development, who led the effort, leaving no rock unturned, as well as chief advancement officer Justin Glasson, Hannah Howe, Julia Howe, and Ayano Tsuchiya, who were also instrumental.

Chief communications officer Gia Storms and her team—including Mitch Marr, Susan Edwards, Nancy Lee, Chisa Hughes, and Arielle Sherman—have done an outstanding job overseeing all of the press for the show. Cheers also to our senior graphic designer Patrick O'Rourke and production and design coordinator Tara Morris for their creativity and hard work on the exhibition graphics. Director of public programs Claudia Bestor and her colleague Janani Subramanian brought many great ideas to the table and adeptly produced all of the public programs. Assistant director of academic programs Theresa Sotto and her team organized wonderful activities for families. Our administrative department—headed by the indomitable Debbie Snyder, deputy director of finance and administration, with valuable contributions by Danny Rosett, Lindsay Martin, Hilary Fahlsing, Jared Hammond, and Margot Stokol—was always ready and willing to assistant with whatever administrative needs came up. Extraordinary thanks must also go to Henry Clancy, director of operations, who oversaw the renovation of our galleries in advance of the opening of the exhibition.

I am indebted to catalogue designer Conny Purtill, who brought his depth of knowledge and special sensibility, along with his unwavering enthusiasm, to the beautiful design of this volume. I am honored to have the written contributions of so many of my esteemed peers and colleagues, who take up wide-ranging topics related to Durham's work in a compelling range of styles and voices: Jennifer A. González, Jessica L. Horton, Fred Moten, Paul Chaat Smith, MacKenzie Stevens, Elisabeth Sussman, and Jessica Berlanga Taylor. It is also a distinct privilege to be able to include several of Durham's own writings—both essays and poems—including "This Is an Eviction Plan (New York in the 1980s)," written for this publication. To me, Durham's writing cannot be separated from his visual art practice, and my hope is that readers will seek out other examples of his texts after reading the selection offered here. I also very much appreciate his willingness to do an interview with me, which brings his singular voice even more into these pages. Editor Michelle Piranio was completely on top of everything and a real pleasure to work with. We are indebted to proofreader Dianne Woo for bringing fresh eyes to the project. Much credit must be given to Tony Manzella, Rusty Sena, and the team at Echelon Color in Santa Monica for making the images in the book so beautiful, as well as Roberto Conti, Marta Conti, and the team at Conti Tipocolor in Florence for their excellent printing. Mary DelMonico of DelMonico Books • Prestel has been our partner on numerous catalogues, and we are grateful for her commitment to our efforts and her early embrace of this title. While I was writing my catalogue essay, Phil and Todd Mercado-Quinn offered the most valuable gift possible: the space and quiet of their home in Ojai. It was the perfect setting in which to read, think, and write, and my essay would not exist without their kind generosity.

Many individuals, institutions, and organizations have stepped forward to support this exhibition and publication. First, we must acknowledge the lenders to the exhibition for generously sharing works from their collections. More than with any exhibition I have ever worked on, these collectors immediately agreed to lend their works and often with great eagerness because of their belief in Durham's work and their genuine excitement to see it garner a larger audience in North America. Durham has had many galleries throughout the years, and all of those who currently work with him have been helpful and forthcoming with information, archival materials, and works of art. I express my gratitude to Christine König, Michel Rein, Franco Soffiantino, Niccolo Sprovieri, and Barbara Wien. In particular, I am deeply appreciative of the support and dedication that Jose Kuri and Monica Manzutto of kurimanzutto have provided to the exhibition and, moreover, to Durham's practice more generally. They have been a constant source of guidance, indispensible partners in gathering information and securing loans, and a font of passion. Many at the gallery deserve my thanks, and every person we worked with during the past three years showed the utmost care and professionalism. My exceptional gratitude goes to Amelia Hinojosa, whose kind assistance and belief in the project have been indispensible. Key individuals helped me in the early stages of the research and at various moments along the way, and I want to acknowledge art historian Jessica L. Horton, who generously shared her research and wisdom without hesitation, Bart de Baere, Isabel and Ricardo Brey, Nicole Klagsbrun, Cisco Jiménez, and Paul Chaat Smith. The Fales Library at New York University was a primary source for our research, and special mention is owed to head librarian Marvin Taylor, who was always happy to help, along with Lisa Darms, Sophie Glidden-Lyon, Emily King, and Brent Phillips. The UCLA Scandinavian Language Department and the UCLA Department of Germanic Languages provided expertise with translations, which we appreciate very much. I also want to acknowledge Cristian Manzutto for his contribution of an amazing film about Jimmie Durham, which offers visitors much insight into the artist and his practice.

We could not have imagined a better tour for this exhibition, and I am grateful to Olga Viso and Fionn Meade at the Walker for signing on almost immediately for the show, and to Vincenzo de Bellis for graciously taking over its organization even before he had officially started working there. I am touched by Adam Weinberg's and Elisabeth Sussman's great enthusiasm for the project, and having Elisabeth as a partner in the exhibition's presentation at the Whitney is a great honor, as I have been a longtime admirer of her practice and dedication to artists. I also want to thank Gregory Burke and Sandra Guimarães at the Remai Modern for bringing the exhibition to Canada. The generosity of donors is absolutely essential to an exhibition such as this, and I echo Annie Philbin's heartfelt thanks to William and Ellen Taubman; Teresa Carbone at the Henry Luce Foundation, which made a very significant grant toward this project; Joel Wachs and James Bewley at The Andy Warhol Foundation, whose travel research grant came at a critical moment and proved indispensable; Maggie Kayne; the National Endowment for the Arts; Lonti Ebers; Jack Kirkland; and Adam Lindemann.

There are two important individuals in Jimmie's life to whom I must express my deep gratitude. First, studio manager Kai Vollmer has been vital to the exhibition every step of the way. His intellect, kindness, and good humor have made him a real joy to work with. And Maria Thereza Alves has been a great support and invaluable resource for the exhibition, but even more, her integrity, composure, and strength as a person, an artist, and a thinker have been an inspiration. Lastly, I thank my partner, Nick Herman, who has spent hours listening to me talk about Jimmie's work and this exhibition and has offered both great insight and meaningful perspectives, while always providing me with a space of calm and well-being, as well as many laughs along the way.

ANNE ELLEGOOD
SENIOR CURATOR, HAMMER MUSEUM

Notes

1. Craig Owens, "Interview with Craig Owens by Anders Stephanson," in *Beyond Recognition: Representation, Power, and Culture*, ed. Scott Bryson, Barbara Kruger, Lynne Tillman, and Jane Weinstock (Berkeley: University of California Press, 1994), 307; statement from Trinh T. Minh-ha's film *Reassemblage*, 1982. Thanks to Litia Perta for reminding me of Minh-ha's assertion in the context of the symposium she organized, "Just Speak Nearby: The Politics & Practices of Art Writing," 356 Mission, Los Angeles, April 21, 2016.

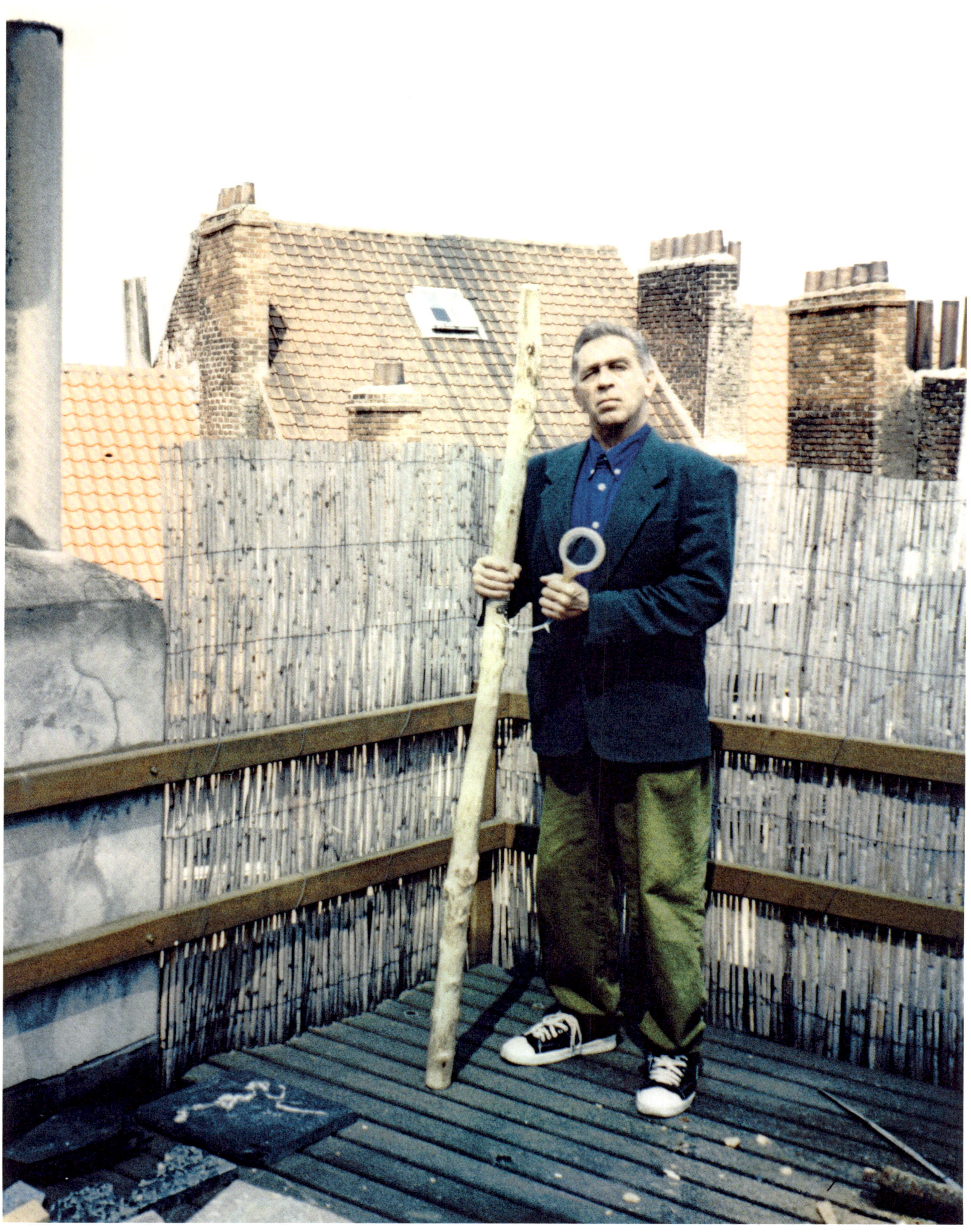

Durham with his first *Pole to Mark the Center of the World*, Brussels, ca. 1995.

JIMMIE DURHAM: POST-AMERICAN

ANNE ELLEGOOD

I feel fairly sure that I could address the entire world if only I had a place to stand.

—Jimmie Durham, "The Ground Has Been Covered" (1988)

I'm an outsider who sneaks in, who continues to sneak in.

—Jimmie Durham, interviewed by Susan Canning (1990)

Prologue

Is it possible to be at once deeply, genuinely American and resolutely, purposefully transnational? To feel an abiding connection to your place of birth yet refuse to set foot there? To be an American whose origins and ancestry mean that you've never actually accepted the statehood this represents? Or the ideas of discovery and progress—of expansionism and entitled sovereignty—that are habitually promoted? To reject the very notion of American identity as it has taken shape over the past five centuries on the grounds that the United States has consistently attempted to erase from history one of its primary founding principles—that the genocide of the indigenous peoples was the necessary collateral damage to creating a "civilized" society—is to refuse to align yourself with misrepresentation, the rewriting of history, and the continued invisibility and exploitation of a group of people based on the social construction of race. This is an ethical supposition. It proposes that the current, widely adopted understanding of America's position in the world—based in rote nationalism, aggressive militarism, and exploitative capitalism—is counterproductive and decidedly hypocritical to its expressed ideology of freedom, equality, justice, and community. This is a position that we might productively call "post-American," and the artist who, in my opinion, most fully embodies such a stance, in his life and his work, is Jimmie Durham.

"I want to say something."[1]

Durham's entire life—as an artist, performer, poet, essayist, teacher, and activist—might best be mapped and understood by his ongoing search for and insistence upon being given a place to stand in order to participate in the discourse. He recognizes this as a lifelong struggle, one that will never be resolved or fully realized, and yet it is an effort to which he has been steadfastly and, one could argue, quite successfully dedicated. To contribute to the discourse means not only being given a place to stand but also being provided—or taking for oneself—a space of visibility. Thus Durham makes objects with an abiding belief in what philosopher Michel Foucault established in the 1970s: that nothing has meaning outside of discourse and that social constructions are the contexts in which meanings are ascribed.[2] Being historically relegated to the shadows and subjected to willful misrepresentation creates a cascading series of misunderstandings and unwelcome interactions, usually prompted by an expectation of justification. Despite his proven dexterity at breaking through the many barriers erected in his path, Durham has articulated such experiences consistently in his writing and artwork, including his incredulousness at the problematic notions of "authenticity" levied at him and other American Indians and his distress at the amount of ignorance about the brutality of American colonization and indigenous peoples' struggles for survival.[3] What is deeply troubling, and even harrowing, is how history has rendered a figure like Durham nearly *indescribable*, so alien to some as to be almost unbelievable.

For more than forty years, Durham has wielded his work to defy this marginalization and to mark his existence, on several occasions by planting a stake "at the center of the world." This phrase is taken from a series of works the peripatetic artist has been making for more than two decades in various locations, beginning in Middelburg, the Netherlands, in 1995 (fig. 1). Titled *A Pole to Mark the Center of the World* (followed by the name of the city in which it was made), each one designates Durham's current location as the "center," while collectively they chart some of the various sites of his exhibitions and residencies. The project can be seen as a simple nod to Western notions of subjectivity and the primacy of individuality, which foster the sense that our position and perspective are always at the center; or, more aptly, it might be understood as a humorous critique of this seemingly relentless self-absorption. It is also inspired by the Cherokee belief in seven directions. Of the works, Durham has said:

> I started out with the idea that Eurasia would have seven centres of the world because Cherokee mythology states that there are "seven directions," and I thought I would make a pole for each direction. The seven key directions we believe in are: up, down, north, south, east, west and inside yourself. There are many more, however: north by northwest, south by southeast and so on—an infinite number of directions. And within myself I'm rather contradictory—as most people are—and I do not follow a single direction.[4]

Many of Durham's hand-carved poles have mirrors attached to them and resemble an object used for a traditional ceremony or ritual. Indeed, in some cases he has created these works during public performances, cutting a sapling down in a particular location and stripping it of its bark. And although he has called it a "cheap trick,"[5] the mirror also inevitably reflects the viewer, thus absorbing her into the work or triggering an awareness that she is part of it. A defining feature of Durham's practice is his deft maneuvering between putting forth objects that on their face are connected to his heritage (he has stated that all art is essentially self-portraiture[6]) and then entangling the viewer in the work so as to deflect his personal history and infuse the object with shared meanings and implications.

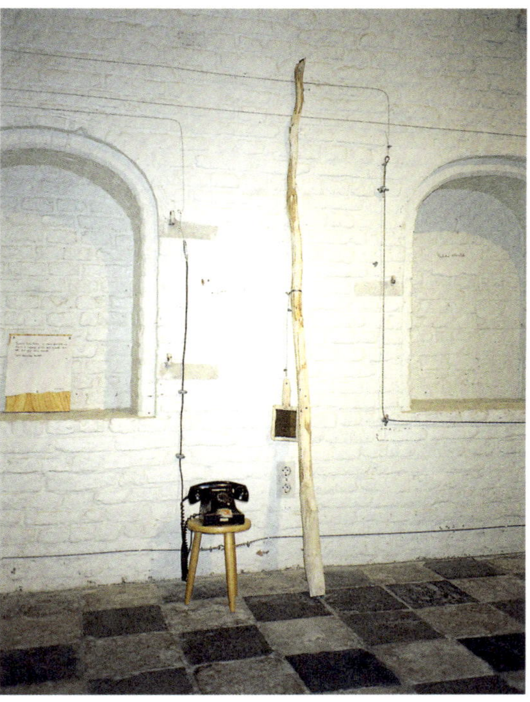

Fig. 1
A Pole to Mark the Center of the World, Middelburg, Netherlands, 1995
Beech, mirror, steel wires
Pole: 78 ¾ × 1 ⅝ to 2 ⅜ in. (200 × 4 to 6 cm); mirror: 3 ½ × 4 ¾ in. (9 × 12 cm)
Collection Vleeshal Center for Contemporary Art, Middelburg, the Netherlands
Installation view, *Centre of the World*, Vleeshal/SBKM, Middelburg, the Netherlands, 1995

For Durham, being at the center is ultimately less personal than it is political. It is a reclamation of sorts, an insistence that he *belongs* at the center, especially after he and his people have been, and continue to be, forced into the margins—or the borderlands, as Chicana poet and academic Gloria Anzaldúa would have it.[7] For Durham, to be at the center is to push his way out of the dark and onto a stage where he will be given the microphone. As he expressed in 1987, "Whenever you folks think about the world, you assume yourselves to be not only at the centre but the standard also, which makes it a little difficult to carry on a conversation with you."[8] Nonetheless, throughout the 1980s—a sometimes fraught yet seminal and transformational chapter in American art—Durham was an active participant in the New York downtown art world, having solo exhibitions at several nonprofit spaces and advocating for other artists through curating and writing.[9]

Durham came onto the New York scene during a period of steady and vocal calls for increased support and visibility for artists of color (or, as they were often called at the time, "minority" artists), who were often placed under the problematic (however initially well-intentioned) rubric of "multiculturalism" and "identity politics." While these efforts at inclusion certainly brought much-needed opportunities for many artists of color, they also successfully maintained the essential framework of difference, which relies on the dynamics of center and periphery, ultimately keeping these categories intact. The result was the segregation of these artists, often in venues that had been founded with the express mission of providing a platform for underrecognized "Others."[10] Furthermore, the very existence of these new spaces and opportunities was construed, falsely, as proof that the artists were now on a level playing field with the mainstream (largely white male) artists who continued to find the most success and validation.[11] Many have argued that multiculturalism became a tactic to camouflage or deflect the fact that dominant institutions continued to keep a diverse contingency of artists out of their programs and collections.[12] Moreover, the large-scale exhibitions at the time that took up the mantle of multiculturalism by foregrounding the work of artists of color and women—both locally and globally—were often criticized for failing to dismantle long-held colonial attitudes within the arts, maintaining outmoded notions of universality, or being more about politics than art (fig. 2).[13] The skepticism was more than just grumbling about politics in art (as if history had not taught us that art has never been a purely formalist, or isolationist, endeavor separate from society or immune from the context of political discourse). Some critics were unabashedly cynical about the work of artists of color and women artists when seen in mainstream institutions, asserting that they were making a kind of "victim art" or were raining on the normative parade with their (presumably unjustified) complaints. Worse, some artists were deemed by critics to be simply creating "bad" art that, to them, would always remain unsophisticated because of its alleged didacticism, overtly transparent, even preachy arguments, and perceived lack of beauty. This friction culminated with the 1993 Whitney Biennial, in which Durham's work was featured, and to which mainstream critics largely reacted with hostile disdain.[14]

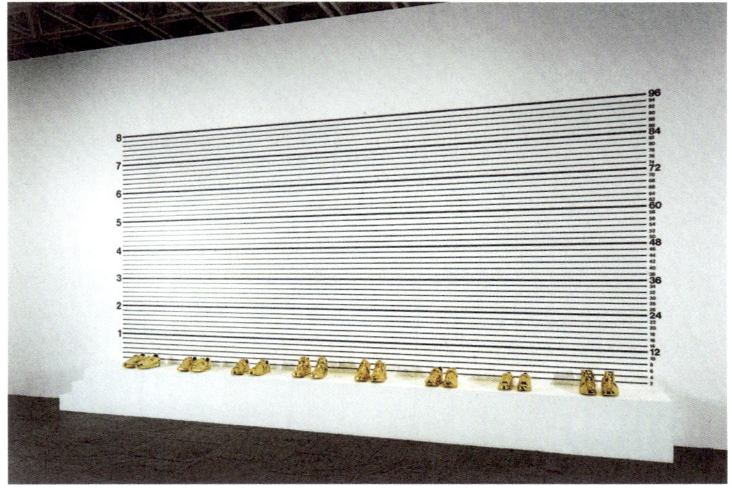

Fig. 2
Gary Simmons
Lineup, 1993
Synthetic polymer on wood with gold-plated basketball shoes
114 × 216 × 18 in.
(289.6 × 548.6 × 45.7 cm)
Whitney Museum of American Art, New York; purchase with funds from the Brown Foundation Inc.
Installation view, 1993 Whitney Biennial, New York

Today this type of rhetoric reads as strangely alarmist, as if outsiders were violently storming the gates of the institution and successfully throwing aside centuries of established hierarchy in the process. Despite the critics' tendencies for overgeneralized and condescending finger-wagging, some of their concerns were valid, even for the artists themselves. Artists of color understood the pitfalls of their work being evaluated simply as polemical statements rather than seriously and fully in terms of *both* subject and form—of the positions put forward *as well as* the materials with which they chose to visualize them. Arguably, this was largely a result of tunnel vision on the part of critics who tended to split form and content as mutually exclusive elements, but nonetheless, artists recognized these types of reactions as yet another form of sidelining and indifference. Even as some critics and viewers complained about art that tackled the history of oppression or recent episodes of societal abuse or neglect, others practically demanded that the work of artists of color contain subjects that made their backgrounds evident. Those who were working abstractly or without obvious referents were just as likely to be ignored.

"I don't think it's about me; I don't think it's about Indians. I think it's about the larger society."[15]

Within this distinctly American context, Durham came to feel the categories to which his work was often relegated were nothing but a dead end for him, so that his work was being seen and understood only through the lens of his ethnic identity, his "Indianness." Even with limited experience of the art world, from very early on he was skeptical of how artists of color were being given only a certain type of access—one that came with the understanding that there were specific predetermined roles for them—and that the contexts for their work would be not of their own choosing but rather provided for them. The 1993 Whitney Biennial remains a poignant example of this tension. Even when artists were allowed to enter into the exalted space of this type of "career-making" exhibition, they had to essentially endure a slew of angry reactions that stemmed from an overly simplified and narrow interpretation of their work, which served to maintain the status quo by insisting on a dichotomy between mainstream and other. "The art world, to the extent that it asks any demands of us, demands that we choose our 'plight' as our subject matter, yet to do so is to remain a curiosity hardly on even the outskirts of discourse" is Durham's succinct appraisal of this dynamic.[16] Speaking to the same concern, art historian Jennifer A. González writes, "In fact, the critical art establishment has shown itself to be only too ready to produce a place (and a market niche) for cultural others as long as they agree to maintain their position of cultural difference."[17]

Despite these pitfalls, Durham's practice was critically and thoughtfully engaged with the politics and problematics of representation, a subject at the center of his life long before he entered the 1980s art world because of his background and work as an activist, particularly his participation in the American Indian Movement (AIM) fighting for human rights at the United Nations in the 1970s. When he returned to art making more fully, in 1980, and was being introduced to the various strands of activity in the markedly heterogeneous art world of this period, he quickly absorbed the trends of the day. By the mid-1980s, his work was deliberately in dialogue with several of the prominent and emerging practices of the moment: the use of found objects in sculptural assemblage coming out of Dada, Duchamp, and Fluxus; the appropriation of text and image to deconstruct how each operates in the spheres of culture and politics to enforce power structures; institutional critique aimed at illuminating ingrained racism and inequities in both the programming and the standard display mechanisms of museums while furthering the argument that context plays an enormous role in interpreting an artwork's meaning; and performance works that insisted on the visibility of certain types of bodies, breaking down common stereotypes in the process. To all of these modalities Durham brought a distinctive and much-needed voice and perspective.[18] By the late 1980s and early 1990s, he was riffing on once avant-garde movements such as minimalism, which by then had been both highly theorized[19] and embraced by the market, with works such as his 1989 black plywood box intended to resemble the fundamental forms of Carl Andre, Donald Judd, and Tony Smith, often referred to as "The Heisenberg Principle," a shorthand for the full title (fig. 3).[20] At the same time, Durham aimed pointed critiques at white male artists who were engaging in a type of anthropological or ethnographic practice or positioning themselves as current-day shamans, including Lothar Baumgarten, Joseph Beuys, and Lawrence Weiner (even though he liked aspects of their work). With acerbic wit, Durham boldly took a position against these highly regarded artists, declaring himself "not" to be the subject of their work (fig. 4).

Not Lothar Baumgarten's Cherokee (1990; page 70), for example, is a work on paper that responds to Baumgarten's site-specific work *The Tongue of the Cherokee* (1985–88), which takes the invention of the Cherokee alphabet by Sequoyah as its subject. Durham's piece juxtaposes two pseudoarchival documents: on the left, some lines in Cherokee from a letter written in the 1880s, and on the right, a handwritten transcription in Finnish, which translates into "Each of us is a direction. Among the Cherokee, the government is formed by a council, to which in fact every Cherokee belongs. In the council, it is each person's duty to listen carefully to what others say and to express their own thoughts precisely and in full." In this and related works, Durham makes evident the irony of artists such as Baumgarten, Beuys, and Weiner speaking for the Other when the "Other" could, in fact, speak for himself.[21]

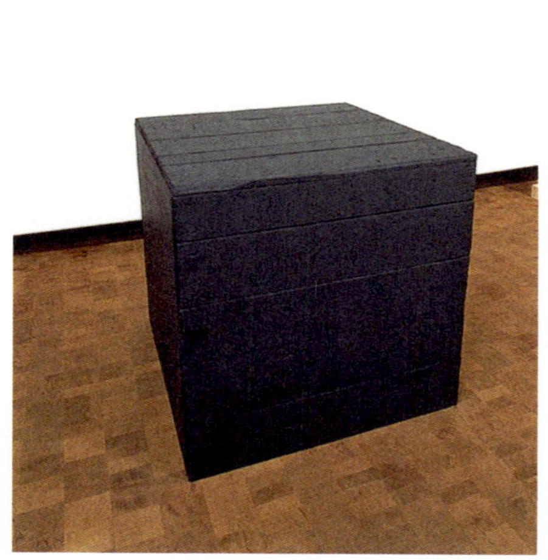

Fig. 3
Werner Heisenberg was a physicist who developed the Uncertainty Principal. To explain the principle he asked us to imagine a box with a kitten inside. The kitten is neither alive nor dead until we open the box. Before that, the kitten is only potentially alive or dead, 1989
Painted plywood with a kitten in it (that may or may not be dead)
33 ½ × 25 ½ × 25 ½ in.
(85 × 65 × 65 cm)
Courtesy of the artist and kurimanzutto, Mexico City

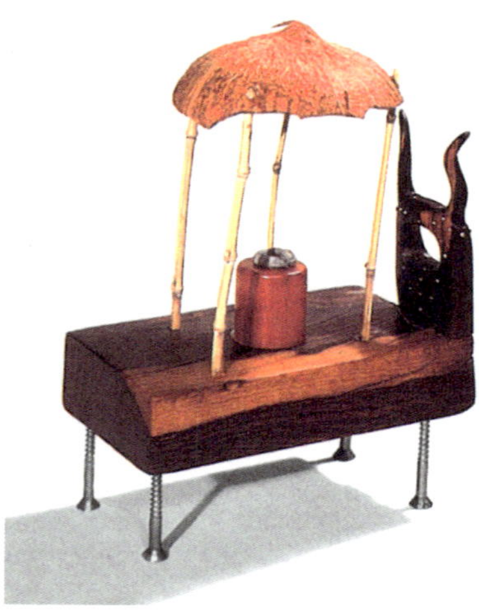

Fig. 4
Not Lawrence Weiner's Trip to the Borneo, 1990
Coconut shell, wood, metal, acrylic paint, screws
7 × 10 ½ × 3 ½ in.
(18 × 27 × 9 cm)
Current location unknown

"Savagism and You"[22]

In 1982 Durham was invited by artist and curator Juan Sánchez to participate in the group exhibition *Beyond Aesthetics: Art of Necessity by Artists of Conscience*, presented at the Henry Street Settlement in New York. He contributed four assemblage paintings that depicted political situations on Indian reservations and included imagery of hardship and slaughter. Durham's experience during this first foray into publicly exhibiting his work in New York led to a pivotal turning point in his practice. The overwhelmingly positive response triggered a realization in him about what he did *not* want to produce as an artist, namely, "images of suffering Indians, which people like."[23] He gave the paintings away and moved toward creating work that was less illustrative of historical events and more ambiguous, equally committed to taking a position but with the intention of opening up a conversation rather than simply making a point that would inevitably result in an endgame.

That same year, Durham participated in the group exhibition *Ritual and Rhythm: Visual Forces for Survival*, also curated by Sánchez, at Kenkeleba Gallery in the East Village.[24] He created what might be described as his first work of institutional critique, *Manhattan Festival of the Dead* (1982; fig. 5). It consisted of a makeshift wooden shelf on which a variety of objects were displayed—including several animal skulls adorned with paint, beads, feathers, and shells—and a hand-painted sign, casually scrawled on a large piece of leather, that hung like a backdrop and read: "Manhattan Festival of the Dead (store)." Several photographs pinned to the structure further enhanced the sense that this was a place of business, a trading post. These photos pictured Manhattan Island, a group of Sioux Indians sitting at a drum, buffalo on the range, and gargoyles on the Chartres Cathedral, all of which were inscribed, "Dear Jimmie, good luck with your new store." Durham sold the individual elements for $5 each—and no doubt gave some away—to friends and colleagues, including art critic Lucy Lippard, who would later write extensively about his work.[25]

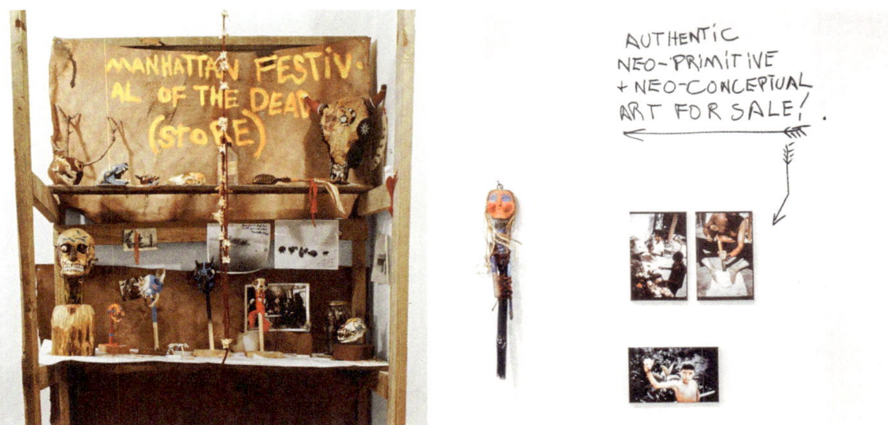

Fig. 5
Manhattan Festival of the Dead, 1982 (detail; see page 40)
Installation view, *Ritual and Rhythm: Visual Forces for Survival*, Kenkeleba Gallery, New York, 1982

Fig. 6
She Rose from Her Warm Bed, 1987 (detail; see page 164, fig. 8)
Installation view, *We the People*, Artists Space, New York, 1987

In part, the installation was a satirical commentary on both the avenues through which Indian cultural production typically finds its audience and the risks of art being seen strictly as a commodity. Durham has often warned against gauging art's value in commercial terms, asserting that art is a social phenomenon that must encourage dialogue and remain open to varying interpretations in order to participate in the ultimate goal of culture: human liberation.[26] On the contrary, "monetarism" in the art world risks perpetuating the belief that "money is the proper reward for making art."[27] With humorous aplomb, he also skewers the very notion of "genuine" American Indian art as a category, taking issue with the proclivity for fetishism and the propagation of false notions of "authenticity" it engenders. Durham would tackle this issue in later writings and artworks, including his installation in the group exhibition *We the People*, which he co-organized with writer and curator Jean Fisher for Artists Space in 1987, in which a caption above images of the artist carving a piece of wood reads, "Authentic neo-primitive + neo-conceptual art for sale!" (fig. 6).

Yet *Manhattan Festival of the Dead* was also an altar of sorts and a place for ritual, staged during the same season and in solidarity with the Festival of the Dead ceremony that takes place in Mexico after the harvest each year. Durham honored deceased animals from the region—dogs, cats, mice, rats, raccoons, fish, and deer—by creating works with their skulls alongside one using a human skull in a revealing gesture that eliminated any discrepancy or sense of hierarchy, physical or cultural, between humans and the natural world (a belief apparent in much of his work and writing before and since). Durham embellished the skulls to create incredibly vital objects, the most haunting of which was, perhaps not surprisingly, the human skull (page 41). It is painted with delicate patterns that seem to burst from its cracks and contours and is embroidered with strings of colorful beads; turquoise is inlaid into the forehead; a seashell rests in one eye socket; and vibrant green, red, and yellow parrot feathers (long since faded) stand in for the neck.

The concomitant presence of irony and gravity in this work encompasses a tenor Durham often brings to his practice. His irony is not the laconic kind that relies on mere sarcasm; rather, it flows like the humorous rantings of the most uncompromising of social critics and cuts deep. Of course, irony and satire are long-standing strategies in the arts, used to their best effect when seducing audiences with humor or titillation before throwing punches at controversial subjects, oftentimes pushed under the rug of history, that are deemed divisive or inflammatory and yet are in dire need of a public forum. These techniques can be powerfully constructive in the way they simultaneously embrace and implicate the viewer. What is remarkable about Durham is his incredible aptitude for levity amid the very serious business of raising social consciousness, bringing them into a coexistence that manages to be utterly enticing while also amplifying the palpable dynamic of anger and urgency in the work. *Manhattan Festival of the Dead* strikes this balance beautifully, as evidenced by the two written texts that accompanied the installation, which I quote in full below:

> **GOOD NEWS FOR ART LOVERS!**
> American Indian Artist May Die
> Act now! At the Manhattan Festival of the Dead you can buy American Indian art at Rock Bottom prices!
>
> But that's not all!
>
> Everyone knows that the value of works of art often dramatically increases when the artist dies. Jimmie Durham, the artist selling his work here at the low, low price of $5 per piece (limit one to a customer.). Mr. Durham is now 42 years old, and the average lifespan of an American Indian man is only 44 years! Mr. Durham also has numerous physical ailments, which could develop into fatal illness. His life has been threatened by several Tribal Chairmen, and he lives in a neighborhood with a high crime rate.
>
> Your $5 investment now could bring you thousands of dollars in just a short time! You would also enjoy the pleasure of having a genuine and beautiful American Indian work of art in your own home! Act Now! Simply sign your name to the sheet provided next to the piece you want to have as your own. At the end of the show you can pick-up your work of art. C.O.D.
>
> **Statement by the Artist**
> In 1973, the American Indian Movement liberated the village of Wounded Knee on the Pine Ridge Reservation. A couple of hundred brave Indians stood off the U.S. Army for 93 days. Nixon's Army had tanks, automatic weapons, jet airplanes, and even chemical weapons there.
>
> In the years that followed more than two hundred A.I.M. people were killed on or around the Reservation by governments forces.
>
> This Festival of the Dead is an honoring ceremony for those people and for people in New York who have been killed by subways, .38 slugs, needles or desperate acts, without any proper ceremonies to help their passage and our passage.
>
> Part of the ceremony is a traditional Cherokee give-away, but since this is a Manhattan ceremony the give-away will cost you $5. Remember these are dead animals from this suffering island. The artwork is ceremonies for them and for us.

Manhattan Festival of the Dead led to a series of sculptures, each incorporating a single animal skull into slightly smaller than human-scale assemblages, including a dog skull in *New York Gitli*; a bear skull in *Wahya*; and a puma (or mountain lion) skull in *Tlunh Datsi*, which translates from the Cherokee into "panther" (all 1984;

pages 42, 43, 45). They were featured alongside other skull sculptures in his first solo show in New York, *A Matter of Life and Death and Singing*, in December of 1984 at the Alternative Museum (fig. 7). In these and several later works, the skull is held aloft by a freestanding construction that serves as a body-cum-pedestal, often incorporating natural materials with man-made industrial elements such as plastic or metal car and machine parts. The careful ornamentation of the animal through the addition of colorful painted sections, beadwork, feathers, and the frequent use of shells or stones for eyes and ears is in contrast to the found objects that sometimes appear to have been taken off the street or pulled out of a Dumpster (in fact, a common way of procuring materials for Durham), such as wooden or plastic police or traffic barricades, tree limbs, and rudimentary structures carved from found wood or readily available construction lumber.

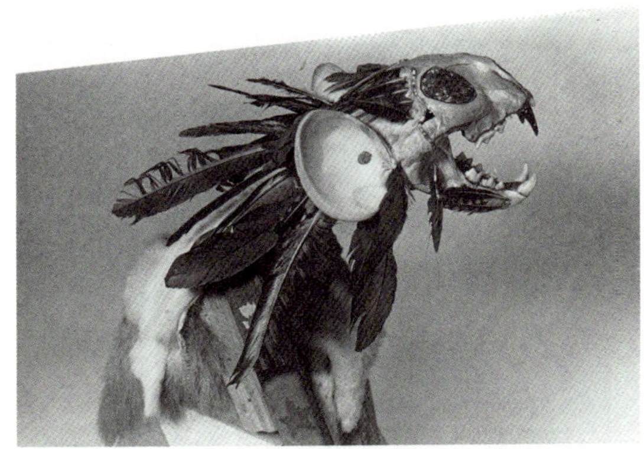

Fig. 7
Exhibition brochure for *A Matter of Life and Death and Singing*, Alternative Museum, New York, 1984

Durham is well aware that his choices of natural matter such as animal bones, hides, and feathers will be understood as the appropriately archetypal ingredients for the work of an American Indian artist. Despite his genuine intention to honor the animals to which he feels an abiding connection, he remains ever cognizant of the fact that the work may be read as "folk art" or "Indian artifacts," and thus deploys these materials to call into question the viewer's expectations about the types of work Indians make. Specifically, he wants to deflect the nostalgic sensibility likely brought to bear on the work by viewers seduced by mythologies of the "noble savage," that most pervasive stereotype of American Indians as primitive and inherently violent but who have nevertheless stoically endured their unfortunate history and have now fully assimilated into and embraced the United States as their home.[28]

At the same time, Durham was trying to interrupt the discourses of modernism and the prevailing articulations of postmodern practices, paradigms from which he felt barred. Exhibitions such as the Museum of Modern Art's notorious *Primitivism* in 1984, which put tribal arts from Africa, Oceania, and North America—including those of American Indians—alongside works by modernist painters such as Pablo Picasso and Paul Gauguin, served only to underscore the connections between modernism and colonialism and to further the misconception that "modernism" in art was exclusively a Western phenomenon. Non-Western and nonwhite artists were thus excluded from the discourse of mainstream modernism, which is, as artist and cultural critic Rasheed Araeen has noted, "in fact the logic of Eurocentric modernity, constituted by the notion of difference between the Self and the Other. The former constitutes history . . . and the latter its margins."[29] Postmodernism's well-meaning desire for inclusion, on the other hand, could at times appear to consider this "goal as an end in itself, as if 'inclusion' was the end of the story," as art historian and critic Kobena Mercer described it,[30] creating the illusion that the Other has been allowed in.

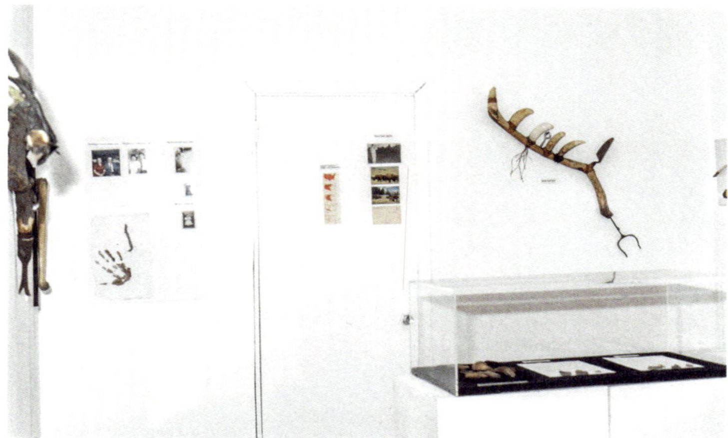

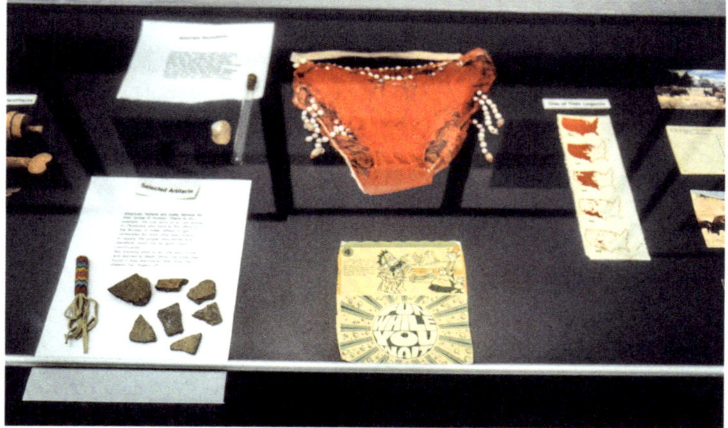

Fig. 8
On Loan from the Museum of the American Indian, 1985 (details)
Installation views, *Dimensions in Dissent*, Kenkeleba Gallery, New York, 1985

In 1985 Durham created what is perhaps his best-known, albeit no longer extant,[31] work of institutional critique, which moves from the terrain of the isolation and commodification of Native artists' work into the realm of museum practice. *On Loan from the Museum of the American Indian* (1985)—first exhibited in the group show *Dimensions in Dissent* at Kenkeleba Gallery and two years later in *We the People*—explored what Fisher called "the ethnographic gaze"[32] and consisted of a variety of found and constructed images and objects displayed on the wall and arranged within glass-topped vitrines lined with black velvet grounds (fig. 8). Presented as an archival, sociological display of the type commonly seen in natural history museums, the work gathered together information about the artist himself and the experiences of American Indians more broadly into an accumulation of what Durham called "fake artifacts," identified by labels in the installation as "scientifacts" and "sociofacts." Inspired by the ongoing discussions about the Smithsonian Institution's new National Museum of the American Indian, which was being planned for the National Mall in Washington at the time, Durham was struck by the singularity held within the title: *the* American Indian. He concluded that perhaps this model American Indian could be him and with biting parody constructed a suitable display.[33] It included photographs of his family members—his parents, labeled "The Indian's Parents (frontal view)," aunt and uncle, grandmother, and sister (page 50); a diagram labeled "Current Trends in Indian Land Ownership" showing multiple maps of the United States that visualize the diminishing amounts of land controlled by American Indian tribes; photographs of land surveyors and buffalo in the landscape (side by side to highlight their distinct relationship to the land); and three ineffectual-looking arrows (one hilariously curvy) made of wood and flint arrowheads typographically grouped with the label "Types of Arrows" (page 51). The vitrines contained shards of stone, wooden handles that would become molds for metal casting, and a racist children's coloring placemat from a diner perpetuating fear of Indians as inherently violent, among several other objects, many with lengthy accompanying didactics. Two striking small-scale assemblage sculptures also hung on the wall, masquerading as artifacts from some unexplained ritual: *Whose Hair Is It?* and *Whale Tooth Stick* (both 1985; pages 52, 53). Two additional elements operated as overt fetish objects—a bloody handprint on paper labeled "Real Indian Blood" (page 48) and a human bone labeled "Indian Leg Bone"—in which parts of the body are expected to stand in for the whole, a fantastical form of representation in which subjectivity is displaced onto an isolated fragment.

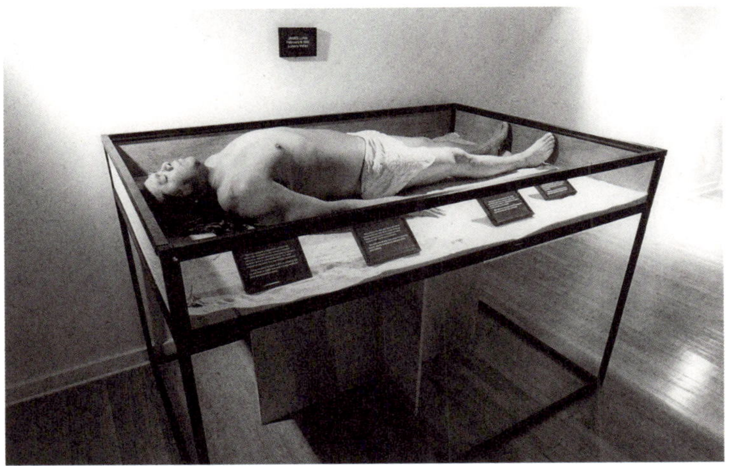

Fig. 9
James Luna
The Artifact Piece, 1987–90
Performance/installation presented at the Studio Museum in Harlem in conjunction with *The Decade Show: Frameworks of Identity in the 1980s*, organized by the New Museum, the Museum of Contemporary Hispanic Art, and the Studio Museum in Harlem, New York, 1990

On Loan from the Museum of the American Indian preceded another important work of institutional critique, *The Artifact Piece* (1987–90; fig. 9) by American artist James Luna, who is Puyukitchum (Luiseno) and Ipi (Diegueno) Indian of Mexican descent. Taking up similar questions of authenticity—Luna once said, "Authenticity is not a goal for Native people, but a prison"[34]—and the historicization of a living people, Luna's installation was first exhibited at the San Diego Museum of Man in 1987. It, too, was composed of vitrines filled with "artifacts," some of them related to traditional practices of his tribe and much of it the accoutrements of a contemporary person characterized by his tastes and interests, including music, comic books, and his driver's license. Mocking the ignorant notion that all American Indians are dead, Luna notoriously put himself in one of the vitrines, lying like a mummified corpse for hours a day. Considering this fictionalized gesture of self-sacrifice, art historian Miwon Kwon describes it as a "strategy of opposition and resistance of a different order."[35] Durham's work also anticipated some of the signature works of a new generation of American artists engaging with a type of institutional critique that employed strategies of performative mimicry and the mirroring of forms of display, such as Andrea Fraser's 1989 video *Museum Highlights: A Gallery Talk* (fig. 10), which takes up the format of the docent tour with an equal measure of intended institutional transparency and nearly slapstick absurdity; Fred Wilson's 1992 act of collection recontextualization, *Mining the Museum* (fig. 11); and Mark Dion's trio of faux natural history displays shown at American Fine Arts in 1992, in which the artist was on-site regularly to add materials such as "marine" life from Chinatown fish markets or soil samples sent from the tropics and configure them into installations based on typology and classification. Despite clear connections between Durham's efforts and projects such as these presented during the same period, his work was rarely included in the debates that surrounded works of appropriation and institutional critique related to authorship, originality, and context. Rather, Durham felt at this time that much of his critique was being overshadowed by preconceived notions of what "Indian art" should look like. "Every time I do a show in New York," he said, "I get the most asinine things said . . . Indians don't do what I just did, or Indians shouldn't do what I just did. I did really ironic things, like 'On Loan from the Museum of the American Indian,' I mean crazy obvious things. Quite a few people thought it was on loan from the Museum of the American Indian and they were not dumb people."[36]

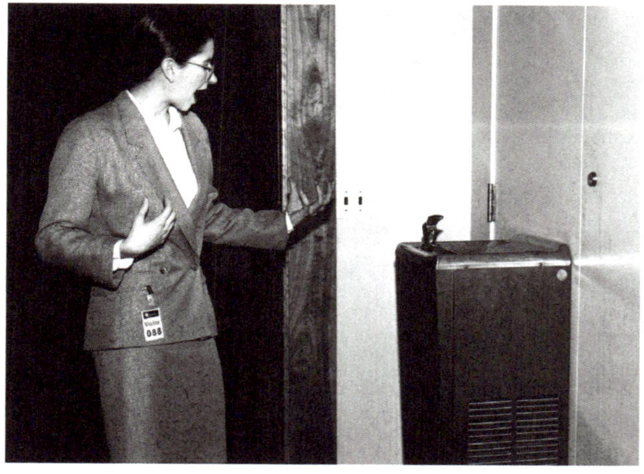

Fig. 10
Andrea Fraser
Museum Highlights: A Gallery Talk, 1989
Video, color, sound
29:00 min.
Courtesy of Galerie Nagel Draxler, Berlin

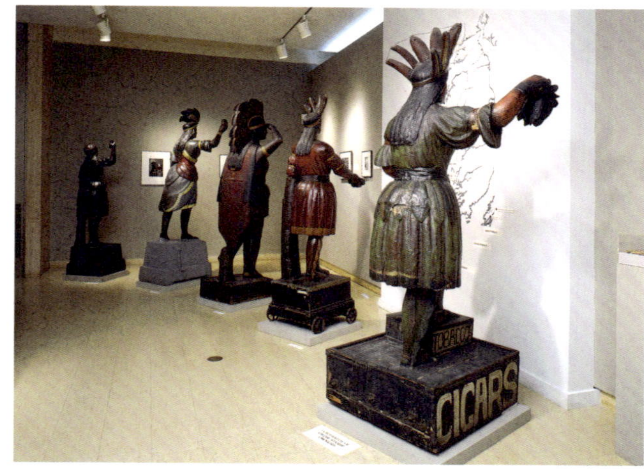

Fig. 11
Cigar store Indians installed in *Mining the Museum: An Installation by Fred Wilson*, Maryland Historical Society, 1992–93

The fetish object par excellence in *On Loan from the Museum of the American Indian* is *Pocahontas' Underwear* (1985; page 49), the bottom half of a costume consisting of bright red feathers and beads that Durham found in the garbage after a neighbor was evicted. This simple—yet relentlessly seductive—object seems to embody the fetish at both its best and its worst. Its vibrant feathers are reminiscent of an object that might stand in for a powerful spirit, yet its association with Pocahontas and placement within the context of Durham's parodic installation push it into the realm of fetishistic fantasy, which denies true representation through acts of displacement and erasure. Pocahontas (whose real name was Matoaka; ca. 1596–1617) is, of course, one of the most widely mythologized American Indian figures in history (fig. 12); her story as it has been told repeatedly in popular culture, most notably by Disney,[37] has been widely disputed by her Powhatan tribe and others. Here, the metonymy of the garment reduces

Pocahontas to her sexuality, as is the case in most of the false historical accounts of her life in which she is deemed a kind of hero for purportedly happily adapting to "civilized" life by joining up with a white man and moving to Europe, as if the marriage of a colonized person to her captor could ever be truly voluntary. These types of historical misrepresentations are perniciously common, but seemingly smaller infractions continue to occur frequently on a less visible but day-to-day basis for so many people of color. As Durham describes it, "I cannot . . . once more explain that not all Indians are from New Mexico, that some Indians have blue eyes and a thousand other stories. I can't defend a reality that everyone knows is not the reality because everyone knows that the Hollywood reality is the reality."[38] Humorous and poignant, *On Loan from the Museum of the American Indian* imitates the complexities surrounding the ways in which artifacts come to inhabit cultural institutions, depicting Indian life in the United States as perceived by a general public to be explicitly of the past, long extinct, and now available to ponder only in the context of the museum as mausoleum.[39]

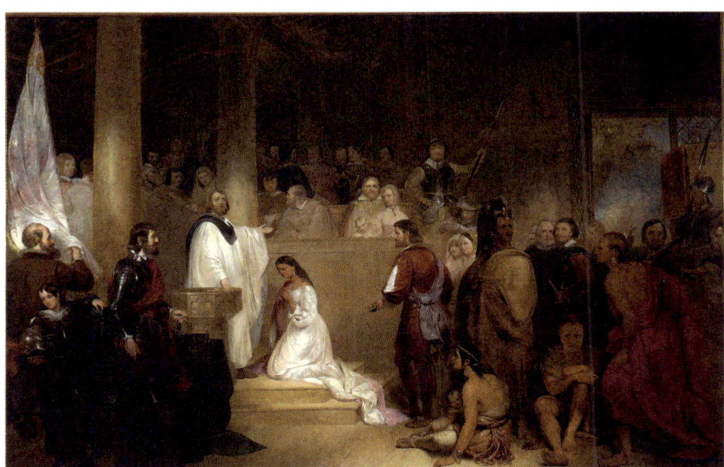

Fig. 12
John Gadsby Chapman
Baptism of Pocahontas, 1839
Oil on canvas
12 × 18 ft. (3.7 × 5.5 m)
Architect of the Capitol (AOC),
US Capitol Rotunda,
Washington, DC

Engaged Withdrawal

Of Cherokee heritage, Durham's family migrated from the southeastern United States to west of the Mississippi River shortly before the forced march known as the Trail of Tears that followed President Andrew Jackson's Indian Removal Act of 1830 (page 37). They landed in Arkansas, where Durham was born more than a century later, in 1940. This communal act of displacement may offer some insight into Durham's need to keep moving, despite his fondness for the landscape of his youth, especially if one believes that the traumas experienced by some can be embodied by future generations and transposed onto their psyches. Durham has written, "We Cherokees were driven from our homeland, and it seems we cannot go back, so we must then search always for ways to be part of some other, some broader homeland."[40] The fundamental difference, of course, is that Durham's ancestors were uprooted and dislocated essentially at the barrel of a gun, while the artist himself voluntarily left Washington, Arkansas, where he was born and raised and has since chosen to lead a peripatetic life (although he might remind us that poverty and other forces beyond his immediate control compelled him, on occasion, to pick up and start again). Despite his proclivity for a type of "homelessness" that might better be understood as a sense of home so expansive that it encompasses the entire world—catalyzed perhaps by a combination of an inherited instinct for flight and the intellectual curiosity and affinity for adventure of an explorer—Durham is transparent in his fondness for his place of origin and how the specificities of its landscape are never very far from him. "Like any normal person I left home as soon as I could," he has written, "and then spend much of my time remembering home. One's childhood memories are so often tied to taste and smell; memory begins sensually."[41]

Durham's self-exile from the United States since 1987 is often presumed to be for political reasons—an outright rejection of the country for its inability to reconcile its colonial past and a response to the way it construes its ongoing imperial activities as imperative. Indeed, as an indigenous person, he already understood himself to be stateless. Earlier, in 1979, he had resigned his position in the American Indian Movement, where he was the director of the International Indian Treaty Council fighting for the rights of indigenous peoples at the United Nations. In an open letter written a few months later and coauthored with Paul Chaat Smith, who also left the movement at the same time, Durham expressed his frustrations with AIM's fragmentation and lack of clearly articulated political goals and admitted that his reasons for resigning "were political."[42] In a 1994 paper given at a conference on internationalism in the arts, Durham wrote, "Like the scientific theories about the first three minutes after the 'Big Bang' that began our universe, our theory must be that both terrorism and censorship, orthodoxy and 'nationality' itself, begin at the moment, at the next moment the thoughtful member must escape, if not physically then at least intellectually, to hold on to the little nation's original idea. This exile then is the 'only true patriot.'"[43] While many acts of exile stem from extreme violence and dislocation—in fact, today we are witnessing an overwhelming moment of mass migration amid our current global geopolitical circumstances—not all are rooted exclusively in loss and displacement. Acts of exile can also be acts of transgressive hopefulness whereby, as Araeen described it, a subject is not a victim but rather someone seeking "a position in which he/she can locate him/herself in the world as a free subject and change it."[44] Indeed, rather than succumbing to victimhood or marginalization, such exiles critically engage with their situation through an act of removal. This can be a position of great power, one that not only expands the boundaries of the body but frees the mind.

Durham's decision in 1987 to move to Cuernavaca, Mexico, along with his life partner, artist Maria Thereza Alves, was not wholly political; it also had to do with his art. He was looking for a more expansive context—a more cosmopolitan environment that valued pluralism and intellectualism. And while he exhibited rarely in Mexico at this time, he would soon begin showing his work actively in Europe, where he would take up topics such as borders and nationality from a different geographic perspective, as well as broad questions related to the ways in which the ideology of Western civilization has affected everything from architecture to religion. Durham has said, "I'm accused, constantly, of making art about my own identity. I never have. I make art about the settler's identity when I make political art. It's not about my identity, it's about the Americans' identity."[45] Identity politics per se was not the politics Durham was after. A politics that could be interpreted only through the specificity of his race—especially when his art was the vehicle for this interpretation—slipped too easily into a reading that positioned him as either the "angry savage" or the "romanticized victim." In his 1993 essay that accompanied an exhibition he curated titled *The Theater of Refusal*, artist Charles Gaines argued that the inability, or unwillingness, of critics to write discursively about the work of artists of color (black artists, in

Fig. 13
The Theater of Refusal: Black Art and Mainstream Criticism, installation view, Fine Arts Gallery, University of California, Irvine, 1993

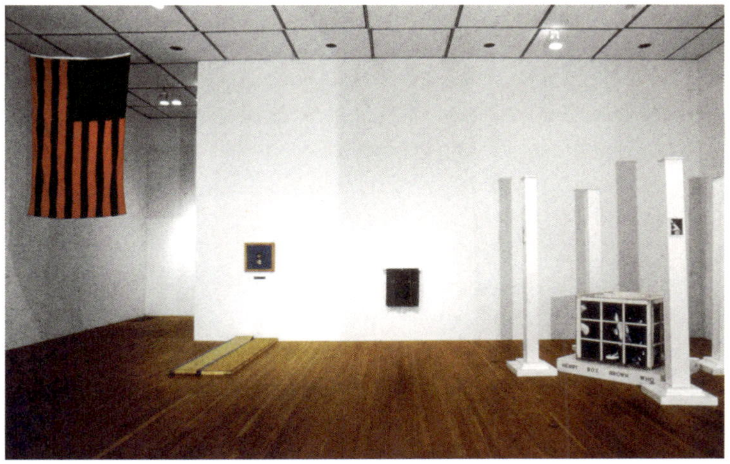

his analysis) added to a reductive and essentializing discourse of marginality, resulting in a majority of these artists being effectively left out of history (fig. 13). Describing the paradox of speaking from one's subject position (a position he sees as essential in the struggle for political power) as a battle of sorts, he wrote, "Marginalization is a sword with two edges: as we use it to attack racism, we wound our villain with each downstroke, but each time we raise the sword for another blow, we wound ourselves."[46] Gaines shares the observations of cultural critic Henry Louis Gates Jr. on the operation of dichotomous structures such as "savage/victim" and our failure to fully address them. For Gates, "In one sense there really is not much difference between negative and positive idealization.... It makes little difference if a black person is represented as a King or god on the one hand or as a devil and a force of evil on the other. Both sets of images serve equally to create an unreality in the life of a black person."[47] Likewise, Durham felt the ever-present dichotomy of savage/victim—or in the more contemporary setting, angry activist/helpless indigent—that informed the readings of his work and yet were often not critically unpacked. Consistent with Gaines's apprehension, Durham both wanted to address the history of marginalization in his work and worried that to do so would, ironically, only serve to encourage some to reinscribe it by trafficking in oversimplified binaries. Durham's move to Europe in 1994 was not so much an act of further remove from his homeland as it was an effort to position himself within an international setting in which he could put forward ideas and participate in the discourse.

Ultimately, the politics to which Durham was, and remains, committed are complex and not easily reduced to supposition or placation. For him, life, art, politics, and activism are utterly entwined. He approaches them simultaneously and at all times with the intention to "attack the machine," as he has described it. He has proclaimed, "It's subversion that I'm after, absolutely. But I don't do art to be subversive. I would want to be the same subversive person no matter what I did.... And it seems to me that's a responsibility we all have because there is this big old thing that is oppressing us. Why would you not work against it?"[48] Importantly, this is what distinguishes art as political statement from the position that all art is by its nature political. Enmeshed in a history of violence and genocide, Durham's work must be understood as an act of resistance.

Unearthing History

In 1977 art historian Douglas Crimp organized the influential *Pictures* exhibition at Artists Space in New York City, one of the first to begin theorizing the work of a young generation engaging in explicit acts of appropriation in order to deconstruct the politics of representation. His essay for the catalogue articulated in great detail what he saw as the most salient characteristics of this form of postmodern artistic production. Recognizing the power that came with wielding control over the production and distribution of images, he wrote, "We are not in search of sources or origins, but of structures of signification: underneath each picture there is always another picture."[49] For Durham, grappling with centuries of historical makeover, a small but meaningful alteration might better describe the archaeology of his particular practice: "underneath each history there is always another history." Since throughout much of history, the recounting of events both monumental and quotidian has been the prerogative of the "captor," the colonizer, the oppressor—indeed, whoever is in power—the layers of history underneath the official record that continue to be in urgent need of unearthing are, as we well know, from the perspectives and in the voices of those oppressed and relegated to the margins. Durham is fully aware that histories are always subjective and incomplete, vulnerable to manipulation. In his own writings, including those integrated into his drawings or adhered to his sculptural forms, he embraces linguistic eccentricities—such as incomplete thoughts, nonlinearity, interruptions, questions about his process, and direct address to the reader—that deflect the mere possibility of a single official narrative. The title of his 1988 essay "A Certain Lack of Coherence" (later adopted as the title of his first anthology of writings) perhaps expresses this elliptical approach best. He is committed to the poetry of prose and the prosaic in poetry, and his writing is marked by a prioritization of wordplay, an impulse toward punning over rhyming, and a favoring of disharmony over familiar cadence. By using these techniques, he enacts an explicit denial of the type of coherence and resolution found in the literature employed by the state, religious institutions, and many historians.

Durham's commitment to incompleteness and to bringing together disparate, sometimes utterly disconnected thoughts is also reflected in his artwork. From early on, he has had a pronounced sensibility for a combinatory methodology in which various materials play off one another so that each specific tactility, surface, color, and shape is mobilized and brought into relief. The simple juxtaposition of small tufts of variously textured hair with piano keys in *Whose Hair Is It?* is playful and amusing, but it also conjures unsettling thoughts about the way such personal, and indeed bodily, materials enter the realm of the museum or the archive. In turn, Durham takes great pleasure in material disguise or misrepresentation, playing with perception through his recognition that wood can look like stone, animal hide can look like paper, and PVC pipe can look like metal. A propensity for drolly undermining the presumed objectivity and usefulness of categorization and classification has long held sway in his practice, enlisted as the primary technique in an array of works: from large installations like *The Museum of Stones* (2011–12; fig. 14), which examines stone's metaphoric and, moreover, its physical relationship to institutions of the state, monumentality, and stability; to sculptures such as *The Dangers of Petrification II* (1998–2007; fig. 15 and pages 170–71) that explore the capacity of materials to stand in for one another, in this case, presenting a variety of found stones that uncannily resemble different foods in precisely organized vitrines; and to beautifully irrational yet modest collaged wall reliefs like *Snake Eyes!* (2006; page 173), which catalogues objects found in the artist's studio by adhering them to a surface and adding humorously misleading captions. Relatively recent large-scale sculptures bring together a remarkable conglomeration of objects into puzzle-like configurations, which can resemble everything from an absurdist machine to an instrument, a storage closet to an abandoned pile of trash. *Something . . . Perhaps a Fugue or an Elegy* (2005; pages 282–83), made for the Venice Biennale that year, contains such unlikely bedfellows as an armadillo shell and a cast-marble head within a twenty-three-foot-long contraption, the front of which bears a sign reading "Start," suggesting a game or a narrative of some sort. The potential frivolousness of the object, however, is quickly belied by the gravity of the things referenced in the title. Viewing the work as a lamentation, the skulls and bones, as well as the variety of discarded objects, take on a melancholy patina, as if the entire apparatus is an homage to the dead and forgotten.

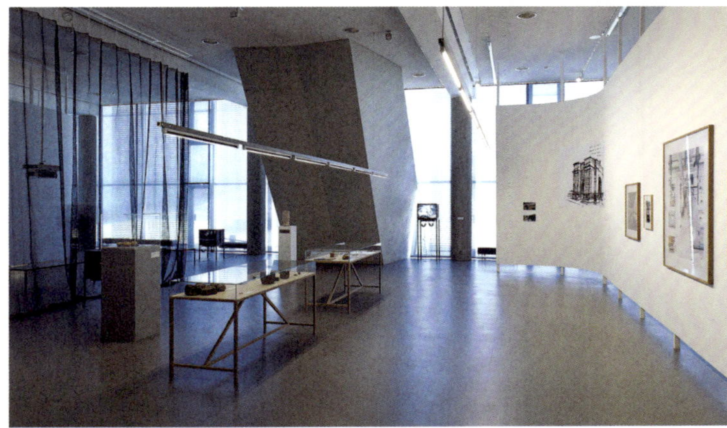

Fig. 14
The Museum of Stones, 2011–12
Installation view, *Animism: Modernity through the Looking Glass*, Haus der Kulturen der Welt, Berlin, 2012

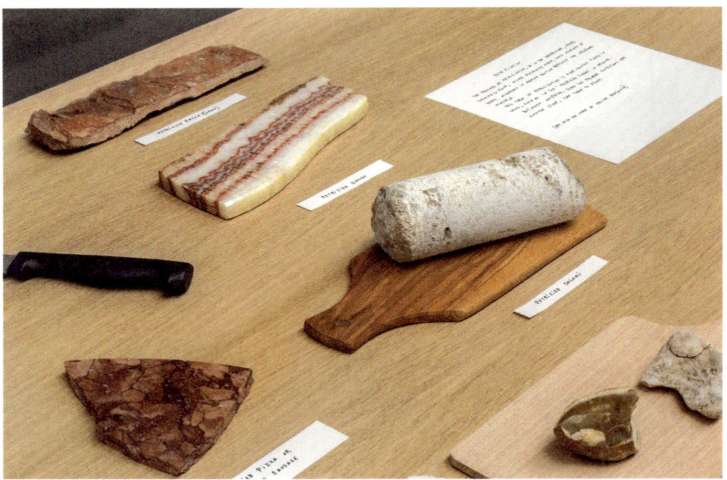

Fig. 15
The Dangers of Petrification II, 1998–2007
(detail; see pages 170–71)

History is storytelling, and Durham's objects have always held enormous narrative potential, not only because of his frequent incorporation of text but also, formally and materially, through acts of assemblage and collage, whereby each individual element reveals the scars of its existence on its surface or holds a latent chronicle of its life waiting to burst forth through the artist's use of juxtaposition. For Durham, history is revealed in material forms and processes. He is astutely aware of the nuanced specificities of his selected materials—their social, geographic, and economic histories—and recognizes that both natural and man-made elements are not merely the sum total of their physical properties but are also discursive forms bound up within social constructions. To use an example put forward by political theorists Ernesto Laclau and Chantal Mouffe, "the fact of . . . a stone depends on a way of classifying objects that is historical and contingent."[50] Durham's consistent use of found objects certainly heightens our awareness of this phenomenon while extending the now well-established Duchampian assertion that context is inextricable from meaning. But Durham's practice is not solely constructed around the use of recycled forms assembled into surprising new configurations; he also embraces the physical transformation of materials through a variety of techniques, from wood and stone carving to casting. Whatever the process of procurement or action taken, his work articulates the historical and contemporary associations implicit in his materials, whether it is a piece of flint valued for its role in weaponry or a piece of a fallen beech tree, felled by nature only many years after it had absorbed into its body the residue of war in the form of flying bullets.

Fig. 16
The Bishop's Moose and the Pinkerton Men, installation view, Exit Art, New York, 1989

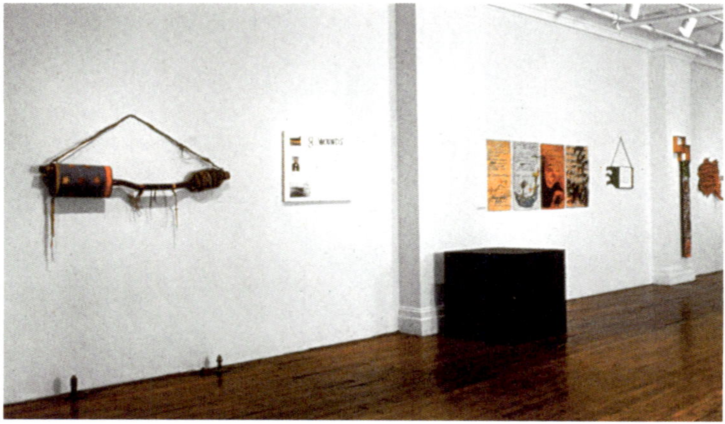

Language, as much as materials, is deployed by Durham with a similar attentiveness and scrupulousness, albeit with the recognition that signs can easily be unmoored from meaning and that, moreover, meaning is constantly shifting. It was in Durham's 1989 solo show at Exit Art, *The Bishop's Moose and the Pinkerton Men*, that he set out deliberately to use text in all aspects of the exhibition, most notably in the objects themselves (fig. 16). In a letter written from Cuernavaca to Jeanette Ingberman, Exit Art cofounder and curator of the show, Durham described his conceptual framework for the exhibition, noting that he planned to use text throughout to deflect a "master narrative" through a "confused combination of metaphor and metonymy," a "word-piece" for the title, and a multilinearity rooted in "footnotes" and "parenthesis."[51] The relationship between narrative and history was activated throughout the exhibition, with works relating to the long reach of the Catholic Church; the troubling entanglement of money, power, and art; and the well-established relationship between natural resources and ethnocide. Palestinian literary critic Edward Said, whose highly influential 1978 book *Orientalism* is foundational to postcolonial studies, has written that "nationalism, resurgent or new, fastens on narratives for structuring, assimilating, or excluding one or another version of history."[52] Durham offers an alternative: a quixotic, absurd, and transparently nonobjective version of history that is nonetheless deadly serious, containing more fact than one would care to admit, and revealing our shared complicity in how the past has shaped our present realities.

Durham has long employed language in all its forms in his art. This could be a short caption adhered to the work that also serves as a descriptive title, as in,

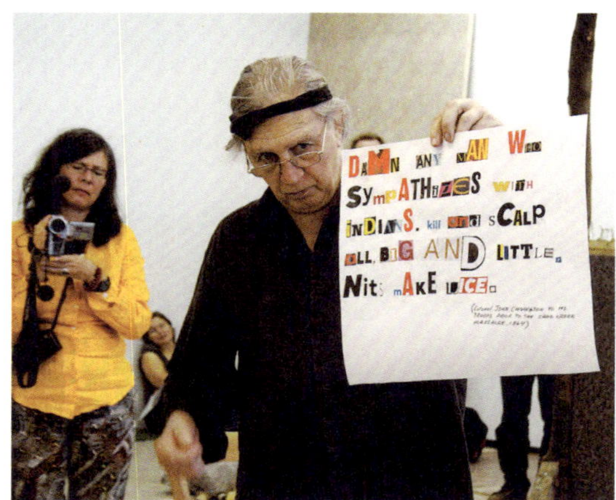

Fig. 17
Durham and Maria Thereza Alves during the public installation of *Building a Nation*, Matt's Gallery, London, 2006

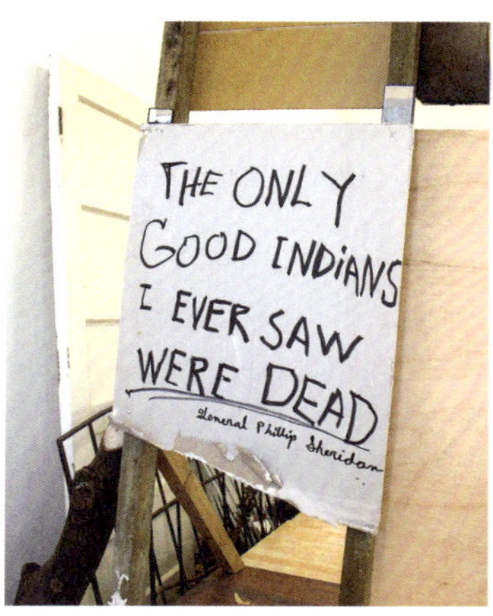

Fig. 18
Building a Nation (detail), installation view, Matt's Gallery, London, 2006

for example, *An Electron Beam Generater* (1989; page 87), in which the misspellings in the title and hand-painted label indicate the absurdity and humor of Durham's version of this sophisticated object. The text might also call attention to some material aspect of the work, as in *Untitled (It's Got Mr. Durham's Teeth)* (1992; page 121), or be more obliquely poetic or contemplative, like *I Forgot What I Was Going to Say* (1992; page 128). In other cases, the texts function as descriptions that outline a particular preoccupation Durham is trying to visualize, as in *Science I* and *Science II* (both 1990; pages 166, 167), which respectively diagram a quark coming into being and observe that atomic particles make up the universe, and *Anti Flag* (1992; page 72), one of the first works in which Durham articulates his fascination with the center of the world, immediately calling attention to the irrationality of this notion by identifying three different locations as the center. Elsewhere, lengthy descriptive texts tell intricate stories or tend to confuse more than elucidate, as in *A Mushroom from the Grunewald Forest* (2006; page 235), whose tone changes from a tale of finding and attempting to identify the eponymous fungus into a rather personal dialogue aimed directly at the viewer. He both writes texts and borrows them, appropriating the words of authors he admires such as José Saramago, or quoting from literary sources as diverse as Victor Hugo, Leo Tolstoy, and the Bible. In his ambitious 2006 installation *Building a Nation*, presented at Matt's Gallery in London, Durham attached to various surfaces statements made by such well-known and historically lauded figures as George Washington, Benjamin Franklin, and Theodore Roosevelt that reveal a vitriolic and hateful disregard for American Indians' lives (figs. 17, 18). These include Roosevelt's declaration from 1886, "I don't go as far as to think that 'the only good Indians are dead Indians,' but I believe nine out of ten are, and I shouldn't like to inquire too closely into the case of the tenth," and children's book author L. Frank Baum's brazenly unapologetic assertion, "The Whites, by law of conquest, by justice of civilization, are master of the American continent, and the best safety of the frontier settlements will be secured by the total annihilation of the remaining Indians. Why not annihilation?"

While Durham recognizes the fractured nature of history, he is simultaneously devoted to historical fact and to participating in remedial efforts to right past wrongs in the narrativizing of events and figures and to make visible that which has largely been obliterated from shared historical memory. He has written:

> I want all of our history. I need every name, every artefact, every effort. I need to know the minute specific of our history because I need to be part of it. But I am part of it, and could not choose otherwise, the way a Jew is part of the Holocaust. In the Cherokee language the word for the world and the word for history are

> the same. Our history is, however, too closely tied to yours for the past three hundred and fifty years. It has become strange, untenable, unbearable and, in unbearable ways, untrue. Our history has become lies within your history. The lies have caused me great suffering from the day I was born, but at least I may (must) react to that suffering.[53]

Durham's art embodies a tension between his alignment with the postmodernist stance that rejects modernism's primacy of narratives of individual artistic genius, whose contributions are revered for their so-called universalism, and his desire to break free of contexts in which his work is evaluated and understood principally as that of the Other and to rid himself of the mandate sometimes thrust upon him to "represent" his group. He worried that postmodernist theorizing in the New York art world during the time he lived there, which purported to work on behalf of expanding the field, was inadvertently making it more narrow. In response to this limitation, Durham has often expressed a desire that his work be "universal." But we must distinguish his use of this term from that deployed in the discourse of Western art and philosophy since the Enlightenment, or in the reductive modality of American modernism in the mid-twentieth century as espoused by critic Clement Greenberg. Like postcolonial and poststructural theorists,[54] Durham has been arguing for a universalism that is not "trapped in the European body," as Araeen describes efforts toward a more inclusive modernity.[55] For Durham, universalism is an idealized space in which categories and imposed limitations are removed, where the contemplation and interpretation of an artwork can carry the kind of nuance that stems from a recognition of—indeed an advocacy for—complexity and the multiplicity of influences and experiences that impact any work of art. Recognizing this conundrum, Durham asserts that "an artist must, of course, look to be universal, without the limits of labels, yet it is easier to do that if you are white."[56] Yet he goes on to explain that he thinks of his viewers as *individuals* capable of interacting with the work critically, an acknowledgment that there is of course no universal, monolithic audience or public, and certainly no convenient one-dimensional understanding of any given artwork.

Conclusion: "Authentically" Post-American

It is tempting to divide Durham's life into neat chapters—the American years, the Mexican years, and the European years; his work as an activist and his work as an artist—and indeed his life and work are often written about or exhibited with these distinctions in mind. And while all of our lives have periods or episodes we could demarcate, and certainly there are particular ideas or approaches that have shifted or come to the fore over time that Durham himself has articulated, the problem with creating these historically convenient categories is that they inevitably set up an oversimplified comparison, even an opposition, establishing the very boundaries and borders that Durham has worked a lifetime to undermine. He has a disdain for categorization, perhaps in part because he has so often been put into categories that spoke louder than he could, enforcing ideas about who he was before he could even enter into the conversation.

Durham is unquestionably many things in addition to being an American, or an American Indian, artist—certainly too many to touch upon meaningfully in this essay. Yet, in evaluating the full scope of his work, as the present exhibition aims to do, one faces the (hopefully productive) dilemma of how to reconcile placing his practice specifically within the context of the history of American art—to see his work as inextricable from his background not just as an American but, perhaps more important, as an American Indian—with the fact that his work is *so* much more. I am far more inclined to think of Durham's work as cosmopolitan, and of him as resolutely international, a born wanderer, a self-taught historian, and an undeniably social animal, never allowing his boots to dry before heading down the nearest road. But what does it mean, then, to claim Durham as an American artist? Why is it important to view his work, at least in part, from this perspective even if such an attempt risks being reductive and absurd? Durham has railed for years against the various categories we've constructed to organize and understand our world for their failure to honor the ways in which complexity, nuance, and confusion are not only facets of reality but *necessities*. In essence, we are all limited by the types of categories to which we are relegated. And yet, there can be political power in coalition building and acts of collectivity, and moreover, there are often meaningful insights to be gleaned from the intellectual or academic exercise of evaluating a practice within a specific context, movement, or historical group.

Fig. 19
Phantom Sightings: Art after the Chicano Movement, installation view, Los Angeles County Museum of Art, 2008

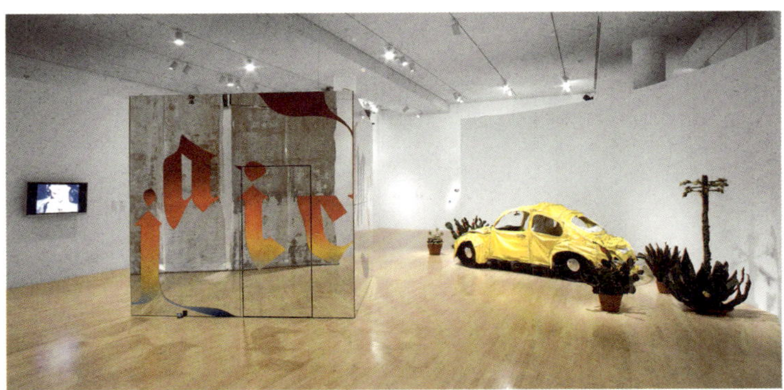

Over the past several years, the prefix *post-* has been placed in front of many identificatory terms within the context of exhibition practice and cultural theory: post-black, post-feminist, post-Indian. As art historians Jessica L. Horton and Cherise Smith have proposed, surely this impulse is not intended to suggest that, as a nation, we have eradicated discrimination.[57] Obviously, simply following current events in the news makes it clear that we are still very far from this goal. Reasons for wanting to articulate a moment in which our cultural and political relationship to identity has shifted are varied. Curators of exhibitions who have explored this position of "post-ness" have argued that notions of identity have become more fluid; that we now recognize and must examine the heterogeneity within any such categorization; that we must reject the false categories that have for so long been used to subjugate people; or that for many artists their individual identity is more important than a collective one (fig. 19). Many of these efforts have intended to create a distinction between the present needs and desires of artists of color or women artists and the multiculturalism and identity politics of the 1980s and 1990s. Anishinaabe author and curator Gerald Vizenor first devised the term "post-Indian" as a rejection of the term "Indian," which he considers to be a falsehood created by the colonizer.[58] Art historian Mark Watson, in his discussion of Durham's *Building a Nation* (figs. 17, 18, 20), takes this notion even further by articulating that "post-Indian" as a denunciation of "Indianness" is inseparable from colonial violence, and yet it is a term with the potential to move beyond the context of America to a transnational or international one. He writes that a post-Indian artwork like *Building a Nation* "explores possibilities for framing histories and relationships outside the largely United States–centered

'Indian' paradigm."[59] He points out, rightly, that the subject of Durham's work is not his identity as an Indian but rather the violence of American colonialism and imperialism, as Durham himself repeatedly has said. Nonetheless, the risk of attaching "post" to these terms is that it is too easy to misconstrue it to suggest that we are living in a period that is *beyond* racism, classism, sexism, and various other forms of discrimination. This is why we may bristle when we hear these terms. Beyond thinking of Durham, the *figure*, as "post-Indian" per se, I find it more useful to think of his *practice* as "post-American."

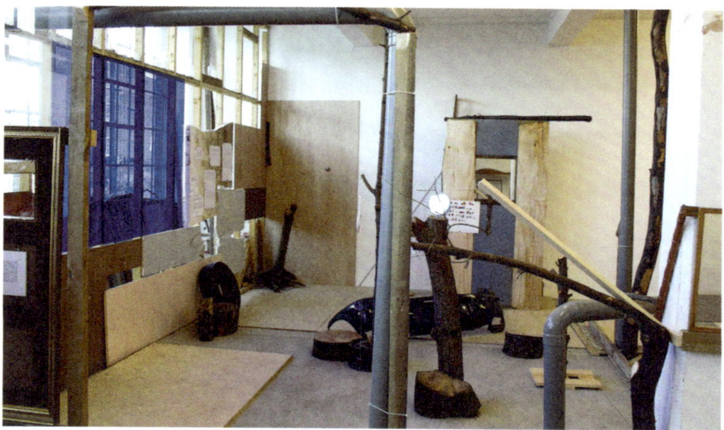

Fig. 20
Building a Nation, installation view, Matt's Gallery, London, 2006

So, with my apologies to Mr. Durham, allow me to pose this question about his position within American art, and why the moniker of "American artist," for him specifically, carries particular weight. Does my earlier claim that Durham is post-American mean he is by default *not* (or no longer) an American artist? I would argue it does not, because one cannot extricate the thing itself from a new imagination of what it could be. Does it suggest that he is anti-American? To equate post-American with *anti*-American is an oversimplification of a dangerous kind, for it employs the type of rhetoric intended to promote hostility and erases the ability to examine how meaningful a post-American stance might be. A post-American figure such as Durham, in my assessment, is highly attuned to and deeply embedded in the history of America, affected by it in profound ways. It is someone who actively seeks to reconstruct his relationship to his country of origin, and in doing so argues persuasively for and works diligently toward the ways in which America should, and must, change, acknowledging that to shape the future, we must first honestly deal with our past. Moreover, a post-American is one who recognizes how the establishment of nation-states and borders has wrought enormous violence and oppression. This does not occur only in the United States, of course; yet we are a nation formed by the intended, and nearly successful, eradication of a people (of, in fact, many nations of distinct groups). As Durham has put it, "The world has pretty much accepted the United States' myths about itself . . . it was the first permanent colony to establish itself *against* and through the denial of local inhabitants."[60] More than being skeptical about national borders (and the near hysterical rhetoric around protecting them we are witnessing in our increasingly divided politics), Durham rejects America as an *ideology* in order to honestly address how its history impacts its actual identity today. While "post" suggests the end of something, it also importantly portends a wholly new mode of being in the world. It is like a call to action, an insistence that we must not give up on the possibility of justice and humanity, and these are the endeavors that lie at the heart of Durham's life and work.

Notes

1. This is the title of a performance Durham did at La MaMa Theater in New York on March 29, 1987.

2. See Michel Foucault, *The Archaeology of Knowledge* (London: Tavistock, 1972).

3. This is evidenced by incidents probably too numerous to count in which, for example, Europeans ask him if he is a "real Indian," as if under the impression that American Indians are extinct; or when someone asked him if his poetry was "real" or "just his," because certainly a Cherokee wouldn't know how to write this most exalted of literary forms. Durham has recounted experiences like these on several occasions to the author.

4. Jimmie Durham in "Various Elements," interview with Kirsty Bell, *Frieze*, no. 150 (October 2012): 185–86.

5. "The 'Nervous State': A Conversation between Jimmie Durham and Mick Taussig," *Performance Paradigm* 6 (June 2010): 7.

6. The full quote is, "When you make things, the result is always a kind of self-portrait, so art ends up telling you whatever politics you have." In "500 Words," as told to Allese Thomson, *Artforum*, July 9, 2015.

7. See Gloria Anzaldúa, *Borderlands/La Frontera: The New Mestiza* (1987; 4th ed., San Francisco: Aunt Lute Books, 2012). Anzaldúa's critically acclaimed semi-autobiographical book, which explores the loneliness of living in the borders between cultures and genders, introduced the concept of the "new mestizo," a state of being that refuses to adhere to these binaries.

8. Jimmie Durham, "Savage Attacks on White Women, As Usual," in *A Certain Lack of Coherence: Writings on Art and Cultural Politics*, ed. Jean Fisher (London: Kala Press, 1993), 124.

9. Durham began exhibiting in New York in 1982 and was in numerous group shows throughout the 1980s and early 1990s in such venues as the Henry Street Settlement, Kenkeleba Gallery, Judson Memorial Church, Artists Space, New Museum of Contemporary Art, Exit Art, and Longwood Arts Center in the Bronx. He also had several New York solo shows in the 1980s, including those at 22 Wooster, the Alternative Museum, Franklin Furnace, and Exit Art, among others. He cocurated two exhibitions with Jean Fisher: *Ni' Go Tlunh a Doh Ka (We are always turning around on purpose)* at Amelie A. Wallace Gallery, SUNY Old Westbury, New York, in 1986, and *We the People* at Artists Space in 1987, both of which included his work alongside that of other American Indian artists and for which he wrote texts. When asked why he would curate exhibitions of all Native artists, given his concern for the ways these methodologies can continue to marginalize artists of color, Durham stated that he and Fisher discussed this at length and felt that considering the total lack of visibility for these artists, they must begin by creating some level of recognition for them. Jimmie Durham, conversation with the author, April 2016. See also Durham's text "This Is an Eviction Plan (New York in the 1980s)" on pages 263–65 in the present volume.

10. One example is the American Indian Community House, founded in New York in 1969, whose mission is to promote cultural activity as well as to provide social services to support well-being.

11. Most mainstream institutions were slow to take artists of color and women artists seriously, unless, of course, they had been founded to address the lack of opportunity by focusing solely on a particular group. The Studio Museum in Harlem, for example, was founded in 1968, El Museo del Barrio in 1971, and the National Museum of the American Indian in Washington, DC, in 2004 (the latter, which had an outpost in Manhattan for some years prior, is devoted largely to the acquisition, preservation, and presentation of artifacts with relatively little programming of contemporary living artists). A.I.R. Gallery (Artists in Residence, Inc.) was established in 1972 in SoHo as the first artist-run nonprofit gallery for women artists in the United States. And there are numerous other examples.

12. See Rasheed Araeen, "A New Beginning: Beyond Postcolonial Cultural Theory and Identity Politics," in *Third Text* 14, no. 50 (Spring 2000): 3–20. For a discussion of how some of these same issues apply to notions of globalism and internationalism, see Mónica Amor, Okwui Enwezor, Gao Minglu, Oscar Ho, Kobena Mercer, and Irit Rogoff, "Liminalities: Discussions on the Global and the Local," in *Art Journal* 57, no. 4 (Winter 1998): 28–49, especially Mónica Amor's "Whose World? A Note on the Paradoxes of Global Aesthetics"; and Kobena Mercer, ed., "Introduction," in *Cosmopolitan Modernisms* (Cambridge, MA: MIT Press; London: Institute of International Visual Arts, 2005), 6–23. For a critique of multiculturalism and using race as a lens for interpretation, see Paul Gilroy, *Against Race: Imagining Political Culture beyond the Color Line* (Cambridge, MA: Belknap Press of Harvard University Press, 2002), and Darby English, *How to See a Work of Art in Total Darkness* (Cambridge, MA: MIT Press, 2007).

13. Notable examples include Jean-Hubert Martin's *Magiciens de la Terre* (1989) at the Centre Pompidou, Paris, touted as the first truly international exhibition; *The Decade Show: Frameworks of Identity in the 1980s* (1990), a collaborative effort organized by the Museum of Contemporary Hispanic Art, the New Museum of Contemporary Art, and the Studio Museum in Harlem; and the 1993 Whitney Biennial.

14. See, for example, Peter Plagens's sarcastic and dismissive "Fade from White," *Newsweek*, March 14, 1993, in which he claims audiences will be turned off by "the lashes of guilt the show dishes out"; http://www.newsweek.com/fade-white-191204. In the *New York Times*, Roberta Smith called the exhibition "a pious, often arid show that frequently substitutes didactic moralizing for genuine visual communication," even as she acknowledged it was a "watershed" in what is ultimately a mixed review. Roberta Smith, "At the Whitney: A Biennial with a Social Conscience," *New York Times*, March 5, 1993, http://www.nytimes.com/1993/03/05/arts/at-the-whitney-a-biennial-with-a-social-conscience.html. Christopher Knight of the *Los Angeles Times* was particularly vehement in his assessment, calling the work in the Biennial "awful," "solipsistic," and "gruesome," among numerous other denigrations. Christopher Knight, "Crushed by Its Good Intentions," *Los Angeles Times*, March 10, 1993, http://articles.latimes.com/1993-03-10/entertainment/ca-1335_1_art-world.

15. Jimmie Durham in "Conversation between Jimmie Durham and Jeanette Ingberman," in *Jimmie Durham: The Bishop's Moose and the Pinkerton Men* (New York: Exit Art, 1990), 32.

16. Jimmie Durham, "A Central Margin," in *The Decade Show: Frameworks of Identity in the 1980s* (New York: Museum of Contemporary Hispanic Art, 1990), 169.

17. Jennifer A. González, *Subject to Display: Reframing Race in Contemporary Installation Art* (Cambridge, MA: MIT Press, 2008), 31. This quote is from her chapter on James Luna, a Native artist whose work *The Artifact Piece* (1987–90) is often considered to have affinities with Durham's *On Loan from the Museum of the American Indian* (1985) for its structure as a quasi-museological display, which she describes as "an ambiguous autofiction, a bicultural autotopography, and a critical autoethnography" (p. 41).

18. At that time, and sadly perhaps even more so today, most professionals in the international contemporary art world (there are many art worlds, of course, but by this I mean the art world generally associated with the ecology of contemporary art museums, as well as contemporary art galleries and fairs internationally) could probably name only a handful of American Indian artists. More than any social group defined by race, gender, or sexuality, American Indian artists remain shamefully invisible within this context. With so few voices participating in the conversation, Durham's absence from American critical debate over the past two decades is a palpable loss.

19. See Gregory Battock, *Minimal Art: A Critical Anthology* (New York: Dutton, 1968).

20. Genuinely interested in physics and other sciences, as is evident in a number of works over time, Durham uses this well-known scientific principle to bring content back into the reductive forms of minimalism, cleverly taking on the tendency to fetishize its objects in the process.

21. For further discussion of this issue, see Hal Foster, "The Artist as Ethnographer," in *The Return of the Real: The Avant-Garde at the End of the Century* (Cambridge, MA: MIT Press, 1996), 170–203.

22. This is the title of one of Durham's "give-away" performances at the Whitney Museum's downtown branch in 1990. Inspired by the Cherokee custom in which the person being honored or celebrated gives gifts to her guests, in these performances Durham would make several small objects and hand them out to audience members.

23. Jimmie Durham in conversation with the author, December 2015, Naples, Italy.

24. Run by Corrine Jennings and the painter Joe Overstreet, the gallery's mission is to provide opportunities for artists excluded from the mainstream, primarily artists of color. Durham was in several exhibitions there in the 1980s. *Ritual and Rhythm* also included the work of Willie Burch, Papo Colo, David Hammons, Ana Mendieta, and Faith Ringgold, among others.
25. The two best-known pieces on Durham by Lippard are "Jimmie Durham: Postmodernist 'Savage,'" in *Art in America* 81, no. 2 (February 1993): 62, and her essay "Little Red Lies," in Durham's *The Bishop's Moose and the Pinkerton Men*, 22–29.
26. See, for example, Jimmie Durham, "Creativity and the Social Process," in *A Certain Lack of Coherence*, 69–73. Written in June 1983.
27. Jimmie Durham, "Second Thoughts," in *Jimmie Durham*, ed. Anna Daneri, Giacinto Di Pietrantonio, and Roberto Pinto (Milan: Edizione Charta; Como: Fondazione Antonio Ratti, 2004), 24.
28. In 1987 Durham wrote the text "Savage Attacks on White Women, As Usual" to accompany the exhibition *We the People*, which he cocurated with Jean Fisher. In the early 1990s, he did a number of performances that explored the mythology of the "savage" Indian.
29. Araeen, "A New Beginning," 6. For further reading on this exhibition, see Hal Foster, "The 'Primitive' Unconscious of Modern Art, or White Skins, Black Masks," in *Recodings: Art, Spectacle, Cultural Politics* (Port Townsend, WA: Bay Press, 1985), 181–210.
30. Mercer, "Introduction," 13.
31. While the complete installation no longer exists, there are individual elements that were kept by the artist, given or sold to individuals, or incorporated into later works, some of which are featured in the current exhibition.
32. Jean Fisher, "In Search of the 'Inauthentic': Disturbing Signs in Contemporary Native Art," *Art Journal* 51, no. 3 (Autumn 1992): 47.
33. Of this museum's name, Durham has said, "It's such a funny title, as though there was one American Indian. . . . The Museum of the African, they wouldn't say that; The Museum of the Jew, they wouldn't say. . . . They wouldn't say it about someone else, this seems so funny to me." "Interview with Rudi Laermans," *A Prior*, no. 9 (2004): 156–84.
34. This opinion by Luna is described in Paul Chaat Smith, "Luna *remembers*," 2005, http://www.paulchaatsmith.com/luna-remembers.html.
35. Miwon Kwon, "Postmortem Strategies," *Documents* 1, no. 3 (1993): 124.
36. "Jimmie Durham: Interviewed by Susan Canning," in *Interventions and Provocations: Conversations on Art, Culture, and Resistance*, ed. Glenn Harper (Albany: State University of New York Press, 1998), 49.
37. The description of Disney's 1995 animated film on the IMDb website reads, unironically, "An English soldier and the daughter of an Algonquin chief share a romance when English colonists invade seventeenth-century Virginia."
38. Published in *Pour une nouvelle géographie artistique des années 90*, ed. Virginia Garreta (Bordeaux: CAPC Musée d'Art Contemporain de Bordeaux, 2002), 119–29.
39. For further discussion, see Amy Lonetree, *Decolonizing Museums: Representing Native America in National and Tribal Museums* (Chapel Hill: University of North Carolina Press, 2012).
40. Jimmie Durham, untitled statement in *Land, Spirit, Power: First Nations at the National Gallery of Canada*, ed. Diana Nemiroff, Robert Houle, and Charlotte Townsend-Gault (Ottawa: National Gallery of Canada, 1992), 145.
41. Jimmie Durham, "Disparate Parts Tenuously Connected Only by My Desire," in *Durham: The Center of the World* (Middelburg: De Vleeshal, 1995), unpaginated.
42. Jimmie Durham and Paul Smith, "An Open Letter on Recent Developments in the American Indian Movement/International Indian Treaty Council," in *A Certain Lack of Coherence*, 46–56.
43. Jimmie Durham, "A Friend of Mine Said That Art Is a European Invention," in *Global Visions: Towards a New Internationalism in the Visual Arts*, ed. Jean Fisher (London: Kala Press, 1994), 115. (The collected papers of the INIVA symposium "A New Internationalism" held at the Tate Gallery, London, in April 1994.)
44. Araeen, "A New Beginning," 9.
45. "Before the Law: Jimmie Durham in conversation with Kasper König," Wiels, Brussels, September 16, 2011, https://www.youtube.com/watch?v=alxRBQ8lzj8&feature=youtu.be.
46. Charles Gaines, "The Theater of Refusal: Black Art and Mainstream Criticism," in *The Theater of Refusal: Black Art and Mainstream Criticism*, ed. Catherine Lord (Irvine: Fine Arts Gallery, University of California, Irvine, 1993), 17.
47. Henry Louis Gates Jr., quoted in ibid., 19. Originally from Maurice Berger, "Speaking Out: Some Distance to Go . . . ," *Art in America* 78, no. 9 (September 1990): 81.
48. "Jimmie Durham: Interviewed by Susan Canning," 42.
49. Douglas Crimp, "Pictures," *October* 8 (Spring 1979): 87. Original version published in 1977 as a brochure for the exhibition.
50. Ernesto Laclau and Chantal Mouffe, "Post-Marxism without Apologies," in *New Reflections on the Revolution of Our Time* (London: Verso, 1990), 103.
51. Jimmie Durham to Jeanette Ingberman, May 20, 1989. Exit Art Archive, MSS 343, Series 1, box 21, folder 21, Fales Library and Special Collections, New York University Libraries.
52. Edward W. Said, "Representing the Colonized: Anthropology's Interlocutors," *Critical Inquiry* 15, no. 2 (Winter 1989): 221.
53. Jimmie Durham, "A Certain Lack of Coherence," in *A Certain Lack of Coherence*, 143.
54. See Edward W. Said, *Orientalism* (New York: Pantheon Books, 1978); Homi Bhabha, "The Other Question: The Stereotype and Colonial Discourse," in *Twentieth-Century Literary Theory: A Reader*, ed. K. M. Newton (London: Macmillan Education, 1997), 293–301; Gayatri Chakravorty Spivak, *In Other Worlds: Essays in Cultural Politics* (New York: Methuen, 1987); and Henry Louis Gates Jr., ed., "'Race,' Writing and Difference," special issue, *Critical Inquiry* 12, no. 1 (Autumn 1985).
55. Araeen, "A New Beginning," 5.
56. Durham, untitled essay in *Land, Spirit, Power*, 143.
57. Jessica L. Horton and Cherise Smith, "Commentaries: The Particulars of Postidentity," *American Art: Smithsonian American Art Museum* 28, no. 1 (Spring 2014): 2–8. In their introduction to this issue of the journal, Horton and Smith look at three exhibitions that argued for various "post-identity" positions: *Freestyle* (2001), at the Studio Museum in Harlem, curated by Thelma Golden and Glenn Ligon; *Remix: New Modernities in a Post-Indian World* (2007), at the National Museum of the American Indian, Washington, DC, and the Heard Museum, Phoenix, curated by Joe Baker and Gerald McMaster; and *Phantom Sightings: Art after the Chicano Movement* (2008), at the Los Angeles County Museum of Art, curated by Howard Fox, Rita Gonzalez, and Chon Noriega.
58. See Gerald Vizenor, *Manifest Manners: Narratives on Postindian Survivance* (Lincoln: University of Nebraska Press, 1999).
59. Mark Watson, "Jimmie Durham's *Building a Nation*: Across Post-Indian, Post-American Modernities," *American Art: Smithsonian American Art Museum* 28, no. 1 (Spring 2014): 18.
60. Jimmie Durham, "A Central Margin," in *The Decade Show*, 163. He continues, "We might all 'know' that the United States was founded upon the invasion and genocide of other nations, nations comprising millions of people who were slaughtered officially. I want to consider that phenomenon not as a moral issue, nor to plead a case, but as an integral yet invisible (dangerously invisible) part of a power-producing apparatus not separated from the overall cultural machinery; it is the center of the machinery . . . we must see that the invasion and the denial of the invasion are the cultural and political foundations of the United States."

Statute I.

May 28, 1830.

Chap. CXLVIII.—*An Act to provide for an exchange of lands with the Indians residing in any of the states or territories, and for their removal west of the river Mississippi.*

Districts to be laid off.

Be it enacted by the Senate and House of Representatives of the United States of America, in Congress assembled, That it shall and may be lawful for the President of the United States to cause so much of any territory belonging to the United States, west of the river Mississippi, not included in any state or organized territory, and to which the Indian title has been extinguished, as he may judge necessary, to be divided

into a suitable number of districts, for the reception of such tribes or nations of Indians as may choose to exchange the lands where they now reside, and remove there; and to cause each of said districts to be so described by natural or artificial marks, as to be easily distinguished from every other.

President to exchange, &c.

Sec. 2. *And be it further enacted,* That it shall and may be lawful for the President to exchange any or all of such districts, so to be laid off and described, with any tribe or nation of Indians now residing within the limits of any of the states or territories, and with which the United States have existing treaties, for the whole or any part or portion of the territory claimed and occupied by such tribe or nation, within the bounds of any one or more of the states or territories, where the land claimed and occupied by the Indians, is owned by the United States, or the United States are bound to the state within which it lies to extinguish the Indian claim thereto.

Title secured to Indians.

Sec. 3. *And be it further enacted,* That in the making of any such exchange or exchanges, it shall and may be lawful for the President solemnly to assure the tribe or nation with which the exchange is made, that the United States will forever secure and guaranty to them, and their heirs or successors, the country so exchanged with them; and if they prefer it, that the United States will cause a patent or grant to be made and executed to them for the same: *Provided always,* That such lands shall revert to the United States, if the Indians become extinct, or abandon the same.

Proviso.

Improvements to be appraised, and paid for.

Sec. 4. *And be it further enacted,* That if, upon any of the lands now occupied by the Indians, and to be exchanged for, there should be such improvements as add value to the land claimed by any individual or individuals of such tribes or nations, it shall and may be lawful for the President to cause such value to be ascertained by appraisement or otherwise, and to cause such ascertained value to be paid to the person or persons rightfully claiming such improvements. And upon the payment of such valuation, the improvements so valued and paid for, shall pass to the United States, and possession shall not afterwards be permitted to any of the same tribe.

Aid in moving, &c.

Sec. 5. *And be it further enacted,* That upon the making of any such exchange as is contemplated by this act, it shall and may be lawful for the President to cause such aid and assistance to be furnished to the emigrants as may be necessary and proper to enable them to remove to, and settle in, the country for which they may have exchanged; and also, to give them such aid and assistance as may be necessary for their support and subsistence for the first year after their removal.

Protection.

Sec. 6. *And be it further enacted,* That it shall and may be lawful for the President to cause such tribe or nation to be protected, at their new residence, against all interruption or disturbance from any other tribe or nation of Indians, or from any other person or persons whatever.

Sec. 7. *And be it further enacted,* That it shall and may be lawful for the President to have the same superintendence and care over any tribe or nation in the country to which they may remove, as contemplated by this act, that he is now authorized to have over them at their present places of residence: *Provided,* That nothing in this act contained shall be construed as authorizing or directing the violation of any existing treaty between the United States and any of the Indian tribes.

500,000 dollars appropriated.

Sec. 8. *And be it further enacted,* That for the purpose of giving effect to the provisions of this act, the sum of five hundred thousand dollars is hereby appropriated, to be paid out of any money in the treasury, not otherwise appropriated.

Approved, May 28, 1830.

 President Andrew Jackson's Indian Removal Act of May 28, 1830, Chapter 148, Statute 1, United States Statutes at Large, National Archives.

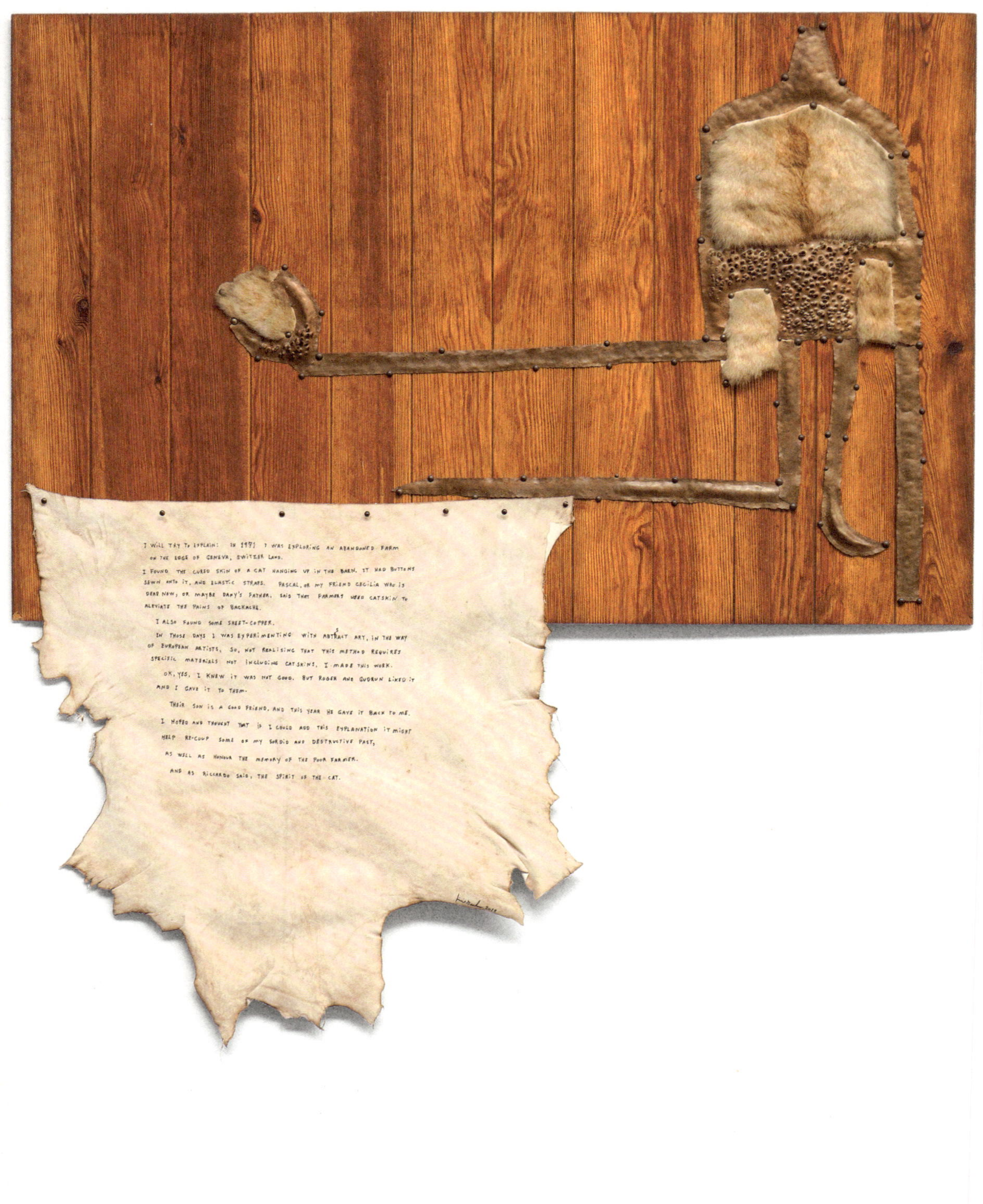

I will try to explain, 1970–2012. Plywood with redwood veneer, copper, Swiss cat fur and leather, goatskin with ink.
Two parts, wood board: 31 ¼ × 48 × 1 in. (79.4 × 122 × 2.5 cm); leather: 28 ¼ × 27 ¼ in. (71.8 × 69.2 cm); 53 ⅛ × 48 × 1 in. (135 × 122 × 2.5 cm) overall.

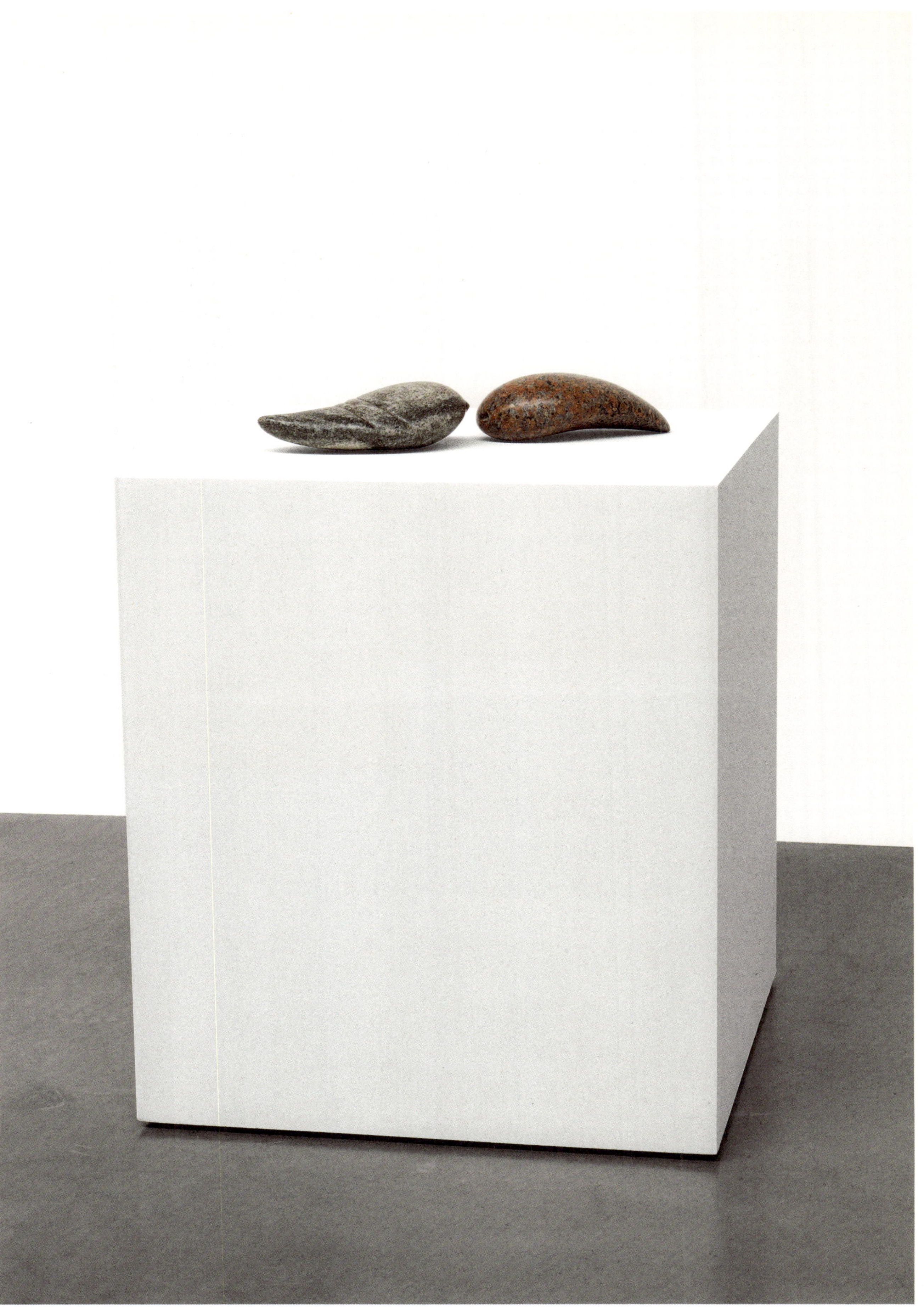

Red Granite and Grey Cristalina Granite, 1971. Red and gray granite. Two parts, 3 ½ × 10 × 5 ⅛ in. (9 × 25.5 × 13 cm); 3 ⅛ × 9 ⅞ × 6 in. (8 × 25 × 15 cm).

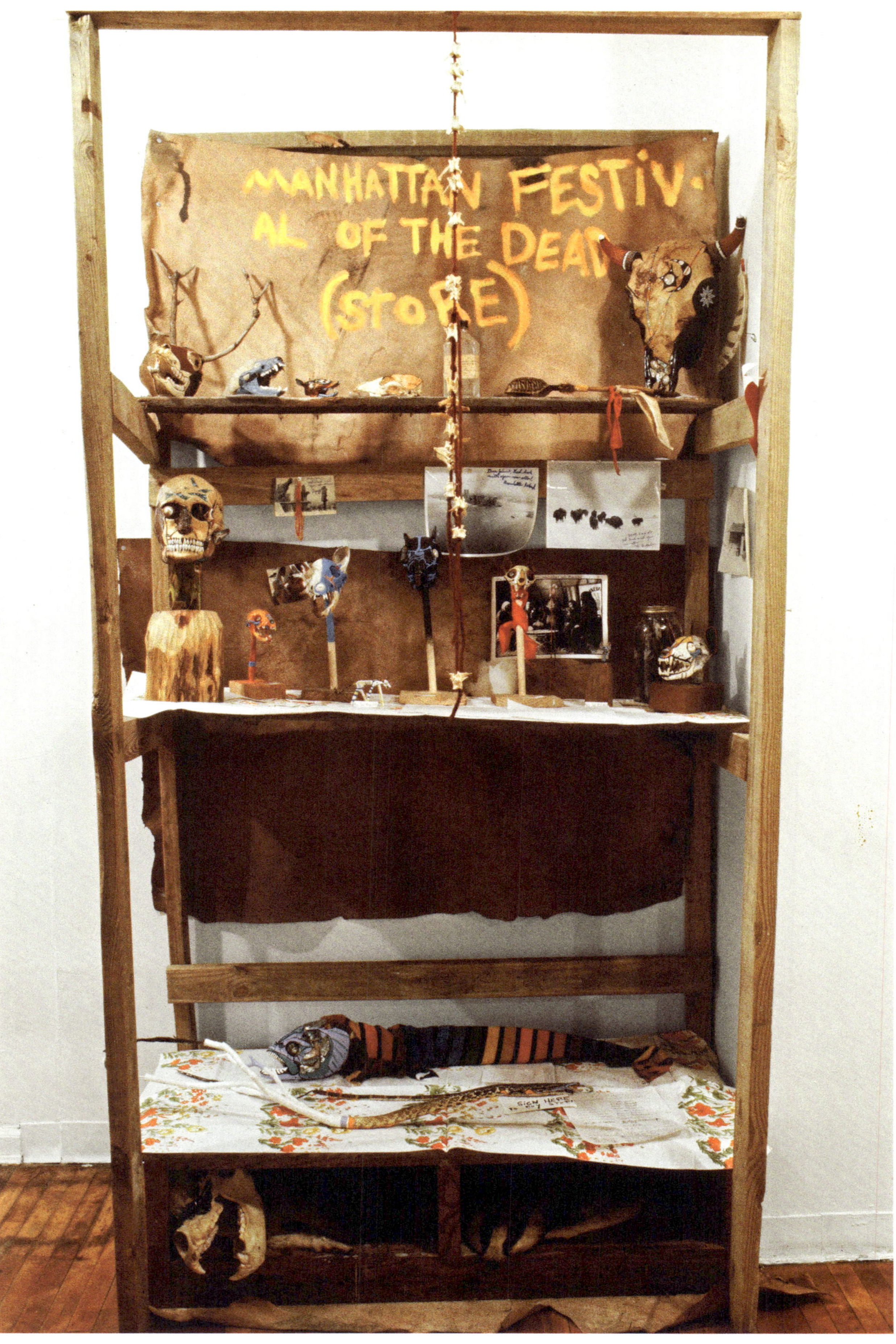

Manhattan Festival of the Dead, 1982, installation view, Kenkeleba Gallery, New York. The complete work is no longer extant; included in the exhibition are: *Karankawa*, 1982 (see opposite and page 80), and Untitled, 1982 (shown above, top right corner). Baby buffalo skull, beads, goat leather, hawk feather, shells, acrylic paint. 16 ½ × 13 ¼ × 7 in. (41.9 × 33.7 × 17.8 cm).

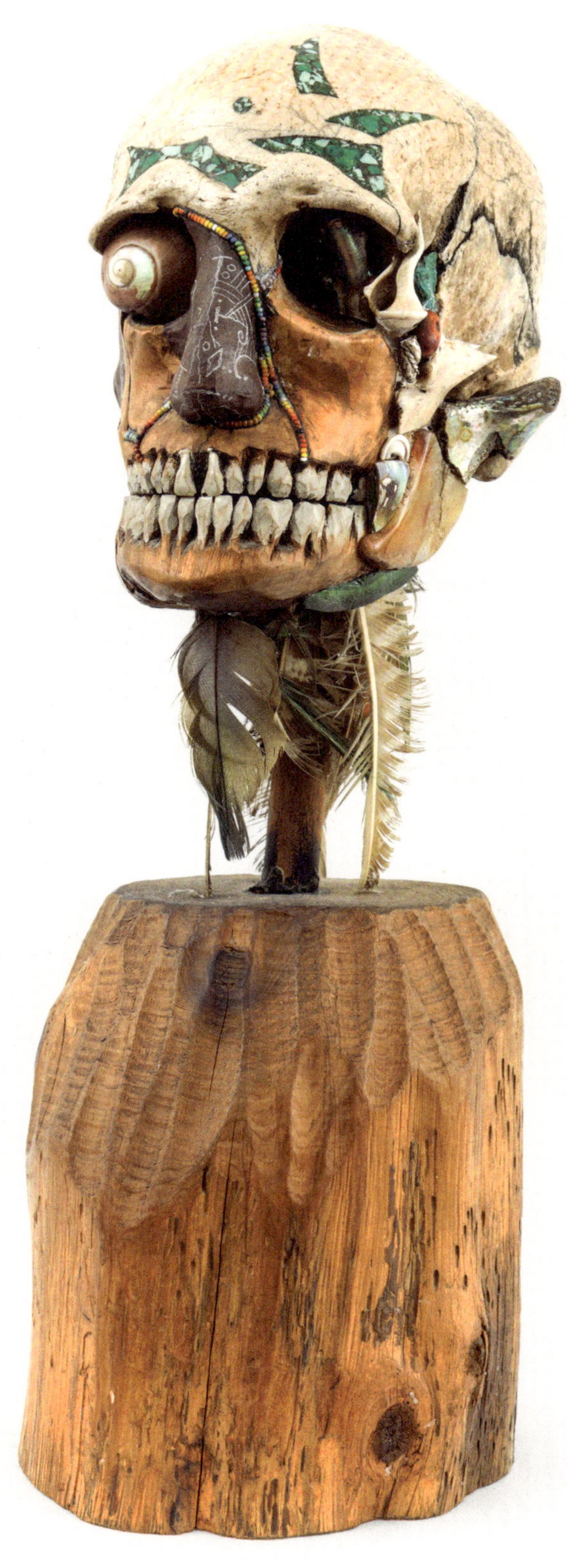

Karankawa, 1982. Human skull, cedar, seashells, abalone shell, alabaster, beads, button, turquoise, cow leather, fish bone, parrot feathers, woodpecker feather, two deer teeth, white and black ink. 19 × 9 × 9 in. (48.3 × 22.9 × 22.9 cm).

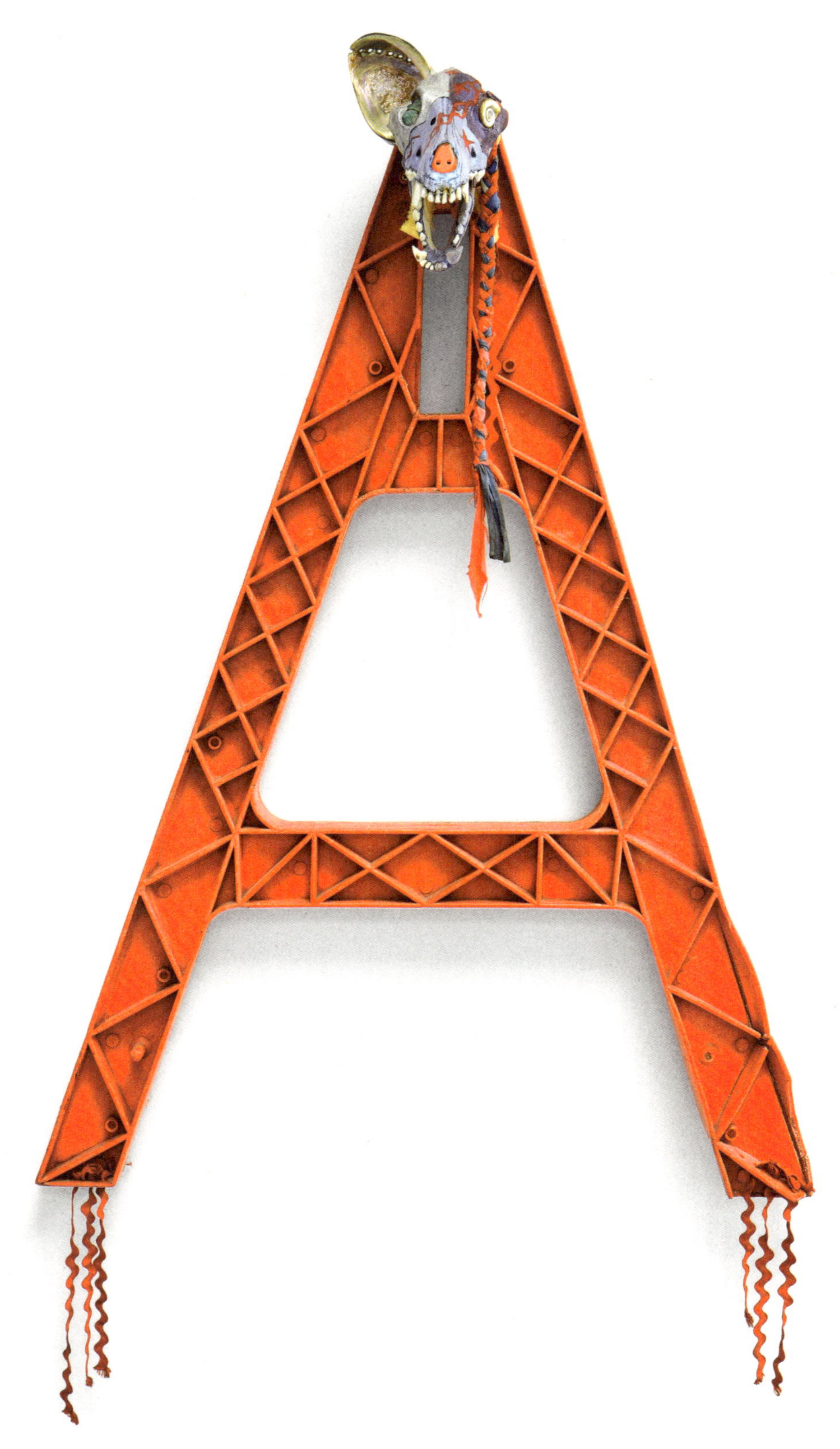

New York Gitli, 1984. Dog skull, plastic, acrylic paint, seashells, leather. 47 ¼ × 27 ½ × 11 ½ in. (120 × 70 × 29 cm).

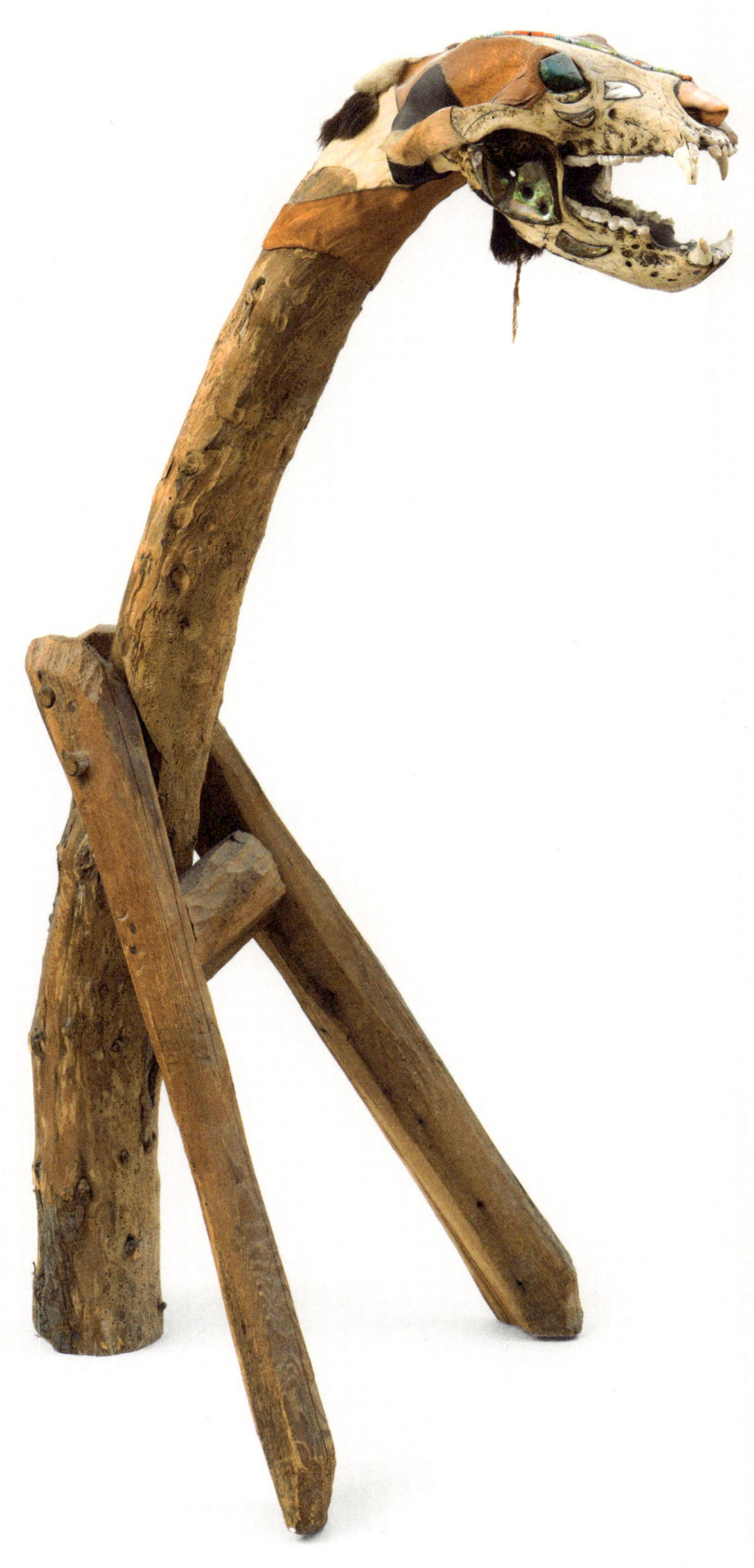

Wahya, 1984. Bear skull, tree branch, carved wood, beads, shells, stones, mother of pearl, leather, horse fur, paint. 53 × 24 × 36 in. (134.6 × 61 × 91.4 cm).

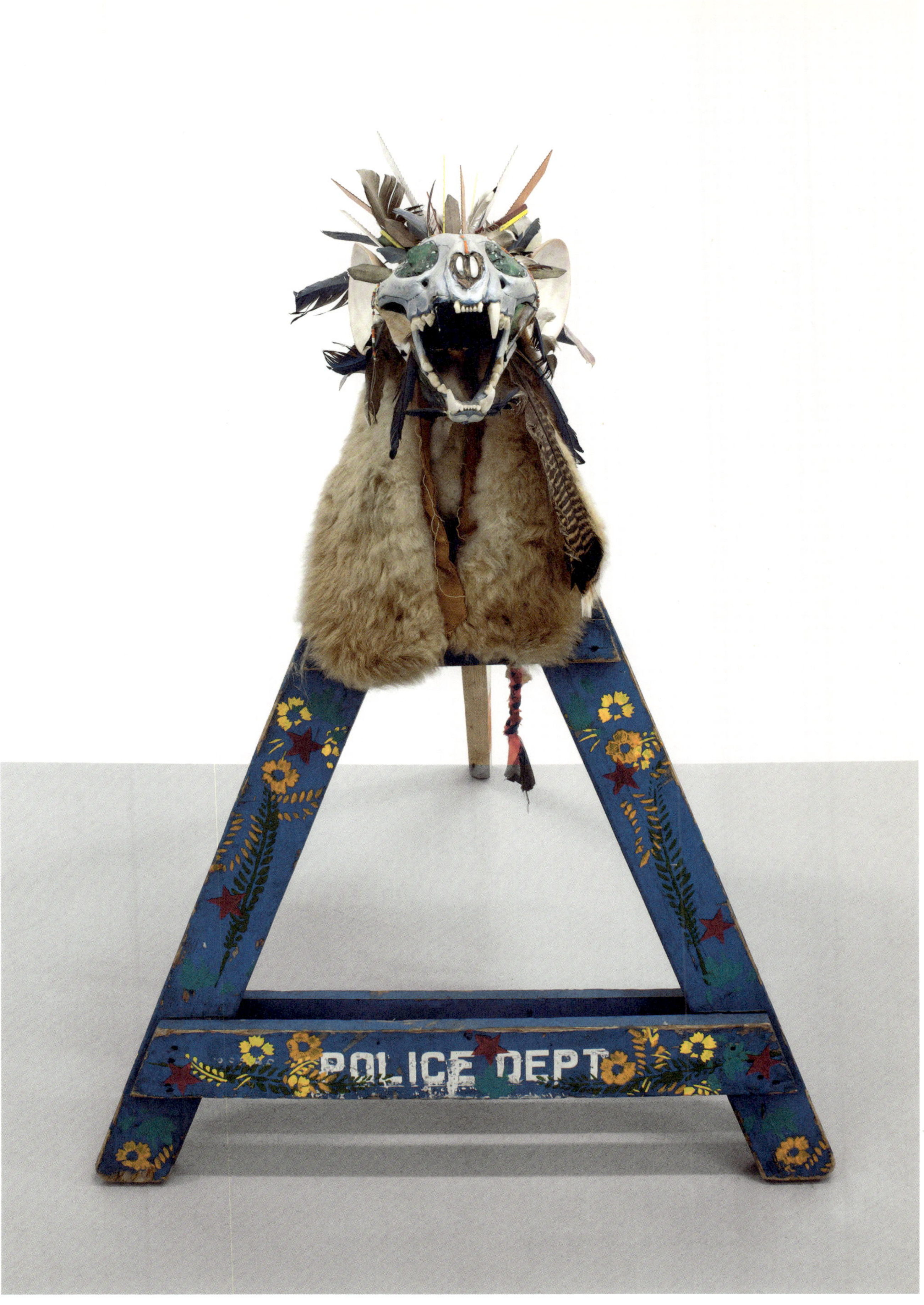

Tlunh Datsi, 1984. Puma skull, shells, turquoise, turkey feathers, metal, sheep and deer fur, pine, acrylic paint. 40 ½ × 35 ¾ × 31 ¾ in. (103 × 91 × 81 cm).

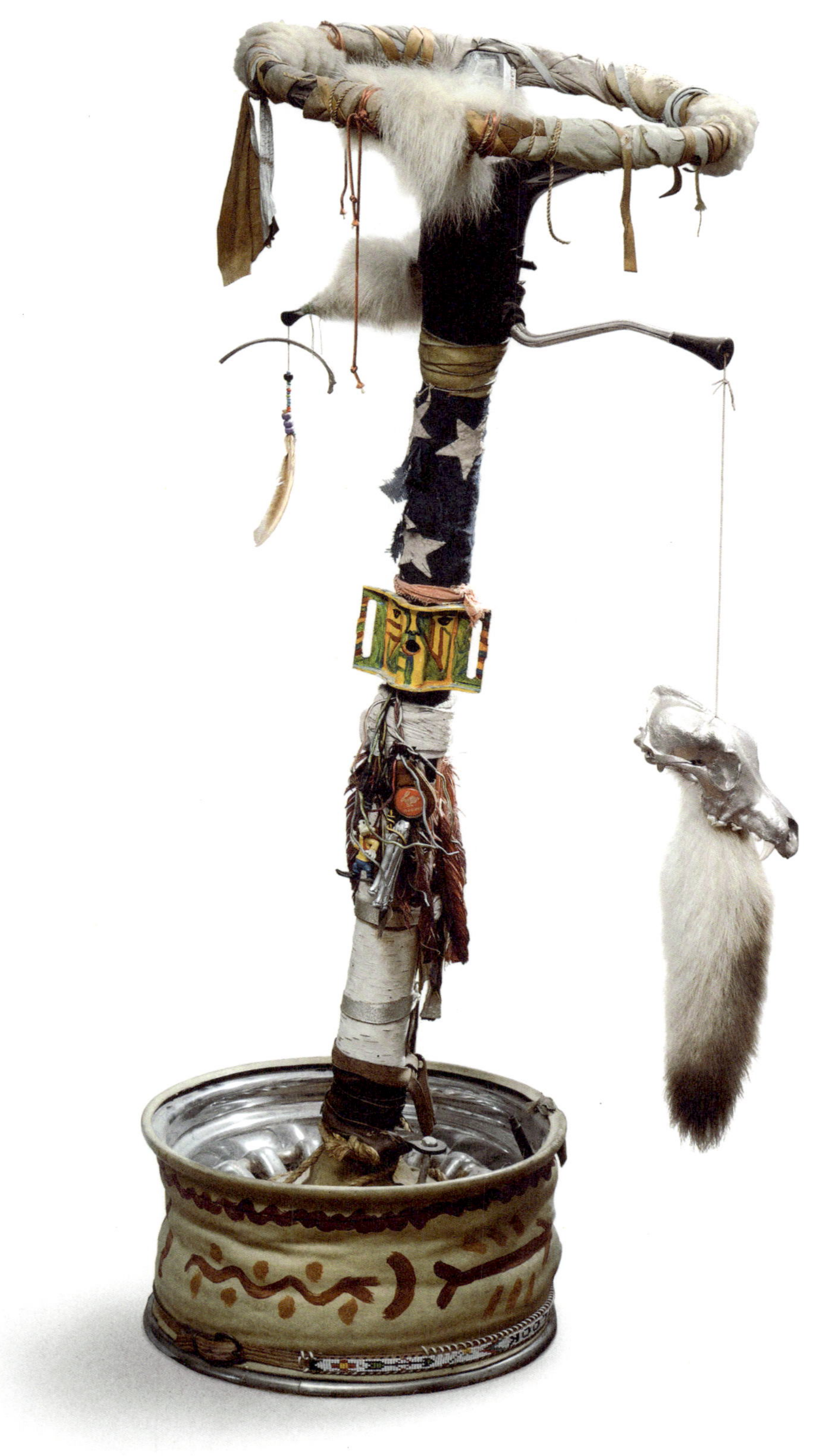

Bedia's Stirring Wheel, 1985. Car steering wheel with shifter, metal car wheel, cotton American flag, cow leather, fur, sheepskin, pigeon feather, dog skull, beads, plastic doll, acrylic paint. 42 ¼ × 18 in. diam. (107.3 × 45.7 cm diam.).

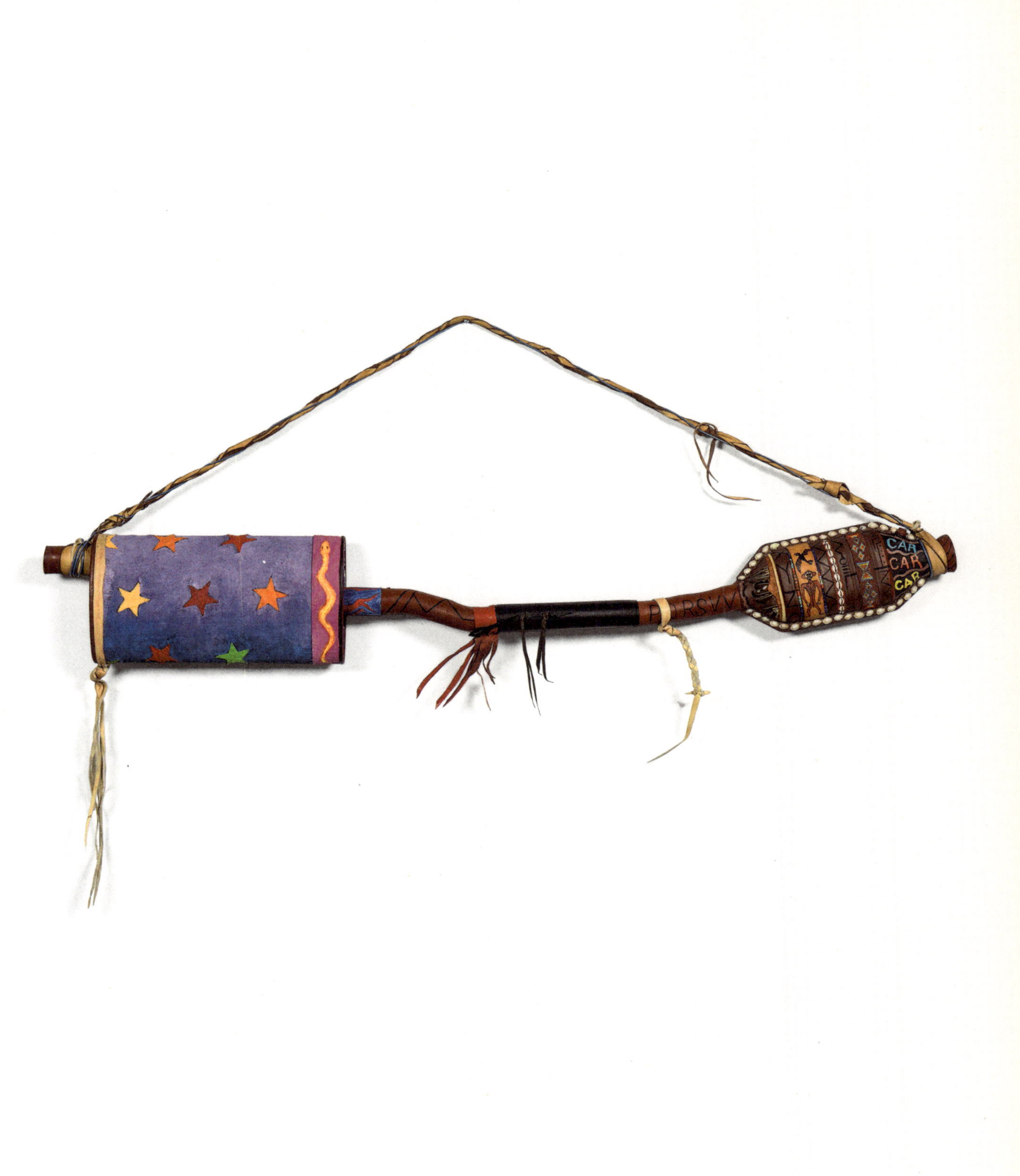

Bedia's Muffler, 1985. Metal muffler, acrylic paint on cotton stars from American flag, leather. 34 × 61 ⅞ × 4 ¾ in. (86.4 × 157 × 12 cm).

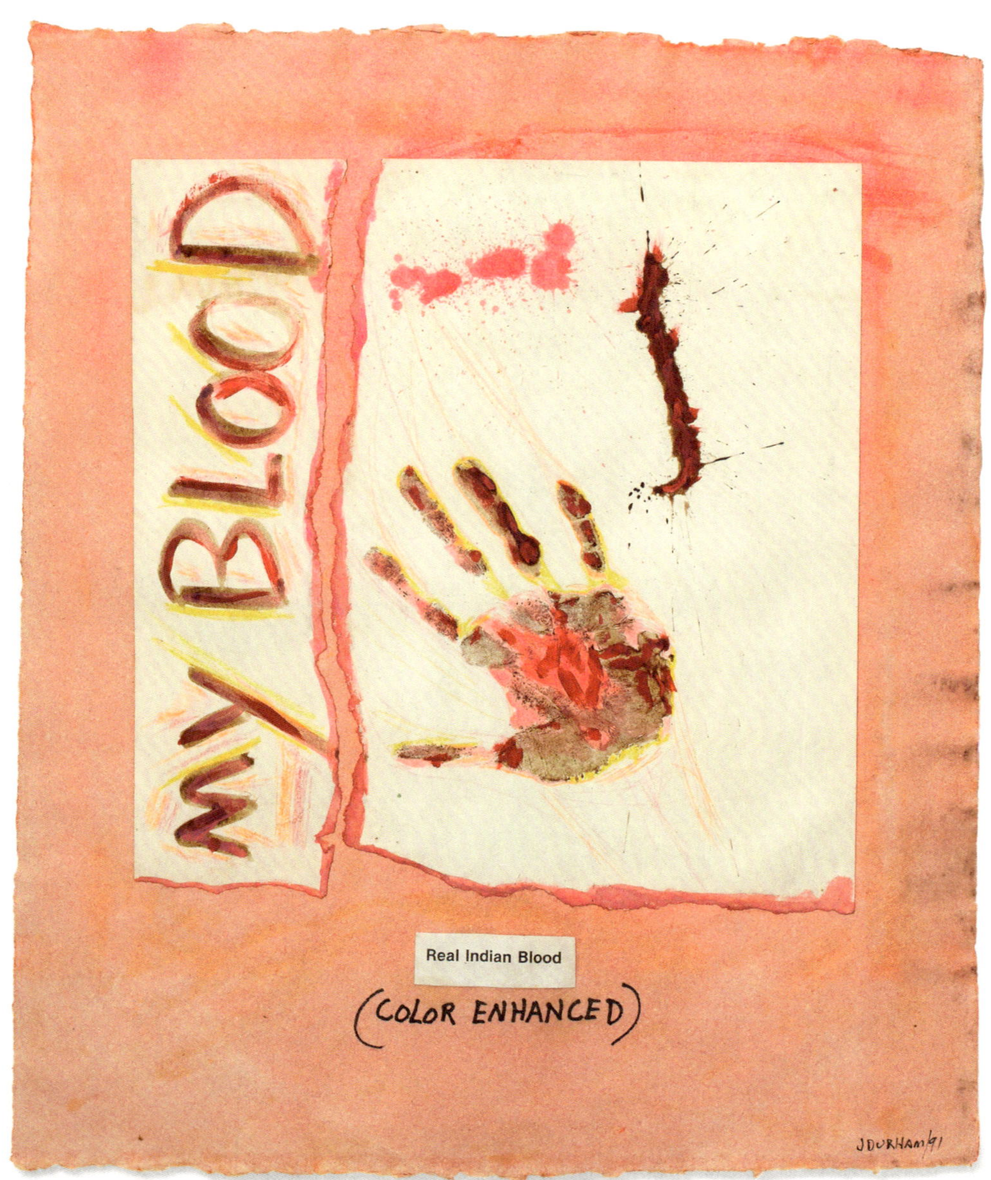

My Blood, 1985/1991. Acrylic paint, artist's blood, and ink on paper. 22 ½ × 18 ½ in. (57.2 × 47 cm).

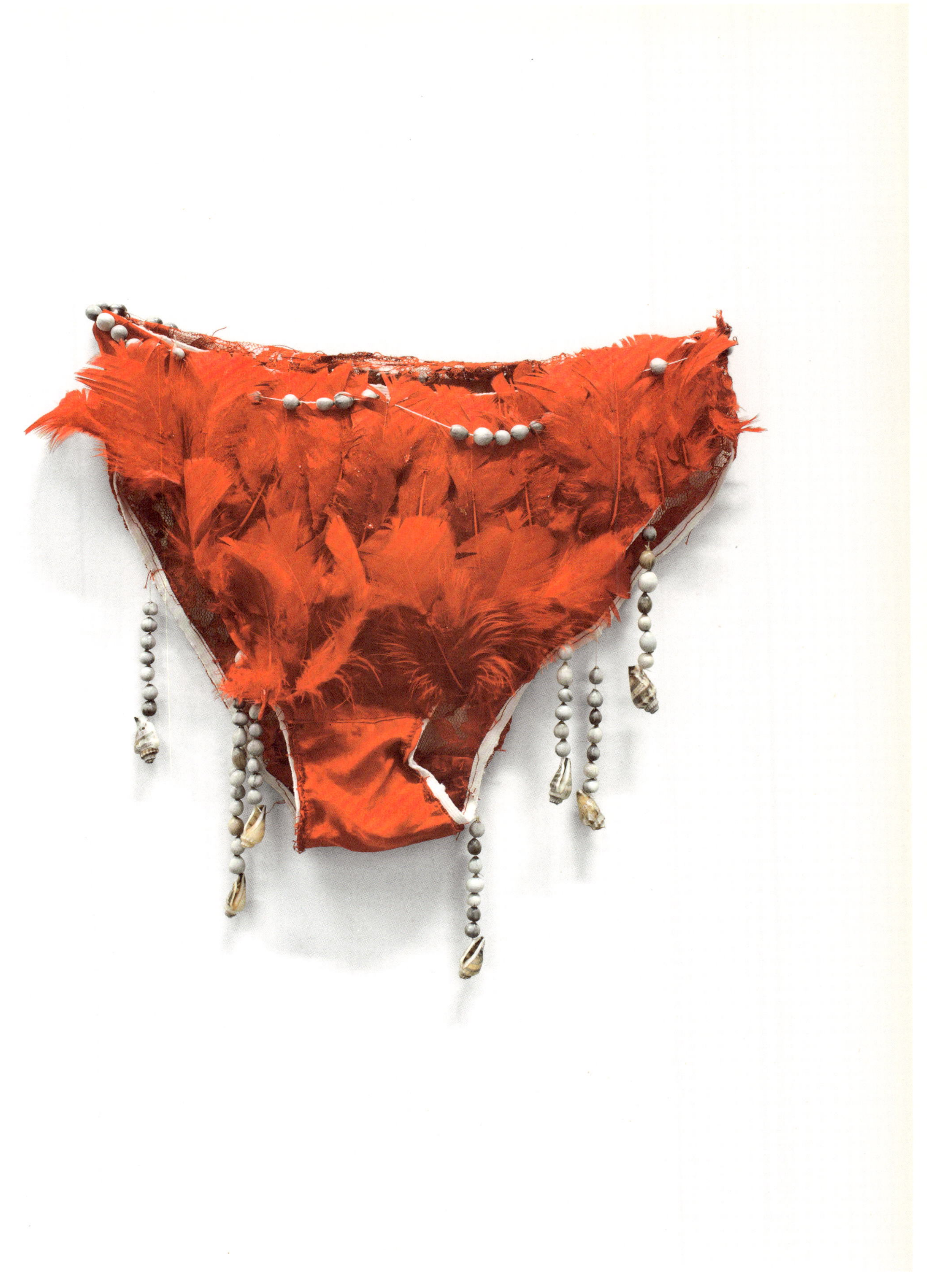

 Pocahontas' Underwear, 1985. Dyed chicken feathers, shells, beads. 13 ¼ × 13 ¼ in. (33.6 × 33.6 cm).

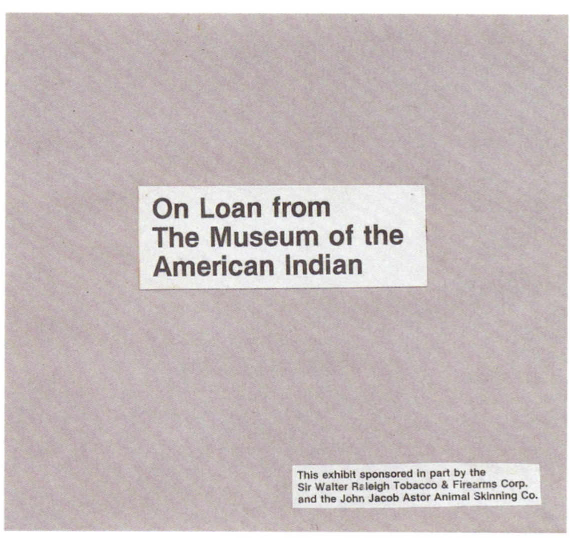

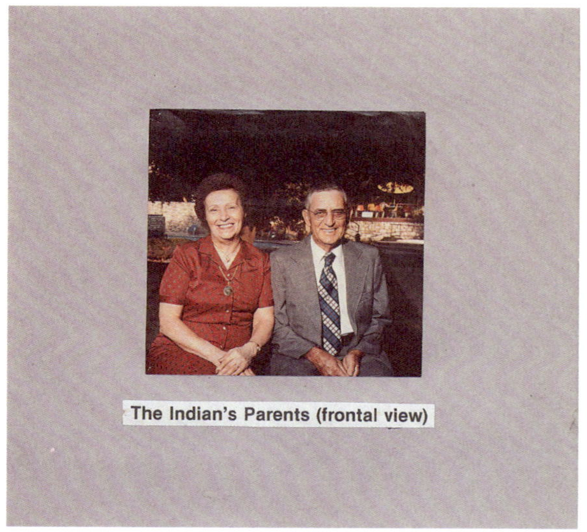

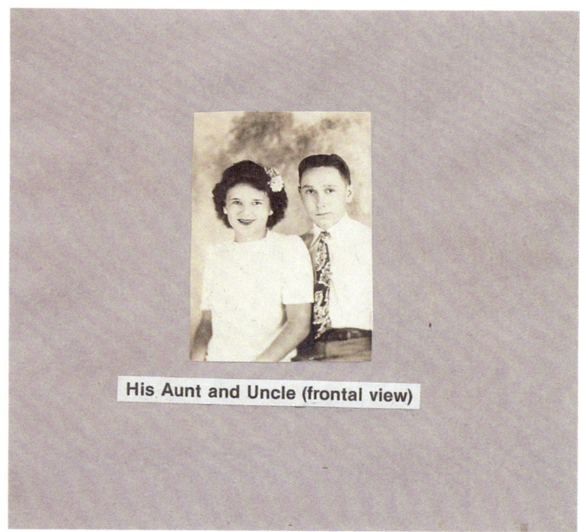

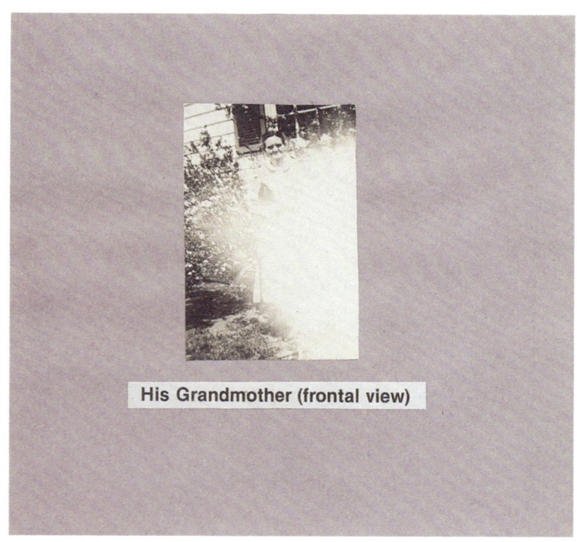

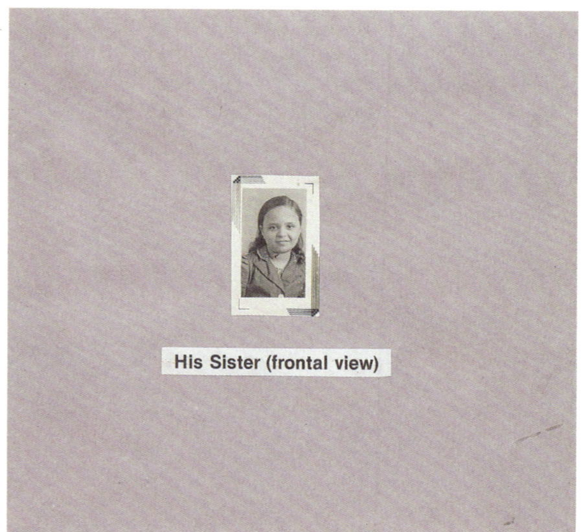

The Indian's Family, 1985. Photographs with collage on paper. 10 × 10 ½ in. (25.4 × 26.7 cm) each of 5.

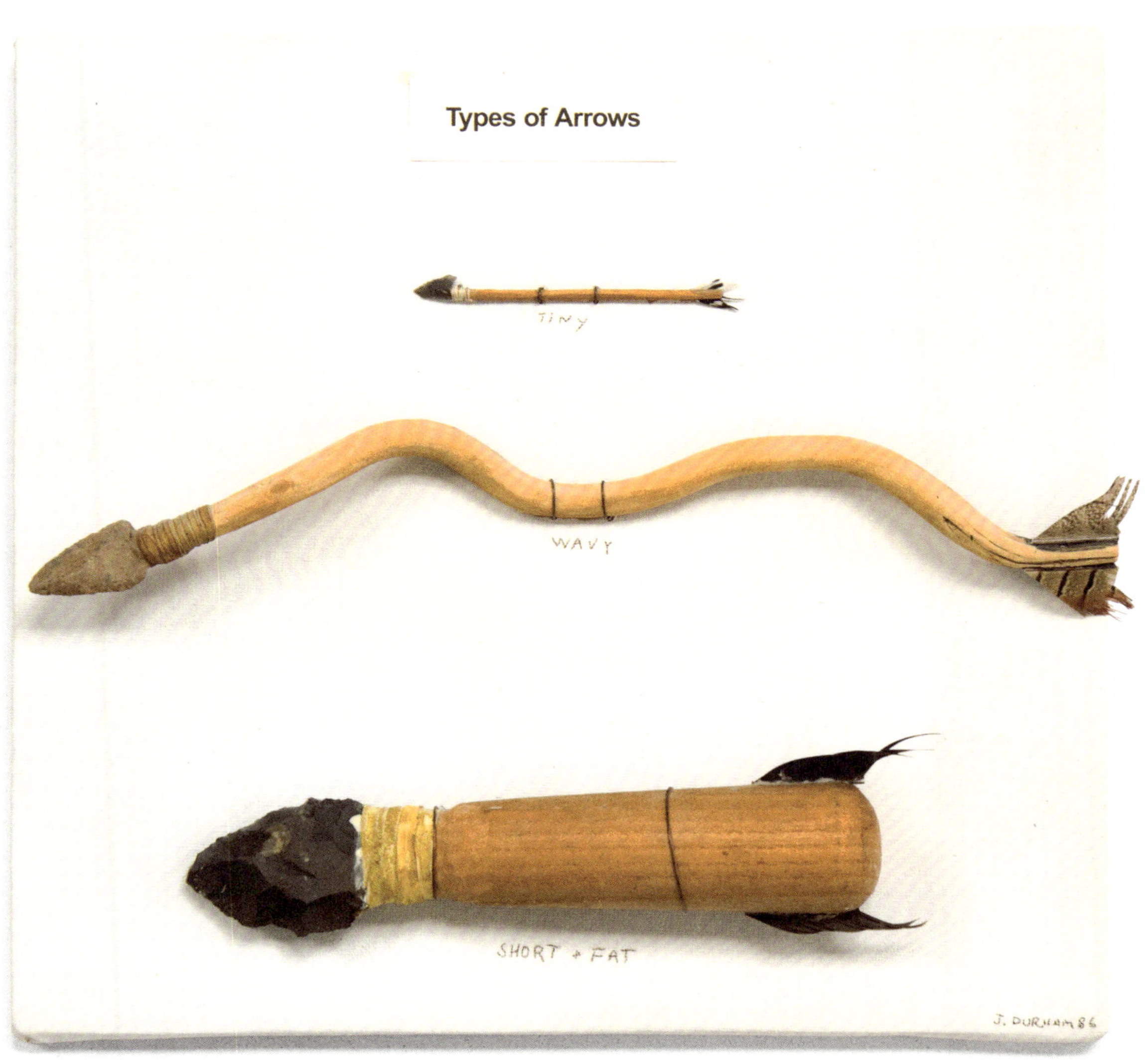

Types of Arrows, 1985/86. Oak, flint arrowheads, cow leather, turkey feathers, canvas over board, ink on paper. 11 ¼ × 11 ¼ × 2 ⅛ in. (28.8 × 28.8 × 5.4 cm).

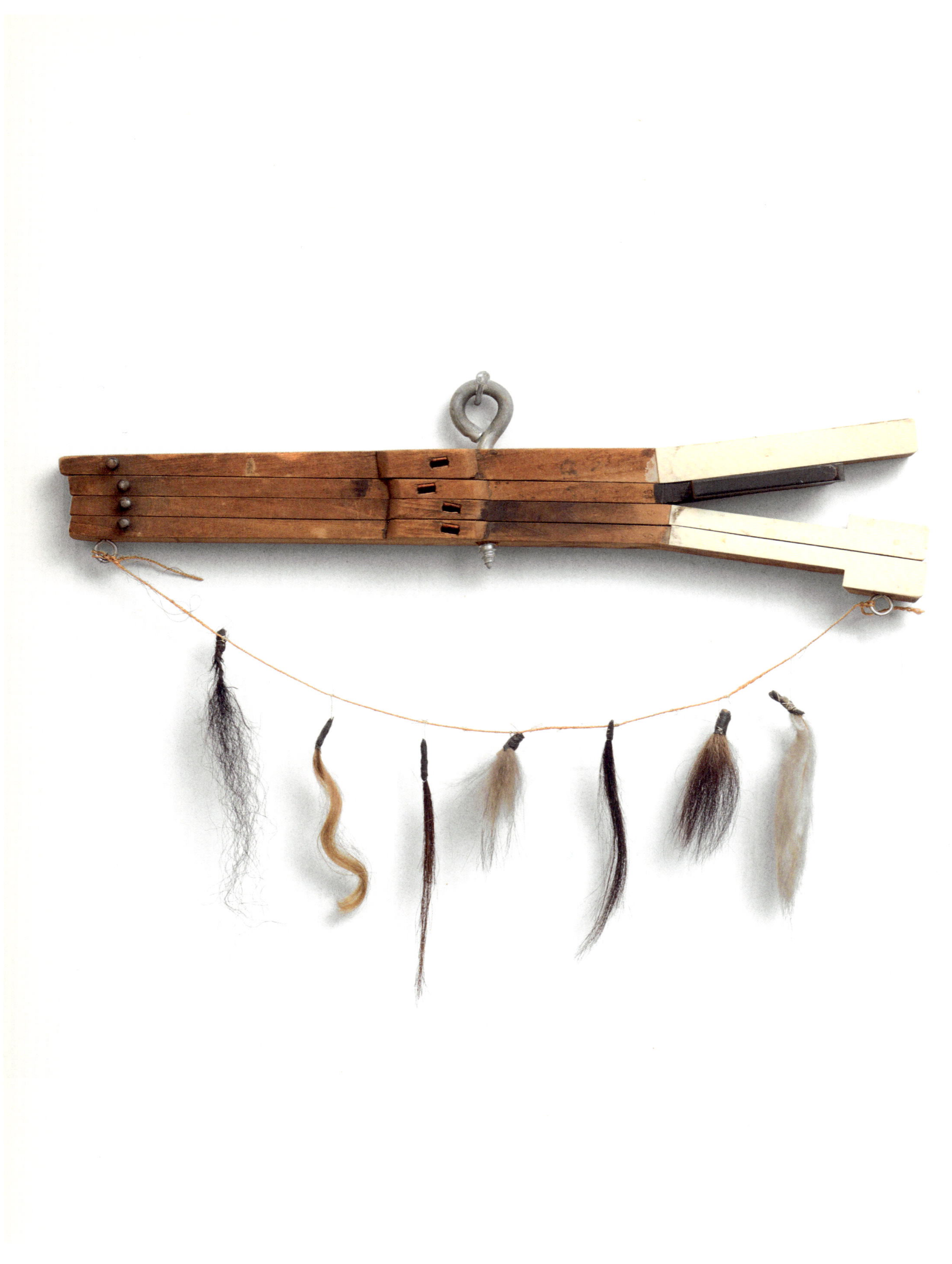

Whose Hair Is It?, 1985. Pine, string, metal screws, ivory piano keys, human, dog, and synthetic hair. 11 ½ × 20 × 2 ¾ in. (27.9 × 50.8 × 7.2 cm).

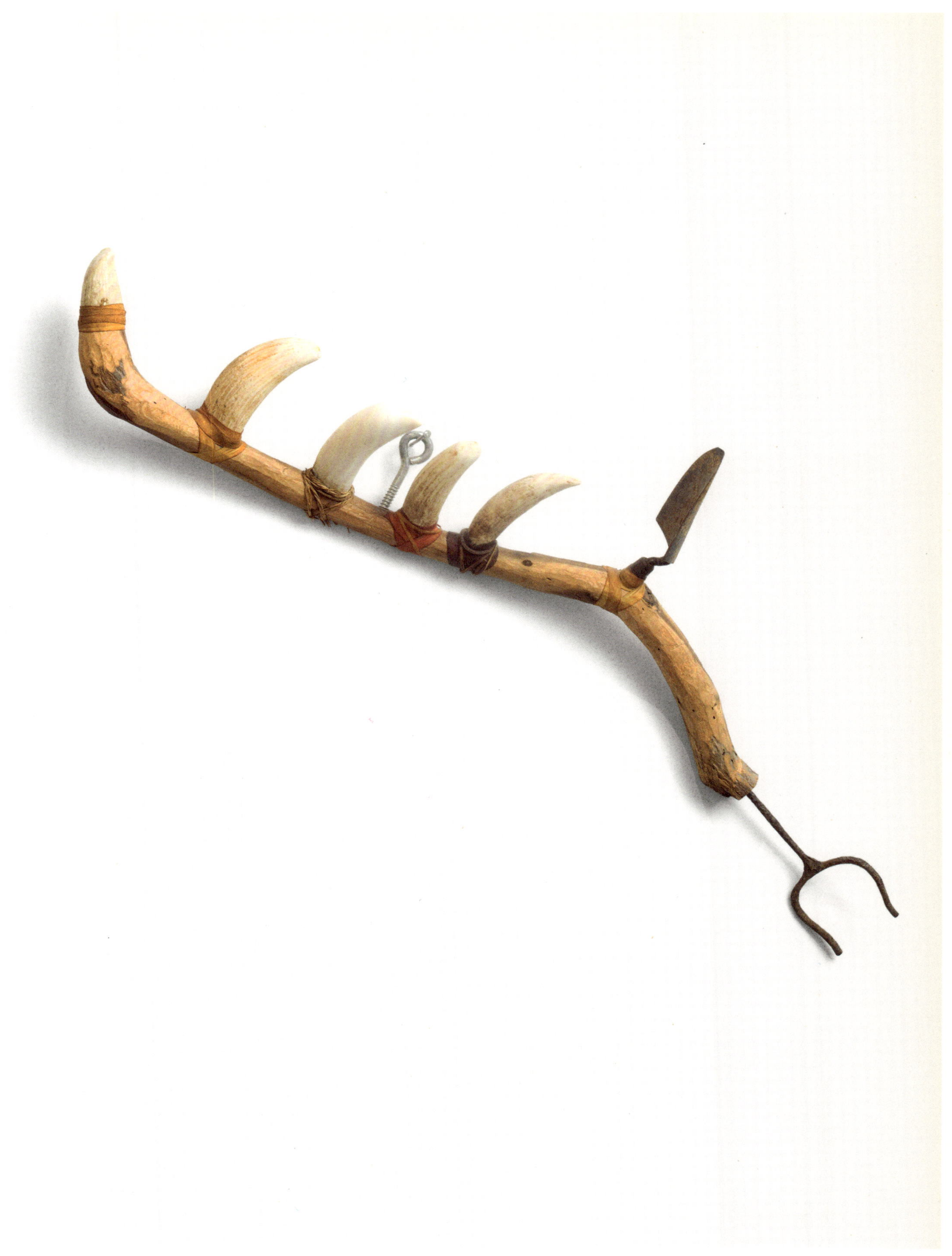

Whale Tooth Stick, 1985. Whale teeth, bodark wood, leather, metal, twine. 46 × 12 × 4 in. (116.8 × 30.5 × 10.2 cm).

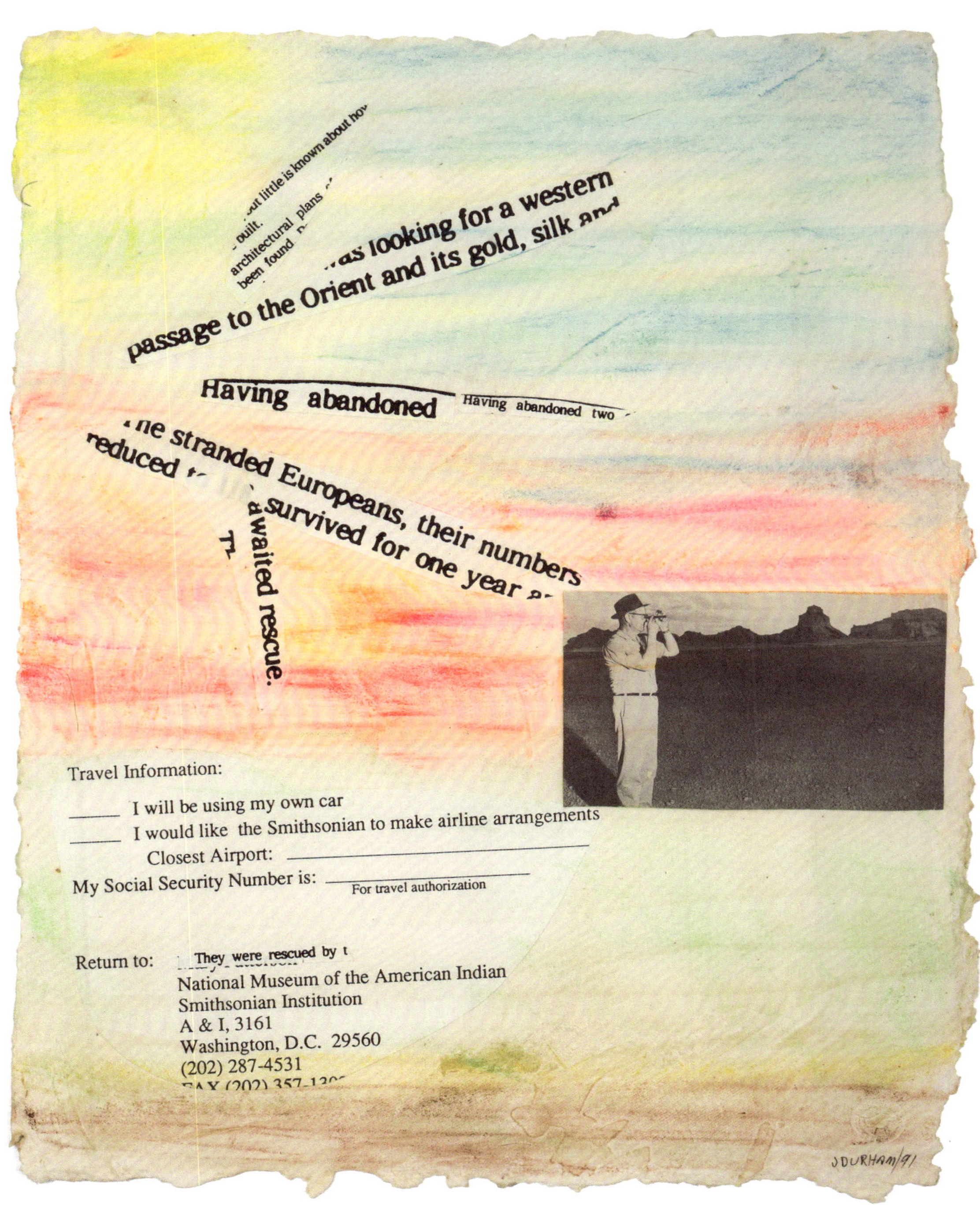

I Would like the Smithsonian . . . , 1991. Acrylic paint on paper with collage. 20 × 16 ½ in. (50.8 × 41.9 cm).

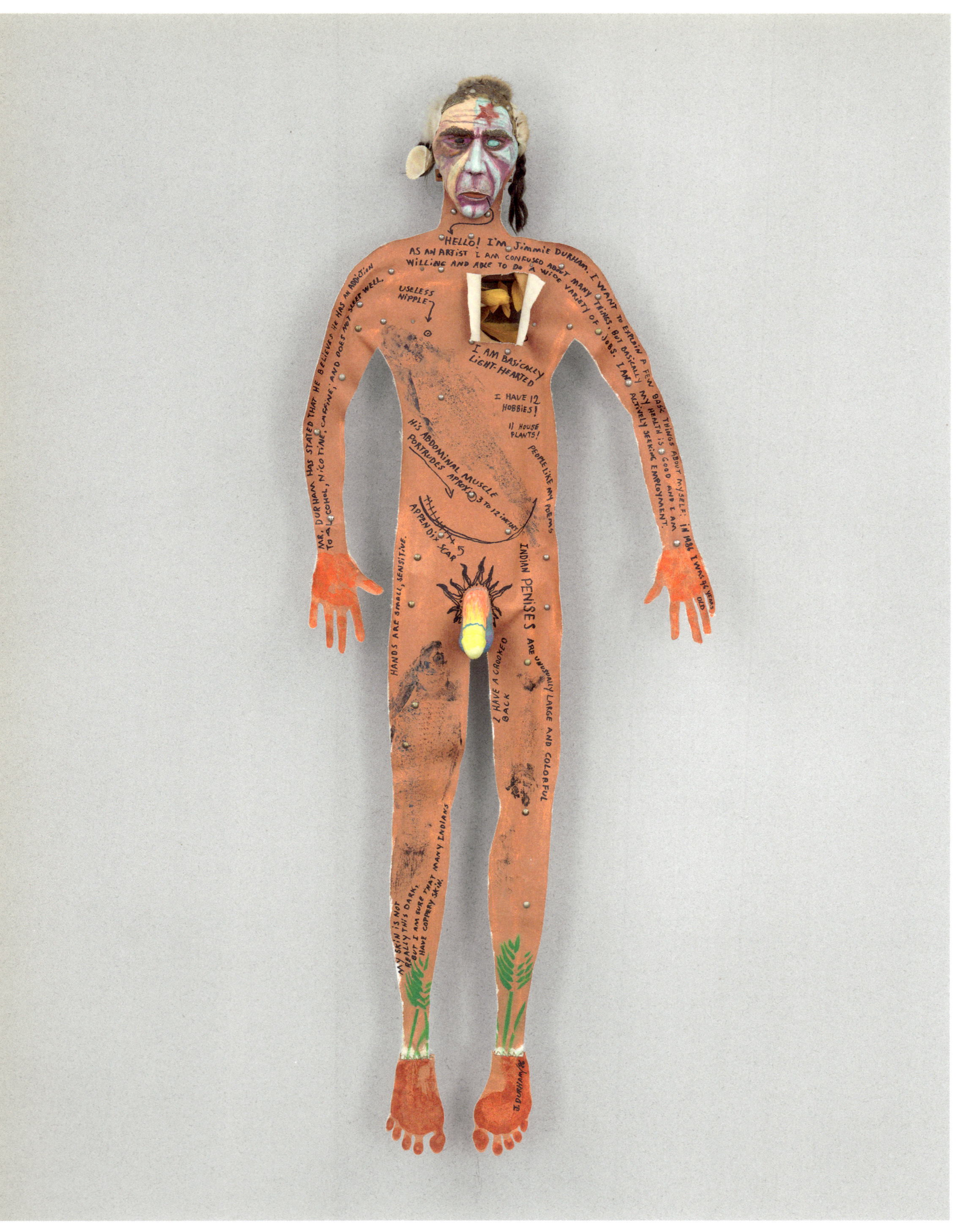

Self-portrait, 1986. Canvas, cedar, acrylic paint, metal, synthetic hair, scrap fur, dyed chicken feathers, human rib bones, sheep bones, seashell, thread.
78 × 30 × 9 in. (198.1 × 76.2 × 22.9 cm).

JIMMIE DURHAM: SELF-PORTRAIT

ELISABETH SUSSMAN

Let's propose that a self-portrait, generically, can be defined as something a painter, sculptor, or photographer makes that represents himself or herself. A photographer, for instance, sets up a situation to take his or her portrait by posing with a close-at-hand but invisible-to-the-viewer shutter that is then manipulated by the photographer and captures the likeness. For the painter and the sculptor, the self-representation emerges out of less literal circumstances and is dependent on the contingencies of materials. This process of self-portraiture is complicated by the artist's questions and decisions about self-presentation, such as whether the self portrayed is the "real" one or an alternative. The artist negotiates the possibilities: psychological, political, and contextual. A dialogue ensues between the artist's intentions and the object that is emerging. Jimmie Durham confronts that basic definition in his singular *Self-portrait* (1986; opposite), in which he proposes himself in tangible form—face, body, head.[1]

Durham's *Self-portrait* is not a painting, a portrait of the artist's face. It is a painted and constructed head and body. He constructed the work so that it hangs on the wall from a nail, about two feet off the floor. The front section, from the head down, is cut following the purported dimensions of Durham's body (shoulders, arms, torso) from a canvas that has been painted red. The canvas front is studded with upholstery tacks that fasten it to a backing, a wooden armature support that can be seen from the side (page 59). The canvas legs are nailed to the support with upholstery tacks, the feet and hands are flat cutouts, and the soles of the feet are painted bright red and stitched onto the legs, which above the ankles are decorated with painted green palm fronds and tattooed with the imprints of fish bodies. This body, then, is a sort of primitivist fantasy of existence that combines animal, plant, and human in one conglomerate whole. So, the yellow feathers that are revealed in the cut-open chest area evoke a bird and a human heart simultaneously (page 60). Yet the carved-wood penis, painted orange, blue, and yellow, unquestioningly announces male identity.

What catches our attention in this frontal view of *Self-portrait* is the face, carved from wood and presumably resembling Durham's own. It is in this face that he chooses to declare that the self he has represented is a Native American. For that face is painted in colors and with symbols that accord with the stereotypical representation of the American Indian: a combination of encounter information transformed into a tall-tale creation for tourists. Beads stand in for eyes. One ear is a mollusk shell. The self-portrait's head of hair consists of braids made of synthetic material and swatches of animal fur.

The politics of this *Self-portrait* (which could be portentous) are actually put forth in epigrams—printed letters painted on the body—that manage to evoke two voices: that of the purported "self," Jimmie Durham, in a disarmingly funny and friendly way, and that of another, an outside examiner, in the clinical tones of a doctor or an anthropologist. What do these texts do? The written words draw on the precedents of texts in 1970s conceptual art, but in *Self-portrait* language is used to create a kind of dialogue or disputation about identity that is wry and poetic, and that tells a story, that nails the body down and makes it communicative. The texts describe the body according to different systems. This is Durham's choice as he, as the artist, makes himself. "He," then, is neither neutral nor natural, as we might mistake white bodies to be, but special, hybrid, mysterious, and

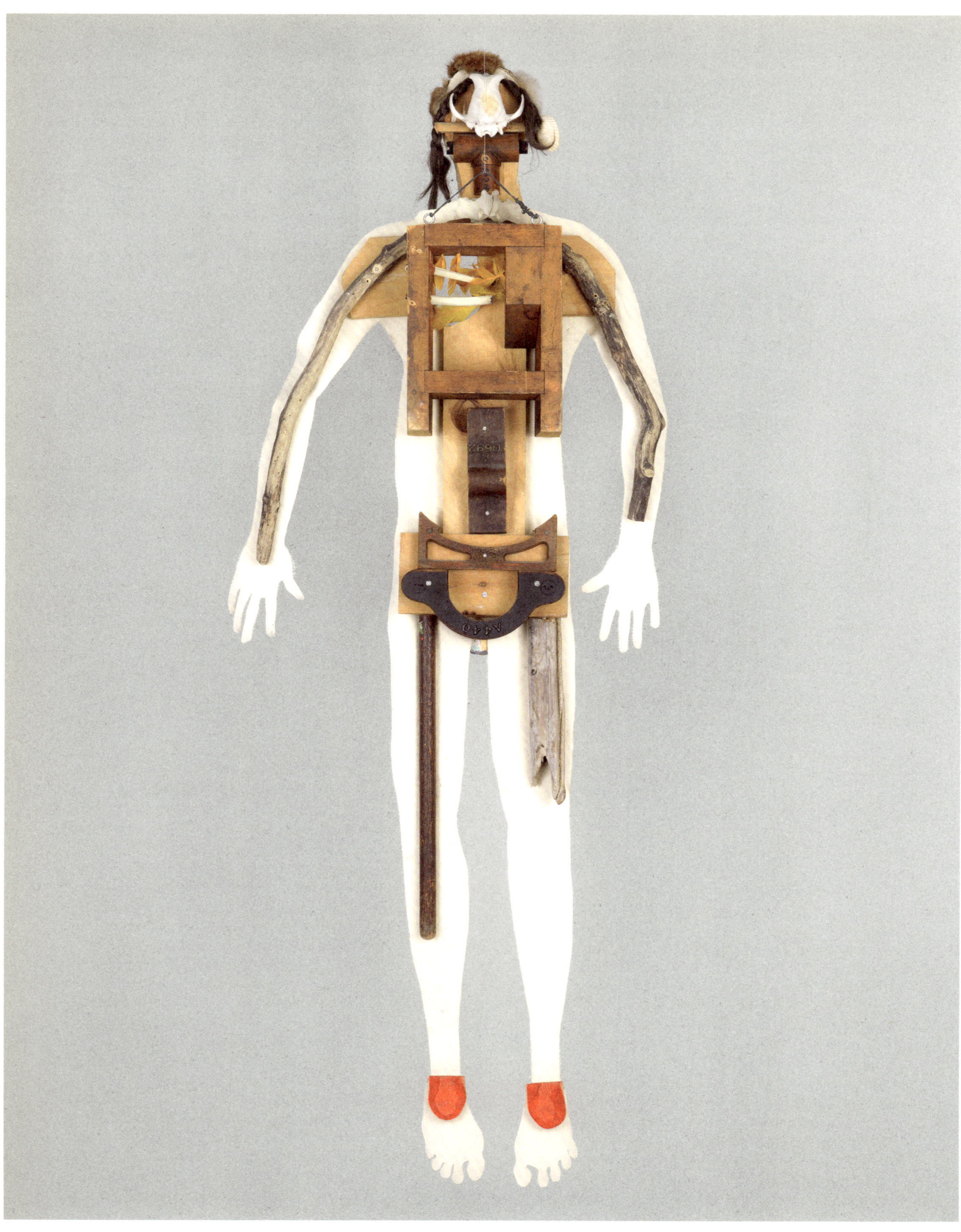

Back of *Self-portrait*, 1986.

needing a descriptive system. Thus this red-painted skin is not the flesh, muscle, and sinew of paintings of classical beauty but a surface and system for a written text. Durham's use of his flesh/body as a tablet for information turns away from the tradition of European painting and, as an alternative, recalls the early hide paintings that as early as 1720 emerged among Native Americans in the Southwest and the Midwestern Great Plains as a means to convey information and illustrate events.[2]

On the right side, as seen from the viewer's position, and connected to the mouth by an arrow in the style of a comic book, are some lines that extend down the shoulder to the hand and introduce the "self" of the self-portrait: "Hello! I'm Jimmie Durham. I want to explain a few basic things about myself. In 1986 I was 46 years old. As an artist I am confused about many things. But basically my health is good and I am willing and able to do a wide variety of jobs. I am actively seeking employment." Nearby, extending up the other arm are lines written in the voice of the clinician: "Mr. Durham has stated that he believes he has an addiction to alcohol, nicotine, caffine [*sic*], and does not sleep well." Which voice are we to believe? The clinical descriptions continue: "Useless nipple," "His abdominal muscle protrudes approx. 3 to 12 inches," "Appendix scar," "Hands are small, sensitive," and "Indian penises are unusually large and colorful" (for emphasis, the size of the letters in "penises" differs from that of the other inscriptions).

But other inscriptions are in the voice of the "self," Jimmie Durham, and are disarmingly cheerful: "I am basically light-hearted" (written near the chest cavity with feathers), "I have 12 hobbies! 11 houseplants!," and "People like my poems." Elsewhere he notes, "I have a crooked back" and "My skin is not really this dark, but I am sure that many Indians have coppery skin." The result of the dichotomy of description is that we no longer have a single self in the tradition of a conventional self-portrait, but rather we are faced with competitive descriptive systems, a fractured entity masquerading as a whole.

If the front of the *Self-portrait* falls apart, so too does the back, the armature that supports the canvas body and the wood head (opposite). The back is not nearly as visible to the viewer as it is to the museum personnel who see the work before and after it gets hung on the wall. Therefore, the back is a secret story reserved for a few. Yet it is intrinsic to the work and seems to be as full of meaning as the carefully constructed "primitive" appearance of the front. The information tablet of the front body and the war-paint mask of the head are in contrast to the doppelgänger of the rear with its canny contraption of found wooden pieces, bones, and animal fur. The front, with its enlightened language(s), is challenged by the truth of its construction, which is revealed in the back as a functional, jerry-built support, a conglomeration of the human and the animal, the natural and the outmoded industrial all held together by tacks, screws, and glue. It could be suggested that this back (which is again not really visible) is a knowing cliché of the material culture of the Native American, which is by necessity of construction hidden behind the language-based representation of the front.

There is an animal skull behind the face, and affixed to the wooden armature of the neck is a segment of animal spine. Human rib bones are inserted behind the feathers in the open wood box, perhaps a factory mold. The chest area, waist, hips, and pelvis are built up with separate old wooden parts that have been connected, each still containing the marks of their former

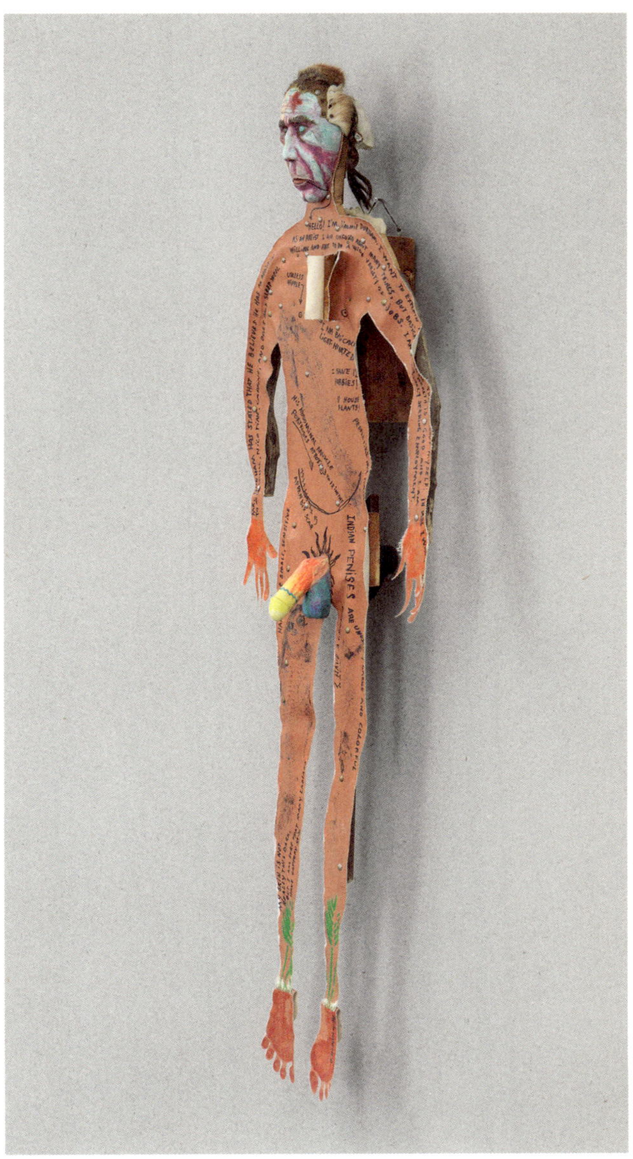

Side view of *Self-portrait*, 1986.

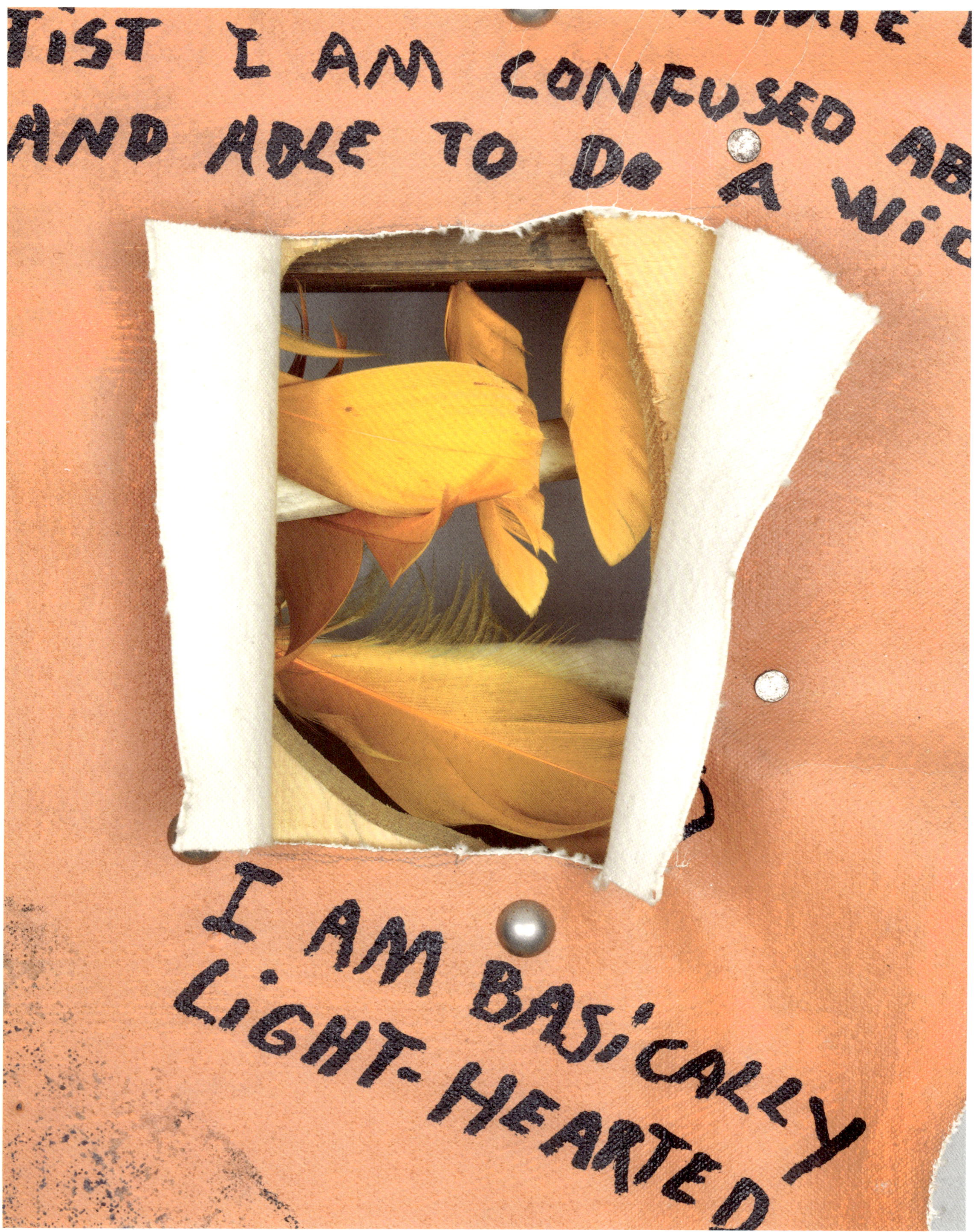

Self-portrait, 1986 (detail).

uses, such as sunken pegs and applied numbers and letters, all now meaningless. In contrast to the old industrial wooden parts are the tree branches that function as the back supports of the canvas arms, and the driftwood and recycled chair legs that support the canvas legs.

Durham's *Self-portrait* speaks through its materials and the way they are put together, and it evokes, if only to joke about the stereotypes, Native American representations and ways of working. But the way that Durham makes things and his address of how to construct a body suggest other traditions as well. Although it may seem far-fetched, Durham's work brings to mind art historian David Rosand's eloquent and astute close interpretation of Titian's painting *The Flaying of Marsyas* (ca. 1570–76). Durham does not at all aspire to the painting tradition of Titian. He was, in fact, amused by the very notion of undertaking something so generically associated with European traditions as a self-portrait. But the close attention given to the materials and to the making of the body and the way that we as viewers come to know the work as we study the materials and their construction make Rosand's words about Titian somehow strangely applicable to Durham: "Depiction," Rosand writes, "depends upon the intensity of the artist's gaze, a focus that is transferred from the model to the image by means of the representing hand. In such a kinesthetic circuit, physiologically as well as culturally based, we, as viewers of images, participate. Involving both creation and perception, the phenomenology of painting inevitably becomes hermeneutic. We discover meaning in the making."[3] If, with the Titian, a close viewing can expose the great painter's hand as he builds up the flesh of Marsyas and can reveal the meanings through the artist's making of the work, a similar thing occurs with Durham's *Self-portrait*: it is the awareness we bring to his making that allows us to see the meanings he elicits as, with knowing irony, he sidesteps artistic virtuosity and deploys the journeyman's craftsmanship and canny reuse of materials.

It can be suggested that in 1986 Durham saw the making of the de-skilled *Self-portrait* in the context of the debates around primitivism that sprang up in relation to the Museum of Modern Art's 1984 exhibition *"Primitivism" in 20th Century Art*. That debate, put very simply, occurred in the pages of *Artforum*, where a review by art historian Thomas McEvilley challenged the curatorial premise of the exhibition, which argued for the affinities between modern art and tribal art, for the "influence" of the primitive object (made by someone who is never named as the maker) on the work of the famed and identified giants of the modernist movement (Picasso et al.). McEvilley's review sharply attacked that presupposition. "The need to co-opt difference," he wrote, "into one's own dream of order, in which one reigns supreme, is a tragic failing. Only fear of the Other forces one to deny its Otherness. What we are talking about is a tribal superstition of Western civilization, the Hegel-based conviction that one's own culture is riding the crucial time-line of history's self-realization."[4] The review sparked letters from the exhibition's curators, William Rubin and Kirk Varnedoe, and long responses by McEvilley. The debate was fierce and followed by the many readers of *Artforum*. Essentially the debate brought into the pages of the prominent and important journal a forced recognition that the definitions and achievements of modernity were totally askew and fixated in the hegemonic story of white, European men. Durham, of course, had been actively involved with the rights and recognition of Native Americans since the 1970s. Therefore, it is totally understandable that in 1984, that is, in the same year as the MoMA exhibition, Durham would state: "I am a Cherokee artist who strives to make Cherokee art that is considered just as universal and without limits as the art of any white man is considered. . . . If I am able to see both Cherokee art and all other art as equally universal and valuable, and you are not, then we need to have a serious talk."[5]

That "serious talk" is Durham's gentle downplaying but quite specific and strong articulation of the loud and public exchanges in the pages of the art magazine. And two years later that talk took material form in *Self-portrait*. When *Self-portrait* was included in the 1989 exhibition *The Bishop's Moose and the Pinkerton Men*, at Exit Art, New York, Durham, in an interview with Jeanette Ingberman, one of the exhibition's curators, returned to the debate of 1984, which, he stated, concerned him deeply: "The first narrative," he said, "is the current discourse around primitivism and the collection of primitivism and the concept and how it operates in society. What is primitive? Who are the primitives? Why do people like primitivism? Why is there neo-primitivism? . . . I play with different ideas of how I can interpret what primitive might possibly be. There's obviously no such thing as primitive."[6] In this context, it is easier to understand all the cross-dialogues of language and materials at "play" (to use Durham's word) in the great *Self-portrait* and why this work is not the work of an anonymous Native artist but one that is authored, declaiming on its body, "Hello! I'm Jimmie Durham."

Notes

1. Jimmie Durham had this to say about the work: "The *Self-portrait* got to be very popular right away as soon as I made it. But I didn't exactly make it on purpose. I made it because a gallery was doing a show of self-portraits and asked me to join. I said 'Well I don't do self-portraits, so I'm not going to do it.' And they said, 'Come on, everybody is going to do it.' It was all minority artists doing things together. So I had the idea as soon as I hung up the telephone: 'Okay, I'll lie down on the floor and Maria Thereza can draw me on the canvas; then I'll carve my face and see what else I will do.'" "Jimmie Durham," Museum van Hedendaagse Kunst Antwerpen, http://ensembles.mhka.be/items/self-portrait?locale=en. Thanks to Anne Ellegood for calling my attention to this statement.

The *Self-portrait* came to reside in the collection of Jean Fisher, the British art critic who had worked with Durham on several group exhibitions devoted to Native American art in the mid-1980s, such as *Ni' Go Tlunh a Doh Ka (We are always turning around on purpose)* at the Amelie A. Wallace Gallery, SUNY Old Westbury, Long Island, in 1986, and *We the People* at Artists Space, New York, 1987. Fisher described *Self-portrait* as "a flayed skin, emptied of any fullness of being, though mapped with ironic inscriptions of its not-quite-sameness." Jimmie Durham and Jean Fisher, "The Ground Has Been Covered," *Artforum* 26, no. 10 (Summer 1988): 101. *Self-portrait* was purchased by the Whitney Museum of American Art in 1995.

2. Howard D. Rodee, "The Stylistic Development of Plains Indian Painting and Its Relationship to Ledger Drawings," *Plains Anthropologist* 10, no. 30 (November 1965): 219–21.

3. David Rosand, "'Most musical of mourners, weep again!' Titian's *Triumph of Marsyas*," *Arion: A Journal of Humanities and the Classics*, 3rd ser., 17, no. 3 (Winter 2010): 39.

4. Thomas McEvilley, "Doctor Lawyer Indian Chief: *'Primitivism' in 20th Century Art* at the Museum of Modern Art," *Artforum* 23, no. 3 (November 1984): 59.

5. Durham as quoted by Lucy Lippard, "Little Red Lies," in *Jimmie Durham: The Bishop's Moose and the Pinkerton Men*, ed. Jeanette Ingberman (New York: Exit Art, 1990), 22.

6. Durham in "Conversation between Jimmie Durham and Jeanette Ingberman," in *The Bishop's Moose*, 30–31.

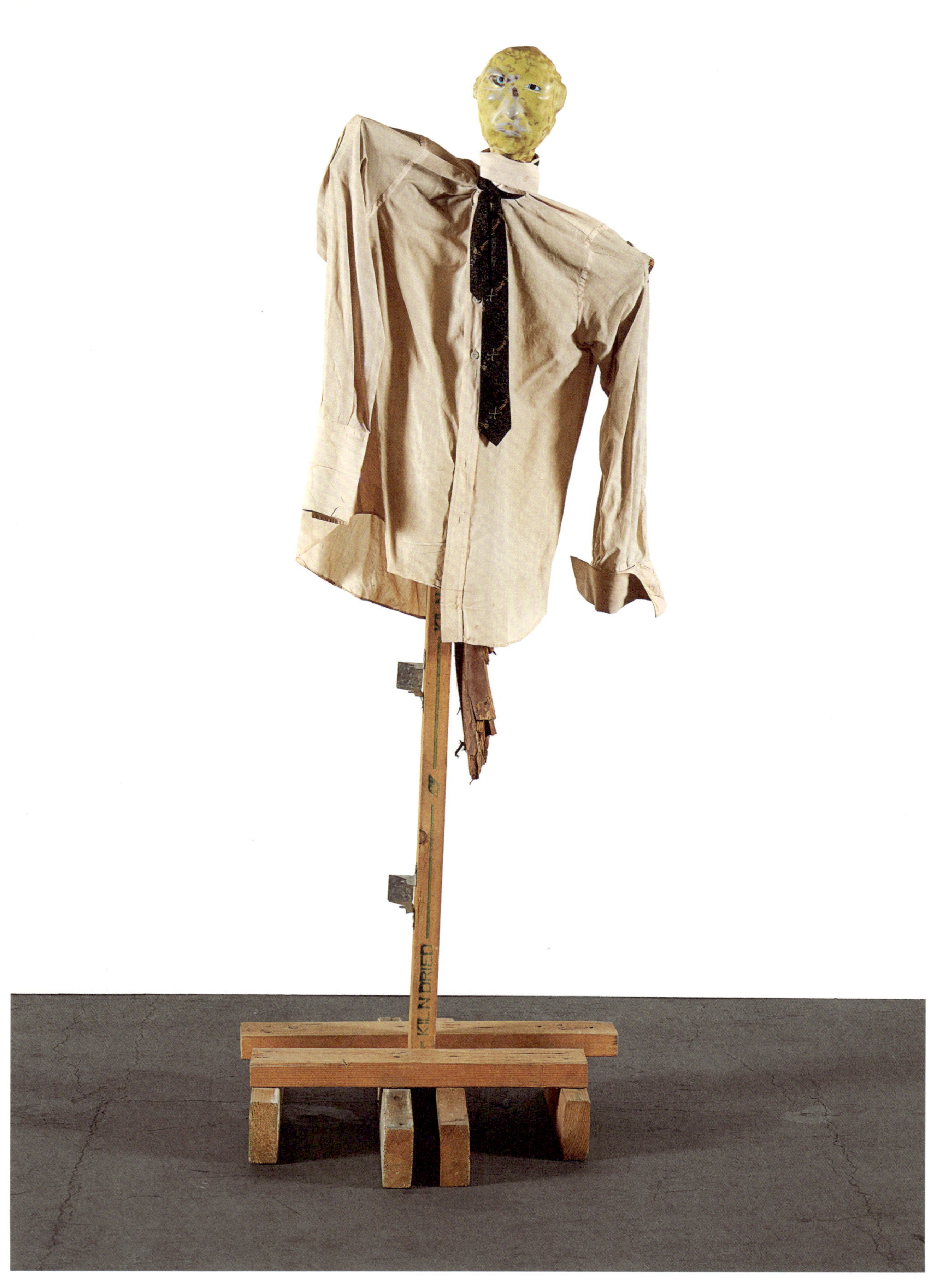

Ahead, 1991. Pine, black walnut, metal, cotton shirt, tie, fiberglass, resin. 65 × 23 ¾ × 25 ½ in. (165 × 60 × 65 cm).

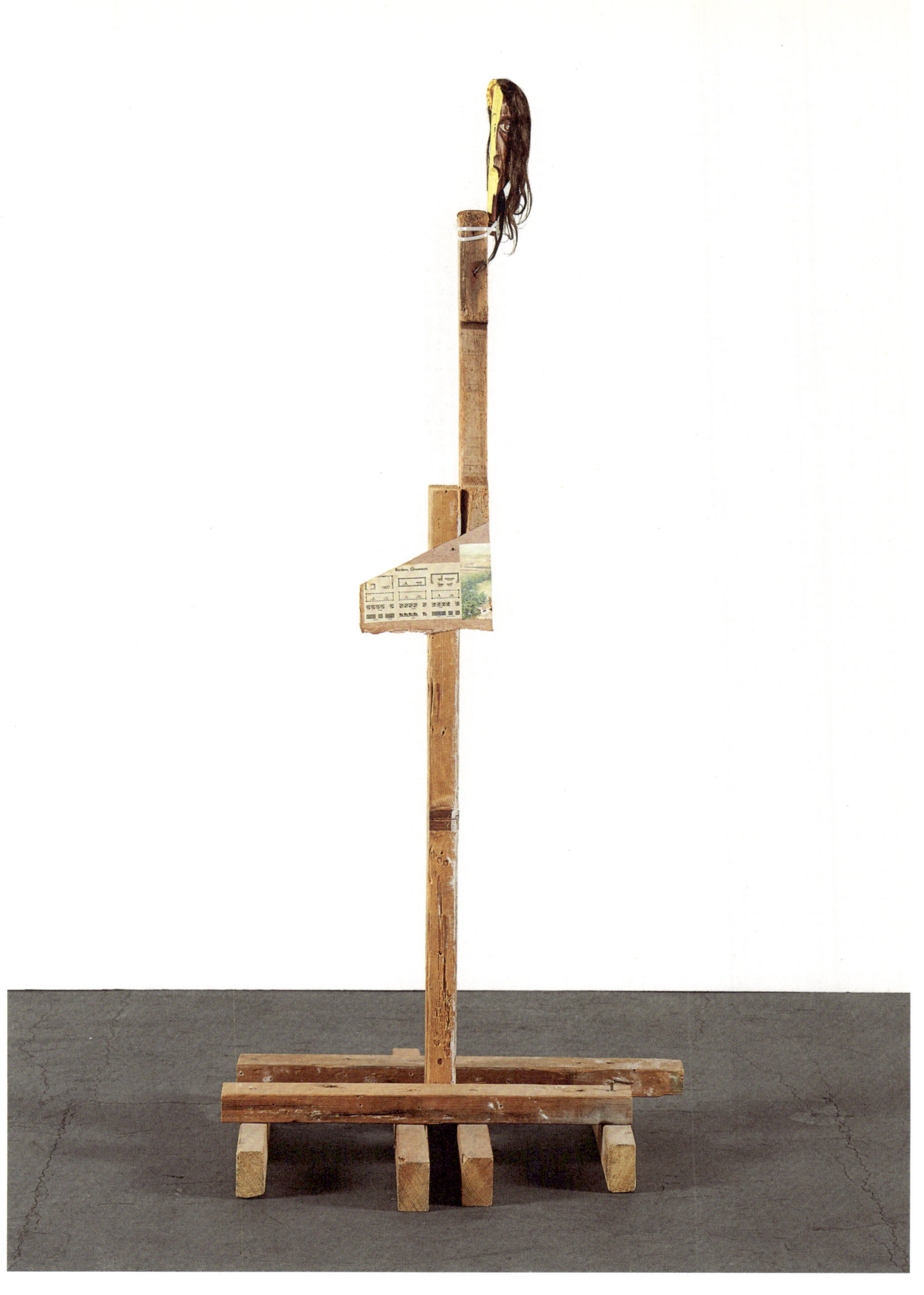

Half Off, 1991. Pine, acacia, acrylic paint, human hair, ink, paper, cardboard. 59 ¼ × 24 ¼ × 24 ¼ in. (50.5 × 61.5 × 61.5 cm).

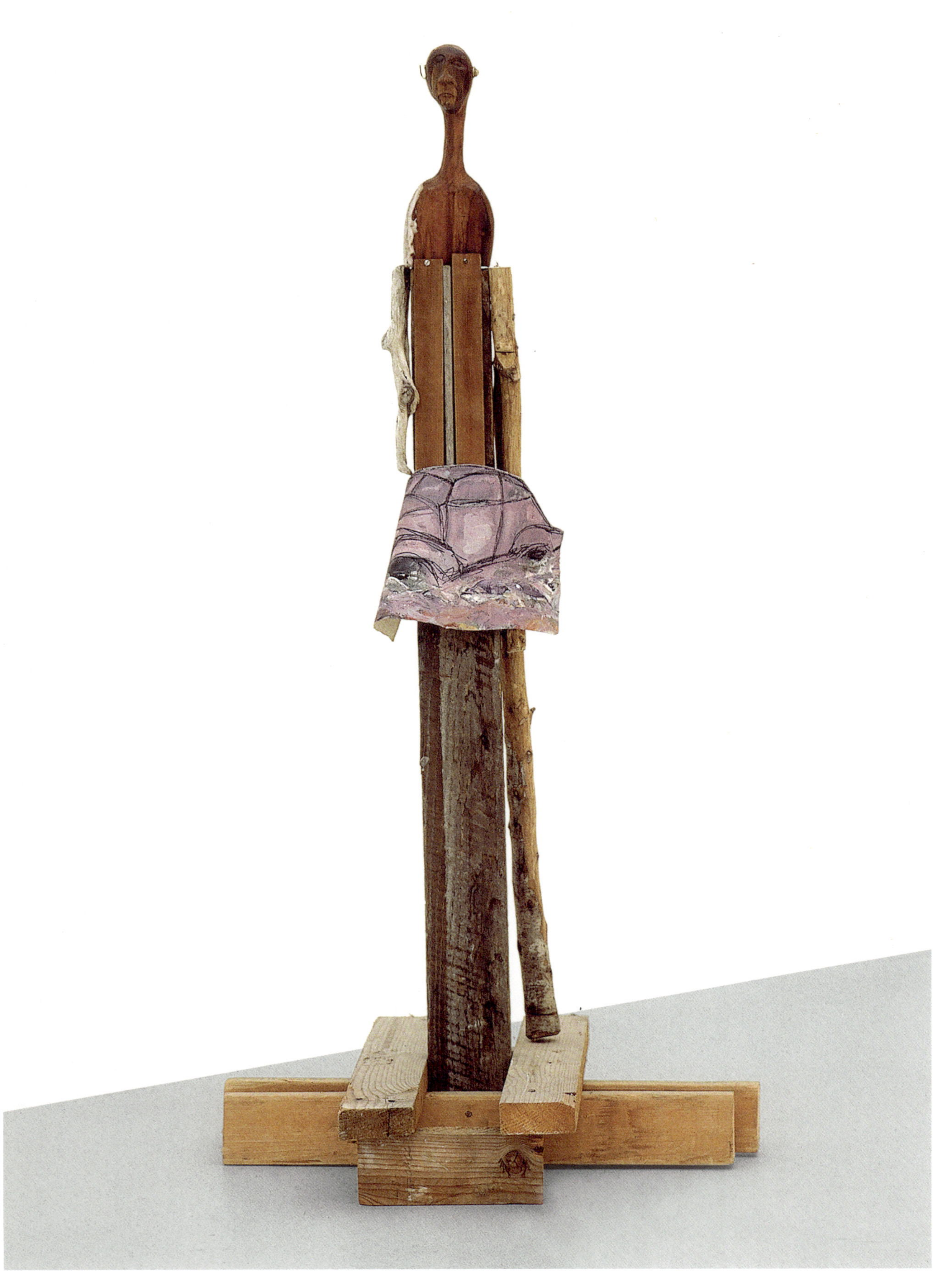

Untitled, 1991. Arkansas plum, ironwood branches, cottonwood, construction lumber, oil on canvas, paint, shells. 59 × 27 ½ × 27 ½ in. (150 × 70 × 70 cm).

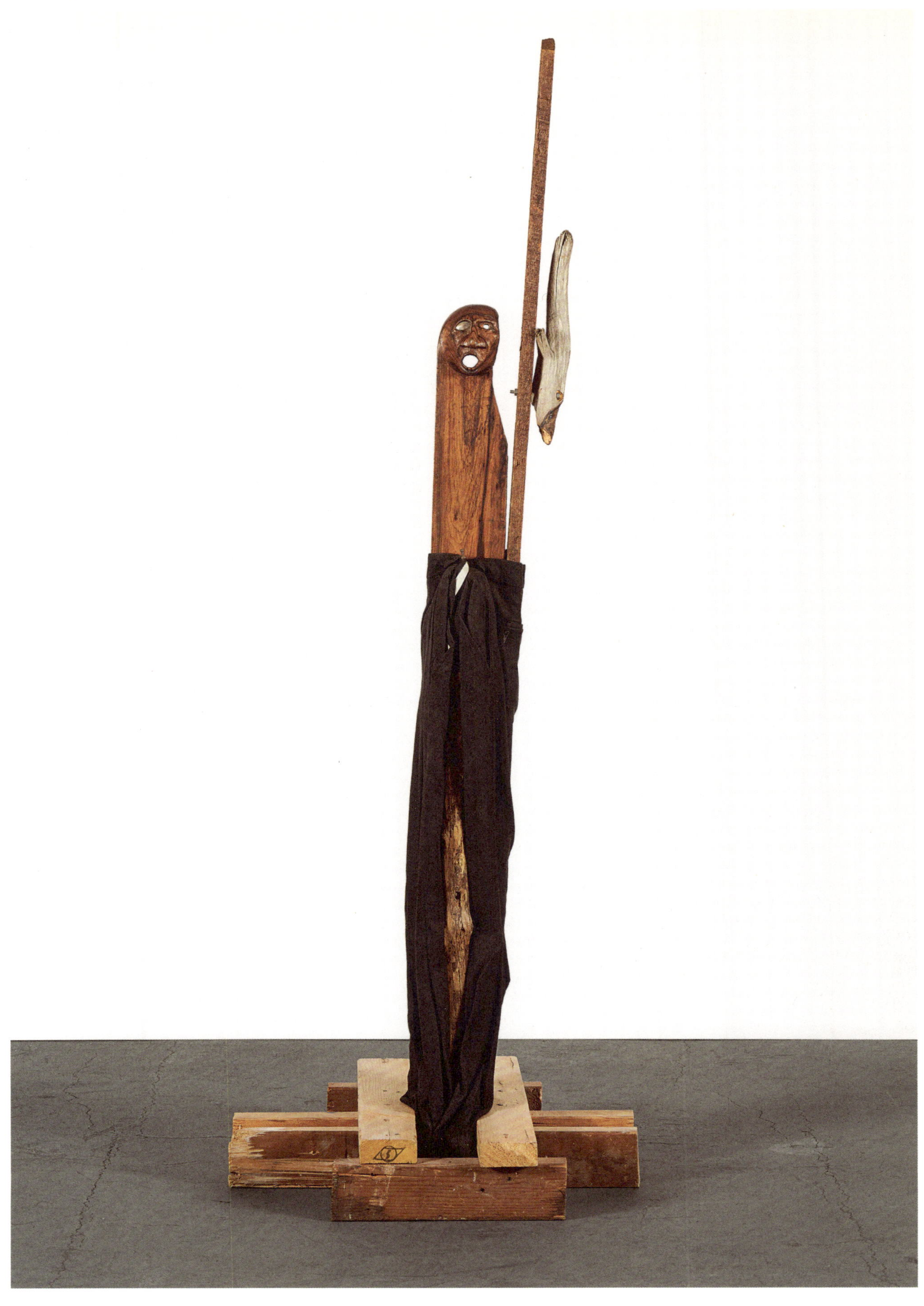

Would and Cotton, 1991. Carved black walnut, oak, cottonwood, pine, cotton pant leg, abalone shell, linseed oil. 72 ¼ × 21 ⅝ × 22 in. (184 × 55 × 56 cm).

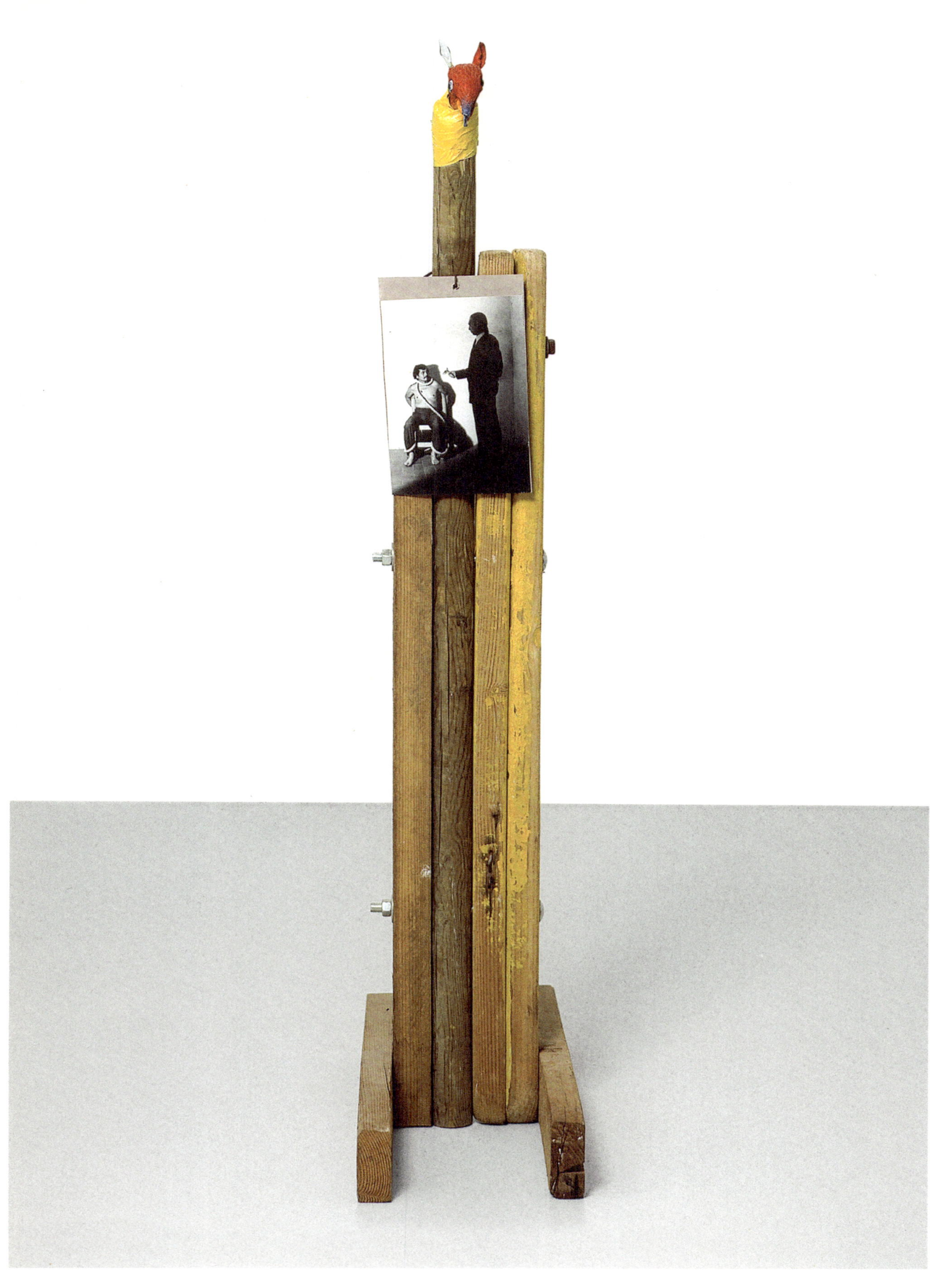

Untitled (Armadillo), 1991. Armadillo skull, oak, acrylic paint, beads, black-and-white photograph. 51 ⅛ × 9 $\frac{7}{16}$ × 24 ⅜ in. (130 × 24 × 62 cm).

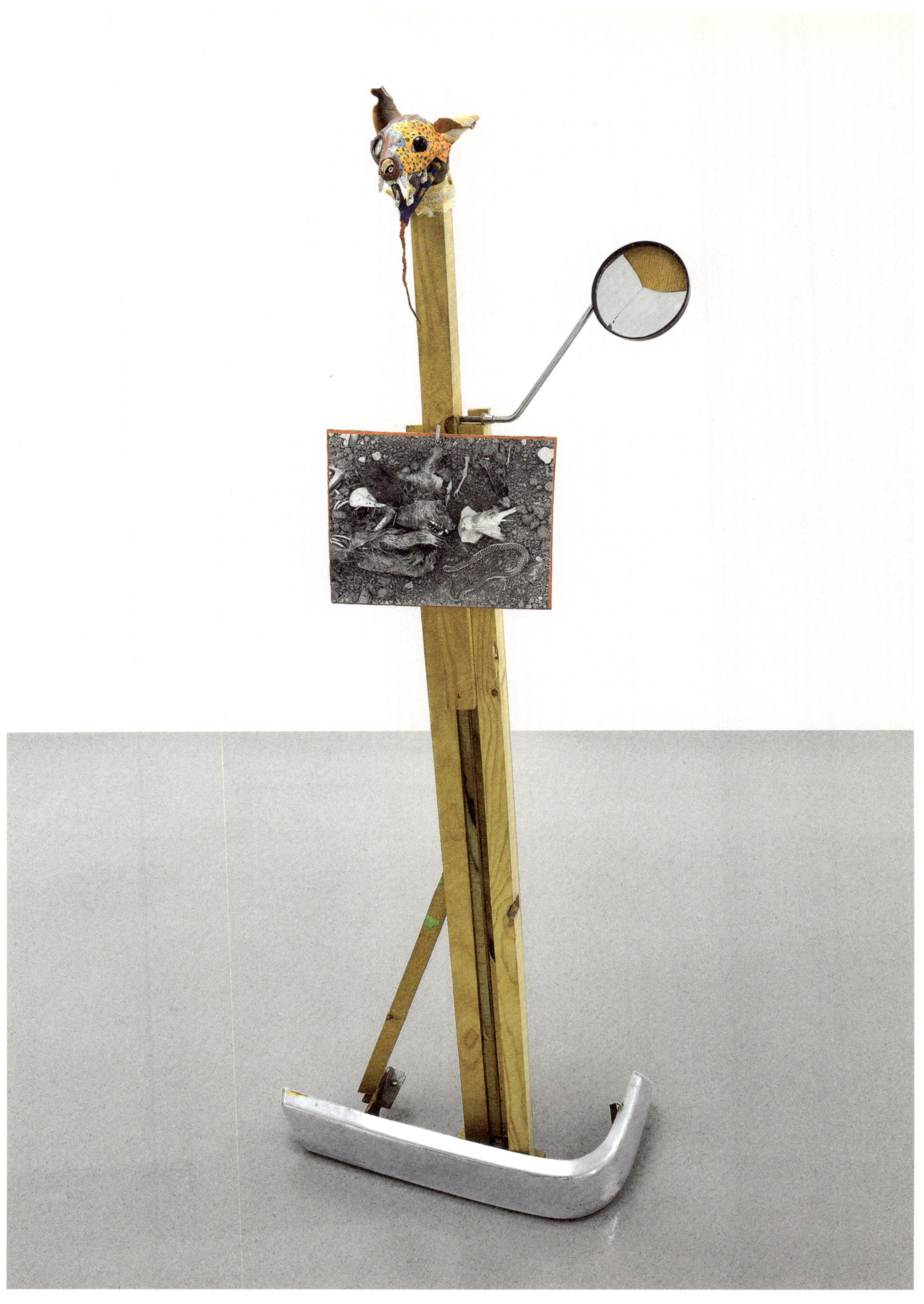

 Raccoon (Skunk), 1989. Skunk skull, pine, acrylic paint, leather, seashells, rearview mirror, car bumper part, black-and-white photograph. 67 × 24 ½ × 20 ½ in. (170 × 62 × 52 cm).

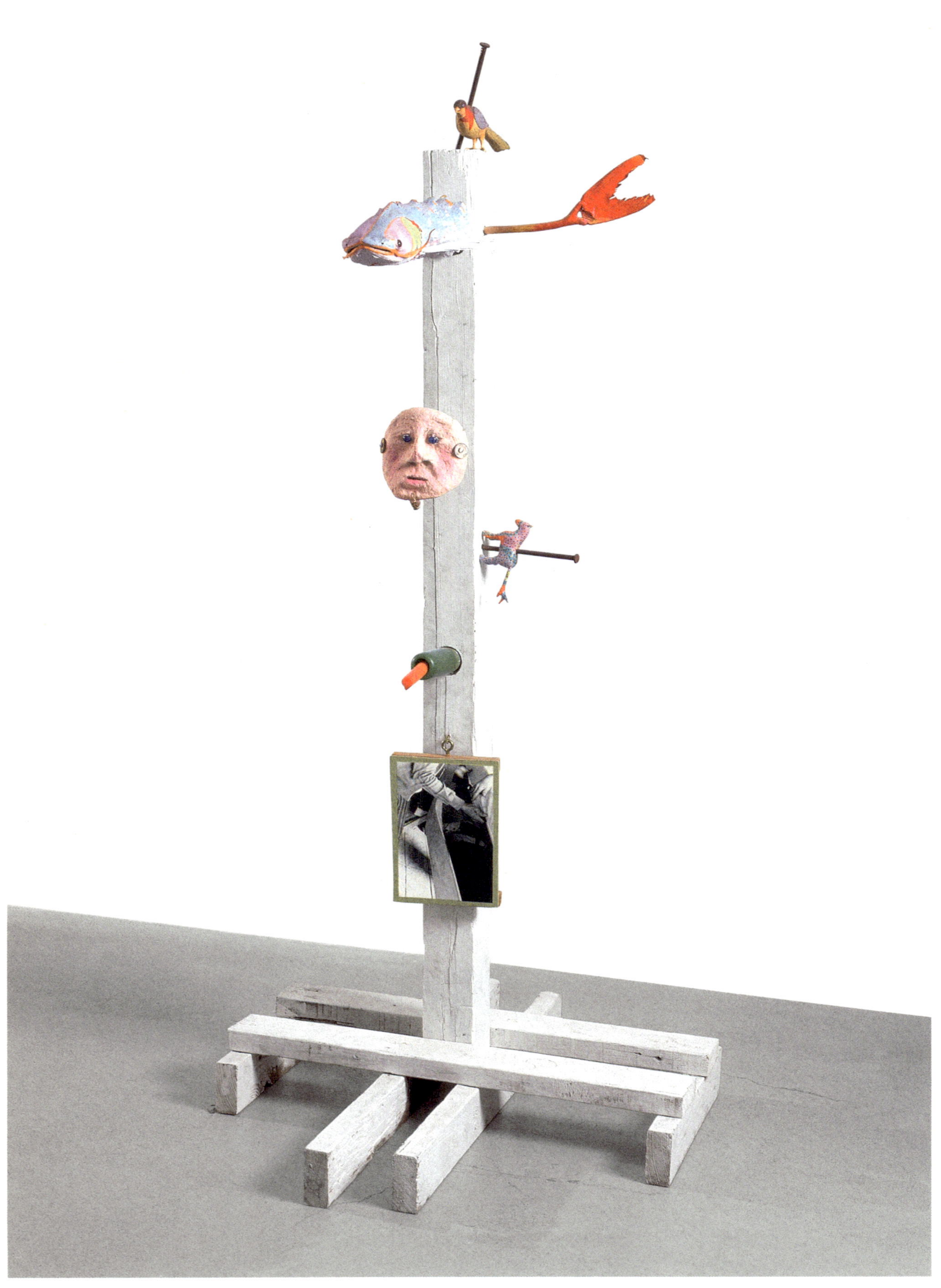

Untitled, 1991. Construction lumber, walnut, palm tree, oak, catfish head, catfish tail, papier-mâché, acrylic paint, plastic, black-and-white photograph.
64 ¼ × 30 ¾ × 28 ¼ in. (163.2 × 78.1 × 72 cm).

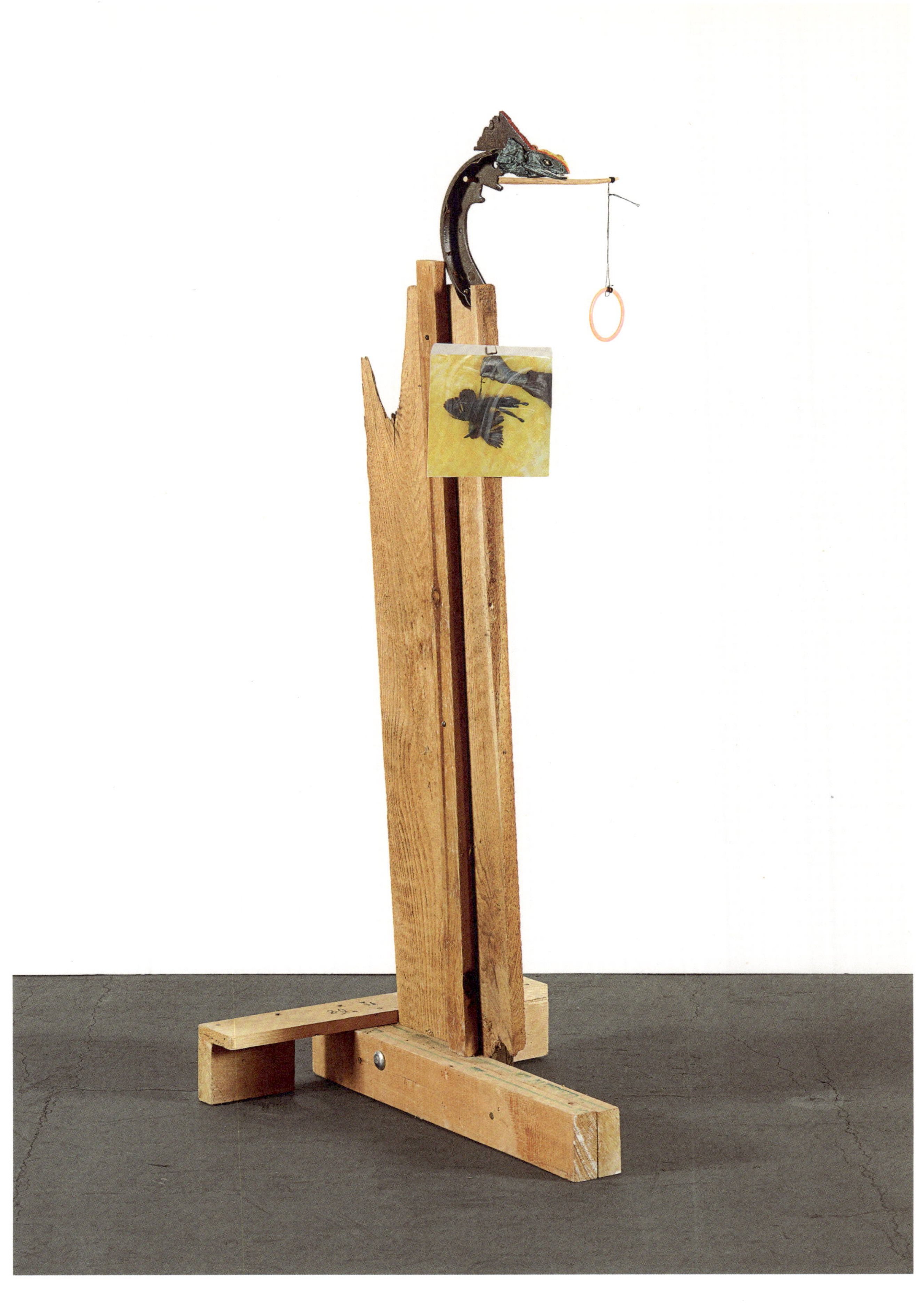

Modern Art with Dead Bird, 1991. Iguana head, beads, acrylic paint, oak, pine, walnut, metal brake drum part, plastic, color photograph.
55 ¾ × 25 ½ × 20 ¾ in. (141.5 × 65 × 53 cm).

Jokainen meistä on suunta. Cherokeilla hallituksen muodostaa neuvosto, johon oikeastaan jokainen cherokee kuuluu. Neuvostossa jokaisen velvollisuus on kuunnella huolella mitä muut sanovat ja ilmaista omat ajatuksensa tarkasti ja kokonaisuudessaan.

JimmiE DURHAM

Not Lothar Baumgarten's Cherokee, 1990. Charcoal and paper collage on paper. 16 × 21 in. (40.6 × 53.3 cm).

LANGUAGE

IS A TOOL FOR

COMMUNICATION,

LIKE

A CITY, OR A BRAIN

Language is a tool for communication, like a city, or a brain, 1992. Lithograph. 22 ¼ × 29 ¾ in. (56.5 × 75.5 cm).

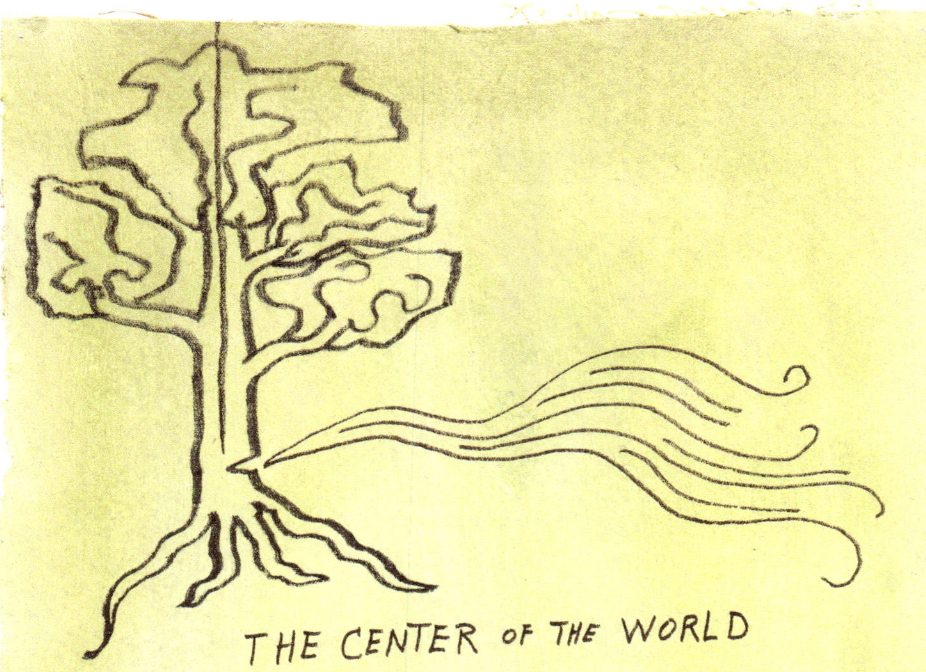

Anti Flag, 1992. Acrylic on unstretched canvas. 21 × 14 in. (53.3 × 35.6 cm).

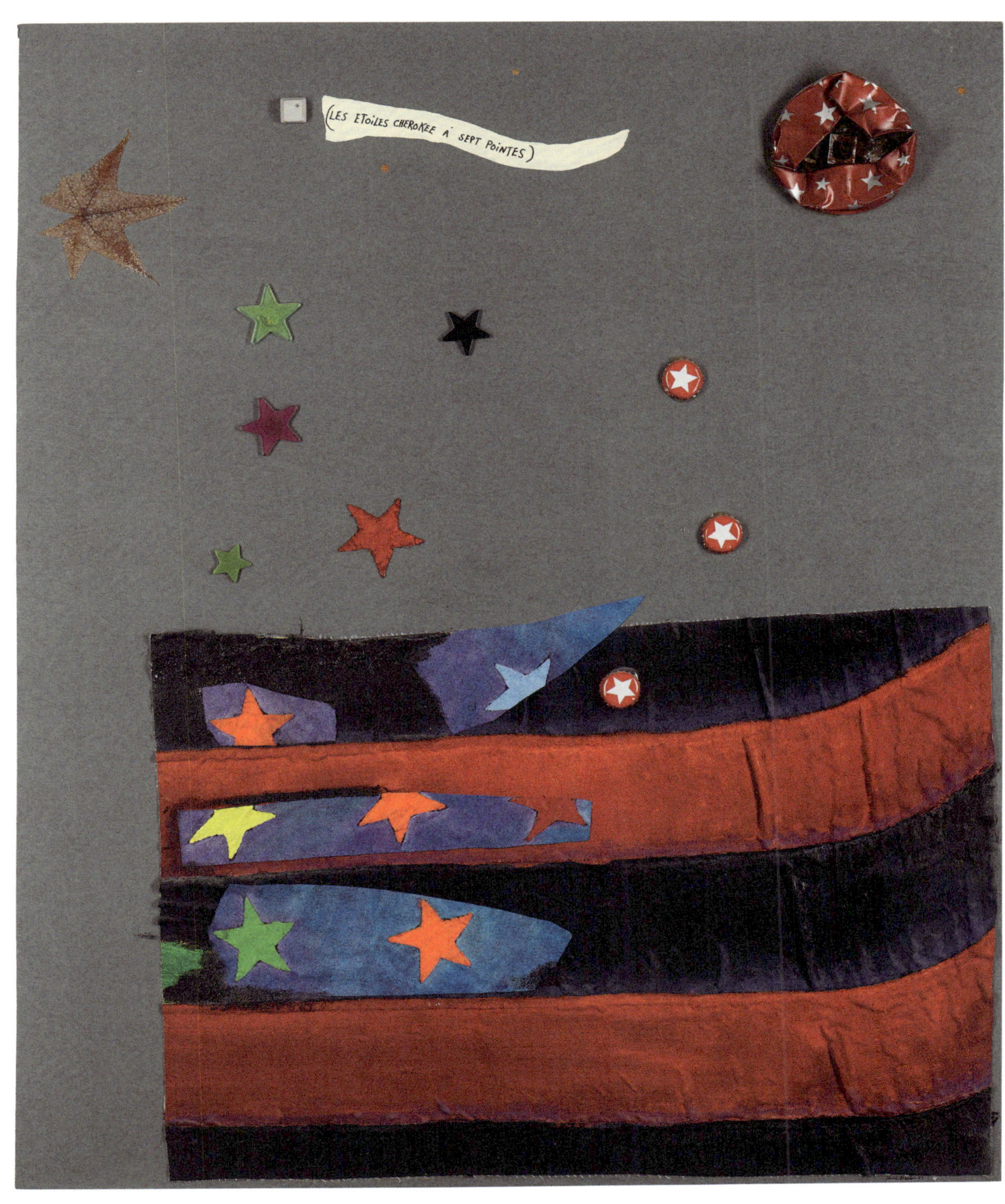

Une étude des étoiles [A study of stars], 1995. Acrylic paint, ink, sweet gum leaf, bottle caps, plastic, metal, computer key, and cotton stars from American flag on wood. 33 ½ × 20 ½ in. (85 × 52 cm).

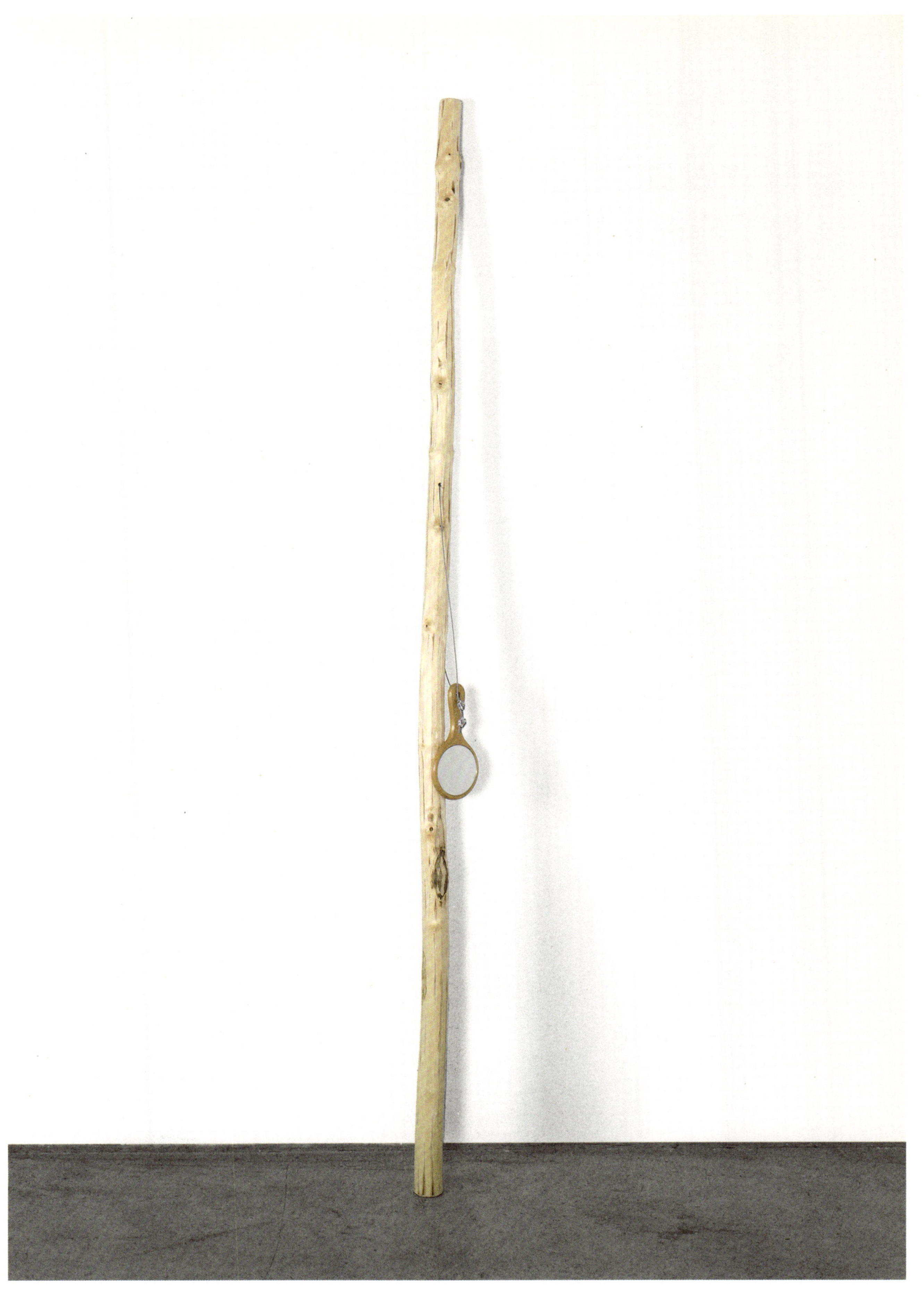

A Pole to Mark the Center of the World in Berlin, 2004. Hawthorn, mirror, cable. 71 ½ × 4 in. (182 × 10 cm).

JIMMIE DURHAM'S STONES AND BONES

JESSICA L. HORTON

In much recent work by Jimmie Durham, stone is a collaborator. During the past two decades, pebbles and boulders have pelted the front of a refrigerator (fig. 1), smashed vitrines and televisions (fig. 2; page 155), splattered paint on a gallery wall, sunk a boat, split an airplane in two (fig. 3), adopted the guise of bacon and pecorino, and masked the physiognomy of the artist (fig. 4). Often in these works, substrate replaces Durham as sculptor, assuming the power to act, transform, and narrate. Uncut stones, usually quarried near their final resting place, have trailed in the wake of Durham's travels through a global circuit of biennials and residencies. Materials indigenous to nearly every place on earth provide ready companionship for an artist on the move.

Stones appear to have supplanted the bones of coyotes, rabbits, deer, and bears that formed the body of Durham's earlier practice in North America. While living in New York City and Cuernavaca, Mexico, in the 1980s and early 1990s, Durham was celebrated for works in which he bound animal skulls, skins, and feathers to sticks and discarded car parts and fused them with garish paint. American critics linked the disturbing beauty of these works to their Indianness, construing the artist as a "postmodernist 'savage.'"[1] After he permanently relocated from Mexico to "Eurasia" in 1994, Durham noted that he did not trust how charming bone bricolage had become: "I see now I'm going to have to find a way out of that."[2] His departure from the Americas is often narrated as an exile from the settler-colonial conditions into which he was born. The artist supposedly turned away from the particularities of Red Power struggles and "issues to do with identity and ethnicity," pursuing cosmopolitan concerns abroad.[3] As two halves of a life are severed, so too is stone cleaved from bone.

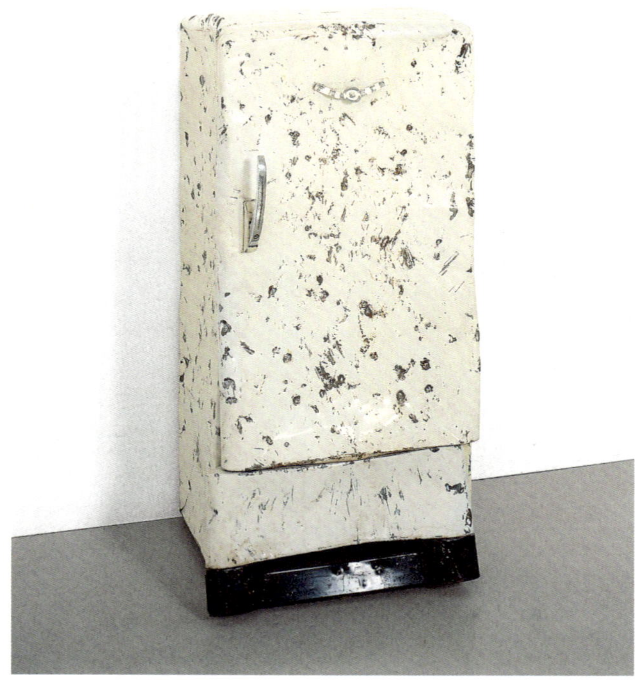

Fig. 1. *St. Frigo*, 1996. Refrigerator. 52 × 23 ½ × 23 ½ in. (132 × 60 × 60 cm). Collection of Ministry of Culture, Lisbon, Portugal.

This essay reunites material kin, revealing the sensuous and conceptual affinities between stone and bone as primary mediums of a creative life. The predicament of indigenous peoples in the United States and around the world has palpably shaped Durham's understanding of modernity as an arena of violent colonial conflict. Yet from the beginning he linked such concerns to the material underpinnings of a common world, willing us to think beyond oppositions of selves and others, oppression and resistance, which structure many anthropocentric power struggles. My understanding of Durham's practice begins with the observation that organic and mineral matter collided, joined, and conversed with human systems of meaning long before the artist's birth in Arkansas in 1940. His bones and stones enter the fray of recent human history and promise to survive its wreckage to bear witness. Interweaving episodes from Durham's activism, writing, and art, this nonlinear account reflects upon the nature of materials that join and exceed a life.

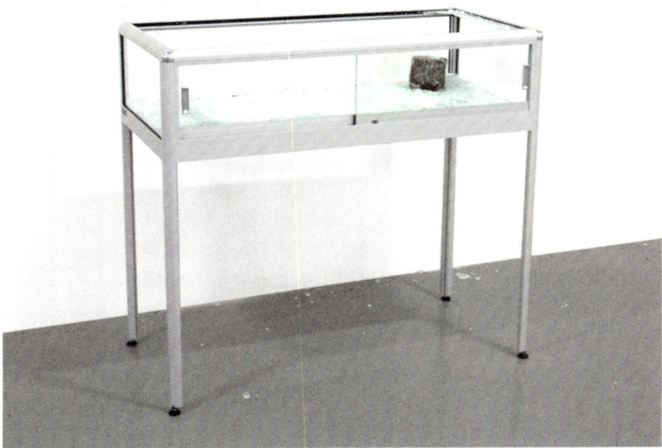

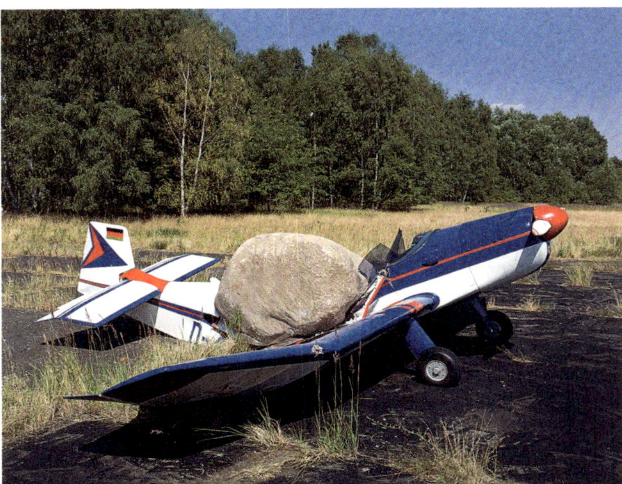

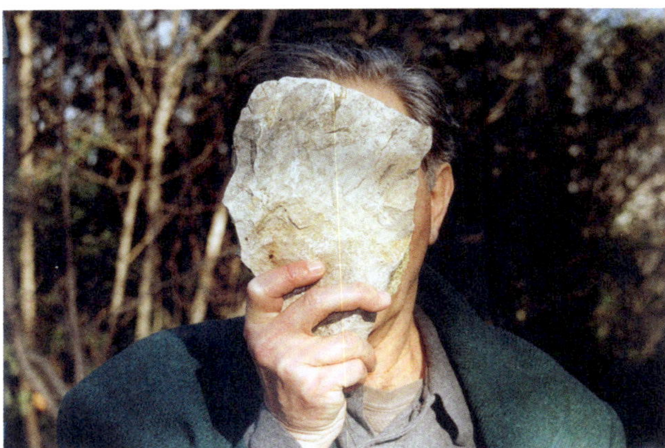

Fig. 2 (top). *A Stone from François Villon's House in Paris*, 1996/2009. Broken vitrine and stone. 39 ⅜ × 39 ⅜ × 27 ½ in. (100 × 100 × 70 cm). Installation view, *Pierres rejetées (Rejected Stones)*, Musée d'Art Moderne de la Ville de Paris, 2009.
Fig. 3 (middle). *Encore tranquillité*, 2008. Fiberglass stone and airplane. 59 × 338 ⅝ × 317 ⅜ in. (150 × 860 × 806 cm). National Gallery of Canada, Ottawa.
Fig. 4 (bottom). Production shot for *Self-Portrait Pretending to Be a Stone Statue of Myself*, 2006 (see page 205). Photo by Maria Thereza Alves.

SIGNS OF UNREST

On May 14, 2000, Durham began to record his amblings around Berlin in the form of a diary called *Nature in the City*.[4] "Most of nature in cities has been organized," he observes. "Cities are as stony, for example, as are hills and plateaux, but the stones are usually ordered into buildings, streets, curbs, monuments. They, like us, must work." Exploited as "natural resources" and employed in the foundations of modern cities, stones are made to bear the weight of human history and authority. Accordingly, Durham and his partner, artist Maria Thereza Alves, set out to track subversive forms of life lurking inside "the prison," the edifice of civilization erected to keep the wilds at bay. Neatly dated entries find them walking through ugly housing complexes and along waterfront malls. They identify yarrow in sidewalks and merle songs among sirens. Durham records his blisters, sunburns, backaches, and fleabites. He encounters a desiccated crow and brings it back to his studio; four months later he goes to clean the bones and finds that bugs already completed the task. Gravestones dated to the 1750s, scarred by lichen, evince "the impermanence of stone" and the attendant hubris of striving for immortality on a mutable earth. Still, the artist pockets a flint knife discovered among gravel that makes him "feel connected to some artist of 40,000 years ago." A diary ostensibly scaled to urban human dwelling is filled with myriad other orders: seasonal winds and creeping fungi, archaeological time and the functions of bacteria in the author's gut. Durham asks, "when un-disciplined life happens . . . don't we feel liberated?"

While *Nature in the City* takes the form of poetic observation, elsewhere Durham actively partners with subversive stuff to sculpt, splatter, or shatter the built environment. In *A Stone from François Villon's House in Paris* (1996/2009), a rock rests amid shards of glass in the bottom of a rectangular vitrine (see fig. 2). The title references a fifteenth-century French poet born into poverty. Villon was incarcerated, tortured, and ultimately banished from Paris after committing a variety of crimes, from robbery to killing a priest with a stone. In Durham's homage, the rock doubles as evidence and iconoclast, indexing the transformative collision resulting from its airborne journey. Here and elsewhere, the artist "frees" materials employed in architecture, the latter broadly understood as a manifestation of oppressive state authority. The vitrine may stand in for house, museum, jail, or city—indeed, any infrastructure and associated ideologies that subject unruly life to enclosure and correction. Art historian Richard William Hill writes that Durham "animates [stone] in ways that both bring to light and undermine its metaphorical associations in monumental architecture with permanence, weight, immobility, and stability."[5] Pebbles and boulders spring to life as agents of insurrection that are allied with, but never subordinate to, human freedom. As raw rock breaks the smooth manufactured surfaces of display cases, refrigerators, and airplanes, so too does it carry geological memories that interrupt modern metrics. Stone evinces the glacial sculpting activities of water and wind as well as the sudden, powerful upheavals of tectonic plates that have shaped the earth over millennia.

Durham's "anti-architecture" is most often understood as a response to his dwelling in stately European metropolises after immigrating in 1994.[6] Yet signs of unrest in the foundations of Berlin and Paris echo a poem the artist published in New York City in 1983, "They Forgot That Their Prison Is Made of Stone, and Stone Is Our Ally."[7] In it the incarcerated American Indian Movement (AIM) activist Russell Means finds solace in the company of vocal walls. They assure him, "Your friends are with you," in "the language of the Sioux—what other language could a South Dakota stone speak?"[8] Conversing with amicable stones helps the leader to keep objectification at bay in the prison, the quintessential disciplinary architecture of the modern state. Means was jailed repeatedly for his involvement in late twentieth-century decolonization struggles, most spectacularly the AIM occupation of Wounded Knee in 1973 (fig. 5). For seventy-one days activists toting rifles and upside-down American flags guarded the town on the Pine Ridge Indian Reservation in South Dakota against the federal authorities. They demanded political and cultural sovereignty from the US government, a value shared with indigenous communities across the Americas who forged alliances during the same period. They asserted the rights of Native American people to live freely on their ancestral lands, as promised in treaties signed in the wake of the Declaration of Independence that were repeatedly broken by the United States.[9] Near the barricades erected by proud AIM resisters, a granite monument alerted tourists to a mass grave filled with the bones of Sioux men, women, and children massacred by the US cavalry in 1890.

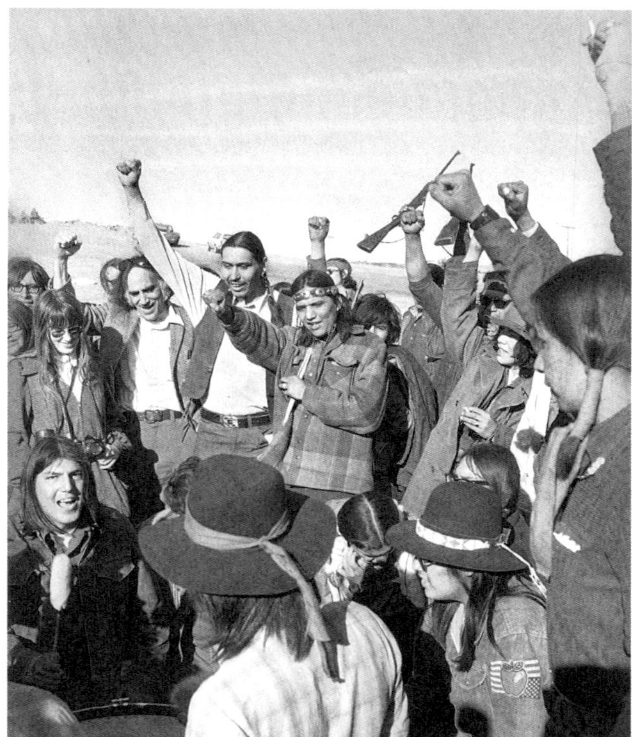

Fig. 5. American Indian Movement leader Carter Camp (white shirt) and attorney William Kunstler (to Camp's right) join AIM activists in celebrating the pullout of federal authorities from roadblocks in Wounded Knee, South Dakota, March 10, 1973.

Durham was living in Geneva during the occupation of Wounded Knee. Disillusioned with American Indian activism and the persistent racism he encountered in the United States, he had left for Switzerland in 1968, pursuing a modernist fantasy of detachment at the free École des Beaux-Arts.[10] News of Wounded Knee, discussed at bars in the company of South American exiles and African liberationists, left him feeling like an "empty [leech]."[11] Durham traveled to Pine Ridge to help with the legal struggles of activists, and then relocated to New York City to become founding director of the International Indian Treaty Council (IITC) in 1974. The new branch of AIM took shape during the incarceration and trials of Means and other Wounded Knee participants, the infiltration of Federal Bureau of Investigation agents posing as activists, and a national media blackout of the movement. In a bid to circumvent the colonial space of the nation, Durham returned repeatedly to Geneva, this time seeking formal recognition for Native Americans as sovereigns before the United Nations. The world conference he helped to organize in 1977 laid the groundwork for the nonbinding United Nations Declaration on the Rights of Indigenous Peoples formally adopted by the General Assembly in 2007.[12]

In 1979 Durham resigned amid bitter factionalism. He circulated a public letter clarifying the goals and failures of the activists, who had sought legitimacy from the very Western legal-political institutions that authorized their colonization.[13] In this and other writings of the period, Durham pictured modernity in a deadlock of nation-state coercion and cronyism. Central to his understanding of recent human history was the European occupation of indigenous land and people. Yet he deemed colonization inseparable from capitalist exploitation of "the real things and processes of our world" upon which all life depends.[14] In other words, the domination, division, and displacement of nonconformist cultures and "nature" resulted from a single imperialistic process with devastating planetary effects. The public framing of AIM—and much subsequent artistic practice—as a matter of "Indian identity" effectively curtailed Durham's efforts to articulate a global arena of common concern through the IITC. Shortly after departing to Mexico in 1987, Durham wrote, "I feel fairly sure that I could address the entire world if only I had a place to stand. But you (white Americans) have made everything your turf. In every field, on every issue, the ground has already been covered."[15]

Through intimate interactions with the physical world, Durham both refined and superseded his own negative critique of human assemblies. His creative ensembles posit the entwined fates of humans and materials while seeking—quite literally at times—to free up the ground. Sioux stones point the way. At first glance, the case of architecture-turned-ally seems to fit a classic mode of speaking back to power. Throughout Durham's poetry of the period, earthly stuff rises from inertia to bolster anticolonial resistance. Addressing the decimation of indigenous brethren by warfare, he wrote, "We held council with the universe. / The stars, eagles, loons and coyotes / Sang, 'Time is with you.' / 'History is on your side.' / Trees gave seeds / And rocks encouraged."[16] At the same time, gatherings of canine and fowl, human and helium, stone and seed indicate a vast network of sensuous solidarities that exceeds opposition to state control. Elsewhere, Durham's description of the world as "a big council meeting" indicates an ecological ethics in which humans are compelled to share authorial power with other beings: "It is obviously one's duty to be a part of it, and that entails listening well and speaking well."[17] Vocal plants, animals, and materials weigh in on human conflicts while simultaneously exposing the conceit of Euroamerican hegemony on an earth where everything—the ground itself—is guaranteed to move. Hence, when Means listens to the friendly words of stone, he is sustained by sources of sovereignty that persist inside and stretch beyond the grip of colonial authority.

While South Dakota stones speak Sioux, participating in a coded indigenous alliance, the boulders that have settled atop vehicles in the wake of Durham's post-2000 travels wordlessly redirect neocolonial flows of global capital. Such works begin with a deceptively simple reversal of expectations about movement and stasis: cars, boats, and airplanes—modern symbols of progress and mobility—appear grounded and defunct, while undervalued substrate exhibits the uncanny ability to fly. For *Encore tranquillité* (2008), Durham orchestrated the lowering of a boulder by crane onto a single-engine airplane in an abandoned airstrip on the edge of Berlin (see fig. 3). The enormous weight of the rock split the vehicle in half. When a photograph of the sculptural pair circulated on the cover of *Artforum* in 2009, readers learned that the antiquated ex-Soviet plane did not meet European safety standards and was slated for sale in Africa.[18] That same year, it was relocated to the foyer of the Musée d'Art Moderne de la Ville de Paris for an exhibition of Durham's work titled *Pierres rejetées (Rejected Stones)*.[19] Now visitors were challenged to reconstruct an encounter that had occurred in the past, scanning the rubble for clues: Did the stone fall from above or sail through the air? Was it local to Europe or a hit man from Africa? Was the plane it targeted still or in motion, occupied or empty? Piecing together the events surrounding the aborted African sale entails heeding the tales told by unpredictable materials.

The work recalls Sioux rock's earlier role as subaltern ally, intervening on behalf of undervalued human lives in longstanding geographies of colonial injustice. Stone plays savior in other senses as well. Upon hurtling cobblestones at the front of a refrigerator in 1996, Durham wrote, "In the end, I called it *Saint Frigo*. . . . I saved its life by making it a martyr" (see fig. 1).[20] A seemingly destructive gesture rescued the appliance from obsolescence and guaranteed its survival as art. The crushing impact of boulder on airplane similarly halted the latter's slide toward the boneyard and transformed it into one half of a transcendent sculpture. The result is more than mere readymade, a class of object that continues to glide smoothly through human systems of value in the wake of Duchamp.[21] Rather, crushed metal and splintered fiberglass expose the material guts—the hidden inner life—of the flying machine. Reduced to misshapen debris, a state of matter that precedes and persists after human fashioning, the object is brought qualitatively closer to the granite mass quarried nearby and settled atop. In the same instant that the materials are coupled and elevated as art, then, they are rejoined with earthly origins and aftermath. Listening to stories told by stuff, visitors hold council with material systems that stretch beyond the physical and temporal bounds of the museum.

The Center of the World at Chalma (1997; fig. 6) makes explicit the latent cartographic dimensions of Durham's materialist project. He scattered a truckload of softball-sized rocks across the floor of the Pori Art Museum in Finland. Photographs of the installation reveal stones spilling across architectural boundaries, filling the gift shop, and gathering on sidewalks. A world map on the wall featured a crooked line drawn by the artist, connecting Pori to Chalma, "a village in the state of Morelos in the southern part of North America." The adjacent wall text told of indigenous peoples who have long traveled there to visit a tree that marks the center of the world: "[T]hose who become discouraged and give up along the way are turned to stone. On the chance that they should be lost souls which might recover themselves upon arrival at the tree, we are asked when on the pilgrimage to kick stones in the direction of Chalma."[22] Museumgoers were invited to orient themselves toward a distant place before booting a chosen rock. Physical participation doubled as an imaginative exercise, projecting oneself into a circuit of human-plant-mineral relations that predates the conquest of North America and the nation of Mexico. At the same time, Durham's hand-drawn path followed well-worn grooves of colonization and globalization, modern trajectories that implicate every visitor in multiple, interlinked "centers" of the world.[23]

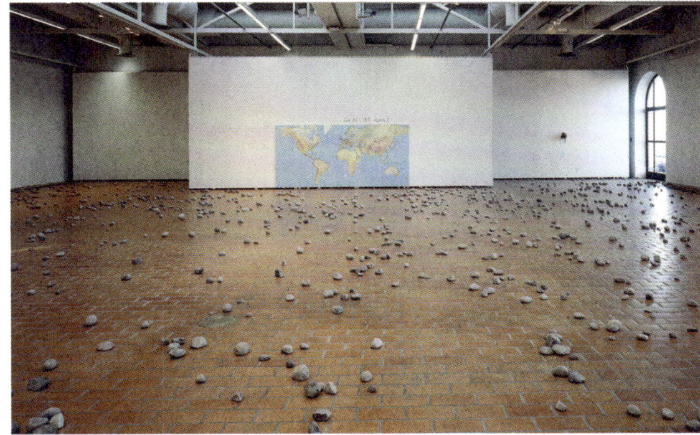

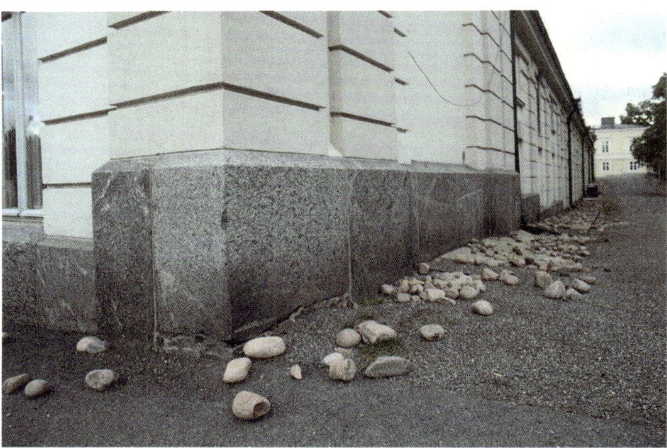

Fig. 6. *The Center of the World at Chalma*, 1997, installation views, Pori Art Museum, Finland.

MAPS AND MEMORIES

Bones, metonyms of fleeting life, are always en route to becoming stones. *The Center of the World at Chalma* asks us to picture this, too, as a reversible process: even fossils can be reanimated in a universe where nothing stays still forever. Following his resignation from AIM, Durham forged an artistic practice on New York's Lower East Side out of femurs and skulls, seeking to free bone from the weight and permanence typically granted death in a Euroamerican context. The human stakes of this project should not be overlooked. Following the atrocities sanctioned by US Indian removal policy in the nineteenth century (see page 37), Native Americans became the stuff of national nostalgia, objectified and left for dead. AIM activists specifically protested the desecration of Indian burial sites by archaeologists and grave robbers, having witnessed their relatives studied by scientists and their ancestral belongings desacralized in markets and museums.[24] In an enigmatic bulletin from 1984, Durham claimed the ability to see dead things as an artistic imperative:

> When I was 13 or so I had to go out into the woods and find my real name. Coyote, who invented death and singing, was the spirit who gave me my name. As is often the case, he also gave me a gift. This is what he gave me as a name gift: that I would always see whatever was dead if it were within my field of vision. For more than thirty years I have seen every dead bird and animal every day wherever I am. So it became necessary to see if that was a usable gift or just a dirty trick that would drive me crazy.[25]

Coyote, a boundary-crossing trickster in Cherokee and other Native American stories, achieved a reputation as a notorious pest in the last decades of the twentieth century, confined by urbanization and surviving on scraps (and the occasional housecat).[26] Durham assumed an analogous role in New York City by using bones and discarded industrial materials as the foundation of a mischievous creative practice. Nailed and glued together with the seams exposed, his patchwork figures made forensic evidence grin and wave.

Among Durham's earliest documented works, *Manhattan Festival of the Dead* (1982; see page 40), at Kenkeleba Gallery in New York, featured an assembly of deer, horse, rodent, human, and other skeletons enlivened with garish paint (figs. 7, 8). Fur ears and stick horns crown smooth skulls, patches of glass seed beads gleam off snouts, and swirling shells peer cannily from hollow sockets. Mounted on rough-hewn stumps and placed on shelves "like a trading post on an Indian reservation," the singing and dancing dead were eagerly purchased by visitors for $5 a head.[27] Durham's anticipation of fetishism, built into the participatory structure of *Manhattan Festival of the Dead*, points to one of the motivating challenges of his career: his every effort to step outside Euroamerican frames of reference risks confirming some audiences' "imperialist nostalgia."[28] Visitors to the gallery apparently missed the work's irony, consuming it the way tourists at Wounded Knee pocketed dream catchers and buffalo-bone necklaces.[29] Soon after, he began affixing animal bones to police barricades and car parts, ensuring that their strange beauty did not so readily indulge primitivism (pages 45, 46).

Critics discussed the "trap" of Native American identity exhaustively in the 1980s and 1990s, crediting Durham's humor

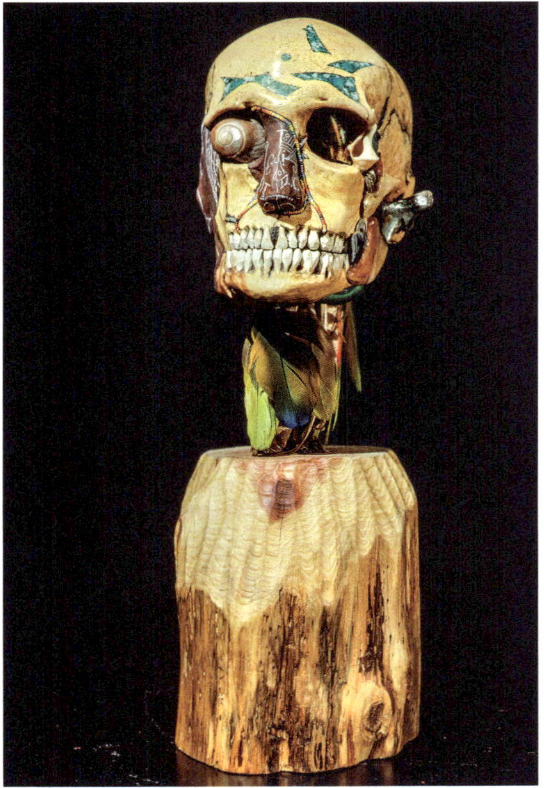

Fig. 7 (top). Untitled, 1982 (detail). Dog skull, shell, wood, acrylic paint, button. 12 ¼ × 3 ⅜ × 5 ⅝ in. (31.2 × 8.4 × 14.4 cm). Included in *Manhattan Festival of the Dead*, 1982.
Fig. 8 (bottom). *Karankawa*, 1982. Human skull, cedar, seashells, abalone shell, alabaster, beads, button, turquois, cow leather, fish bone, parrott feathers, woodpecker feather, two deer teeth, white and black ink. 19 × 9 × 9 in. (48.3 × 22.9 × 22.9 cm). Included in *Manhattan Festival of the Dead*, 1982.

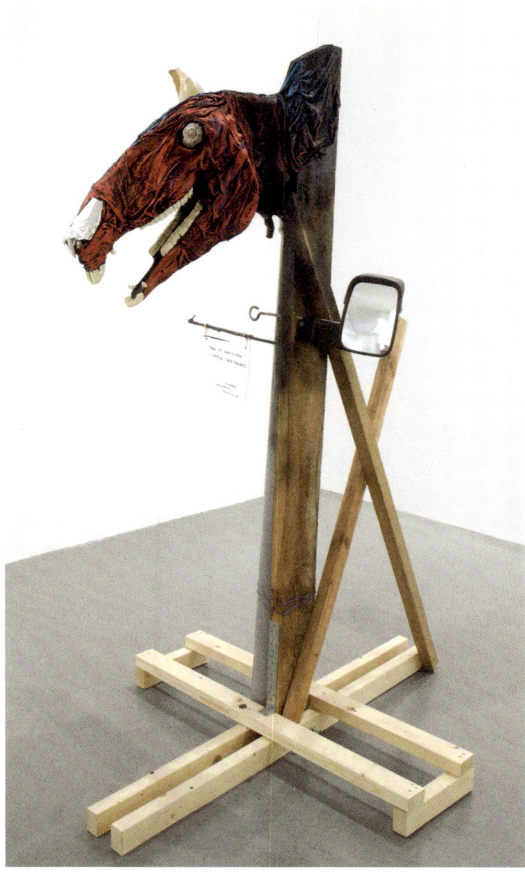

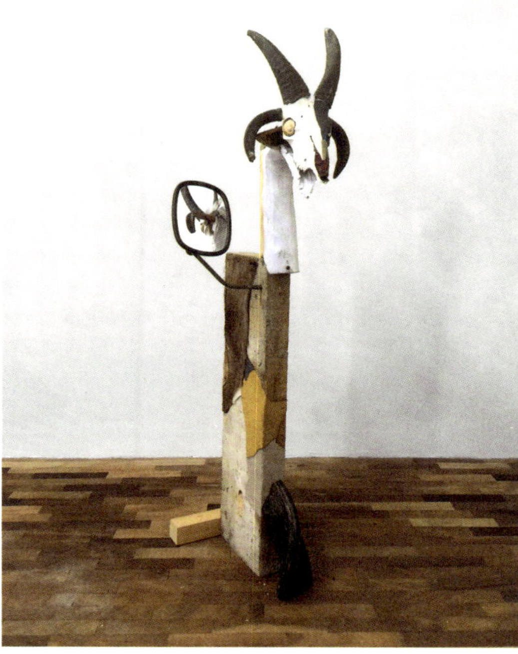

Fig. 9 (top). *Mulholland Drive*, 2007. Wood, horse skull, sheet metal, rearview mirror, acrylic paint, seashell. 88 ½ × 71 × 43 ¼ in. (225 × 180 × 110 cm). Private collection, Switzerland.
Fig. 10 (bottom). *The Isle of Man*, 2016. Four-horn sheep skull, obsidian, seashell, mussel shell, acacia seed pod, Murano glass, leather, olive, pine, poplar, truck rearview mirror, acrylic paint, silicon glue, white glue, epoxy glue, metal screws, nails. 52 × 16 ½ × 21 ¼ in. (132 × 42 × 54 cm). Courtesy of the artist and kurimanzutto, Mexico City.

as a strategy of evasion. He was deemed "the 'coyote' or 'trickster,' mischievous and cunning—an artist who uses irony to strip away the ornamental packaging that bounds American Indians in, what remains for many, a colonial present."[30] Art historian Richard Shiff elaborated: "The jokes insure that his art avoids all claims to self-mastery, as well as any possibility that this particular 'Indian' identity will ever be mastered by the colonizers."[31] In such accounts, Durham assumed the role of a trickster appropriated from indigenous precedents to serve the ends of postmodern and anticolonial critique. This is how the artist is commonly remembered in the United States today: a mocking miscreant who set out to interrupt white hegemony, first as an AIM activist, then as a bone bricoleur. The trouble with such an interpretive framework is that it begins on occupied ground and never quite transcends the negativity assigned to Native subjects in American history. Durham appears locked in an unending relation of opposition from the margins, exiled even before departing the United States. The impression was compounded when, while living in Cuernavaca, he vehemently criticized the US Indian Arts and Crafts Act of 1990 for managing the "authenticity" of indigenous art and identity. His noncompliance with the law resulted in the cancellation of several planned solo exhibitions in the United States in the midst of the Columbus Quincentennial.[32] At the same time, meetings between organic and manufactured materials stabilized into symbols of Cherokee resistance. In other words, Durham's bricolages calcified apace with the artist's reputation. He largely banished bones following his transatlantic relocation in 1994, only to reintroduce them more than a decade later in works such as *Mulholland Drive* (2007; fig. 9), composed of a decorated horse skull mounted on plywood and PVC pipe, and more recently a four-horn sheep skull in *The Isle of Man* (2016; fig. 10). Durham notes in *Nature in the City*, "the only place for such things in Europe is exotic anthropology. Still, it is unusual to find a dead crow in the city."[33]

By attending to the kinship between stones and bones, we may recover a worldly significance for the latter, beyond their negative role in anticolonial critique. Durham's poetry again provides a prompt. In "Tarascan Guitars" (1983), stones appear as witnesses to murder and eyes to see past it. The artist writes, "In Texas, at that old Comanche place called White Flint, / I found the skull of an armadillo. / Maybe some new hunter killed an armadillo with a .22 rifle. / I asked rocks and other things around. / It was probably that way, they said."[34] He describes restoring agate and seashell to empty eye sockets, preparing the armadillo to "dance like a flower to the music of his brothers" at a festival of the dead in Mexico. The poem continues, "If we do not let our memories fail us / The dead can sing and be with us. / They want us to remember them, / And they can make festivals in our struggles."[35] The view offered by surrogate eyes is a long one. As stone, shell, and bone meet and mingle, their assembly intersects and exceeds the life span of any single conflict, be it between an armadillo and a gunman, or Native Americans and the state. The aggregate memory of such materials is oceans wide and eons old. By "listening well" to the counsel of dead things, humans may in turn stretch our capacity for recollection to include the dancing earth.

Rejoining stones and bones finally allows us to meaningfully connect the scattered geographies of Durham's itinerant life. Texas, Mexico, Geneva, Berlin, Japan, Sydney: these are just a few of the cities, states, and nations traversed by the artist

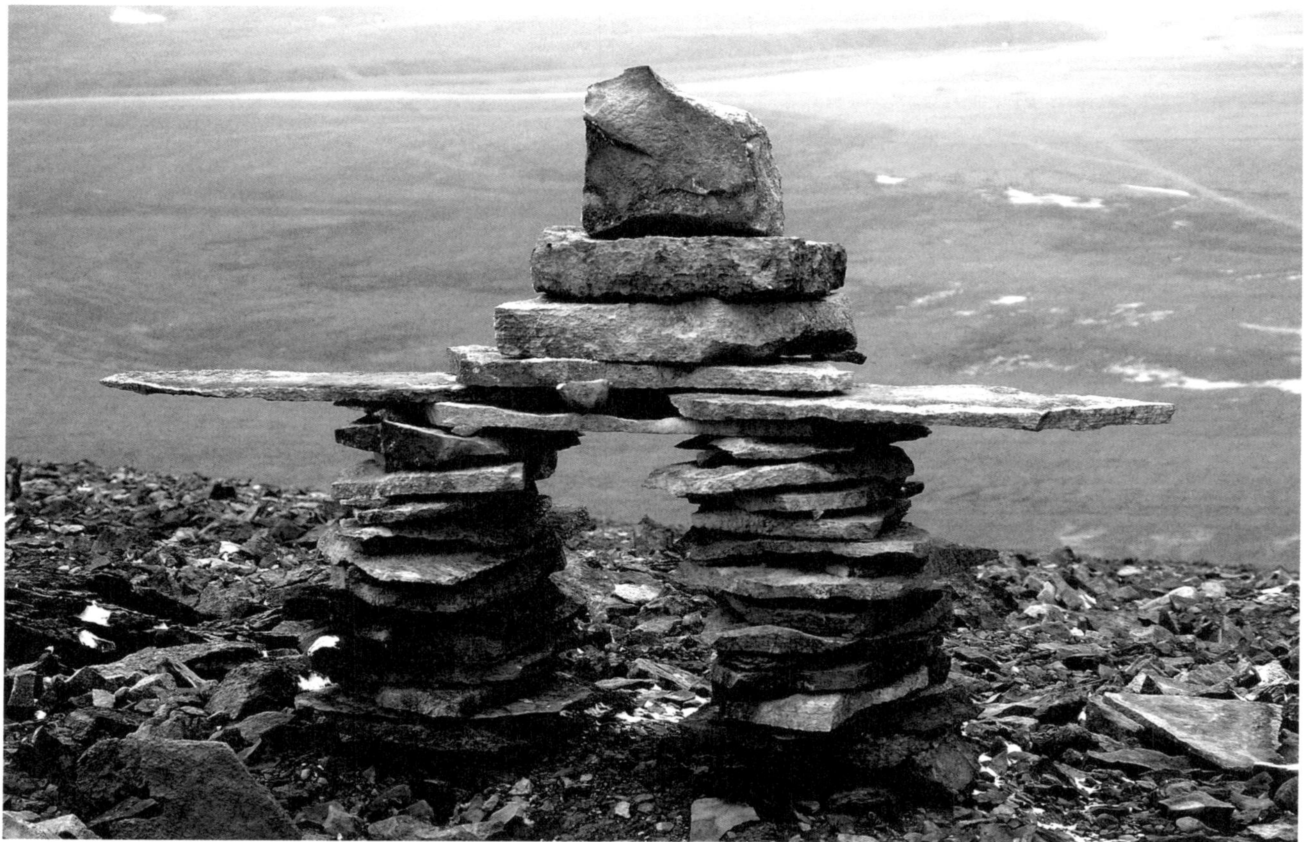

Fig. 11. Inuit *inuksuk*, Resolute Bay, Nunavut, Canada, 2008.

and teeming with material collaborators that are indigenous to everywhere. With such a worldly address in mind, I am compelled to double back, acknowledging the quiet debt this project owes to long-standing Native American cartographic practices. The pebbles and boulders Durham leaves behind recall rock piles assembled by indigenous travelers to mark key points in journeys before and after the colonization of the Americas.[36] Inuit people assemble stones in the shape of hominids called *inuksuit* (the singular *inuksuk* means "to act in the capacity of a human"); these formations are utilized as message centers alerting travelers to shelter and food caches needed to endure on ice (fig. 11).[37] While today's hikers commonly refer to stone trail markers using a term derived from Gaelic, *cairn*, a Quechua word, *apatsixta*, translates as "burden depositor," conveying an understanding that travelers' fatigue can be transmitted to substrate and left behind.[38] As stones and bones scattered in the wake of Durham's journeys hold council with the living, they testify to the colonial violence of much recent human history while bolstering the survival of alternative collectivities and stories. More than acting "against" architecture, material allies map a common ground that persists, undivided.

Notes

1. Lucy R. Lippard, "Jimmie Durham: Postmodernist 'Savage,'" *Art in America* 81, no. 2 (February 1993): 55, 63–68.
2. "Interview: Dirk Snauwaert in Conversation with Jimmie Durham," in *Jimmie Durham*, ed. Laura Mulvey, Dirk Snauwaert, and Mark Alice Durant (London: Phaidon, 1995), 25. Note that Durham refers to his new home as "Eurasia" rather than Europe, emphasizing the constructed nature of modern geopolitical boundaries.
3. "Chronology," in *Jimmie Durham: Pierres rejetées (Rejected Stones)* (Paris: Musée d'Art Moderne de la Ville de Paris/ARC, 2009), 43. This tendency is due in part to Durham's disinterest in exhibiting in the United States following his move from Mexico to Europe in 1994. Museum van Hedendaagse Kunst Antwerpen (M HKA) director Bart De Baere and curator Anders Kreuger challenged this division in their 2012 retrospective *Jimmie Durham: A Matter of Life and Death and Singing* (Antwerp: M HKA, 2012), setting out to "respect chronology" as well as "the meaningful coils and twists of his development, the variation of themes, the revisiting of ideas and images" (p. 14). Nonetheless, their primary concern was Durham's relevance in Europe.
4. Jimmie Durham, *Nature in the City: A Diary* (Berlin: BüroFriedrich, 2001), n.p.
5. Richard William Hill, "The Malice and Benevolence of Inanimate Objects: Jimmie Durham's Anti-Architecture," in *A Matter of Life and Death and Singing*, 75. See also Richard William Hill, "The Question of Agency in the Art and Writing of Jimmie Durham" (PhD thesis, Middlesex University, 2010).
6. See, for example, Isabel Carlos, "Storytelling versus Architecture," in Carolyn Christov-Bakargiev et al., *Jimmie Durham: Report from the East Atlantic* (Amsterdam: Artimo Foundation, 2005), 139; and Hill, "The Malice and Benevolence of Inanimate Objects," 75.
7. Jimmie Durham, "They Forgot That Their Prison Is Made of Stone, and Stone Is Our Ally," in *Columbus Day: Poems, Drawings and Stories about American Indian Life and Death in the Nineteen-Seventies* (Albuquerque: West End Press, 1983), 86.
8. Durham, "Chapter Two," in *Columbus Day*, 7.
9. Speeches and other documents by AIM leaders are published in Alvin M. Josephy Jr., Joane Nagel, and Troy Johnson, eds., *Red Power*, 2nd ed. (Lincoln: University of Nebraska Press, 1999).
10. Durham, "Chapter Two," 5.
11. Luis Camnitzer, "Jimmie Durham: Dancing Serious Dances," in *Jimmie Durham: The Bishop's Moose and the Pinkerton Men*, ed. Jeanette Ingberman (New York: Exit Art, 1990), 9; Durham, "Chapter Two," 5.
12. Durham later surmised that although AIM's efforts in Geneva rallied certain countries on behalf of the movement—notably, Cuba and Syria—"no one had even come close to achieving UN action or resolution on a matter inside the US." Durham, "An Open Letter

on Recent Developments in the American Indian Movement/International Indian Treaty Council," in Durham, *A Certain Lack of Coherence: Writings on Art and Cultural Politics*, ed. Jean Fisher (London: Kala Press, 1993), 47. Note that 143 member countries voted in favor of the declaration in 2007, while the United States, Canada, New Zealand, and Australia initially voted against it. They later endorsed the document under pressure from the international community. The declaration is available on the UN website: www.un.org/esa/socdev/unpfii/documents/DRIPS_en.pdf.

13. Durham, "An Open Letter," 46–56.

14. Durham, "American Indian Culture: Traditionalism and Spiritualism in a Revolutionary Struggle," in *A Certain Lack of Coherence*, 16.

15. Jimmie Durham and Jean Fisher, "The Ground Has Been Covered," *Artforum* 26, no. 10 (Summer 1988): 101.

16. Durham, "Middle," in *Columbus Day*, 30.

17. Jimmie Durham, untitled statement in *Land, Spirit, Power: First Nations Art at the National Gallery of Canada*, ed. Diana Nemiroff, Robert Houle, and Charlotte Townsend-Gault (Ottawa: National Gallery of Canada, 1992), 145.

18. Durham, "1000 Words," *Artforum* 47, no. 5 (January 2009): 189.

19. At this point the boulder was replaced by a fiberglass replica.

20. Jimmie Durham, "Stones Rejected by the Builder," in *Jimmie Durham*, ed. Anna Daneri, Giacinto Di Pietrantonio, and Roberto Pinto (Milan: Charta; Como: Fondazione Antonio Ratti, 2004), 124.

21. In *He said I was always juxtaposing, but I thought he said just opposing. So to prove him wrong I agreed with him. Over the next few years we drifted apart* (2005), Durham intervened in the legacy of the readymade by dropping a classical marble head on a urinal.

22. The author thanks the Pori Art Museum for providing archival photographs for study.

23. After moving to Eurasia, Durham began a series of works to mark multiple centers of the world. See Richard William Hill and Beverly Koski, "Jimmie Durham: The Centre of the World Is Several Places (Parts I & II)," *FUSE Magazine* 21, nos. 3–4 (1998): 24–33; 46–53.

24. Vine Deloria Jr., *God Is Red: A Native View of Religion* (Golden, CO: Fulcrum Publishing, 1994), 13–18.

25. This fragment from Durham's bulletin has been widely quoted and is usually attributed to its reproduction in Lippard, "Postmodernist 'Savage,'" 66.

26. Elsewhere Durham credits Coyote for contributing to the creation not only of his bone work but of Cherokee people: According to "an absolutely true and scientific account of [Cherokee] origins . . . Coyote impulsively bit every animal present at the council, and regurgitated the flesh in the form of humans." Jimmie Durham, *Mataoka Ake Attakulakula Anel Guledisgo Hnihi (Pocahontas and the Little Carpenter in London)* (London: Matt's Gallery, 1988), n.p.

27. Jimmie Durham, "Attending to the Words and the Bones: An Interview with Jean Fisher," *Art and Design* 10, nos. 7–8 (1995): 48.

28. Renato Rosaldo coined "imperialist nostalgia" to describe a process whereby "the agents of colonialism long for the very forms of life they intentionally altered or destroyed." Rosaldo, "Imperialist Nostalgia," *Representations*, no. 26 (April 1, 1989): 107–8.

29. Durham, "Attending to the Words and the Bones," 48; Durham in conversation with the author, Rome, Italy, October 2011.

30. Laura Turney, "Ceci n'est pas Jimmie Durham," *Critique of Anthropology* 19, no. 4 (December 1999): 431.

31. Richard Shiff, "The Necessity of Jimmie Durham's Jokes," *Art Journal* 51, no. 3 (Fall 1992): 79.

32. For commentary on the law and its effects, see Gerald R. McMaster, "Borderzones: The 'Injun-uity' of Aesthetic Tricks," *Cultural Studies* 9, no. 1 (January 1995): 74–90; Shiff, "The Necessity of Jimmie Durham's Jokes"; and Kay WalkingStick, "Democracy, Inc.: Kay WalkingStick on Indian Law," *Artforum* 30, no. 3 (November 1991): 20–21.

33. Durham, *Nature in the City*, n.p.

34. Durham, "Tarascan Guitars," in *Columbus Day*, 48.

35. Ibid.

36. Stephen C. Jett, "Cairn Trail Shrines in Middle and South America," *Yearbook: Conference of Latin Americanist Geographers* 20 (1994): 1.

37. Norman Hallendy, *Inuksuit: Silent Messengers of the Arctic* (Vancouver, BC: Douglas & McIntyre, 2000), 22.

38. Jett, "Cairn Trail Shrines," 5.

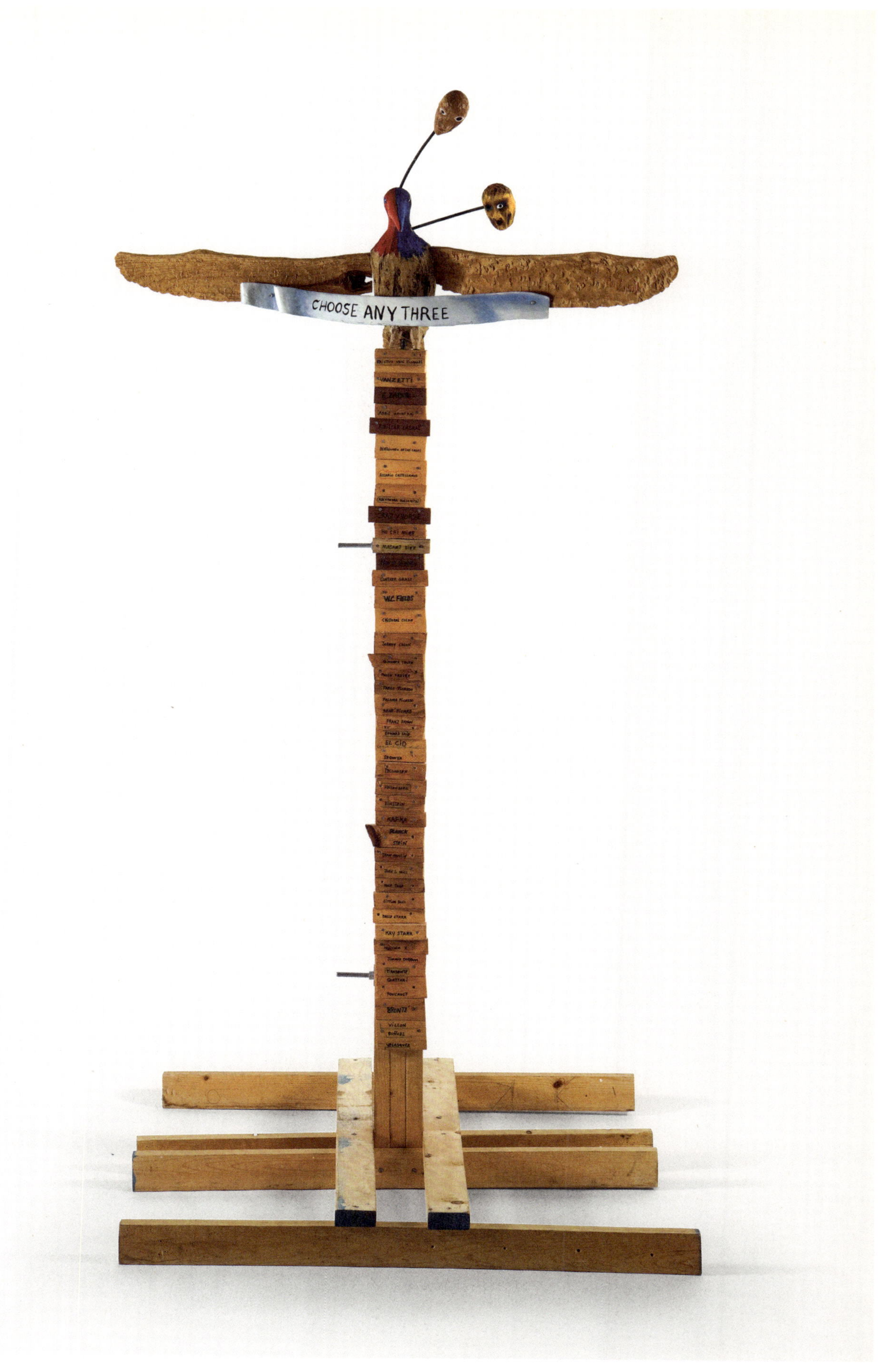

Choose Any Three, 1989. Carved ash, magnolia, pine, metal, glass, acrylic paint. 99 ¼ × 49 ¼ × 48 in. (252 × 125 × 122 cm).

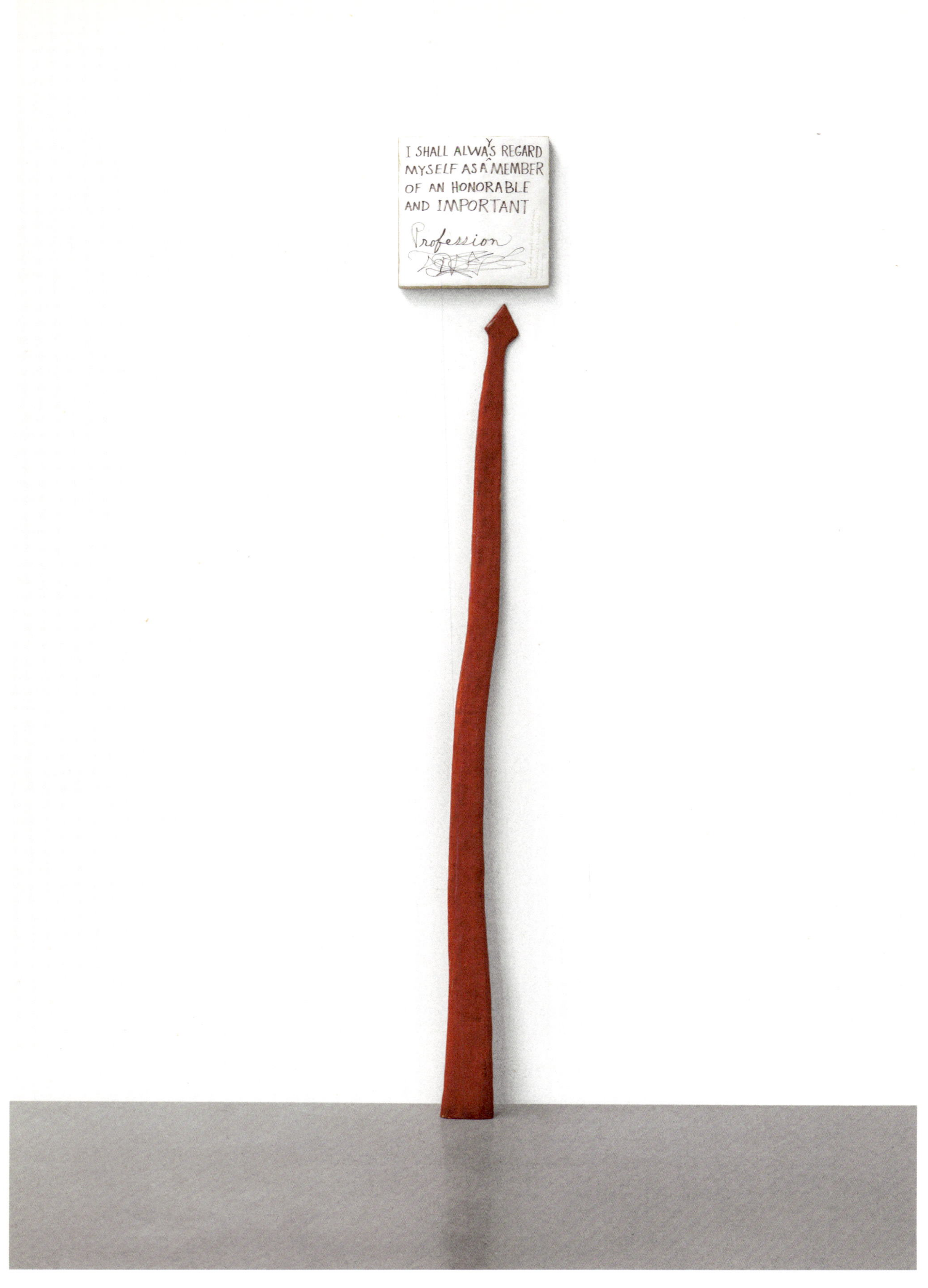

Articles 2 and 3 from the 1986 Pinkerton's Agency Manual, 1989. Mahogany, polyester resin with red dye 2, ink on wood panel.
Sculpture: 56 × 5 ½ in. (142 × 14 cm); text: 9 ¾ × 9 ¾ in. (25 × 25 cm).

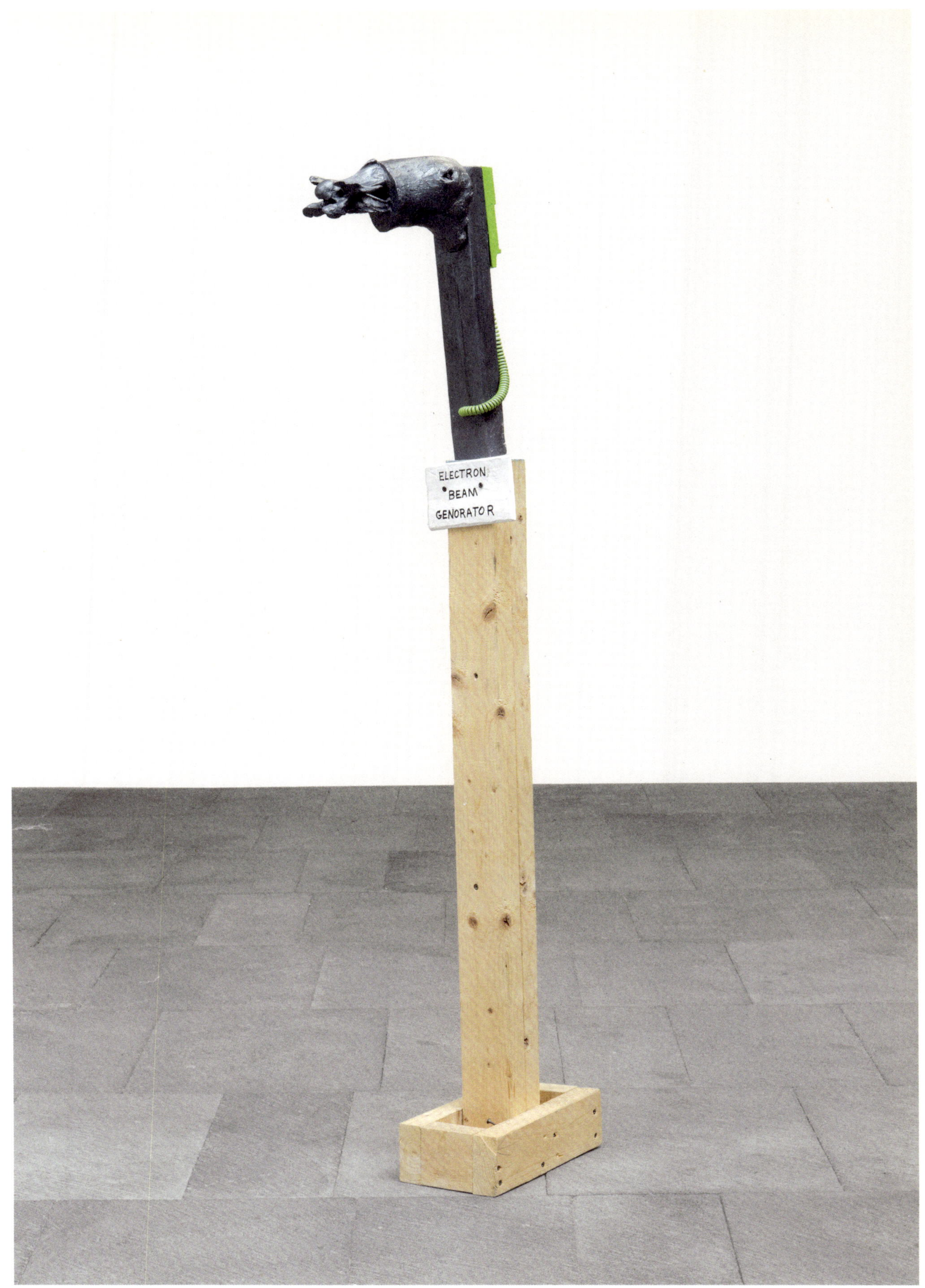

An Electron Beam Generater, 1989. Pine, cow vertebrae, plastic telephone part and cord, acrylic paint. 59 ¾ × 6 ¾ × 20 ½ in. (151.5 × 17 × 52 cm).

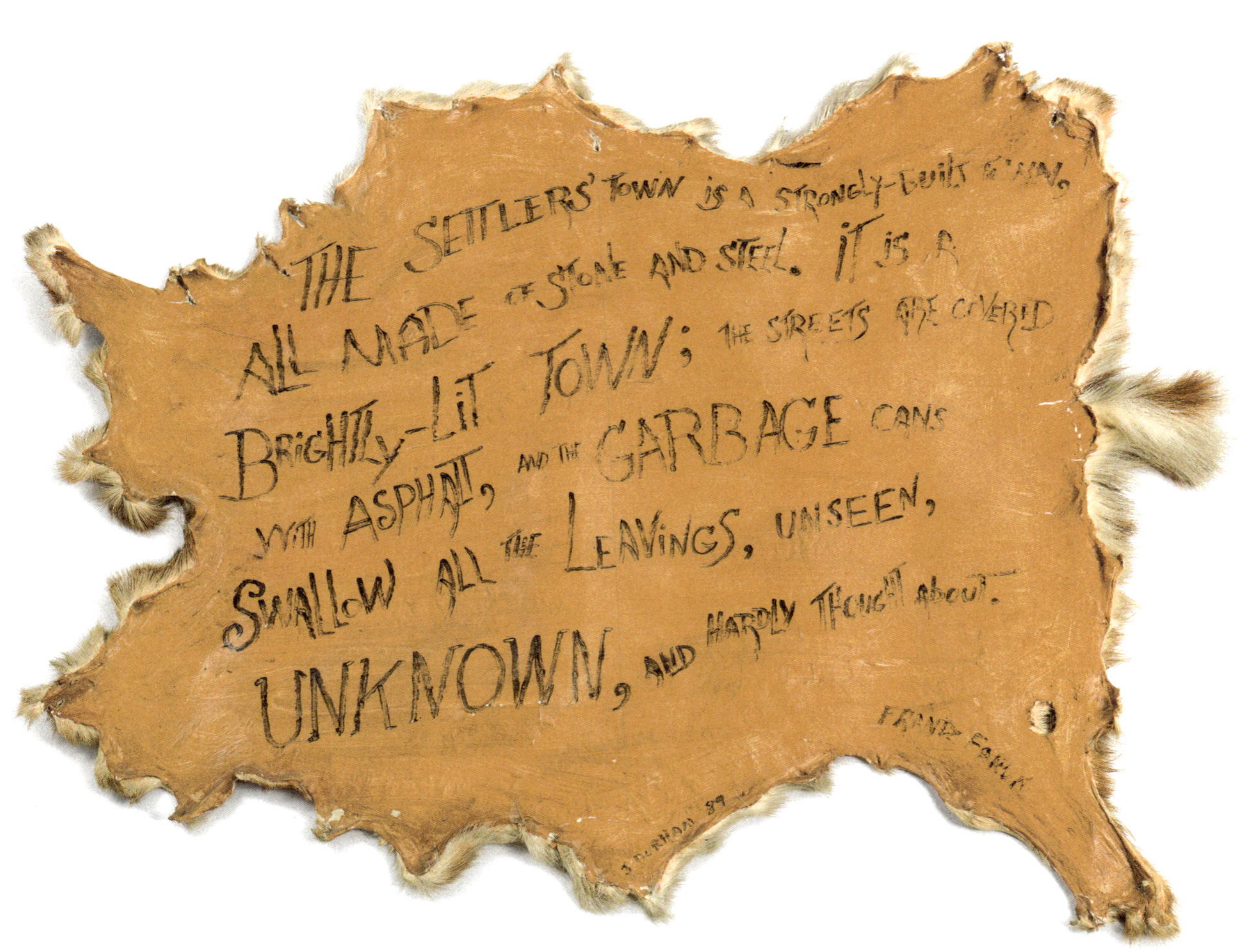

Tradition, 1989. Deerskin, acrylic paint, ink. 34 × 34 × 1 in. (86.4 × 86.4 × 2.4 cm).

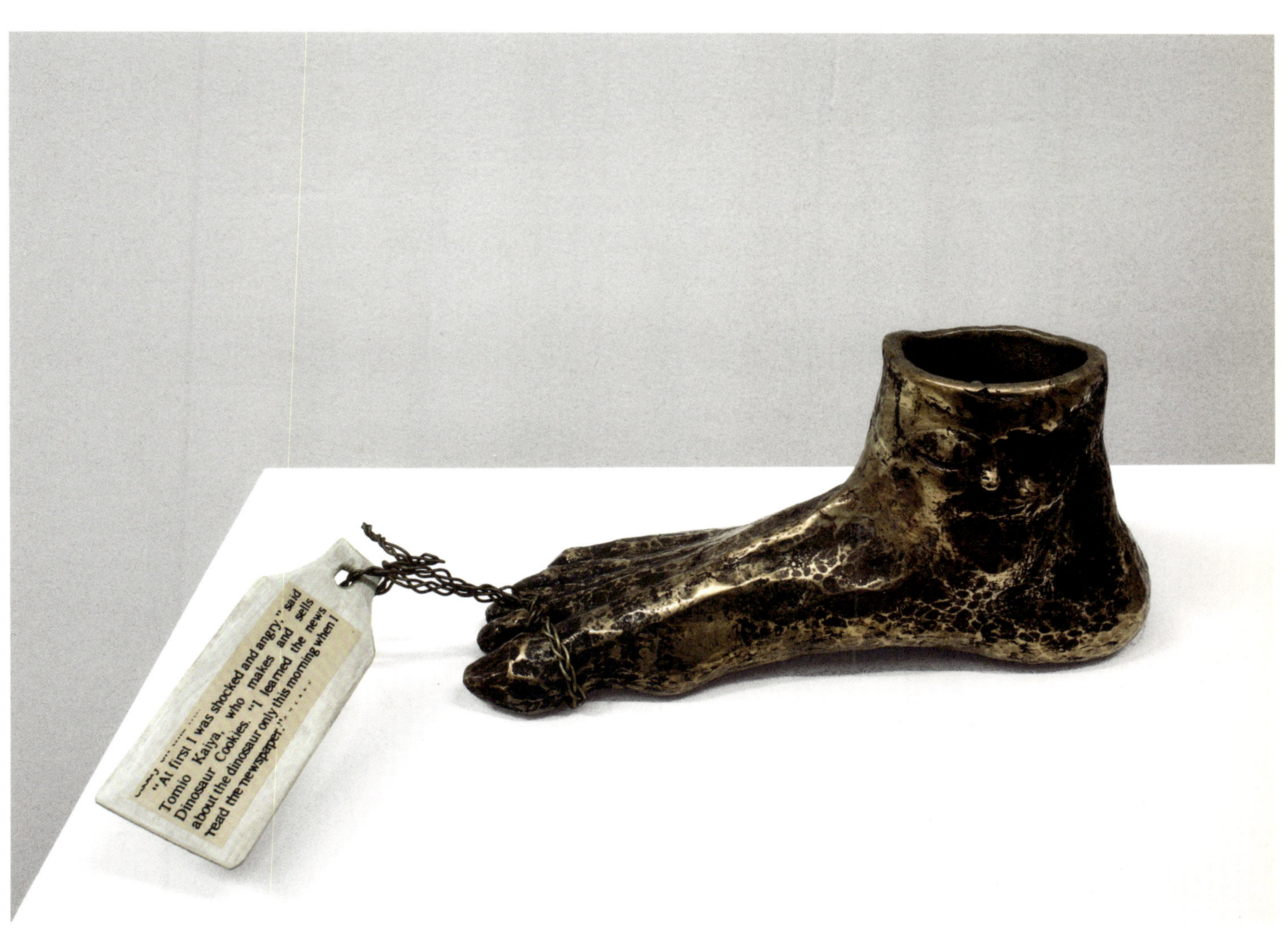

Footnote, 1989. Bronze, metal chain, acrylic paint on wood, ink on paper. 4 × 12 ¼ × 2 ¾ in. (10 × 31 × 7 cm).

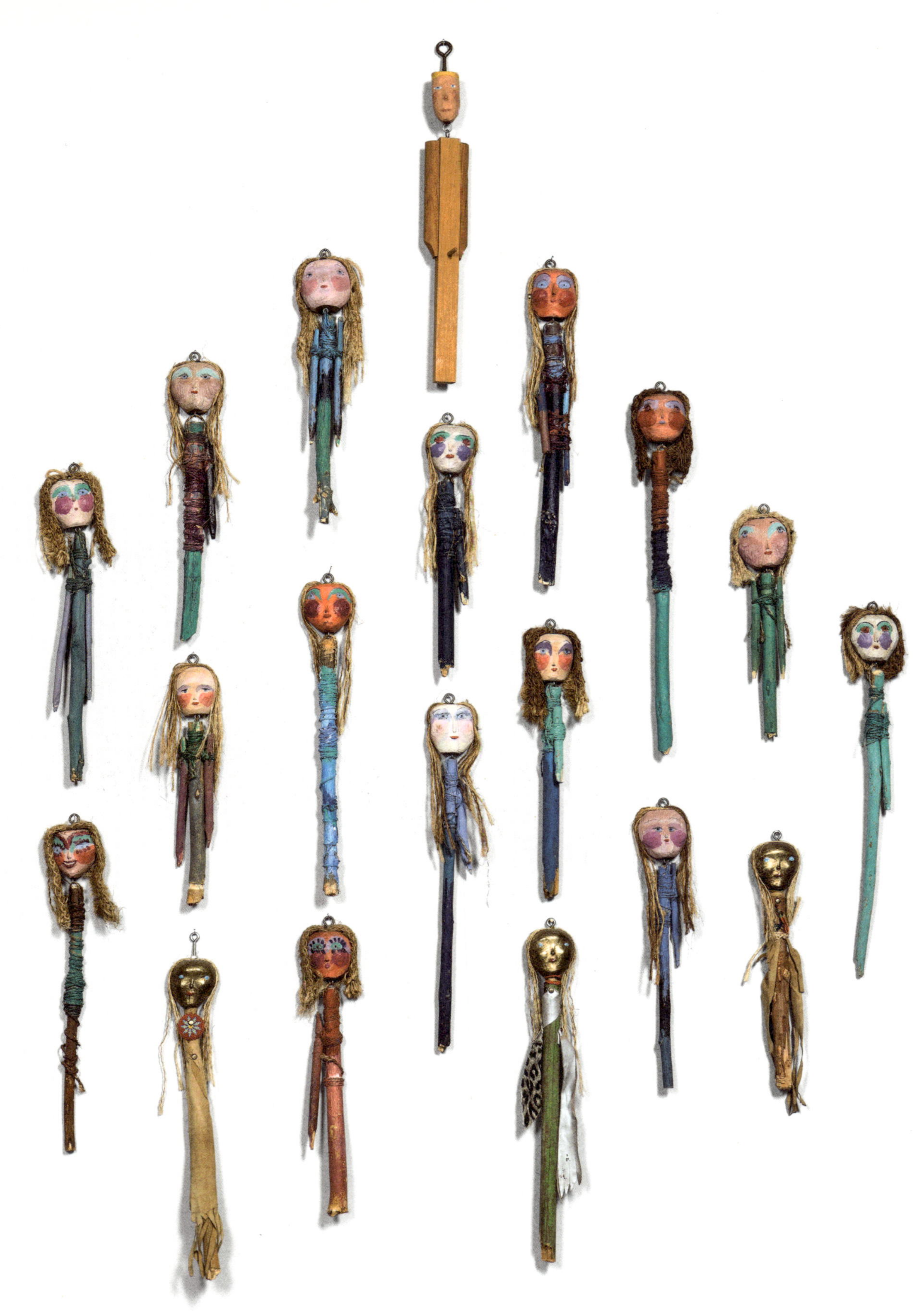

New Clear Family, 1989. Tree branches, carved wood, cotton cloth, leather, twine, string, beads, acrylic paint, metal. 17 ¾ × 4 in. (45 × 10 cm) each of 19.

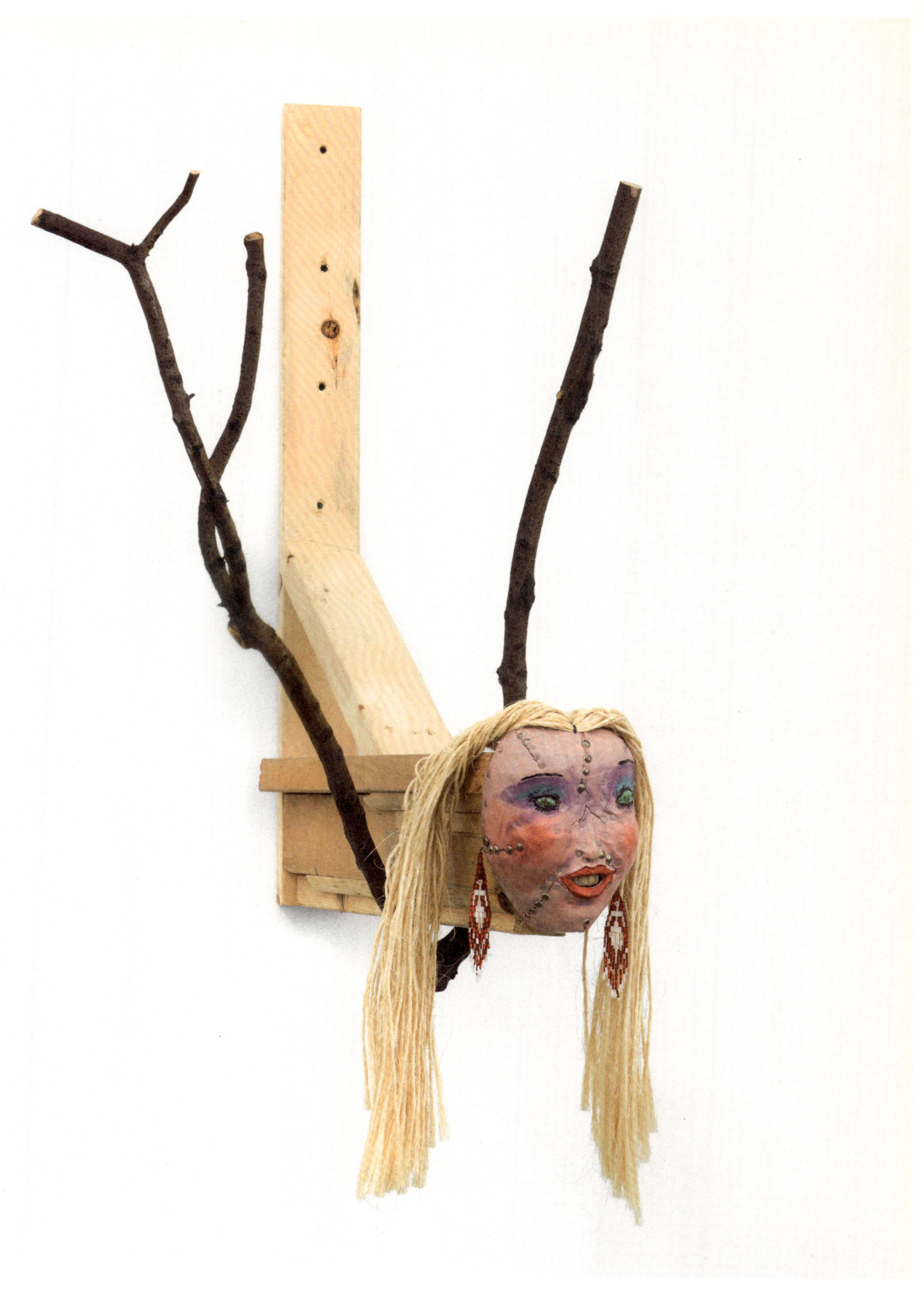

Over the River and Through the Woods, 1989. Plum tree branches, pine, stones, acrylic paint, beads, pigskin leather over carved pine, upholstery tacks, twine.
25 × 9 × 9 in. (63.5 × 22.9 × 22.9 cm).

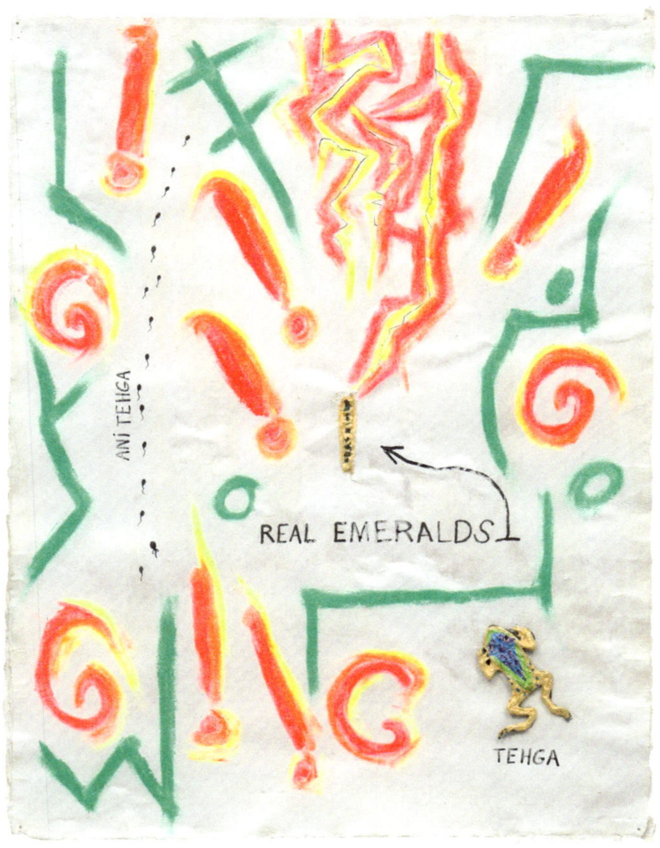

Six Authentic Things, 1989. Acrylic paint, enamel spray paint, ink, and pencil on paper, with turquoise, gold, emeralds, obsidian, flint.
29 × 23 11/16 in. (73.7 × 60.1 cm) each of 6 (framed).

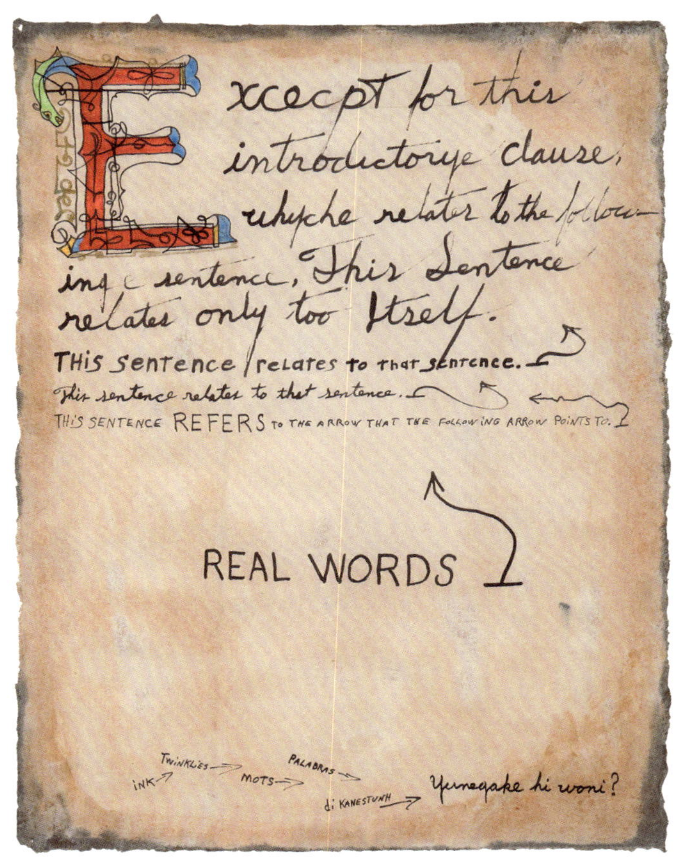
Except for this introductorye clause, whyche relates to the follow-ing sentence, This Sentence relates only too Itself.
THIS SENTENCE RELATES TO THAT SENTENCE.
This sentence relates to that sentence.
THIS SENTENCE REFERS TO THE ARROW THAT THE FOLLOWING ARROW POINTS TO.
REAL WORDS
INK
TWINKLIES
MOTS
PALABRAS
di KANESTUNH
Yunegake hi woni?
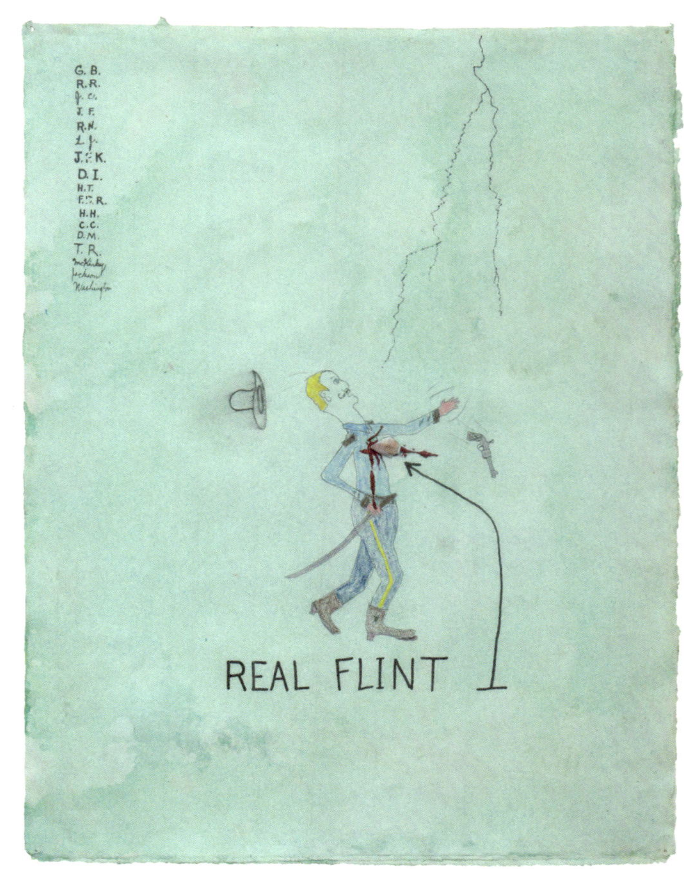
G. B.
R. R.
J. F.
R. N.
D. I.
H. T.
H. H.
C. C.
D. M.
T. R.
McKinley
Jackson
Washington
REAL FLINT
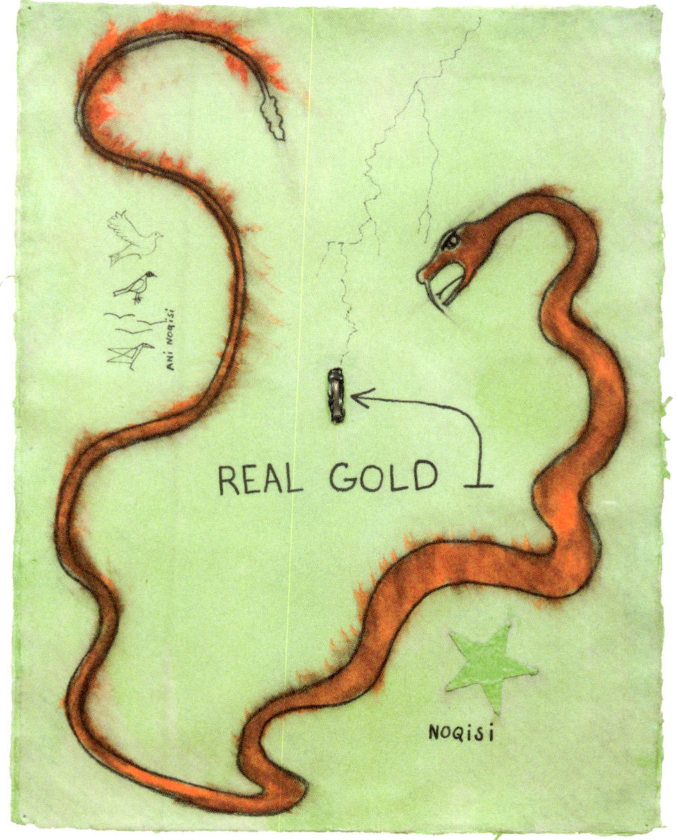
ANI NOQISI
REAL GOLD
NOQISI
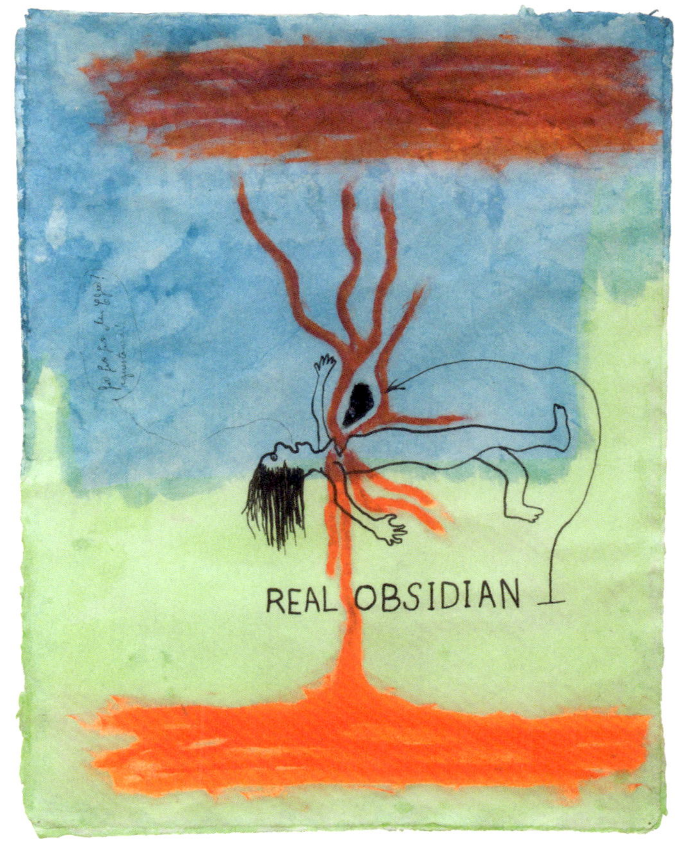
REAL OBSIDIAN

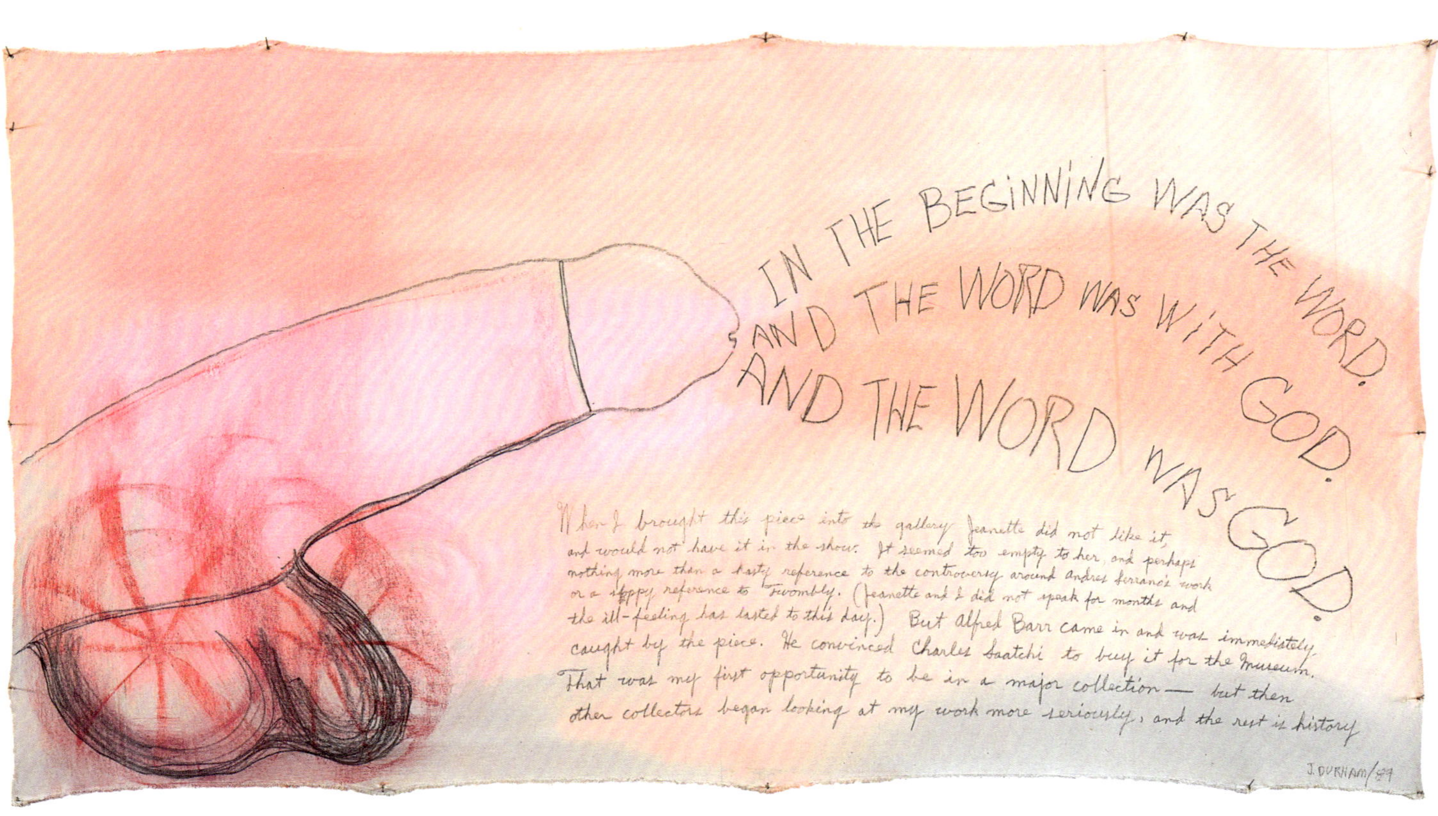

The Testament According to John, 1989. Acrylic paint and graphite on canvas. 36 ¾ × 67 ¾ in. (93.5 × 172 cm).

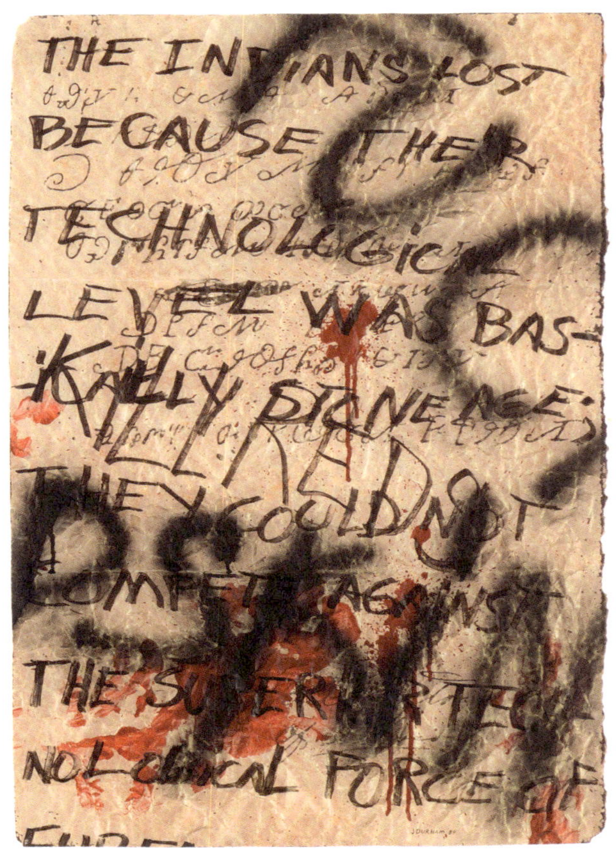

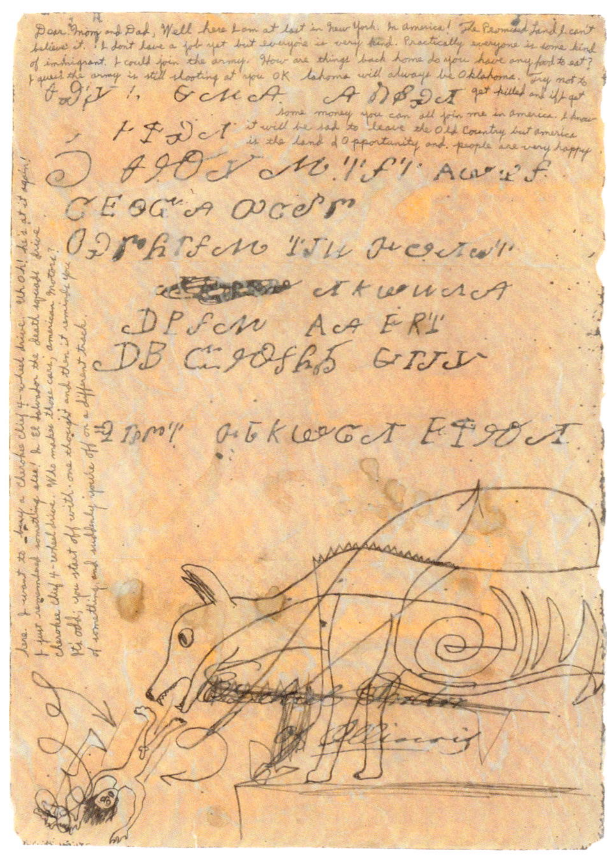

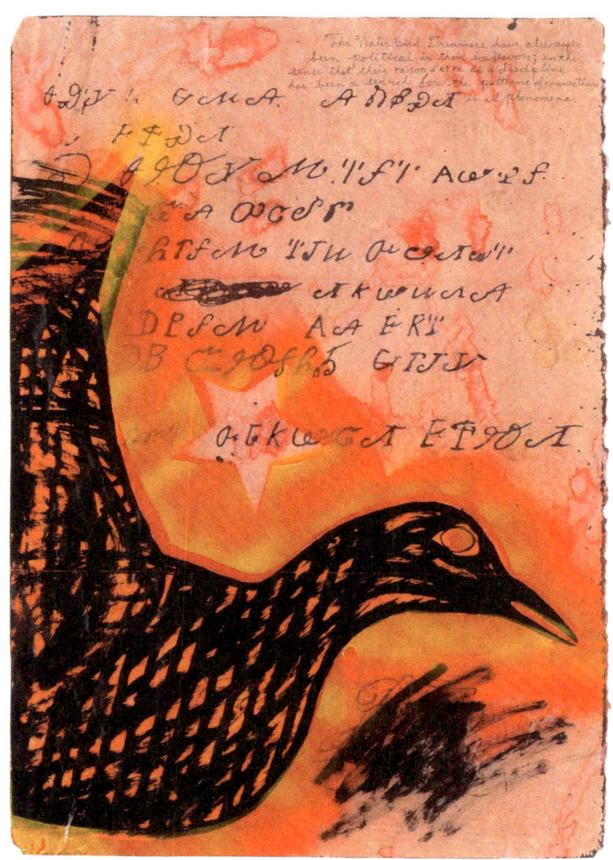

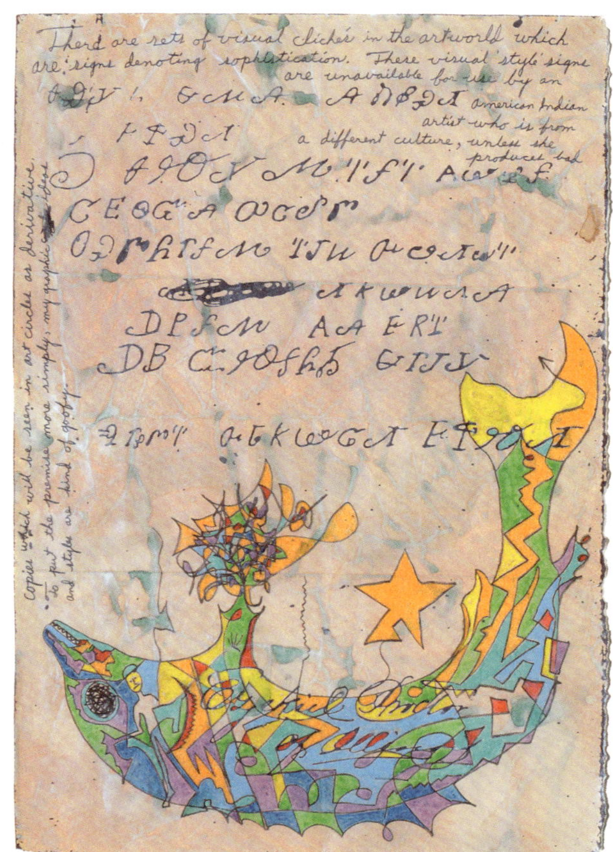

Zeke Proctor's Letter, 1989. Acrylic paint, ink, and enamel spray paint on paper. 32 ⅛ × 22 in. (81.6 × 55.9 cm) each of 4.

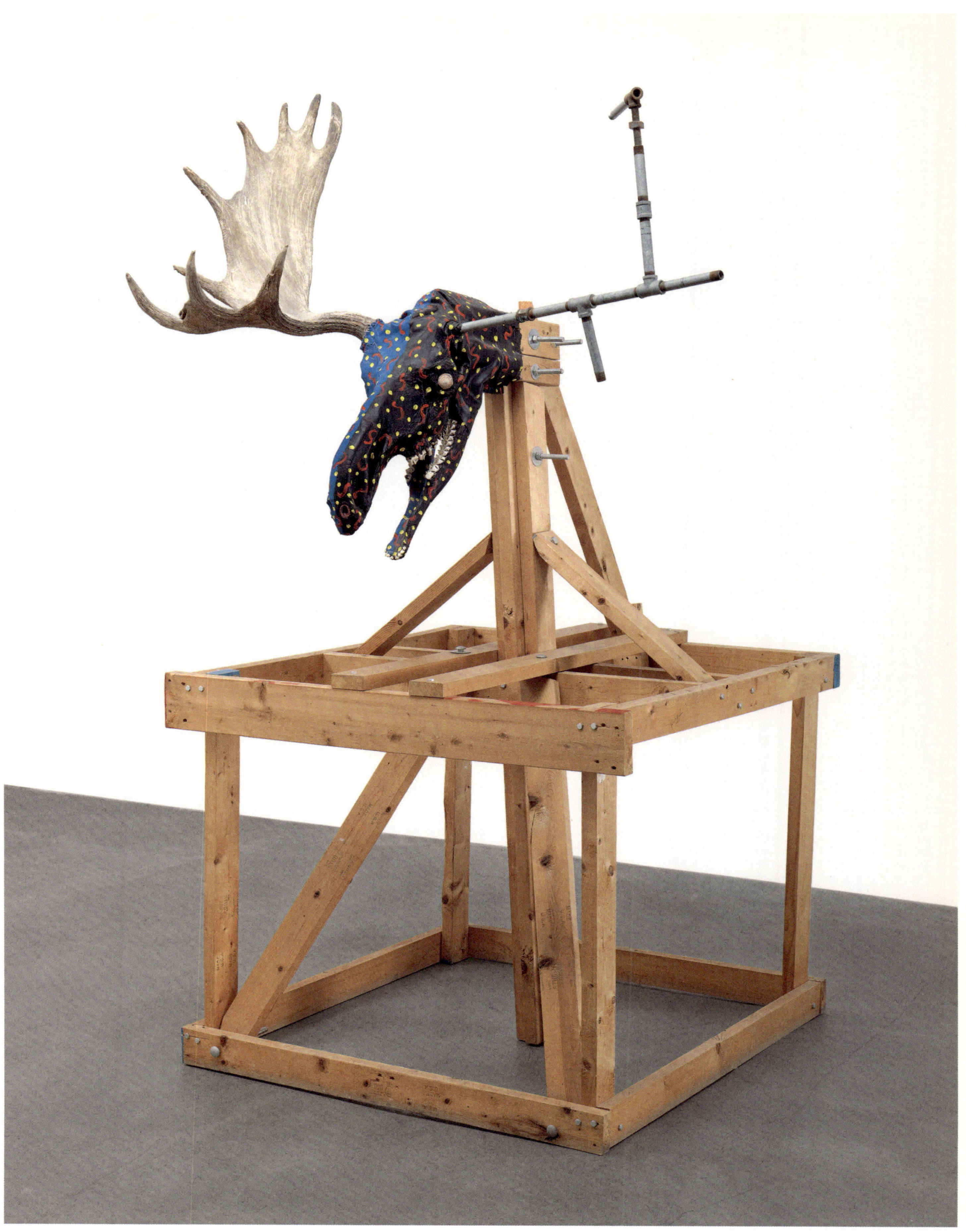

The Cathedral of St. John the Divine in Manhattan is the World's Largest Gothic Cathedral. Except, of course, that it is a fake; first by the simple fact of being built in Manhattan, at the turn of the century. But the stone work is also re-inforced with steel which is expanding with rust. Someday it will destroy the stone. The Cathedral is in Morningside Heights over-looking a panoramic view of Harlem which is separated by a high fence., 1989. Moose skull with antler, metal pipes, construction lumber, acrylic paint, seashell, sunglasses lens, metal hardware. 96 × 60 × 54 in. (243.8 × 152.4 × 137.2 cm).

Jimmie Durham
New York City, 1974

What the White People Thought When They Saw Manhattan Island For the First Time

Oh goddamnshitlordhavemercy lord save us oh hell oh goddamn bring a blanket bring a comb oh shit look (don't look, Priscilla) lord god look at that lush wild heathen dancing green and black rock and rolling sumac sugar sweet maple place! Fucking barbarian place quick bring fire guns weapons underwear! Bring bricks and collars quick. Oh lord our unbodied savior save us from disheveled destruction save our children from long dancing hair and jimson weed. Men bring shears bring shovels bring shades and windows to pull them down pull up trousers pull up weeds pull up laughing filthy deeds and throw them in the furnace of our virgin mom Sweet Jesus C. look at that! Hurry with buildings. Squash down wild fucking stuff. Bring concrete cement bring elevators cages boxes anything! Mash down this joyous exhibition with inhibition, sane but huddled masses, families and klans come with chains. Tame domestic servants bring Europe quick!

Jimmie Durham
New York City, 1976

Columbus Day

**In school I was taught the names
Columbus, Cortez, and Pizzaro and
A dozen other filthy murderers.
A bloodline all the way to the General Miles,
Daniel Boone and General Eisenhower.**

**No one mentioned the names
Of even a few of the victims.
But don't you remember Chaske, whose spine
Was crushed so quickly by Mr. Pizzaro's boot?
What words did he cry into the dust?**

**What was the familiar name
Of that young girl who danced so gracefully
That everyone in the village sang with her—
Before Cortez' sword hacked off her arms
As she protested the burning of her sweetheart?**

**That young man's name was Many Deeds,
And he had been a leader of a band of fighters
Called the Redstick Hummingbirds, who slowed
The march of Cortez' army with only a few
Spears and stones which now lay still
In the mountains and remember.**

**Greenrock Woman was the name
Of that old lady who walked right up
And spat in Columbus' face. We
Must remember that, and remember
Laughing Otter the Taino who tried to stop
Columbus and who was taken away as a slave.
We never saw him again.**

In school I learned of heroic discoveries
Made by liars and crooks. The courage
Of millions of sweet and true people
Was not commemorated.

Let us then declare a holiday
For ourselves, and make a parade that begins
With Columbus' victims and continues
Even to our grandchildren who will be named
In their honor.

Because isn't it true that even the summer
Grass here in this land whispers those names,
And every creek has accepted the responsibility
Of singing those names? And nothing can stop
The wind from howling those names around
The corners of the school.

Why else would the birds sing
So much sweeter here than in other lands?

Jimmie Durham
ca. 1983

Cutting Off Their Feet at Acoma Pueblo

**We were standing in line to get a foot cut off.
That was bad. Now, it's hard to say what was the hardest
part, but that standing in line waiting your turn,
listening to the whack! thunk! other guys screaming,
that was hard.**

**I remember standing there remembering all the times
when I was a boy running and running. But the guys
who broke the line and ran, they really got hacked up.**

**You tried to feel it before your turn, so you'd
be kinda prepared. You concentrated on the joint at your ankle,
imagining it separated from your foot. I
thought, first this big tendon, then the smaller tendons,
a little skin and muscle, all done.**

**But those Spaniards. The reason I cried was the
first blow of the axe just got me in the lower leg, broke
into the bone. I cried because it hurt really bad, but
mostly I thought it would never stop, it hurt so bad, and my foot
wasn't even chopped off yet.**

**It still hurts all the time. Slivers and chunks of
bone still left in there, so if you accidently lay the
wrong way at night you get a really sharp pain, and then
you wake up and think about your foot.**

**They have a festival of the Conquest now in Santa Fe,
and they're always after me to come, but I never do.**

Jimmie Durham
1984

The Gulf of Mexico

**I want you all to go and stand
By the little Rio Grande.
It is not a wall, you know,
Doesn't it flow into the Gulf of Mexico?**

**Comanches, Apaches, Papagos, and Yaquis
Live on both sides, swim in the middle.
At sunset rock doves come down
To drink and fly across the Rio Grande.**

**We must all stand up beside our little rivers now.
If Texas had been less vicious
Their great barrier would have been further north,
Would have been the Pecos or Nueces,
Or they would have chosen the San Jacinto River
Or the San Bernard, or even the River of the Arms of God.**

**Should clouds be wasted, and little fish
Assumed complicit? I want you all to stand up now,
And stand on innocent land falsely accused.
It is not united states; it is united by tears.**

**The rocks broke up patiently year after year,
And here are parts of pre-historic trees.
Many kinds of little creatures, and the pretty Rio Grande,
Assisted in the transformation of solid objects
Into soil.**

**Out in the Gulf of Mexico drops of water have strained
To break the surface minute by hour by
Millions of years to fly as clouds and water the Rio Grande.**

**The scorpion in the sky is innocent and echoes
Kindly the little scorpions which have responsibility under rocks,
So that all these sacred processes return.
Will policemen arrest the Gulf of Mexico?**

Jimmie Durham
1984

Song of Myself

Many people,
Especially the women - - -
A lot of women
Call me Dr. Jimmie.

References can be easily provided.
“Let Jimmie take over”
I’ve heard that on the radio!

Muhammad Ali said he was so tough
He wounded a stone.
He made a brick sick,
He said.

Not me; I fix ’em up.
Most good singers are named
Jimmie: Jimmie Cliff, Jimmie Reed, Jimmie Baldwin,
Jimmie Rodgers, Jimmie Hendrix.

Me too, I sing. Dance. Move.

Jimmie Durham
Middelburg, the Netherlands
October, 1995

The Center of the World
(The Direction of my Thought)
– Direct from my New Home in Eurasia –

(Visité)
        "Here" is a word you might like,
In French:
        IN   VI   SI
        BI   LI   TE
"Invisibilité"

        Drawn by the stone called
"Graphite" across white paper
By your/my hand, it is a pretty word,
And looks like and sounds like "visité".
It looks to be

(No words look not I look)
(See, if you receive these words
Through the front of your head;
That is 'visually', instead of laterally;
[And I want to be on your side]
You see the nécessité of a, _a comma_
To see: "Words look not, I look")
It looks to be jumping quietly up,
And only half-way back down: "invisibilité".

On arrival all my words were already
(All ready [read]) arranged carefully.

I knew what I intended to say.
I had rehearsed well and knew
Rules of poetics and discursive.
Still do; the longer I am away
The more memory can create.

(For example, when I hear your story
It sounds familiar, and the next day
I imagine I had happened in it.)

Surely you must know this rhyme
Is not mine - - - (either):

I might say, "Now we see through a glass, darkly,
But at home I will see my own reflection."
You will know how long I had planned
To say it.

This happens often on television:
One guy holds a gun, and says, "Give me
One good reason why I should not kill you!"
I always cry, because <u>of course</u> he knows
I know no reason:
He just wants me to watch tomorrow.

In the Orient, I mean, in Portugal;
That is only to say, in the Far East
Of the Atlantic - - -
In the East Atlantic Ocean

Close to the end of the world
At one time, in Portugal;
José Saramago wrote, "Do you say I am lying?"
"No", he answered, "when precision limits us
We choose words which lie for us."

Where shall we go, to the netherworld,
Like Orpheus? (Give me one good reason
Why I should not kill you!) No, I mean
Like Gilgamesh; Orpheus is sentimental.

"Don't look back!" He says. Too silly
(And who was that guy in the labyrinth?
I am at a point where I cannot find
A reason for my words, nor the thread
– Of the discourse of course –)

Suppose I were to say, to write (And you
Know that I have been planning
To say that for several ~~lonely~~ nights)
That I write these strings of old words
In the Netherlands?

Wait. I am writing (saying words
Inside my head so that my hand
Across the page will draw toward
Some other person irrevocably lost
In the future) in the city of Middelburg,
Where the telescope was invented!

Jimmie Durham
Berlin, 2002

The Wedding, July 1, 2002

**I was not invited to the wedding but did not attend.
There were dates, most likely, dried apricots
And little cakes.
The bride was blown to bloody bits.**

**Not being there, I was worse than innocent;
No bystander. The radio told me about it.
North of Kabul, the younger sister of the bride,
Yes, the younger sister was squashed down
Into the bloody sand.**

**So was her mother and the groom (Boom! No more room!)
"The people of Afghanistan are prepared to make sacrifices."**

**Pieces of dirty metal entered the groom's right hand,
And rudely entered his neck, and the groom's chest
And his stomach, legs, head, and feet; flying so
Quickly he was dead before he heard the sound.**

**I was far away, almost everyone who did not attend
The wedding was far away and as I write
Distance ourselves, become more far away.**

Jimmie Durham
On the road somewhere
after Innsbruck to Berlin
January 10, 2013

Askance

Lance
Ulance
Bulance
I am
Iambic balance
Ambiguous glance
Fer De Lance.

Oh for heaven's sake, wake up!
A Fer De Lance is a poisonous snake!

Jimmie Durham
Virchow Clinic, Berlin
October 29, 2014

After My Surgery

**It all began with high blood pressure
I suppose.**

**The doctor gave me some pills
but global warming continued to rise.**

**Then after my surgery a severe depression
and panic in global markets.**

**During the radiation therapy for cancer
several nations invaded Iraq again.**

**After my stroke my computer broke
and Afghanistan was once again broken.**

**In Calabria my shoulder broke
An epileptic seizure brought on another stroke.
Or maybe the stroke made an epileptic seizure
And I broke my hip.**

**So many countries in Central Africa
Began to shatter.
Syria and Turkey
Had another matter broken.**

Jimmie Durham
Virchow Clinic, Berlin
November 2, 2014

How We Were Made

With stands of oak and hickory with magnolias
And other kinds of oak
Then a lone black walnut tree
Because they do not tolerate being close to other trees.

Maybe he flies from the black walnut tree.
Or maybe he flies into it.
When you see this
You drop your thoughts.
Sometimes maybe you drop to the ground.
You do not try to explain.
You try to look more and more.
Sometimes he would be on the trunk
Of the black walnut tree.
And his hammering would make a noise more than your heart.

This is the giant woodpecker.
Bigger than an eagle.
Bigger than your knowledge no matter how many times you see it.
They are gone now.
And pretty much the giant trees in the forest
That they sustained.

Maybe I was 11 years old - - -
At the edge of a clearing a black panther.
You might say not for very long,
But now I am in my mid-70s
I still see it.

In our forest back home
We had chenquapins.
We had glass-clear salamanders,
The length of the first digit
Of my childish finger.
And large salamanders called sirens,
With front legs, snaky bodies and feathery gills.
Hellbenders in the creeks.
Wrinkled ugly salamanders,
Large enough to eat a poodle.

**This forest had long-nosed soft-shelled flat turtles.
Every couple of summers
Some white person would capture one.
And all the newspapers would say it was an animal from Mars.**

**Miniature owls that would whisper
To each other at night.
Also in the water,
There was a fish that had been there since Jurassic times.
If you caught one in a boat and pulled it in,
It might very well bite your ankle half off.
This is the bowfin.
Gars could get seven feet long
Simply to frighten children.
With giant teeth
And scales that could be used for arrow points.**

**I was supposed to be in London
Participating in a conference about extinction.
I am in the hospital
But the real reason I did not go:
I know too much about extinction.**

Jimmie Durham
Berlin, 2015

A Stone

There was a guy.
Don't know his name:
No one remembers his name.

We do not forget
We do not remember

His ways
When he awoke mornings, sleeping habits.
More than any of us for a long time.
I remember families slowly leaving Siberia better
And not even that at all.

He left a stone he had worked on,
Had made into a tool.
He chipped

/Quite a bit of chert
(I've carried that bird chirping phrase
In my mind since about nineteen
Sixty-five, waiting for an opportunity,
So now break into the story
Of the stone we found with
An explanation of the kind of stone
It is. It is chert.)
Quite a bit, as I wrote, of chert
Will spark if struck with iron.
Flint is chert, jasper, all the agates.

Chert and humans make fire.
Break bones also, of larger animals
So that the fat marrow can be roasted
In the fire. For thousands of years
Humans have made tools from chert.

Incredible dexterous craft, making
An axe or knife from stone.
This we found is old old old.
By weight it's one thousand one hundred
And thirty-seven grams. Thirty-seven
Thousand years old, maybe more.

Too heavy to fight with or strike
A goat or ox for my weak old arms.
Sharpened to a striking, not cutting, edge
On one side, it maintains the rounded shape
It had before the human encounter,
Horribly comfortable and fitting
Into a large rough hand. /

No, not chipped, not carved, we have no verb
To say the action of quickly, carefully
Taking away flakes of stone from stone.
Speaking of that, I could make up a name
For him and its soft falsity
Would offend us. We know
We don't know his name.

With nonchalant precision
This guy made this stone heavy---
Added more than all the grams and kilos.

We told god what to tell us, didn't we?
Truly, humankind has fallen.
Any colt will tell you horsekind has fallen too,
And all the kinds of moving life,
Living to devour, living by devouring,
Watching always fearful of the bite.

We live by death of course
We want god's advice,
Tell him what we want to be.

I've been in the hollowed out marble mountain
Of Carrara and stood on the hardened lava
In Mexico metres above a city
Covered like Pompeii, tried to figure out.

In Europe, Mexico, Arkansas and on the beach
I've found stone tools left often desperately
Dropped my mind imagines, used just like
The Large Hadron Collider by Voltaire's old house
By Geneva, by people who want

I'm not sure how to say what we want.

What I mean, I know the rocky road.
I've seen, held, been held back by many stones.
Hell, man, I live on one.

What I mean, Ho Chi Min, Crazy Horse,
Redbird Smith.,,, used to be, everyone changed their names
To fit better into new situations, new places.

His old name, this old guy, maybe
It was not the real part.
Still by this stone I recognise him,
I know how we want.

Jimmie Durham
2015

The Kid the Cop Shot

**Often it is about the sound,
Alignment of syllables in mental spaces.
Throat or glottal stops more than meaning.**

**Music needs no exegesis,
Why should poetry always mean?**

**I mean mean linguistically.
The long tongue of the law.
Shorthand for off-handed-ness**

**Or Loch Ness, recall Arne Naess in Bucharest or,
The kid the cop shot;
Means little, another day another dollar.**

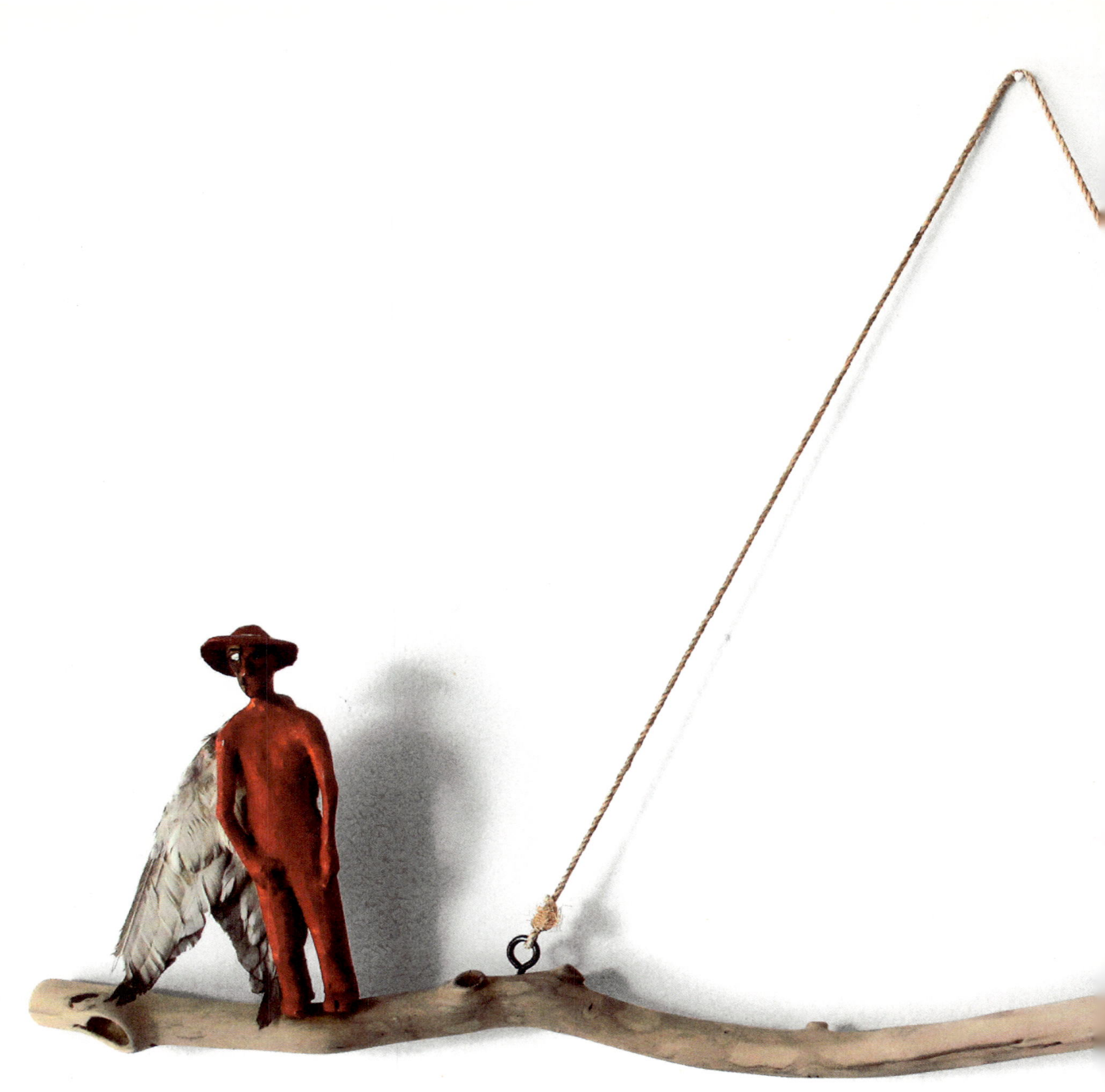

The Arrogant Little Peasant, 1989. Carved ash, elm branch, acrylic paint, pigeon feathers, jute string, metal, ink on paper. 13 ¾ × 46 × 4 in. (35 × 117 × 10 cm).

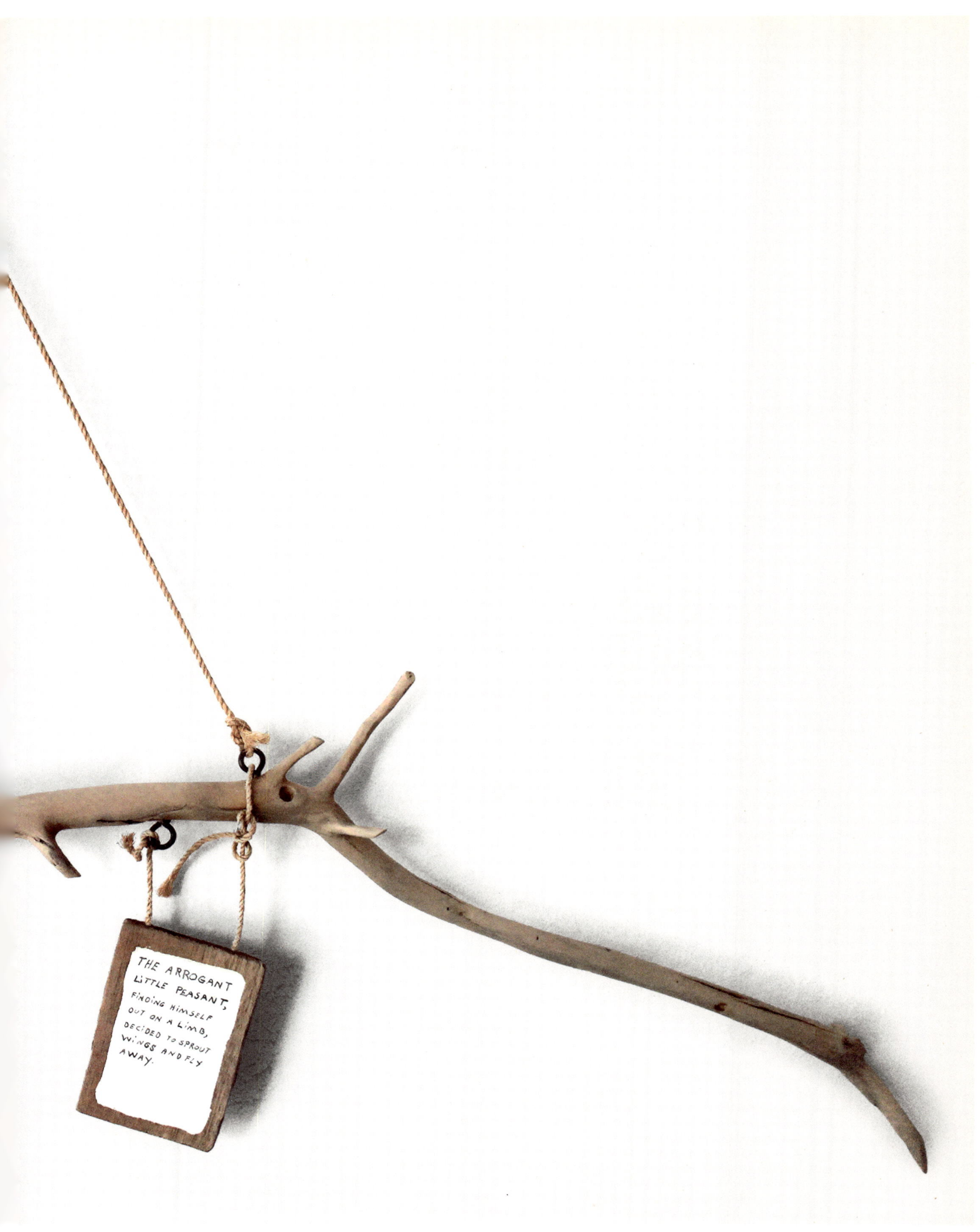
THE ARROGANT
LITTLE PEASANT,
FINDING HIMSELF
OUT ON A LIMB,
DECIDED TO SPROUT
WINGS AND FLY
AWAY.

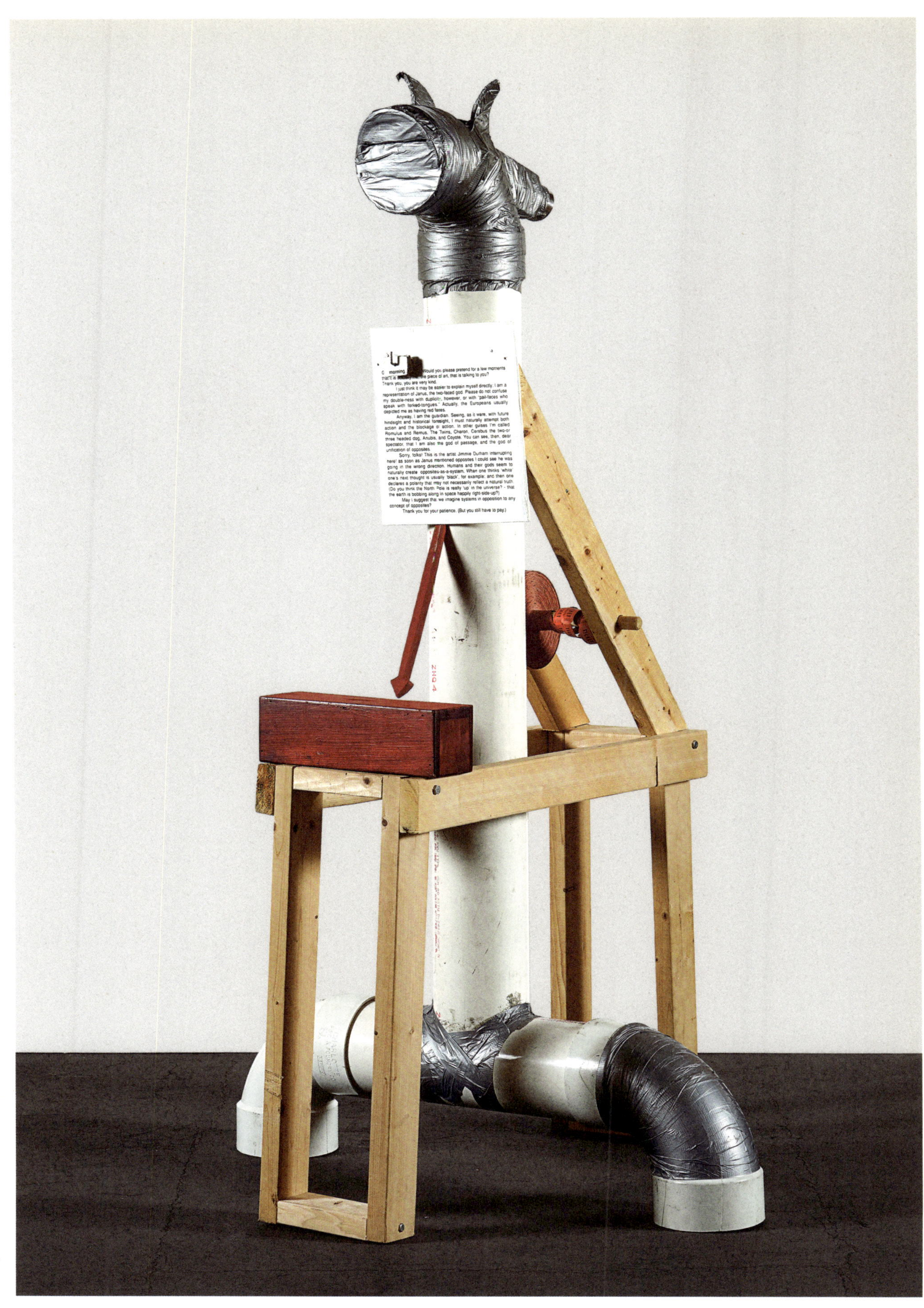

The Guardian (free tickets), 1992. Construction lumber, found wood box, PVC, acrylic paint, duct tape, paper tickets, ink on paper mounted to wood. 76 ¾ × 40 ¼ × 34 in. (195 × 102 × 86 cm).

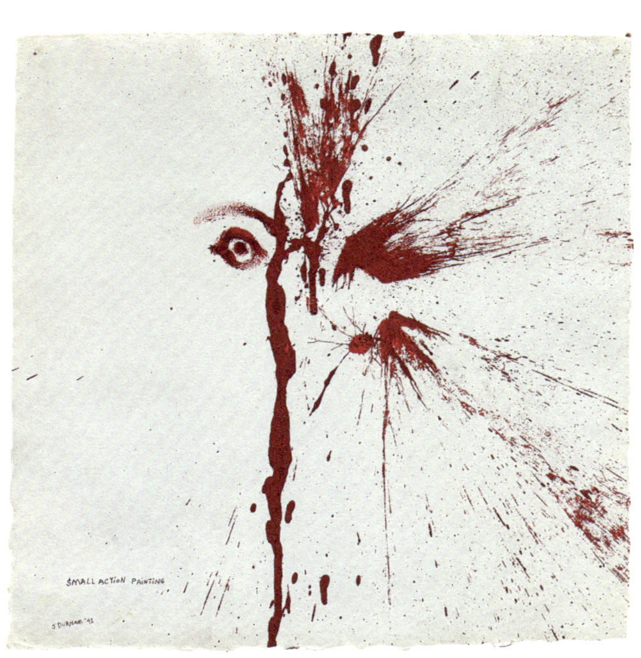

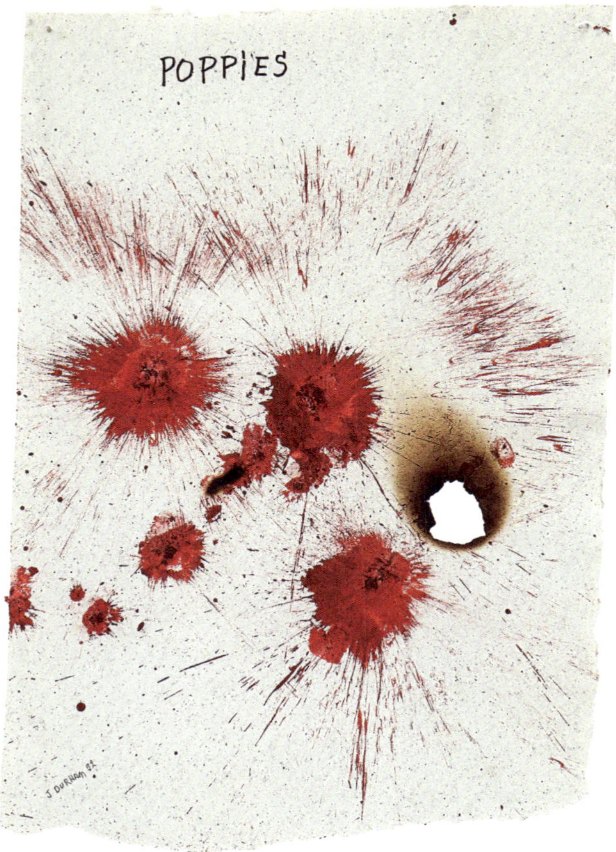

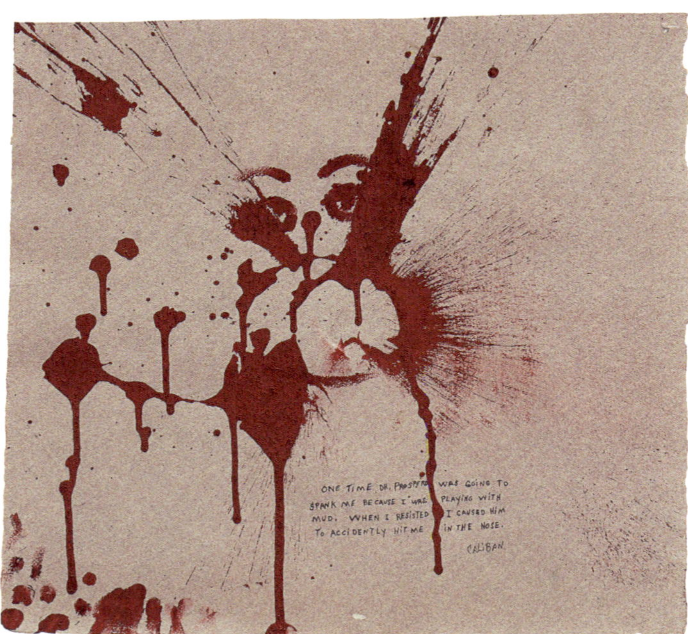

Top left: *Small action painting*, 1992. Acrylic paint and ink on paper. 20 ½ × 20 ¼ in. (52.1 × 51.4 cm).
Top right: *Poppies*, 1992. Acrylic paint, ink, and burn on paper. 19 ¼ × 13 ¼ in. (48.9 × 33.6 cm).
Bottom: *Not Caliban's Nose*, 1992. Acrylic paint and ink on paper. 17 ¾ × 19 ¼ in. (45 × 48.7 cm).

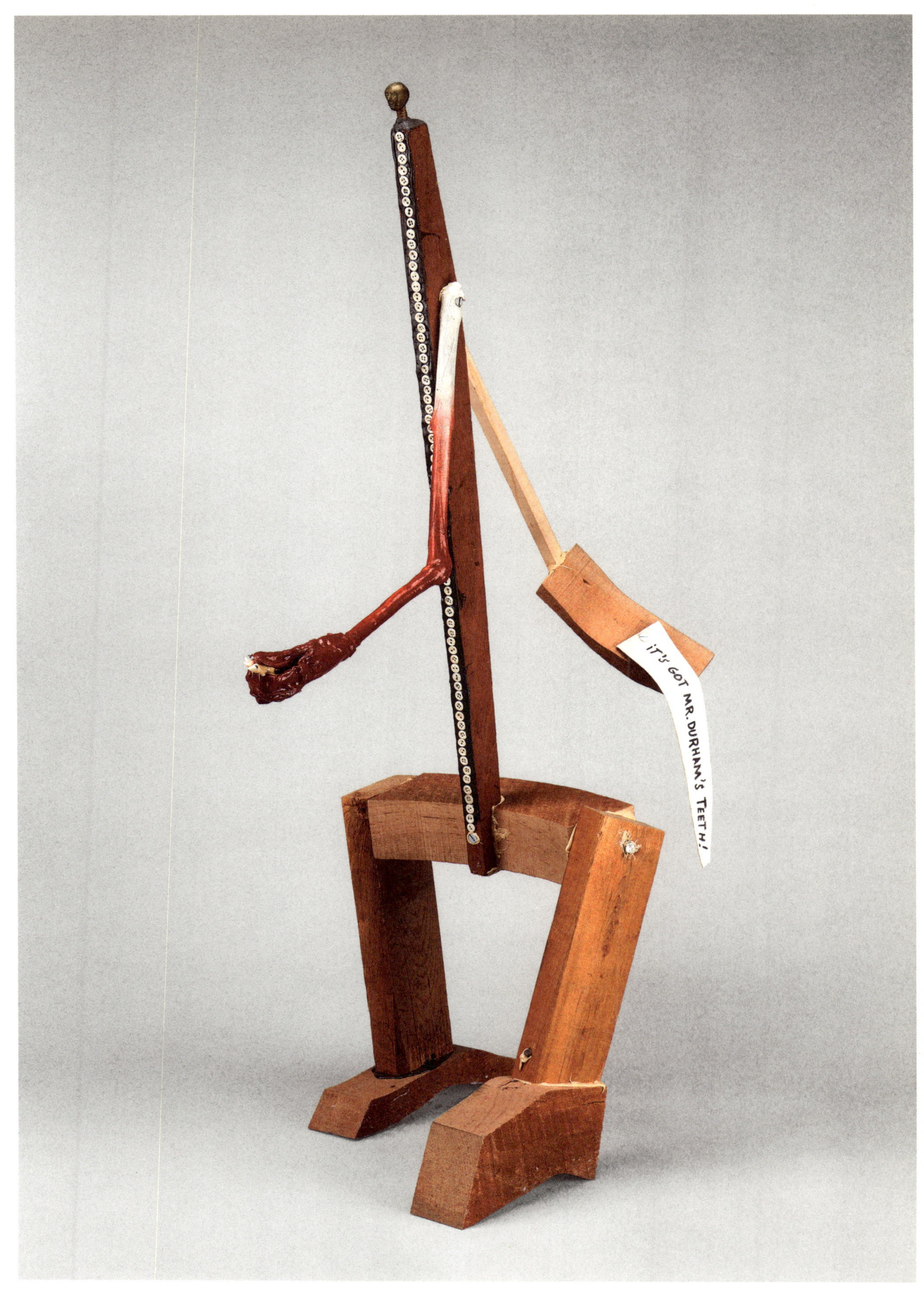

Untitled (It's Got Mr. Durham's Teeth), 1992. Oak, beech, leather glove, acrylic paint, Jimmie Durham's teeth, seashell buttons, epoxy resin, ink on canvas. 44 ¼ × 13 ¼ × 26 in. (108 × 31.2 × 62.4 cm).

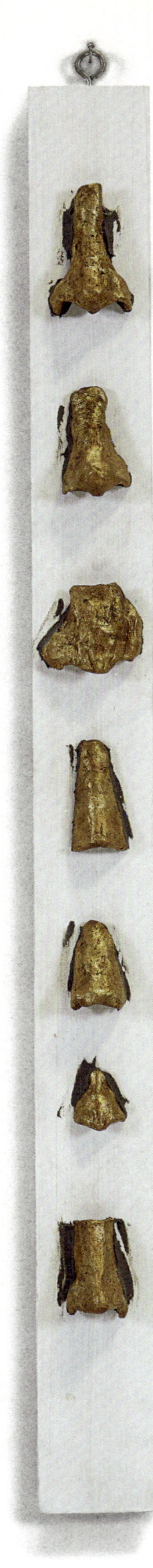

Some noses, 1992. Cast brass, acrylic paint, wood. 37 × 3 × 2 ¾ in. (94 × 7.5 × 7 cm).

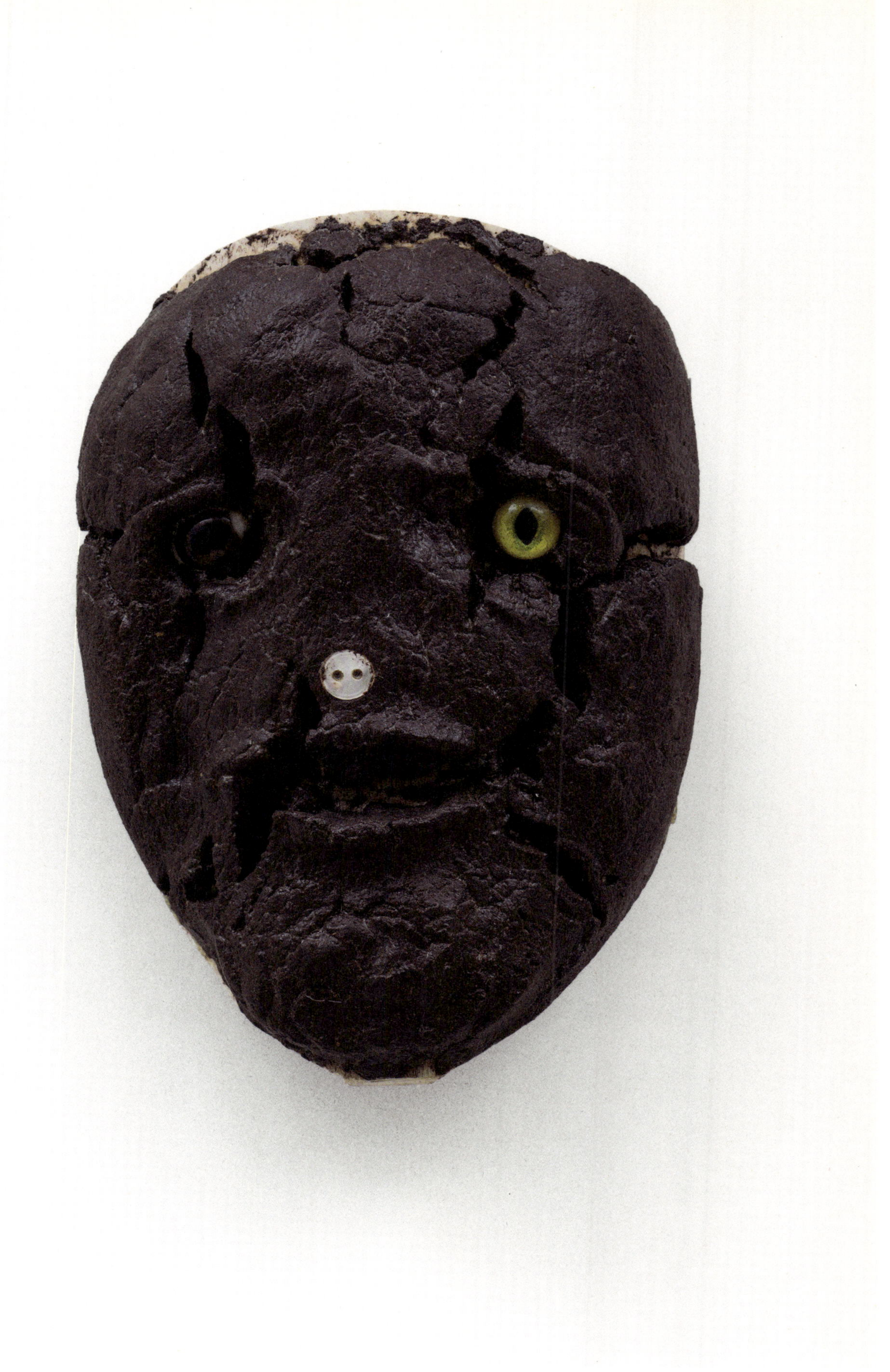

Untitled (Caliban's Mask), 1992. Mud, glue, glass, button, PVC. 9 ½ × 6 ¼ × 2 in. (24 × 16 × 5 cm).

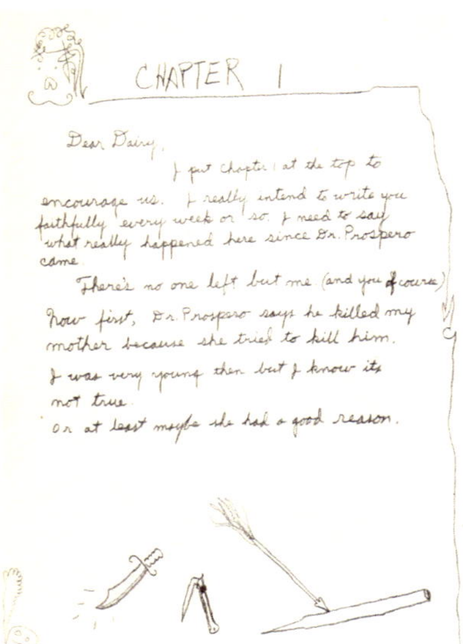

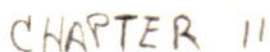

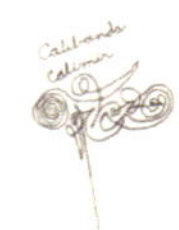

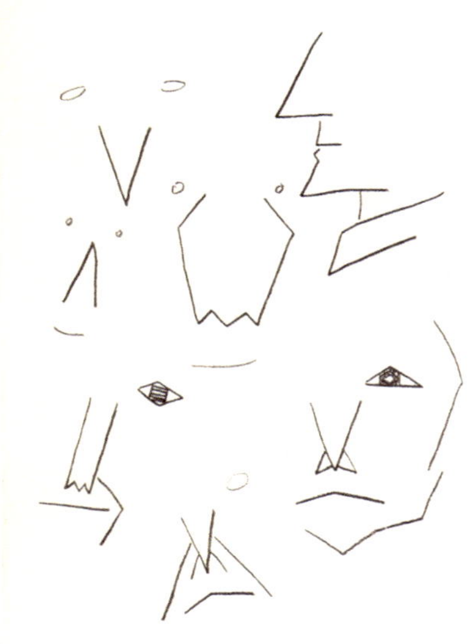

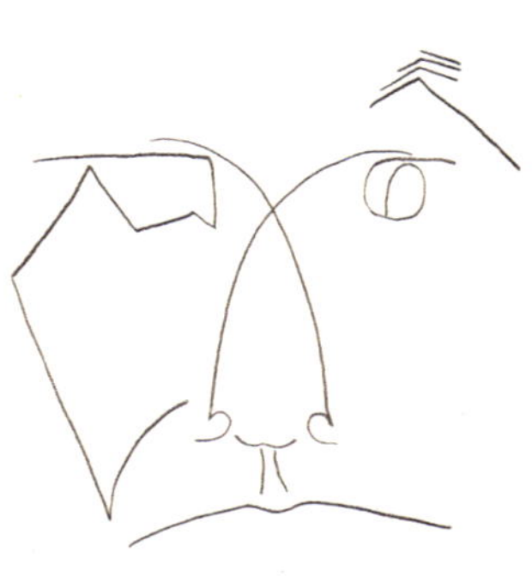

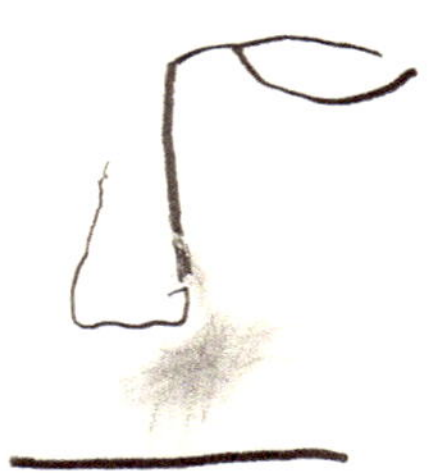

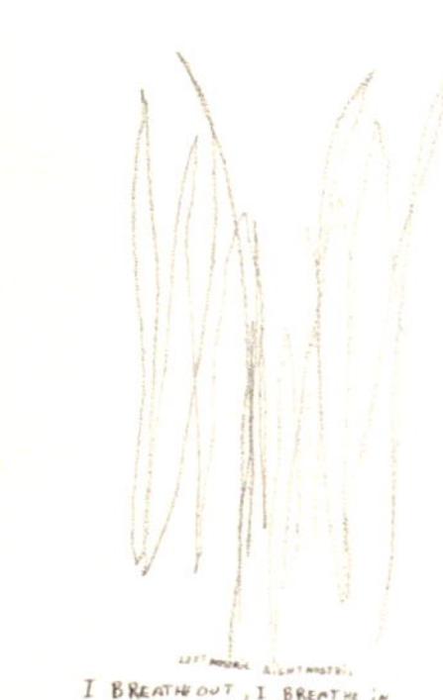

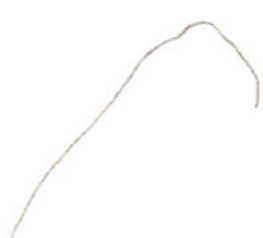

Caliban Codex, 1992. Pencil on paper. Twelve sheets, 21 × 15 in. (53.3 × 38 cm); two sheets, 22 ¼ × 15 in. (56.5 × 38 cm).

Dear Daisy,

I didn't tell you before but its Dr. Prospero who taught me to speak right and to write. as he says, his language is marvelously subtle and complex. Every day I learn a new set of words.

HEAVY, OR DARK (OPPOSITES →)	LIGHT
EARTH	SKY
LAND	HEAVEN
GROUND	CELESTIAL BODIES
DIRT	SUN
DUST	ANGELS
CLAY	PHOTONS
MUD	CELESTIAL REALMS
MUCK	GOD
MIRE	LIGHT
ME	PURITY
FILTH	MIRANDA
GARBAGE	ETHER
WASTE	BEAMS
~~D~~ DETRITUS	RAYS
DRECK	X RAYS
DROSS	ULTRA VIOLENT LIGHT
CESS	GASES
CRAP	FIRE
SHIT	
CA CA	
DOO DOO	

Your friend Caliban,
the heavy duke

Chapter IIIIIII

Daisy guess ~~s~~ what?! I've decided to be an artist! Don't worry, Daisy, I'll still write you. But I want to make a ~~true~~ complete portrayal of myself. and I'm good with my hands so why not?

I don't know what I look like. Since Dr. Prospero came there's nothing here that reflects me.

I don't know what my nose looks like, for example. I can't touch it because Dr. Prospero says its not nice to touch yourself.

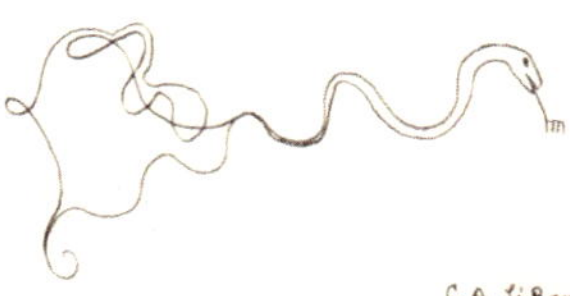

C.A. LiBon

CHAPTER IIIIIIII

Today I asked Dr. Prospero if my nose looks like his.

He can be so mean sometimes! Then he said I didn't know how to draw anyway.

So heres my new idea: if my nose doesn't look like anyone else's, and if I myself don't recognize it, aren't I free of my nose? But I have to stop thinking about it.

(Calibanos)

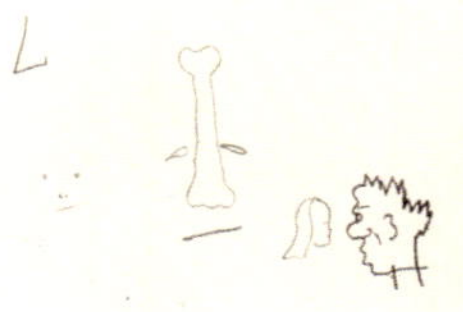

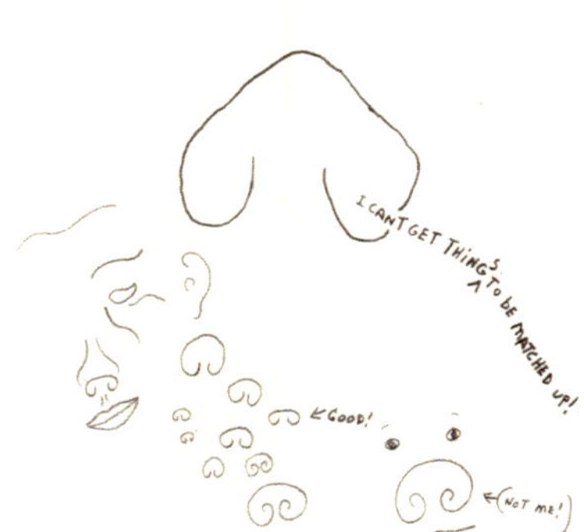

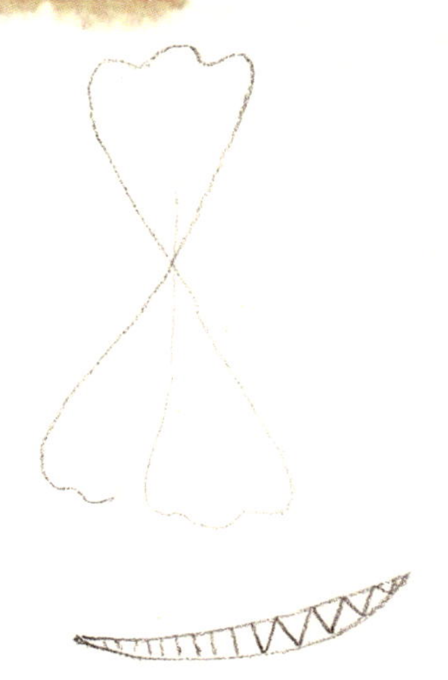

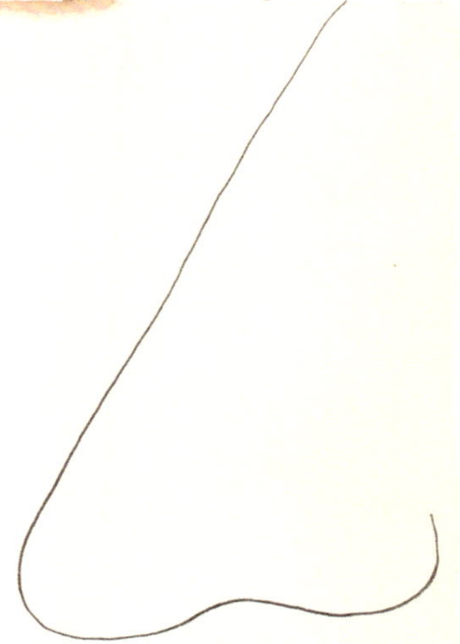

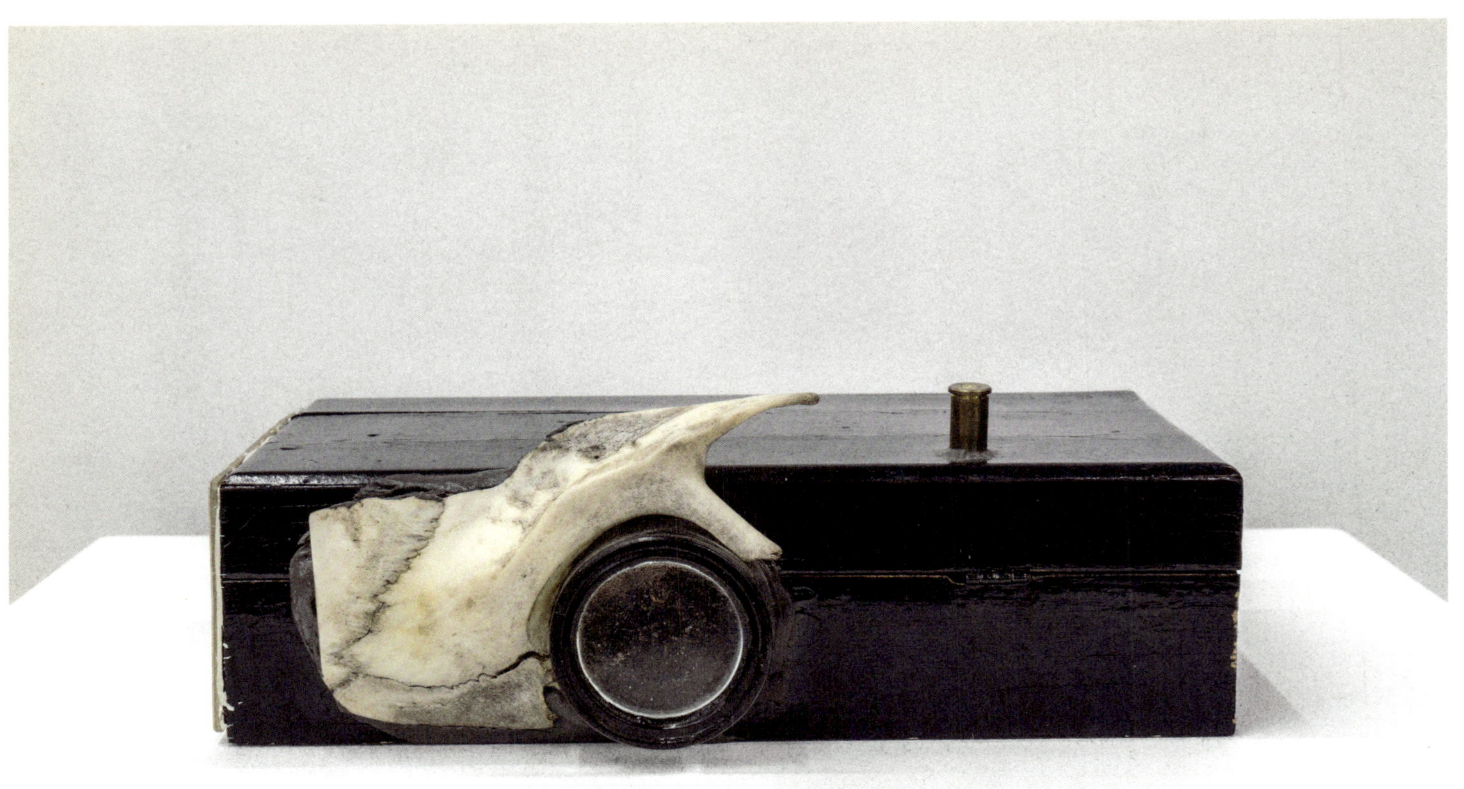

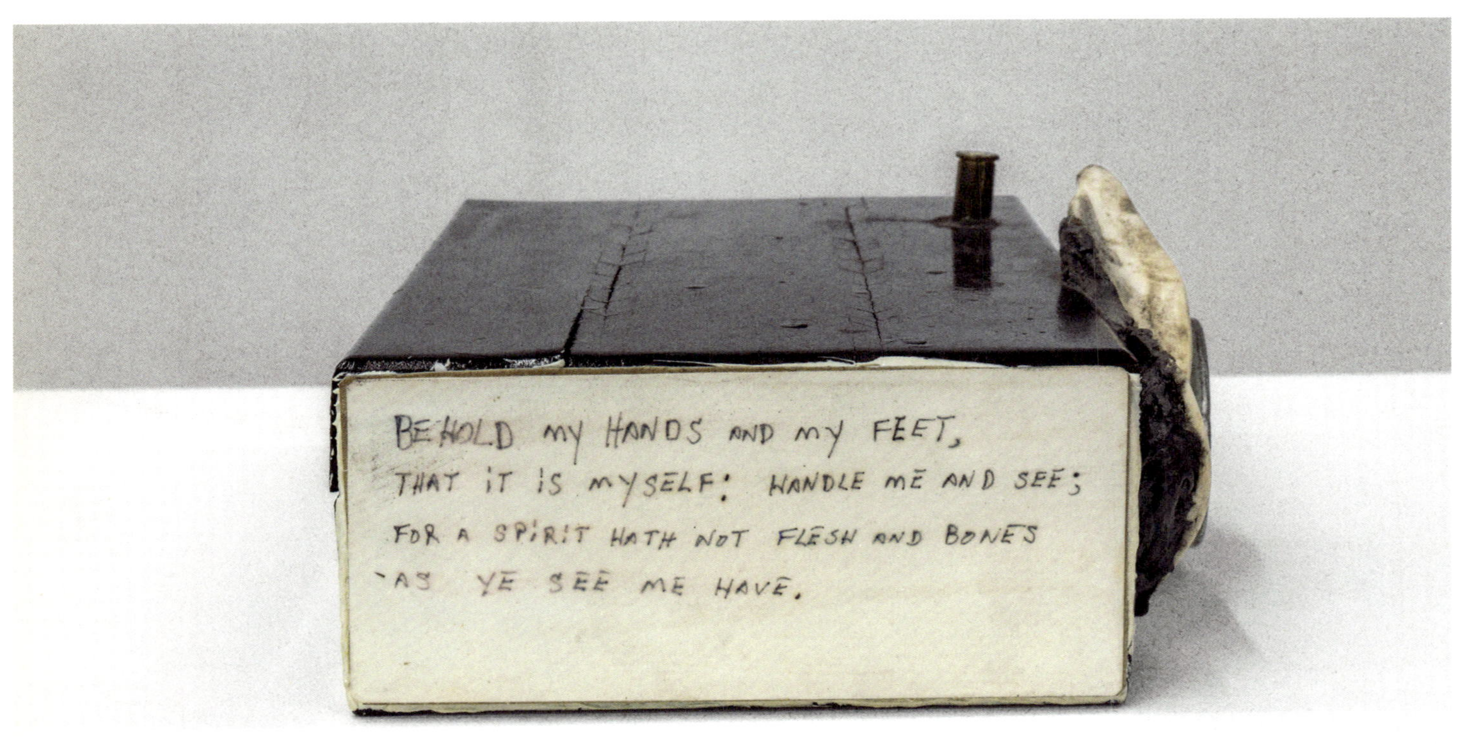

Behold my hands and my feet, that it is myself: Handle me and see; for a spirit hath not flesh and bones – as ye see me have., 1993 (front and side views).
Painted wood box, cow eyebrow ridge bone, glass lens, bullet shell from 45-caliber pistol, ink on paper. 4 × 6 × 10 in. (10.2 × 15.2 × 25.4 cm).

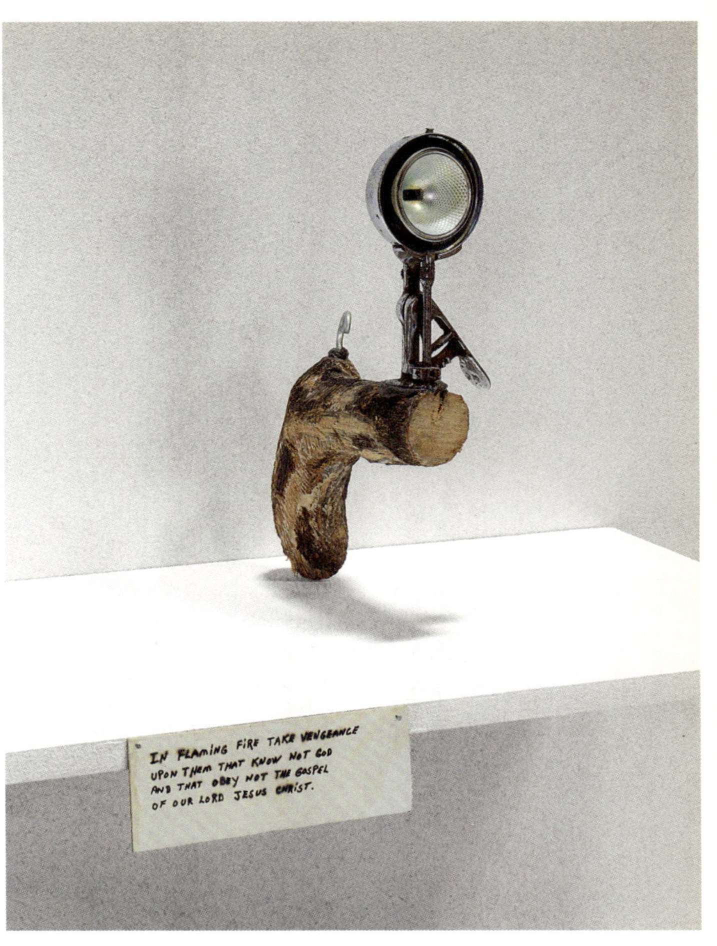

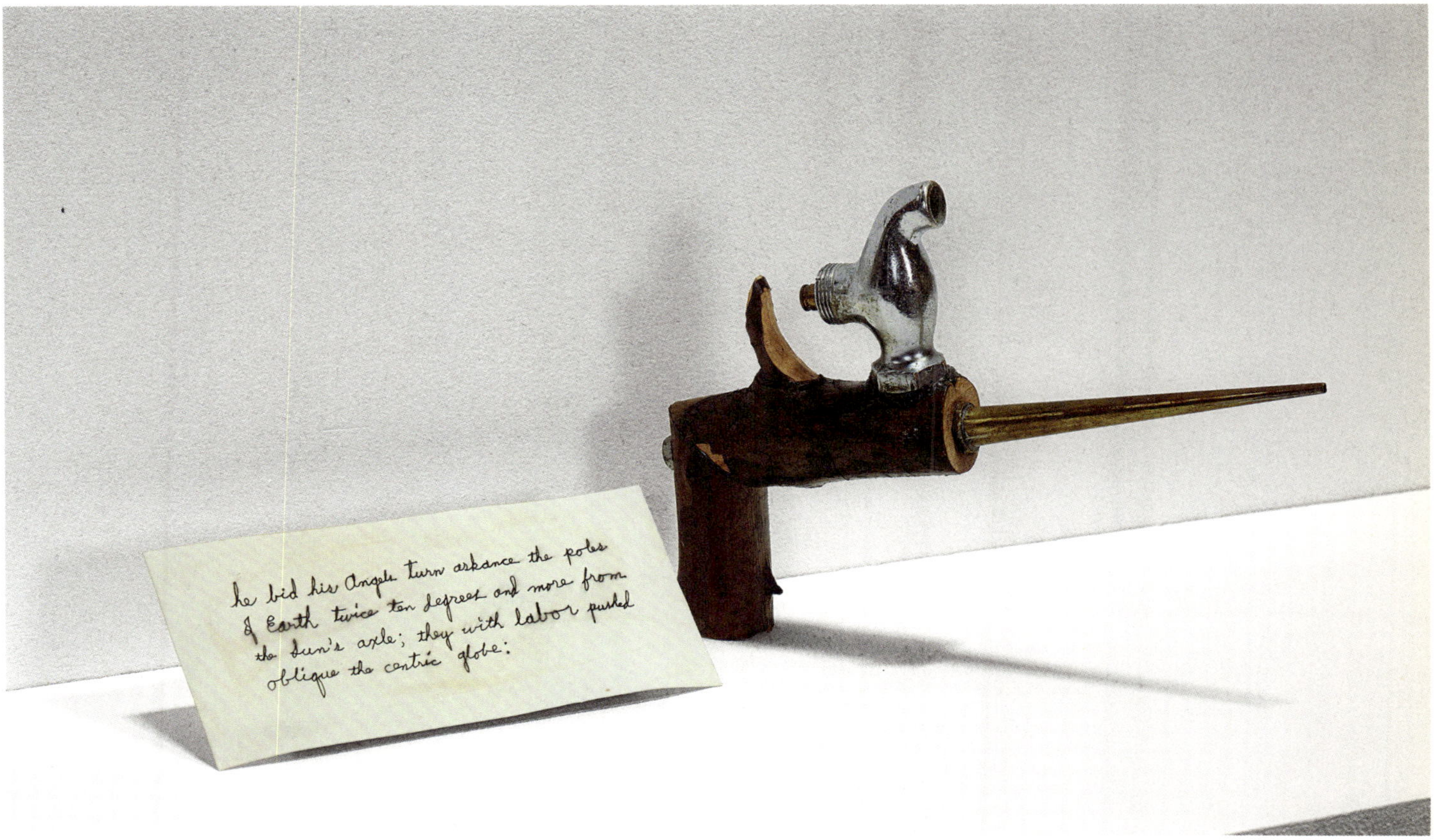

Top: *In flaming fire take vengeance upon them that know not God and that obey not the gospel of our Lord Jesus Christ.*, 1993. Metal ice-cream scoop, plum wood, ink on paper. Sculpture: 10 ¾ × 3 ½ × 8 in. (27 × 9 × 20.3 cm); text: 2 ¼ × 1 ¾ in. (5.5 × 4.7 cm).
Bottom: *He bid his Angels turn askance the poles of Earth twice ten degrees and more from the sun's axle; they with labor pushed oblique the centric globe:*, 1993. Wood doorknob, metal, oil can part, ink on paper. Sculpture: 9 ½ × 1 ½ × 5 ¾ in. (24 × 3.7 × 15 cm); text: 3 ¼ × 7 × 2 in. (8.5 × 18 × 5 cm).

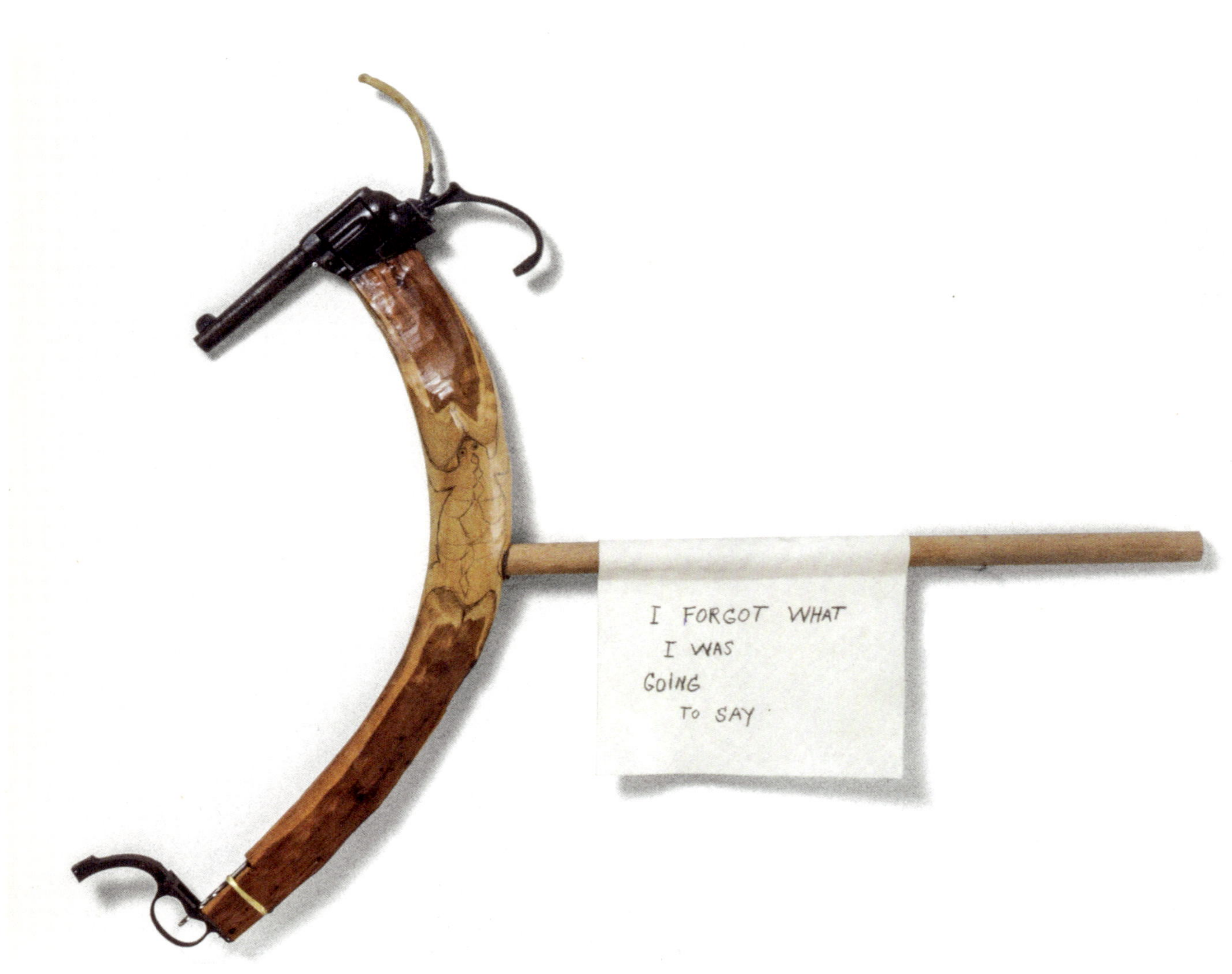

I Forgot What I Was Going to Say, 1992. Metal gun parts, carved yew tree from Ireland, wood dowel, bone, acrylic on canvas. 24 ½ × 26 ½ × 2 ½ in. (62.4 × 67.2 × 6 cm).

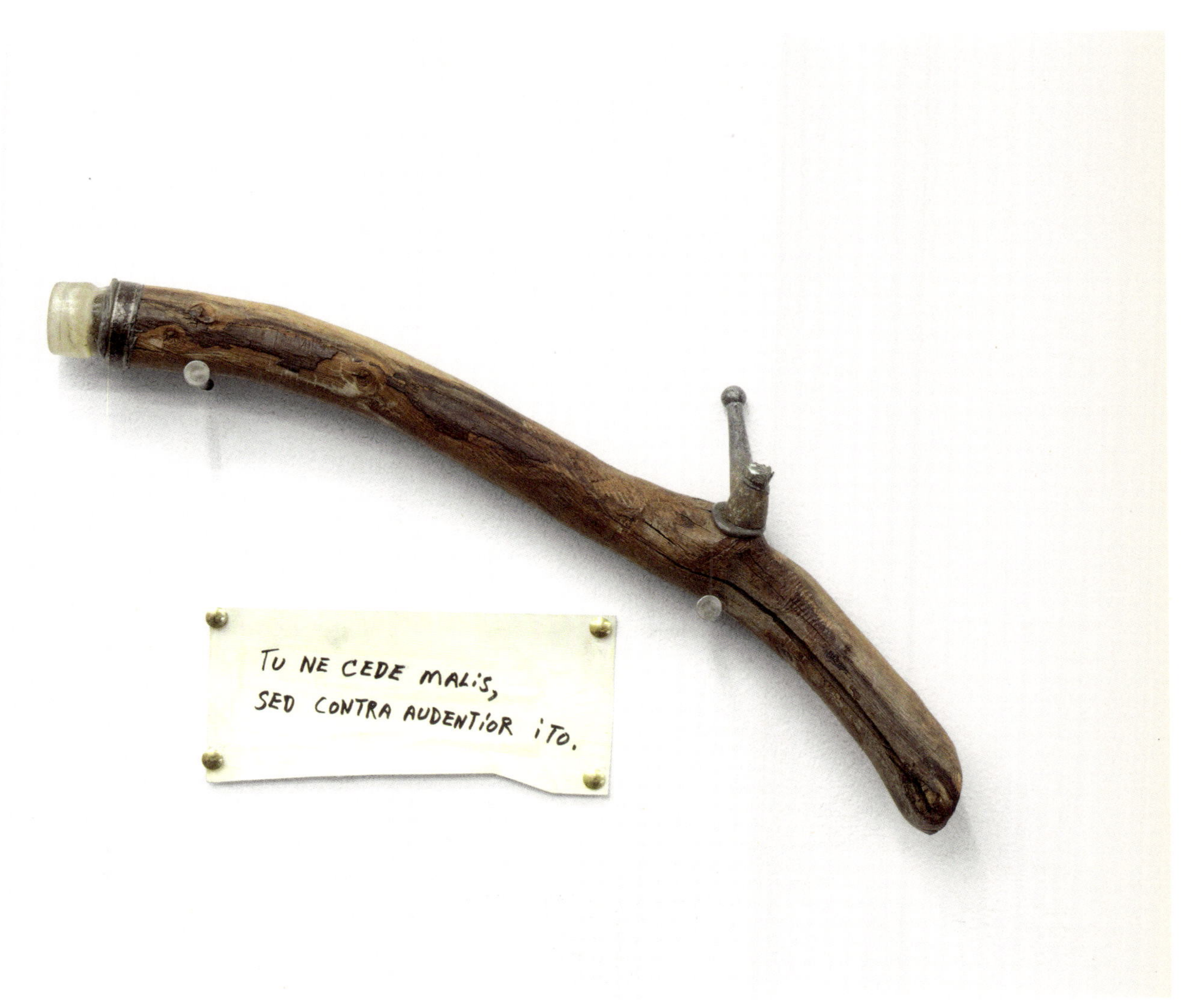

Tu ne cede malis, sed contra audentior ito., 1993. Carved guava branch, glass, metal, ink on paper. Sculpture: 9 × 17 × 2 ½ in. (22.9 × 43.2 × 6.4 cm); text: 3 ⅜ × 7 ¹⁄₁₆ in. (8.5 × 18 cm).

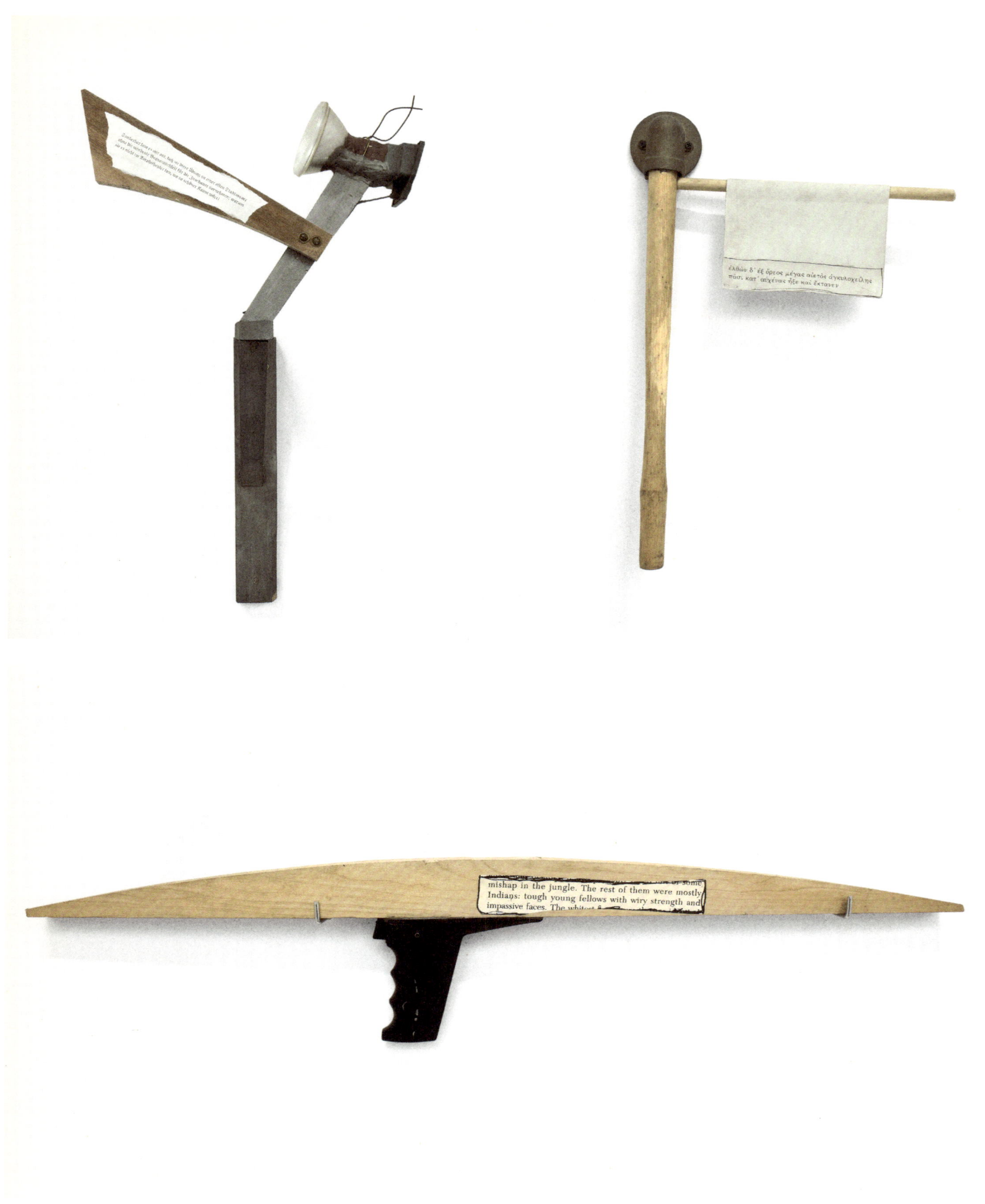

Top left: *Sonderbar kam es mir vor, daß sie diese Übung an einer alten Stadtmauer ohne die mindeste Bequemlichkeit für die Zuschauer vornehmen; warum sie es nicht im Amphitheater tun, wo so schöner Raum wäre!*, 1993–2012. Maple, pine, glass and metal headlamp, leather, slide viewer, metal wire, ink on paper. 39 × 15 × 15 in. (99 × 38 × 38 cm).
Top right: ελθων δ΄ εξ ορεος μεΎας αιετος αΎκυλοχειλης πασι κατ΄ αυχενας ηξε και εκτανεν, 1993. Wood axe handle, wood dowel, metal, ink on paper on canvas. 19 × 12 ¾ × 1 ½ in. (48.5 × 32.5 × 4 cm).
Bottom: *Mishap in the jungle. The rest of them were mostly Indians: tough young fellows with wiry strength and impassive faces. The whitest*, 1993. Plywood, plastic handle, paint, ink on paper. 6 ¼ × 31 × 1 ⅛ in. (16 × 79 × 3 cm).

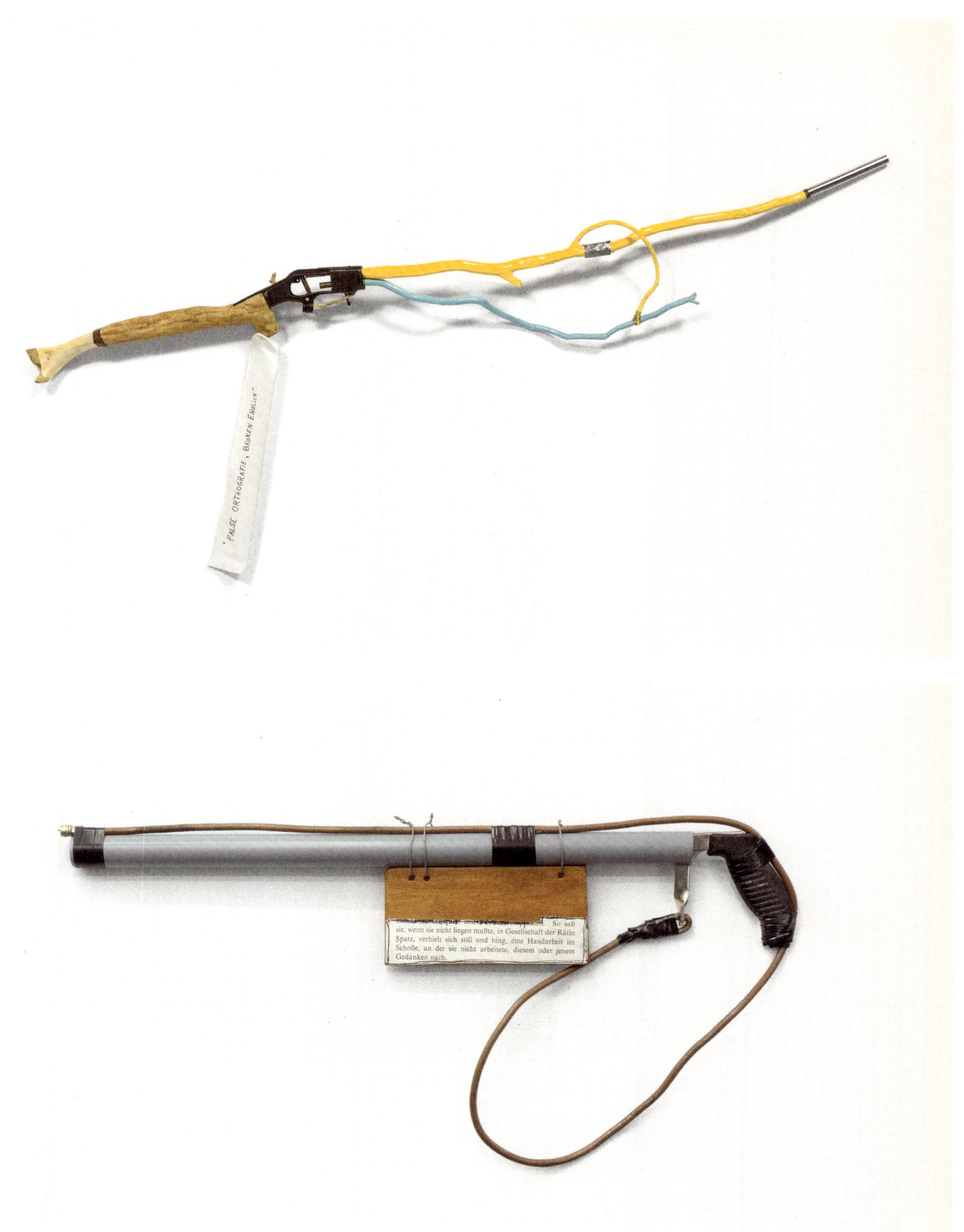

Top: *False Orthografie, Broken English*, 1993. Guava branch, rifle part, goat bone, coyote rib bone, spent bullet casing, acrylic paint, metal, canvas, tape. 69 × 25 × 4 ½ in. (175.3 × 63.5 × 11.4 cm).
Bottom: *So saß sie, wenn sie nicht liegen musste, in Gesellschaft der Rätin Spatz, verhielt sich still und hing, eine Handarbeit im Schoße, an der sie nicht arbeitete, diesem oder jenem Gedanken nach.*, 1993. Plastic tube, plastic handle, wood, cord, tape, metal, ink on paper. 15 × 28 × 4 in. (38.1 × 71.1 × 10.2 cm).

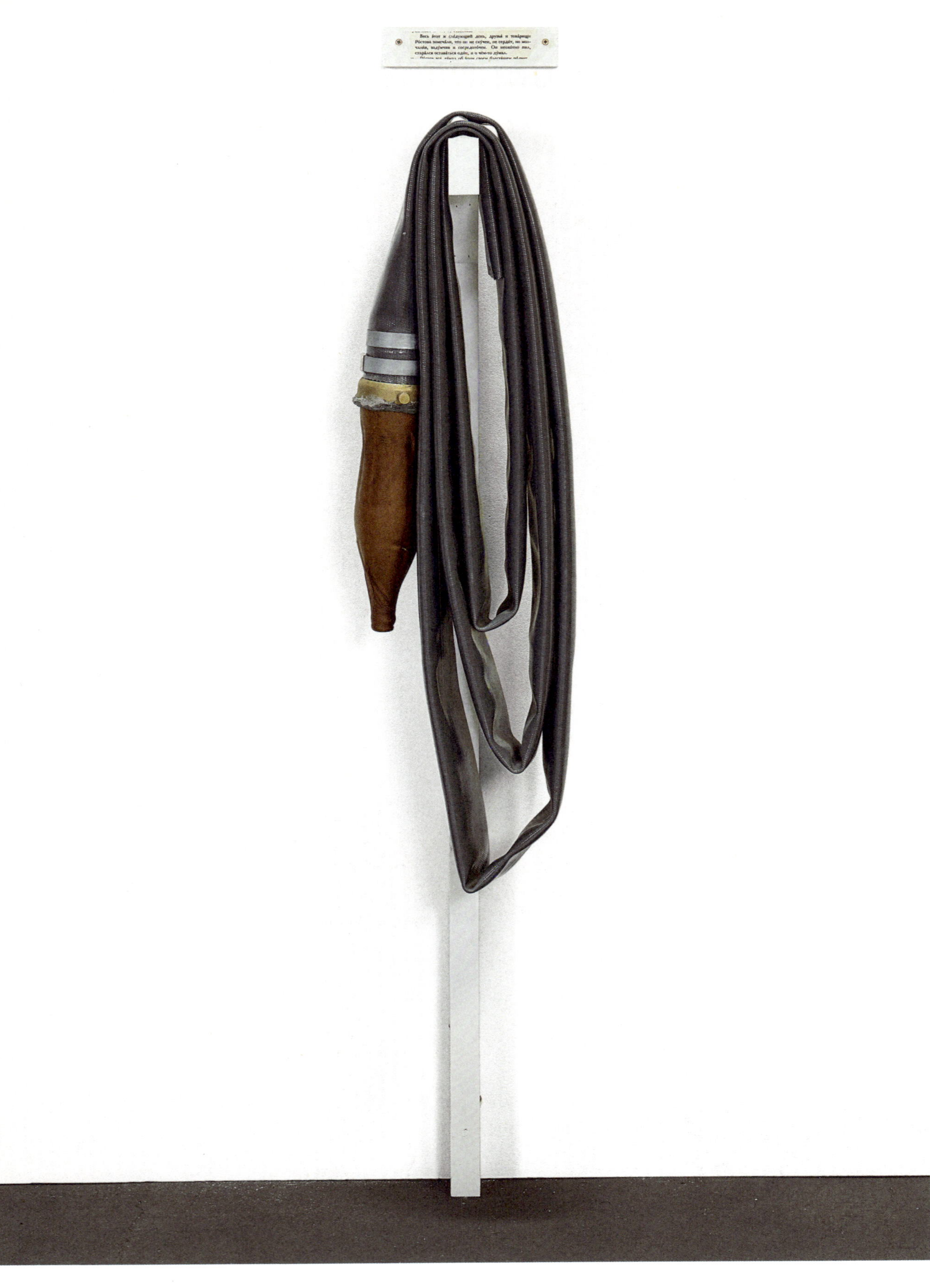

Весь этот и следующий день друзья и товарищи Ро́стова замечали, что он не скучен, не сердит, но молчалив, задумчив и сосредоточен. Он неохотно пил, старался оставаться один и о чем-то все думал, 1993. Fire hose, Coke bottle coated in leather, wood, acrylic paint, ink on paper. 59 ⅝ × 17 × 9 ⅝ in. (150 × 43.2 × 23 cm).

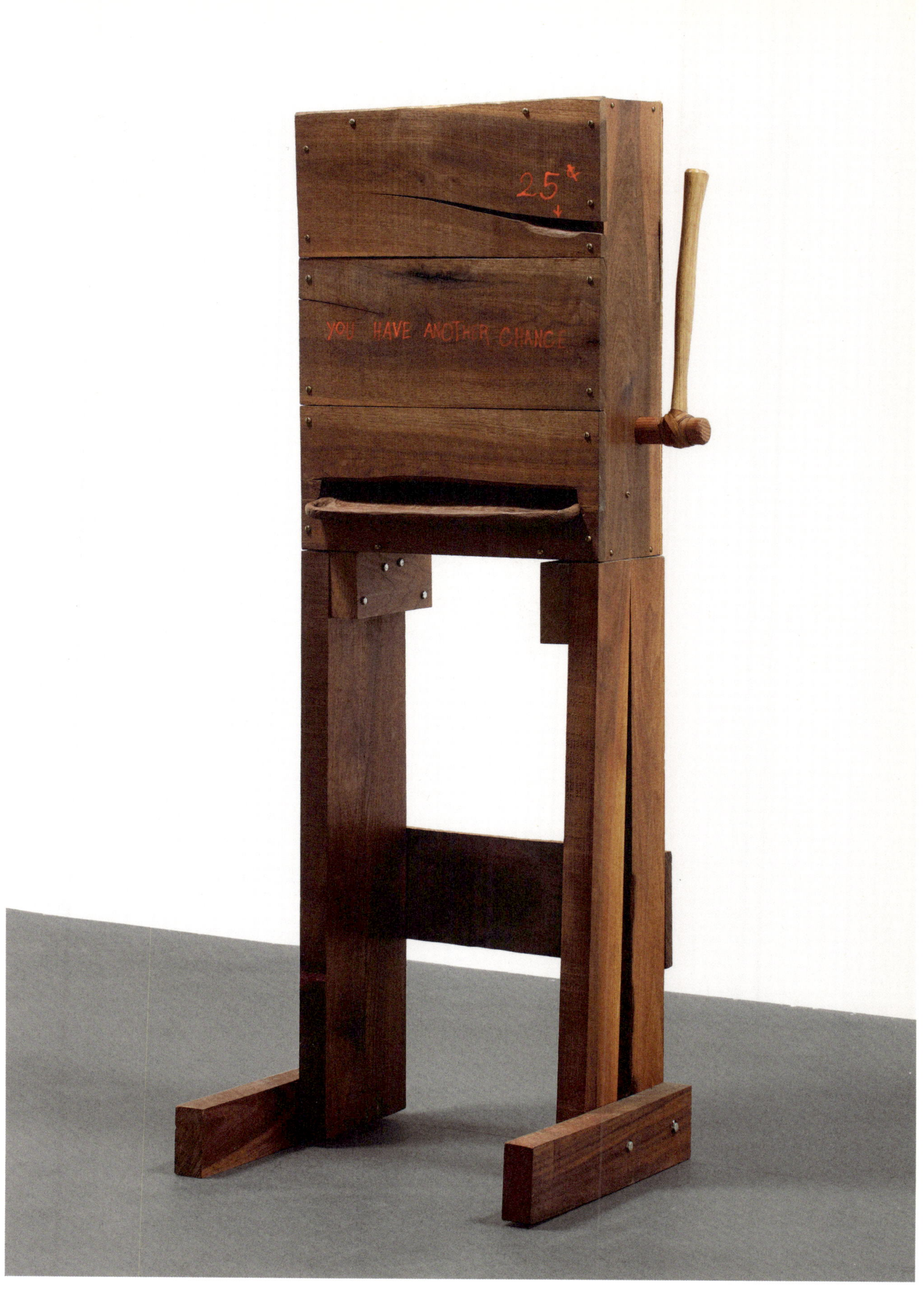

Another Chance, 1993. Black walnut and acrylic paint. 64 ¼ × 24 × 20 in. (153 × 57.6 × 48 cm).

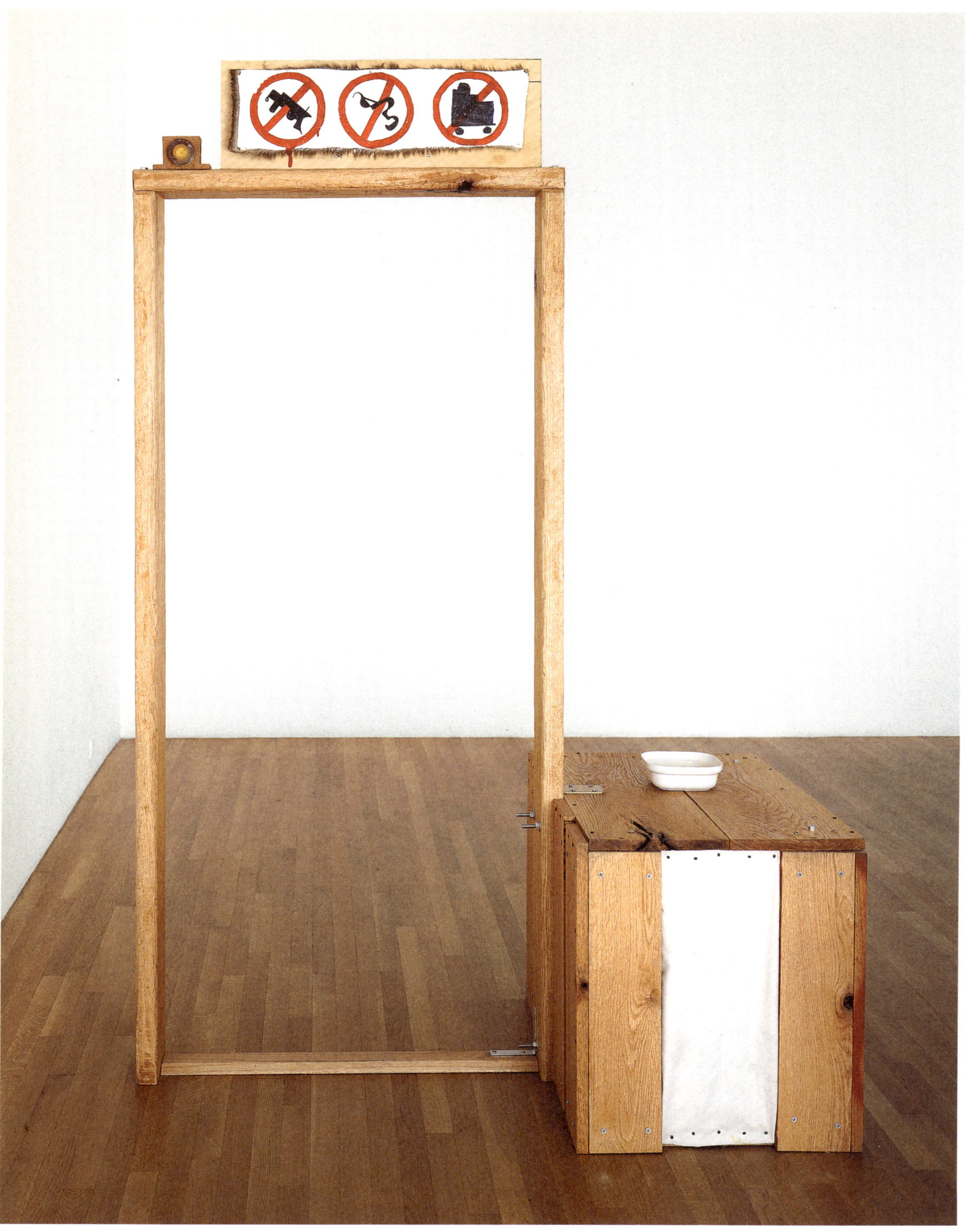

Forbidden Things, 1993. Oak, raw canvas, polyester resin, acrylic on untanned deerskin, plastic bowl. 89 × 56 ¾ × 32 ⅜ in. (226.1 × 114.1 × 82.2 cm).

RADIO FREE EUROPE

PAUL CHAAT SMITH

I first met Jimmie Durham in 1974, and over the years he's given me advice on many things. Some of the advice was good, some of it was terrible. I will share with you now the two best things he ever told me.

First, always take a taxi to the airport. It's more money but worth the splurge. Second, always strive to make work for people smarter than you are.

The taxi thing I understood and implemented right away. The other one took a while. How can you make work for people smarter than you are, I wondered. Won't these brainiacs simply laugh at your feeble efforts? Wouldn't a better strategy be to become smarter yourself, so you could then make work for your peers? And if that's impossible, surely it's better to make work for people dumber than you, because, really, what are they going to say? I struggled with these and many other questions, trying to understand Durham's riddle.

Eventually I figured it out, for myself anyway. The reason I write for people smarter than me is because it keeps you humble and keeps you on your toes and keeps things interesting. It raises the stakes. To write for smart people, you have to risk looking stupid.

Umm, maybe we should interrogate the smart/stupid thing a bit.

I received this advice in Cuernavaca, in 1991, I think. It could have been 1990, but I am pretty sure it was 1991, plus the exact year doesn't matter and anyway I really like palindromes. Durham had relocated to Mexico, and Robert Allen Warrior and I were about to write a book about the American Indian Movement (AIM). We spent many hours struggling over the question of audience: was the book intended for Indians or white people? We came to realize two things: first, we were terrified of writing the book and were stalling (also, we just thought it would be fun to blow our advance on a dicey trip to Mexico), and second, we were asking all the wrong questions. The American Indian Movement was a huge, complicated mess, and if our book was going to be any good it had to acknowledge that going in, and perhaps if we did that we might advance interesting conversations about what happened and what it meant. In other words, we would write for people who knew things we didn't, who had the same questions we did, who had different questions, and we would respect them enough to present the book as an inquiry rather than a definitive conclusion. Specifically, this meant saying some harsh things about AIM, because this social movement, like all movements that mattered and that dreamed as large as AIM did, had tremendous strengths and tremendous weaknesses.

So we decided not to act as gatekeepers. We decided to make the book about the questions that kept us up at night. And the payoff was that people we didn't know and would never even meet craved the same conversations. They didn't want platitudes.

Writing for people smarter than yourself is just clumsy shorthand for imagining an audience that knows things you don't but is generous enough to think you might have something to contribute, and that by joining forces we all might come out of it a little better off than when we started.

What I mean to say is that I'm talking about things that keep me up at night, things I haven't figured out. Because this stuff is hard, and I need people, like you perhaps, who are smarter than me to make sense of it.

It's 1984. You live in a big city on an American coast. New York or Boston or DC or San Francisco or Los Angeles or Seattle. Reagan is president, professional liars on television keep telling you it's morning in America; in other words, life is terrible and appears to be getting worse.

The only bright spot (as if you would ever use such a term) is that you are not alone. Bad times create great music, and there's lots of it out there. Three bands command your attention. All three are brimming with talent and have released excellent records, and when they visit, their live shows are the talk of the town.

Everyone knows that one of them is going to break out. It's a lock: before you know it, the barely known band you saw last year in a local bar opening for a slightly more well-known band will be headlining stadiums all over the world.

You thought it would be X, the Los Angeles quartet, because their sad American plainsongs sounded like those sad American times. Also, their members had the most perfect names: John Doe, Exene Cervenka, D. J. Bonebrake, and Billy Zoom. You thought it would be the Replacements because you needed a little joy to wash down all the bitterness. Here's why you thought it would be REM: they were pretty good too.

Well, we know who won. REM's breakthrough album was called *Murmur*, and we all instantly renamed it *Mumble*, on account of none of us being able to understand a word Michael Stipe was singing. And because of the way time and memory impose their fascist methods on how we understand both past and present, it all seems inevitable now, yeah, sure, of course, REM.

At the time, it was anything but. People, scientists, tell us that if the whole quantum physics thing checks out, there are multiple universes with different outcomes. And that in one of them, the Replacements did achieve their record company's dream and became America's Rolling Stones. And in another, X sold more records than Guns N' Roses, and lead singer John Doe was elected to the US Senate in 2002. These scenarios are just as plausible, and just as unlikely, as REM, with their dirgelike tunes and mumbling lead singer, emerging from the postpunk pack and enjoying decades of massive popularity. Really? That's who becomes the most celebrated band of the 1990s?

In 1984 I lived in New York, and I followed these career trajectories closely. Well, not as closely as I might have: when I saw Stipe perform onstage in a dress, it never crossed my mind that he was telling us he was gay. I was also closely following another scene that, in the words of a Replacements song yet to be written, was achin' to be, and that scene was contemporary Indian art. Just as alternative rock (were we still calling it New Wave in 1984?—not sure) needed a breakout star, a hit record, a band to seize the moment and create new possibilities for ten thousand other bands, Native art (had we started calling it that in 1984?—can't remember) needed someone to break out of the alternative gallery ghetto and start headlining at MoMA.

Did we have such an artist? Yes, we did, in fact we had several. There was Jaune Quick-to-See Smith (no relation). Edgar Heap of Birds. James Luna. Kay WalkingStick. And there was Jimmie Durham. They were as talented and amazing and different from one another as the Replacements, REM, and X were. All would be successful artists enjoying successful careers. Yet only one would reach the stratosphere. And, of course, we know who that would be. This project, *Jimmie Durham: At the Center of the World*, is a victory lap of sorts, validation for Durham's magnificent and deeply weird career.

In thinking about breakouts, it's helpful to know that the Replacements' "Left of the Dial" namechecks Georgia, a nod to REM's university hometown of Athens. That at the time, they and X and the Replacements were rivals and yet joined in a common cause, with shared tastes and experiences and audiences. That although the outcome wasn't inevitable, it remains instructive.

My analogy is a fragile thing, and you've probably seen through it already. For one thing, I was a passionate rock music fan who never knew (or wanted to know) the people in the bands themselves. I was just another twentysomething in New York who found meaning wherever I could. The artists were another matter. Durham (full disclosure) was a friend and mentor whom I had already known for a decade. And during the 1980s, I would know all of them and write about their work. It was a small crowd. There weren't ten thousand artists like that; that's another difference from the postpunk scene. It was unlikely there were even another dozen Indian artists out there who had a chance to break through. We already knew everybody there was to know.

Durham is from Arkansas and Switzerland and Houston and New York and Cuernavaca and, more recently, from Naples and Berlin. I don't think it would surprise anyone who knew him in the mid-1980s that he would end up living in all those places. He was always pretty clear about not being a fan of the United States, finding New York merely tolerable, and talking openly about his art school background in Europe. And, of course, he's always refused to be defined by any of those things.

The fundamental stance of all of these artists, the ones art historian Jessica Horton has named the AIM Generation, is the same: that making work that engages Indian topics does not make one simply and only a Native artist. They insist they are also American, and global, artists. (WalkingStick's recent show at the Smithsonian's National Museum of the American Indian couldn't be more direct. It's called *Kay WalkingStick: An American Artist*.) And they all, as both a political and a career goal, very much wanted to be part of the mainstream art world.

What is different, then, about Durham? Aside from the possibility that he simply is the best artist of his generation.

He left. They stayed.

The question that keeps coming up in Native art circles is whether it takes moving to Europe, or, in the case of Brian Jungen, fashioning a career that largely avoids group shows of Indian artists and even the venues that showcase them.

So I'm interested in what Durham's success tells us. Does it tell us that the Indian situation is so messed up, so trivialized, so unimportant that the only way to have a significant art career worthy of a touring exhibition among America's elite museums is to abandon the United States and operate from Europe? Should we encourage younger Native artists to consider doing the same? Abandon the whole Indian art thing and try something, well, less Indian?

Durham's most famous line, from his long list of unforgivably charismatic and brilliant quotes, is: "I feel fairly sure that I could address the entire world if only I had a place to stand."

Turns out, that place is Europe, and Europe alone. Here's my problem with that: Europe has embraced Durham (which is good!). And because he vowed never to set foot in the United States again, he has become a remote figure to the American and Native art worlds.

This is a drag. And it's kind of weird, because we're talking about an artist whose ideas and whose works are so accessible and so relevant to the historical moment that it seems to me a kind of betrayal of his practice not to be speaking directly to the largest of audiences.

Like many of us, Durham has been rereading James Baldwin. I think this speaks to how seriously Durham takes his role as a public intellectual, and how powerful that voice can be in times of crisis. We need his voice to reach a broader audience. We need his voice to reach an American audience.

This is hard, because one thing I know about Durham is that he finds American cluelessness "intolerable." He finds it intolerable to be around so much cluelessness about, well, everything. And at the very high end of that intolerability scale is the kind of conversations you are forced into as a Cherokee artist.

Here's what a lot of Native artists, who get the American clueless thing very well and are forced into stupid conversations all the time, want to know: so you're telling me Europe is so much better? Crimes, well, what about World War II? Or, you know, all those colonizers? Durham has answers for all this, of course. They just aren't good enough, and I think he knows this.

Another Durham quote applies here, the one that says, "Europe is an Indian project." How cool is that?

But what it suggests to me is that Jimmie Durham, stone-cold Cherokee Indian, even named for the famous country singer Jimmie Rodgers, like so many other Cherokee sons of the 1940s, is a lot of things, and one of them is this: Jimmie Durham is an Indian project.

Perhaps all I'm really saying is that even more than needing him, we really miss him. The Red Nation wants him back.

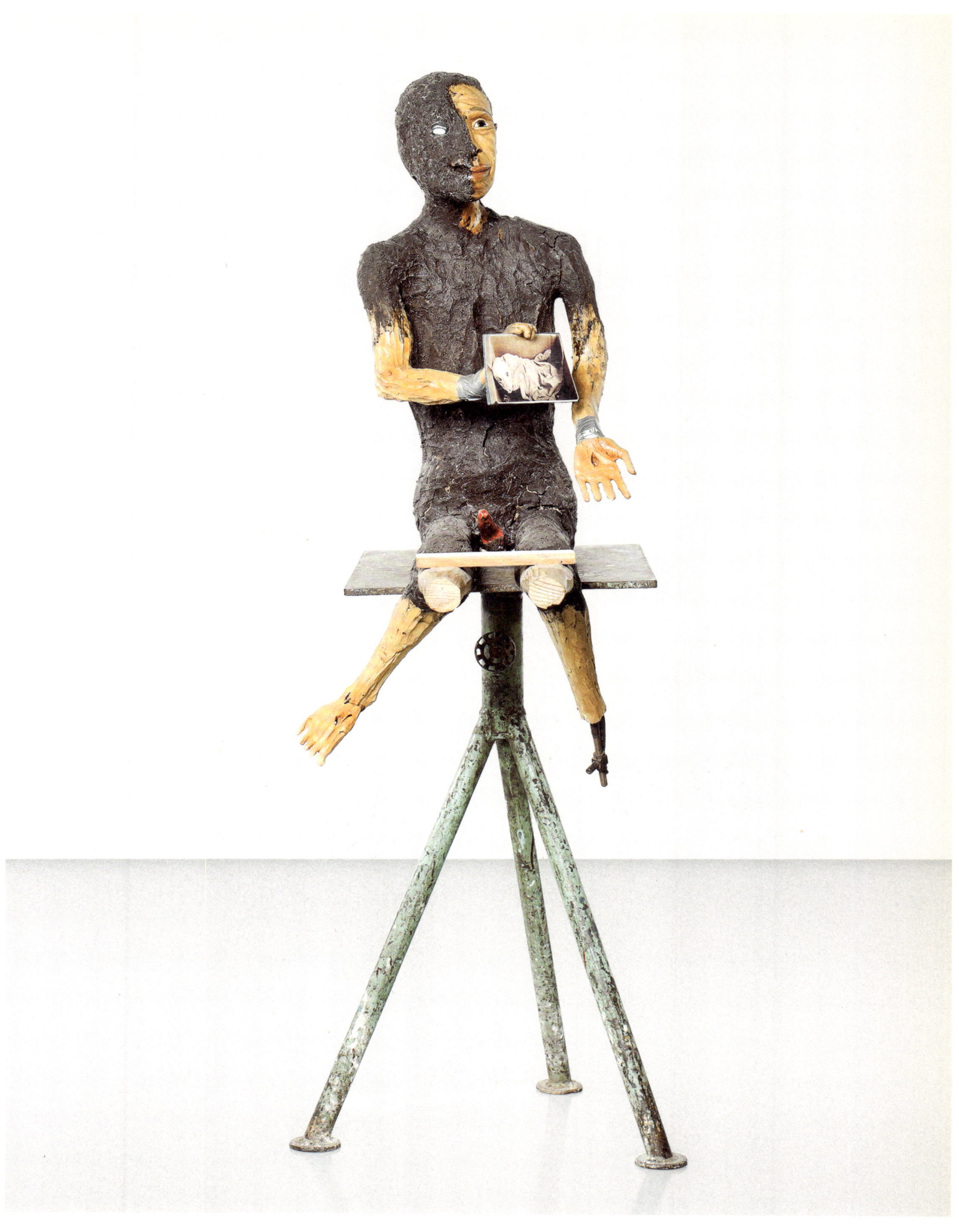

Jesus (Es geht um die Wurst) [Jesus (It's all about the sausage)], 1992. Ash, acacia, guava, duct tape, dirt mixed with blood and white glue, acrylic paint, color photograph, cardboard, magnetite stones, metal. 58 ¾ × 15 ¾ × 43 ¼ in. (152 × 40 × 113 cm).

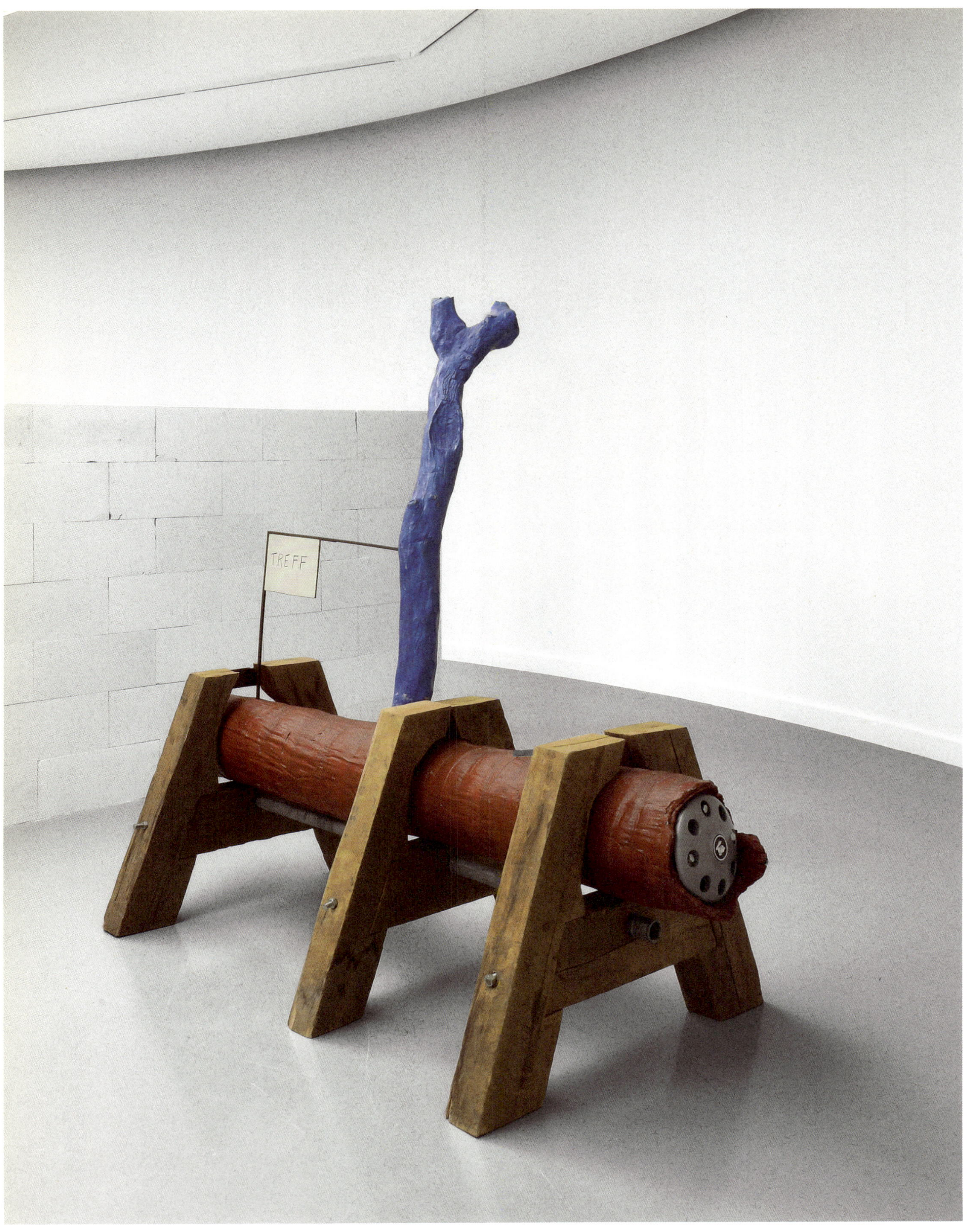

Treff [Encounter], 1992. Guava, Mexican cedar, palm trunk, iron, hubcap, black-and-white photograph, acrylic paint, ink on paper. 84 ¾ × 80 ¾ × 42 in. (215 × 205 × 107 cm).

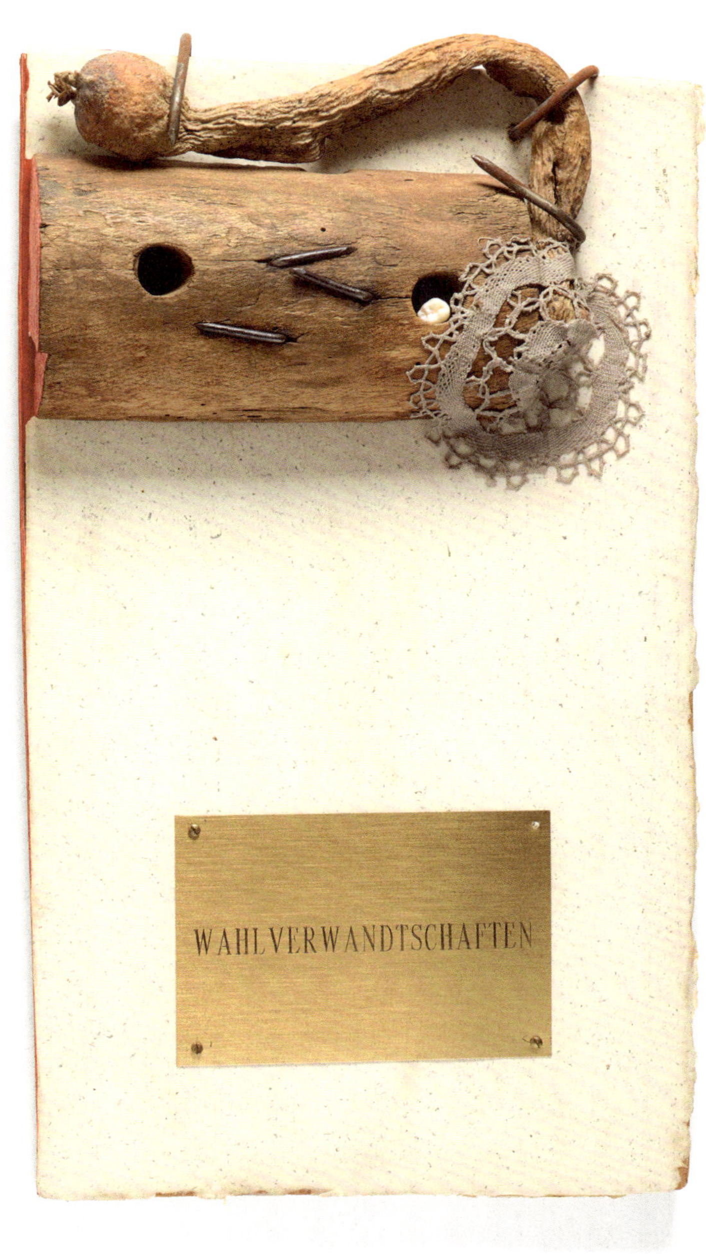

Wahlverwandtschaften [Elective affinities], 1992. Wood, nails, fabric doily, dried plant, tooth, brass plaque, acrylic paint, and paper-pulp collage on board. 18 ¼ × 10 ¾ × 2 ⅝ in. (46.3 × 27.3 × 6.7 cm).

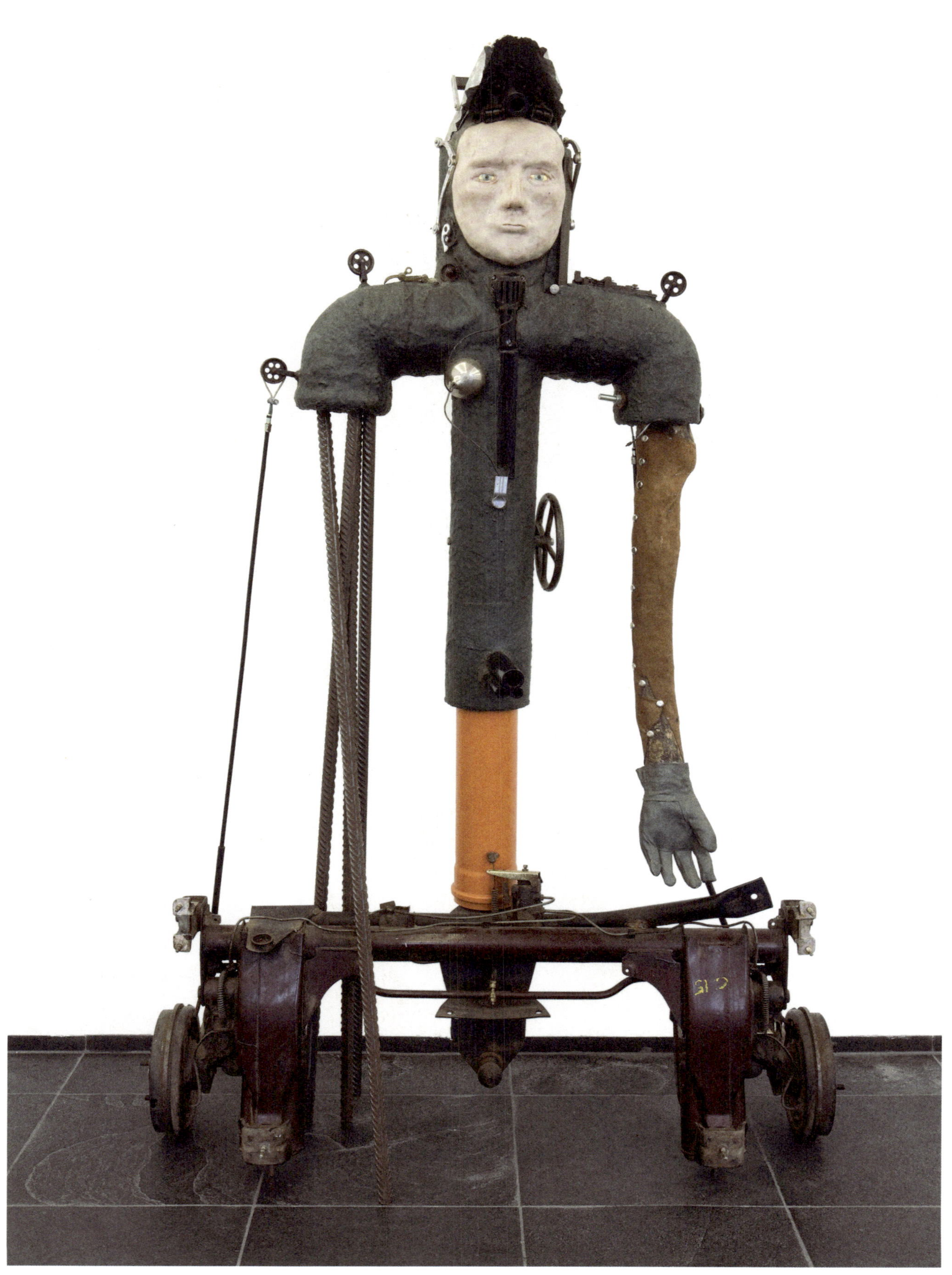

Cortez, 1991–92. Fiberglass and resin, PVC, metal car parts, leather, glass, acrylic paint, rebar, sheet metal, pulleys, handles. 88 ½ × 57 × 20 ½ in. (225 × 145 × 52 cm).

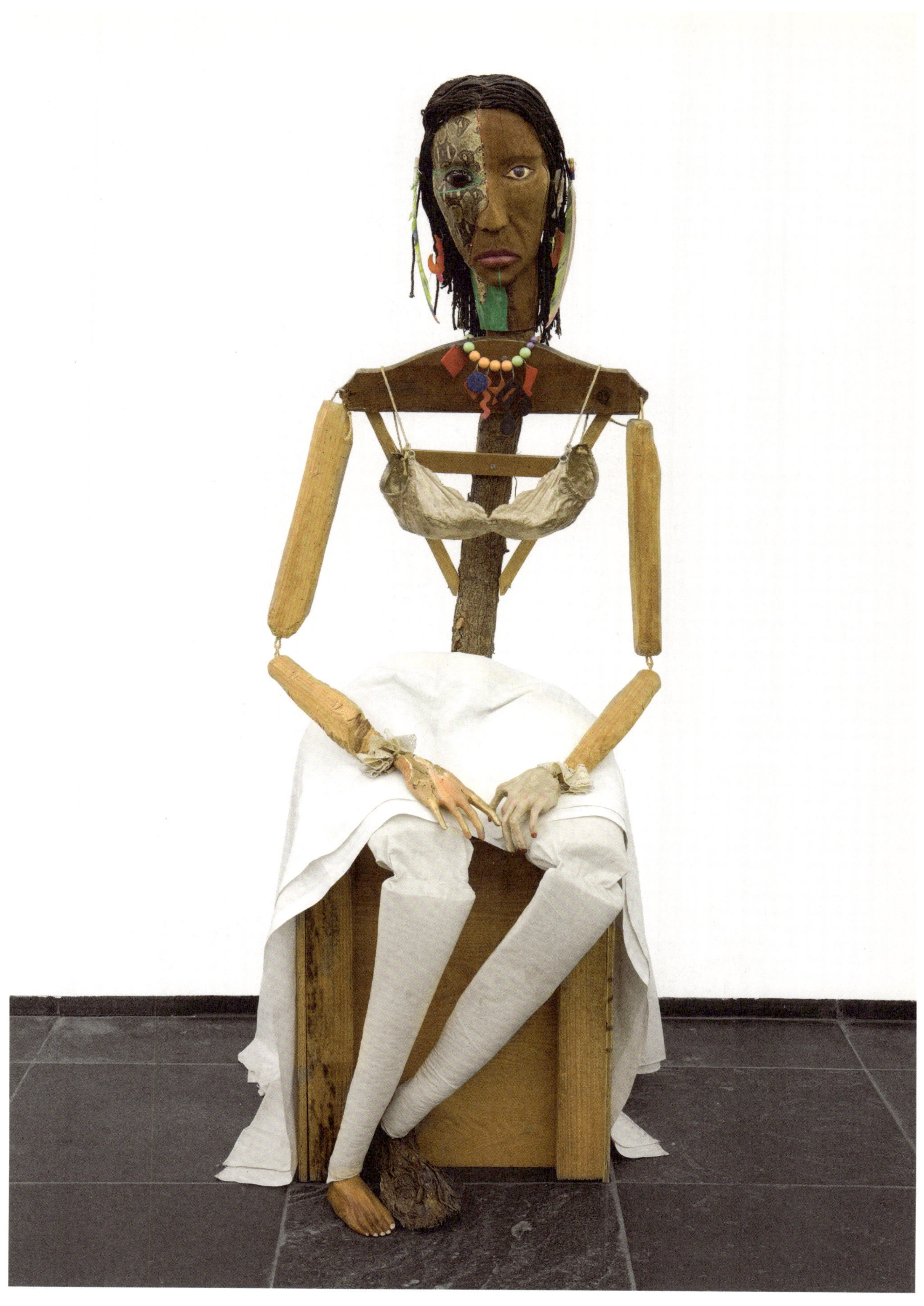

Malinche, 1988–92. Guava, pine branches, oak, snakeskin, polyester bra soaked in acrylic resin and painted gold, watercolor, cactus leaf, canvas, cotton cloth, metal, rope, feathers, plastic jewelry, glass eye. 70 × 23 ⅝ × 35 in. (177 × 60 × 89 cm).

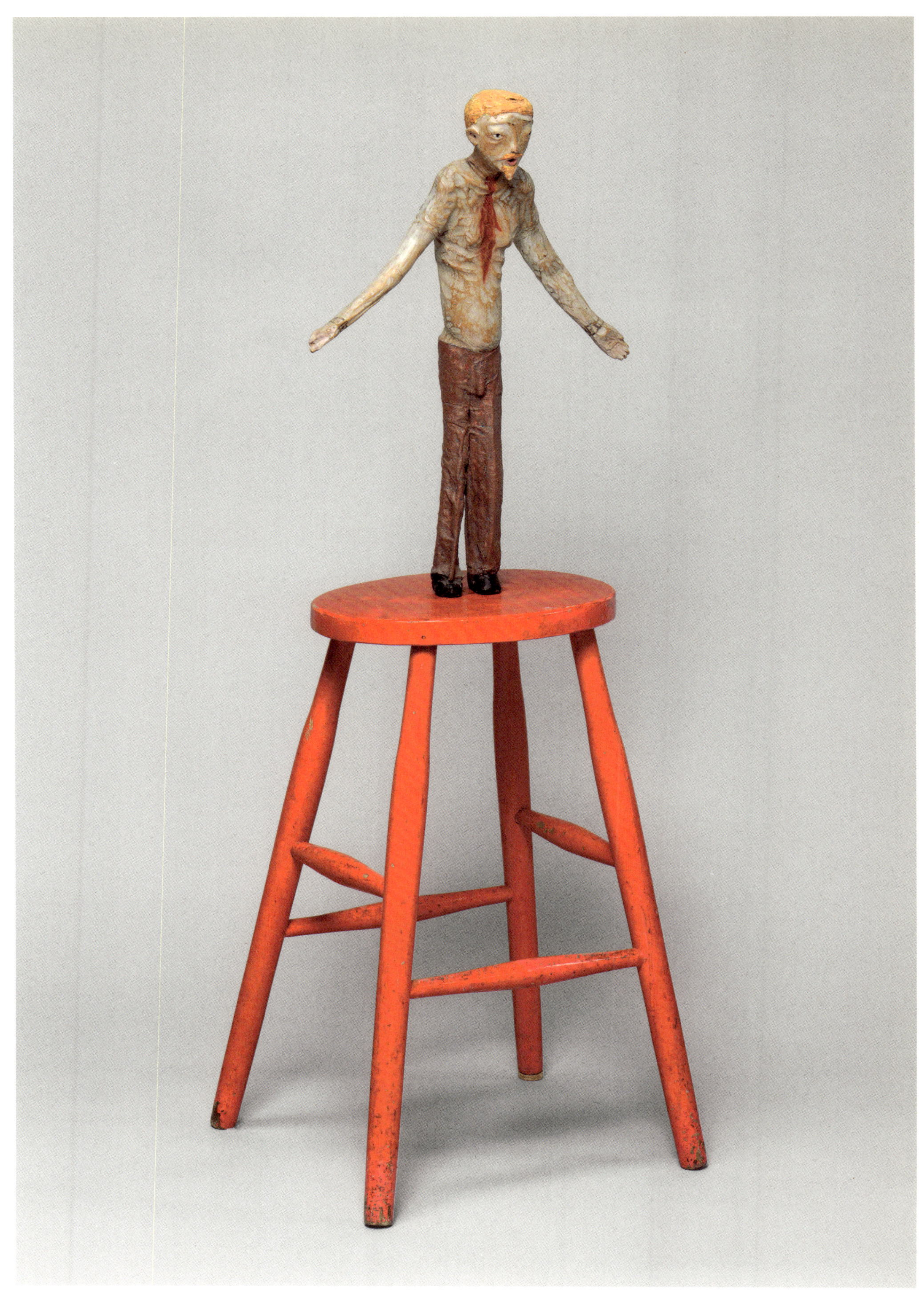

The Two Johns, 1988. Carved ash from Cuernavaca, synthetic hair, acrylic paint, cotton cloth, found painted stool. Figure: 24 × 21 ¼ × 2 ¼ in. (61 × 54 × 6 cm); stool: 23 ⅝ × 15 ¾ × 15 in. (60.5 × 40 × 38 cm).

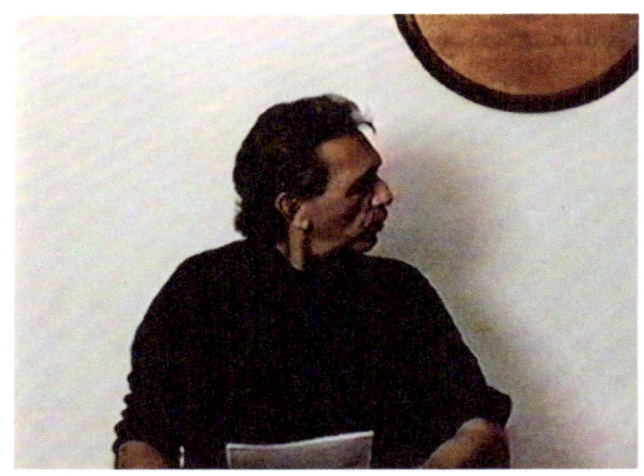
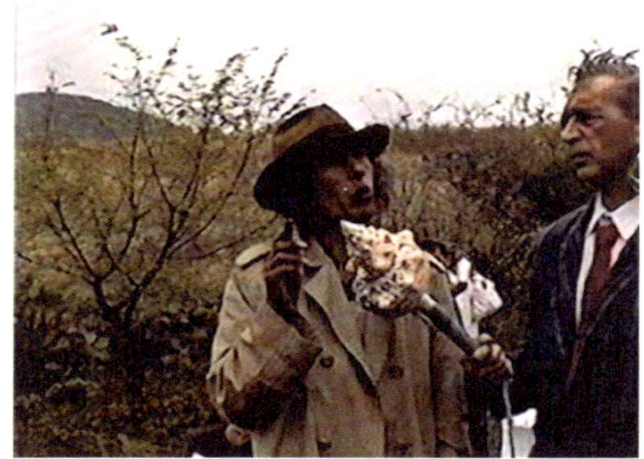
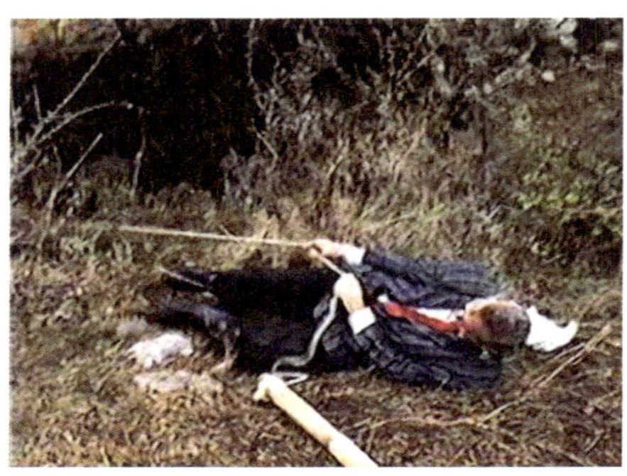
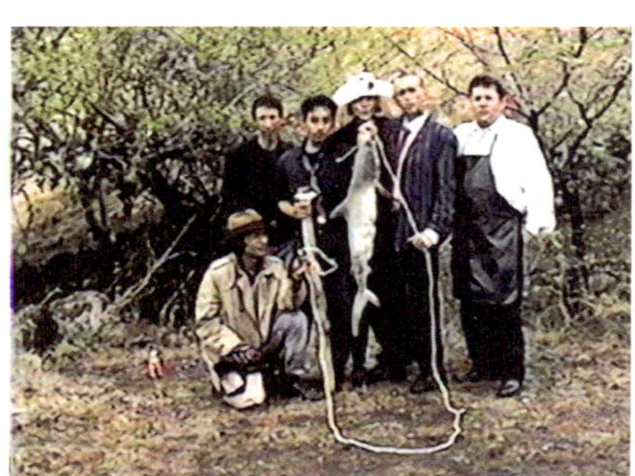
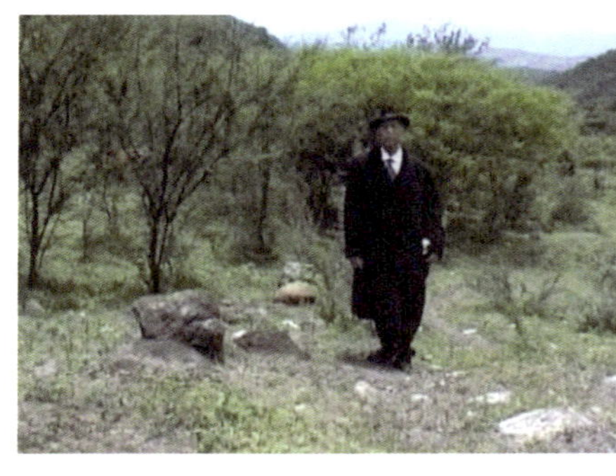
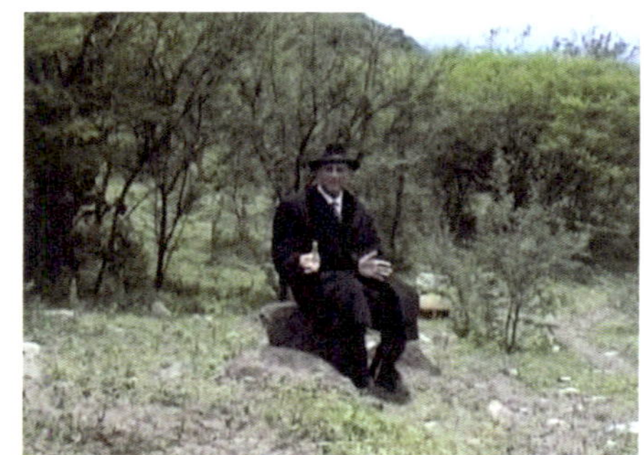
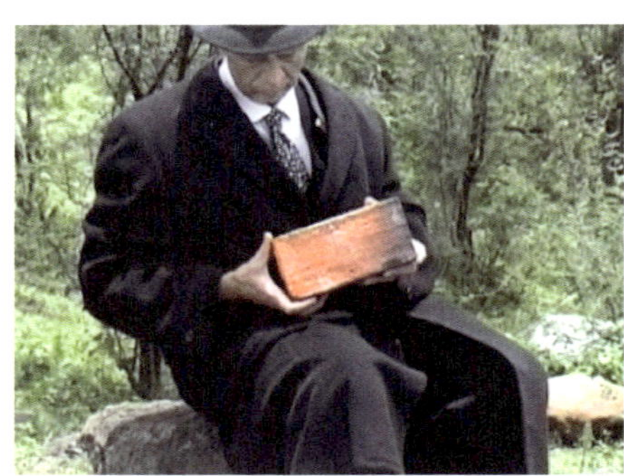
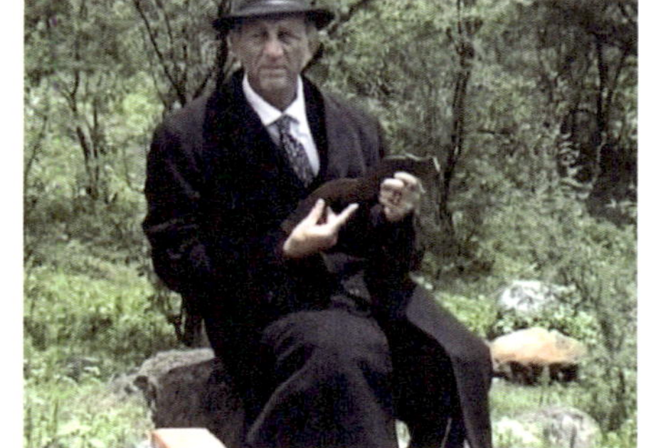

Top: *The East London Coelacanth*, 1993. Video, color, sound. 10:20 min. Filmed in Xochicalco, Morelos, Mexico.
Bottom: *The Man Who Had a Beautiful House*, 1994. Video transferred to DVD, color, sound. 7:27 min. Filmed in Xochicalco, Morelos, Mexico.

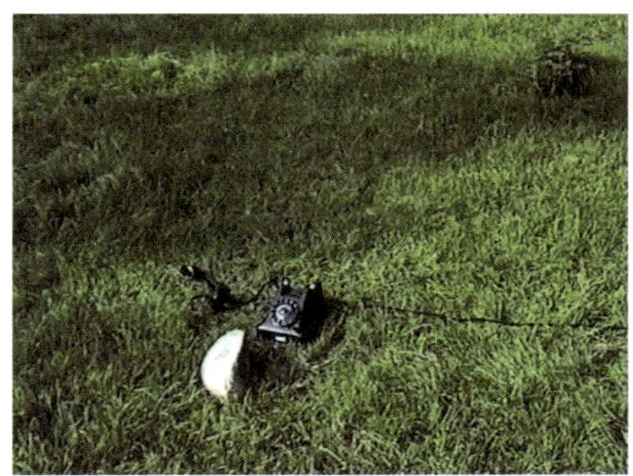
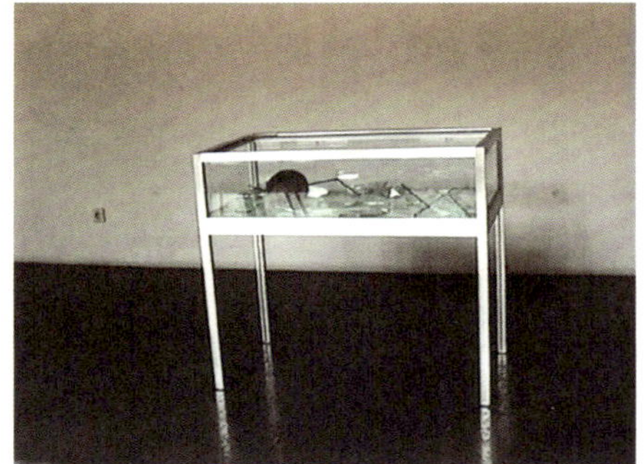
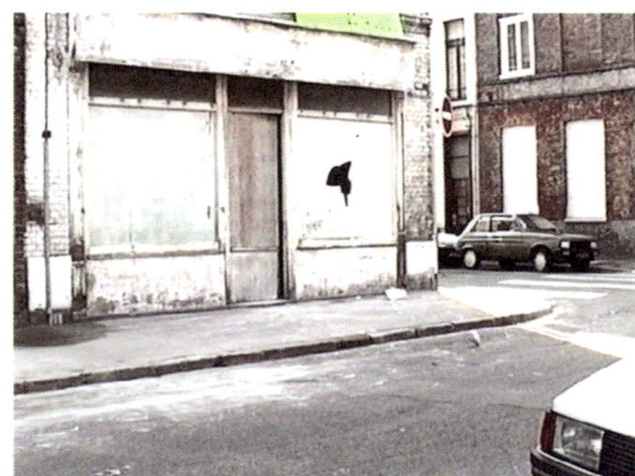
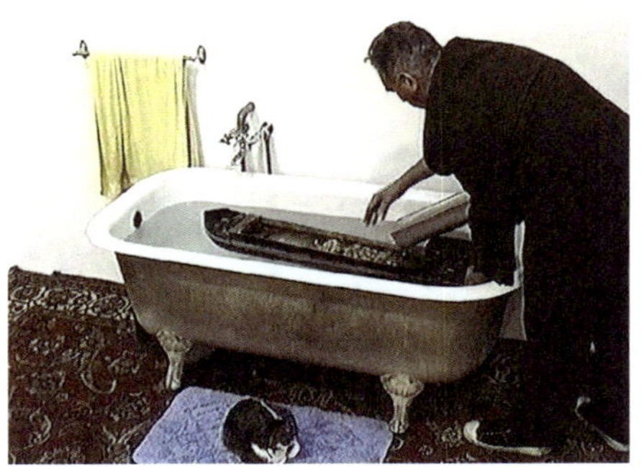
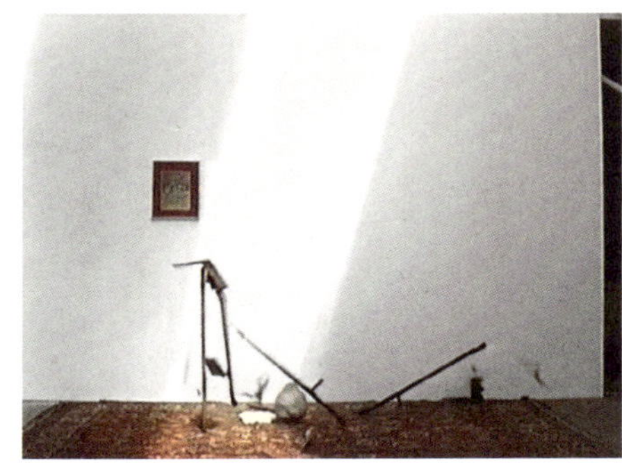
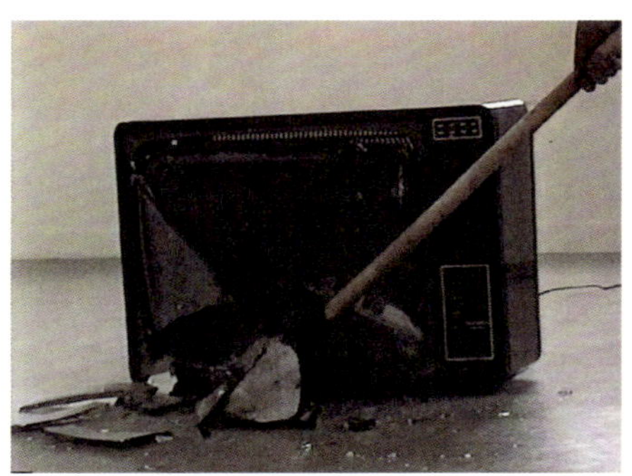
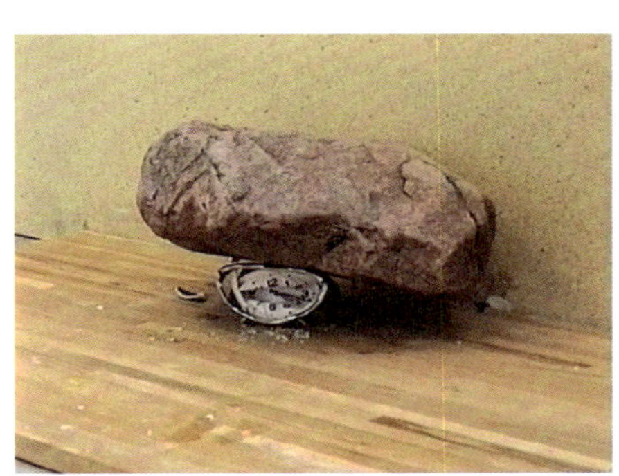
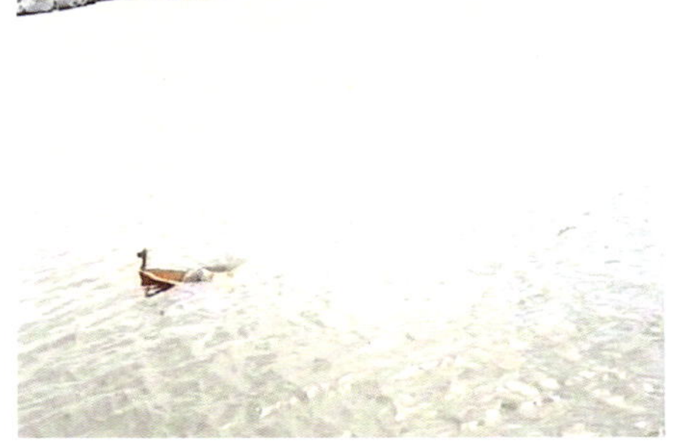
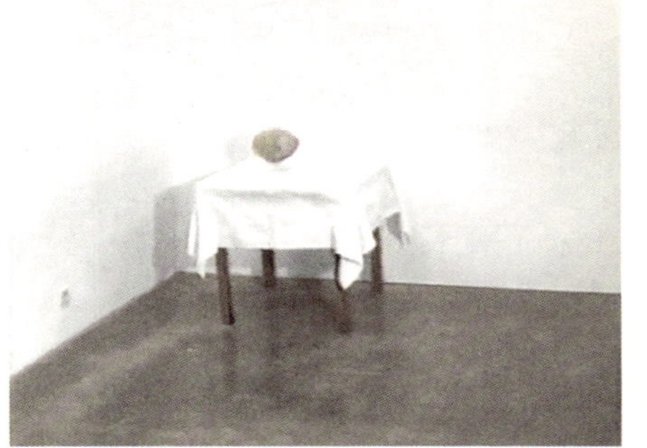
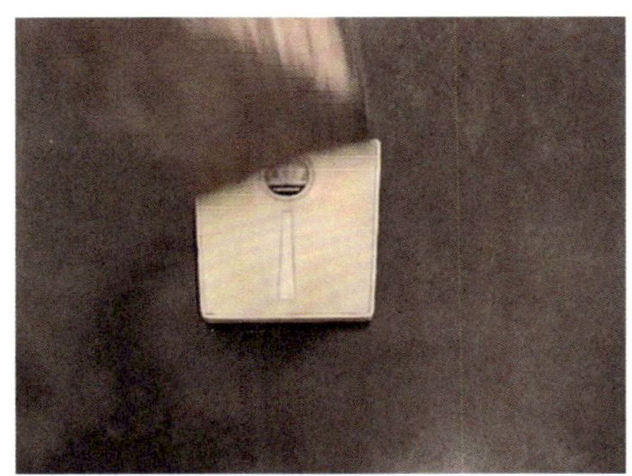
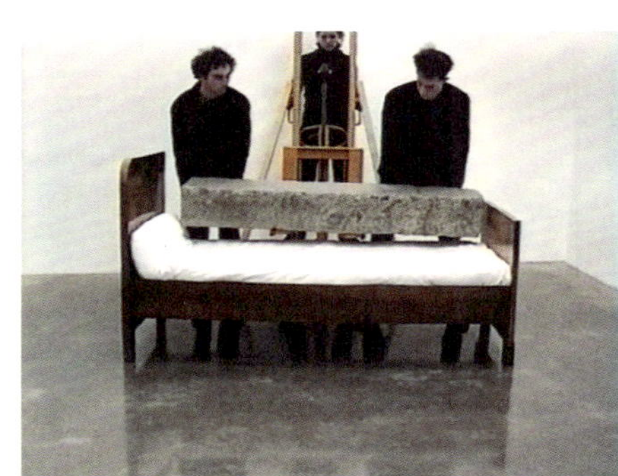
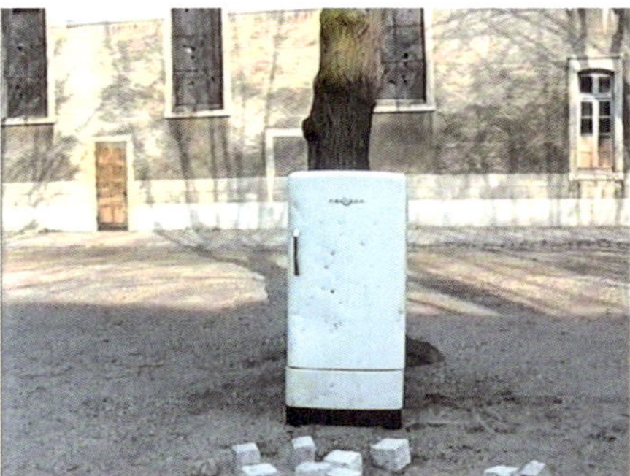
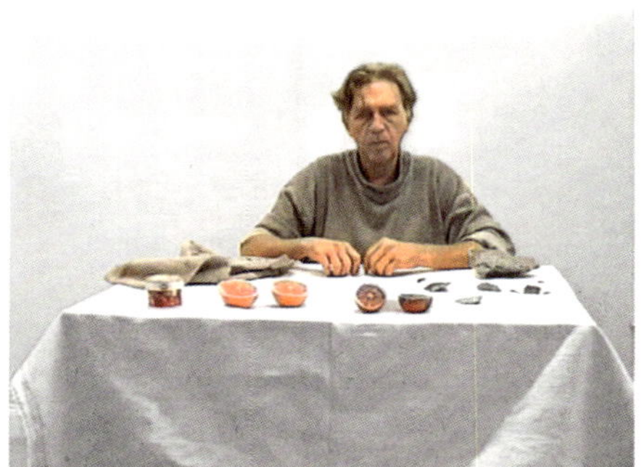

Collected Stones: 13 short videos (Incident at Middelburg, 1996; A Stone from Metternich's House in Bohemia, 1996; 13 Rue Fenelon, 1996; Enough!, 1995; A Heavy Stone, 1996; HTV, 1996; Pink Granite at Work, 1997; Un Projet à Lille, 1996; Nature Morte, 2000; Towards Light, 1999–2002; A Stone at Home in Bed Asleep, 2000; Stoning the Refrigerator, 1996; Brazilian Bloodstone, 1997), 1995–2002. Single-channel video, color, sound. 21:39 min.

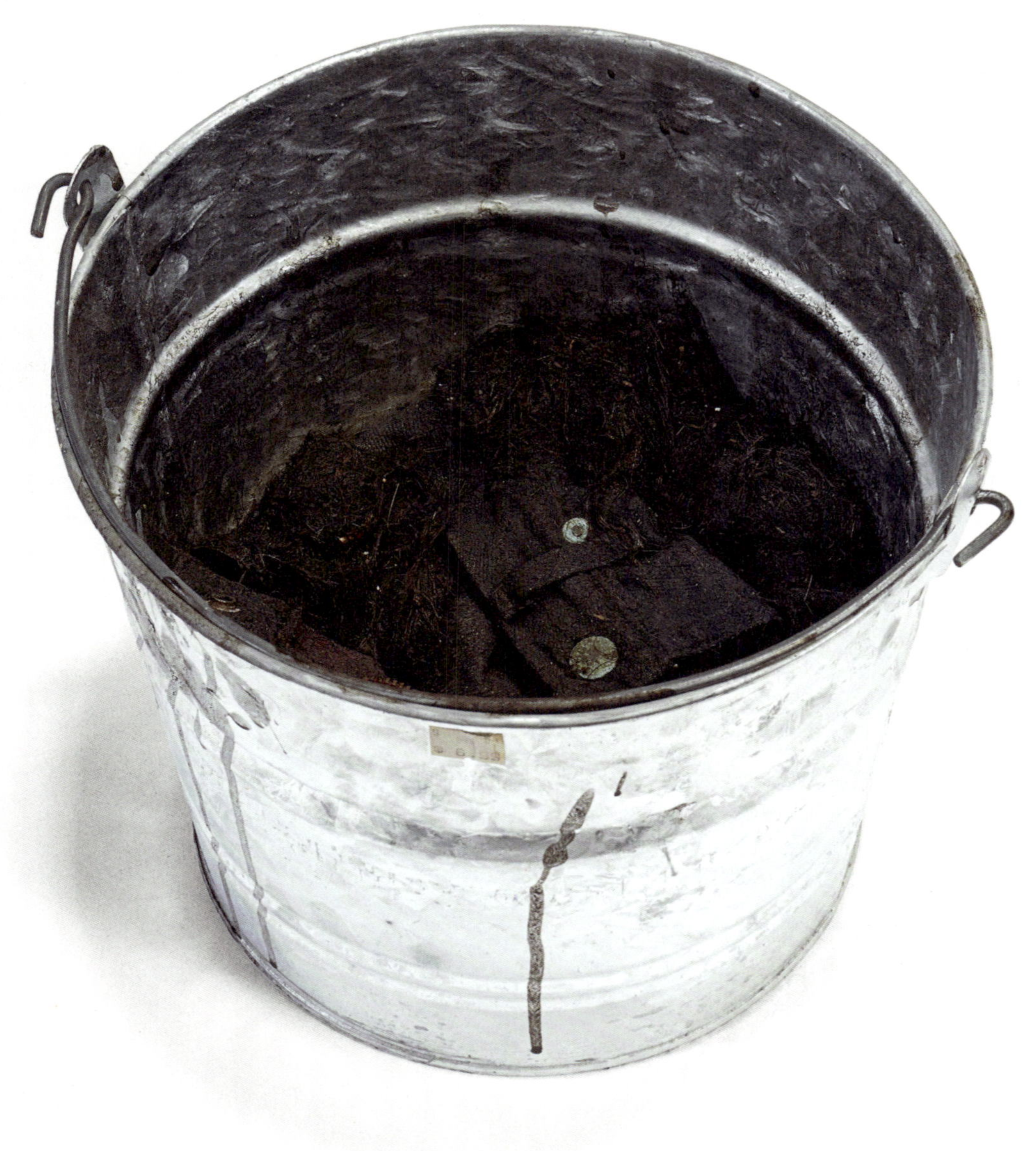

Dirt, Human Hair and Cotton in Steel Bucket #4, 1995. Dirt, human hair, cotton in stainless-steel bucket. 10 ¼ × 12 × 10 ½ in. (26 × 30.5 × 27 cm).

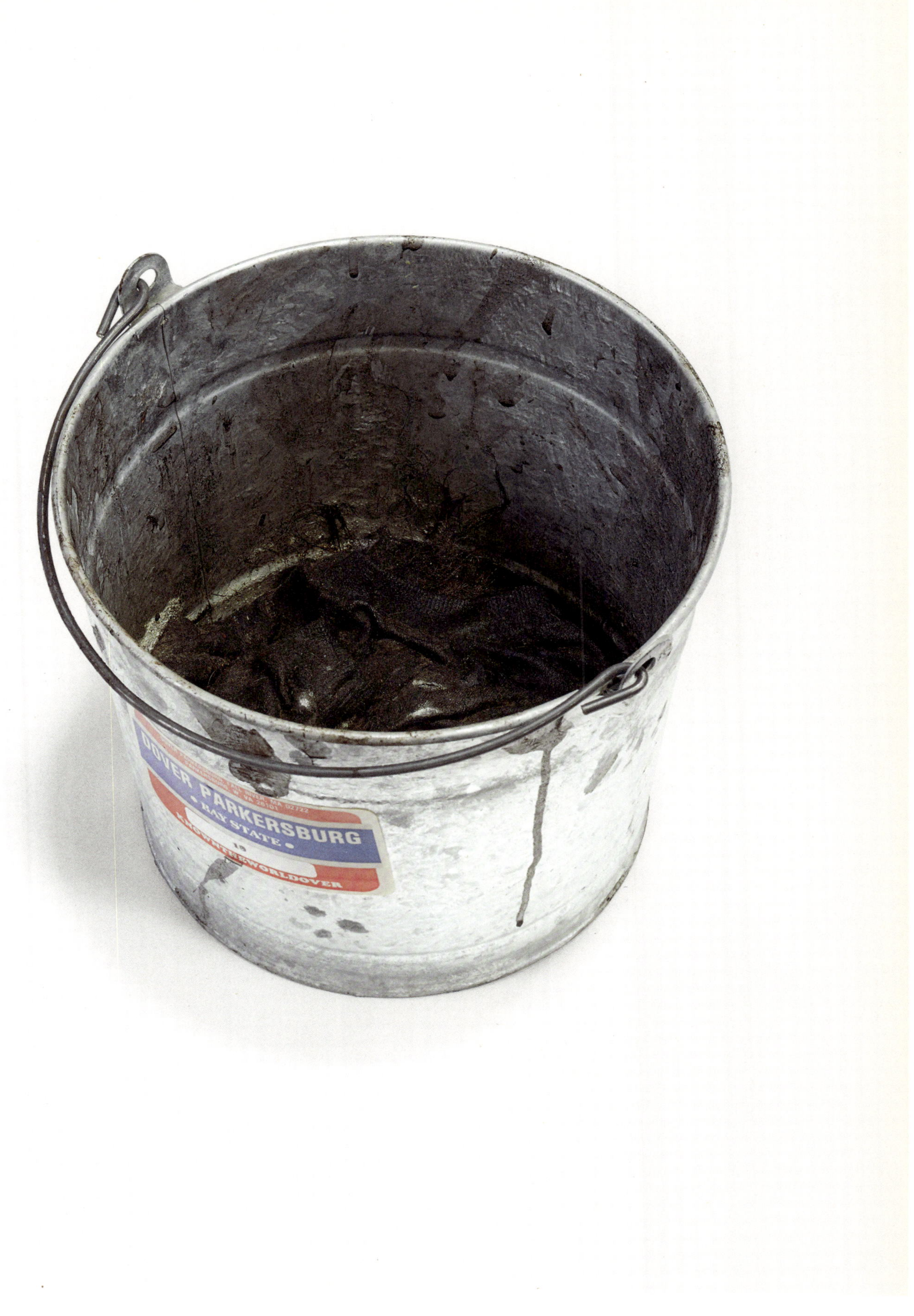

Dirt, Human Hair and Cotton in Steel Bucket #2, 1995. Dirt, human hair, cotton in stainless-steel bucket. 9 ½ × 11 ¼ × 10 ½ in. (24.5 × 29 × 27 cm).

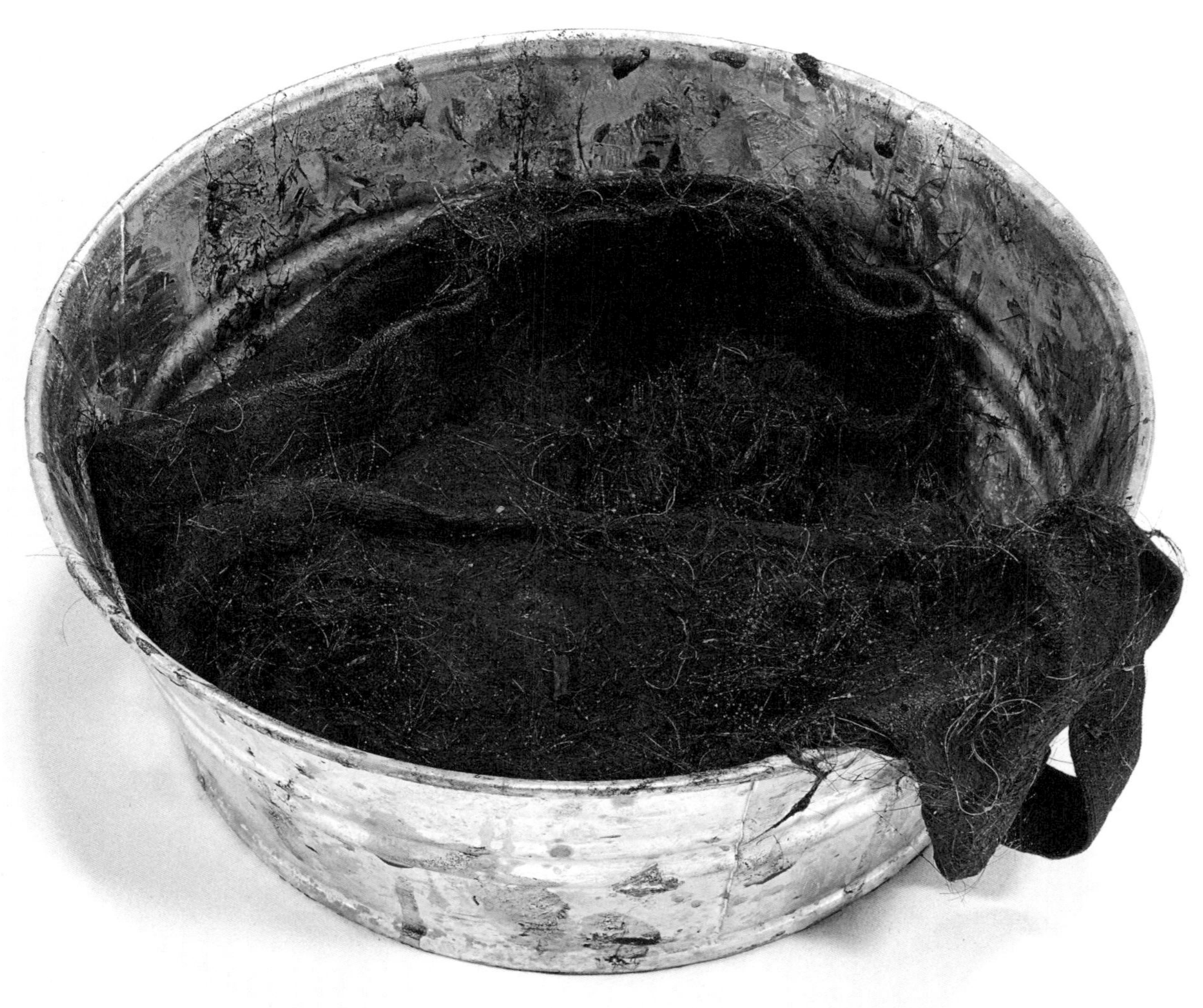

Dirt, Human Hair and Vegetable Fiber in Steel Bucket #2, 1995. Dirt, human hair, vegetable fiber in stainless-steel bucket. 4 × 9 ¼ × 8 ¼ in. (10.5 × 23.5 × 21.2 cm).

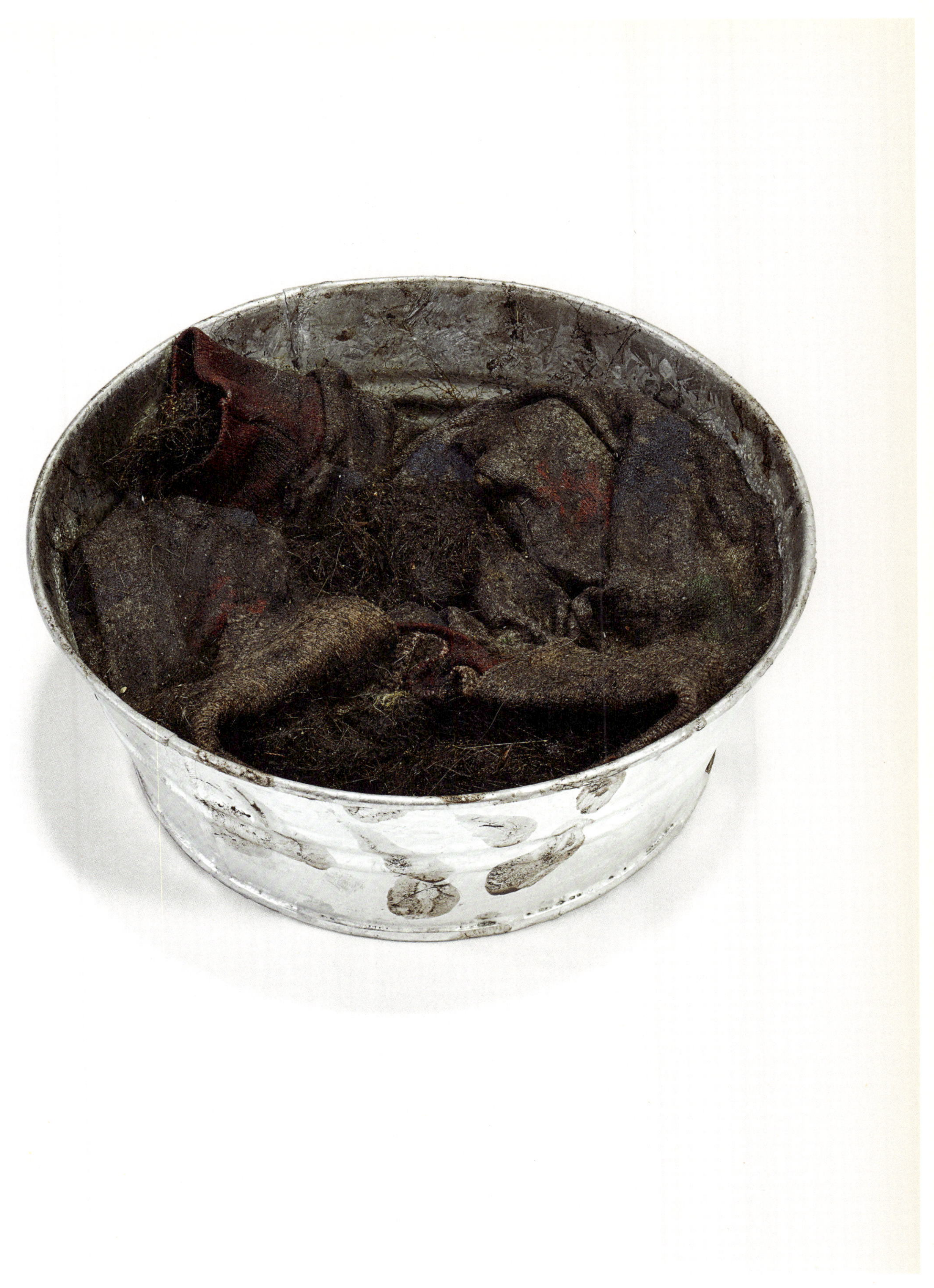

Dirt, Human Hair and Vegetable Fiber in Steel Bucket #3, 1995. Dirt, human hair, vegetable fiber in stainless-steel bucket. 3 × 8 ¼ × 8 ¼ in. (8 × 21 × 21 cm).

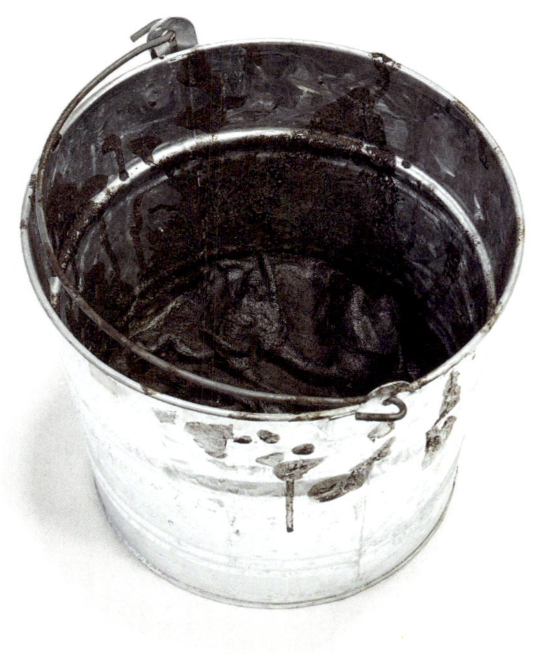

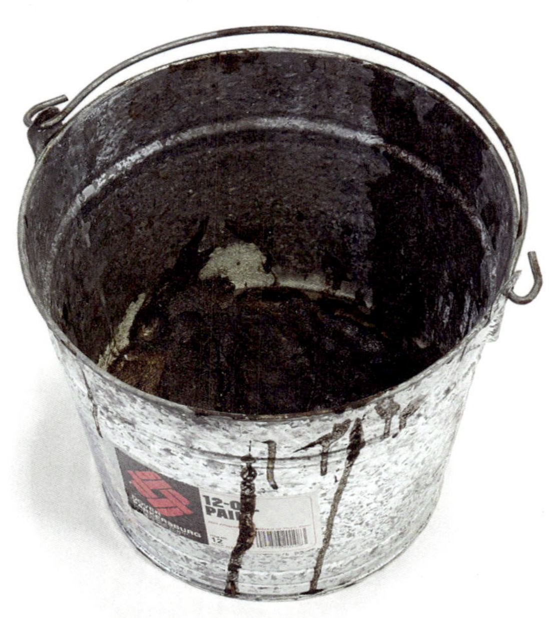

Top: *Dirt, Human Hair and Cotton in Steel Bucket #3*, 1995. Dirt, human hair, cotton in stainless-steel bucket. 10 × 11 ¾ × 10 ½ in. (25.8 × 30 × 26.7 cm).
Bottom: *Dirt, Human Hair, Squirrel Hair and Cotton in Steel Bucket*, 1995. Dirt, human hair, squirrel hair, cotton in stainless-steel bucket. 10 ½ × 12 ¾ × 11 ½ in. (26.5 × 32.5 × 29.3 cm).

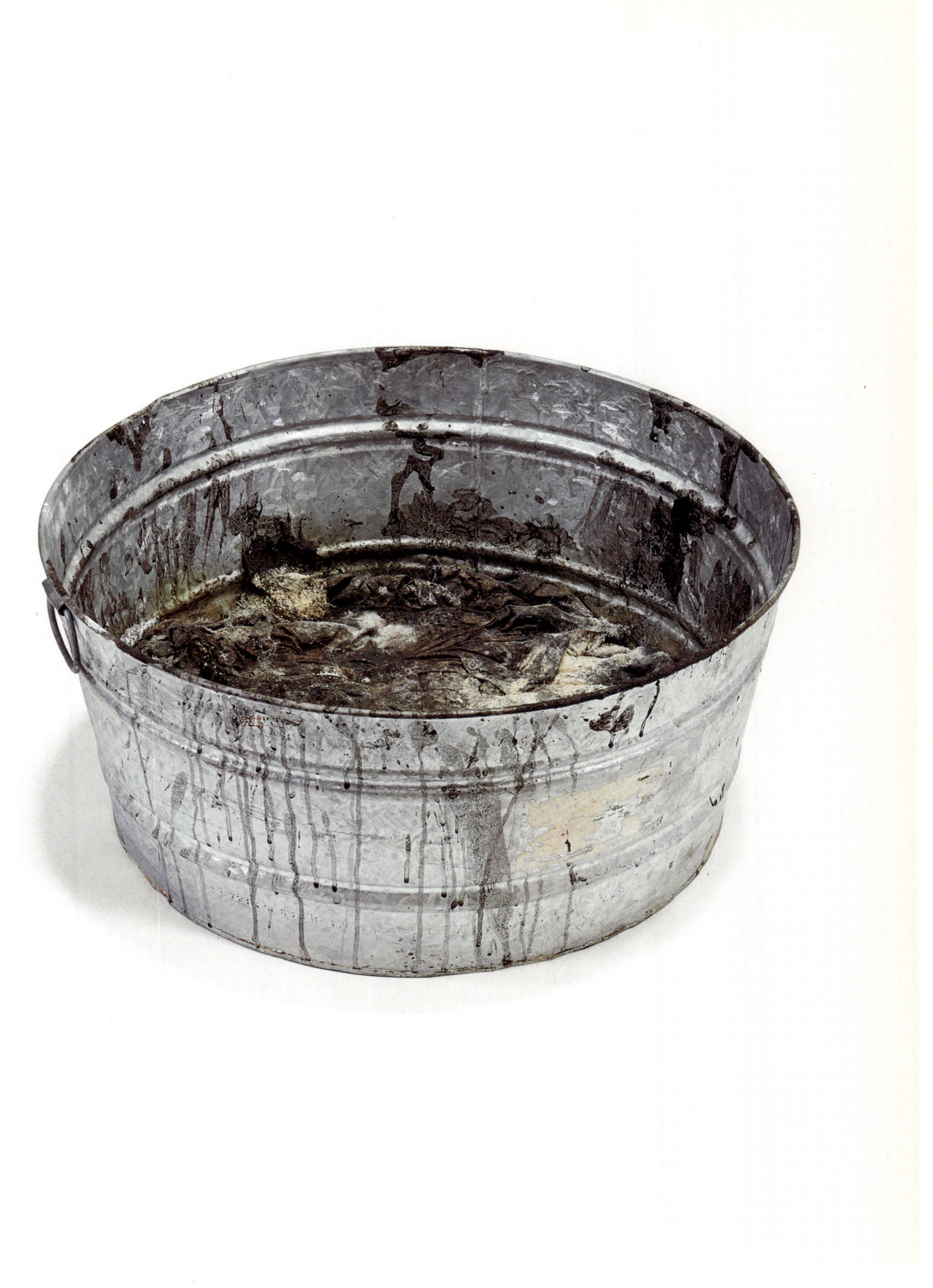

 Dirt, Human Hair and Vegetable Fiber in Steel Washtub, 1995. Dirt, human hair, vegetable fiber in stainless-steel washtub. 11 ½ × 24 ½ × 24 ½ in. (29 × 62 × 62 cm).

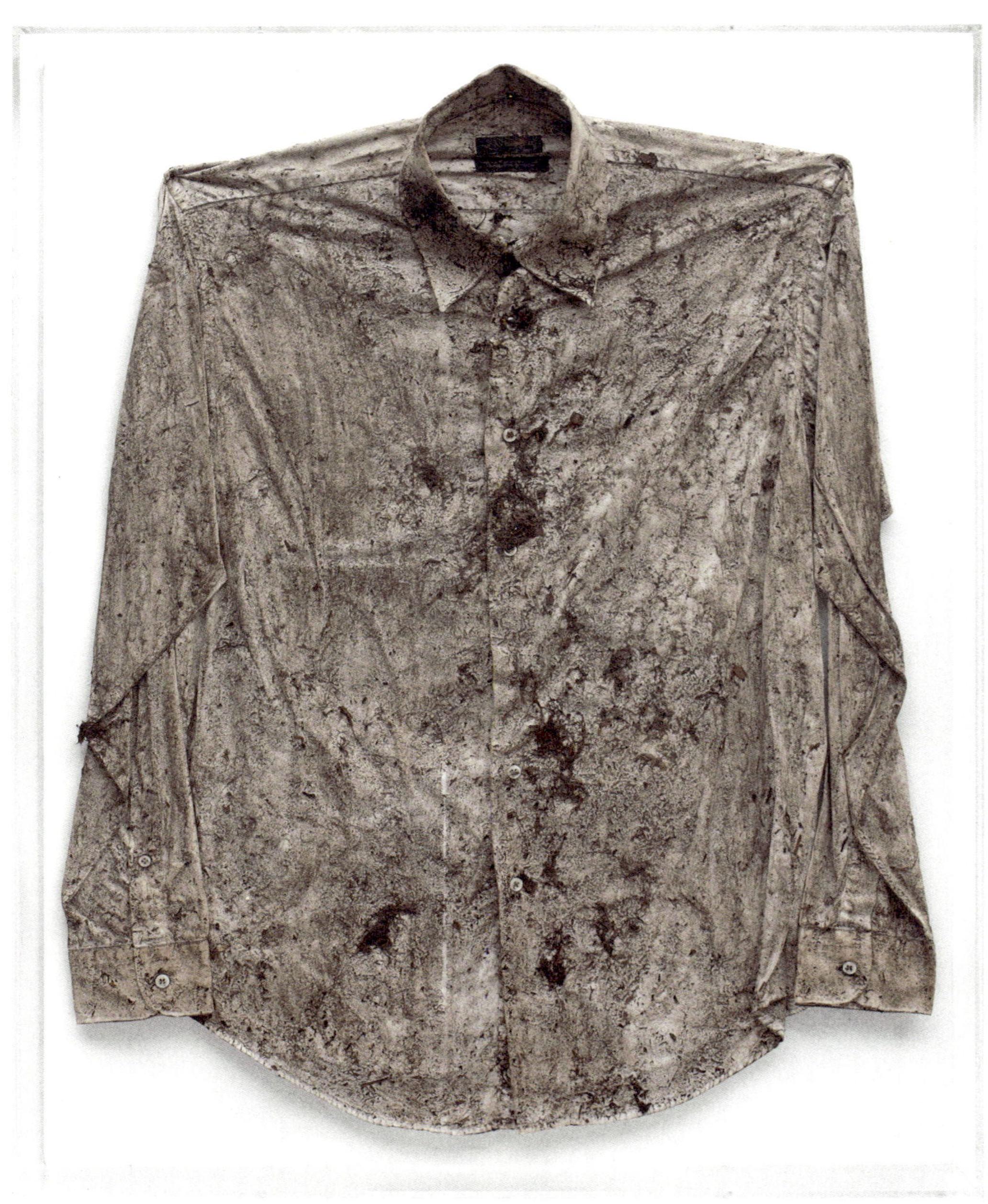

Le Lesson d'anatomie no. 4 [Anatomy lesson no. 4], 1996. Reims cotton shirt, artist's hair, dirt. 29 ½ × 26 ⅜ × 1 $^{3}/_{16}$ in. (74.9 × 70.1 × 3 cm).

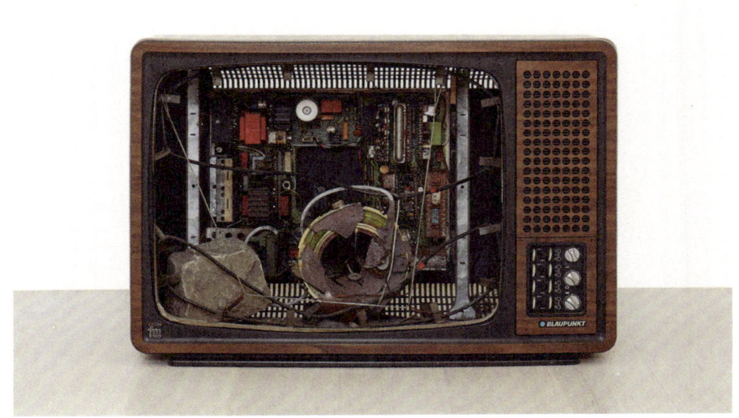

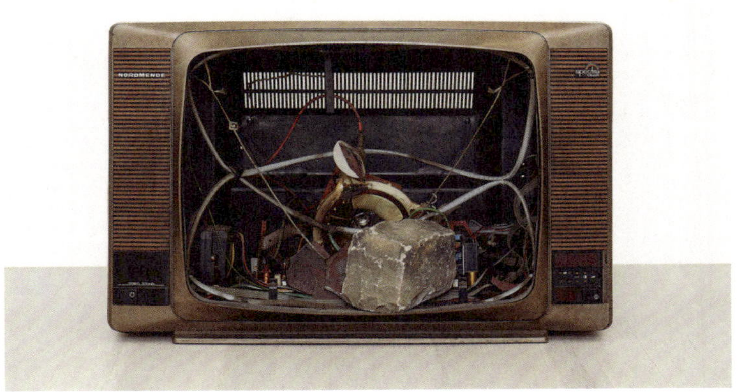

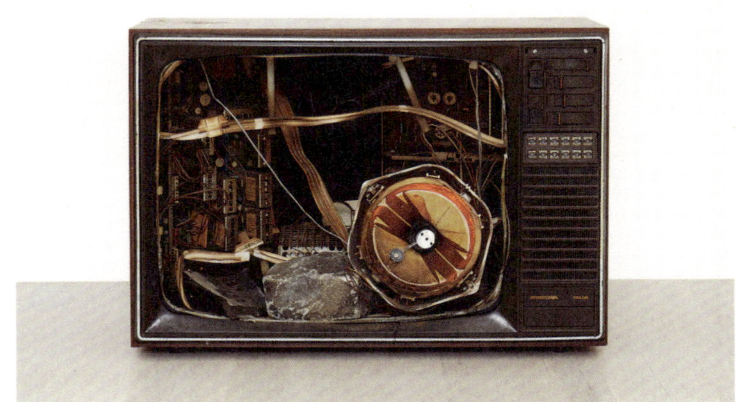

Resurrection, 1995. TV (plastic, glass, wire), flagstone. Approx. 17 ¾ × 26 × 17 ¾ in. (45 × 66 × 45 cm) each of 3.

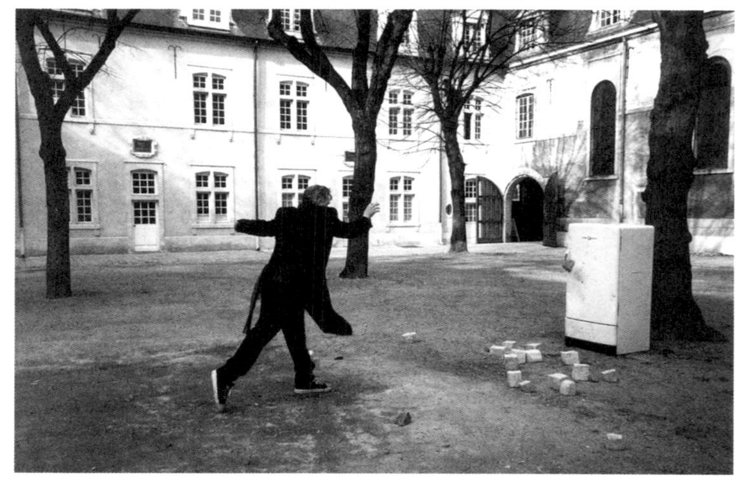

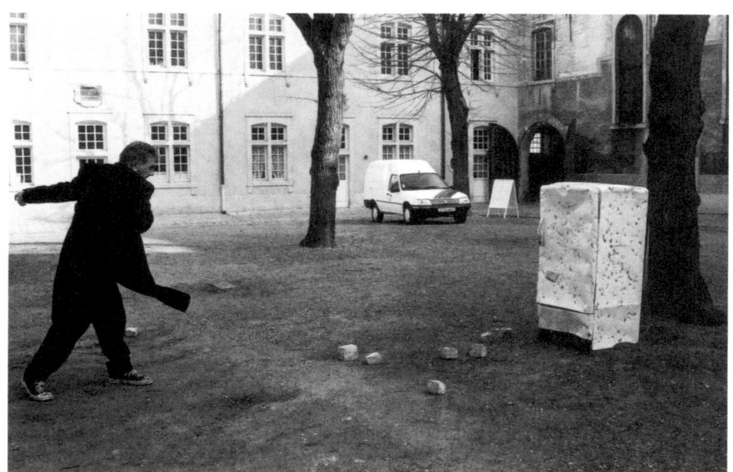

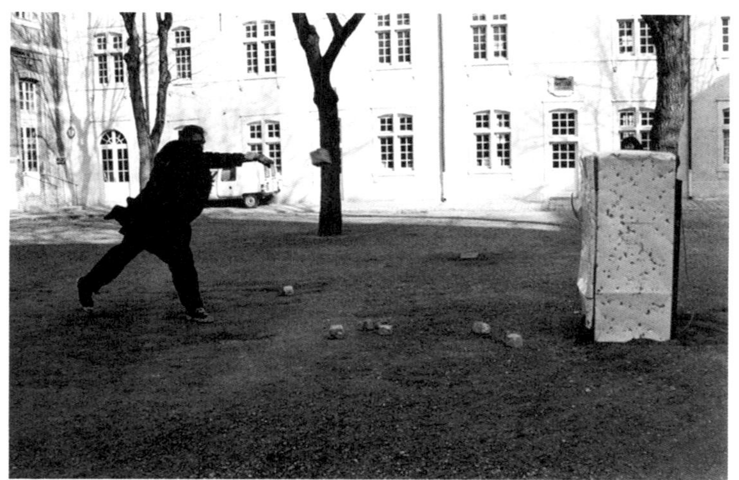

Stoning the Refrigerator, 1996. Video, black and white, sound. 3:27 min.

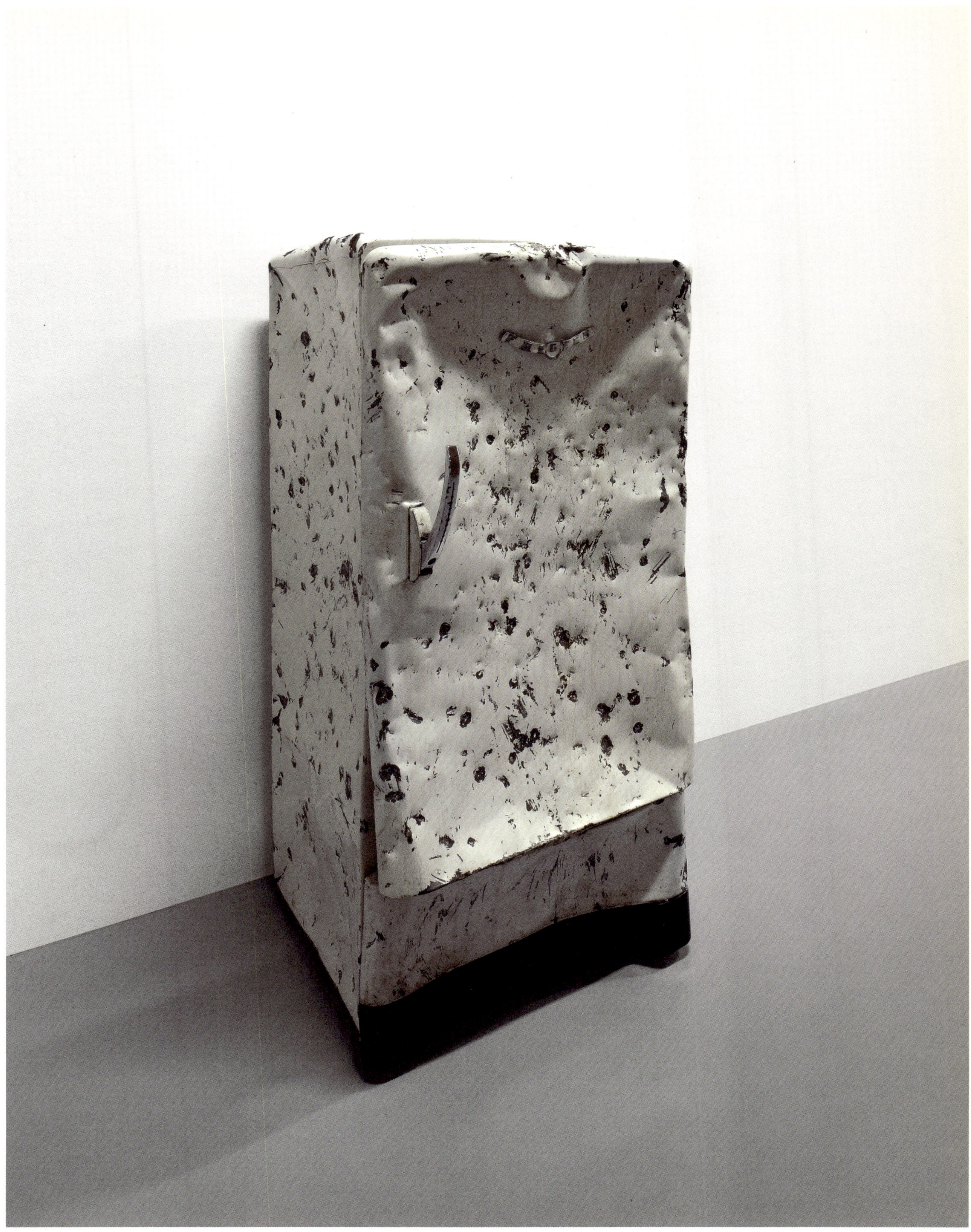

St. Frigo, 1996. Metal refrigerator. 52 × 23 ½ × 23 ½ in. (132 × 60 × 60 cm).

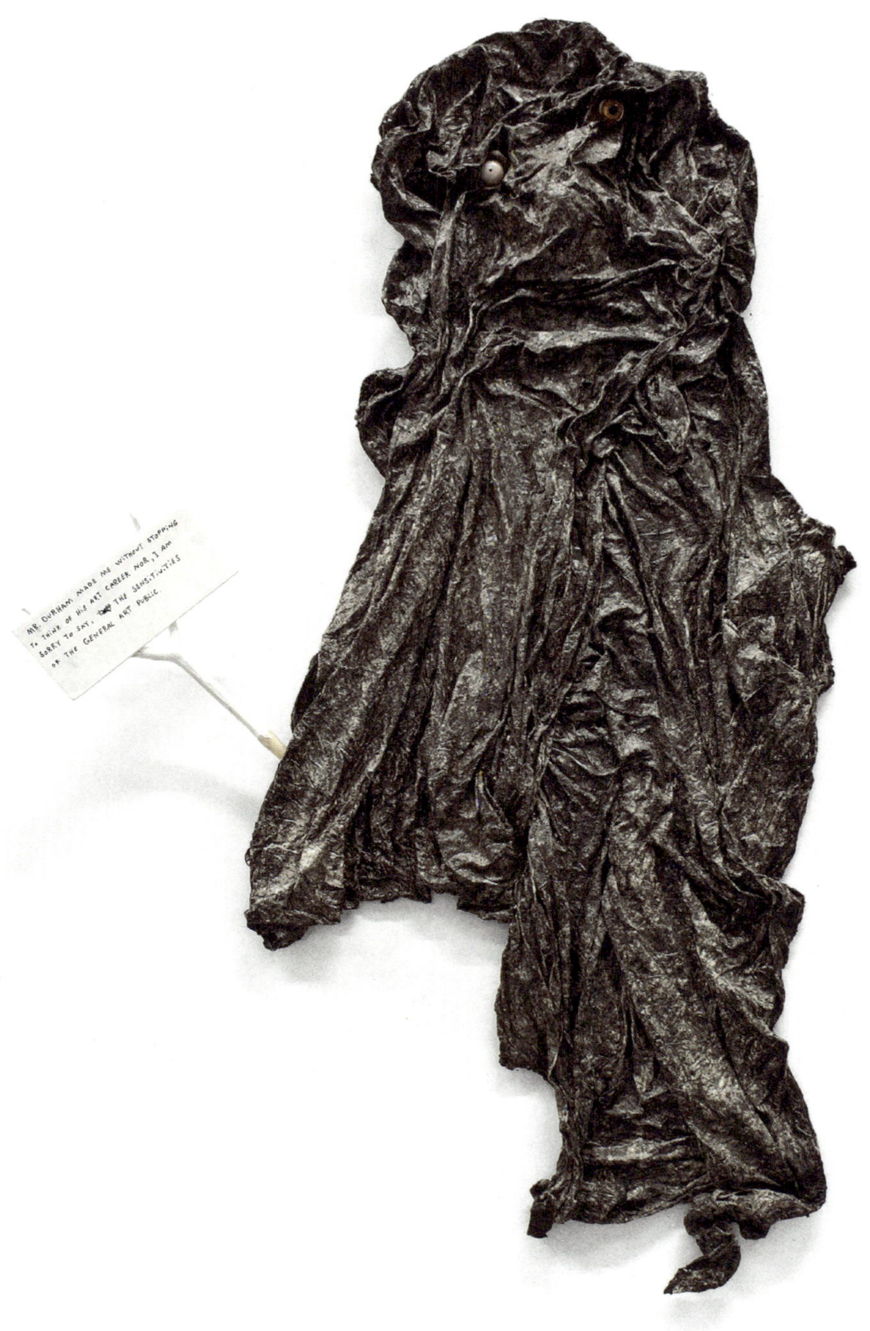

Confessional, 2006. Hair and dirt on canvas, acrylic paint, agate, animal taxidermy glass eye, ink on wood. 73 × 35 ½ × 6 in. (185 × 90 × 15 cm). [Text: Mr. Durham made me without stopping to think of his art career nor, I am sorry to say, ~~this~~ the sensitivities of the general art public.]

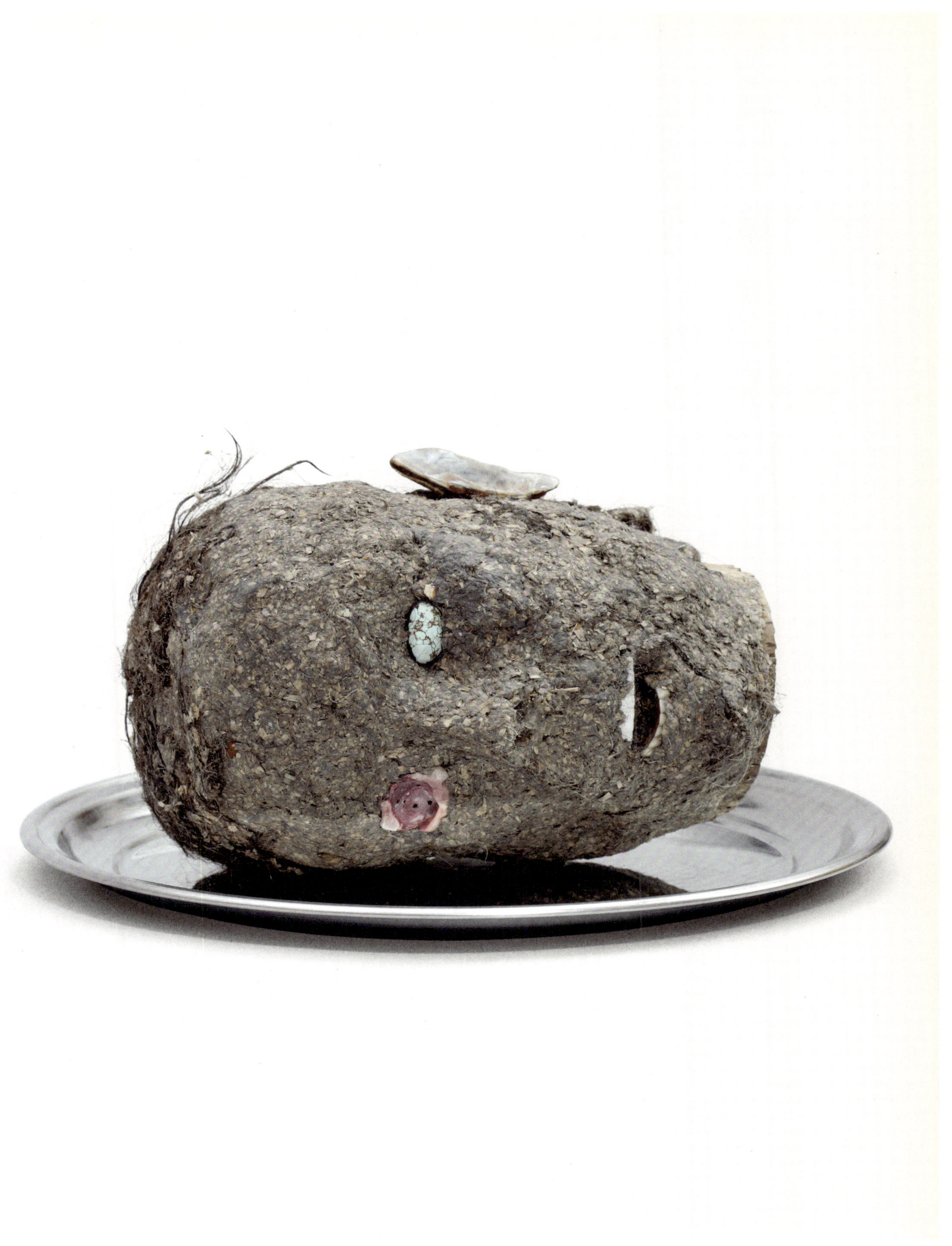

Head, 2006. Wood, papier-mâché, hair, seashells, turquoise, armadillo shell, human dentures, metal tray. 10 × 16 × 16 in. (25 × 40 × 40 cm).

"I'M STILL SITTING AT THE TABLE": THE CUERNAVACA YEARS

JESSICA BERLANGA TAYLOR

I.

Cuernavaca has always been known for its beautiful weather year-round. The explorer and naturalist Alexander von Humboldt, upon arriving there in 1803, called it "the city of eternal spring."[1] Its original name in Nahuatl, Cuauhnahuac, signifies "next to trees" or "surrounded by trees," and also "the valley of eagles." Mispronunciation by the Spanish conquerors resulted in its current name of Cuernavaca. As the capital of the state of Morelos, it has always been cosmopolitan due to its proximity to Mexico City, and has a long history of attracting foreign visitors and inhabitants. A weekend and holiday destination since Aztec times, during the nineteenth century it hosted such personalities as Maximilian I, archduke of Austria and emperor of Mexico from 1864 to 1867, and his wife, Carlota, who came to relax among the bougainvillea, palms, massive ficus, jacarandas, tall pointed araucarias, flamboyant or "flame" trees with their intense orange flowers, and amate trees (fig. 1).[2] Emiliano Zapata had his army and headquarters here during the Mexican Revolution of 1910. In the 1930s the Hotel Casino de la Selva, with its famous hyperbolas, or "umbrella roofs," designed by architect Félix Candela, was built amidst the natural springs and exotic plants. Josep Renau, José Reyes Meza, and David Alfaro Siqueiros were among the artists invited to paint murals in the Casino.[3] English author Malcolm Lowry was inspired by his brief stay in Cuernavaca in 1936 to situate his novel *Under the Volcano* in the city of Cuauhnahuac, guarded by the surrounding Popocatépetl and Iztaccíhuatl volcanoes.

In the 1950s Europeans and North Americans continued to arrive, and together with Mexican artists, activists, and intellectuals promoted critical thinking and alternative religious, social, political, and cultural models. German architect and sculptor Mathias Goeritz immigrated to Mexico after World War II and designed the altar for the Cuernavaca Cathedral. He had already created a series of stained-glass windows for the Metropolitan Cathedral in Mexico City, and this had led to serious debates between the two cultural factions that historian Ariel Rodríguez Kuri has termed "the neobaroque or restorers" and "the modernists or renovators."[4] In the second group was Sergio Méndez Arceo, named bishop of Cuernavaca in 1952, a notorious figure known as the "Red Bishop" for his support of socialism. He practiced liberation theology, insisting that the Catholic Church needed to fight all forms of injustice and its institutionalization; he was also the force behind the Basic Ecclesiastical Communities formed in the 1970s by people who wished to go deeper into their conscience, promote the study of the Bible, and take political action in defense of human rights.[5]

A few years earlier, Belgian monk Gregorio Lemercier (who became known around the world for his prayer "Lord, forgive my sins as I forgive yours") had founded the Benedictine monastery of Santa María de la Resurrección in Santa María Ahuacatitlán, a few miles from Cuernavaca.[6] Lemercier was a champion of psychoanalysis, and by 1959 the monks were undergoing group analysis with nonreligious therapists—first following the humanist approach of Erich Fromm, who was living in Cuernavaca and had founded the Mexican Society of Psychoanalysis, and then that of Sigmund Freud.[7] In 1966 Lemercier opened the Emaús Psychoanalysis Center at the monastery, which he supported by giving workshops in

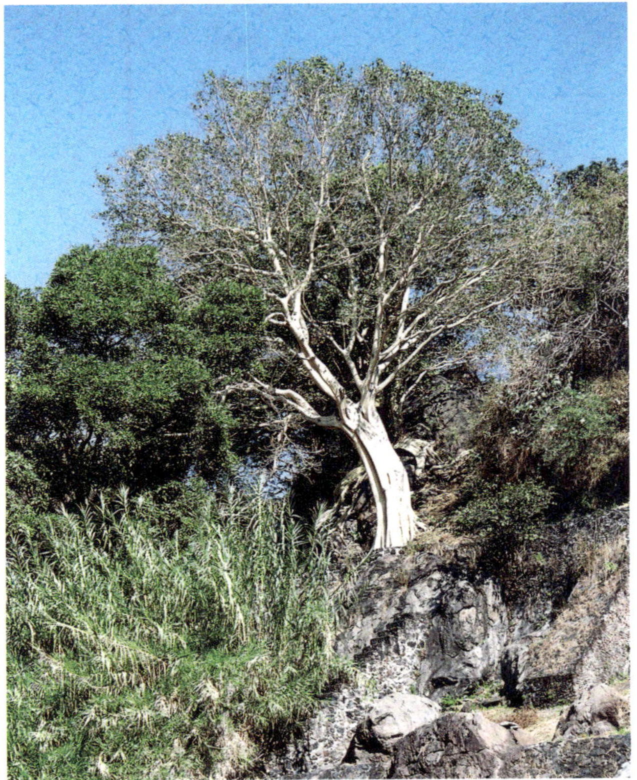

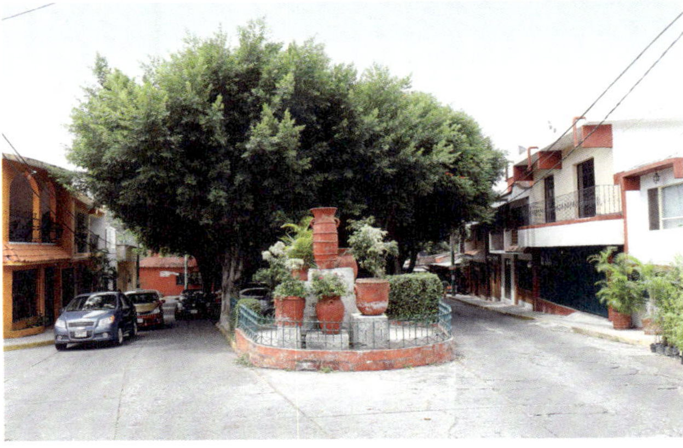

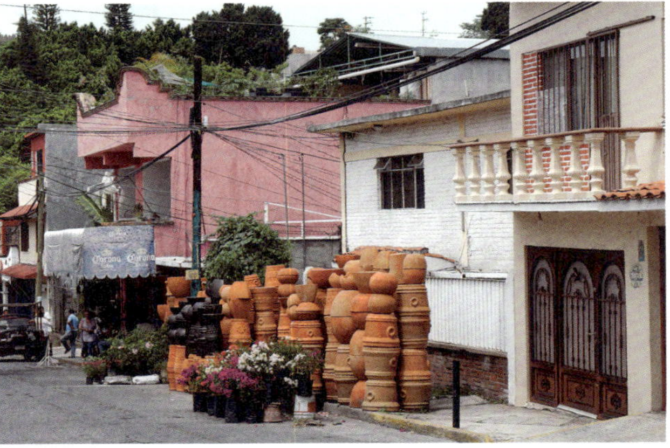

Fig. 1 (top). Antonio Berlanga, amate, Chapultepec Park, Cuernavaca, 1995.
Fig. 2 (middle). Antonio Berlanga, fountain at entrance to Durham's street, El Salto de San Antón, Cuernavaca, 2016.
Fig. 3 (bottom). Antonio Berlanga, local pottery and plants, El Salto de San Antón, Cuernavaca, 2016.

silver, serigraphy, carpentry, ironwork, and marquetry. When Austrian philosopher and Catholic priest Ivan Illich arrived in Cuernavaca in 1961, Méndez Arceo offered him his diocese for the Intercultural Documentation Center (CIDOC),[8] a research center that documented the Vatican's participation in "third world" countries. Illich strongly opposed Western ideas of "progress and development," and his center attracted many like-minded intellectuals and politicians, including Fromm, sociologist Peter Berger, educator and theorist Paulo Freire, and anarchist philosopher Paul Goodman, to name a few. By the 1970s the center was known worldwide as a hotbed of avant-garde concepts and radical politics, some of which are now considered to be in the public domain: "counterproductivity, radical monopoly, colonization of the informal sector, conviviality, differentiation between prescriptive law and proscriptive law, coalitions among 'similarly affected citizens,' vernacular values, to name a few."[9] This was the rich political and cultural climate of the city where Jimmie Durham and his partner, artist and photographer Maria Thereza Alves, lived from 1987 to 1994.

II.

I met Jimmie Durham in 1987, when I was eight years old. My father, Antonio Berlanga, a photographer, would take me with him to visit Jimmie and Maria Thereza[10] at their house in the Salto de San Antón neighborhood of Cuernavaca (fig. 2).[11] We would drive up to their home in our 1974 VW Kombi, weaving around pottery sellers (fig. 3), potted plants, and children playing football. It was noisy and the sky was always blue. Clay statues of Saint Francis painted a light brick color and about my height lined the pavement, the saint's open palms holding a birdbath. My favorite ones had one or two tiny clay birds perched on the edge of the bath, always about to fall in. And Saint Francis's robe was tied around his waist with a piece of knotted rope. Once, just before entering Jimmie and Maria Thereza's house, my mother explained that the last thunderstorm of the rainy season in Mexico was called *el cordonazo de San Francisco*, signaling the start of the dry season.[12] I also saw hummingbirds for the first time flying in and out of the bougainvillea bushes and the magnolia trees.

What I recall most of those visits is space—empty space and light filtering through large floor-to-ceiling windows overlooking the *barrancas*, or ravines. And a mysterious, quiet presence, a man with the brightest blue eyes I had ever seen, sitting on a wooden stool at his desk, usually carving tiny wooden figures. I don't think we ever spoke, but we exchanged looks while Maria Thereza and my father talked about photography. Sometimes he would turn around as I crept up and would open his hands and show me from a distance some very strange-looking figures. I found them fascinating but frightening. This usually lasted only a few seconds, and I would run to my dad or onto one of the terraces to look at the waterfall pouring onto basalt prisms and the tangled mass of cacti, grass, and plants covering the ground underneath (fig. 4).

I didn't know, of course, that he was sculpting. Writing in Cuernavaca about the preoccupations of his work, he observed, "There is a sense in which I am naturally a sculptor—I made objects before I learned to talk—so that I am always playing with, talking with objects and their relationships to me and to the rest of the world. But when I say 'me' I mean [a] confused, complicated, political being."[13]

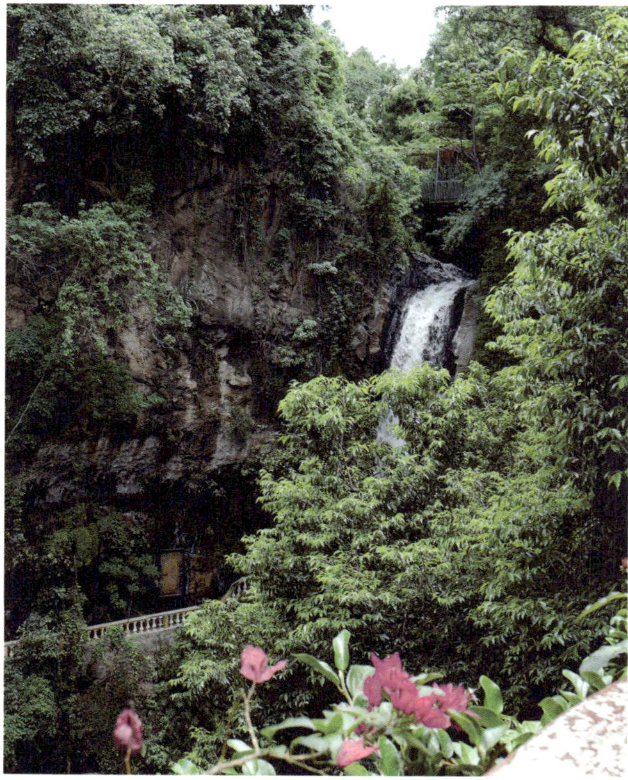

Once I rushed into the house, past the flamboyant trees outside the main entrance, hardly noticing the fiery orange of their flowers wilting in the heat, crushed to a thick pulp on the cement pavement, and came upon a very large doll in the middle of a big empty room. I liked it because it was a woman wearing a skirt, with black beady eyes, a lopsided red mouth, and a body made out of pieces of wood (fig. 5; page 143). She looked like the tiny figures the quiet man with the brightest blue eyes I had ever seen sometimes carved. Except she was huge and not so frightening. It was just the two of us. La Malinche and me.[14]

III.

At 7:15 a.m. on September 19, 1985, Mexico City experienced one of the worst moments in its history. An earthquake with a magnitude of 8.0 on the Richter scale and two major aftershocks killed at least five thousand people. More than four hundred buildings collapsed and around three thousand others were seriously damaged.

I was sitting on the edge of my bed in Cuernavaca, thirty-five miles away from Mexico City—a bunk bed I shared with my younger brother, who was still fast asleep. I was six years old and getting ready for school. My parents rushed in, swooped us both up, and took us out into the garden. I was amazed at what was happening. Everything was alive. Waves of water spilled out of the swimming pool, and as the earth shook even the sky looked as though it were about to fall.

Fig. 4. Antonio Berlanga, waterfall and basalt as seen from Durham's terrace, El Salto de San Antón, Cuernavaca, 2016.

Fig. 5 (below). Durham's sculpture *Malinche* (1988–92; see page 143) with Carlos Ortega (standing) holding the face of *Cortez* (1991–92; see page 142) and Julián Villaseñor, 1993.

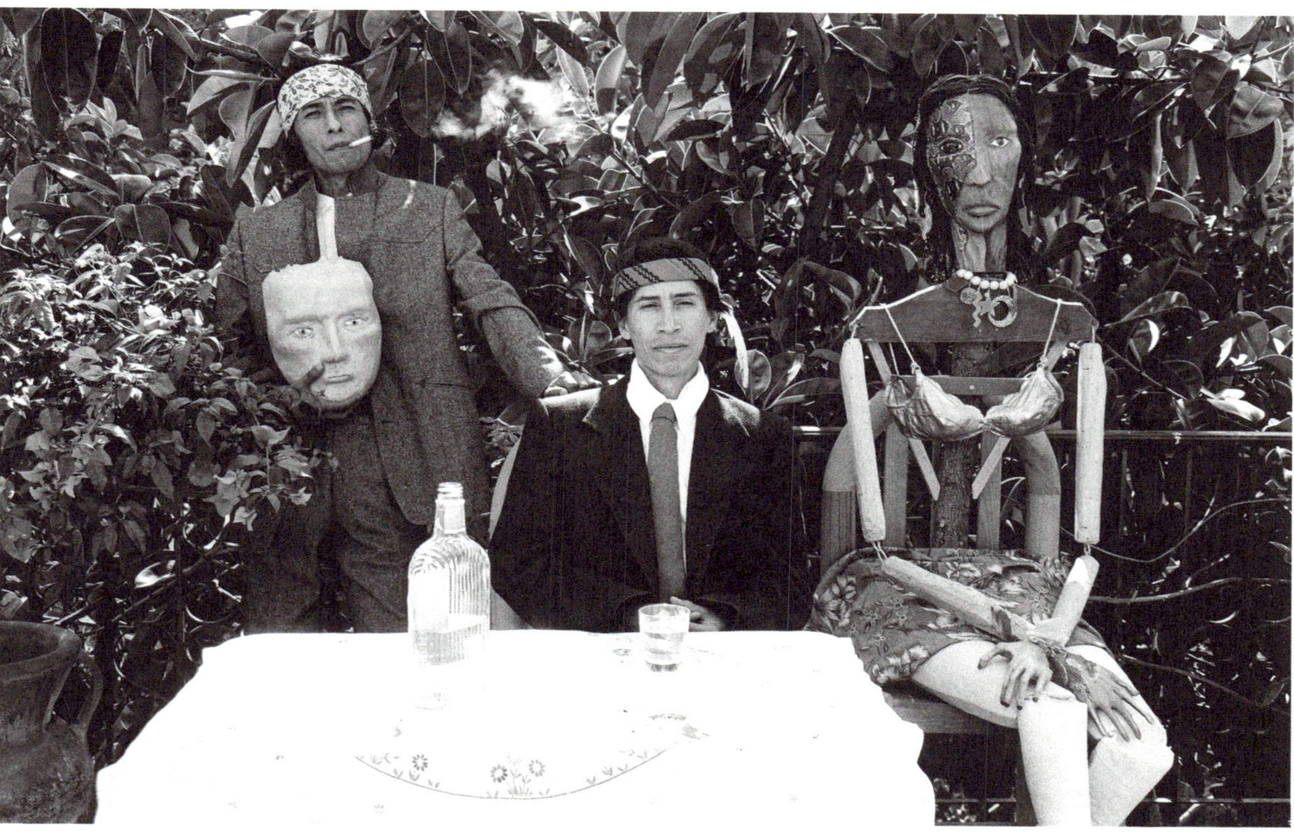

For a child, safely in her father's arms, it was a fascinating event. But for most people, the traumatic experience has never quite ended.

As a consequence of the destruction, thousands of people moved to the valley of Cuernavaca, where the population almost doubled. According to artist Cisco Jiménez, a native of Cuernavaca, before the earthquake the city had "an important and dynamic rural population. You saw people wearing the traditional huaraches, or open sandals, and straw hats. After 1985, there began a process whereby a large middle class was formed with bourgeoisie customs."[15]

By the mid-1980s an important industrial presence had been established in and around the city, and it remained a destination for international celebrities ranging from Italian aristocrats and Polish-born painter Tamara de Lempicka to American jazz musician Charles Mingus and Argentinean writer Manuel Puig. It was also a time of intense political activity. As Jiménez notes, "There was a change in society, it became more polarized after the creation of the Cardenista Front Party, and later the Party for Democratic Revolution (PRD). Morelos became a bastion for the Revolutionary Institutional Party (PRI), and that generated a lot of violence."[16] A few years earlier, in 1976, Illich had closed the CIDOC after difficulties with the Vatican due to the center's continuous critiques of the Church. The Emaús Psychoanalysis Center also shut down between 1979 and 1980; Lemercier had already resigned his priesthood and was married, and Méndez Arceo retired in 1983 as a very controversial figure in the history of the Church in Mexico.

IV.

The move to Cuernavaca was, Durham recalls, "a beautiful experience, but also a horrible one. Much of my life has been like that."[17] Virtually penniless at the time and suffering from ill health after living in New York City, he wanted to get out of the United States. Cuernavaca offered good food and gardening, which helped him recover his health.[18] In his book on Cuernavaca, Francisco Javier Arenas challenged Humboldt: "Cuernavaca is not eternal springtime, traveler. This is untrue. It is a sanatorium with no doctors, where those whose bodies and souls are tired go to."[19] In a 1990 interview, Durham explained that his relocation was not about retiring in any sense: "I moved to Cuernavaca because I couldn't afford to live in New York. But I am not hiding in Cuernavaca. I write for publications in London and New York and I am very active in Mexico. I would feel the same way if I lived in New York. I would want to deal with Mexico, I would want to have a discourse with whatever is out there, everything that is out there."[20]

Cuernavaca had little communal activity in the late 1980s, but a few artists, journalists, writers, and political activists got together from time to time. Durham began to attend these gatherings, some hosted by Cedric Belfrage, a British journalist, film critic, and political activist who had translated Uruguayan journalist and poet Eduardo Galeano's *Open Veins of Latin America: Five Centuries of the Pillage of a Continent*. Belfrage, who in 1948 cofounded a radical US weekly newspaper called the *National Guardian*, had left the United States after refusing to declare his involvement in the American Communist Party to the House Un-American Activities Committee presided over by Senator Joseph McCarthy. Belfrage would later be accused by some of being a Soviet agent as well as working for the British Security Coordination as a double agent. It was at these meetings, which Galeano sometimes attended, that Durham met British sculptor John Spencer and, on one occasion, Elizabeth Catlett, an African American graphic artist and sculptor who focused on conveying social and political messages rather than aesthetic forms; through her, Durham and Alves met a number of African Americans in Cuernavaca. I remember seeing Catlett's work in my father's studio, ready to be photographed, in particular the face of a young African woman looking to the left. Barely smiling, her carved form seemed to be emerging out of the panel.

Jimmie did a performance in 1993 with Jiménez, painter Carlos Ortega, and ceramist Julián Villaseñor, among others. Called *The East London Coelacanth*, it was directed and filmed by Maria Thereza at their home and in the archaeological area of Xochicalco (site of the House of Flowers), in Morelos, and was about a pseudoarchaeologist (played by Jimmie) searching for the fossil of the eponymous fish (fig. 6). The performance is a mix of historical facts and fiction—a series of conceptual and contextual mishaps and a play on failure that present the artist as a provocateur, an agile figure who can be amusing, charming, and obstinate. He even appears naïve, though is anything but, for he questions issues of identity and authenticity, and raises anthropological discussions around the savage, the exotic other, imperialism, and globalization.

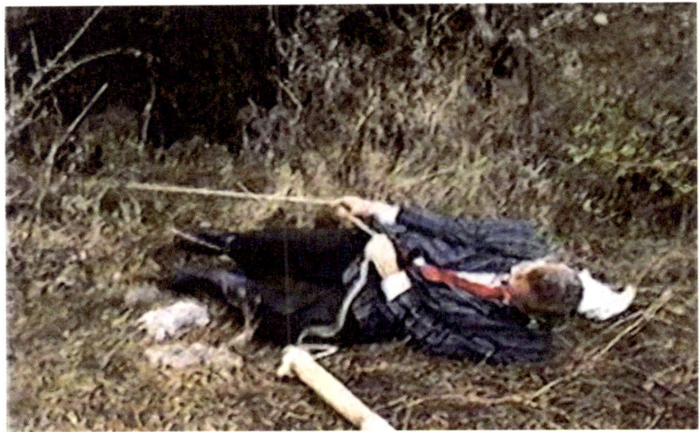

Fig. 6. Still from *The East London Coelacanth*, 1993 (see page 146 top).

V.

Except for an exhibition in Monterrey in 1991, curated by Olivier Debroise, which also included works by Gabriel Orozco and Diego Gutiérrez, there was not much interest in showing Durham's work or in having him teach or lecture in Mexico. Neither he nor Alves had galleries in the country. Jimmie recalls, "José Luis Cuevas was the big artist at the time and the galleries didn't take themselves very seriously; artists didn't either. Those who did were quiet and isolated. Their work wasn't a conversation. We met Graciela Iturbide in Mexico City, a wonderful photographer, but we hardly left Cuernavaca unless it was to fly out of the country. Most of our friends were local people, some of whom we met at an arts space." That arts space, called La Estación,[21] was located in a popular, very old downtown neighborhood called Amatitlan, from the Nahuatl, meaning "a place abundant in amate trees." Jiménez, who was eighteen years old at the time, showed there: "That's where

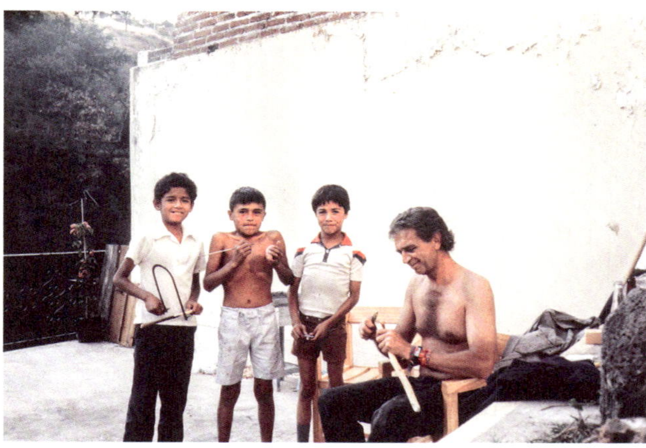

Fig. 7. Durham and local boys making dolls that would eventually be used in *She Rose from Her Warm Bed*, Cuernavaca, 1987.

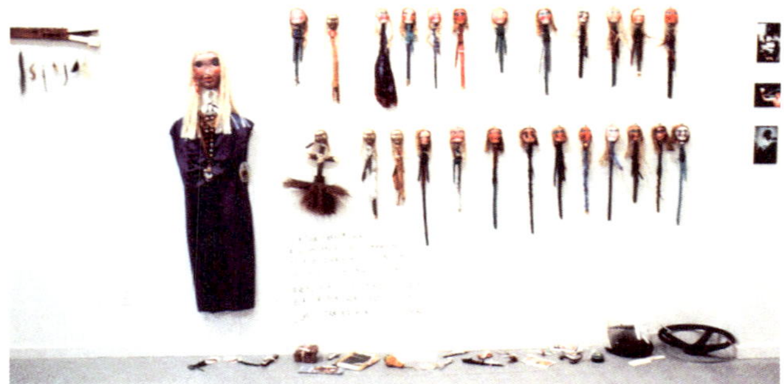

Fig. 8. *She Rose from Her Warm Bed*, 1987, installation view, *We the People*, Artists Space, New York, 1987.

I first met Jimmie and Maria Thereza. What Jimmie did was totally perplexing to me. That's what I remember thinking back then. Objects that weren't art, they were something else and usually not taken seriously by more than three or four people. And to make matters worse, Jimmie would announce the coming of postmodernism and the death of painting—things that were considered sacrilegious here."[22] No one was aware that Durham was showing at the 1992 Documenta in Kassel and the 1993 Whitney Biennial, that he was exhibiting in London, Los Angeles, and San Francisco, nor that the small carved dolls he created with the children from the *barrancas* had been shown in New York in 1987 as part of his work *She Rose from Her Warm Bed*, exhibited at Artists Space (figs. 7, 8). "What can I get for you from New York?" he would ask the children. "A teddy bear," they all replied. They all wanted teddy bears—teddy bears and tennis shoes.

VI.

The *barrancas* across from Jimmie and Maria Thereza's house were full of children. From one of the two terraces of their house, I sometimes saw them bathing in the beautiful waterfall that Arenas described as displaying "all the colors of the world, a rainbow that is like the color of the gods who bathe their worries in these waters. Yet there, all the *teotecuhtlis* (leaders), their spirits, wander one by one, visiting every corner."[23]

Durham and Alves developed relationships with the children. "They were so good-spirited and so much in need, these children," Jimmie remembers. "We started a school with the boys, the girls weren't allowed. It eventually all fell apart after the exhibition in New York, where we sold some of their carved dolls and split the money. The boys started getting weird, one by one. The mums also started making trouble, and we soon learned that local people were beating the children up for going to the school. A man called Julián Villaseñor had started a pottery school with local boys past the Hacienda de Cortés. Something happened to him." There is a difficult pause, then: "I hate all animals, they break your heart. Children are even worse." If ravines are geological accidents produced by the forces of a river, I guess these kids created beautiful cracks in Jimmie's spirit.

VII.

"What is that wood that's hard and fleshy, with a sensuous look to it?" Jimmie asks. "There were trees all over the *barrancas*. The fruit was delicious, all the children would eat it." "Guavas!" I exclaim. The trees are so common that people born in Morelos are called *guayabitos*, little guavas. "I used a lot of that wood in the work I created in those years," he continues. "I always wanted more of it. Everything was scraps, bits and pieces from local trash, cars, wood strap for houses, anything I could find, plastic, polyester resins." He would go to a store that sold only plastic, where the owner once told him, "My parents are Indian. Not me." Visiting nearby Tepoztlán, Durham realized that many of the items sold as handcrafts, such as the infinite variety of painted masks made from coconut shells, were produced exclusively for the tourists. In downtown Cuernavaca's *zócalo*, or main square, Durham was interested in the vendor displays on the streets of the hot, dusty city. One man sold objects made of wool and straw, and even offered to sell Durham his thirteen-year-old granddaughter. "How degraded everything is, and how beautifully we can move around it," Jimmie says, with his eyes almost shut.

VIII.

It is April in Mexico, 2016. The hottest time of year. Jacarandas are blooming in Cuernavaca, their tiny purple flowers covering the ground everywhere. The last rays of sun filter a violet light, and if the hazy white skies of spring allow, one can see the Popocatépetl and Iztaccíhuatl volcanoes. I mention this to Jimmie and he smiles, he *really* smiles. "Ahhh, rosewood, that dark, expensive wood." We agree I'll send him photos of the jacarandas.

IX.

"You know, I'm still sitting at the table I had in Cuernavaca, made from mesquite," Jimmie says. Now I smile. A table that has traveled all over the world: Cuernavaca, Ireland, Berlin, Naples. The table where he writes poetry. The table from which he *is speaking* poetry. This whole conversation is a poet's creation. To synthesize a vision, not of the world, of a cosmos in flux, through a jacaranda tree or through the flamboyants at his door; to describe fish-shaped, hairy objects (mango seeds) he found lying on the streets in Cuernavaca as mysterious and beautiful. Most of his time in Mexico was spent making art. "When I can't write poetry, I do sculpture. And when I can't do sculpture, I write poetry. My whole being goes into sculpture or poetry. Very few people say I'm a poet. A lot say I'm an artist." We both laugh when he recalls someone asking him, "Are these real poems or did you write them yourself?"

X.

In 1994 Mexico was in turmoil. The Zapatista Army of National Liberation (EZLN)[24] in Chiapas was growing and getting international attention. "All of a sudden, *Norteños* were all Zapatistas," Jimmie explains.[25] And the country woke up to the crash of the Mexican peso in January of 1995, with Carlos Salinas de Gortari as president. A special production about Indians of the Americas produced by the Discovery Channel was shown on television in Mexico in 1994, with Jimmie in it. A short while later, armed men in helicopters began circling their house, over the *barrancas*. Jimmie and Maria Thereza left Cuernavaca and headed for Europe.

XI.

"One more story," Jimmie says, as we begin our good-byes. "Hummingbirds, *colibrís*, travel so much. They spend their winters in Argentina, some go to Colorado. We had one on our terrace for three years. He never left. He had a lot of good flowers."

Notes

1. Humboldt spent only a few hours in Cuernavaca but wrote a number of books related to Mexico: *Personal Narrative of Travels to the Equinoctial Regions of the New Continent, during the years 1799–1804*; *Political Essay on the Kingdom of New Spain*; and *Views of the Cordilleras and Monuments of the Indigenous Peoples of the Americas*.

2. The amate tree (*amatl* in Nahuatl, meaning "paper") is important to the area of Morelos and central Mesoamerica, and considered by the indigenous people in Mexico to be one of the things that are "necessary to live." With a creamy white bark and roots that grow over the earth before going deep into the soil, the amate has been used for making a special type of paper since pre-Hispanic times. The interior of the bark is crushed to a pulp and sometimes boiled in water, and then thin rectangular layers are formed and laid out to dry in the sun. Pre-Hispanic cultures used it to create their books or codices, many of them burned by the Spanish. The Nahuatl language is an agglutinative one, meaning that words and phrases are formed by combining prefixes, suffixes, and root words that each express an idea. *Atl* means water, so other meanings can be added to the *idea* of the amate. For example, *maitl* means hands. So paper plus water plus hands creates a powerful idea and image of the use and meaning of the amate tree.

3. In 2001 the property where the Hotel Casino de la Selva stood was bought by Costco Wholesale Corporation. According to Huberto Suárez, this transaction "not only destroyed the architectural work of the Spaniard Félix Candela and of Jesús Martí, as well as some of the murals painted by Mexican masters, but also led to the cutting down of more than 800 trees—most of them centuries old and home to three migrant bird species that procreated there before continuing their journey south. Two megastores were built on top of the watertable that fed Cuernavaca, which suffers serious water supply problems, as does the rest of the state of Morelos. On the other hand, more than 180 ancient sites, believed to be related to the Olmec culture, were buried before being studied and classified." Huberto Suárez, "La destrucción del Casino de la Selva, 'Un crimen de lesa humanidad,'" *Réplica* 21, June 16, 2004, http://www.replica21.com/archivo/articulos/s_t/344_suarez_casino.html. Unless otherwise noted, all translations are my own.

4. Ariel Rodríguez Kuri, "La proscripción del aura: Arquitectura y política en la restauración de la Catedral de México, 1967–1971," *Historia Mexicana* 56, no. 4 (2007): 1313–14. On January 17, 1967, the choir and the Altar of Forgiveness at the Cathedral of Mexico City suffered serious damage caused by an accidental fire. According to Kuri, the incident provoked "one of the most important intellectual and artistic polemics of the 1960s" (p. 1313). Two groups were formed around the actions taken to restore the damages, which he designated, respectively, "the neobaroque or restorers, who were keen to restore the choir and the altar to their original state; and the modernists or renovators, who thought it was time to redefine the space of the main nave, in not only liturgical terms but also aesthetic" (p. 1313).

5. George W. Grayson, *Prospects for Democracy in Mexico* (New Brunswick, NJ: Transaction Publishers, 1990), 114–20.

6. Thomas Merton, poet, activist, and superior of the Order of the Trappist Monks of the United States, holds Lemercier up as an example to all of Latin America. Cited in *Proceso*, one of Mexico's most important weekly publications on political and social analysis; http://www.proceso.com.mx/147639/el-camino-de-gregorio-lemercier.

7. See Lya Gutiérrez Quintanilla, "Gregorio Lemercier y su monasterio del psicoanálisis en Cuernavaca," *Diario de Morelos*, March 20, 2013, http://www.diariodemorelos.com/article/gregorio-lemercier-y-su-monasterio-del-psicoan%C3%A1lisis-en-cuernavaca. "Lemercier thought that for some, with 'neurotic traits,' monastic life had become a refuge from the failures of an ordinary life. Through psychoanalysis, they would understand the authenticity of their calling and they would also see the way toward healing and accepting these neurotic traits, before becoming monks." Ana María Ashwell Mallorquín, quoted in ibid.

8. In Spanish, Centro Intercultural de Documentación.

9. Javier Sicilia and Jean Robert, "Iván Illich," *Letras Libres*, March 2001, http://www.letraslibres.com/revista/entrevista/ivan-illich. In 1971 Illich had already published one of his most controversial works, *Deschooling Society*, a radical criticism of institutionalized education. Javier Sicilia is a distinguished Catholic poet, journalist, and activist who founded the Movement for Peace, with Justice and Dignity, shortly after his son was murdered in Morelos in 2011.

10. Maria Thereza worked with my father in his studio (where we also had our home) and would develop and print her work in the lab. Throughout the years, one of the photographs that always sat on one of the long wooden tables in the studio was of Maria Thereza standing outside a funeral parlor called Karonte at midnight. It had just rained and there were puddles of water, the light from the street lamps playing on the surfaces. My father did a double exposure, so she looks like a ghost. He then superimposed a photograph Maria Thereza had taken of herself nude as the Virgin Mary, with a blue cape draped over her head, which was part of a triptych in her installation *No soy su madre* (I am not your mother). The composite photograph was toned in selenium except for the image of Maria Thereza as the Virgin Mary.

11. Usually referred to simply as "El Salto." In the 1920s President Plutarco Elías Calles had asked for the removal of any religious references in the names of streets and neighborhoods in the country. The Nahuatl name for El Salto was Analco, meaning "on the other side of the water."

12. According to one legend, Saint Francis wished to play with the clouds, but, not wanting to get wet, he first struck them with his rope belt so they shed all their water.

13. Jimmie Durham, statement for *Land, Spirit, Power: First Nations at the National Gallery of Canada*, National Gallery of Canada, Ottawa, 1992, available online through the Centre for Canadian Contemporary Art Canadian Art Database: http://ccca.concordia.ca/c/writing/d/durham/dur001t.html.

14. La Malinche was an Indian woman from the Gulf region of Mexico, a polemical figure in the history of the country. She was the interpreter, counselor, lover, and intermediary for Hernán Cortés, with whom she had a son, Martín Cortés, the first mestizo (a person with European and indigenous roots). Many Mexicans consider her a traitor.

15. E-mail to the author, April 18, 2016.

16. Ibid.

17. All statements by Jimmie Durham are from a conversation with the author in April 2016, unless otherwise noted.

18. El Salto was full of fruit trees, since the whole area used to be an orchard, according to Carlos Domínguez Ayala, whose family moved there in the early 1930s.

19. Francisco Javier Arenas, *Un viaje por México: Estado de Morelos* (Mexico City: Talleres Gráficos Olimpo, 1968), 94. Arenas was a writer, attorney, and congressman from Morelos, who died when the Hotel Del Principado collapsed in the 1985 earthquake.

20. "Jimmie Durham Interviewed by Susan Canning," in *Interventions and Provocations: Conversations on Art, Culture, and Resistance*, ed. Glenn Harper (Albany: State University of New York Press, 1998), 45.

21. La Estación was an artists' collective founded by Anastasio Acevedo in Cuernavaca in the 1990s. Alves was involved in La Estación quite early on; others associated with it included artists Carlos Ortega and Cisco Jiménez, and curator and critic José Manuel Springer. Maria Thereza Alves, e-mail to Anne Ellegood, May 27, 2016.

22. E-mail to the author, April 18, 2016.

23. Arenas, *Un viaje por México*, 96.

24. Another liberation theologist, Samuel Ruiz García, bishop of San Cristóbal de las Casas, Chiapas, was the mediator between the EZLN and the PRI.

25. *Norteños* refers to men from the north of Mexico and also from the United States.

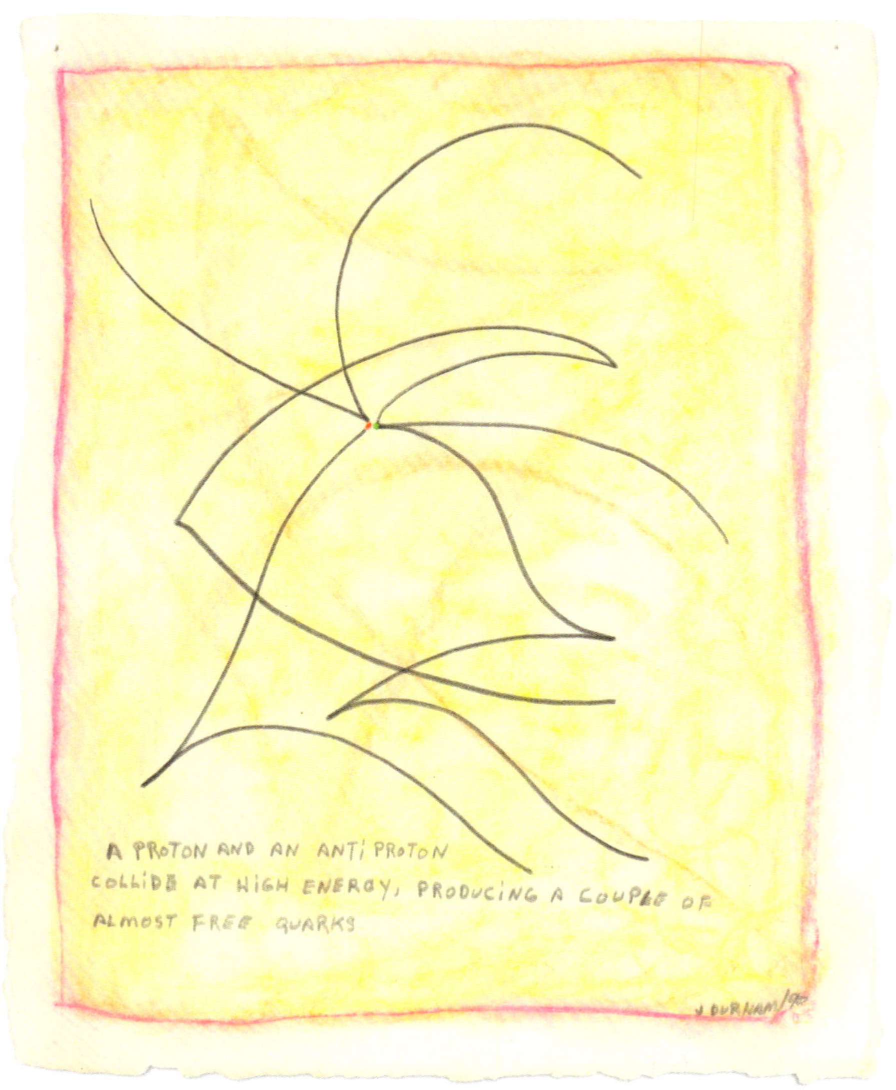

Science I, 1990. Dry pastels and pencil on paper. 20 × 16 in. (50.8 × 40.6 cm).

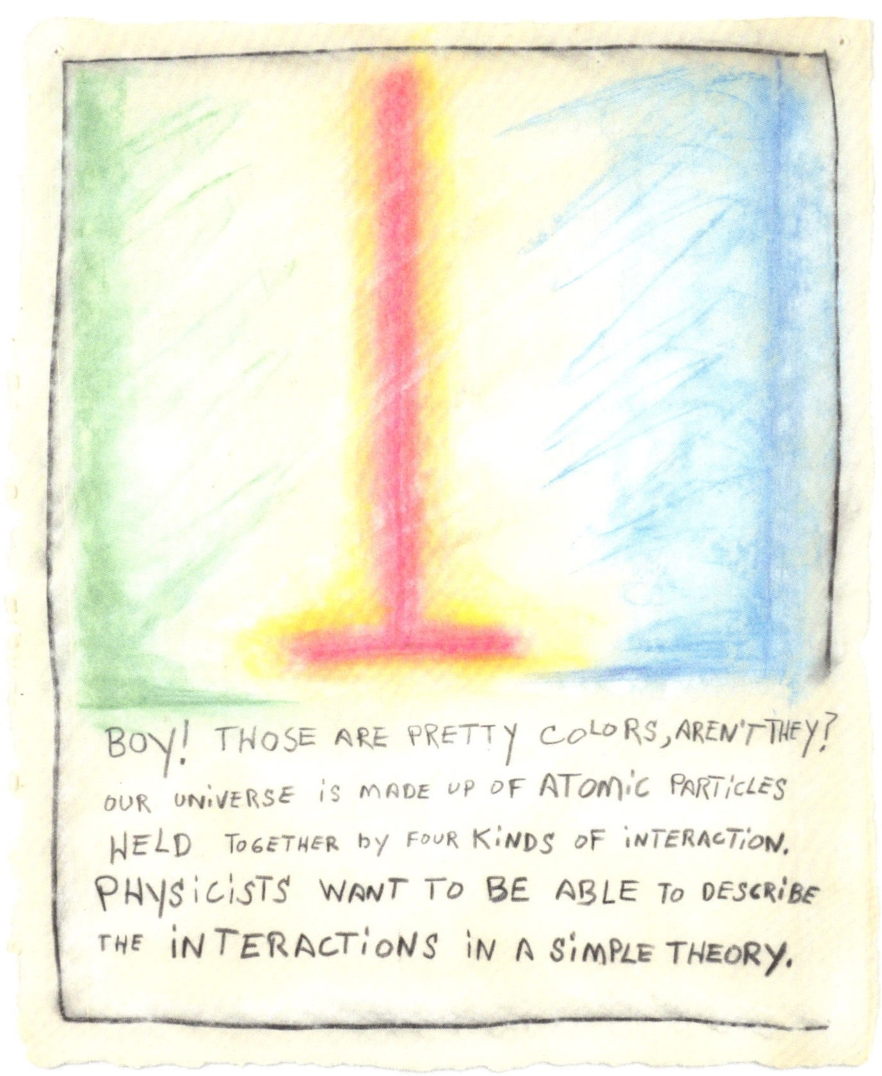

Science II, 1990. Dry pastels and pencil on paper. 20 × 16 in. (50.8 × 40.6 cm).

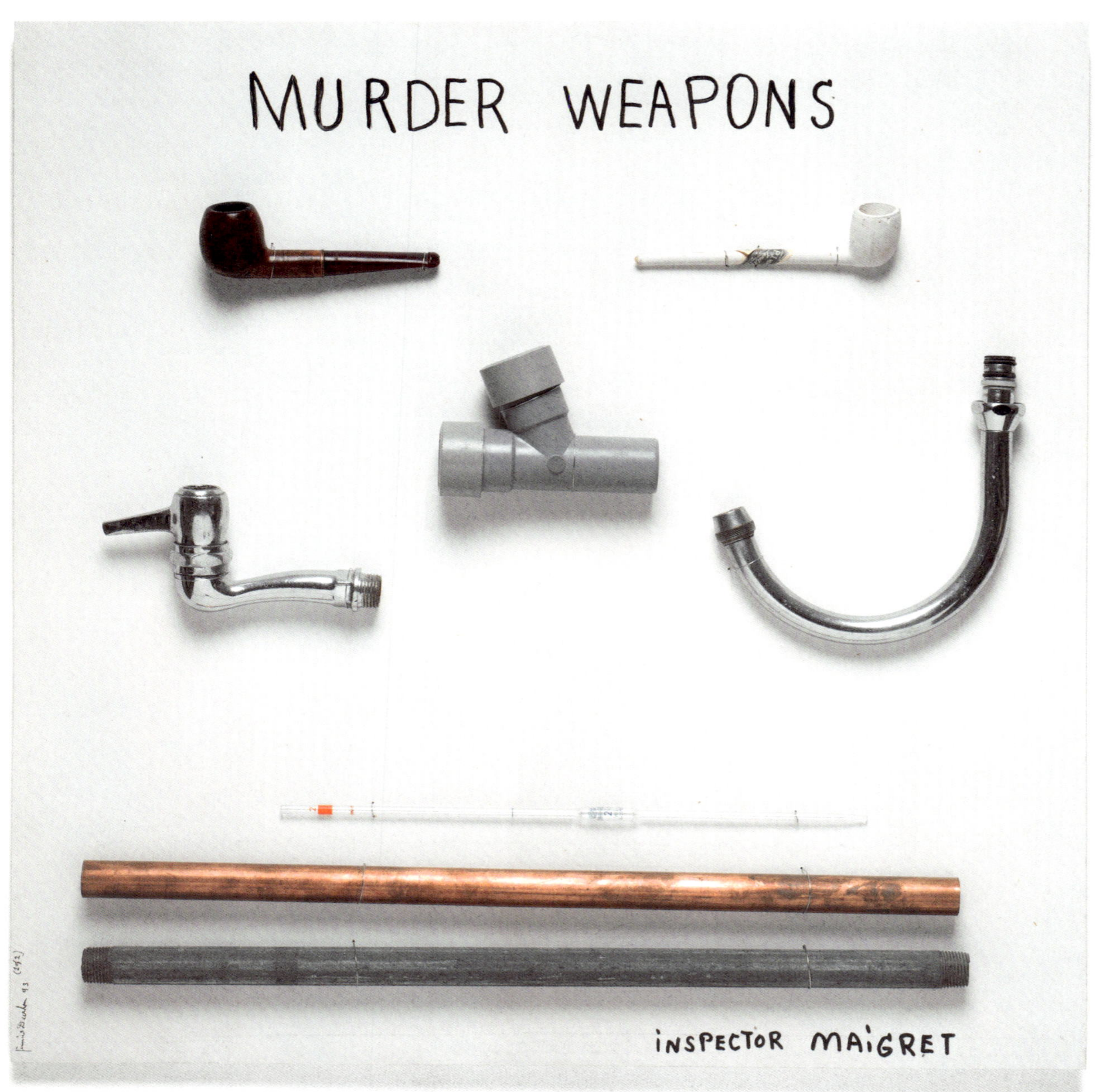

Types of Murder Weapons by Maigret, 1993. Metal, copper, plastic, wood, ink on wood board. 24 × 24 × 2 in. (61 × 61 × 5 cm).

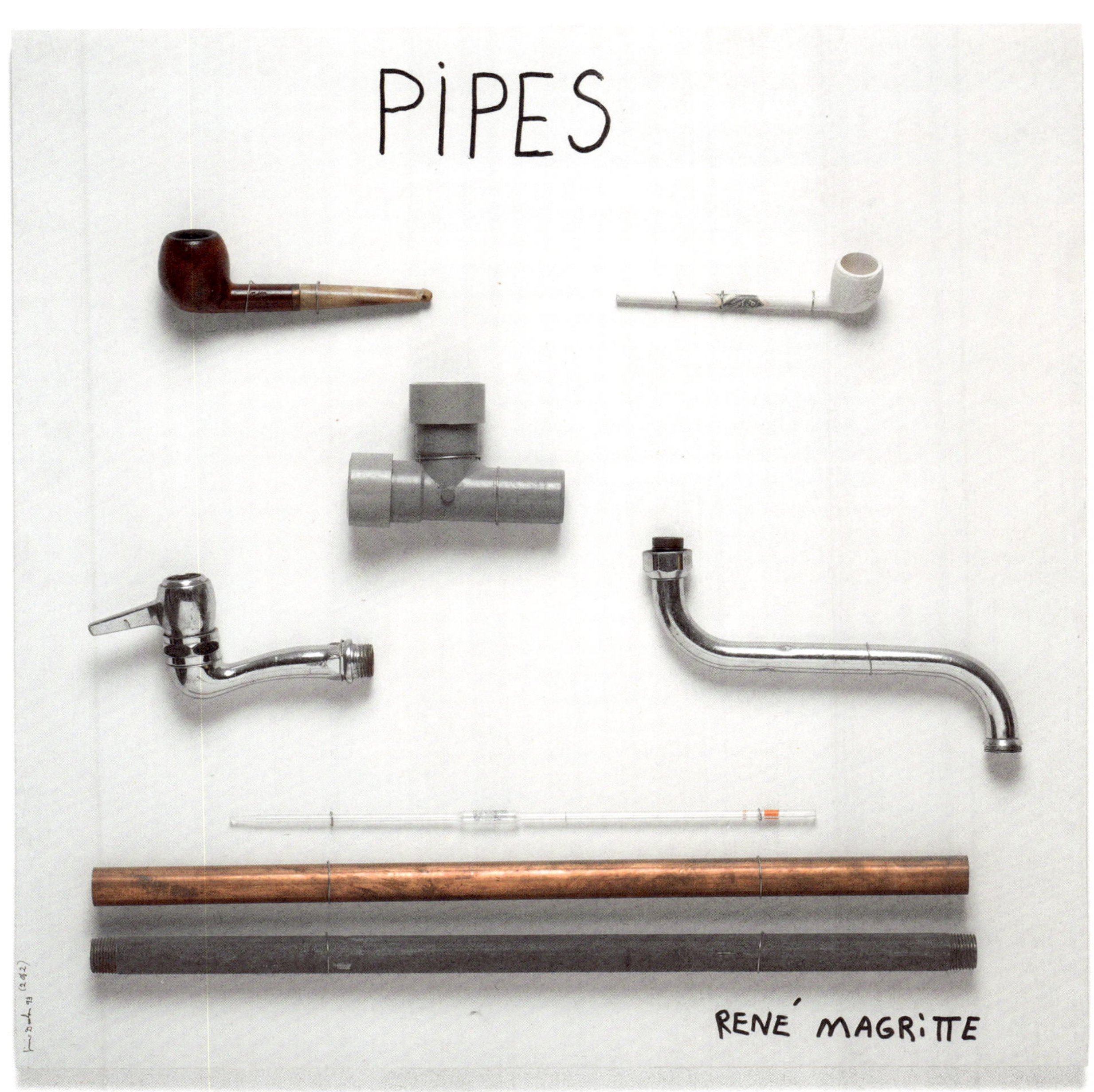

Types of Pipes by Magritte, 1993. Metal, copper, plastic, wood, ink on wood board. 24 × 24 × 2 in. (61 × 61 × 5 cm).

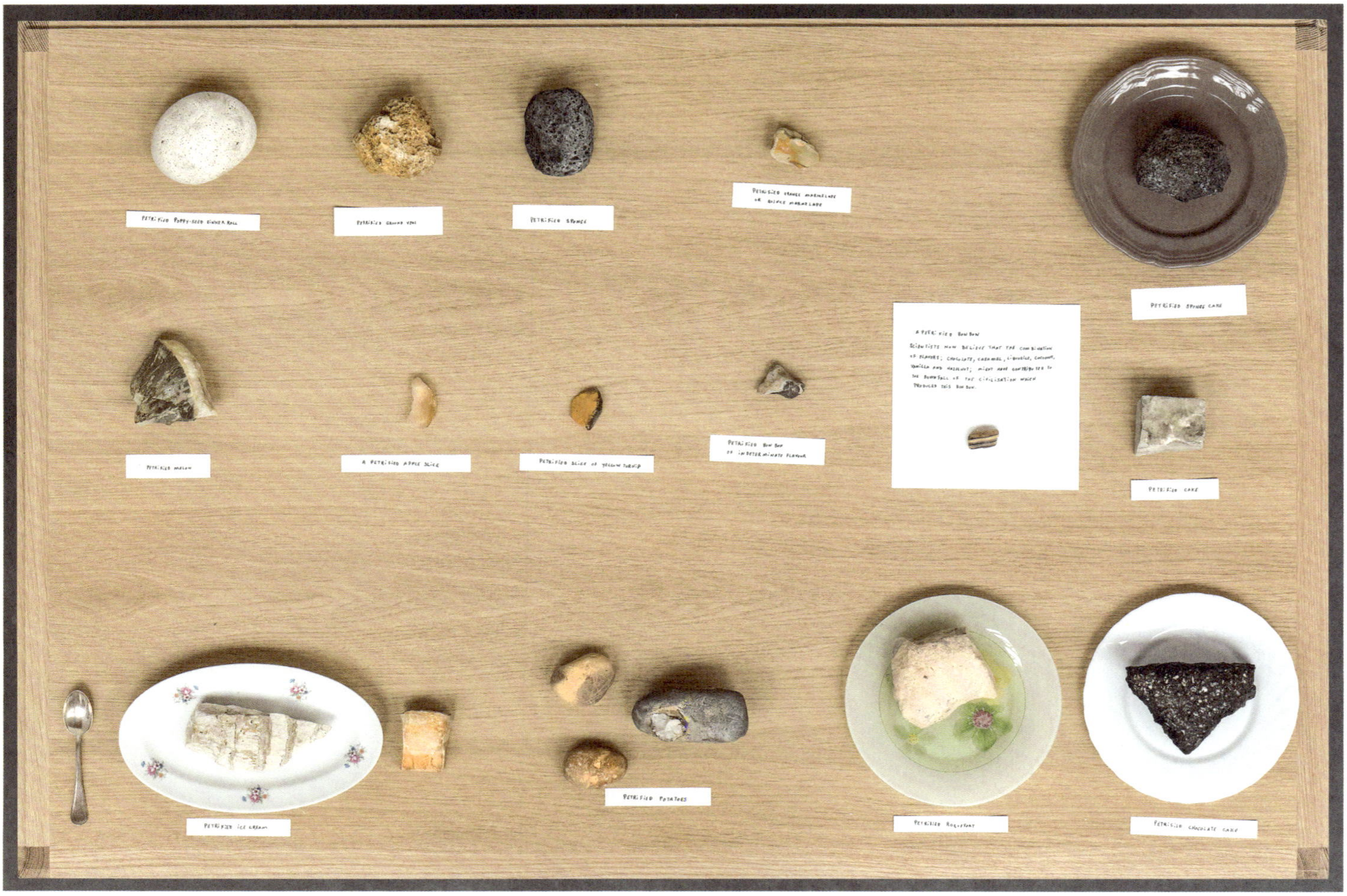

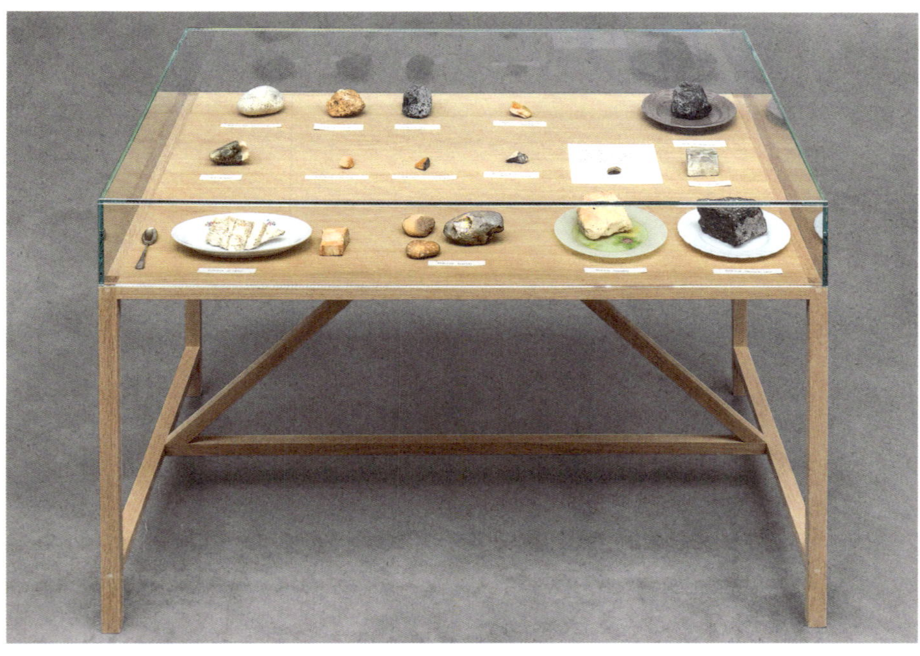

The Dangers of Petrification II, 1998–2007. Wood and glass vitrines with objects: stones, two knives, spoon, four ceramic plates, ceramic bowl, three wood chopping boards, ink on paper. 39 ¼ × 51 × 29 ½ in. (100 × 129.5 × 75 cm) each of 2.

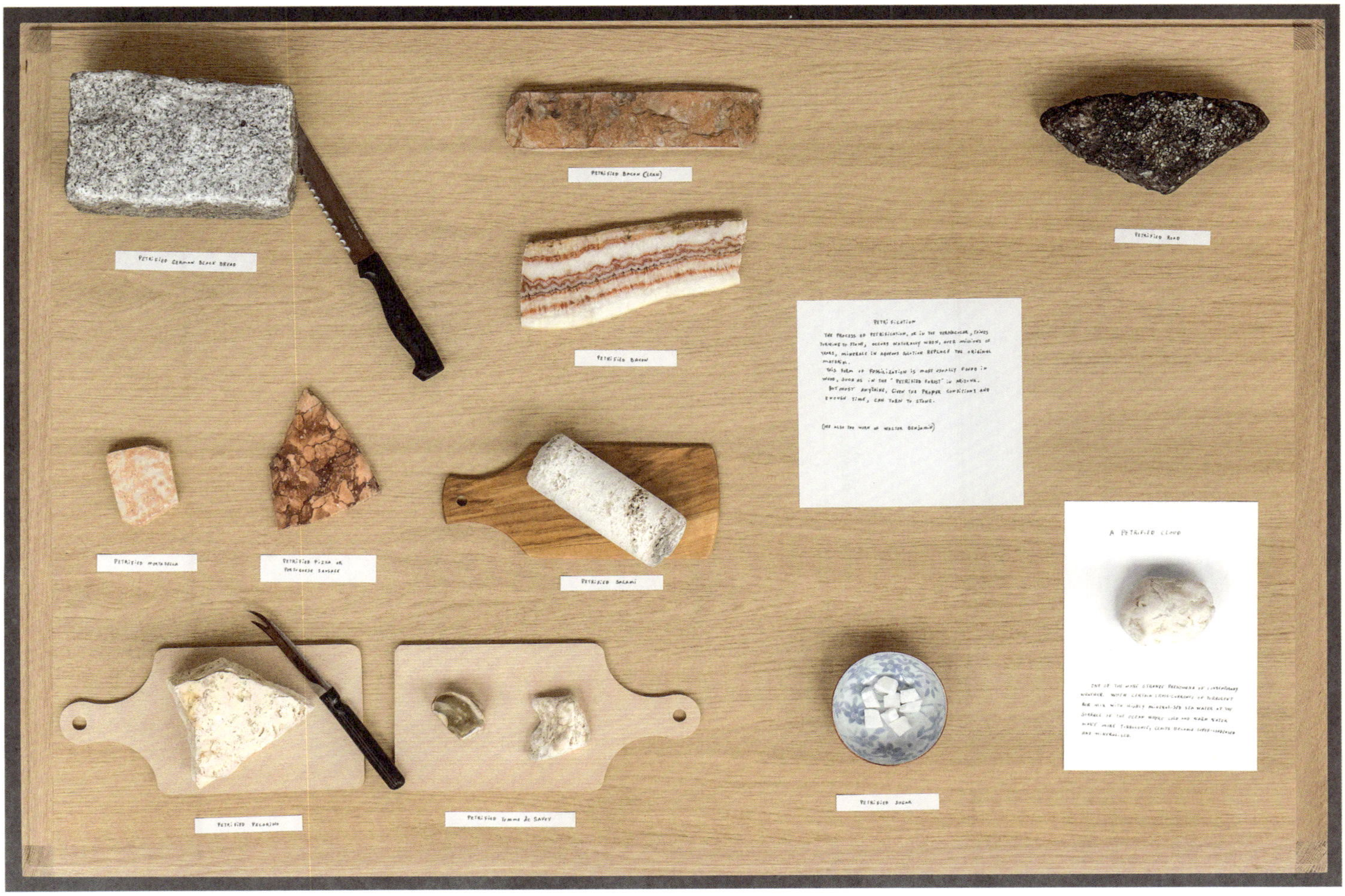

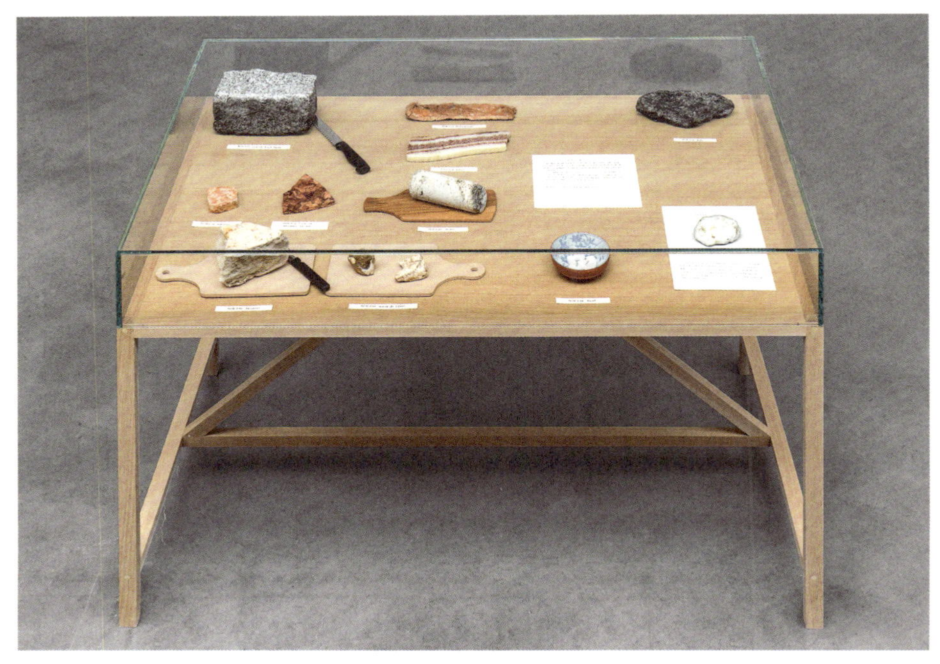

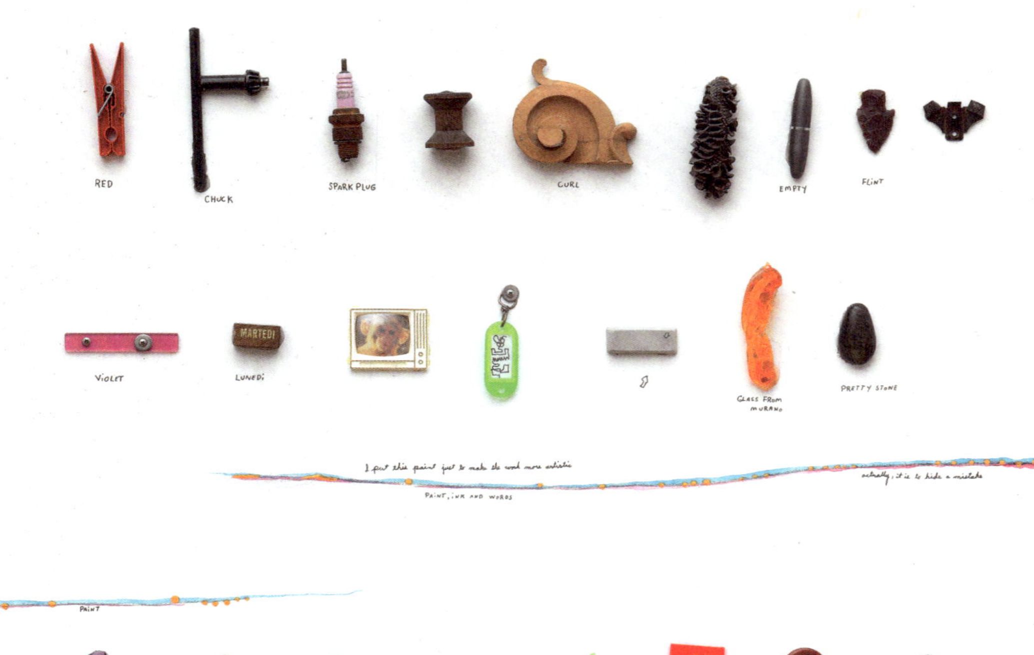

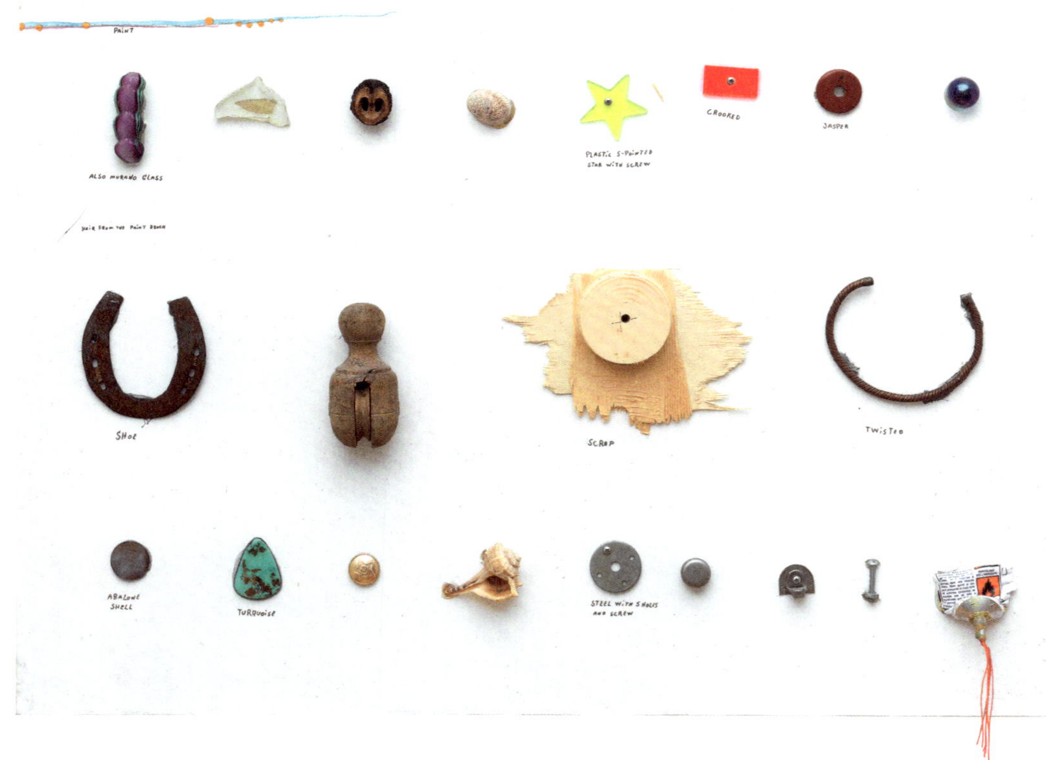

THERE'S PLENTY MORE WHERE THESE CAME FROM, 2008. Objects from the artist's studio, acrylic paint, and ink on wood panel. 40 × 27 ½ in. (101.5 × 70 cm).

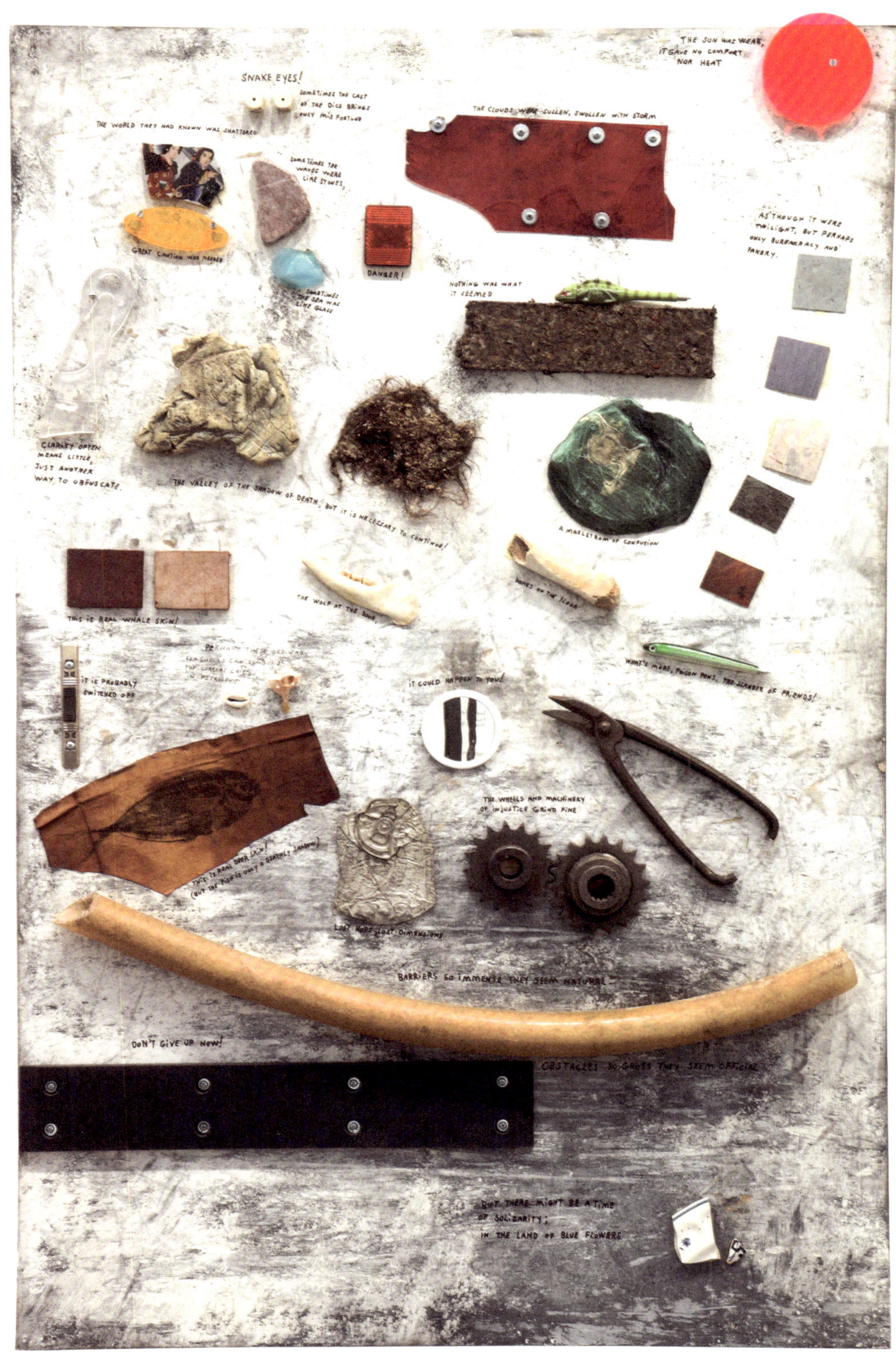

Snake Eyes!, 2006. Objects from the artist's studio on canvas with graphite and primer over wood panel: stone, plastic, bone, metal, aluminum, seashells, deerskin, hair, ceramic shards. 49 ½ × 32 in. (125 × 81 cm).

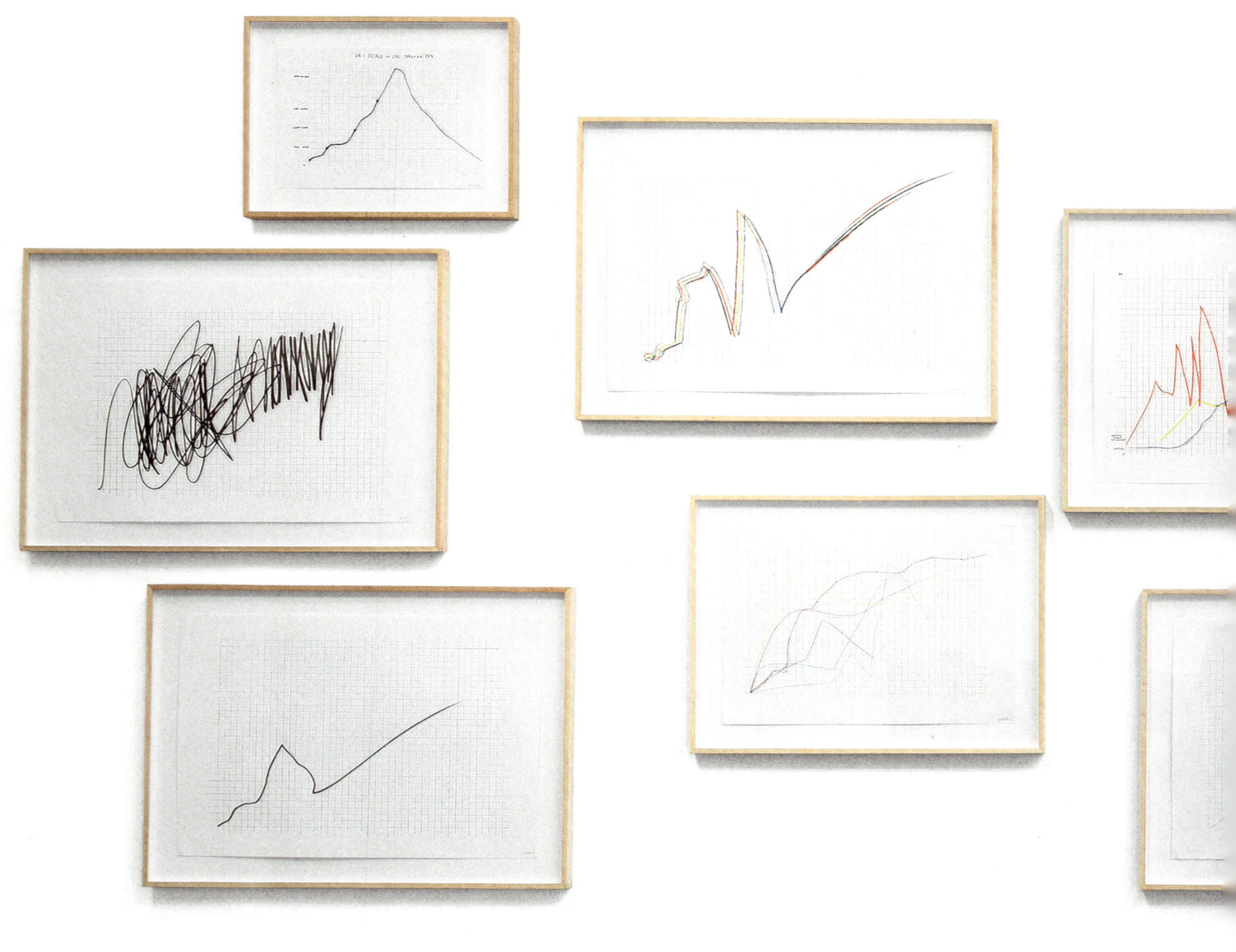

Untitled (On a Scale of One through Ten, Recalcitrant Trends, Ill Wind, Seven Lines Indicating Various Colors and Trends, The Turquoise Line Is Probably Indicative, Red and Blue Meeting, Water, Lightning and Anger, Clearly, Not Everything Functions, Indications of the Frequent Escape Mechanisms of Clarity, from Normality . . . , More a Process Than a Beginning and an End), 2013. Suite of eleven drawings; graphite and pencil on paper.
Two sheets, 11 ½ × 16 ½ in. (29.5 × 42 cm); two sheets, 16 ½ × 23 ¼ in. (42 × 59 cm); seven sheets, 20 × 28 ¾ in. (51 × 73 cm).

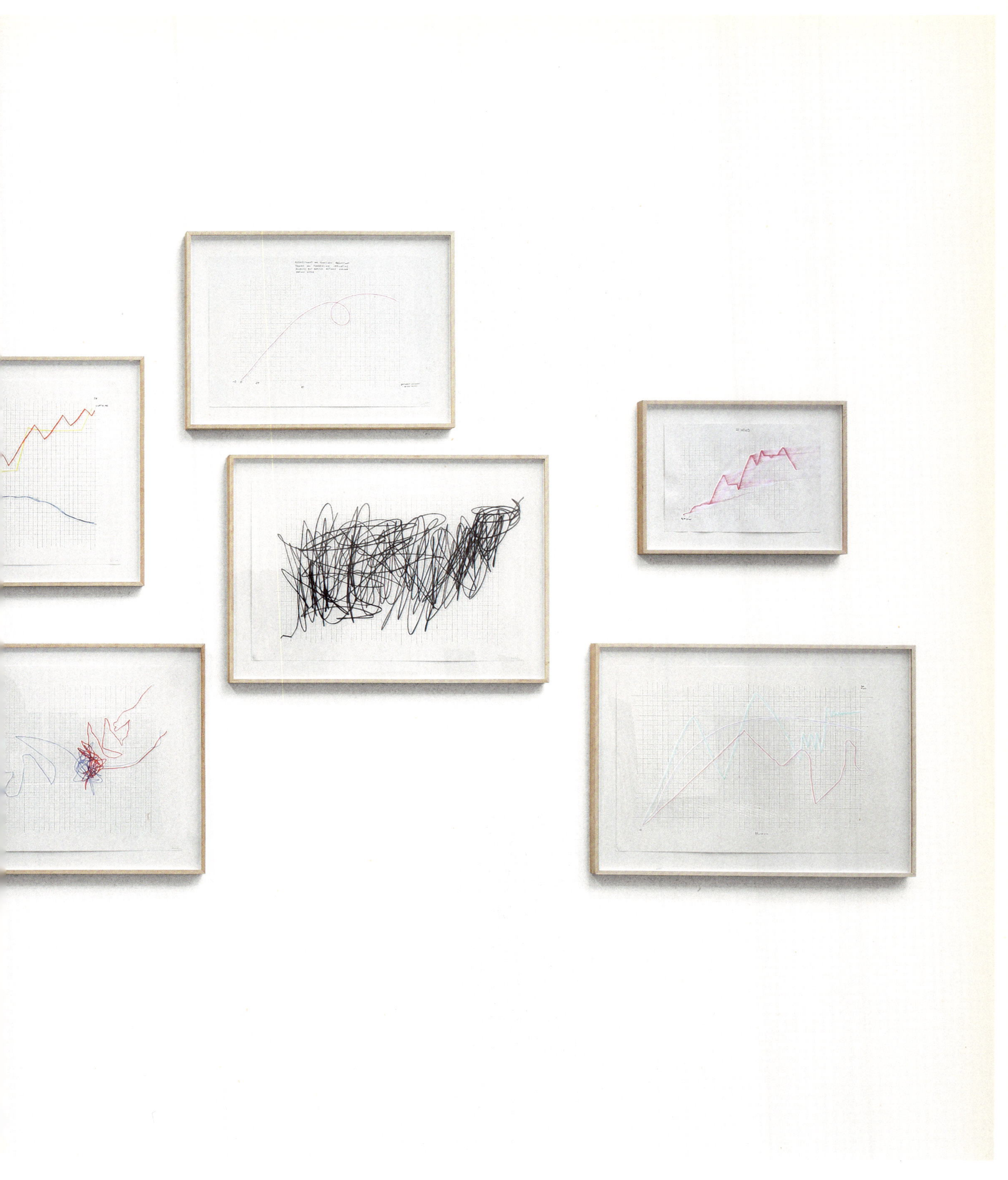

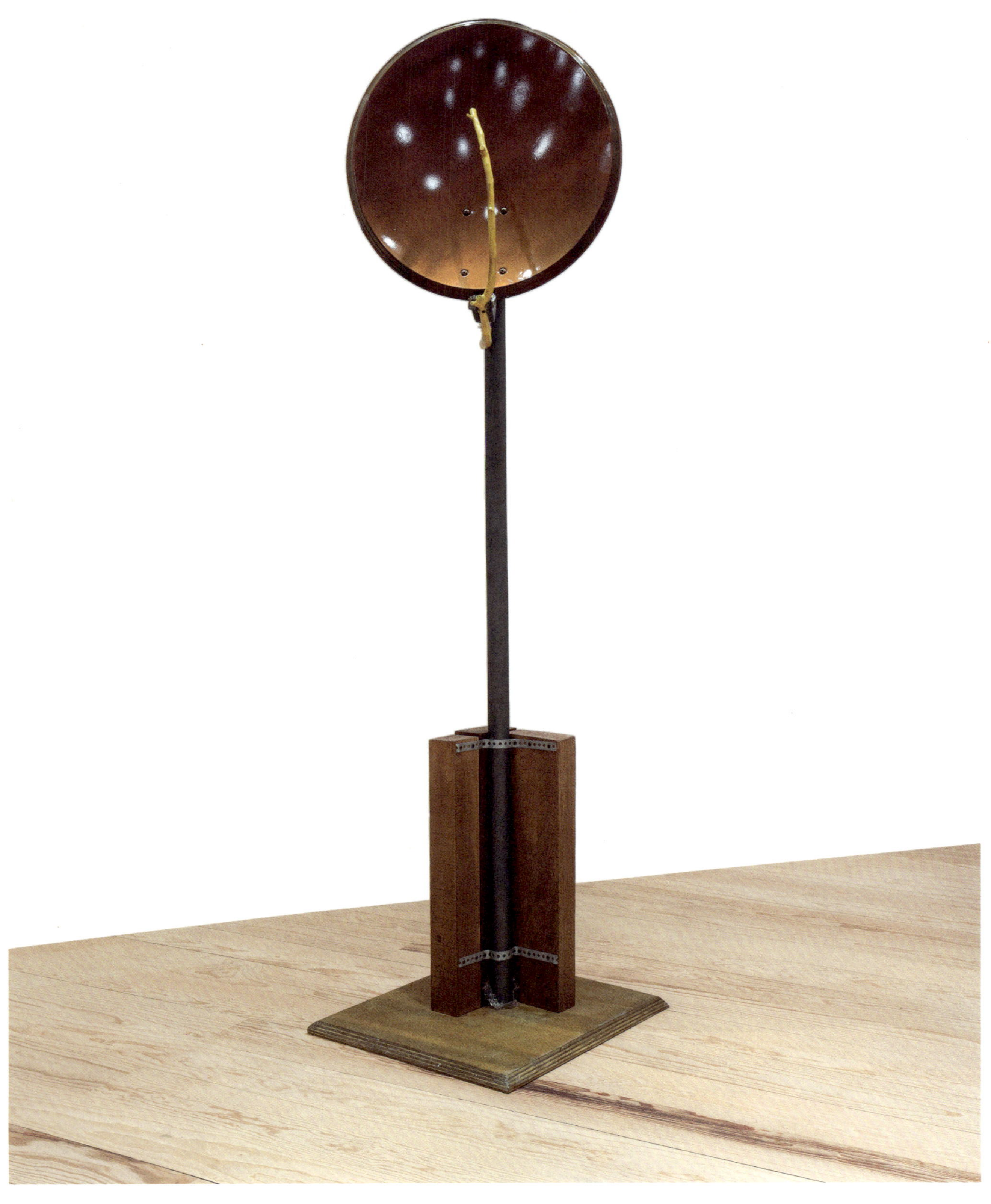

Hertz Receiving Apparatus, 2013. Satellite dish, steel pipe, mahogany, carob tree branch, plywood, acrylic paint, chameleon paint. 80 ¾ × 21 ¼ × 19 ¼ in. (205 × 54 × 49 cm).

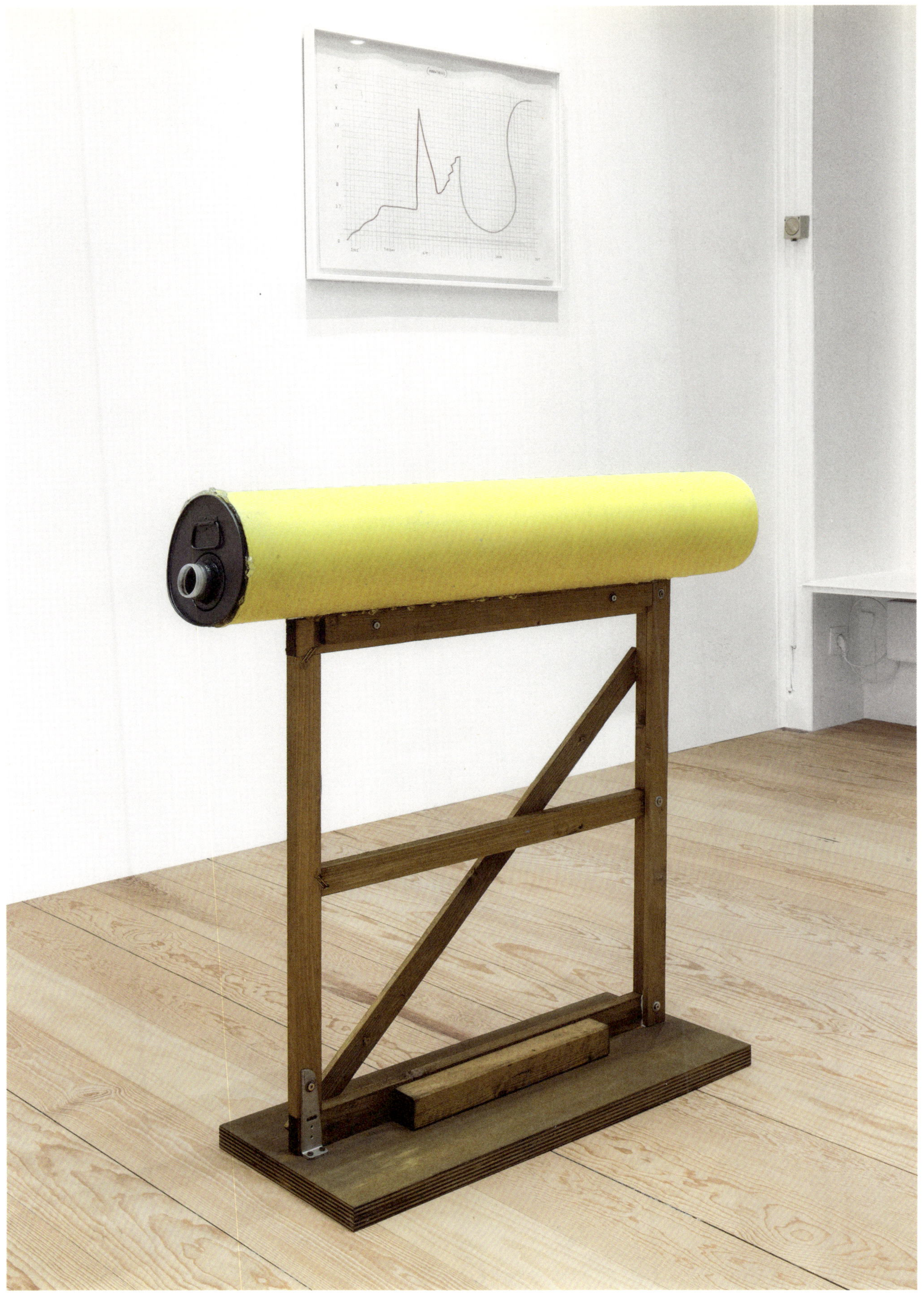

 Yellow Higgs Transmitting Apparatus, 2013. PVC, metal, wood, acrylic paint. 34 ¼ × 37 × 11 ¼ in. (87 × 94 × 29 cm).

The Effect of Gamma Rays on Certain European Plants—Volume III, 2014. Bronze, acrylic paint, wood. 52 ¼ × 17 ¾ × 17 ¾ in. (130 × 45 × 45 cm).

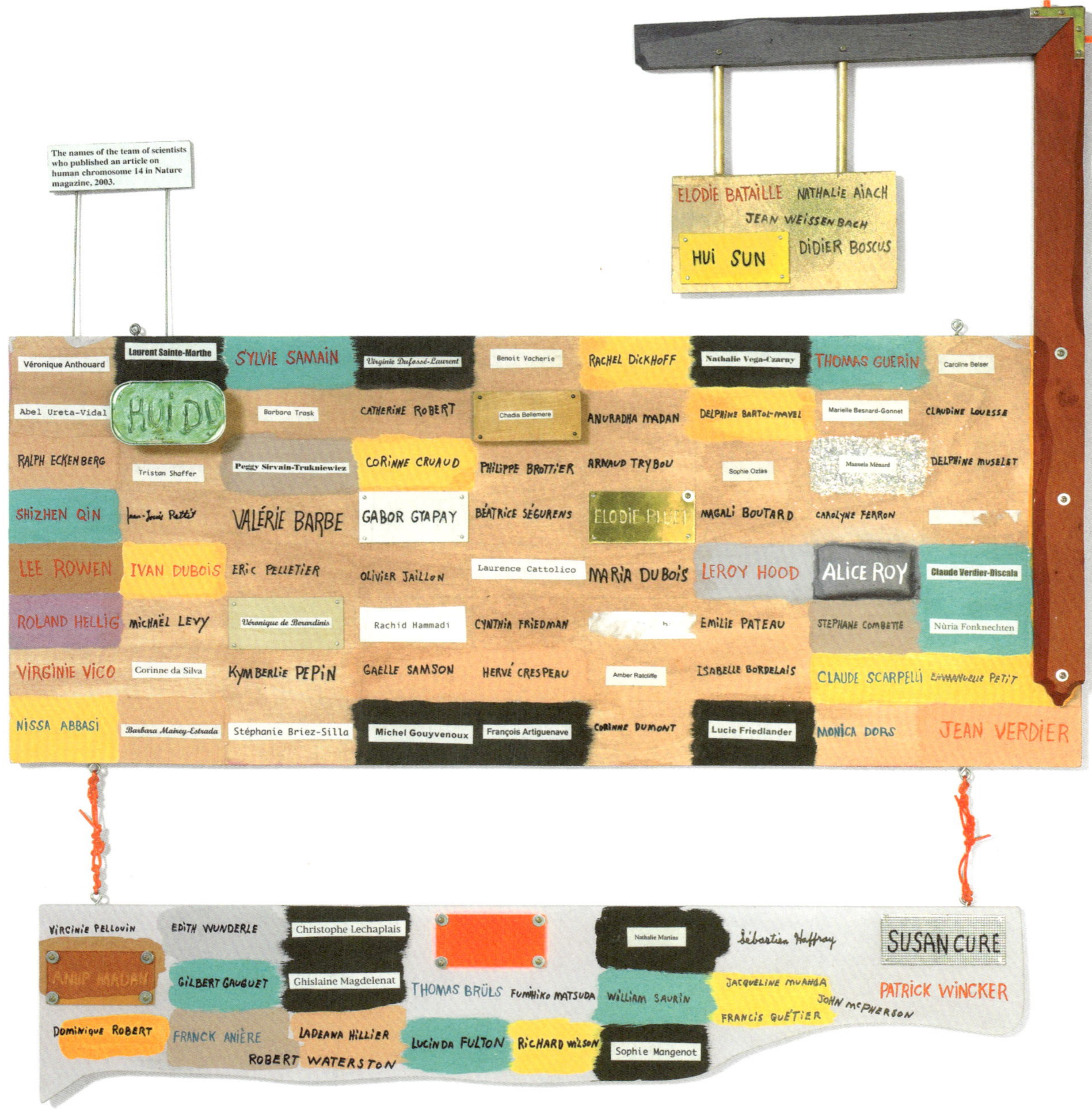

The names of the team of scientists who published an article on human chromosome 14 in Nature magazine, 2003.
Plywood, oak, acrylic paint, ink, metal, electrical wire, sardine can. 51 × 39 ¼ in. (130 × 100 cm).

SOME IRRUPTIONS AND INCOHERENCES FOR JIMMIE DURHAM

FRED MOTEN

1.
The propensity to dance in America is both corrosive and preservative, both uncountable and accumulable. There's a genocidal braid of sets of qualities and instances that can't be seen as one another's originals, that might just be an object you can change. It's an object that's always changing. The alternative is everywhere as air, but we're careless with what we breathe and how we breathe, hence this massive problematic of use, which is a kind of worship, if you can change without improving. If we embrace obscenity and contradiction, just in the way we move with them, it's not only because sometimes the terror of resisting earthly terror feels good, it's also because the terror of feeling good is not optional. But there's a cloned, dronelike, two-faced officer, a doubly unconscious coin made out of any impossible body, money made out of untroubled performance and unalloyed critique, who says "privilege" and then, when you turn him over, "precarity," while acting like the realities these words are meant to index can be separated because, evidently, you can't see two sides of your art historical self in the mirror. The piety of not thinking, which is given in acting out this one-sided two-sidedness, is surreptitiously piped into the general reservoir of normatively thoughtful bullshit, making it more noxious than it already is. Minted, self-assertion sways like a bunch of empty uniforms, shows like Calvinist branding on disavowed flesh, sounds like screeches, tweets, and chidings, at once pseudopolitically and hyperpolitically marketing the suffering that exceeds being bought and sold, that can't be calculated because it can't be individuated or packaged in a tranche of torture-backed, countercaressive securities. Such critique is an interminable citizenship test in the world its performers say they want to disappear. They dance, too, harder and faster, precisely because they are the ones who are supposed to know. They negate everything, with neither joy nor pain, and we are left with them, because we are them, watching them arresting what we are, because that's what we are, suspended between the careless negation of what ~~we~~ are and the careful affirmation of what we ~~are~~. Is that what ~~we~~ are, is that what we ~~are~~, this propensity to dance given in the terrible imperative not to celebrate?

2.
Is Jimmie Durham an artist? The legitimacy of his claim to the category is undeniable if he just wanted to be somebody, to the extent that any such claim can be legitimate for anybody, if there is some body, if there is any body. And it's just as undeniable that in his enactment of the category he simultaneously refuses its imperative to preserve itself in separation. To be an artist, in Durham, for Durham, is not to be one, as well. To suggest that he works, or that he is in movement, or that he is movement against the separate single being of the artist is to suggest a more general resistance to severalty, to what one might call, in an echo of what the Dawes Act cruelly echoes, the allotment of identity, which Durham is constantly, which is to say endlessly unsuccessfully, escaping. Maybe Jimmie Durham is an activity. Maybe Jimmie Durham is a practice. Showing that we are not what we are, that we are not, that we ~~are~~; saying that to say that is to affirm we as the persistent, militantly preservative practice of no-thingness, of the inveterate changing of every object and every nation, of an open-ended sculpturing of every exhaustively open end, Durham re-presents we

as a matter of thought that the prison church of privilege and precarity tries but fails to interdict. That we as cuts we ~~are~~ just enough so we don't have to worry about being-consistent or being-coherent is what we study, is all of how we come to nothing in study, finding more than everything in the findings we make. The practice persists, is preserved, only insofar as it is open, radically nonexclusionary, insistently improper as an overturning that laughs at itself to keep from crying. The vast range of violence the antenational international perpetrates on the verb "to be" in the unholy name of the nominative case of the first person plural pronoun is a clue that is, at once, both immanent and transcendent.

3.
What we be trying to talk about all the time, amongst and against ourselves and all up in the air and under the ground and water, is antegrammatical—a general beyond of the analogy, whose very invocation remains a kind of sterile double entry. The hold, the trail, the trailer, the project, the general antagonism—all that's just the mobile locus of an intensification of every feeling, which is why the way the alternative survives the ongoing genocide is so unfadeably chorographic and choreic, manifest in a dance of vicious colonial mapping and nervous anticolonial muscularity. But all that's special about this or that exclusion is the refusal of this or that exclusion. If the notion that this or that modality of suffering is special requires disavowing the intensity of the entanglement of privilege and precarity (when that entanglement is so crucial to our necessary comportment toward the open end of world and time), then special needs to get let go in a continual enactment of that ceremony we keep finding, where being singular plural is dispossessed in a plain of sēms.

4.
Celebration lets being-special go, but under an absolute duress. Escape from the struggle for freedom is required. Celebration in art can't be redemptive because what we have to celebrate is so immeasurably small and large. Art asks how to hand on or hand out the feel and the sense of that which is against the grain of aesthetic theory's tendency to call the authorities in itself on itself. If I could only get myself to police myself, aesthetic theory wistfully sighs. In lieu of that, the ascription of radical irregularity is the ground not only of art's exclusion but also of the exclusion of every practice of the alternative, which is what we ~~are~~. We have to celebrate the offness that's been written on us, which we accentuate in nonperformances of nonportraiture, in we as, as in how we be pretending to be the pretending to be called Rosa Lévy. We on in putting on, in nothing, which turns out to be all red and black in the absence of the artist, a pencil 'stache and juicy lips, Duchamp's interminably descending rock bottom, impersonation itself in drag. In overloading an already overcrowded rogue's gallery of self-portraiture, Durham makes it seem like art might actually be able to rewrite itself out of making pictures of its selves in severalty all day long. Maybe we write ourselves out. Maybe that's what we ~~are~~, he says, when we as like that.

5.
To ask the question of how we get past the imposition of severalty and the self-portraiture that is its imperative and residue is already to bear something more and less than the artist's way of being. For the artist is given in severalty, beholden to what Durham calls the state's violent "immortality," which comes into relief as a spectral projection against the backdrop of patterns of exile and return, of precedent postresidential resistance to the brutally perennial settler state, which proliferates in a bunch of little states of settlement, found(ed) by artists in flurries of anti-Loisaida self-picturing on the death march from urban village to East Village.[1] "We are parasites of the rich," an artist friend of Durham's once said.[2] In recounting that passively aggressive self-assertion, Durham teaches us that severalty is where racialization and aesthetic theory converge. The individuation of the artist is already a kind of massacre. And so we seek out the landed blessings of the landless, neither as a repertoire of countermeasures nor as a collection of countersubjective standards but just because to want to dig the transverse earth is what we ~~are~~. We as this changing object called object changers.

6.
This is all about land and use, but it's also all about language and/as material. Does the artist own the materials he uses and, in so using, improve upon? Does the poet own his language and, in so owning, purify the language of the tribe (as T. S. Eliot once said in a beautifully fucked-up Western called *Four Quartets*)? On the other hand, is there a work of dispossession in Durham, of resistance to severalty, and even of a resistance to sovereignty given past the claim upon it and moving on in and as a violent unsettling that is at once earthly and divine? If there is, it's only insofar as the work of dispossession cannot be contained. It places the artist, having come into his own in and through allotment, in grave danger of having to suffer the immeasurable grace of his disappearance, of her dispersal. See, I'm interested in the work and feel and material presence of dispossession, disappearance, dispersal, and disbursal in Durham's art, which is not his, and I'm thinking that this is something as palpably, audibly, flavorfully visible—as spirit, as breath, as irreducible and ineradicable aroma—in the objects he changes, in the changing of himself as object, and in the objections his changes raise and play not only on the very idea of objecthood itself but also on subjectivity, the object's evil twin, its "evilly compounded, vital I."[3] That's why it's so cool and crucial to check out the itinerary of his thinking on use, on development, and how it turns not only in his writing on artist-driven gentrification but also on the problematic of the very idea of the artist and his world. Durham moves, is on the move, his indigent indigeneity in voluntary exile from voluntarism's slough and epicenter. But what's at stake is not the way he carries himself or keeps carrying himself away; what's important is the way he carries his selflessness, the way he keeps changing that object, like a mobile sculpture in the act of its own making and unmaking, wrapped in the mantle of its own dismantling, continually asserting this refusal of self-assertion, constantly refusing representation and self-representation with a particular wave, an emphatic and insistently gentle kind of greeting and good-bye. The presence of the one who says here I am in not being here is dispersed and more and less than full, given in the air and dirt and water and flesh of a whole other, pre- and postcolonial mathematics. In this old-new math, it's not about figuring out ways to count the uncountable. It's about standing together, in refusal of standing, in praise of all. And let's say that for

right now, for just this moment, that the name of all is Jimmie Durham. Now, I'm not saying that we ~~are~~ Jimmie Durham. That's a beautifully terrible thing to say. I'm just saying that in saying that the name of all is Jimmie Durham I'm saying that all don't quite add up. Jimmie Durham practices (the theory of) non-numerical material.[4]

7.
Dense and airy earth, let's rearrange the neighborhood again, in curacy. The earth has a future at the end of the world right now. Right over here there's a museum for durational art formed in walking by panthers of care on a wingtip cruise. There's a vast unincorporated evangelical mission of blur. We trying to get people to practice and people already been practicing. They already knew but maybe just didn't feel it or didn't let it be a bright feeling, a way of strolling glow mutuality. When shift happens we notice the duration of the living. "The music is happening, I don't need to play," Monk says. Duration in Durham is like *Mary Lou's Mass*, monks say, while walking down the street as art taking displacement. Charged with the uncollectible, the museum will have taken aim, like a society for community safety, a defense mechanism of absolute openness for aesthetical Cherokees. Durham's durationally extrarational art wants to be beautiful, a certain lack of coherence in creativity and the social process, that ongoing interruption of naturalization that we keep waiting for, the museum as a bunch of lumpen parties, a serially intergalactic swarm of midnight jams. The beautiful that's inseparable from the terrible, that's too nasty to be sublime, too flavorful to be tasteful, too syncopic to be fixed, too red, blur, and black for things to persist in residence. The state is a mechanism for the monopolization of violence, its placement in or under reserve, in and as the strict regulation of generativity. And Western thought and culture have been where this monopolization is theorized and defended, in the name and by way of sovereignty, self-possession, and self-determination. Freaked out over the generativity that destroys order, troubled by savory metastasis, underconceptual cancer, pre- and postconceptual sensing, not grasping but letting go in ripped-up anapprehension, embodied viscera sense inevitable fade while the earth laughs sunlight.

8.
Bricolage is too charming, Durham says, too comfortable to keep close, too closed for the necessary discomfort.[5] So how do you go from pleasingly putting lots of things together to having nothing quite add up, to letting nothing be so thoroughly in the work that a certain unworking of the work gets done? The work of letting be the nothing in the work that undoes the work till it and the artist are eased with being nothing. The museum of that is walking around in exile and humility, endlessly having to have something to say for itself so it can help you make you strange to yourself. Estrangement, here, is all up in the rub or glance, not in the work, because to be strange to yourself, to be able to have been disabled in the museum, to walk in but not walk out (as you), and then to walk on, aesthetically, is to be unable to have found the work. An eccentric little piece of nothing gestures to the work's not being there. It's like if you can't see it, then you can't see yourself in it. Indians love his work, Durham says, because they don't look at it. He says they have no use for it and perhaps it is in this that the work is useful.[6] Out of this nettle, danger, we pluck this flower, safety, which is way too terribly like picking all the goddamn cotton in the world. There's this problematic of how to refuse and to refuse, as well, their refusal, which often takes the form of fusion, of being collected in exclusion, of being brutally, violently wanted—in a libidinal economy of absolutely have to have—when absolutely no one wants you. Because the One can't want these explosive, "eccentric little pieces of nothing," these tchotchkes made for money by the ones who refuse to be money, these little bits of stealing in stolenness.[7] Viciously, this has all but all been admitted. To let in is to confess, whereas to incorporate is to deny. The whole thing is radically untenable, and then there's the fact that we have to take responsibility for it. Europe is our project. America is our thing. You have to say that a million times before blowing them up becomes a necessary option. Jimmie Durham laughs, repeat after me.

Notes
1. Jimmie Durham, "The Immortal State," *A Certain Lack of Coherence: Writings on Art and Cultural Politics*, ed. Jean Fisher (New York: Kala Press, 1993), 191–92. See also Durham, "A Friend of Mine Said That Art Is a European Invention," in *Jimmie Durham*, ed. Laura Mulvey, Dirk Snauwaert, and Mark Alice Durant (London: Phaidon Press, 1995), 140–47.
2. Durham, "Artists Must Begin Helping Themselves," in *A Certain Lack of Coherence*, 62.
3. Wallace Stevens, "The Poems of Our Climate," in *The Collected Poems: The Corrected Edition* (New York: Vintage, 2015), 206.
4. Durham, "Material," in *Waiting to Be Interrupted, Selected Writings, 1993–2012*, ed. Jean Fisher (Milan: Mousse Publishing; Antwerp: M HKA, 2014), 351–55.
5. Durham, "Interview: Dirk Snauwaert in Conversation with Jimmie Durham," in *Jimmie Durham*, 25.
6. Ibid., 9.
7. Ibid., 10.

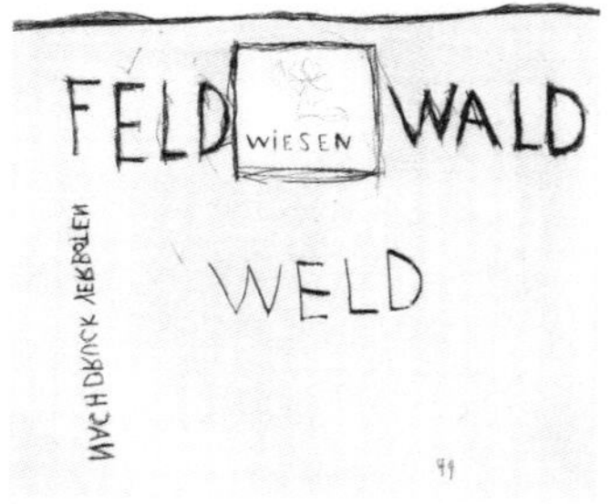

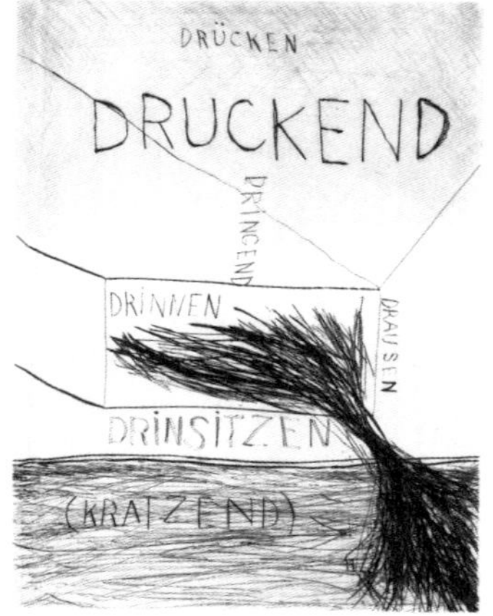

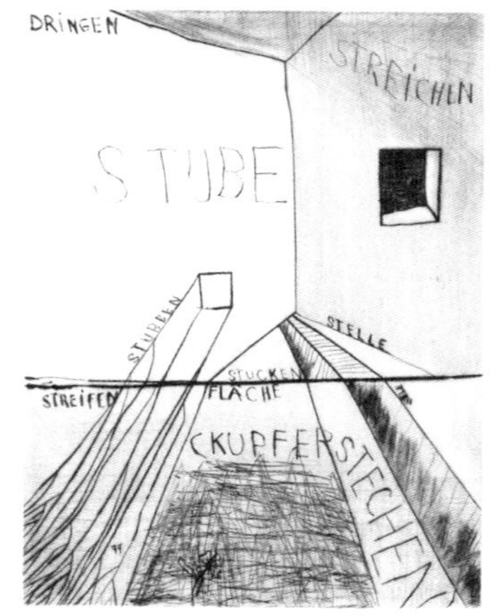

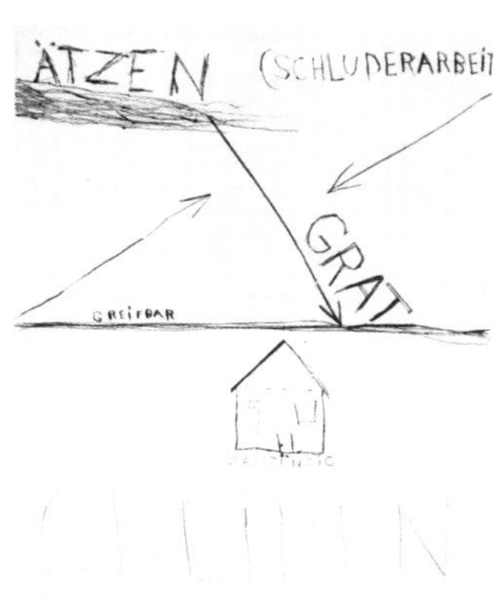

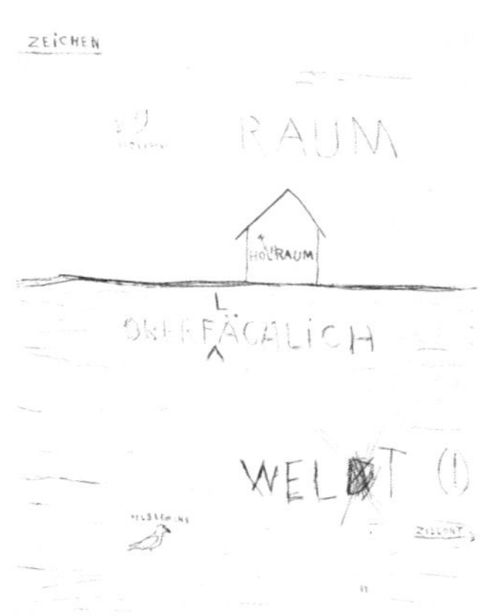

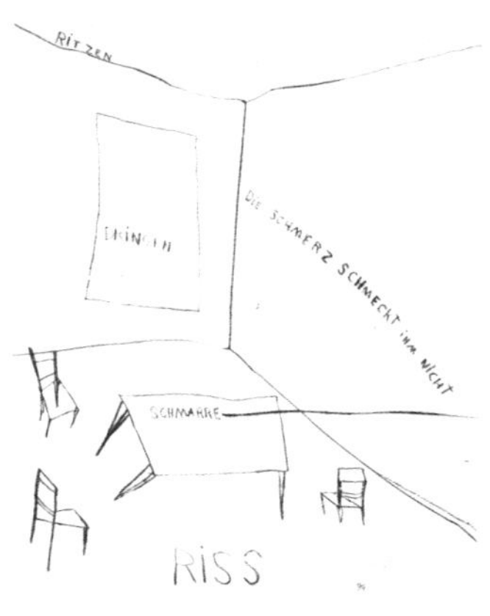

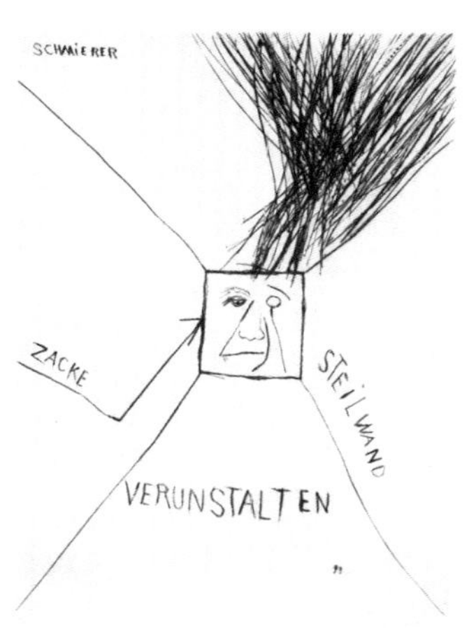

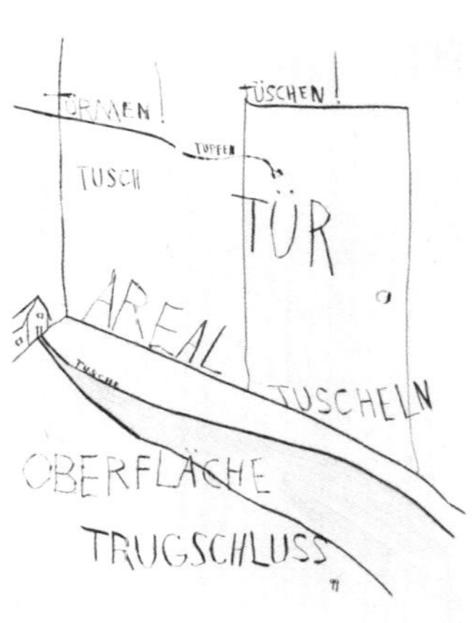

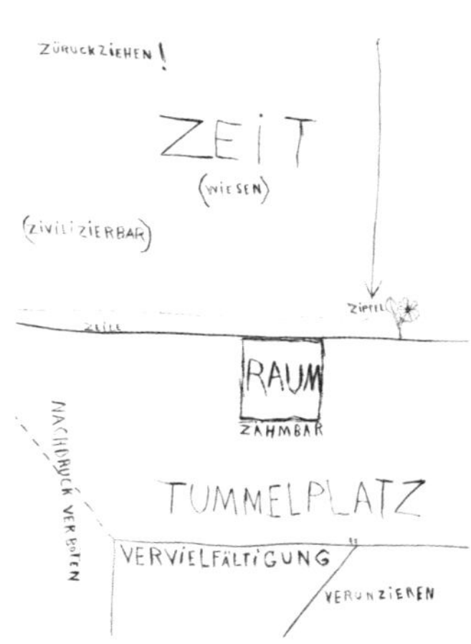

Mäßige Materialfehler [Moderate material defects], 2000. Etchings on paper. 16 ½ × 12 ½ in. (41.9 × 31.7 cm) each of 9.

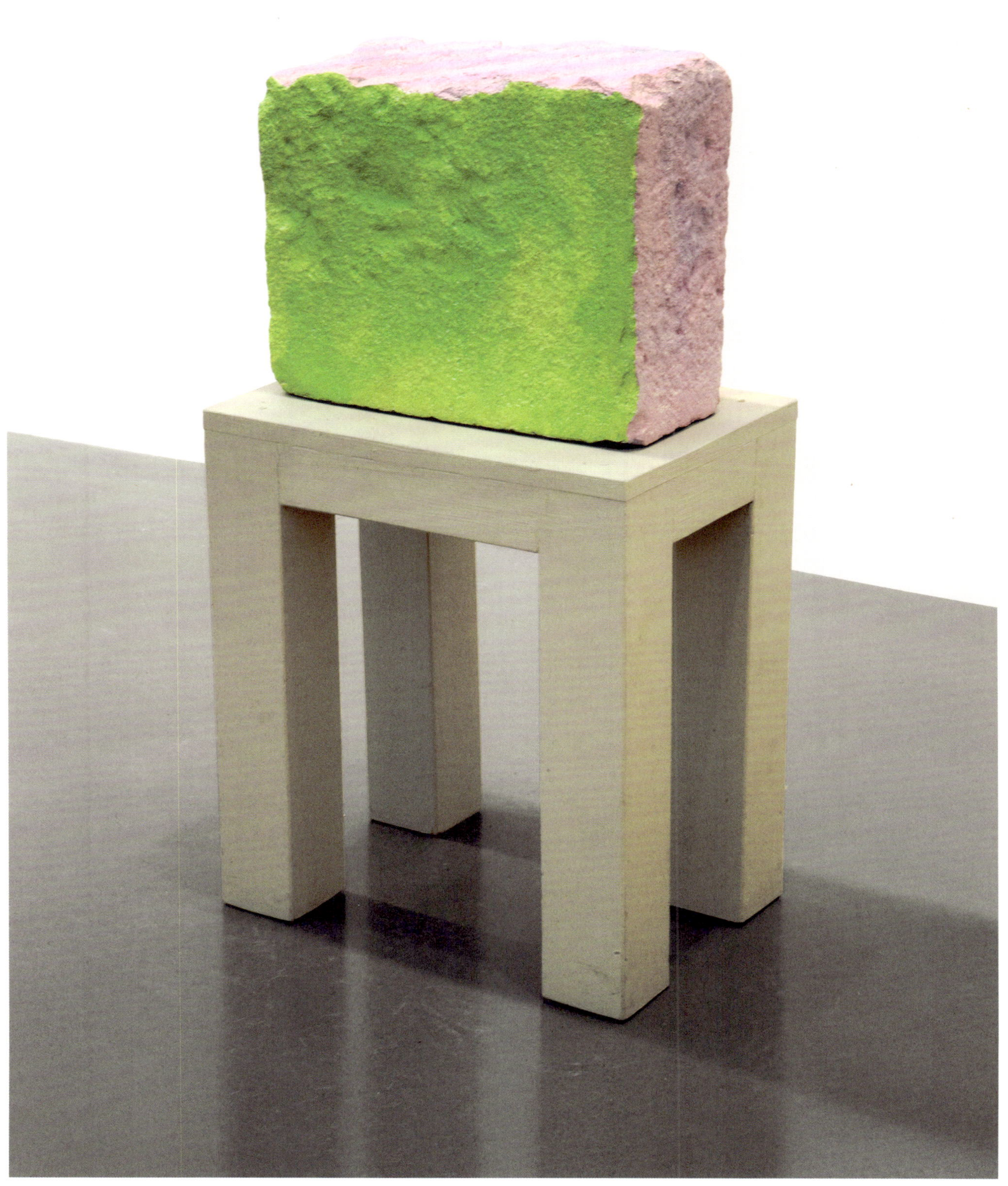

 A Stone Rejected by the Builder (1), 2006. Stone, wood, acrylic paint. Stone: 34 × 41 × 20 in. (86.3 × 104.1 × 50.8 cm); table: 55 × 48 × 35 in. (139.7 × 121.9 × 88.9 cm).

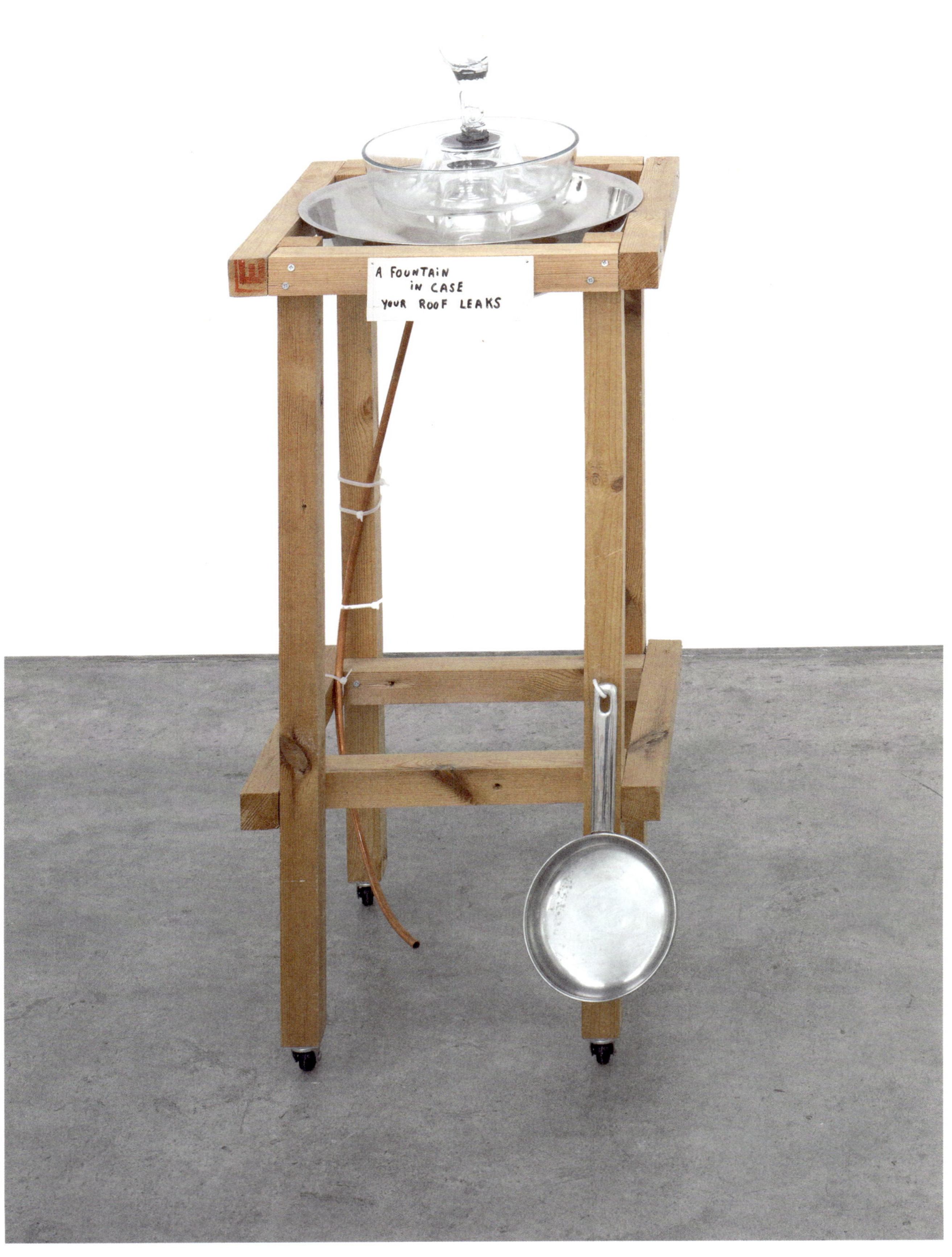

A Fountain in Case Your Roof Leaks, 1996. Pine, broken glass, stainless-steel salad bowl, metal skillet, plastic tubing. 48 ½ × 19 ⅝ × 19 ⅝ in. (123 × 50 × 50 cm).

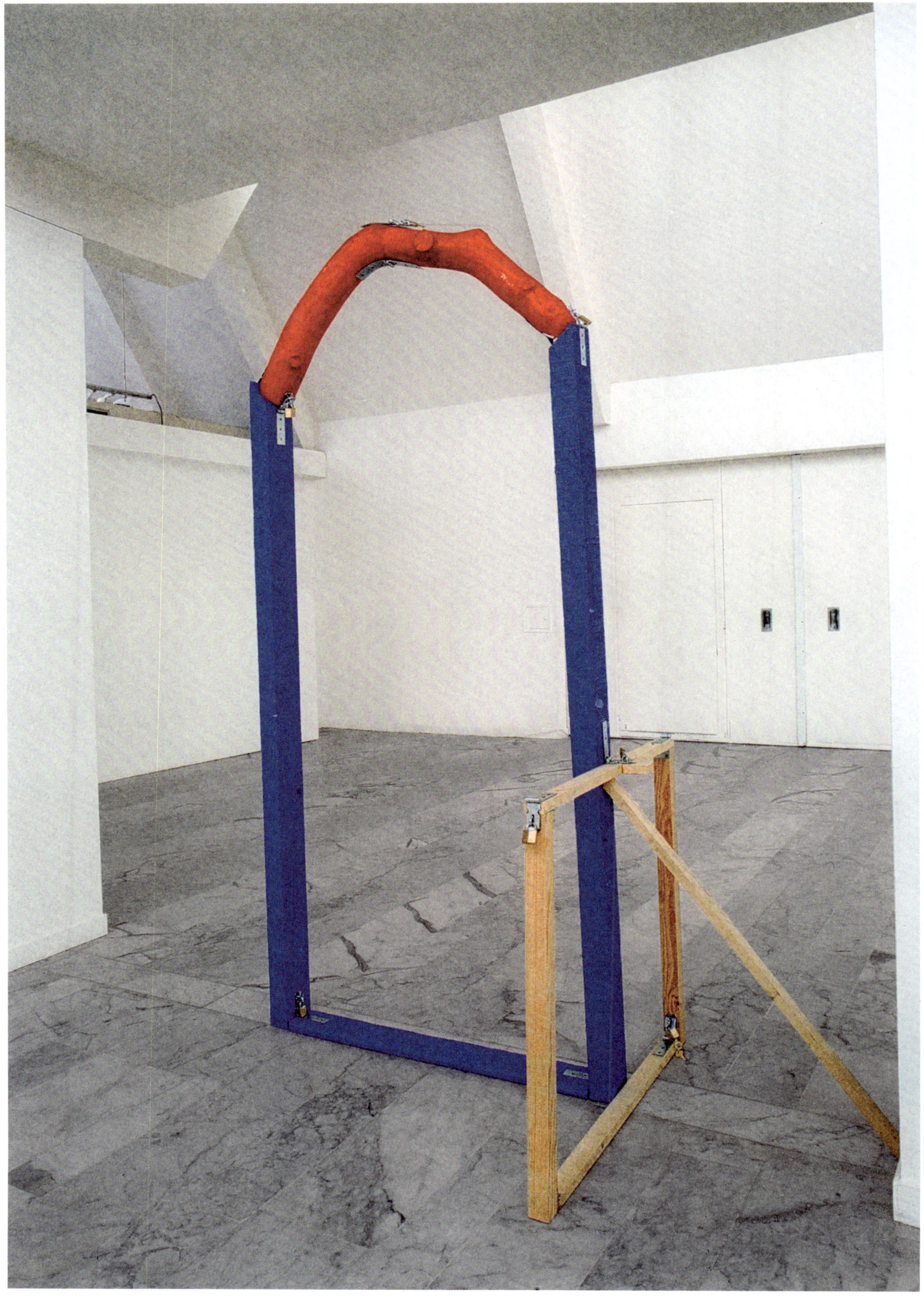

Arc de Triomphe for Personal Use, 1996. Pine, acrylic paint, metal hardware, padlocks, keys. 78 ¾ × 31 ½ × 31 ½ in. (200 × 80 × 80 cm).

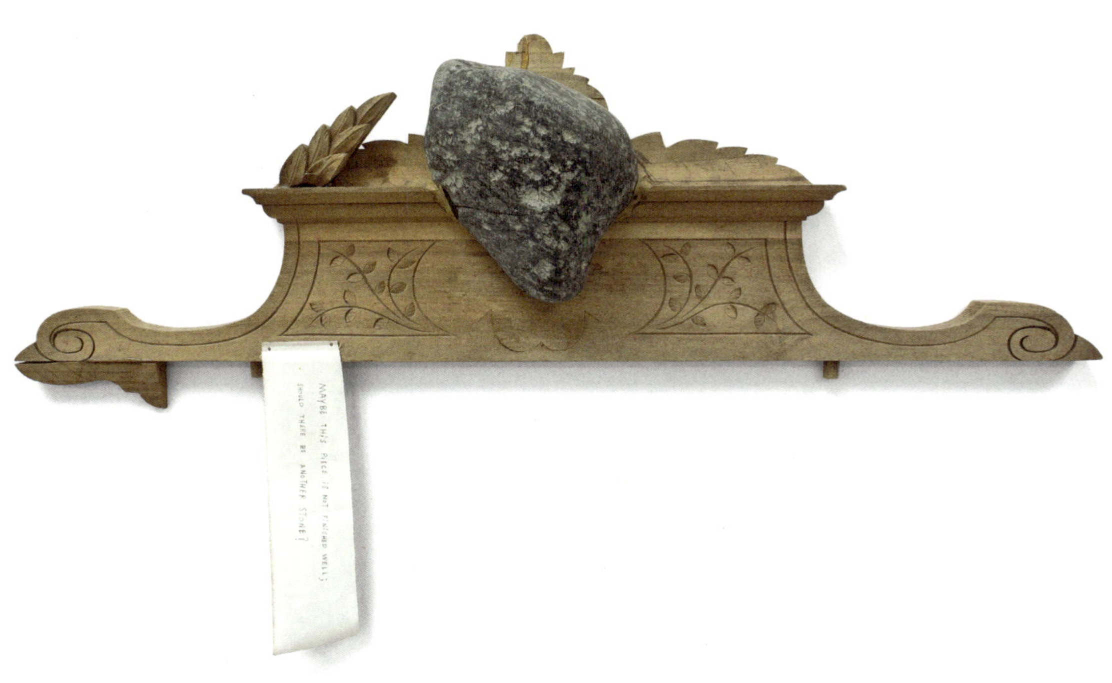

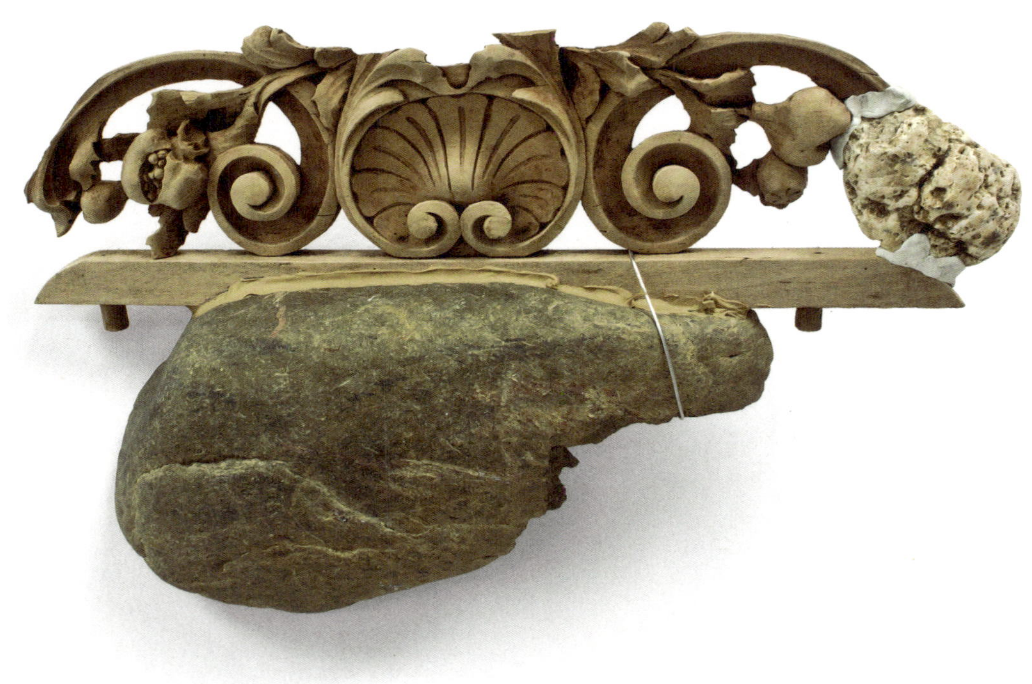

Top: *Suggested Proposal for a New Architecture n°3*, 2003. Carved walnut, stone, ink on paper. 10 ½ × 34 ½ × 4 in. (27 × 88 × 10 cm).
Bottom: *Suggested Proposal for a New Architecture n°2*, 2004. Carved walnut, stones, metal wire. 14 ½ × 23 ½ × 6 in. (37 × 60 × 15 cm).

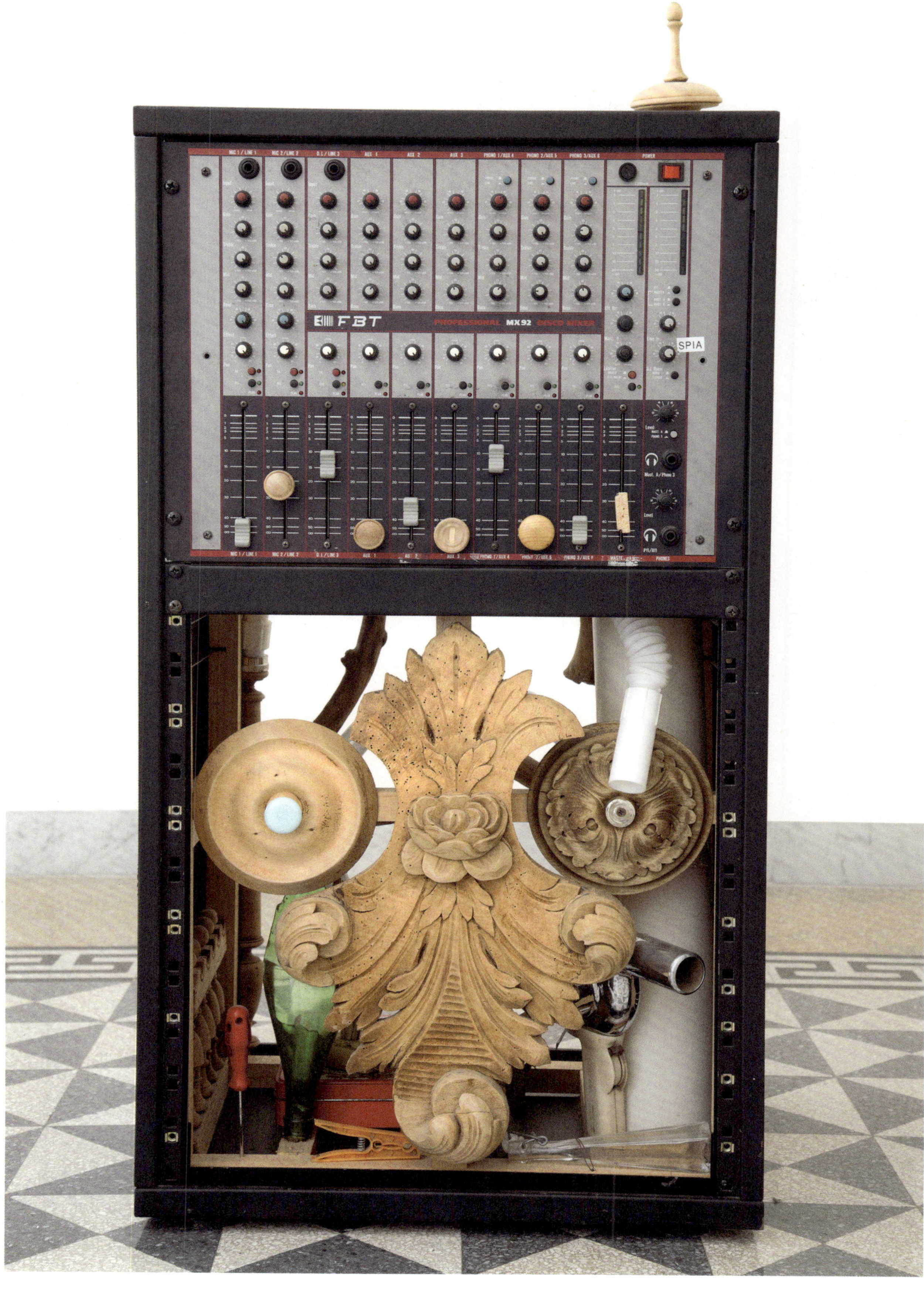

You Cannot Book a Judge Under Cover, 2006. Carved walnut furniture parts, PVC, branch, glass bottle, plastic bottle, ice-cream scoop, clothespins, hair dryer, painted tin box, wire bedspring, cords, screwdriver, metal hardware, plastic and metal tubing in a found sound mixer. 47 ¼ × 31 ½ × 31 ½ in. (120 × 80 × 80 cm).

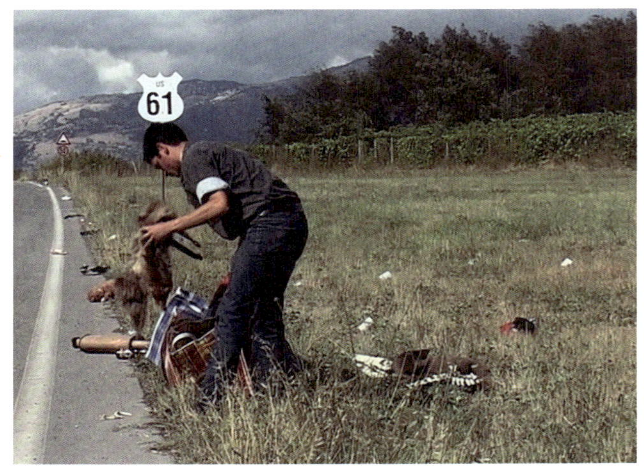

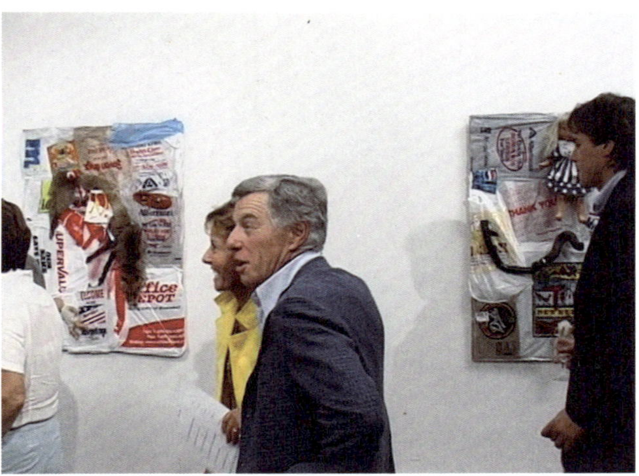

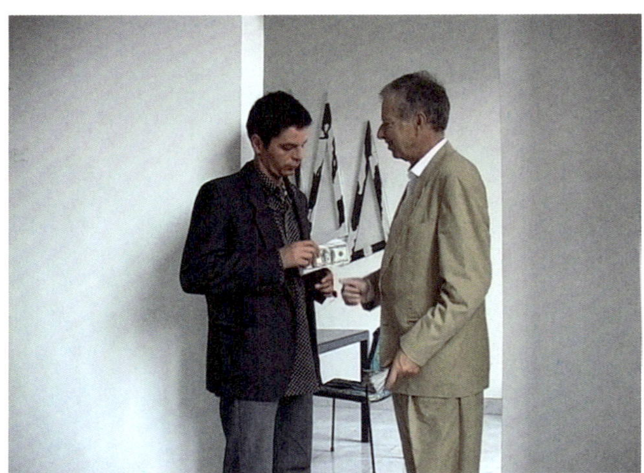

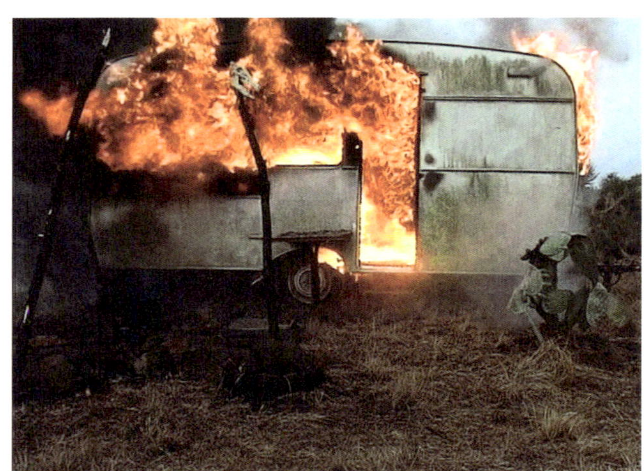

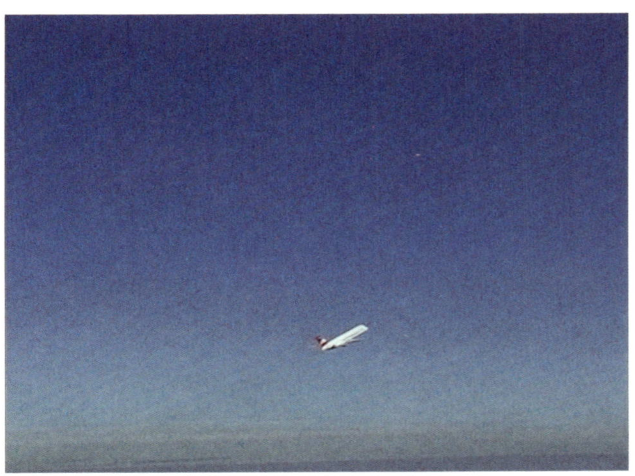

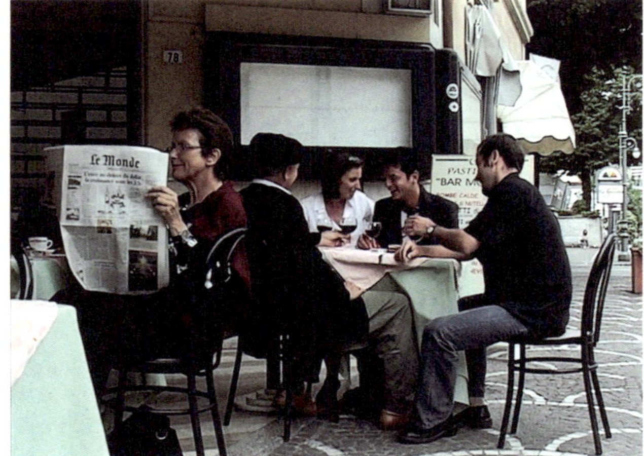

La Poursuite du Bonheur [The pursuit of happiness], 2003. 35mm film transferred to DVD, color, sound. 13:00 min.

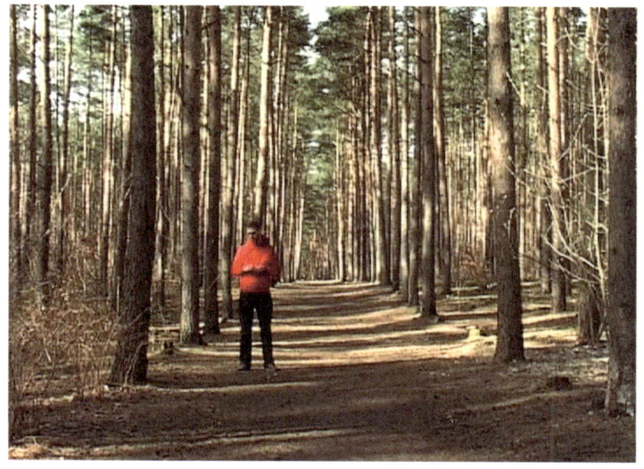

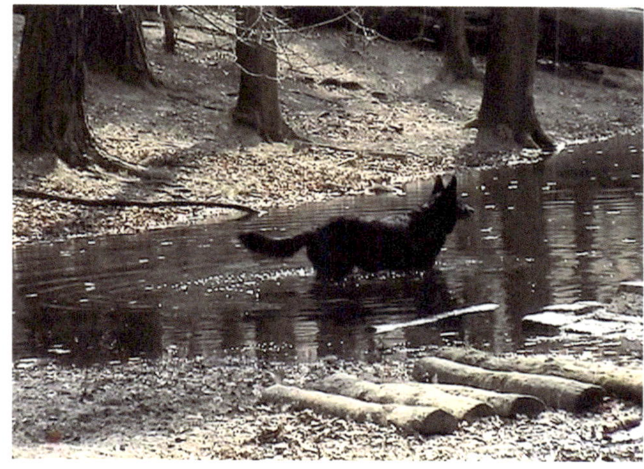

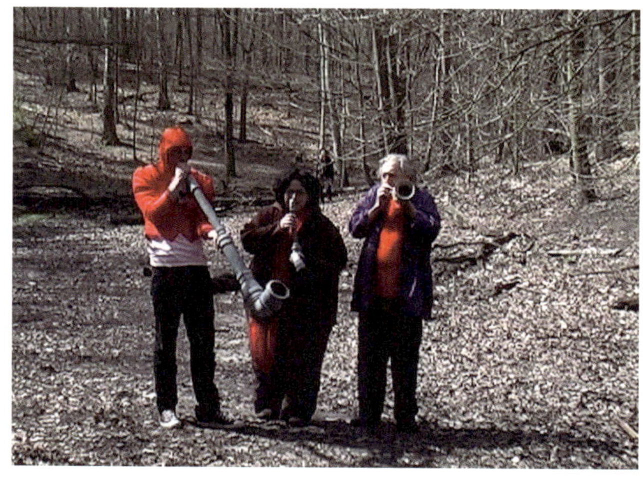

With Maria Thereza Alves, *Grunewald*, 2006. Digital video transferred to DVD, color, sound. 13:35 min.

CATEGORICAL REFUSAL: UNWINDING THE WOUND

JENNIFER A. GONZÁLEZ

France is an invention of Paris.
Jimmie Durham, "On the Edge of Town" (1992)

We live in a world of competitive naming. Colonial efforts to erase indigenous claims and solidify territorial rights have resulted in city names like New York, Los Angeles, and Johannesburg. Airports are named after presidents; streets are named after entrepreneurs; nations are named after explorers. So perhaps it should be no surprise that a wide variety of distinct peoples indigenous to the "Americas" are called "Indians." Although this is among the most ludicrous and tenacious of naming errors, the monikers "Indian" and "American Indian" adhere to so many important moments of political struggle, institutionalization, and group identification that their disappearance appears unthinkable, even if some people have longed for the disappearance of their referent.

As a thinker, maker, and writer, Jimmie Durham takes up the gauntlet that our material and linguistic world has thrown down. He resists living with things at face value; he rejects categorical imperatives in language. When many of us look at a wooden fence, we see a fence; Durham sees an oak tree, planted by settlers who brought its seeds from across the ocean, deracinated and divided into uniform parts and redistributed across the land. When many of us look at Notre-Dame Cathedral, we see a religious monument; Durham sees stone, extracted from the earth, carved, shaped, and culturally constrained in towering vertical rows. "Stone suffers from architectural weight," he observes, "the weight of metaphor and the weight of history."[1] Paris, beautiful Paris, is also an elaborate graveyard of ivory-colored rock that once was at home in the earth. Just as our physical infrastructure is a literal carving up and redistribution of our material world, so language is a carving up and redistribution of thought across the continuous manifold that is reality. Language is the fluid, mercurial, and barbed-wire limit of that reality, the silver-tongued knife slice, the finely measured frame of meaning. Words such as *nation*, *race*, *culture*, *nature*, *animal*, and *aesthetics* have done a great deal of semiotic labor over the centuries, as well as a great deal of social damage.[2] If words like *nation* and *race* have produced (and continue to produce) artificial and hierarchical separations in the continuity of humanity, we might ask: Are some words crimes? Do some words leave wounds on the world?

In his 2014 essay "Silly Crimes of the Academicians," Durham recounts how scholars, museum curators, critics, and the art market are guilty of such linguistic misdeeds.[3] Looking back to the early 1990s, when his work was beginning to be shown widely, he points to the way the art world pigeonholed artworks according to rubrics of race or ethnicity—euphemistically creating the label "identity art" to encapsulate a diverse set of practices by artists outside of the white mainstream.[4] As a gesture of containment, this designation effectively limited the semantic scope of works that were seen to be culturally specific projects (e.g., "Indian"). As Durham points out, however, European artists had been representing European bodies and European "identity" for centuries—why was this not also considered identity art? He writes,

> It is certainly true that very many Native American artists have been making paintings of Native Americans. Similar, I suppose to paintings of guys like those by Chuck Close, Elizabeth Peyton, David Salle, David Hockney and others, but these artists are exempt from the charge of identity art.[5]

Indeed, the charge that "identity art is over" was flung, like an epithet, at Durham by a young white woman when she visited his New York studio in the early 1990s. Close to the time of the 1993 Whitney Biennial, in which artist Daniel Joseph Martinez distributed his wearable museum tags reading "I can't imagine ever wanting to be white," there might have been a defensive tone to her remark. Regardless, the comment was meant to define Durham as an artist making "identity art" and to indicate that his practice was passé. Such was the experience of many artists at the time, whose works were narrowly read in relation to a long-standing social taxonomy that linked the art object with the ethnic, gender, or sexual "identity" of its maker.[6] Critics frequently could not see past such categories to properly read the art.

What is immediately apparent in Durham's work, however, is the way it rewards close reading. In an early installation, *Bedia's First Basement* (1985; fig. 1), with what seems to be a tongue-in-cheek reference to contemporary Cuban artist José Bedia, Durham transformed the basement of the building housing 22 Wooster Gallery, in SoHo, into an archaeological dig.[7] A basement is a socially and culturally constructed domain of containment, an architectural device for keeping the earth out, for enclosing bodies and things underground. It serves as the final bulwark against the earth's encroachment, yet it is simultaneously a part of the earth, a crypt. In *Bedia's First Basement*, Durham filled a two-foot plot of fresh earth, surrounded by a border of found bricks, with small artifacts such as cowrie shells, broken pottery shards with Native American motifs, bullet casings, cigarette butts, buttons, beads, and the bones of small animals, all laid out in a careful pattern as if recently exposed by the archaeologist's brush. Elsewhere, circles of earth contained sculptural gatherings of horse and deer bones, a hawk skull, and bird wings enlivening simple stick figures that were nevertheless fixedly dead. Taken together, these material traces revealed a political moment in which pollution and violence met with natural elements and traditions in a collective burial of late twentieth-century modernism and indigenous history.

Affixed to the wall was a typewritten, one-page text that told a layered story of the past from the perspective of an imagined future in the year 3006. Its playful parody of labels found in museums or heritage sites invites us to ponder how our present will be legible to an alternative future in which the "Sir Walter Raleigh Tobacco and Firearms Corp." and the "John Jacob Astor Animal Skinning Company" are the sponsors of the investigation leading to the discovery of the First Basement, supposedly built to imprison "Chief Injun Joe," the "last" Indian in Manhattan, who later used the basement as his apartment and place of worship. Another wall text, this one written by hand, attracted attention with large letters reading "Of Special Interest" and purported to give details about the ancient inhabitant's drum and bed:

> His Drum: Why is his drum so small? The last Indian in Manhattan wanted to be civilized, and take his place in society, but he did not want to go "cold turkey," so every few months he would get a smaller drum, and would sing shorter songs.
>
> His Bed: Why is his bed so small? Lo, the poor little Indian was so poor he had to buy it at a ½ off sale.

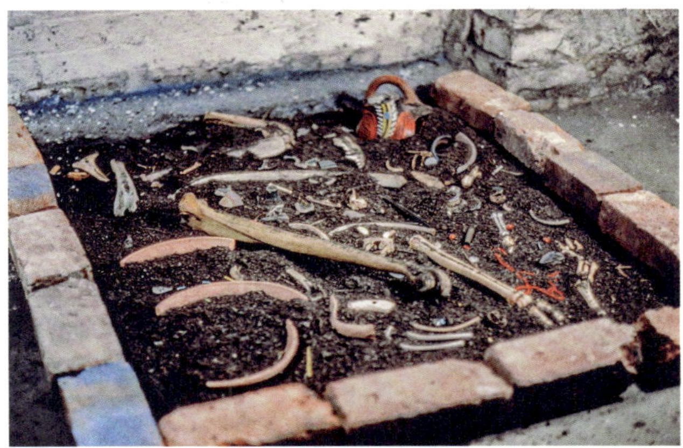

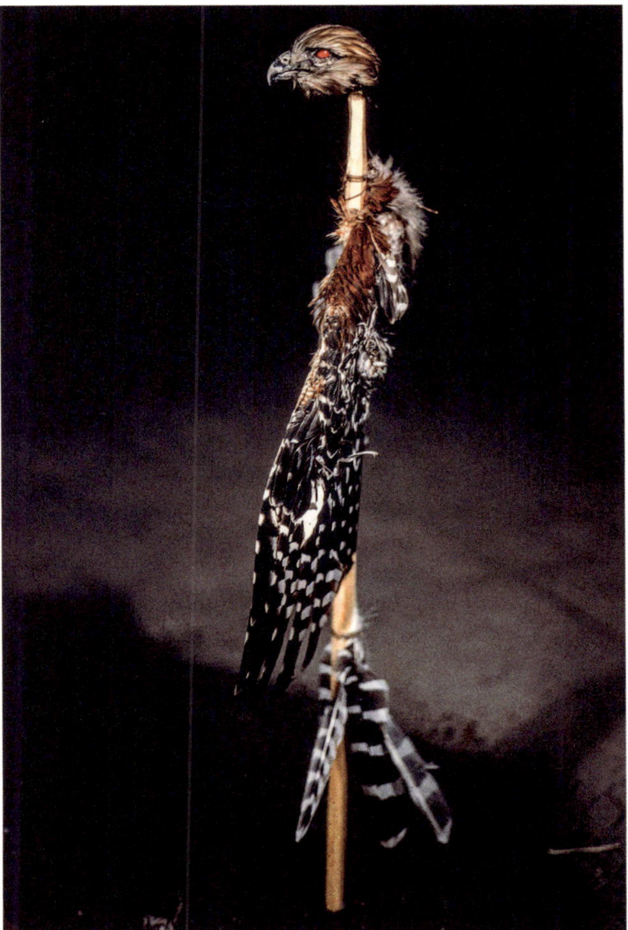

Fig. 1. *Bedia's First Basement*, installation views, 22 Wooster Gallery, New York, 1985.

Durham's apparent humor reminds us not to take the installation too seriously, not to read the sculptural objects as a form of nouveau shamanism, and yet it also references the long history of racist Indian jokes that are not so funny and the dire economic conditions that many indigenous Americans face. Pinned to the wall opposite was a cutout magazine advertisement for General Dynamics detailing the military manufacturer's employment relationship with the Navajo, which included an image of the Navajo chief looking off into the distance like an Edward S. Curtis portrait under the headline: "The last thing he wants is a

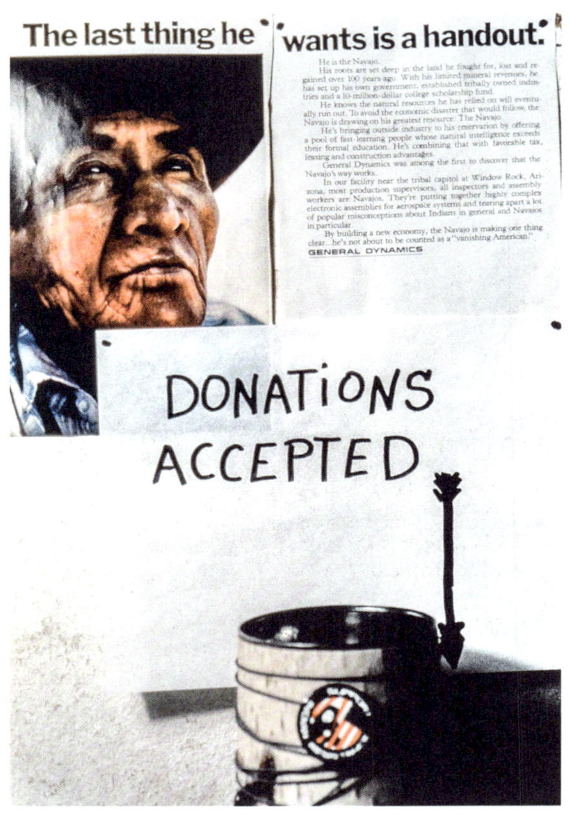

Fig. 2. *Donations Accepted*, 1985. Collage. Dimensions unknown. Installation view, *Bedia's First Basement*, 22 Wooster Gallery, New York, 1985.

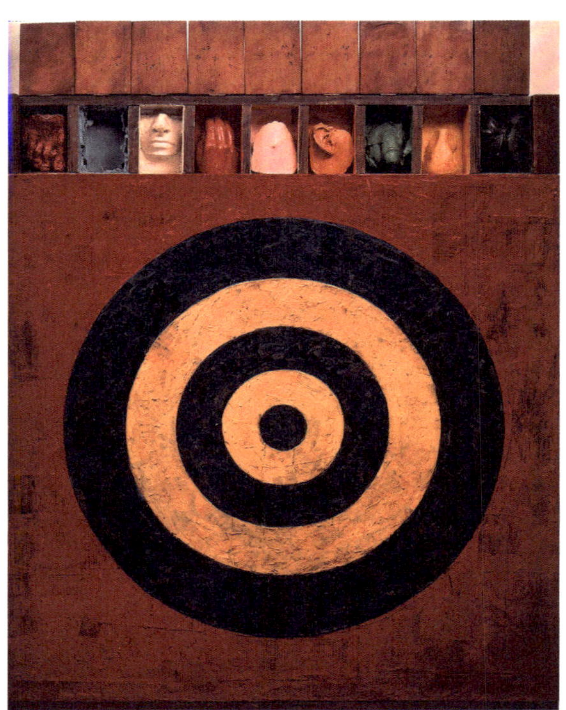

Fig. 3. Jasper Johns, *Target with Plaster Casts*, 1955. Encaustic and collage on canvas with objects. 51 × 44 in. (129.5 × 111.8 cm). Collection of David Geffen, Los Angeles.

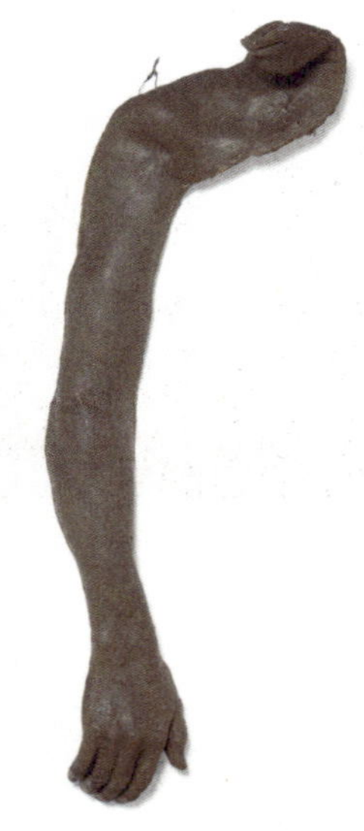

Fig. 4. Bruce Nauman, *From Hand to Mouth*, 1967. Wax over cloth. 28 × 10 ⅜ × 4 ⅜ in. (71.1 × 26.4 × 11.1 cm). Courtesy of Sperone Westwater, New York.

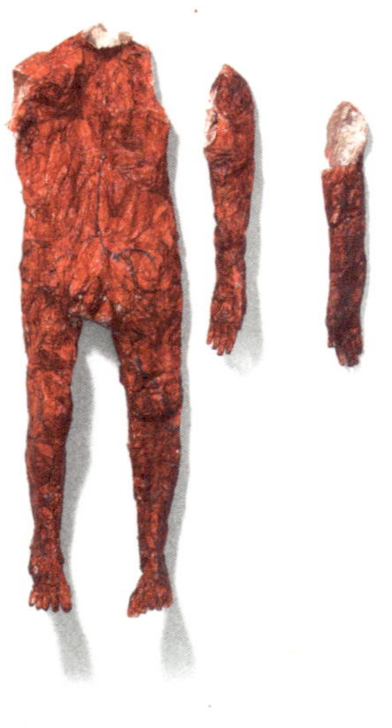

Fig. 5. Kiki Smith, *Untitled (Red Man)*, 1991. Ink on Gampi paper in four parts. Dimensions variable. The Broad Art Foundation.

handout." Below, Durham put another sign reading "Donations Accepted" with an arrow pointing to an empty can (fig. 2).

Irreverent, rhetorically ludic contradictions and oppositions productively operate throughout Durham's works, not only in the early years but also in an ongoing and self-referential way. *Bedia's First Basement* offered viewers not a simple "Indian identity" but a layered interrogation of US history, archaeology, architecture, memory, economic disempowerment, and survival, while also confirming Durham's commitment to a combinatory practice in which words become a central sculptural element. "I realize that I have never made a separation between writing and making sculptures," he recently commented.[8] With the uncomfortable poetics of the surrealists, or the materialist alchemies of Joseph Beuys, Durham's sculptures are conjoined artifacts that live in the limbo of their incompatibility, in their forced mating. "The word in Cherokee that is used for 'carpenter' means a 'fixer,'" Durham writes, "someone who joins things together in a clever fashion. The word is also used colloquially to mean a married couple. And also to mean a poet—someone who joins words together."[9]

Written on the body, words can also start to unravel the very idea of subjectivity as internally coherent. Durham's *Self-portrait* (1986; page 56)—first exhibited in the group show *Self-Portrait* at Kenkeleba Gallery in the East Village—becomes an exercise in revealing the curiosity, projection, and fascination of others as much as his own secrets. Durham's life-size canvas cutout is embellished with handwritten texts indicating such characteristics as "appendix scar," "hands are small, sensitive," and (written on the leg) "I have a crooked back." The head and brightly painted genitals in carved wood are the primary three-dimensional elements and may make reference to Jasper Johns's cast objects, for example *Target with Plaster Casts* (1955; fig. 3). Durham's drooping, suspended body made of reddish-brown painted canvas—"My skin is not actually this dark . . ."—echoes the sculptures of both Bruce Nauman and Kiki Smith (figs. 4, 5). Durham engages historical and contemporary sculptural references while simultaneously pursuing questions of American Indian authenticity and stereotype. Significantly, the body is excessively *overwritten* by the improbable combination of intimate revelations and cultural mythologies.

Self-portrait appeared again in an installation titled *The Bishop's Moose and the Pinkerton Men* (1989),[10] which included a drawing on stretched cloth titled *The Testament According to John* (1989; page 94) showing what appears to be a phallic cannon with testicles (whose etymological root is very close to that of *testament*) from which a stream of Scripture bursts forth: "In the beginning was the word. And the word was with God. And the word was God." Here "the word"—as a dominating force that seems to carry its own momentum in the colonizing project of the Americas—is decoupled from its strictly biblical reference and becomes all-powerful as a form of enunciation.[11] The drawing furthermore invites us to read words differently in the rest of the installation. For example, *Section 8 of the 1986 Pinkerton's Agency Manual* (1989; fig. 6), a work on poster board, includes large scrawled words: "Wounds: a wound is a break in the skin. Wounds are subject to infection and bleeding." The original Pinkerton's National Detective Agency, founded in 1850, was active especially between 1866 and 1892 as a hired antiunion strikebreaking organization. Both John D. Rockefeller and Andrew Carnegie, major figures in the art world

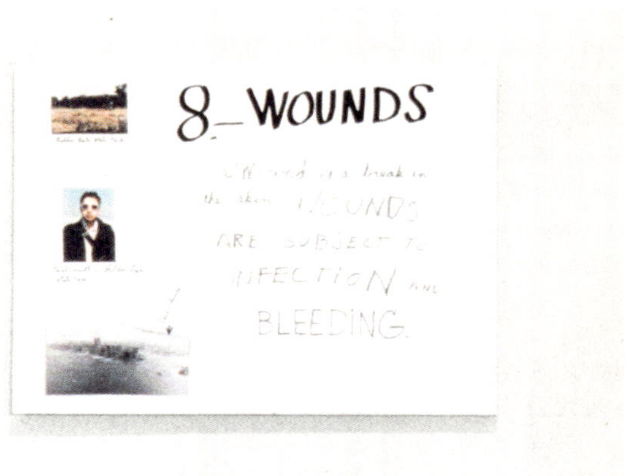

Fig. 6. *Section 8 of the 1986 Pinkerton's Agency Manual*, 1989. Photograph, drawing, and mixed media on canvas. 22 ¾ × 30 ¼ in. (57.6 × 76.8 cm). Installation view, *The Bishop's Moose and the Pinkerton Men*, Exit Art, New York, 1989.

who amassed collections and founded major museums, used Pinkerton's agency to break up union strikes in their coal and steel industries. In Durham's piece, three photographs have been placed like a kind of visual footnote on the left side of the poster, respectively captioned: 1) Golden Gate State Park; 2) Paul [Chaat] Smith in Golden Gate State Park; and 3) Paul's House. For those who feel like investigating, it is possible to learn that Smith's 1992 essay "Every Picture Tells a Story" begins with an account of Ishi, the "last" Yahi Indian who was brought to Golden Gate Park to see an airplane fly.[12] "Every Picture Tells a Story" develops into a thoughtful analysis of photography's role in Smith's extended Comanche family and in the general history of photographic and film representations of Indians in the United States.[13] Suddenly the wound and its bleeding have a second set of connotations. Durham's couplings are not, or not only, materialist puns but can also be seen as tools or devices that cross cultural, historical, and ontological divides, a fertile concatenation of grammars in which each element has its semantic role to play.

In the 1993 Whitney Biennial, for example, the artist presented a series of small sculptures resembling makeshift weapons from a lost time (fig. 7); the display was clearly reminiscent of Claes Oldenburg's *Ray Gun Wing* of the 1970s (fig. 8), but the objects felt more homegrown and carefully crafted. Each small artifact combined found elements made of metal (sometimes parts of actual guns), electronic parts such as camera lenses

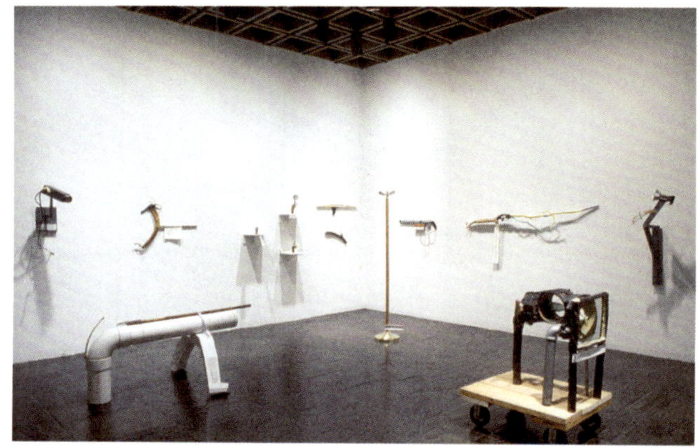

Fig. 7. View of Durham's installation, 1993 Whitney Biennial, New York.

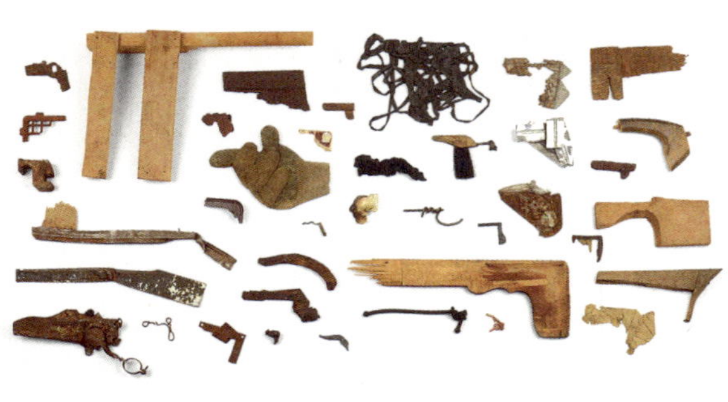

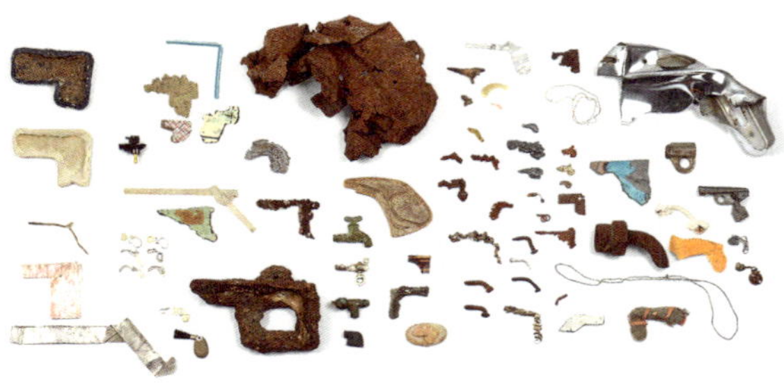

Fig. 8. Claes Oldenburg, *Mouse Museum, Ray Gun Wing, Vitrine V* (top), and *Mouse Museum, Ray Gun Wing, Vitrine VI* (bottom), 1977. Mixed media. Dimensions variable. Museum moderner Kunst Stiftung Ludwig, Vienna.

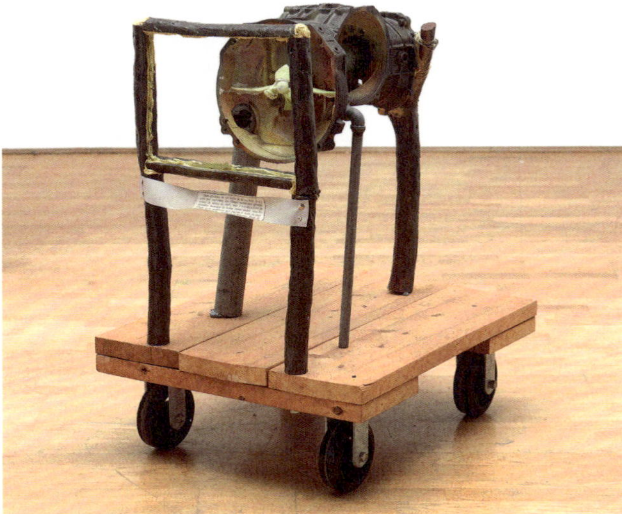

Fig. 9. *Dans plusieurs de ces forêts et de ces bois, il n'y avait pas seulement des villages souterrains groupés autours du terrier du chef, mais il y avait encore de véritables hameaux de huttes basses cachés sous les arbres, et si nombreux que parfois la forêt en était remplie. Souvent les fumées les trahissaient. Deux de . . .*, 1993. Aluminium machinery part, wooden planks, tree branches, caster wheels, Coca-Cola bottle, bone, galvanized steel, glass, and other materials. 38 ⅛ × 30 ⅜ × 26 in. (97 × 77 × 66 cm). Tate, Purchased with funds provided by the 2010 Outset/Frieze Art Fair Fund to benefit the Tate Collection, 2010.

or lightbulbs, animal bones and carved wooden parts, string, and bits of wood putty as well as text, sometimes attached as a label or integrated into the very structure of the object as a linguistic interruption. The most explicit version of the latter appears when the artist separates the trigger from the barrel of a gun using a curved wooden brace to which a small canvas with the words "I forgot what I was going to say" is attached with a wooden dowel. The installation was among the more publicized of Durham's works at the time, and its understated historical references allowed it to escape some of the vitriolic criticism that targeted the politically activist nature of other artworks in the biennial.[14] But most critics did not analyze, for example, the beautifully spare carving of a horned toad lizard in the center of the wooden brace in *I Forgot What I Was Going to Say* (page 128), or wonder what its talismanic pause between forgetting and remembering might signify. How does wood interrupt steel? How can a gun forget to speak? Who is going to pull the trigger, and what is stopping them? On another wall, a long musket-shaped branch with a bottle-cap muzzle and window-crank cocking device appeared with a phrase, in Latin, from Virgil's Aeneid: *Tu ne cede malis, sed contra audentior ito* (Yield not to misfortunes, but advance all the more boldly against them) (page 129). Glued onto another wood and metal specimen was a small bit of paper with the text ". . . mishaps in the jungle. The rest of them were mostly Indians, tough young fellows with wiry strength and impassive faces." And on a leather tag attached to a handgun-sized artifact with a bone handle and pointed wooden muzzle was the following text:

> The Sioux Indians occupy and claim nearly all the lands from above latitude of about 43° from the Mississippi to the Rocky Mountains. They are numerous, powerful and entirely savage. The railroad would drive the savage Sioux and their buffalo North and we can then succeed in bringing the removed and small tribes to habits of industry and civilization.
> —Asa Whitney

Of course, Asa Whitney (1791–1874), a wealthy merchant and transcontinental railroad promoter, was a member of the same New York family as Gertrude Vanderbilt Whitney (1875–1942), founder of the Whitney Museum of American Art. The railroad was probably among the most destructive technologies for northern plains people, who subsisted on the migration patterns of the buffalo. The artist's citation allows us to see how the railroad's inception had precisely this destruction, and not just financial gain, as its goal.

In addition to the gunlike objects, Durham included some other sculptures that looked like surveillance cameras or broadcast devices, implying that these too might be weapons with destructive power. Duchampian in character, these works have odd concatenations that suggest a mechanism without a machine. One object, looking like a television or radio console, consists of a framed rectangle of wood through which one might imagine sounds or images appearing via a sculptural device made up of a slingshot at the back (sender), a Coca-Cola bottle in the center (transmitter), and a speaker-shaped aluminum machine part with a fan attached (output device) (fig. 9). Tacked like a caption under what might be the rectangular "screen" area is a piece of cloth printed with French text from Victor Hugo's novel *Ninety-Three* (1874):

Dans plusieurs de ces forêts et de ces bois, il n'y avait pas seulement des villages souterrains groupés autours du terrier du chef, mais il y avait encore de véritables hameaux de huttes basses cachés sous les arbres, et si nombreux que parfois la forêt en était remplie. Souvent les fumeés les trahissaient. Deux de . . .

(In many of these forests and woods, not only were there underground villages grouped around the chief's burrow, but also one could find true clusters of low-rise hamlets hidden under the trees, often so numerous that the forest could be full of them. Often smoke would betray their presence. Two of . . .)

Like the voice-over of an anthropological account, or an excerpt from an explorer's diary, Hugo's text is written from the perspective of an outsider, an invader. The novel's title echoes the year of the Whitney Biennial; its narrative is one of revolution and counterrevolution. Taken together, the objects in Durham's installation demonstrate how violence arrives and is perpetuated through the terms of European languages: English, Latin, and French. Stories told via the broadcast mouthpieces of modernity, phrases about impassive faces in fiction, encouragements in Latin, and capitalist plans for expansion and extermination become the real subject of the work.

Durham is nearly always site-specific in his choice of materials and references, explicitly indicating the institution, the city, or the infrastructure of his exhibition's location through carefully researched citations and locally gathered materials: stone, wood, bone, and metal. In this way, he explores the entanglements of culture, history, language, and materiality that create our present moment. These entanglements are complicated, layered, and embedded in our psyches and habits, the way plumbing and electrical cable networks are embedded in cities. Like so many veins and arteries, the material scaffolding that supports urban infrastructures requires a conceptual scaffolding to be sensible. "We know the world and communicate with the world basically through metaphor," writes Durham. "Language is metaphor. Civilisation sells the idea that its truth, its narrative, is literal and real, not metaphoric."[15] Civilization invites us to read a river or stream as a "resource," to see a tree as "timber," a man as an "Indian," and the dispossessed as the "stateless." Sometimes language wounds and must be disentangled, or *unwound*, from those referents held fast in its grip. Durham asks: "What, for example, if we had a world law against the buying and selling of land? If, as so many stateless peoples say, the earth is the earth and not a commodity?"[16]

Notes

1. Jimmie Durham, *Between the Furniture and the Building (Between a Rock and a Hard Place)* (Cologne: Verlag der Buchhandlung Walther König, 1999), 85.
2. For example, François Bernier's 1684 essay "A New Division of the Earth, according to the Different Species or Races of Men Who Inhabit It" reveals just how long Europeans have been interested in creating divisions among people and geographies, and draws our attention to the fact that the racialization of humans is inseparable from the carving up of the planet. Bernier, "Nouvelle division de la terre, par les differentes espèces ou races d'hommes qui l'habitent," *Journal des Sçavans* 12 (1684): 148–55; trans. T. Bendyshe (London, 1863–64).
3. Jimmie Durham, "Silly Crimes of the Academicians," unpublished essay; printed in the present volume, pages 254–55.
4. For further discussion see Jennifer González, "Introduction," in *Subject to Display: Reframing Race in Contemporary Installation Art* (Cambridge, MA: MIT Press, 2008), 11; and Joe Baker and Gerald McMaster, eds., *Remix: New Modernities in a Post-Indian World* (Washington, DC: National Museum of the American Indian; Phoenix: Heard Museum, 2007).
5. Durham, "Silly Crimes of the Academicians."
6. See Jean Fisher, "In Search of the 'Inauthentic': Disturbing Signs in Contemporary Native American Art," *Art Journal* 51, no. 3 (Fall 1992): 44–50.
7. As Durham recalls, the owner regularly had shows in the basement, though the gallery was upstairs. 22 Wooster later became Colin de Land's legendary gallery American Fine Arts.
8. Quoted in Daniel Kunitz, "Jimmie Durham," in *Modern Painters* 24, no. 8 (October 2012): 96.
9. Durham, *Between the Furniture and the Building*, 21–22.
10. For a rich discussion of this exhibition, see *Jimmie Durham: The Bishop's Moose and the Pinkerton Men*, ed. Jeanette Ingberman (New York: Exit Art, 1990).
11. The subtext that was handwritten on the lower half of the drawing reads: "When I brought this piece into the gallery Jeanette did not like it, and would not have it in the show. It seemed too empty to her, and perhaps nothing more than a hasty reference to the controversy around Andres Serrano's work or a sloppy reference to Twombly. (Jeanette and I did not speak for months and the ill-feeling has lasted to this day.) But Alfred Barr came in and was immediately caught by the piece. He convinced Charles Saatchi to buy it for the Museum. That was my first opportunity to be in a major collection—but then other collectors began looking at my work more seriously, and the rest is history." An apocryphal story perhaps?
12. The essay was first published in *Partial Recall: Photographs of Native North Americans*, ed. Lucy Lippard (New York: New Press, 1992).
13. Durham met Paul Chaat Smith when he returned to the United States to join the American Indian Movement, in which they worked closely together for several years. Smith is now an associate curator at the National Museum of the American Indian in Washington, DC.
14. See Luis Camnitzer, "The Whitney Biennial," *Third Text* 7, no. 23 (1993): 128–30; and Hal Foster et al., "The Politics of the Signifier: A Conversation on the Whitney Biennial," *October* 66 (Fall 1993): 3–27.
15. Jimmie Durham, "On the Edge of Town," in *A Certain Lack of Coherence: Writings on Art and Cultural Politics*, ed. Jean Fisher (London: Kala Press, 1993), 251.
16. Jimmie Durham, "Against Internationalism," *Third Text* 27, no. 1 (January 2013): 32.

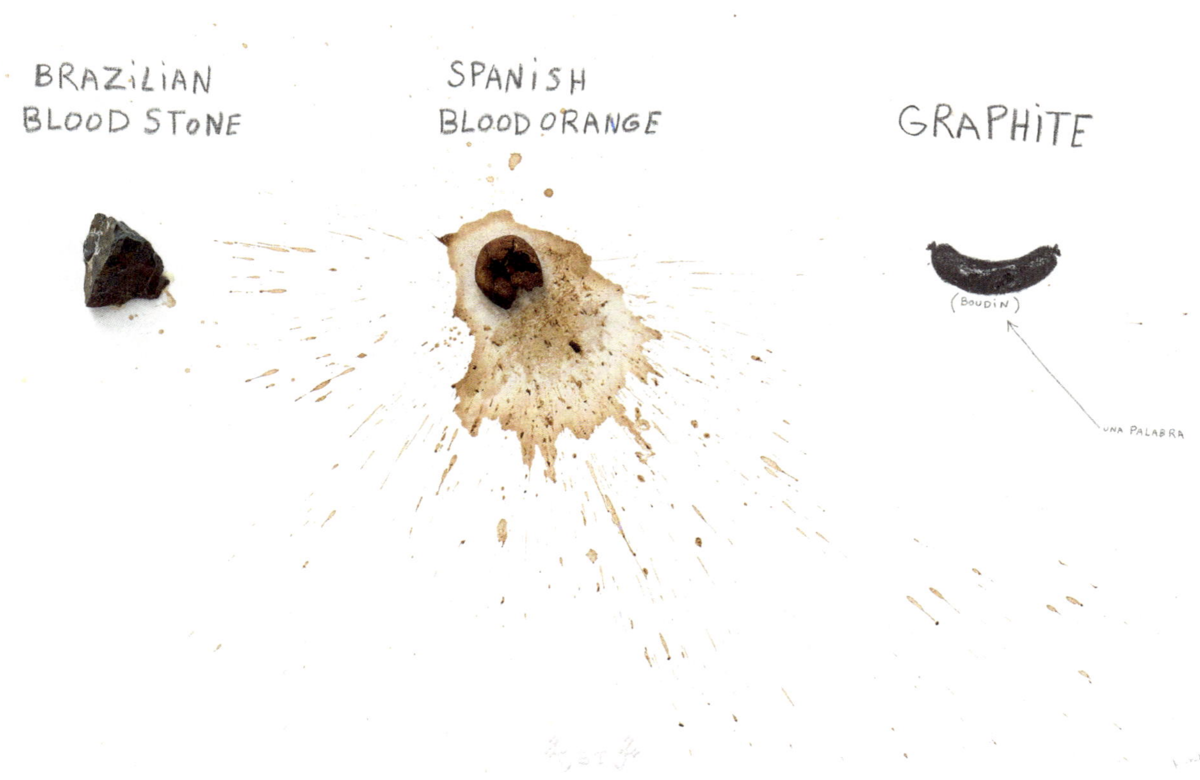

Brazilian Bloodstone, 1997. Brazilian bloodstone, orange, graphite, acrylic paint on wood panel. 32 ⅝ × 47 ¼ × 2 ¾ in. (83 × 110 × 7 cm).

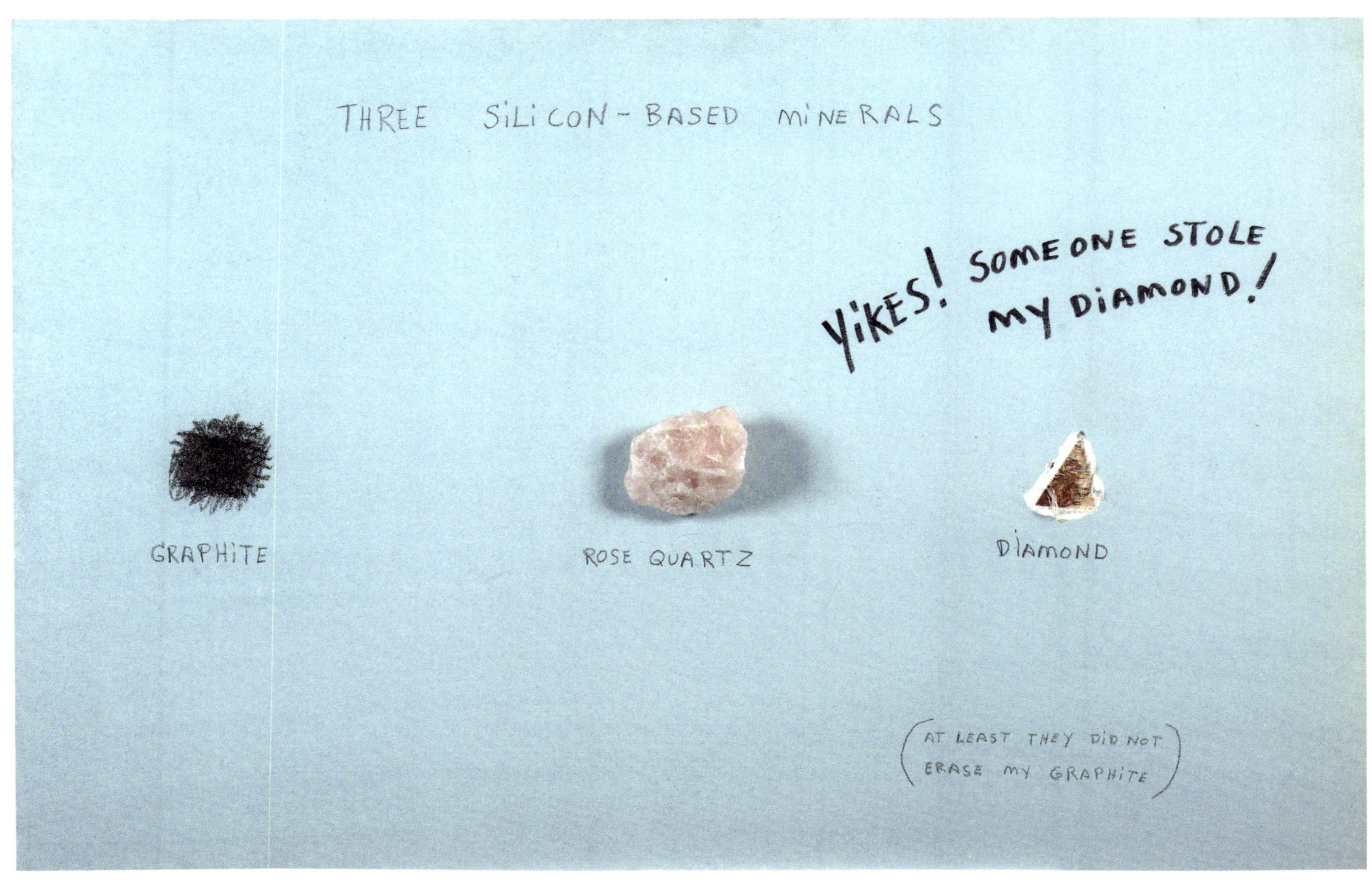

Someone Stole my Diamond, 1998. Rose quartz, acrylic paint, graphite, ink on wood panel. 32 ¼ × 49 ¼ × 2 ¾ in. (82 × 125 × 7 cm).

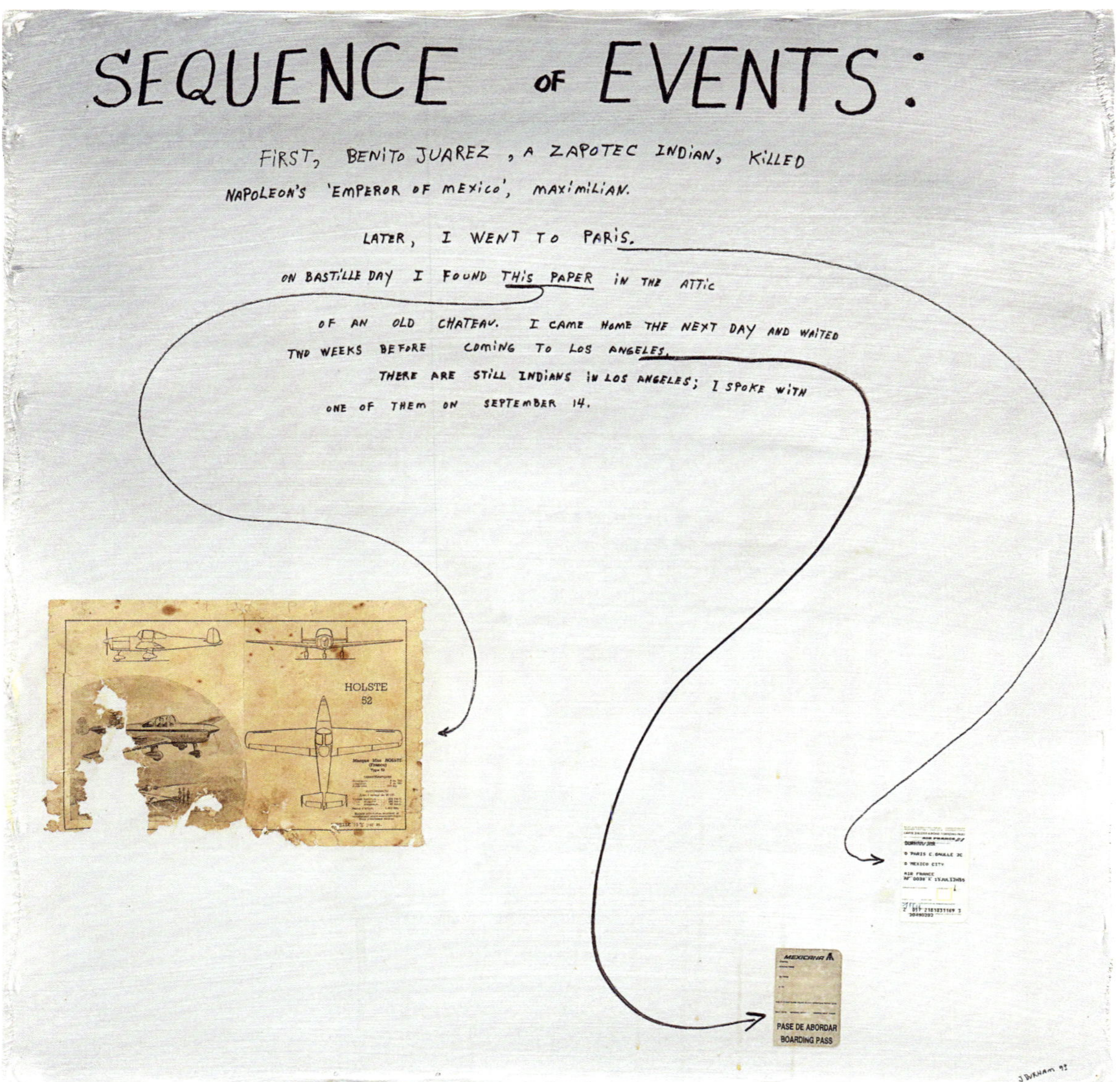

Sequence of Events, 1993. Acrylic paint and collage on wood panel. 36 ¼ × 36 ¼ in. (92 × 92 cm).

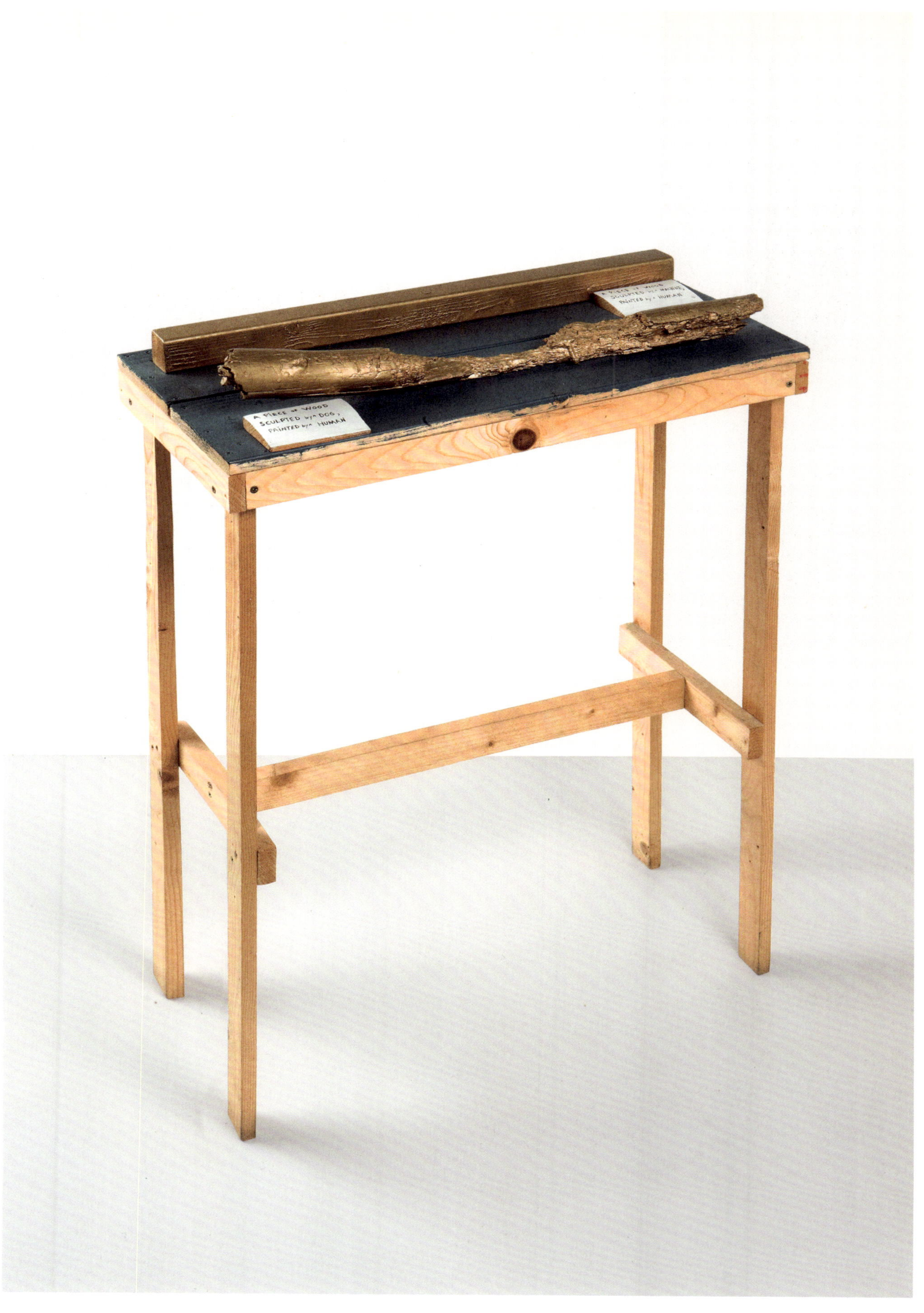

Hommage à Filliou (A Piece of Wood Sculpted by a Dog, Painted by a Human. A Piece of Wood Sculpted by a Machine, Painted by a Human), 2003.
Pine, purpurin dye, acrylic paint, ink. 39 ¾ × 29 ½ × 13 in. (100 × 75 × 33 cm).

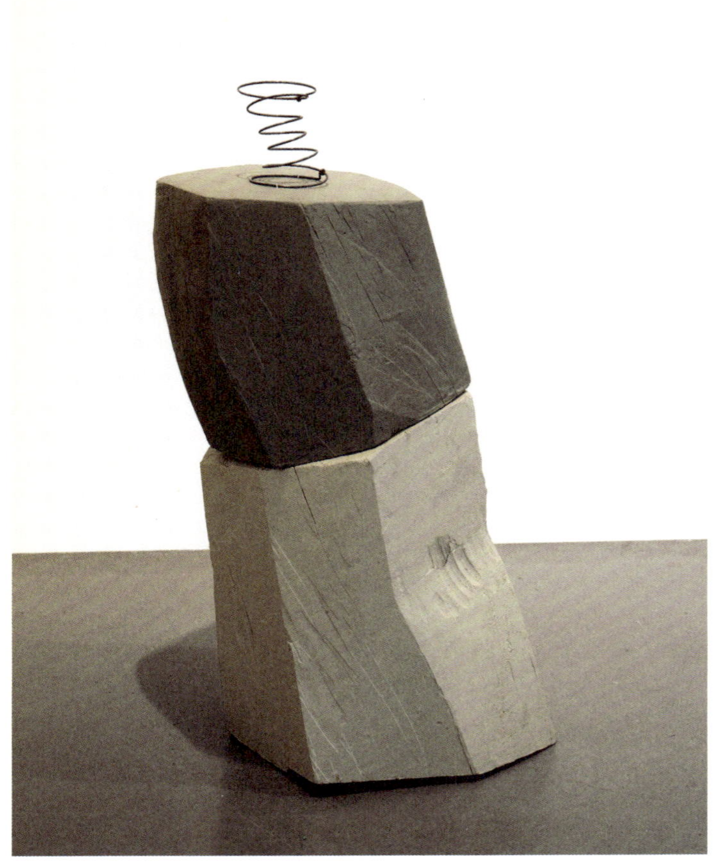

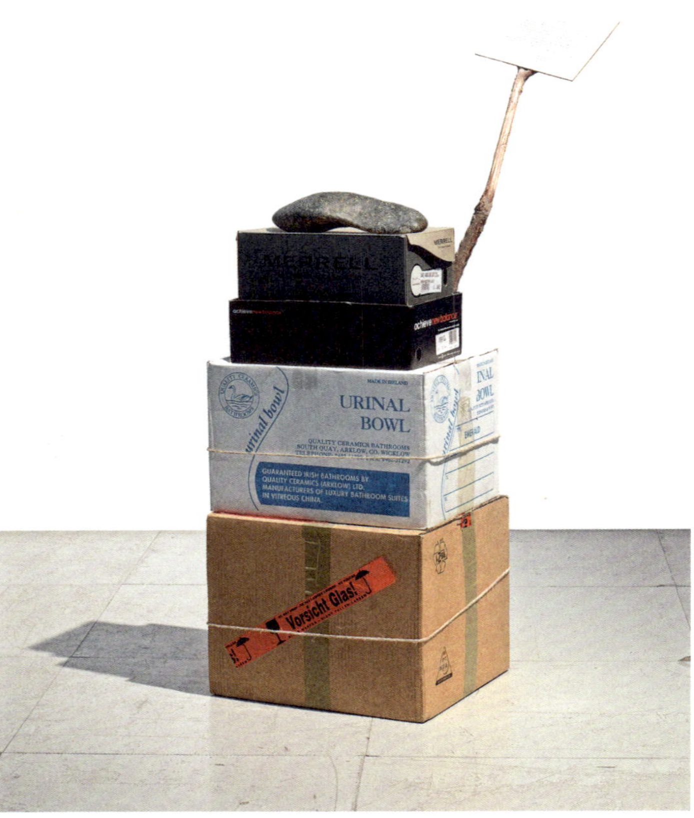

Left: *Homage to Constantin Brancusi #1*, 2007. Poplar, acrylic paint, bedspring from Alexander Calder's studio. 47 ¼ × 19 ⅝ × 19 ⅝ in. (120 × 50 × 50 cm).
Right: *Anti-Brancusi*, 2005. Cardboard, wood, serpentine stone, rope, ink on paper. 48 × 17 × 31 ⅛ in. (122 × 43 × 79 cm).

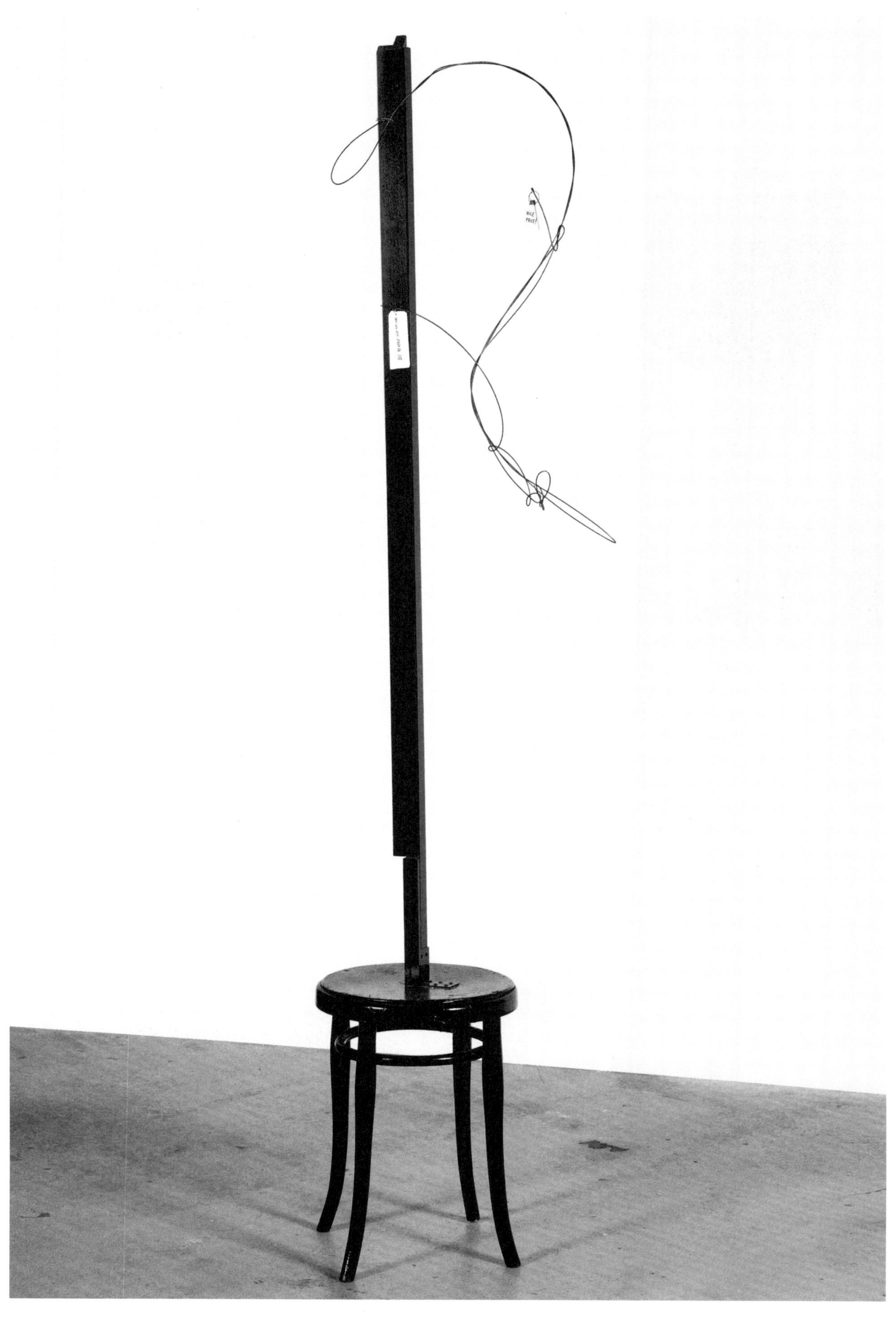

Homage to Alexander Calder, 2007. Wood, aluminum chair (with back removed), aluminum labels, acrylic paint, wire from Alexander Calder's studio.
84 5/8 × 33 × 13 3/4 in. (215 × 84 × 35 cm).

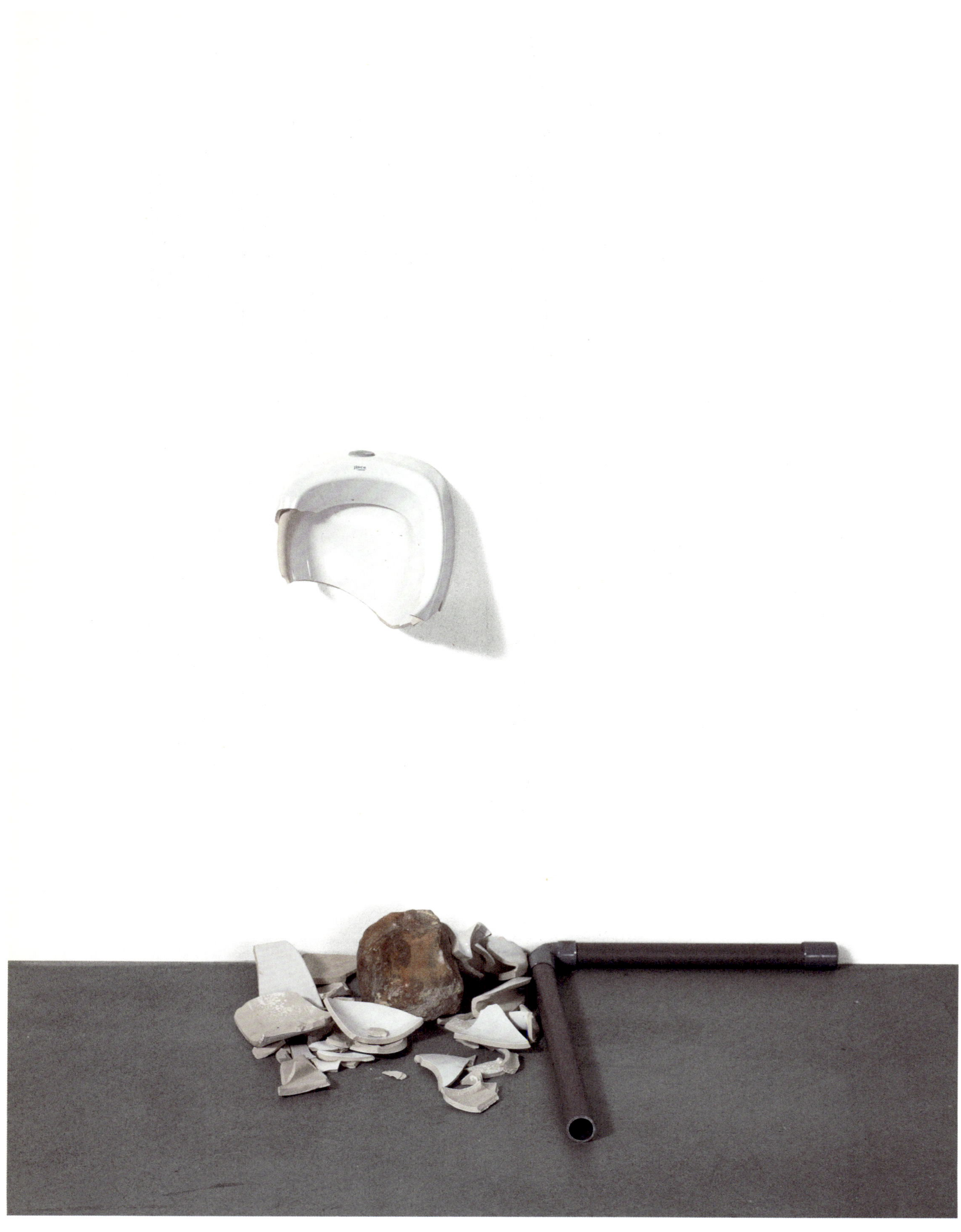

Homage to David Hammons, 1997. Porcelain, stone, PVC. Dimensions variable.

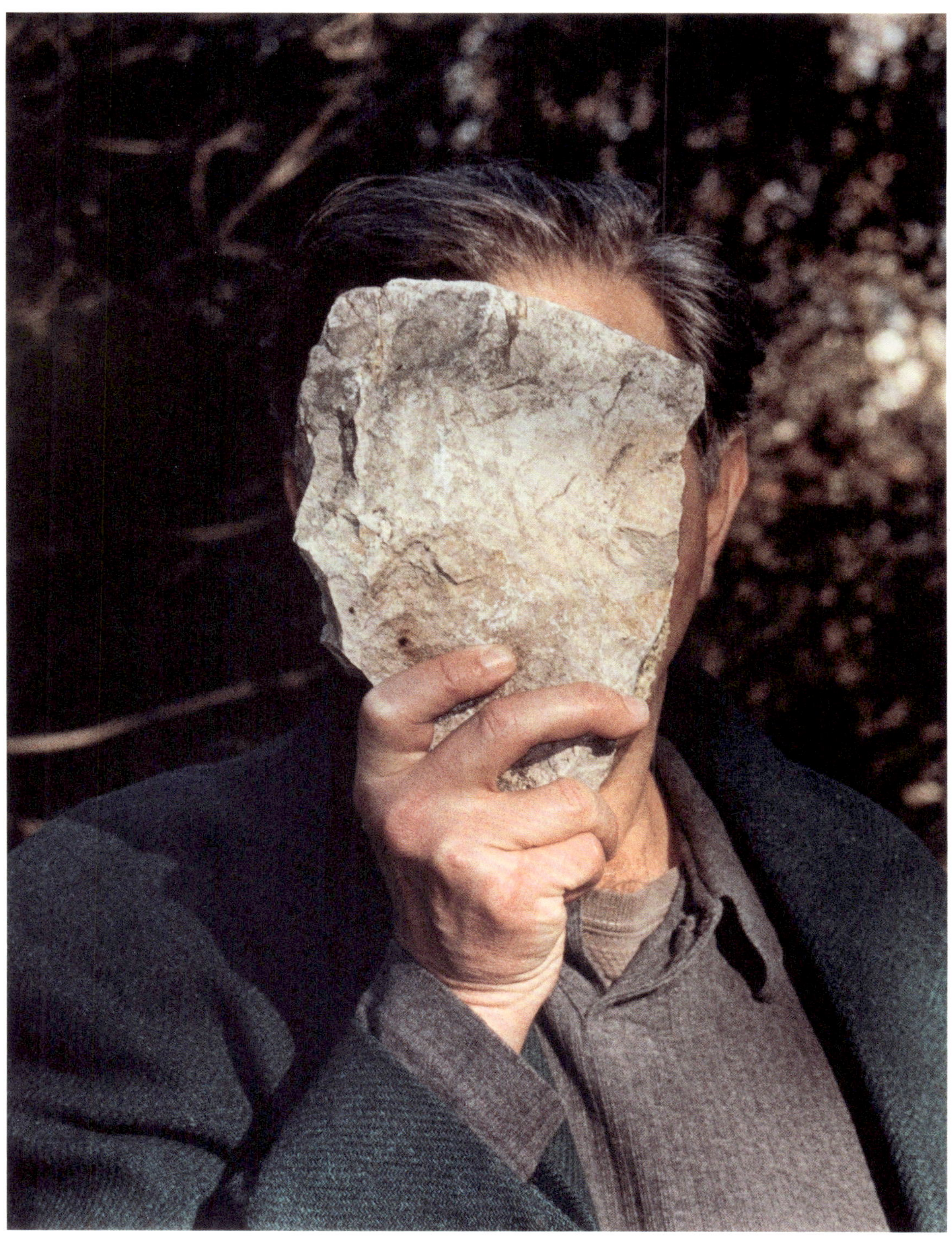

Self-Portrait Pretending to Be a Stone Statue of Myself, 2006. Color photograph. 31 ¾ × 24 in. (80.7 × 60.9 cm).

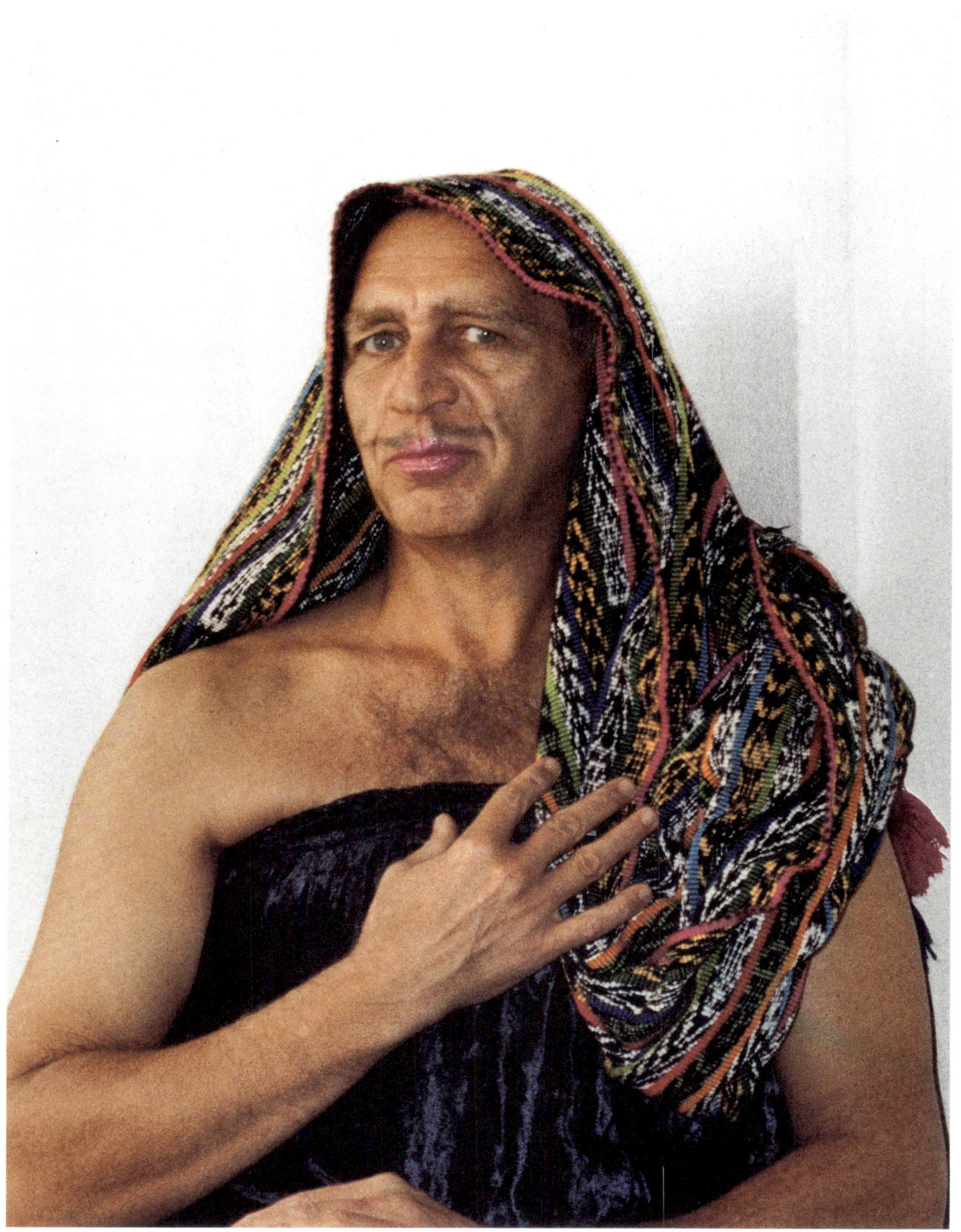

Self-Portrait pretending to be Rosa Levy, 1994. Color photograph. 32 × 24 in. (81.2 × 60.9 cm).

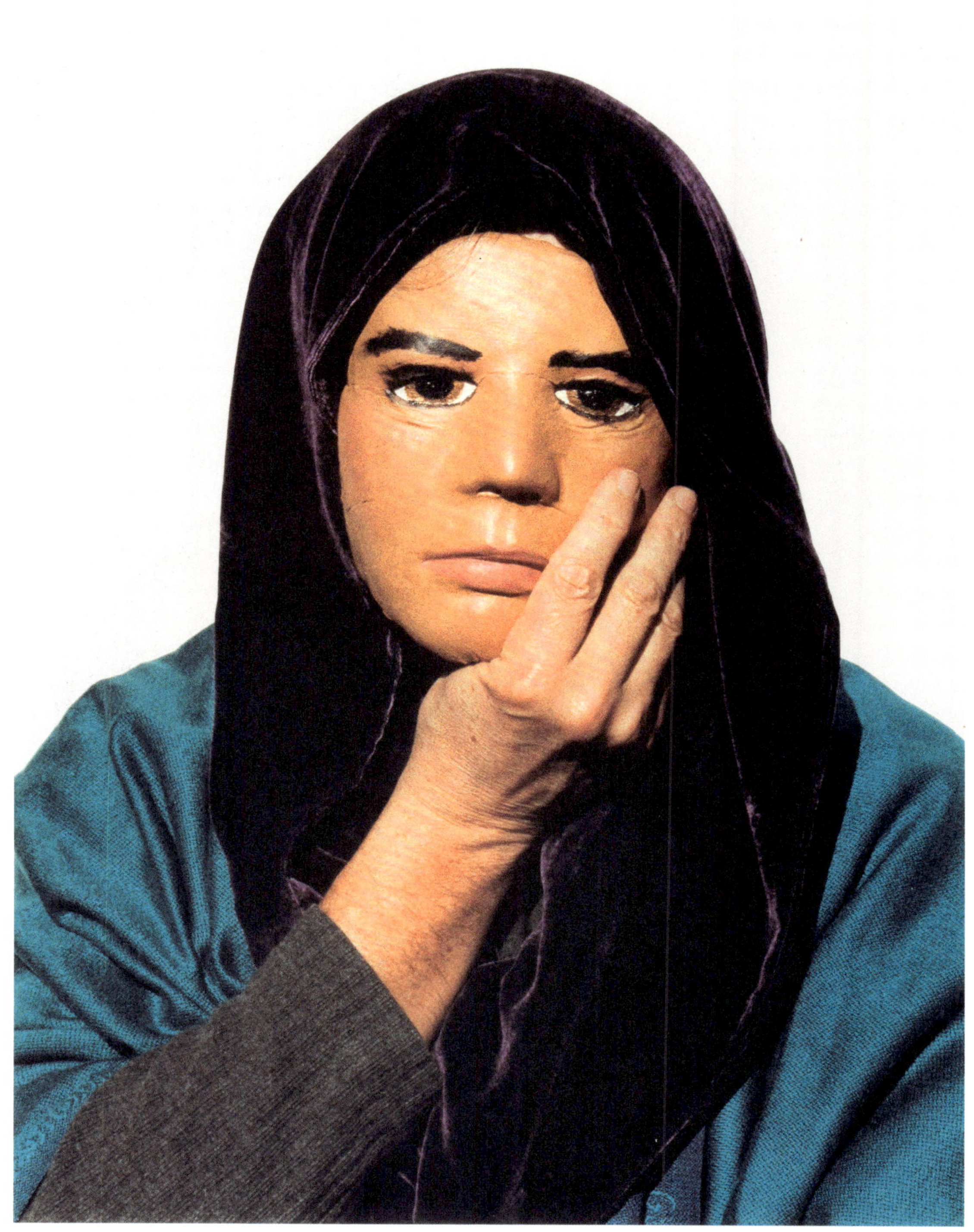

Self-Portrait Pretending to Be Maria Thereza Alves, 1995–2006. Color photograph. 32 × 24 in. (81.2 × 60.9 cm).

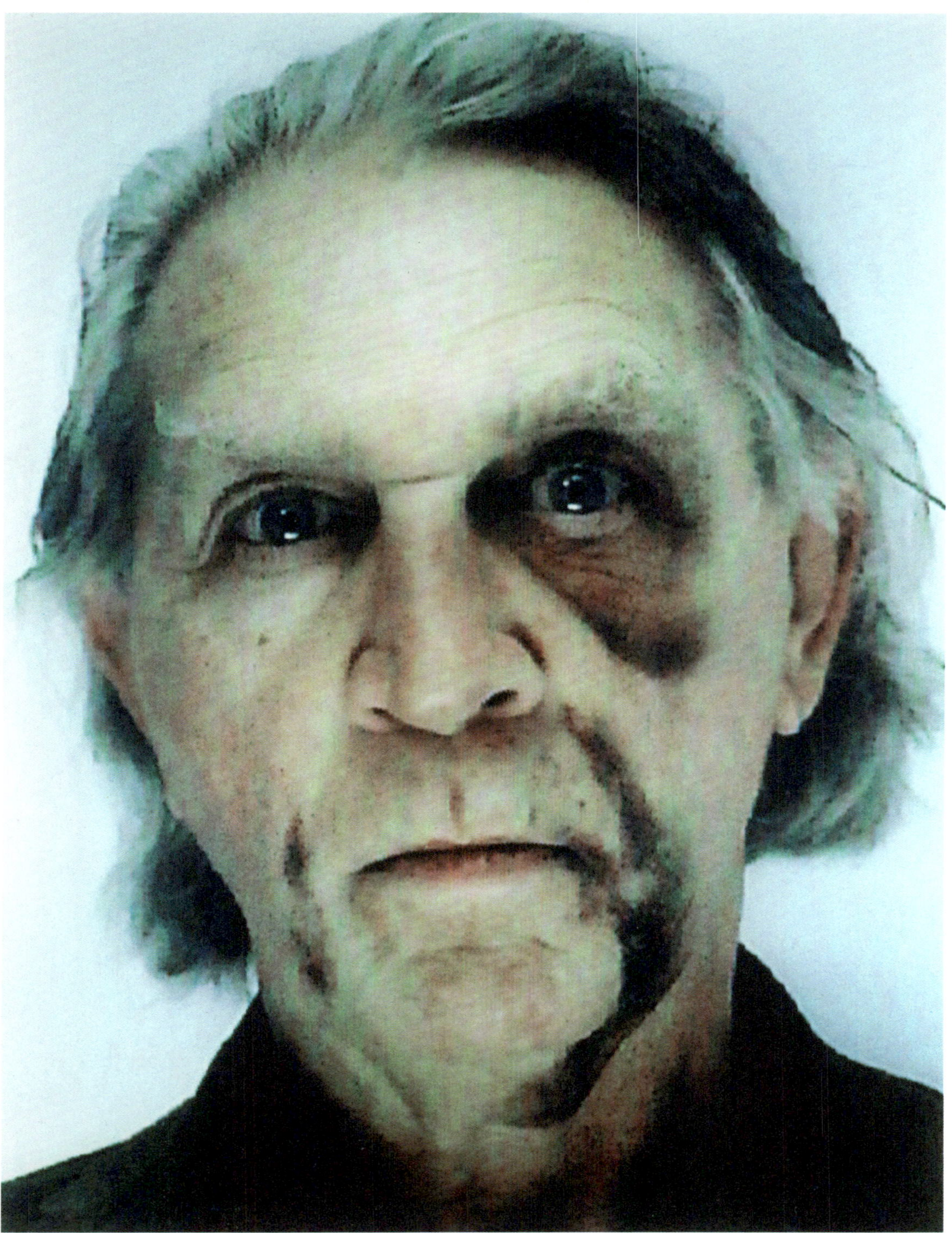

Self-Portrait with Black Eye and Bruises, 2006. Color photograph enlarged from photomaton print. 38 × 23 ½ in. (79 × 60 cm).

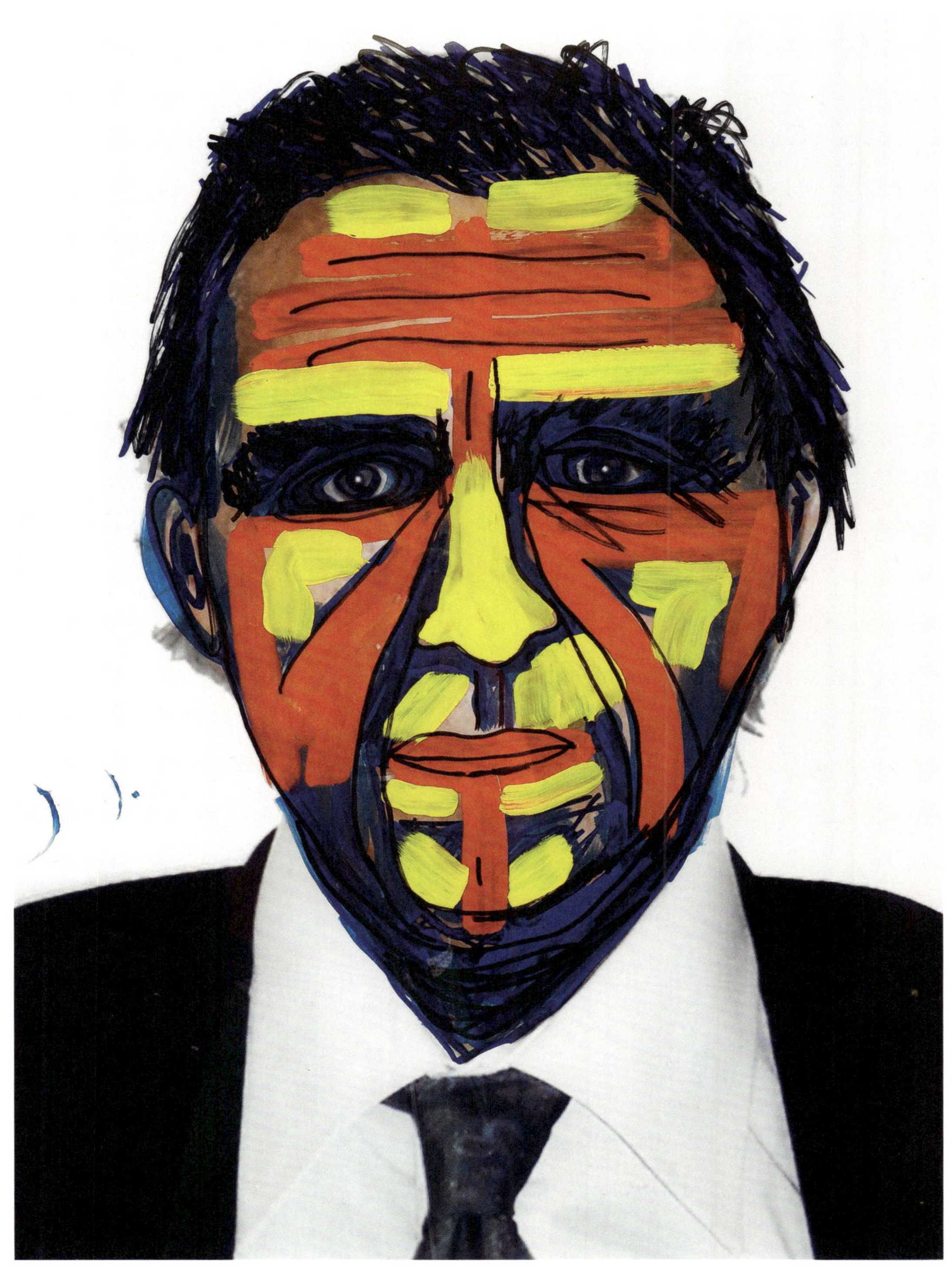

Painted Self-Portrait, 2007. Acrylic paint and marker on color photograph. 27 ½ × 23 in. (70 × 58 cm).

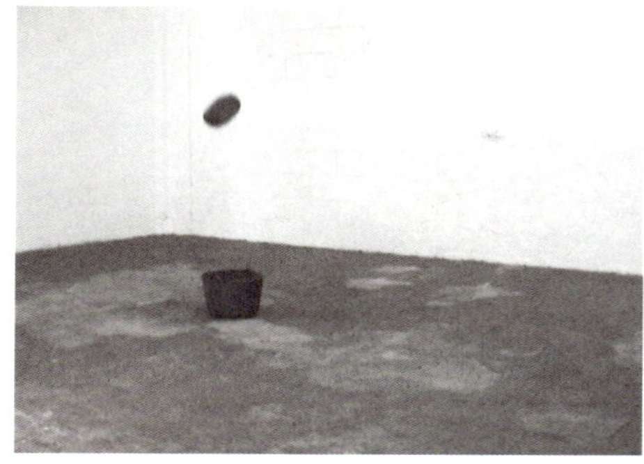
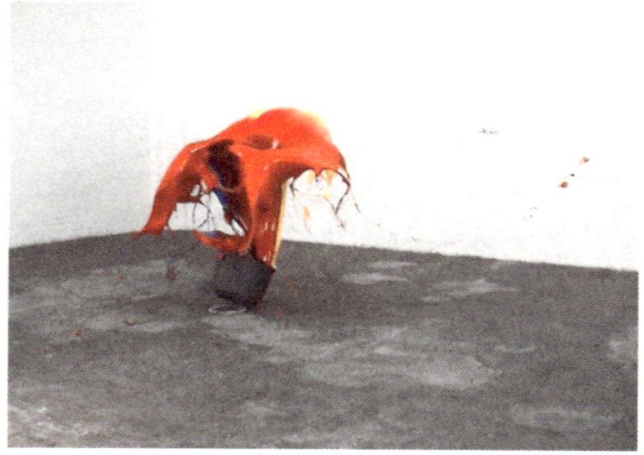
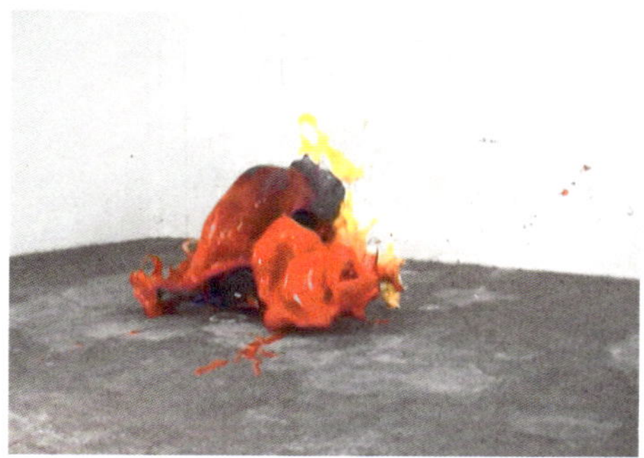
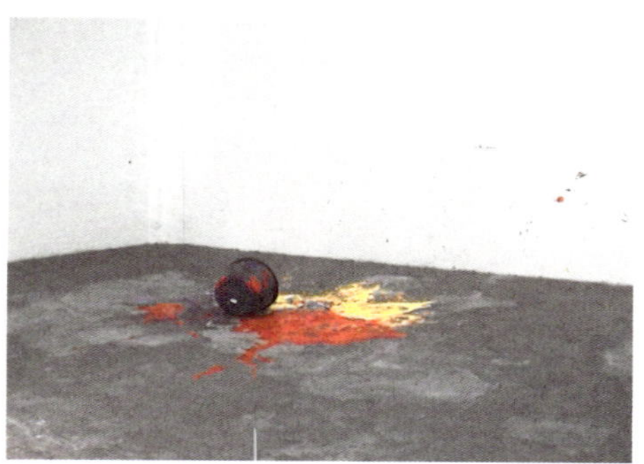
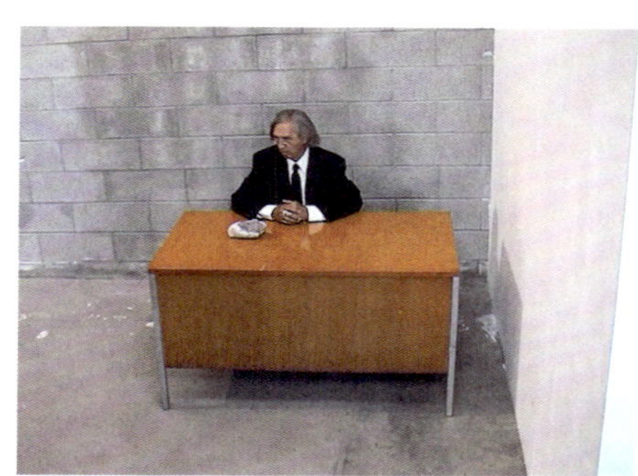
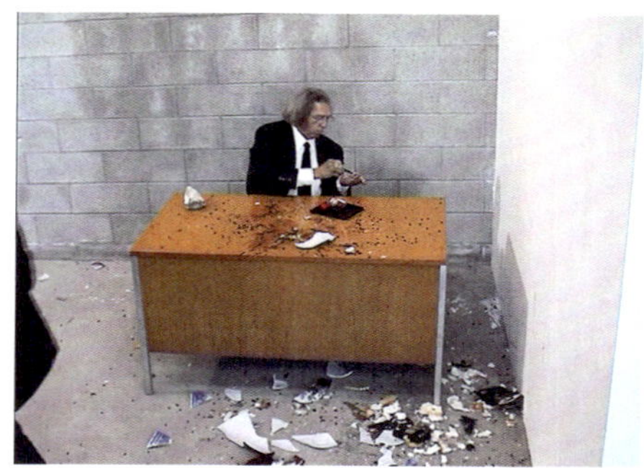
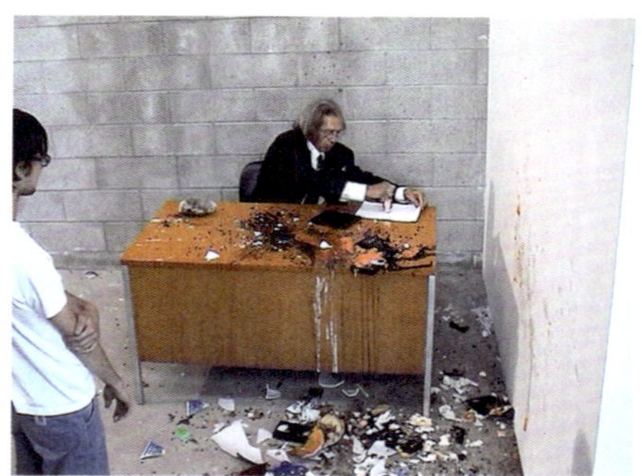
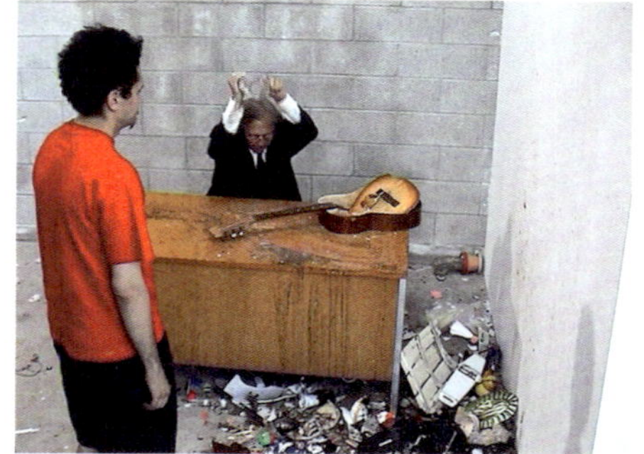

Top: *Fleur de Pas Mal*, 2005. Digital video, color, sound. 00:28 min. (loop).
Bottom: *Smashing*, 2004. Digital video, color, sound. 1:31:54 min.

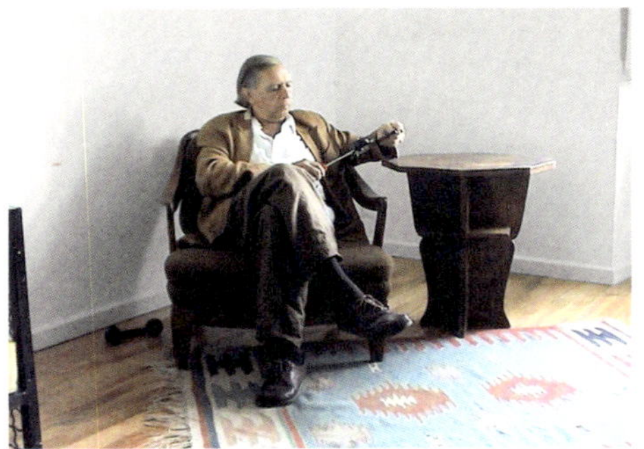
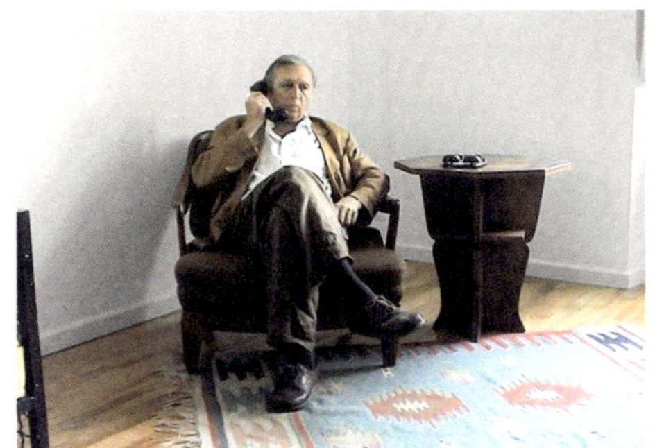
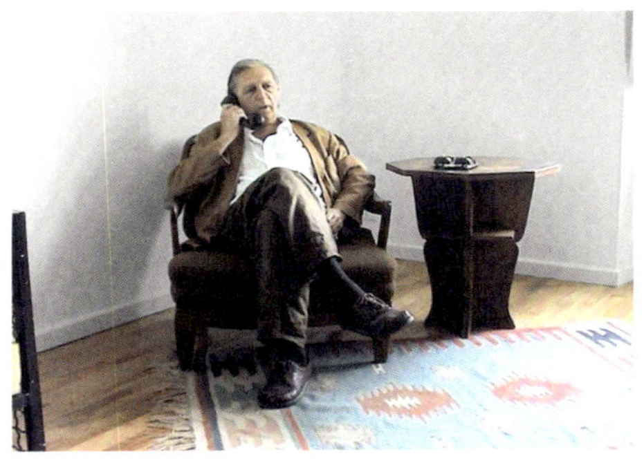
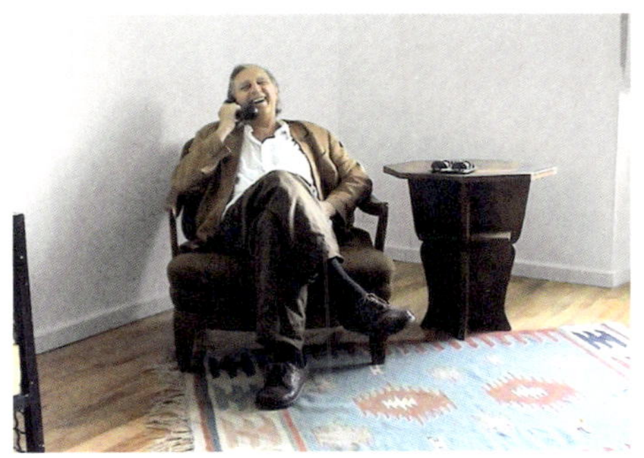
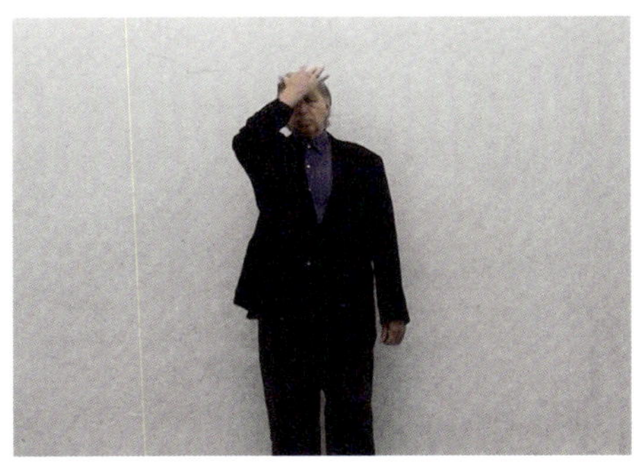
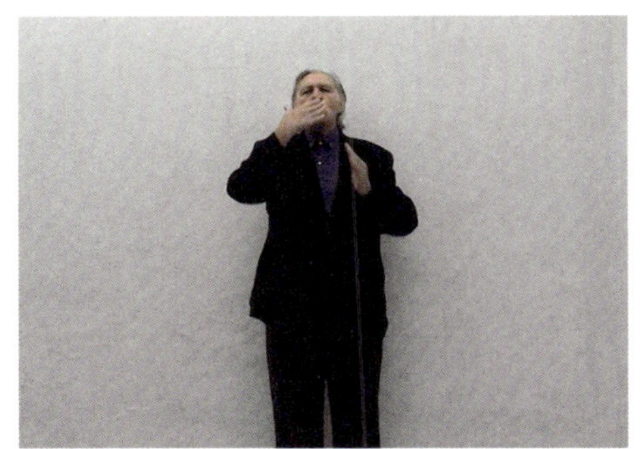
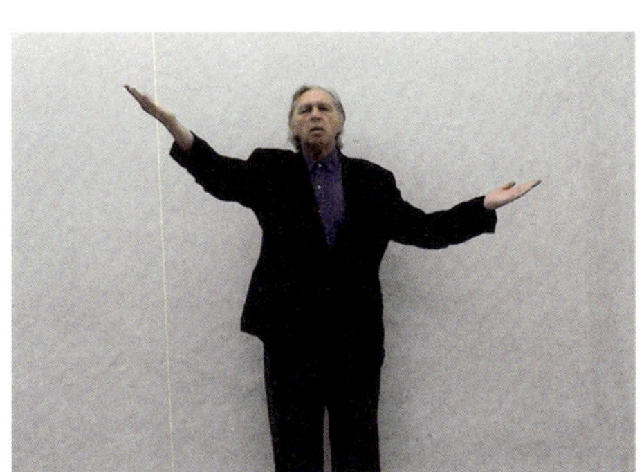
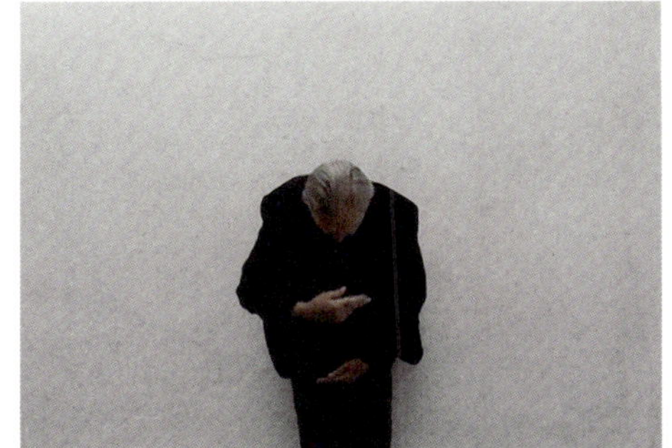

Top: *The Telephone Call*, 2006. Digital video, color, sound. 2:35 min.
Bottom: *A Proposal for a New International Genuflexion in Promotion of World Peace*, 2007. Video SD, color, sound. 00:26 min. (loop).

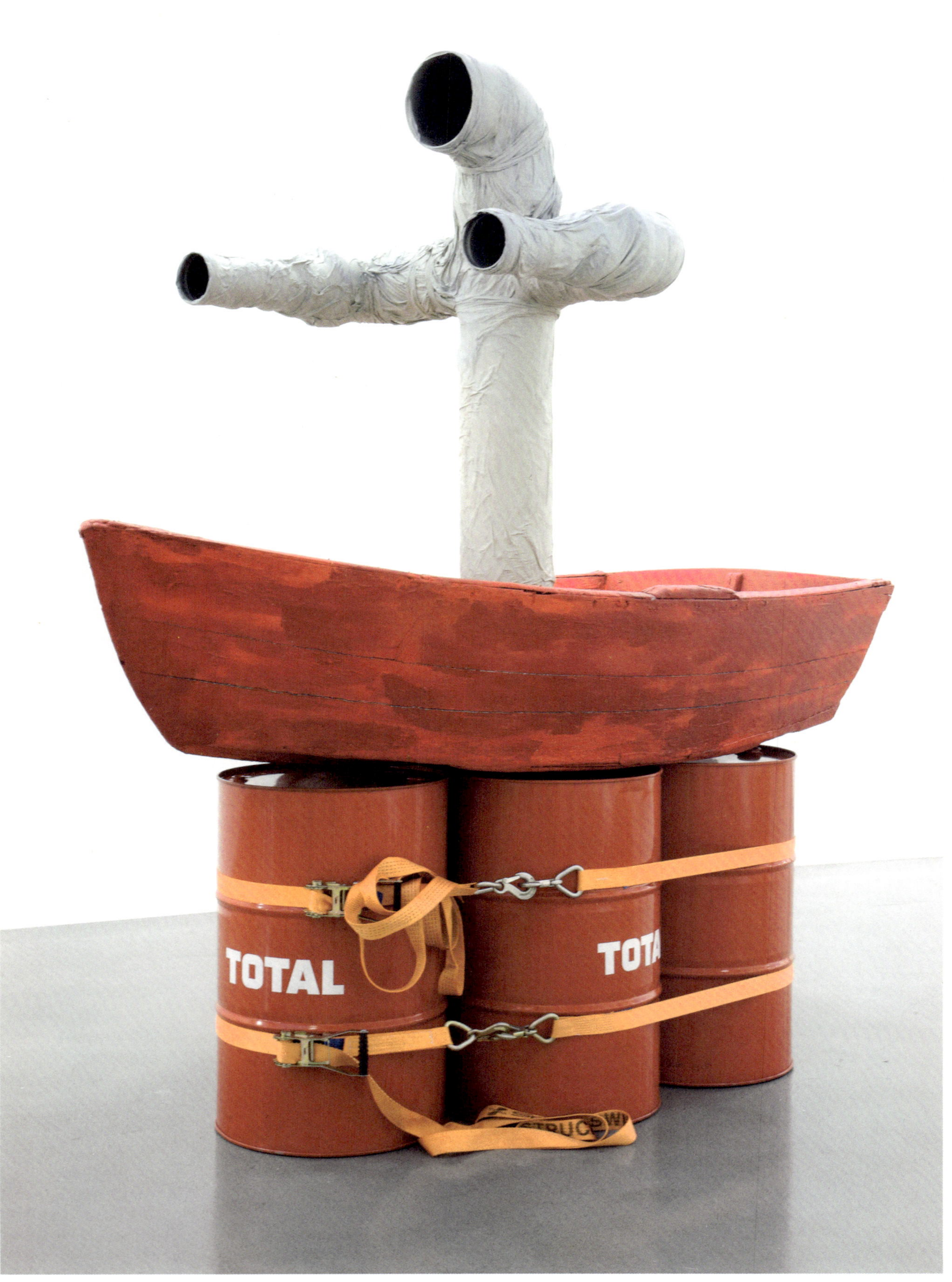

L'Essence, 2007. Oil barrels, linen canvas, wood boat, PVC, acrylic paint, polyester and metal fasteners. 138 × 118 × 45 ¼ in. (350 × 300 × 115 cm).

A CONVERSATION

JIMMIE DURHAM
AND
ANNE ELLEGOOD

April 18, 2016, Naples, Italy

ANNE ELLEGOOD I wanted to start by quoting from your 1988 essay "The Ground Has Been Covered," in which you say, "I feel fairly sure that I could address the entire world if only I had a place to stand." I've always been struck by how poignant that statement was, and still is. And it occurs to me that you've spent your life creating different places to stand and different positions from which to address the world. This has made you a peripatetic person but also a very active person, always finding new avenues for addressing people but also, importantly, for starting conversations—through your visual art, through writing, through teaching. I'm curious if you feel that over your lifetime, and since you made that statement in the 1980s, you've been successful in creating places to stand and start conversations?

JIMMIE DURHAM I often ask myself that, but I really don't know. In many ways it's a relief to be out of the Americas and to be in Europe, which, hard as it is, is much easier to be in. Many people read my writings in Europe, but I always have the feeling they're not *really* reading my writing. They're not really engaging with me intellectually. It's the same as when people look at my artwork. Europeans have been taught very strongly what to expect from me, from any American Indian. They expect back-to-nature, romanticism stuff, and hardly believe anything else. Artists here assume that I'm an artist who does a certain kind of stuff, which is not really very interesting to them, even though they like me as a person. I get that feeling constantly. And I got that feeling in the US, too, but not so constantly.

AE I wonder if when you were living in the States, rather than the romantic, back-to-nature assumption—although we know that exists too, particularly in popular media—you faced the flip side of that problem, which is the assumption that your work is always going to be angry and political.

JD Oh yeah, exactly.

AE So in the American context, you are the "savage Indian"—a phrase you've used in your artwork, writing, and performance—and in Europe, the stereotype is the more idealistic one. Do you think that's because in Europe there is little knowledge about American Indian history?

JD I think there's too much fake knowledge. What people know about American Indians is strongly there, and it's always false. It's very hard for people to break out of it. In [the film] *Dances with Wolves* there are horrible, evil people. But all Indians in the US were horrible, evil people because all of us cooperated with the US at different times. It's colonialism that made people crazy. The US was killing everybody and everybody was going really crazy.

AE And yet, there is a real problem of invisibility for American Indians in the US. There is the historical oppression and marginalization in the social and political contexts, but invisibility has also existed in the art world. In part, this is a result of creating categories of people and practices that can end up keeping artists of color grouped together. This still happens today—with artists of color, as well as women artists, queer artists, and any group you can think of—but it seems to operate even more narrowly with American Indian artists, so that the contexts made available are often those in which their work is exhibited and evaluated almost exclusively with other Native artists. We're failing, as a contemporary art community in the US, to become truly integrated.

JD It certainly seems that way, yeah.

AE But your life and career are unusual because you've tried to resist these narrow categorizations and your work has consistently been shown within a larger context. To return to your insistence on being given a place to stand, on participating in culture internationally, what are your ambitions for that going forward?

JD That my writing might be taken seriously, that my work might be seen as art, as sculpture. There was—and still is for all I know—a sculpture center in New York State called Storm King, and every five years there used to be a sculpture exhibition—like Münster in Germany [Skulptur Projekte Münster]. I've never been invited to be in any sculpture shows in the US. When they think of sculptors, they might think of Martin Puryear, but they don't think of me, they don't think of David Hammons. Münster has been curated by Kasper König, whom I've known since 1991. It was a dream he'd put me in there. But he doesn't see me as a sculptor. He sees me as an Indian artist. [chuckles]

AE So you're rarely invited to be in shows that are medium-specific or constructed around formal investigations?

JD I do a lot of sculptural work, yet I'm never considered a sculptor. It seems very strange to me.

AE It *is* very strange. I think of you first and foremost as a sculptor.

JD Me too.

AE You've talked about how you see art as an investigation, as an intellectual endeavor, and that one of your strategies within your art making, as well as your writing, is to create narratives, but narratives that get interrupted, can be confusing, and embrace tangents. Is this sense of being unfinished, or nonlinear, a counterpoint to the idea of a "master narrative" or the expectation of a completely resolved object?

JD Yeah, this has led to some negative views in terms of how my work is received. But there's a good side too . . . regular people almost always really like my work.

AE Why do you think that is? Are they responding to the materiality?

JD The materiality, but also the unfinishedness and not presenting them with a bunch of facts to show off my knowledge of this or that. You still have to try to engage with people, and I think they very often feel engaged.

AE I think of your work as a series of propositions, suggestions, and provocations. You've often described art as a social phenomenon and stated that the still common assumption that art is the output of a virtuoso in isolation is a false premise.

JD It's a very strong false premise. All of my life there have been artists who pretend that they're being modest when they say, "I don't care about the public. I do my work for myself. I don't do my work for other people." But this seems stupidly arrogant, and also untrue, because we work socially, no matter what we do. Humans are social animals. We don't know how to do things for ourselves. That's why it's such horrible punishment to be given solitary confinement . . . people go crazy.

AE Prior to moving to Europe in 1994, you were in Cuernavaca but still showing regularly in the US, and you had started to show consistently in Europe, too. But you've not been in the US since the mid-1990s or exhibited there very much at all over the past twenty years. What does it mean to you to be doing this show in the US after all this time? How did I finally convince you to do it? [laughter]

JD [laughter] That part I don't know. I've been so busy since the 1992 Documenta. I told myself upon moving to Europe that I would do everything anyone asked me to do, and I did that for years and years, and I loved doing it. It took me everywhere, all over Europe. We had a little bit of that in New York City in the early 1980s, but not so much, because there were not many venues where my work could reach the public. Artists of color—or whatever we may call ourselves—were basically doing things with each other.

AE When you moved to Europe, you continued to show in the US for a short while; you had the show at [Nicole] Klagsbrun in 1995, which was your last show with the gallery. At a certain point, was it a deliberate choice to say, "I'm going to stop showing in the US now," or did it just happen?

JD It just happened, because I was quite busy. For that last show I did with Nicole, I liked the work very much, and I really liked presenting something so unexpected, but I felt she didn't like it. [chuckles]

AE The title was *Ropa Vieja*, or "old clothes," with the subtitle *Spring Collection*.

JD I got the idea from an Aztec sculpture I saw in 1964 in Mexico City, at the entrance to the anthropology museum. It was a big stone carving of the Rain God [Tlaloc]—a big chunk of stone, but extremely intricate on the surface. I'm not sure if it is still there, because I've not been back to that museum since the '80s or '90s. Somebody may have stolen it. [chuckles] But I like when the shape is not really what you should look at. So I made a bunch of things inside buckets, different-sized buckets that were completely uninteresting on their own. And then I put dirt and mud and old clothes in them. And a lot of my hair, some animal hair, this and that and the other. I didn't want the work to have any signs of being art. And I didn't want it to have any signs of something that we know to be interesting, even though I find all those things that I put together extremely interesting . . . just like I find garbage to be extremely interesting.

AE And why did you title it the way you did?

JD *Ropa Vieja* is from a Puerto Rican–Chinese dish that we ate all the time in New York. It means "old clothes" and it's basically beef or pork with any kind of thing left in the refrigerator. My father would call it slumgullion.

AE And there were other works in which you used clothing.

JD There were a few things for which I used parts of clothes as forms. I had a white shirtsleeve and filled it with about half an inch of hard plaster. And other ones that used a single trouser leg.

AE These works feel very emotional to me, like battered or abused bodies.

JD Yeah, that's true, isn't it? It's already more than it intended to be. Everyone sees more than the object wants to be seen as. I never saw these works as in any way disgusting, but still kind of horrifying. I don't mind making art that's hard to look at. A painting that Maria Thereza [Alves] and I really like is by Artemisia Gentileschi here in Napoli, of someone cutting off someone else's head [*Judith Slaying Holofernes* (ca. 1612–20)].

AE So your works with clothing are a commentary on humanity, or maybe a warning about the impact of a lack of humanity. But you felt like the work in *Ropa Vieja (Spring Collection)* was not well understood.

JD No one in New York seemed to notice the show at all. [chuckles] For the first show I did with Nicole [*Janus and His Double* (1992)], all sorts of people came and they liked it.

AE That show opened after you were in Documenta that year.

JD Bart De Baere came to Mexico and invited me after he saw the Exit Art show in 1989.

AE One of the things that fascinates me about the way you often work is that it's site-specific in a sense. You go to the place you've been invited to exhibit and make the work there, or most of it. You might bring some materials with you, but you also find materials there and create the work with the context of that place in mind.

JD Almost always, because I have a better chance to be smart that way. And I need all the help I can get. [laughter]

AE Your working process is perfectly symbiotic with how you've chosen to live your life, not surprisingly I suppose. You have chosen not to root yourself too firmly in one place and have moved around quite a bit over the years. But once you go to a place and spend time there—whether you're an actual resident, as in Berlin and now Naples, or it's a short-term visit—you have this incredible way of immersing yourself in that place and learning a lot about it. You are paying attention and you're curious . . .

JD . . . about many things. Yeah, that's true . . . I'm just absorbing it. When we lived in Belgium, we lived in a neighborhood with quite a few Portuguese people around and quite a few Moroccan and Turkish people. We were good friends with most of the Turkish people, and the Belgian people wanted nothing to do with us because they were a very strange bunch of people. They were all completely racist.

AE Why did you go to Brussels?

JD We first moved to Ireland and didn't like it, and I had a show coming up in Antwerp. I didn't want to live in Antwerp, because it was too close to too many art friends, and I wanted to be a little separate from them. [laughter] No one is happy in Belgium. They don't like each other and they don't like anybody else. And it was quite pronounced in those days. Most of the young Arab and Turkish people assumed that Maria Thereza was one of them because she didn't look Belgian. So they would very often hit her on the side of her head as they walked by, for not wearing her hijab. Most people have a binary world, one way or another.

AE What was your intention with the group of works you made for Documenta?

JD I wanted to do something very complex that might draw you in but didn't have a point where you say, "Now I get it," and then walk on. I hate that kind of work, it makes me crazy that people can say, "Oh, I get it now."

AE I'm interested in the juxtaposition of *Treff*, which translates into "an encounter," and *Jesus (Es geht um die Wurst)* [Jesus (It's all about the sausage) (both 1992)] because they're very different types of objects in terms of subject matter and affect, although not in terms of their materiality.

JD They really are different, except to me they are similar because all of their stuff is from right around my house [in Cuernavaca]. The blue piece of wood is guava and the red tree trunk is a palm tree trunk. It was close to my house and very heavy, and I brought it in thinking, "I don't think you can do anything with a palm tree trunk." [chuckles] But it's so magic-looking.

AE There is a photograph by Maria Thereza on *Treff*. How did that come about?

JD Usually, as in this case, she didn't like the print for some reason, or didn't like the photo. And I would say, "Can I have it?" And then, sooner or later, I would have a use for it.

AE I read somewhere that the face of your work *Jesus* is based on a friend. Is that true?

JD It was, because it's easiest to carve if you have someone in mind.

AE Did he sit and model for you?

JD Yes, because he visited fairly constantly. We were very close. He's the potter who moved to Canada. Julián Villaseñor. I told him when I finished, "This looks like you, if you were a little monkey." [laughter]

AE Why do you often create two distinct sides to a face, as in this work? Your first exhibition at Klagsbrun took Janus—the two-faced god who is said to look forward and backward simultaneously—as its subject. *Malinche* [1988–92] has snakeskin on half her face. And in the works you made for the Luggage Store show [*John Rollin Ridge, Zorro and The Joad Family Players* (1991)], many of the human forms also have double-sided faces. Is this to resist the idea of a singular subjectivity? To show the complexity of people?

JD I think it's probably that, yeah. People and animals. I do it almost all the time. When I started using animal skulls, they almost always had two sides. Because we are so accustomed to thinking that we can *represent* a face, and of course you cannot unless you have the flesh and bone and blood of that animal or person. You can't represent it because you're not using the right materials! [chuckles]

AE The brown substance that covers half the face and much of the body on the Jesus figure is remarkable, beautiful yet also disconcerting.

JD It's dirt, blood, a little hair, and white glue. My idea was that it should be organic.

AE With mud covering half the face while the other half is exposed pale wood, it provokes a comparison between black and white skin tones, which is intriguing given that Jesus is always depicted in Western culture as white, and we all know that is not accurate.

JD I think I got that idea from a wooden sculpture by [Juan Francisco] Elso Padilla, a Cuban artist who died young [1956–1988]. He did a very famous sculpture of José Martí in which he was covered in plaster, which was then stripped away strategically. He gave me the idea to cover the body strangely so it is not what you expect to see.

AE And your friend Julián, is he Mexican? Is he indigenous?

JD He's mostly indigenous; somebody is Scottish in his family. [chuckles]

AE That's why you like him. You have that in common.

JD Yeah. [chuckles]

AE And tell me about the image of the possum that Jesus is holding.

JD It was a magic find near the Headlands [Center for the Arts] near San Francisco. Out there in the grassy part, there was this desiccated possum that had died and dried up. It was a mummified possum. But I didn't feel like taking this mummy possum back to New York. So, I left it there after I took a photo.

AE Somebody recently told me that that possum you found is still at Headlands. In their library or somewhere.

JD Wouldn't that be nice?!

AE The possum is a good example of the way that materials often find you, rather than the other way around.

JD Yeah, this happens quite often. If I need a little piece of string, all I have to do is go out and start looking on the ground and the world brings me pieces of string. And the first one might not be very good, but you say, "Thank you," you appreciate it. But it's not quite what you need, and the world keeps bringing more pieces of string until in the end, it won't stop and you have too many pieces of string!

AE You have a very special relationship to animals, in part, because you don't adhere to the hierarchy between humans and animals so ingrained in our culture and sciences. You have also said that dead animals have spoken to you. Is this type of experience part of the process of finding skulls and bones for your work?

JD It must be, because I never looked for animal skulls, even though sometimes, like in New York when I was doing a whole show of animal skulls, I needed a bunch [*A Matter of Life and Death and Singing*, Alternative Museum, 1984]. But I didn't look for any skulls. You're walking along and there's an animal skull, in New York City!

AE And people also sometimes gave them to you. Usually family members?

JD Usually family, but also people who lived in other parts of New York would give me a deer skull or this or that. And I bought the bear skull. Not because I really needed a bear skull. It was in a shop window in New York and it said, "Look!" So I went in and asked, "Is this bear skull for sale?" And it was, quite cheap of course.

AE When you did a residency at Calder's studio in Saché, France, in 2007, you became close to an old cat there, which you felt was being mistreated by the caretaker.

JD Yes. And out in the woods behind the house, there was a family of foxes. A mother with two kits. I fed them scraps all the time. It was a fox hunting area, so they knew they were safe with us. [laughter] And after a while a giant pheasant started coming to the house, lying around the front door. So she got fed. Every morning and every evening she would show up.

AE So you were feeding the cat, the pheasant, and the foxes. You had a whole menagerie of animals you were taking care of!

JD I always do, because animals know I'm a sucker.

AE Tell me a little bit about your studio in the Grunewald forest outside Berlin, the building that was commissioned by Hitler for [sculptor] Arno Breker. When I first met you, in 2006, I visited you there and it was unlike any studio I had ever seen.

JD It's a building that Hitler made for his favorite artist, Breker. It was made in 1940, the year I was born. Breker didn't stay in Berlin because he was afraid it was going to be bombed, but his apprentice used it, and he and his wife stayed there. After the war, nobody used it until the 1950s and then the Fluxus artist Wolf Vostell took it over. He used it for a little while and then moved to Spain. So I was only the third person to ever use it. The main studio was a seven-meter cube. Just a beautiful space.

AE Was it strange working in this place? Did you feel like it had a haunted quality to it?

JD I think Wolf Vostell took the bad spirits away!

AE I want to talk about your Exit Art show in 1989 called *The Bishop's Moose and the Pinkerton Men*. You had moved to Cuernavaca by this time. And you had already exhibited quite a bit in New York, mostly in group shows and a few solo shows, but the Exit Art show was the most ambitious show you did in New York. How did the works develop?

JD I found a book in the garbage about various Ludlow characters [typefaces]. And I had already found a Pinkerton Detective Agency manual on the same street in the Bowery. And I knew that the Pinkertons had been involved in the Ludlow Massacre in Colorado [1914].

AE So it started with this strange coincidence. And you also found the moose's skull?

JD In the Cathedral of Saint John the Divine's garbage. We were living on Amsterdam Avenue near the cathedral when I found it. It had belonged to the father of the bishop, Paul Moore, who shot the moose. But over the years it had gotten quite rotten—sand and sawdust were coming out everywhere and the nose was busted. So it was in the garbage, and I took it and walked it to my place. It was a great big thing. I couldn't even get it in the front door. So I had to run upstairs, get a saw, and saw off one of the antlers.

AE So that's why one of the antlers is missing and replaced with metal!

JD With a steel pipe. I like that way of doing things anyway, I like asymmetry. There's such energy in lack of symmetry.

AE Were aspects of the work at Exit Art a deliberate shift from your past processes?

JD Yeah, I wanted to develop some ideas that I had vaguely started in past shows. I didn't want to have one overarching idea or theme; I felt each work could be separate but they would still hang together.

AE So, as opposed to your show at the Alternative Museum, for example, where there was a specific body of work—you wanted this show to be more eclectic, so people would have to look for connections. There are a lot of topics in the exhibition—science, history, language.

JD I enjoyed all those different topics and complexities. I didn't have one idea, but because I found the bishop's moose head, it became a central idea. Except there was another work in the center called *Choose Any Three* [1989]. The names listed on that work are not connected to each other, so you can choose. They're just random, out of my brain.

AE I've seen the handwritten list of those names you wrote in a letter to Jeanette [Ingberman] describing the works in the show and wondered how you came up with it.

JD You write one name, and then . . .

AE . . . another name comes to mind.

JD So there is [Christopher] Columbus and [Johnny] Colon, and there are several writers and artists.

AE And there are several revolutionaries and activists—and also scientists, intellectuals, and even actors and comedians like W. C. Fields.

JD You don't know why your brain does this. [chuckles]

AE So it was an associative process, stream of consciousness. One thing that is both very funny and poignant is that you've inserted your name among all the names, between Malcolm X and Tiradentes. You're in good company!

JD Yeah, I thought that was funny.

AE You've used many different languages in your work. One work might have a text attached to it in English. Another might be in French, Italian, German, or Portuguese, which are, not surprisingly, all languages spoken in countries where you've lived or worked. You've also used Cherokee, like in a beautiful drawing called *Zeke Proctor's Letter* [1989]. And I recall you explaining that beyond the obvious fact that you are Cherokee, you like to use the language because very few people speak it.

JD Yeah, because the use of language is not always to understand the sentences being said. Something else is always being said anyway . . . there are many subtexts.

AE Were you interested in making viewers aware that they couldn't read, or perhaps even recognize, the language?

JD That's what I wanted. I knew it could be frustrating.

AE Let's talk about your poetry. Before you started making visual art, you were a poet. You also got into performance, both of which you have continued to do, while also being a visual artist.

JD Whenever possible, yeah, because I can do a lot of things.

AE That's true! How did you start writing poetry?

JD I was in the US Navy aboard a ship, and we had a library, a very bad library. All paperbacks. Ayn Rand, Ian Fleming, really horrible things! But they had a book called *The Treasury of English Lyric Poetry*. And I never knew that there could be poetry. It was beautiful. And I saw that there's something really free and charming about using language as poetry. When I read that book, it changed me, and I became a poet, even though I wasn't writing any poetry yet.

AE How long was it before you wrote your first poem?

JD When I got out of the military. Sometime in late 1963, I suppose.

AE Do you remember it?

JD Yes, it was quite short and quite bad, but I wrote it because once I got to Houston I went to a bookstore and they had a book of Basho's haiku. I didn't want that formal tightness, but I liked the idea of a weird, succinct poem. My first poem has never been published. It goes like this: "Out on the porch, sit in your chair, whittle your brain, 'til a poem is there." Very bad!

AE It has a certain charm.

JD But I saw how you can play with words. And the next one after that was: "Ever been out along sundown, and found something staring, peeking at you through branches, like it had night in a sack over its shoulder and was about to throw it right in your face."

AE I see real progress between the first and the second one. [chuckles]

JD I did, too!

AE So you're starting to write poetry, you're experimenting. And around this time you met Vivian Ayers [Allen]?

JD Soon after, I met Vivian. I saw in this bookstore a copy of her literary magazine *Adept*. And I sent her a letter, kind of an essay, a short essay about what language was, what poetry was. To me, not to the world. It was probably stupid and pretentious. But she called me and invited me over for supper. We became close friends.

AE And you started writing for *Adept*. Were you writing in both essay form and poetry?

JD Yeah. But I don't know that the essays were essays, exactly, because I didn't know about essays. But they were kind of like diatribes—about Indians in the US and black people in the US and so on.

AE And were you doing live readings as well?

JD I was. With Vivian. We were in what was the black part of Houston in those days. There were two universities in Houston, one for white people and one for black people. I hate Texas. [chuckles] There was some sort of protest on campus, and the cops came down really hard. There were armed cops all over the campus, all of the time. And it was very dangerous because they were white cops, not black cops. So it was like a college being occupied by the state. We did a lot of different kinds of community-based things.

AE Your commitment to activism started early, and I'm interested in how it relates to your artwork. You came back from art school in Geneva to join AIM [the American Indian Movement] in 1973. And then you worked with AIM in various capacities, eventually as the director of the International Indian Treaty Council, which brought you to New York to open and run the office. And then in 1979 you quit AIM and quit the Council and began to exhibit your work again. Although you weren't making very much art during the time you worked for AIM, you were already an artist. You'd gone to art school. You'd been creating different kinds of objects throughout your life. Sometimes it is suggested that you stopped being an activist and became an artist, or vice versa, as if these two things are exclusive of each other. So I feel it's important to acknowledge that in fact you are both—you have always been both—and both are central to who you are as a person, as an artist, and how you choose to live your life.

JD I don't see why there would be a separation. There's not enough time in any day to do what needs to be done. I always made things, and I remember Paul [Chaat Smith] when we were in the AIM legal office in Sioux Falls said, "You're always doing things with art. Why don't you show some of it here?" So I had an art show. I was absolutely complimented, and I felt so good about that. I was always carving something. Very often pieces of bone instead of wood because there is so much bone on the Pine Ridge Reservation. I carved all my life. I made necklaces and all sorts of trinkets. I would give them away as soon as they were made because people would ask for them. And it is an absolute honor when somebody asks for something and you just give it to them.

AE Did your father teach you to carve?

JD Yeah. Everybody in my family carved and made things. Not just carving. We made everything all the time. Slingshots to murder birds with, traps to trap animals with. My father was a very good furniture maker. He made all sorts of carvings for the children. Just before my father died, my mother gave me a box he had made. I had never seen it before, but it was a very well-made box with lettering on the front made out of sticks. She told me it was the first thing he ever made for her.

AE Do you want to say anything else about your work as an activist, your interest in political struggles and civil rights, and how you see this connecting to your artwork?

JD My mother was the revolutionary. But my thoughts about this also come from having known Paulo Freire. His idea was that everything you do has to be toward human liberation because none of us is free. It's also related to Augusto Boal, whose books I read. I knew him briefly. He also said that art should always be on the side of human freedom.

AE Let's return to the materials in your work. The primary materials you have used over time are wood, stone, and bone. Stone has functioned metaphorically in your art, especially as it relates to monumentality and architecture. But it seems to me that wood is less metaphoric and somehow more matter-of-fact. Wood inevitably makes you think about time—you can literally see time embedded in it.

JD Wood is more obvious to us. It is closer to us.

AE You use wood as a historically and geographically specific material. I've been so impressed with your memory of materials, like where a particular piece of wood came from and how you got it. You can't remember dates, but you remember the life of all your materials! And your knowledge of these materials is quite extensive, understanding them in the contexts of biology, ecology, and agriculture but also in terms of labor, identity, and commerce. I was thinking about how you came from the forest, so there's also a biographical connection that has to do with your early lived experience. How do you think about these three materials and why do you return to them so consistently?

JD When I use wood, I think about trees. On the earth now, trees are so political. After I first met Maria Thereza, she went home to Brazil for a little while. She brought me back some pine nuts from a tree that grew on her grandmother's property . . . beautiful big ones. And that tree no longer exists. All over Brazil, these trees don't exist anymore. Which is so silly. When I was in Brazil, just a couple of years ago, I found a fallen jackfruit tree. It's not protected because it's not native. It's from India and other places, and during slavery it was brought over to plant so the slaves would have something to eat. It produces a giant sweet fruit and you also eat the nut inside, so it's very nourishing. It's marvelous wood and a marvelous fruit. But nobody likes it. Nobody plants it. And they don't want to eat it. And you can certainly cut them down and everybody will be happy, because they remind people of slavery.

AE This is the type of historical context that you bring to your chosen materials, in addition to your knowledge of its physical properties. So, a piece of jackfruit wood in one of your sculptures would carry this history with it. This is fundamental to understanding your practice.

JD The politics of humans with trees is a constant for me, I think. Around the outskirts of Maria Thereza's hometown in Brazil, Ubatuba, there are families living in little houses and they're all wood-carvers, and they sell things to the tourist shops. They live in the forest and they're not allowed to cut down any trees. They depend on the government to provide wood for them. Brazil's trees are certainly very protected, especially from poor people. [chuckles]

AE You did an exhibition in a gallery in Rio in 2010, after the Bienal [de São Paulo], and the works included a lot of local wood.

JD It was my first time in Rio. I loved it. We stayed a month. The gallery gave me a studio out in the poor area called Santo Cristo. Beautiful town. I got all sorts of local Brazilian wood. We found places that demolish houses and would take all the scraps. They were all things that had already been used, and each one told its own story, so every piece in the show had a text to accompany the object. So, for example, there was a piece of old mahogany that had been part of a piece of furniture, and it was telling the story of how this man came to cut it. He'd worked for the railroad and he found this piece of wood and brought it home and made it into part of a table. Then he and his wife did this and did that, and then he died. Many years later his wife died, and this piece ended up in the garbage and then it became part of my artwork. A nice woman said, "But how do you know all that?" [laughter]

AE What about stone?

JD I did concentrate more on stone after coming back to Europe. But stone is not us the way a tree is us, it's not grown from the same family of living things. In Cherokee everything that is alive is people—pine tree people, oak tree people, dog people, et cetera. And you're all people in this together. But stone is a stranger. It's got a mysterious quality we can't quite get to. We don't know how stone is done. We say we know the process of crystals, but any sort of hard crystal is beyond our ability to understand time. I can say ten million years. It doesn't mean I know what ten million years are at all!

AE Time is embedded in stone, like wood, but it's less fathomable to us because the expanse of time is so great.

JD When we talk about astronomy and physics, we say all these outlandish things that mean nothing to us. We just hope they might someday. We now have some black holes that are so many hundreds of millions of light-years away from us—that doesn't mean anything because the distance it takes light to travel even one year is such a long distance.

AE But we're fascinated by it!

JD We're fascinated by it partly because it's beyond us.

AE The specificity of objects and materials in your work is also connected to your interest in history. There's another quote I really love from your essay "A Certain Lack of Coherence," in which you say, "I want all of our history. I need every name, every artefact, every effort. I need to know the minute specific of our history because I need to be part of it. . . . In the Cherokee language the word for the world and the word for history are the same."

JD Those are very down-to-earth words, not secret words. Everything about us is down-to-earth. I think it's very important to try to know history. And it's absolutely impossible. Because it's never what we think it is. Absolutely never. Real history has the same complexity as that of animals, including humans, and trees. But we still must think about it because it is our lives. Our past is our future. And our past is where we live.

AE You talk about your desire to reclaim certain materials, and it also seems you have a desire, or even feel a responsibility, to reclaim certain histories in an effort to make them visible again.

JD A friend wanted me to show him Sioux Falls. It's a dumpy little place. And I found some wild asparagus growing there. I said, "Look, Tom, this is wild asparagus." And he said, "Yeah, but look how dirty and degraded this place is. I wouldn't eat it." And I said to myself, "I'll eat it just because of how dirty and degraded this place is."

AE You like your actions to have some purpose.

JD Yeah, exactly that. So I think I'm a little goofy and sentimental about places and the materials found in those places.

AE One way to tell the history of a place is through its materials and its objects. Your work makes us think about how certain materials have been used by different societies so that they maintain their specificity, rather than becoming just a set of physical properties. But you also use text to relay histories related to significant people and events. You bring these different types of history—revolving around both materials and actions—together.

JD It's great fun to bring them together. It's very meaningful.

AE Another aspect of the life of materials that gets conjured in your work is the migration of plants and trees, which is also often the path of human migration, right?

JD Absolutely. So, our history of evolution is there. There are so many ways that we use trees: for fire, for spears, for shelter, for everything. And for many hundreds of years, for every kind of machine part. There used to be very little metal, but a lot of wood.

AE For your 2012 show here in Napoli, *Wood, Stone, and Friends*, most of the pieces were a combination of wood, stone, and metal. And many of the metal elements were found in this building, which is now your home, when you bought it.

JD Old machines and parts from the leather factory that was here.

AE Those works are almost like hybrids of wood and metal and stone, where the materials rely on one another, and one material begins to resemble another.

JD We still combine those materials, just not as often as we used to. We take a piece of steel and put some wood on one end and sharpen it up and carve our roast with it. I once did a drawing of an arrowhead and a soldier [part of *Six Authentic Things* (1989)]. And I wrote a poem about it: "This stone led wood directly to a soldier's heart. . . ." It went on and on, but that was the basic idea. I was playing with the doubleness of it—which was the leader and which was the follower?

AE I love that drawing. Let's talk about the idea of exile. You once said that your decision to leave the US was not a rejection of your people or certain aspects of the country, but rather a refusal of a *situation*, a situation that was imposed upon you, and many others, from within the limits of that place, which I think is a really compelling way to describe it. When people talk about you living in exile, it doesn't feel to me like exactly the right word. I realize it's a self-imposed exile, you weren't kicked out of the US, I don't think. [chuckles] Do you feel that to say you're living in exile is an apt description?

JD I don't think so. Because I really do think that when I became an adult, I became a human being, an active human being. At that point, you don't have race, you don't have nationality. You have humanity, and you have animals.

AE You have become a citizen of the world, rather than of a single place.

JD That's what I like, yeah. That's what I like very much.

AE From a very young age you never felt that being in one place made any sense to you.

JD Yeah, quite true. I was known to run away from home when I was six, but I wouldn't really mean to run away. One time, I was coming home from school, and I saw a dog that I didn't know and he was obviously going somewhere, so I followed him to see where he was going and then we lost each other somehow. And then I was lost. And I saw so many things that I didn't know about. It was fascinating! It was night when I got home. Everybody was worried. My poor mother, I gave her such trouble! But my father and his brothers, and my brother and our cousins would often go hunting or fishing far away. All sorts of faraway places to a child, but places they knew quite well.

AE Did you do a lot of hunting when you were a kid?

JD Yeah, because my father was fantastic at hunting and fishing. I was always slightly cross-eyed, I still am, and I can't see things exactly where they are.

AE So you weren't very good at it?

JD I could kill a rabbit with a shotgun, but most tin cans felt very safe from me. [chuckles] Maria Thereza and I were hiding out in the Sandia Foothills outside of Albuquerque once, at a friend's home, and nobody was around and we had a pistol. We had some tin cans, so we went out back and started shooting at them. Neither of us could hit those tin cans.

AE Maybe that's why animals like you: "He's a terrible shot. Don't worry about him!"

JD Yeah, probably.

AE I want to ask you about a few particular exhibitions. When you were living in New York, and Maria Thereza was studying at Cooper Union, you met Juan Sánchez and he invited you to be in a show he was organizing at Henry Street Settlement. The work you were making at that time included a lot of imagery of life on the reservation and was more didactic than you ultimately wanted your work to be.

JD It could be didactic. And I don't know how I came to start doing that work.

AE And when you saw the reaction to that work, you decided to take a left turn?

JD Yeah, I really did, because New Yorkers loved all that work, and I could see them being entertained. Our work was always about our troubles on the reservations, and I didn't want them to be entertained by our troubles.

AE The two projects that you did soon thereafter are *Manhattan Festival of the Dead* [1982] and *On Loan from the Museum of the American Indian* [1985]. To me, these are works of institutional critique, quite distinct from the collages you showed at Henry Street. At that point, you were already giving things away in your give-away ceremonies, and you had already been thinking about the role of art in public space while in school in Geneva through your street performances. In *Manhattan Festival of the Dead*, one of the extraordinary things is that you sold the objects for $5, which was clearly a commentary on the market and art as commodity. You made a bunch of objects and set up the work like a trading post, and then you added a text that says something like, "I would give these away, but we're in Manhattan so you have to pay five bucks." [laughter]

JD When I was living in Austin and Houston, making little things, selling them in a gallery, making a lot more money than I'd ever made before, I suddenly saw that it's kind of wasteful. These are not much, but they're more than money. I know I can work for money, but to make something and get some money back for it, that's not nice. I never did like that.

AE When you made *On Loan from the Museum of the American Indian*, the Smithsonian's Museum of the American Indian was in Manhattan, and there was a lot of press around it. Were they preparing to open the museum in DC?

JD Yeah, they were preparing to move. When I first came to New York in 1975, I was invited to a government meeting with everyone from the newly invented American Indian Community House in Manhattan. I'm very cynical, so I thought it was the government's way of making us happy off the reservation, off our land. [chuckles] So I was invited to a meeting by the government, by the Bureau of Indian Affairs I suppose, to talk about what the Smithsonian should do with its stuff. And I remember they said they had half a million or a million pairs of moccasins, and asked what should they do with them. And I thought, "Holocaust museum. That's what you should do with them." They had all this stuff that belongs in a holocaust museum, they just don't ever admit it. And now they have a holocaust museum—a genocide museum, a slavery museum.

AE *On Loan from the Museum of the American Indian* is presented as a kind of museological display, with vitrines and descriptive labels, typical of historical or natural history museums.

JD I went to the Heye Foundation a couple of times and they had the most horrible, disgusting displays. Big dioramas with tiny little Cherokees doing tiny little Cherokee stuff. I thought, "Why not do that for French people, or German people?" But I would often take visitors there because as bad as it was, on the second floor there was an entire shrunken missionary. And he was so beautiful. [chuckles] When you shrink a person you have to roast the skin with hot gravel inside. It's quite a technology. Isn't that nutty, isn't that crazy?

AE You said that the name—Museum of *the* American Indian, in the singular—struck you as really funny. As if the museum is based on one Indian.

JD It's so funny. So I assumed it was me!

AE *On Loan from the Museum of the American Indian* is related to later works that also play on the institution of the museum. You did a great installation with Maria Thereza for the Bienal de São Paulo in 2010, *The Bureau for Research into Brazilian Normality*.

JD I spent a long time walking around São Paulo. They have a lot of apartment complexes with the most ridiculous names: French and American towns like Las Vegas and Santa Monica, and people like King Louis or Princess Elizabeth. So I wrote down all these silly names and then they went on the wall. It was a great big, long list of names. I also wanted to make a modern-day *bandeirante*. A *bandeirante* is a São Paulo pioneer, Indian killer, gold hunter, and slave hunter. They're the heroes of São Paulo, even now, those little bastards. There are statues of them everywhere. There's one in São Paulo—he's holding up a bag of gold, and on the plaque under it, it talks about how he gave firewater [strong liquor] to the Indians, to trick us into things. I made one for the Bienal with a mannequin and a fake Gucci suit and a Rolex watch, and I wanted him to wear a pistol and have a rifle in his golf cart, because they're all such criminals. The staff hated this work so much that they left it for vandals every day, and twice the Rolex watch was stolen. Of course I bought the watches on the street. [chuckles] São Paulo hated it. Brazilians are like people from the US. They're very self-righteous and very defensive about their marvelous countries. Especially when it's us Indians criticizing.

AE Jumping continents now, I'd love to hear about the permanent work you did in Tana, Norway, at the Sami Courthouse [*Seven Directions* (2003)].

JD Since '73 there have been forced concessions for the Sami from the Norwegian government. So in Tana they got their first Sami courthouse, and they wanted public art for their new courthouse. The Norwegian government didn't trust the Sami artists. Why not, I don't know. And the Samis would not have trusted a Norwegian, so the Norwegians found me! I was there a month and it was never dark. The king and the queen came for the opening. They came in separate helicopters because what would poor Norway do without a king and queen?! But the judge had become a good friend of mine, and he got up and gave the most incredible, insulting diatribe. It was just beautiful. "You can't take this away from us now. And you must sit there and listen."

AE Was the work made of materials you collected locally?

JD Most of it was local. I brought a seashell, a spent bullet, and a flint arrowhead from my family. I had a bunch of steel cable that went over a stone outside and then it started going inside and then it changed into different kinds of wire and went across the waiting room in the courthouse and then came down onto a wall and then over to another wall. It was completely senseless. What I hoped was that it would be interesting to people and their families who had to be in the courthouse. If it had been political or pictorial, it would get boring pretty quickly, especially if it was about the Sami culture, because then you would just be seeing your own culture!

AE What was the response of the local people?

JD Everybody loved it. The day of the opening I decided to dress up for the king and queen. I had a nice pinstripe, tailor-made suit, and a white shirt, and a tie, and a Cherokee headband. I had really long hair then, and I tied it back with this headband. I went out of my house to go to the opening ceremonies. And all these other guys were coming out of their houses, also dressed up super fancy in their Sami clothes. They were so pleased that I would wear a headband, that I would, as they saw it, be on their side.

AE Before we end, let's talk about the title of the show, *Jimmie Durham: At the Center of the World*. Since 1995 you've made a number of works that are poles—or staffs—to mark the center of the world, in a range of locations. You've made at least ten so far, in places like Berlin, Middelburg, and Gwangju. During a trip to Siberia, you cut down a tree and made a pole to mark the center of the world, right?

JD Yeah. On New Year's Eve it was 60 below. That's really, really cold! The next day, the local people invited us on a picnic out in the forest, and that's when I cut the tree down. And this part of Siberia is more than five times the size of France, and it never had a Gulag, because it doesn't have a railroad.

AE So you were basically in the middle of nowhere but also at the center.

JD Really in the middle of nowhere! Beautiful people out there. And they got very rich—this was in the early 1990s—because they were all scientists. Three different Native groups and they were all scientists.

AE I think of this impulse to stake your position in the world as a political act. Being at the center is not a self-absorbed notion that you are the center of the universe, but rather an insistence that you belong in the center and not on the margins. That you have something to offer. Your poles to mark the center of the world also suggest that the center is always shifting.

JD Every country in the Americas, whether they say it or not, believes that Indians don't matter much anymore, because there are not very many of us left. Anyone who is not in a power position, to me, they are our hope, they're not hopeless. If you can't liberate them, you can't liberate anybody. So, because we're not in the history of the Americas but the history of the Americas is *because* of us, of course we're the center of the world. Of course we are! Most animals have a stupid hierarchy based on stupid males doing stupid things. And certainly humans have that, and if we were not so stupid and sexist, we would be better off. Everything we do ought to be feminist.

AE Well, I would agree with that! Any last thoughts? Any hopes and dreams you want to share?

JD By my own reckoning, I have about fifty more years of life.

AE You told me you were immortal. Now it's only fifty years? [laughter]

JD Well, we can talk again in forty-five years!

AE I look forward to it. Thank you, Jimmie.

JD Thank you, it was nice.

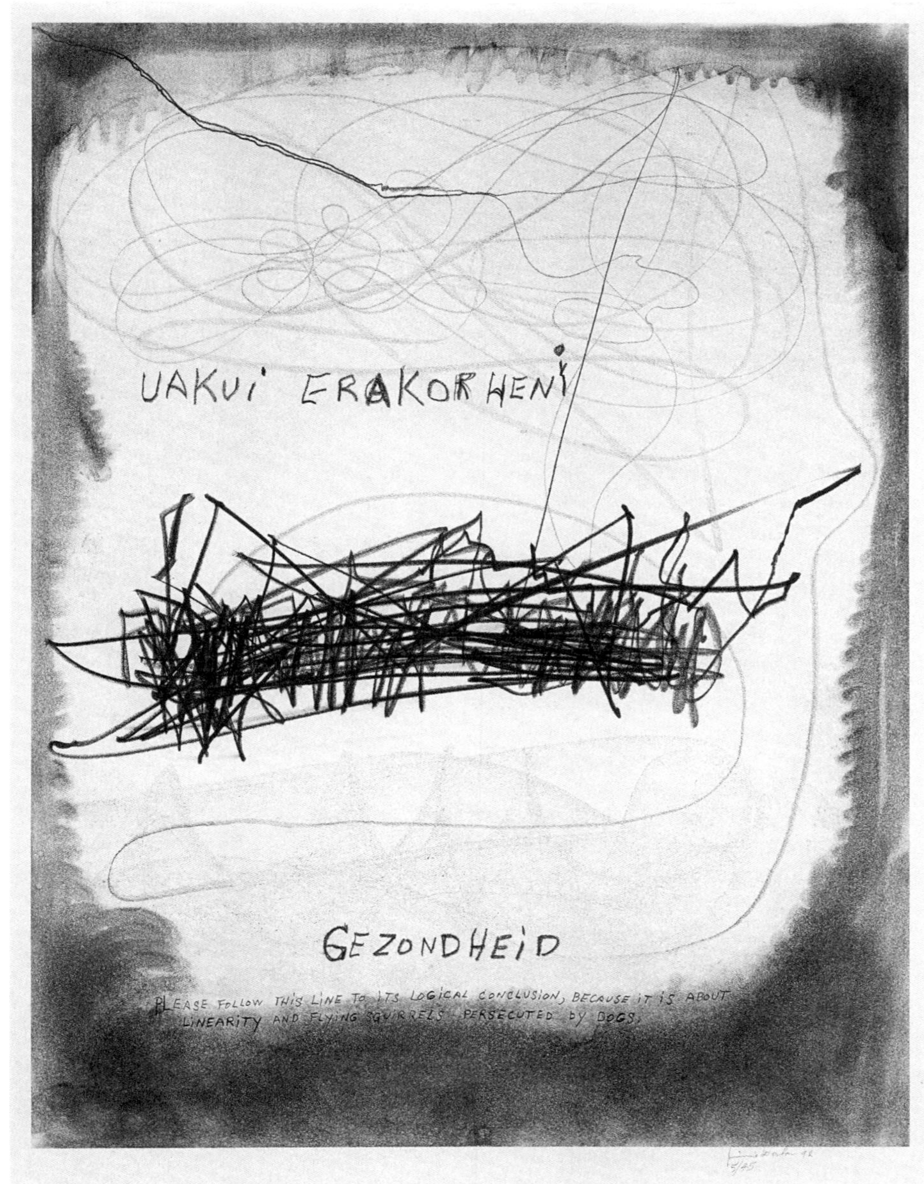

Gezondheid, 1992. Silkscreen and graphite on paper. 25 ¼ × 19 in. (64 × 48 cm).

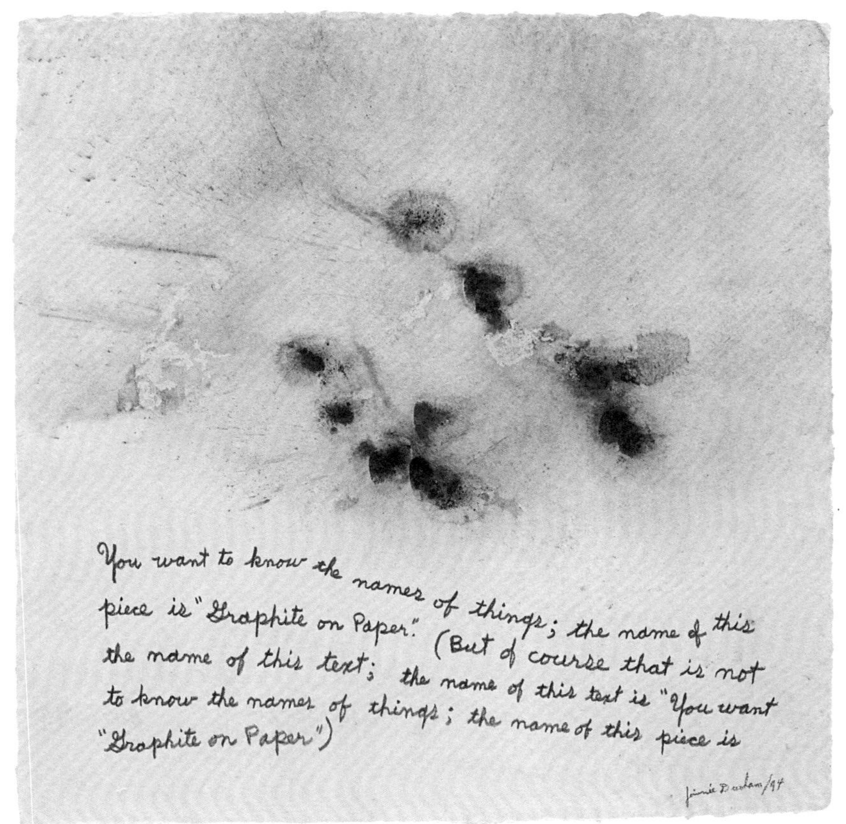

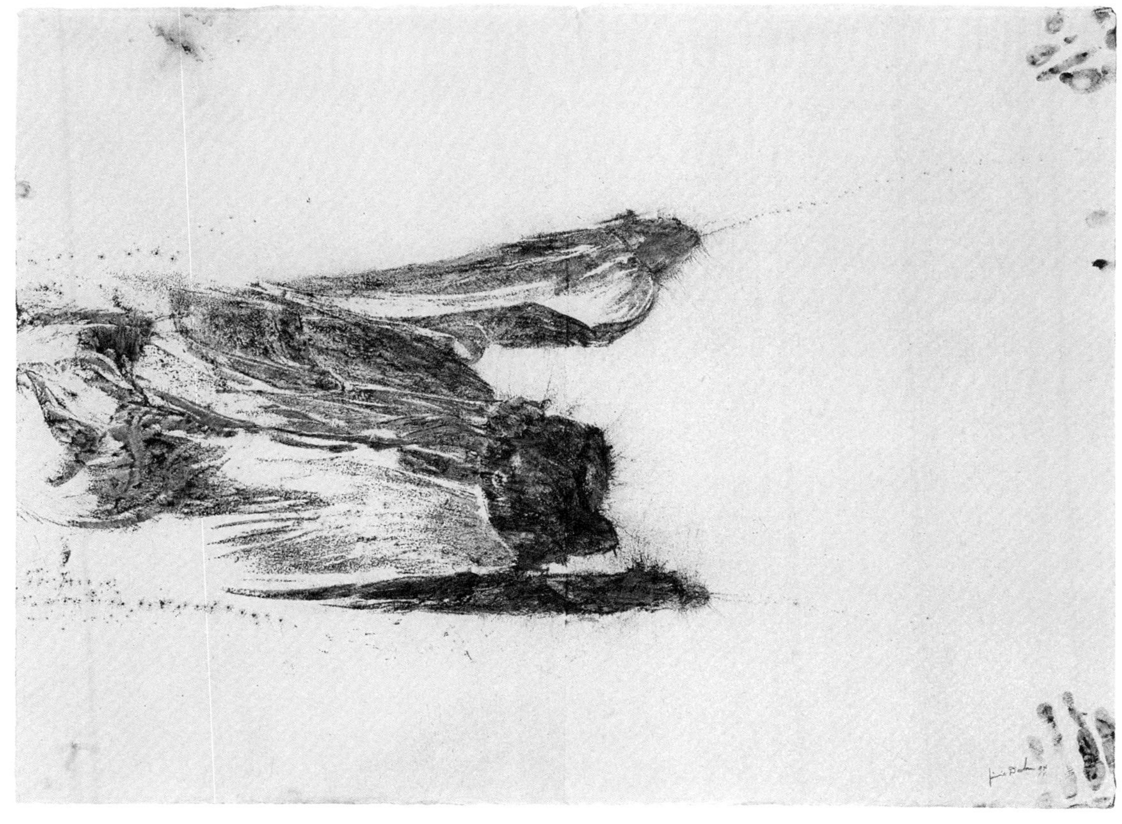

Top: *Graphite on Paper*, 1994. Paint and graphite on paper. 20 ¾ × 20 in. (52.5 × 51 cm).
Bottom: *Graphite on Paper #2*, 1994. Graphite on paper. 22 ¼ × 30 in. (56.5 × 76 cm).

Untitled (Grafite, Soil), 1994. Dirt, hair, white glue, graphite on canvas over plywood. 17 × 22 in. (43.2 × 55.9 cm).

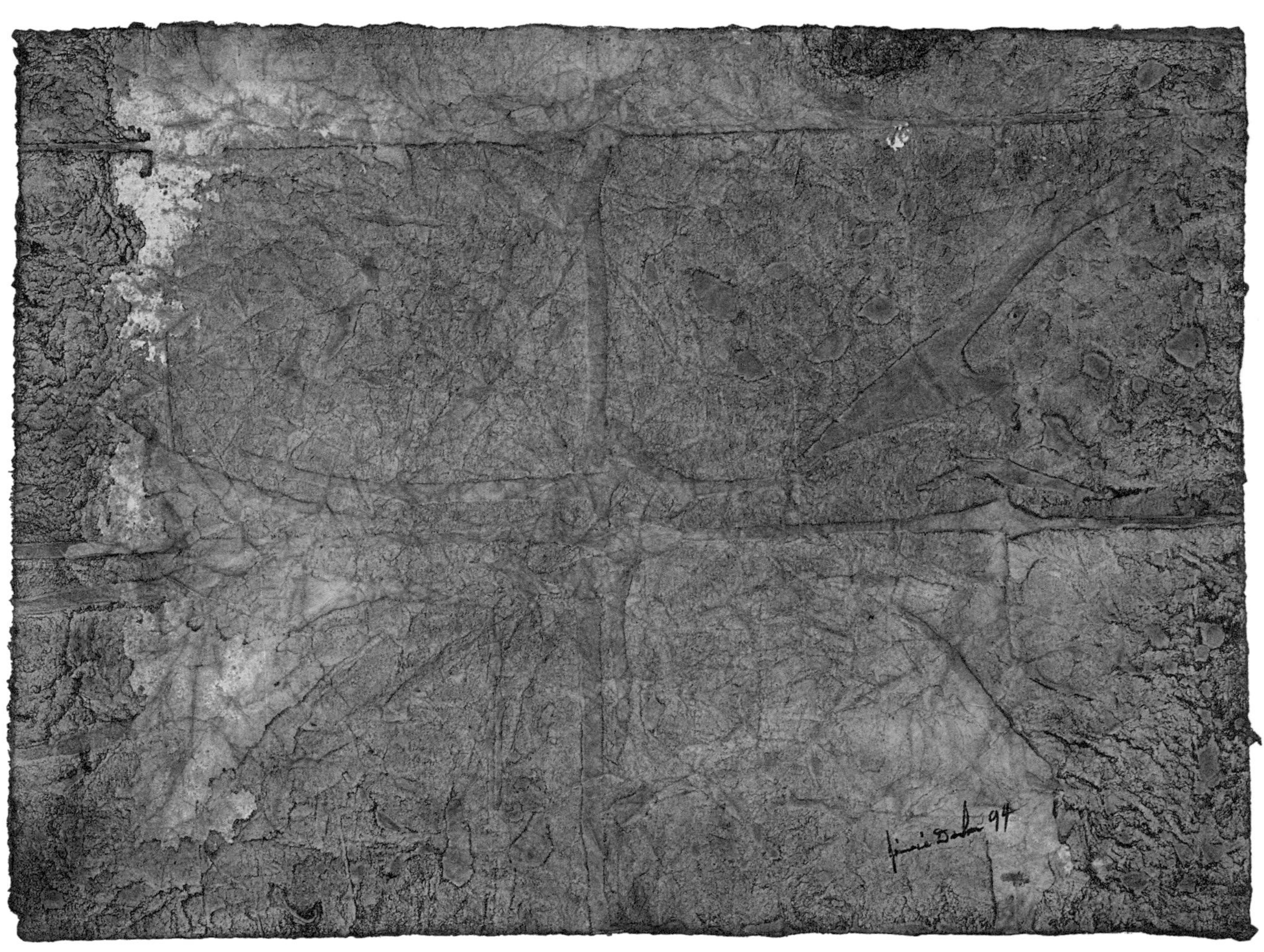

Graphite on Paper #1, 1994. Graphite on paper. 17 × 22 ¼ in. (43.2 × 56.5 cm).

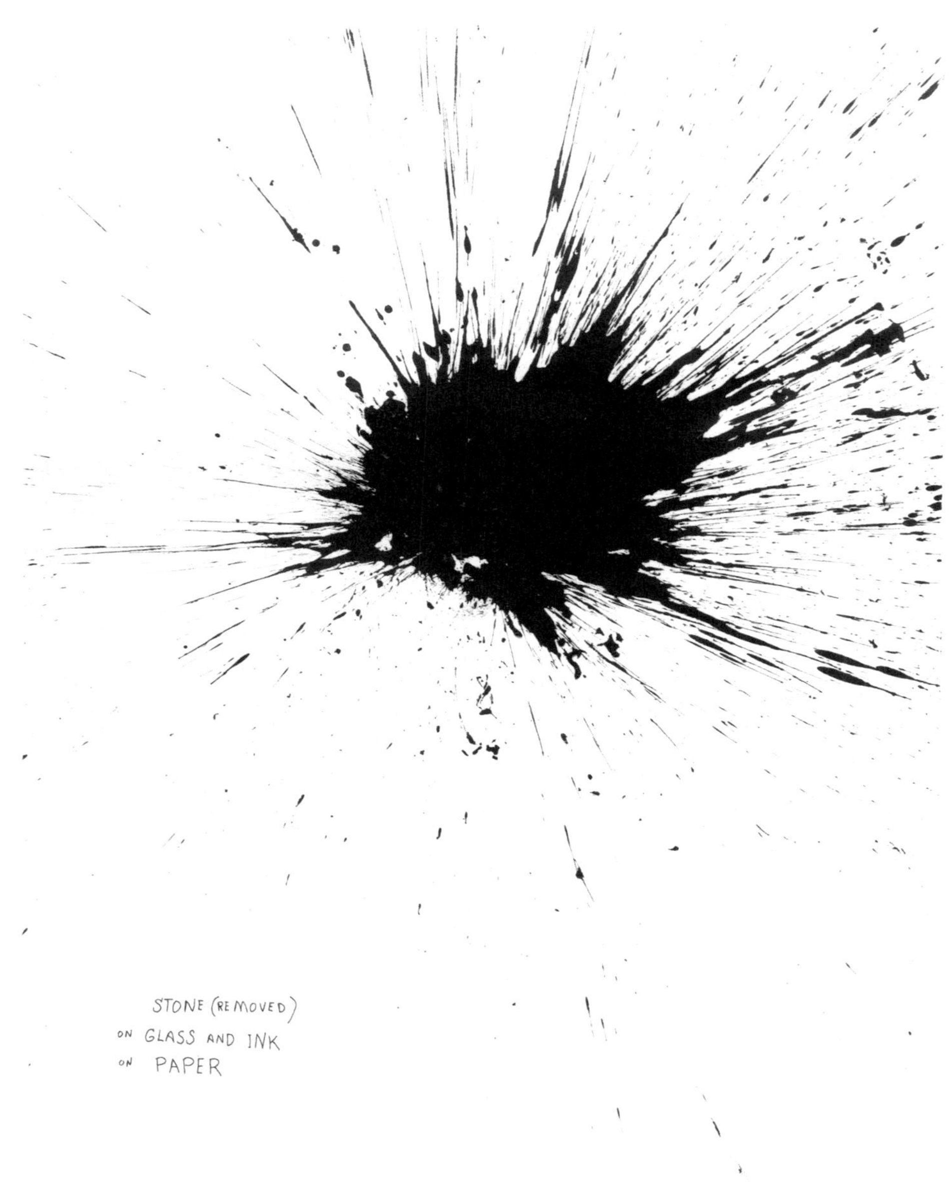

Stone (Removed) on Glass and Ink on Paper, 2002. Ink on paper. 40 × 31 in. (101.6 × 78.7 cm).

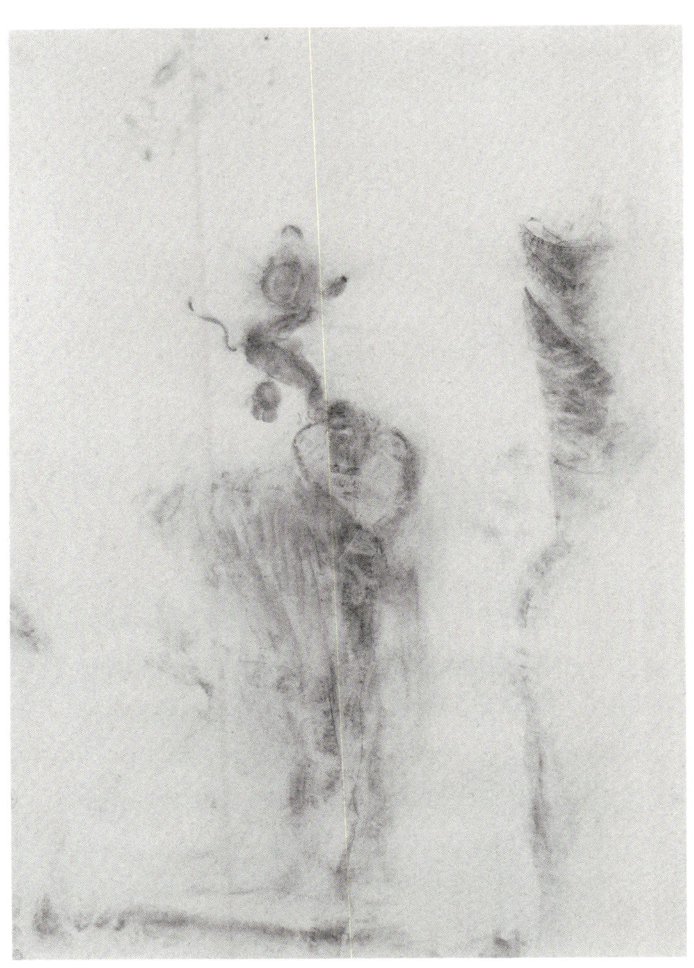

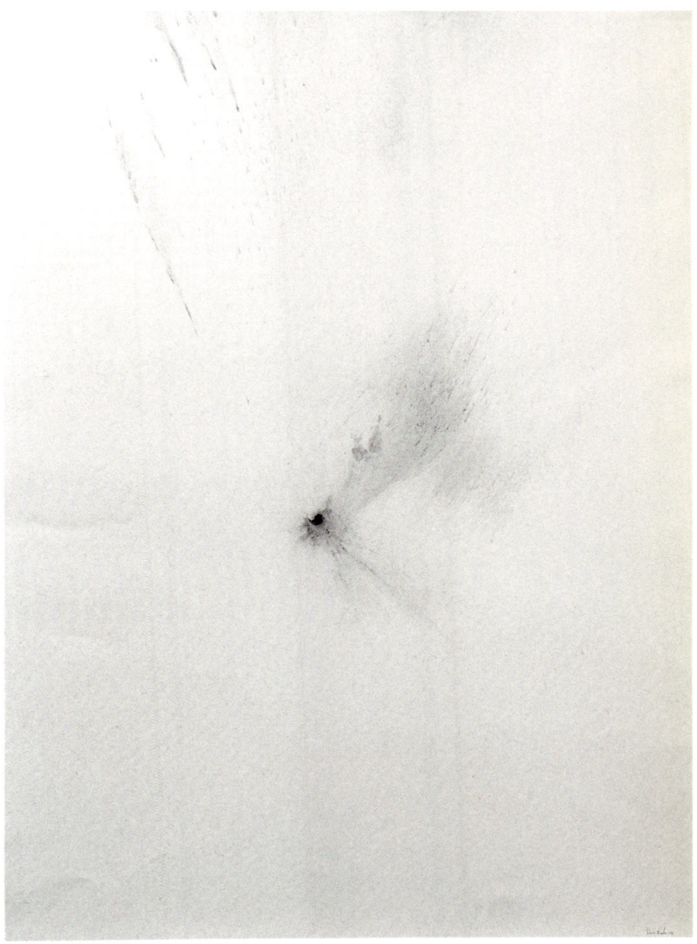

Left: Untitled, 1998–99. Black chalk on paper. 42 15⁄16 × 31 5⁄16 in. (109 × 79.5 cm).
Right: *Untitled 4 ("Stoning" series)*, 2004. Graphite on paper. 27 ½ × 19 ½ in. (70 × 49.5 cm).

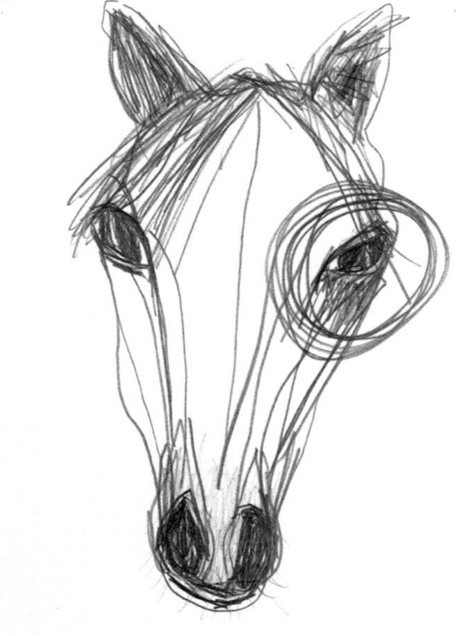
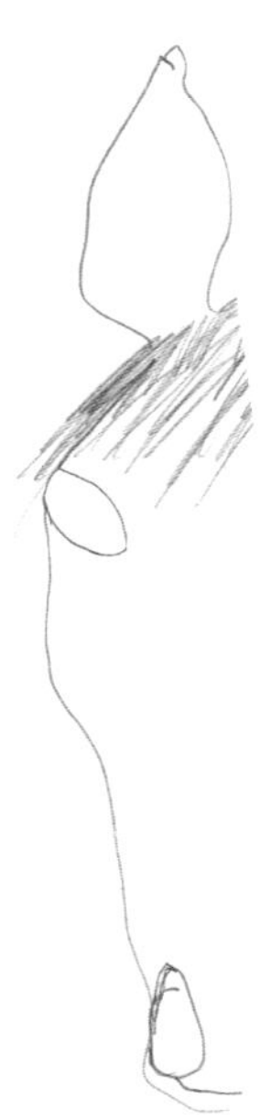
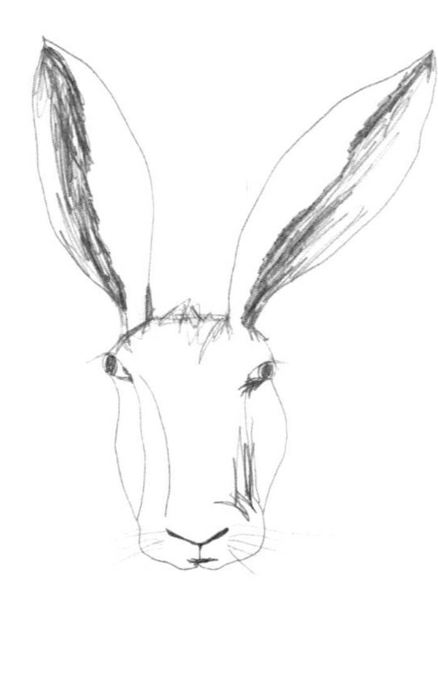
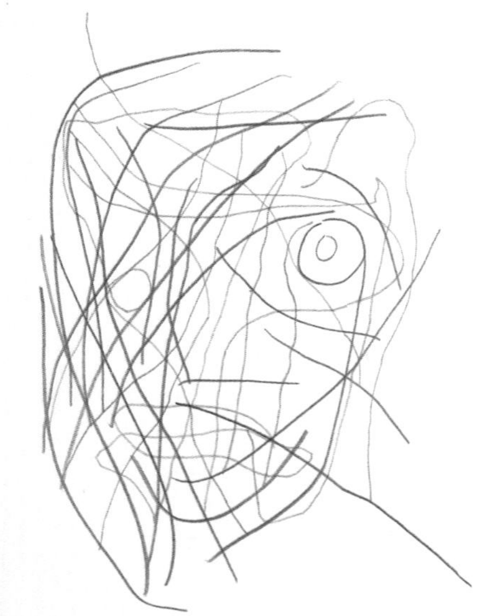
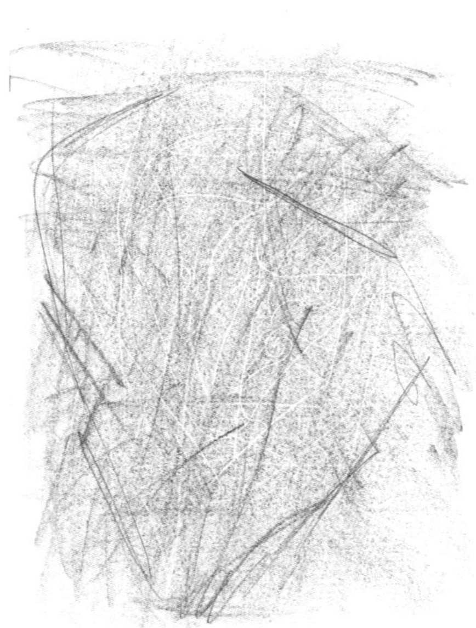
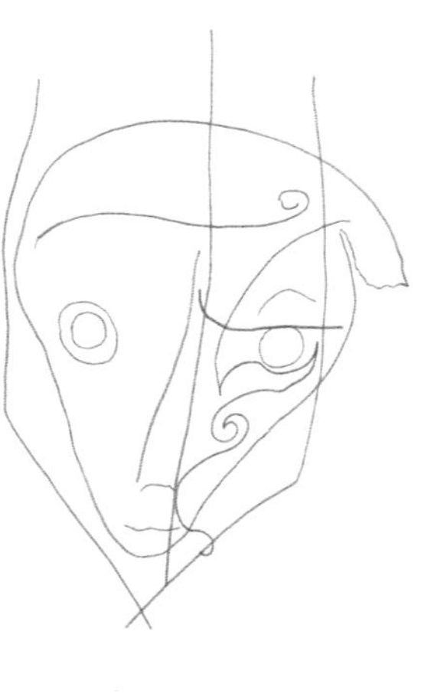

Top row: *Drawn Lines and Faces*, 1998. Graphite on paper. Six sheets (irregular), 21 ¼ × 74 ½ in. (54 × 189 cm) overall (framed).

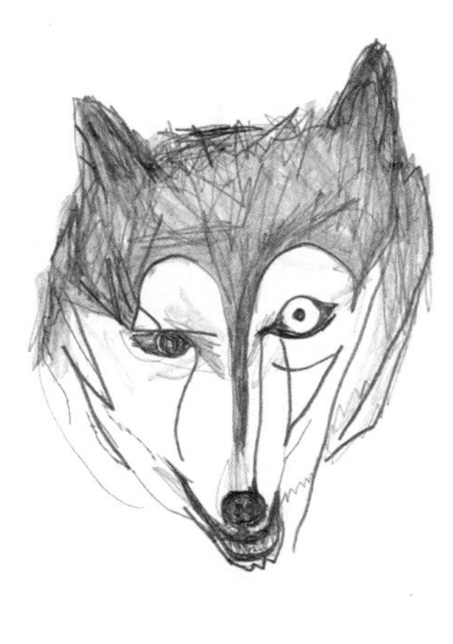
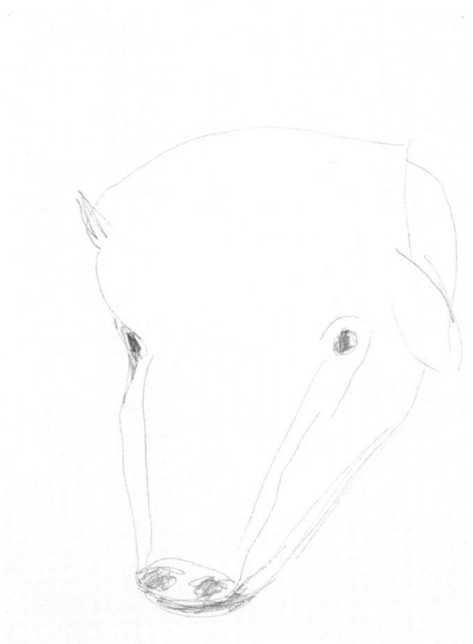
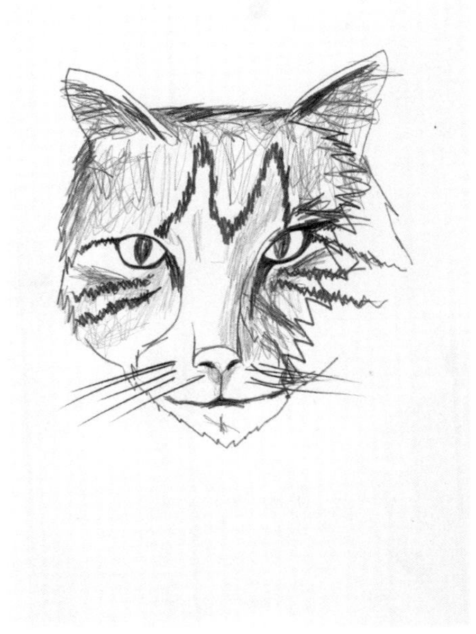
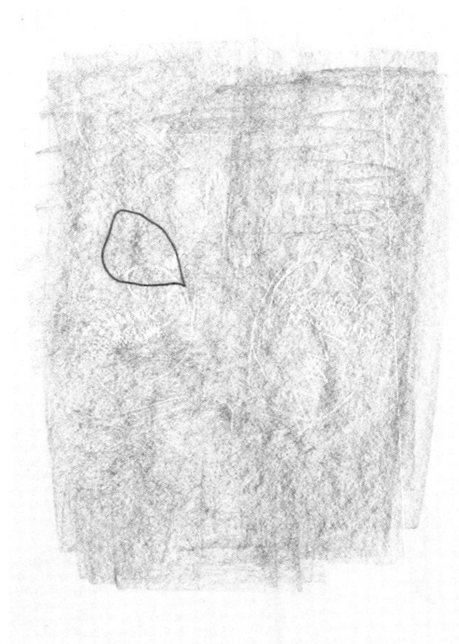
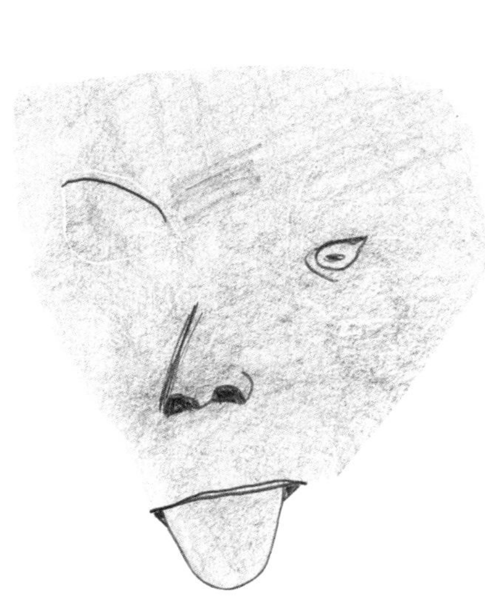
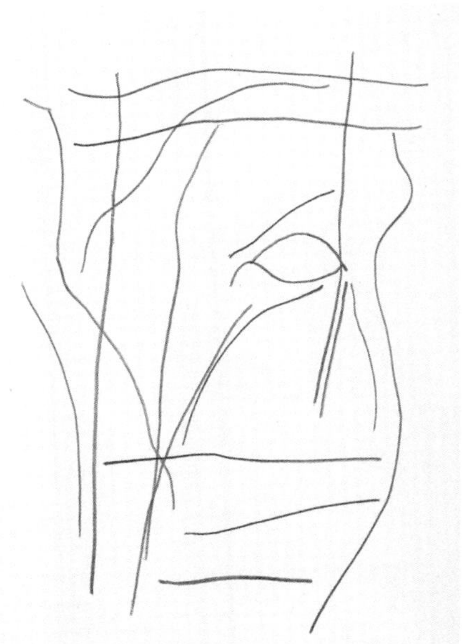

Bottom row: *Three Faces*, 1998. Graphite on paper. Six sheets (irregular), 21 ¼ × 74 ½ in. (54 × 189 cm) overall (framed).

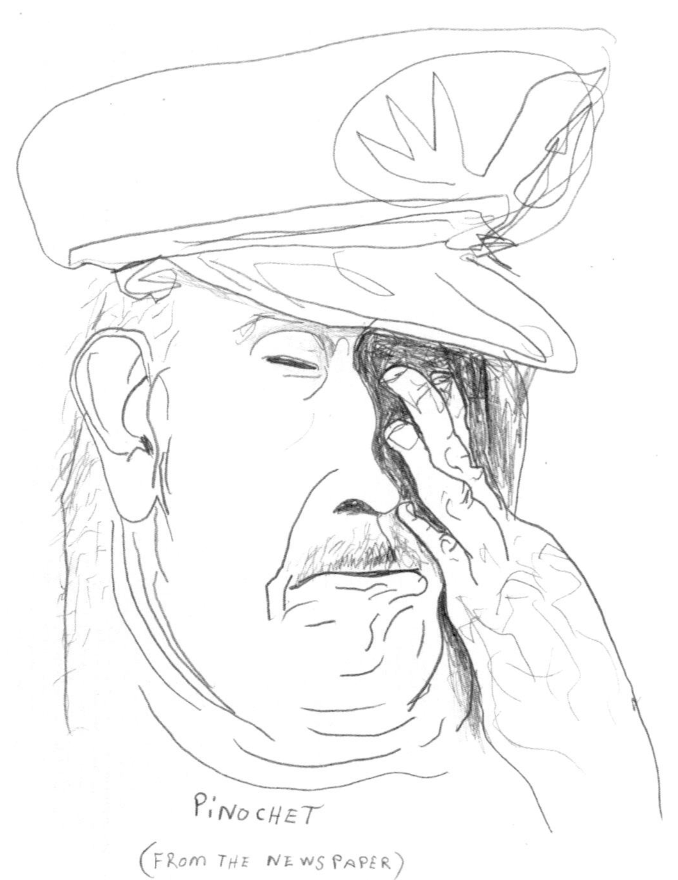

Pinochet, 1998. Graphite on paper. 16 ⅛ × 11 ⅝ in. (41 × 29.5 cm).

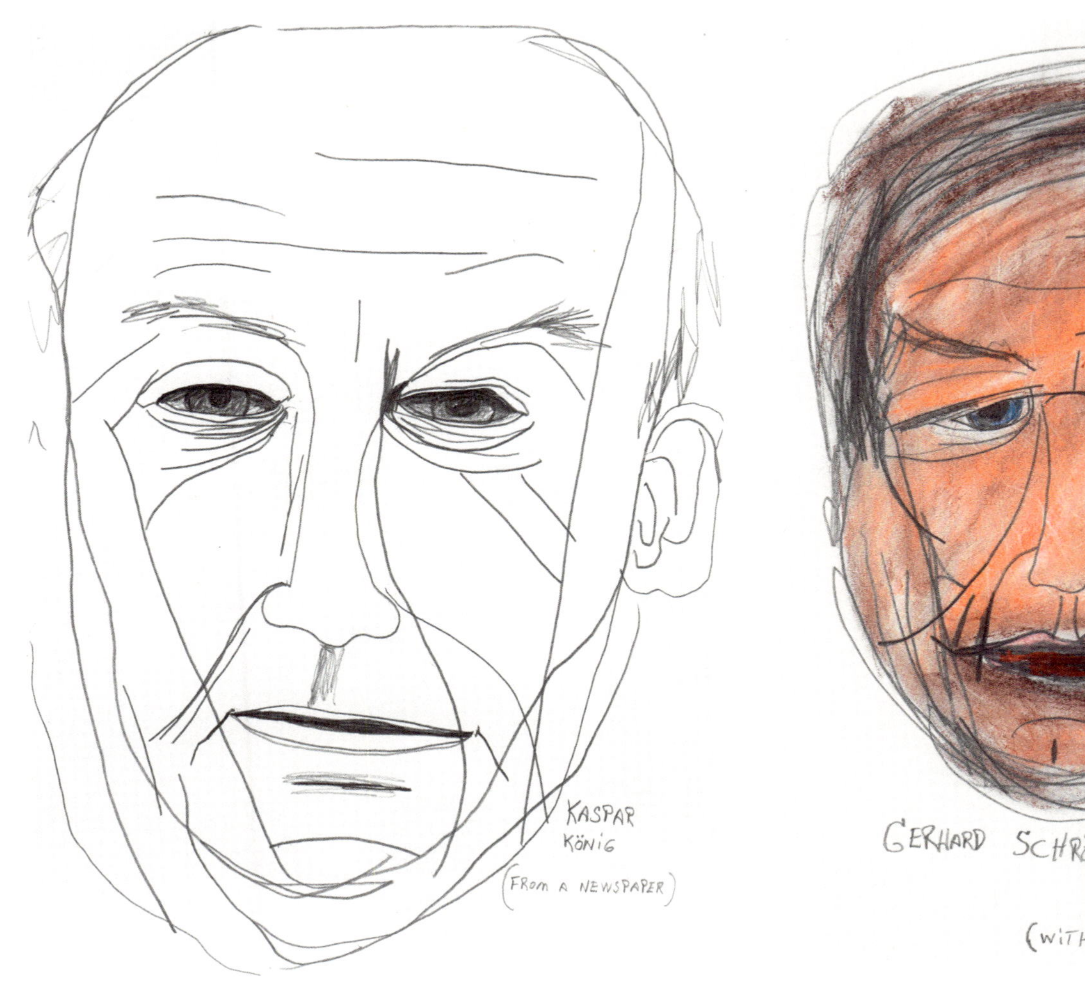

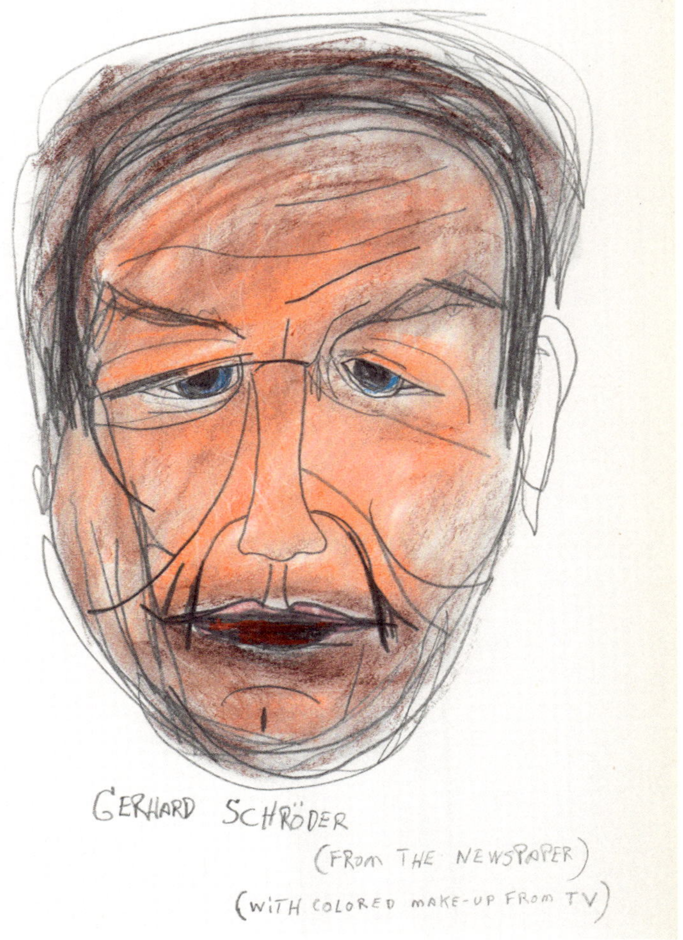

Left: *Kaspar König*, 1998. Graphite on paper. 16 ⅛ × 11 ⅝ in. (41 × 29.5 cm).
Right: *Gerhard Schröder*, 1998. Graphite and pastel on paper. 16 ⅛ × 11 ⅝ in. (41 × 29.5 cm).

THE
PENIS
MIGHTIER
than the sword

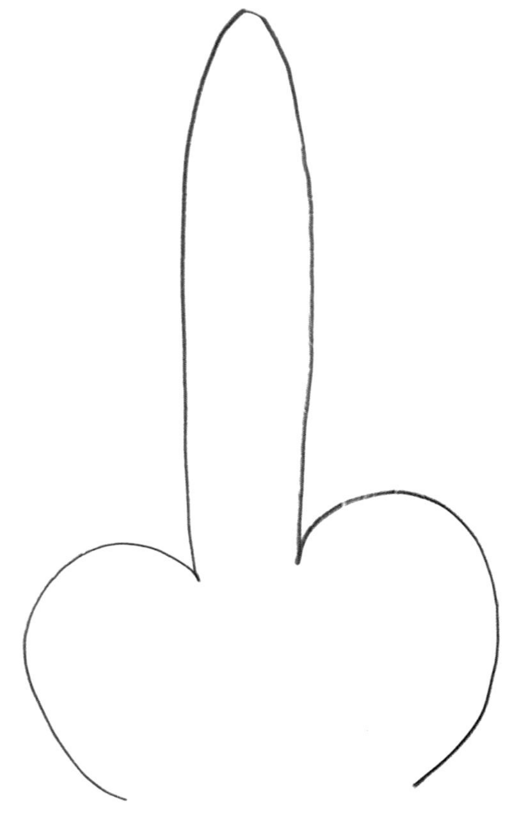

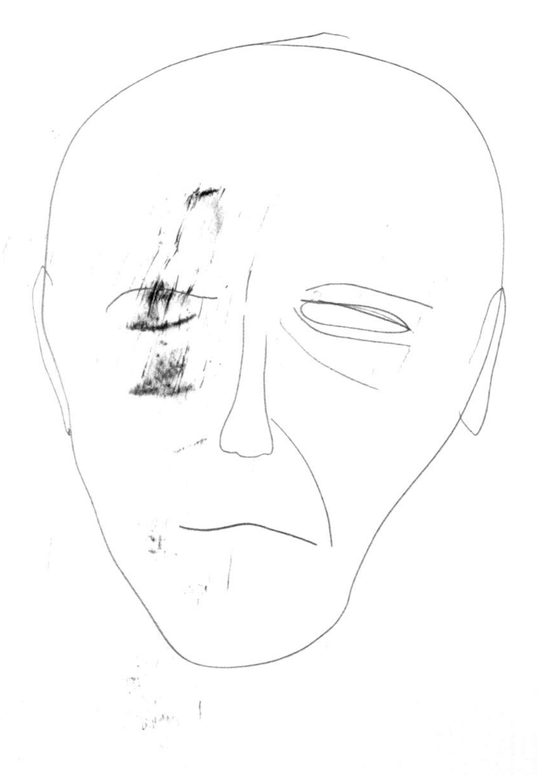

Top row: *Untitled (The Penis Mightier)*, 2007. Graphite on acid-free cotton paper. 30 ¼ × 23 in. (77 × 58 cm) each of 3.

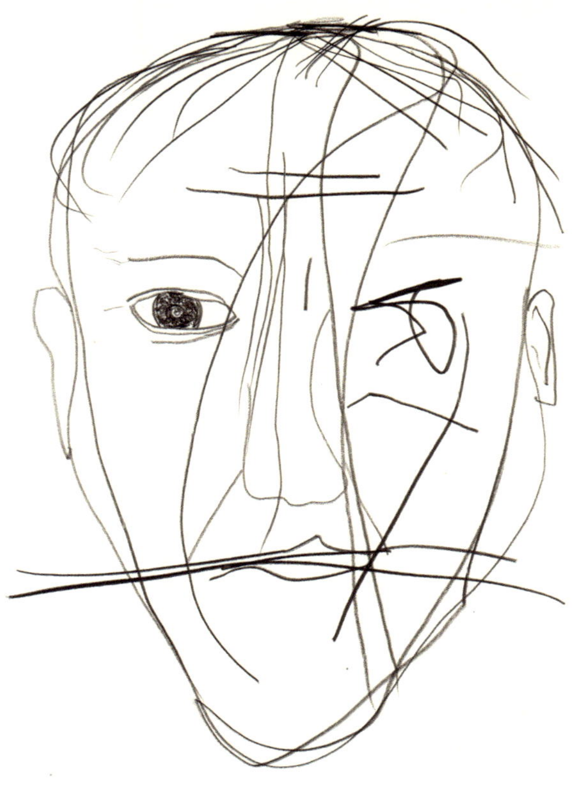

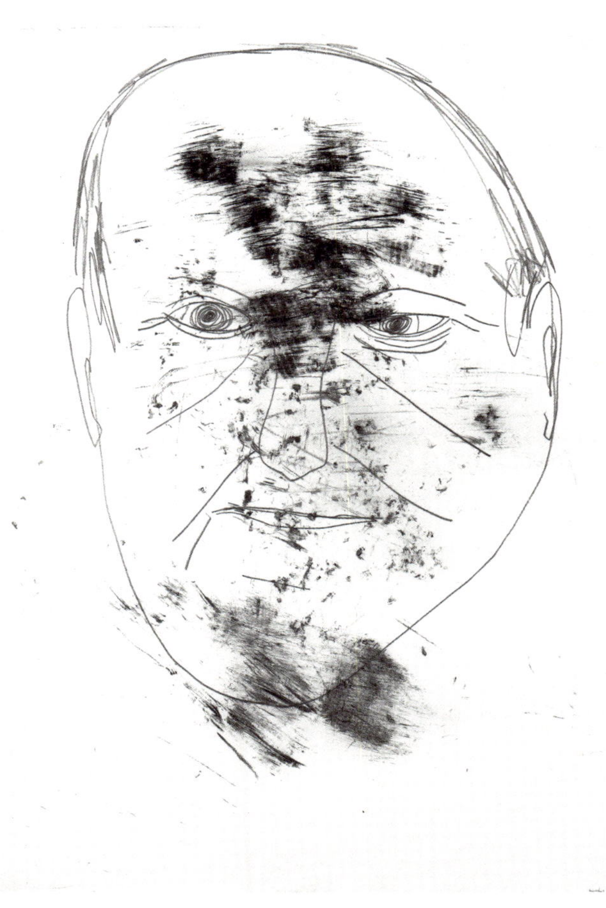

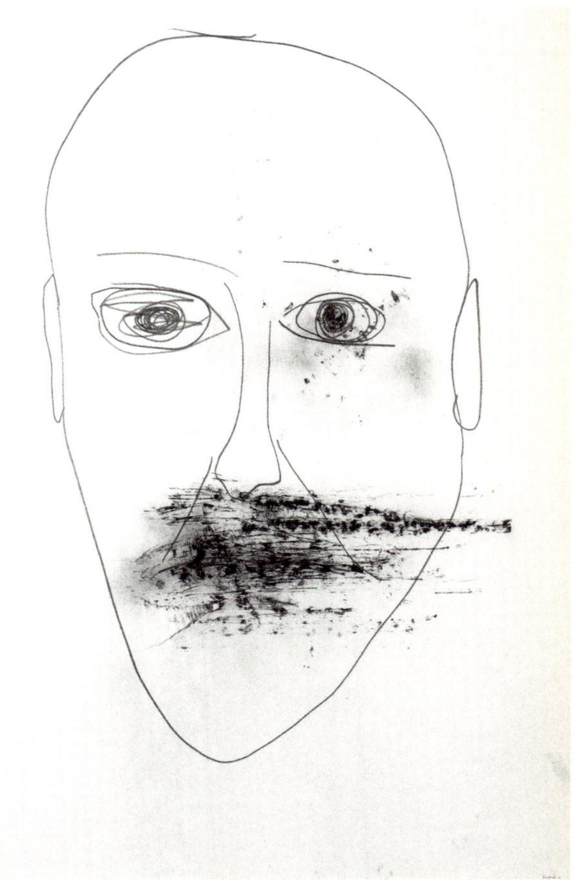

Bottom row: *Untitled (Damaged face drawings)*, 2006. Graphite on paper. 39 ½ × 27 ½ in. (100 × 70 cm) each of 3.

PREHISTORIC STONE TOOL

THIS SIMPLE FLINT HAMMER WAS MADE ALMOST 40,000 YEARS AGO IN THE AREA OF THE RIVER SEINE CLOSE TO PRESENT-DAY PARIS. OF COURSE, KNOWING SO LITTLE OF THE LIVES AND CULTURE OF PEOPLE WHO PRODUCED THIS TOOL, IT CAN BE ONLY CONJECTURE AS TO ITS USE. HOWEVER, WE CAN HEY! OW, OW, AIEE! STOP! STOP! WHY ARE YOU HITTING ME? PLEASE! STOP! OH NO! STOP! OUCH!

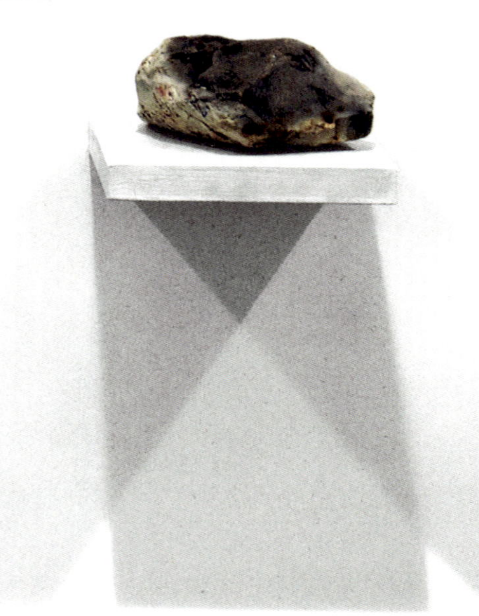

Prehistoric Stone Tool, 2004. Acrylic paint and ink on wood panel and flint stone. Wood panel: 35 ½ × 25 ⅝ in. (90 × 65 cm); shelf: 7 ⅞ × 7 ⅞ in. (20 × 20 cm).

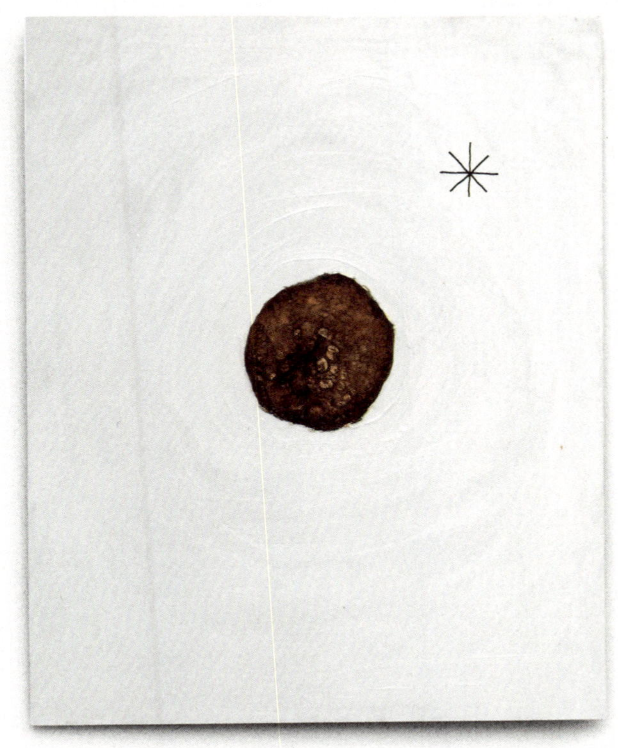

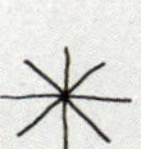

A Mushroom from the Grunewald Forest, 2006. Dried mushroom, acrylic paint, ink on two wood boards. Two parts, 33 ½ × 26 ¼ × 4 in. (85 × 67 × 10 cm); 21 × 26 ¼ × 4 in. (53 × 67 × 10 cm).

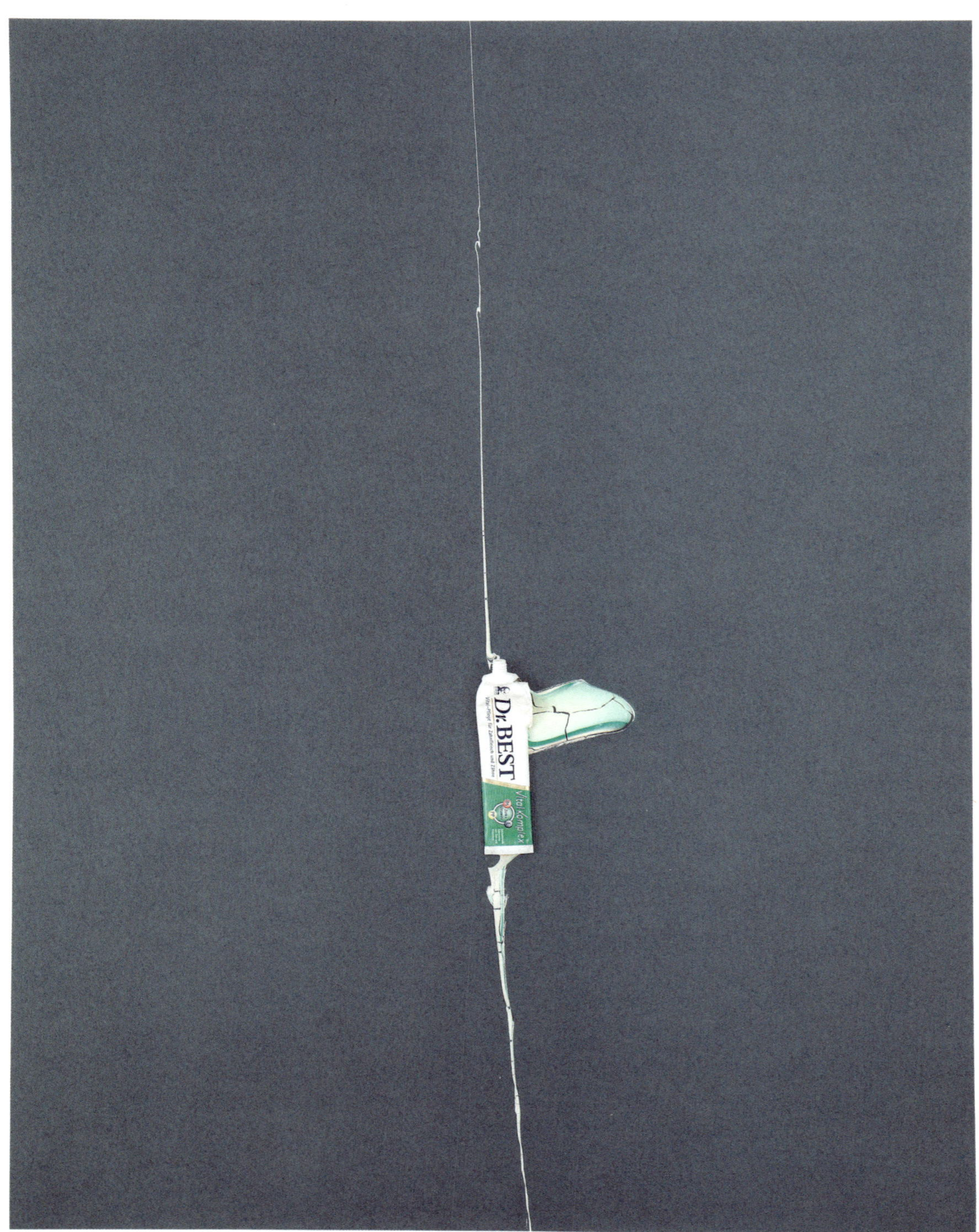

Gray granite (removed) on Dr. Best's, 2001. Acrylic paint and toothpaste on wood board. 43 ¼ × 33 ½ in. (110 × 85 cm).

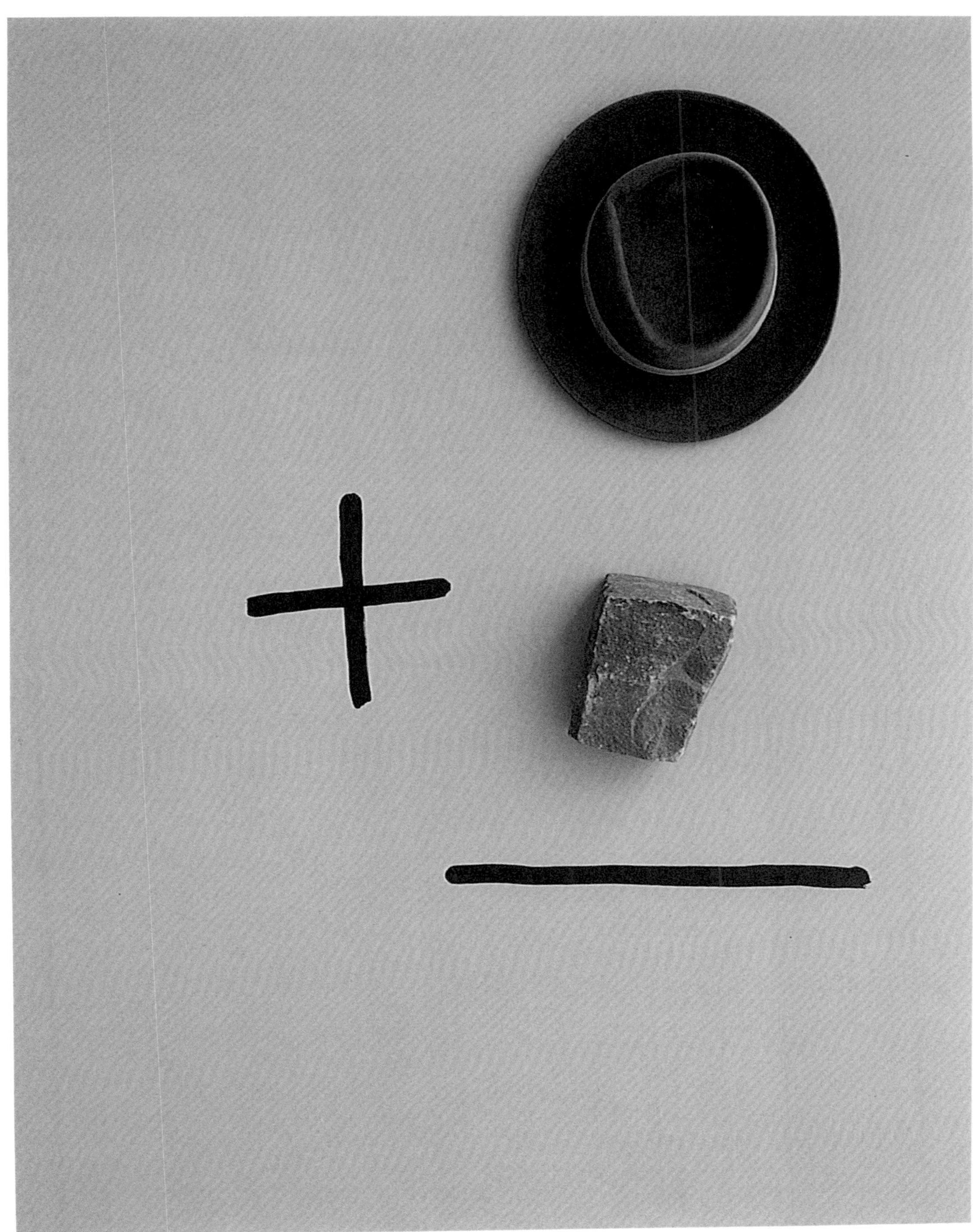

No Men Clature in Paris, 2002. Felt hat, cobblestone, acrylic paint on wood panel. 43 ½ × 33 ⅝ × 5 ½ in. (110.5 × 85.5 × 14 cm).

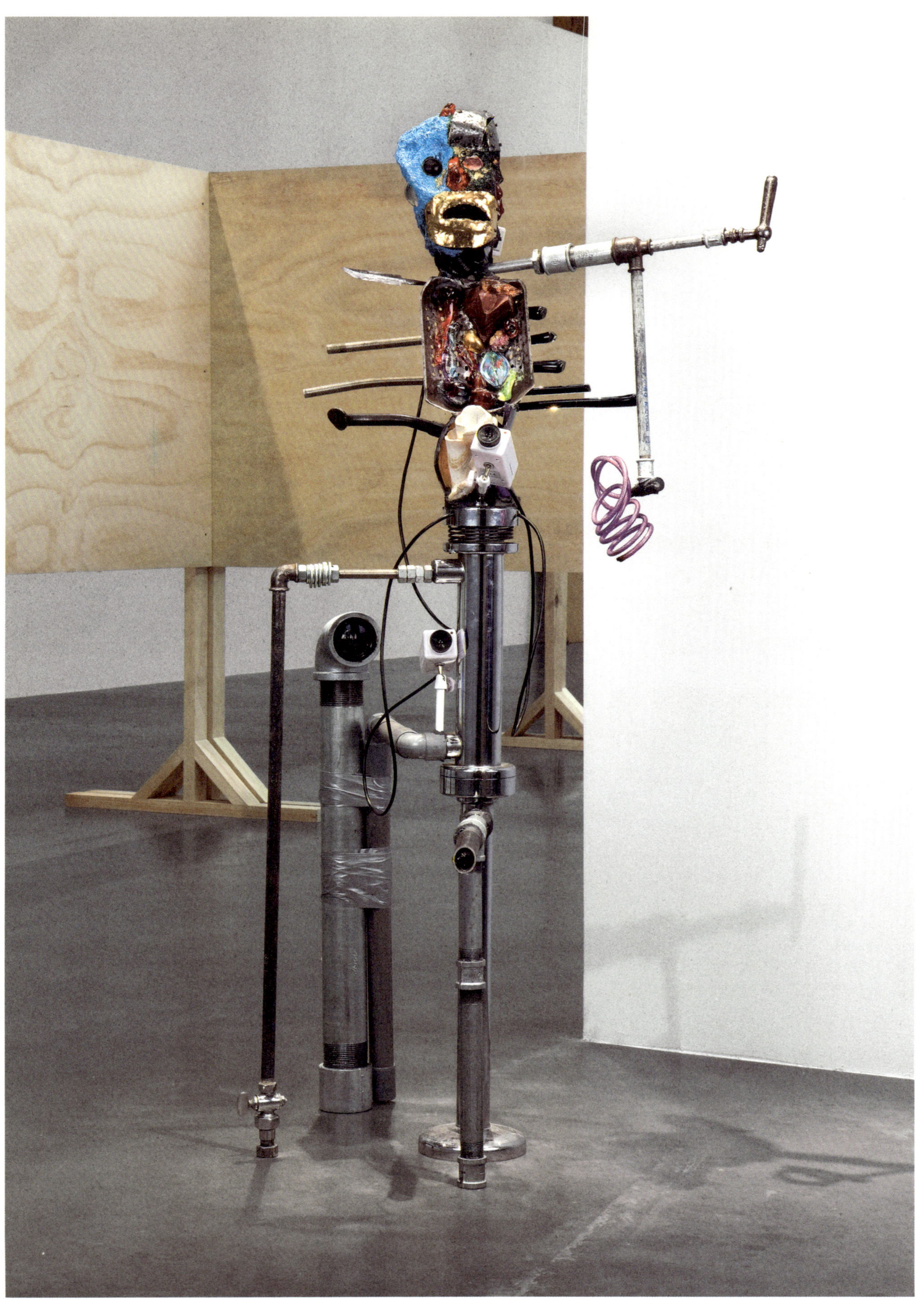

The Doorman, 2009. Steel, gold, Murano glass, olive oil can, acrylic paint, obsidian, seashell, wood, bike lock, surveillance cameras, electrical wires, duct tape.
64 × 32 × 27 ½ in. (162 × 81 × 70 cm).

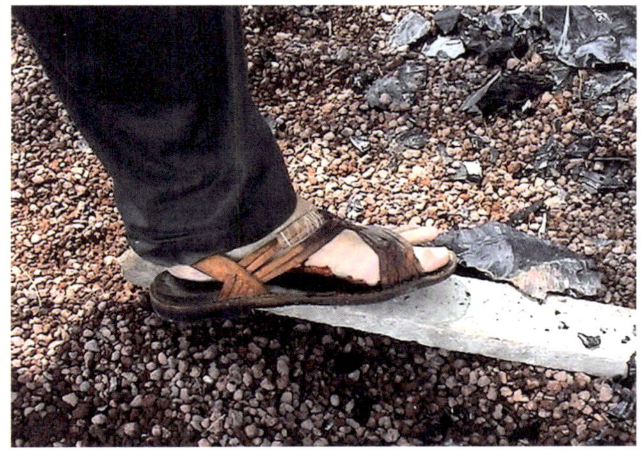
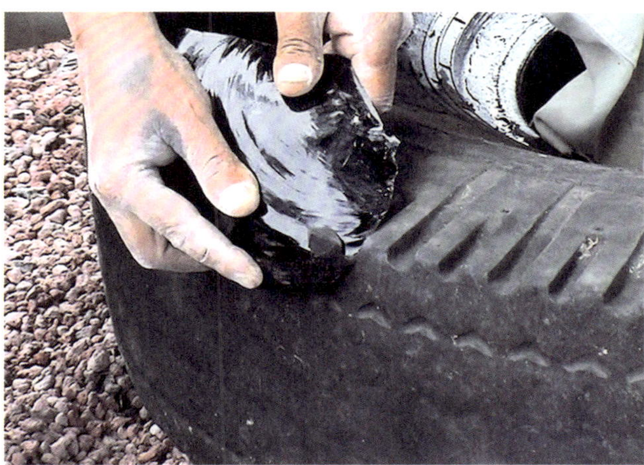
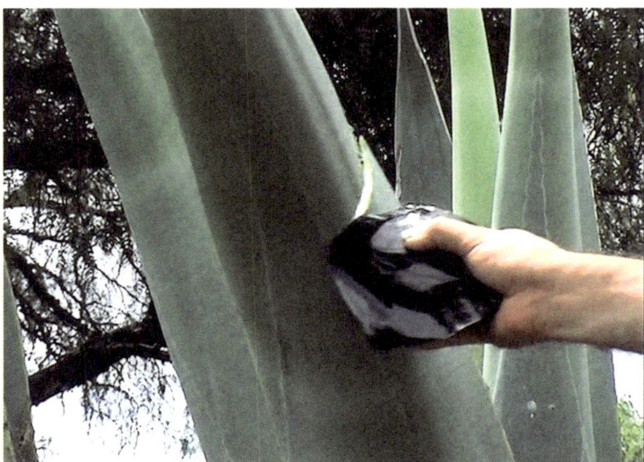
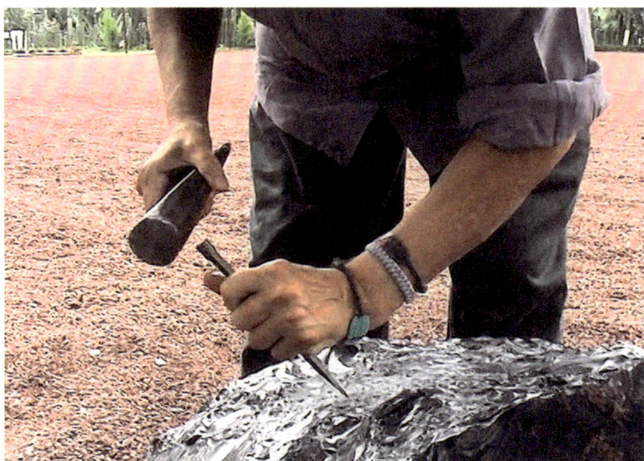

Obsidiana, 2009. Single-channel video transferred to DVD, color, sound. 5:43 min. (loop).

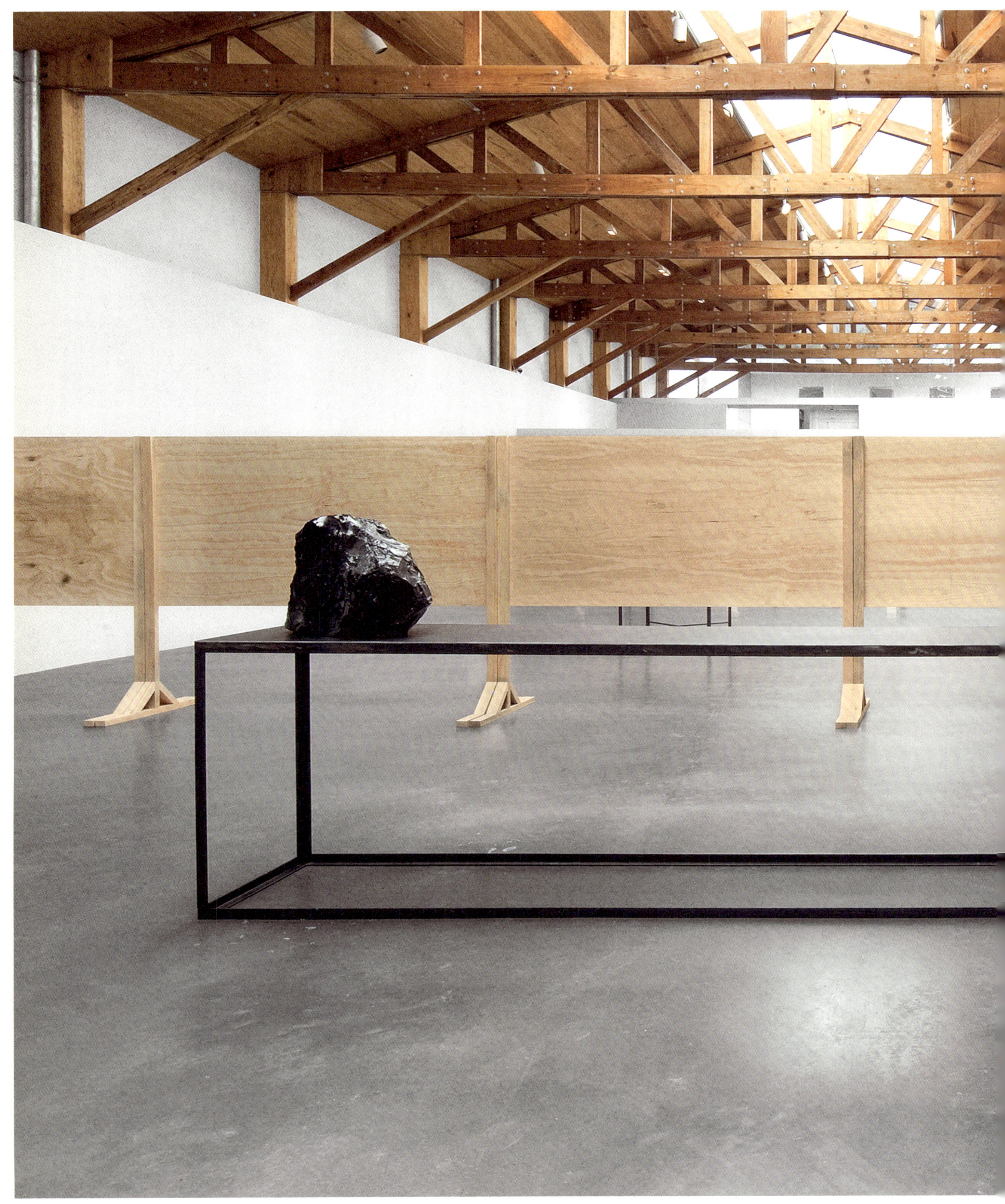

Upon reflection, I was no longer sure of my position, 2009. Obsidian, German silver (copper, zinc, and nickel), steel table, obsidian mirror with colored tin frame. Mirror: 13 ½ × 10 × ¾ in. (34 × 25 × 2 cm); table: 39 ½ × 197 × 23 ½ in. (100 × 500 × 60 cm); obsidian: 18 ½ in. (47 cm) diameter; German silver: 17 ¾ in. (45 cm) diameter.

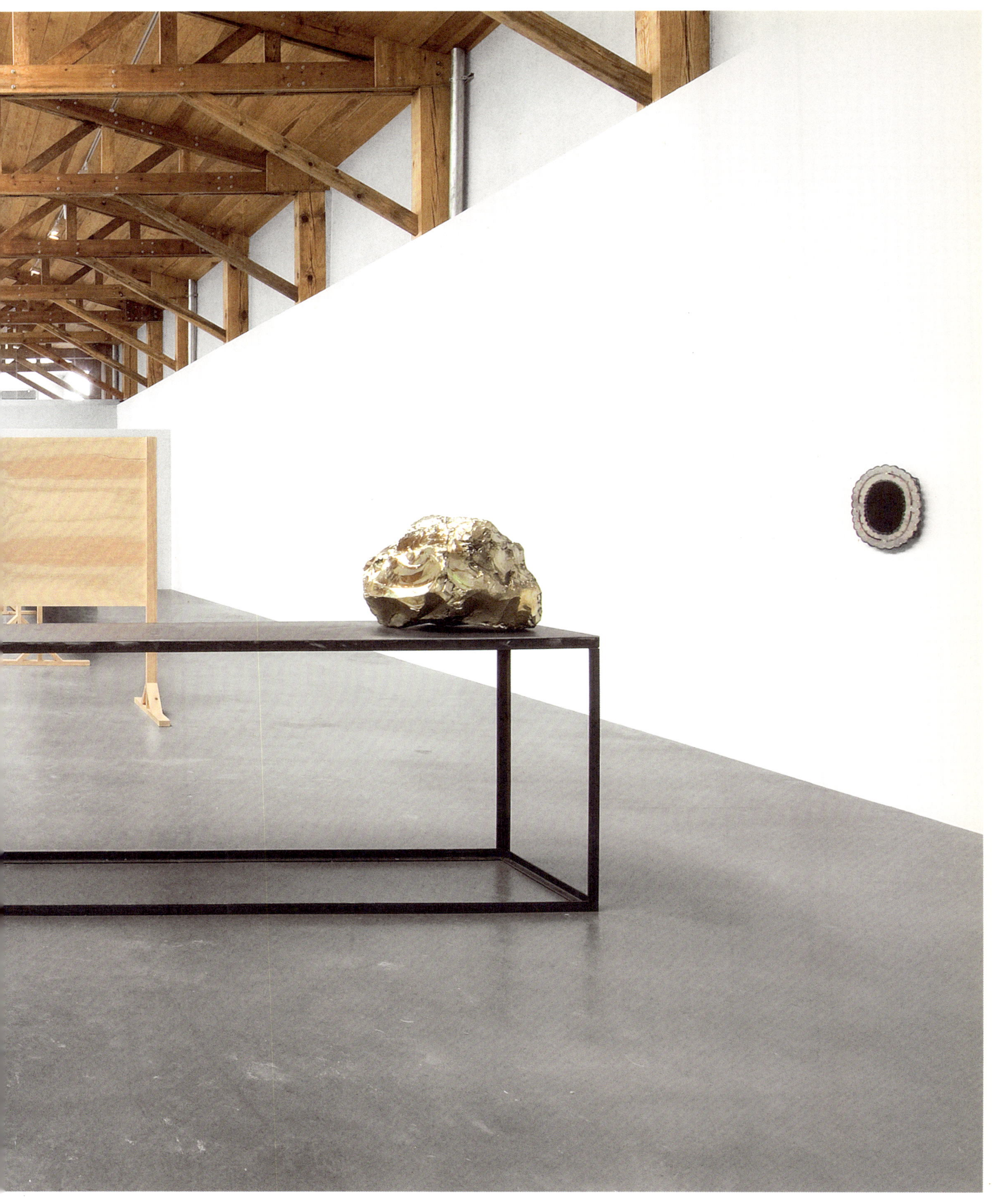

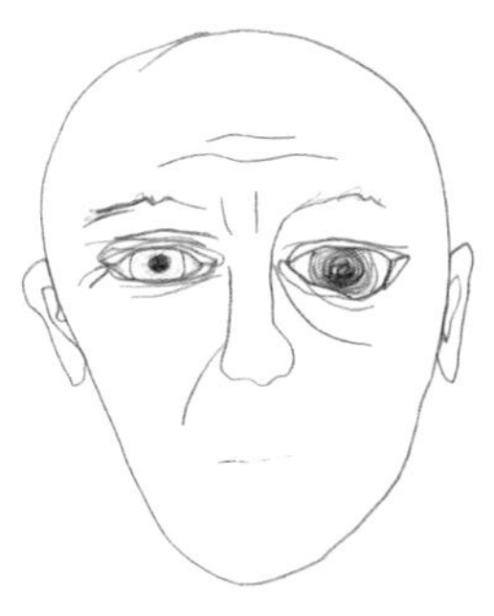

OBSIDIAN IS SO SHARP
THAT WHEN YOU ARE CUT
BY IT YOUR BODY DOES
NOT RECOGNIZE THE TRAUMA.
TO STOP THE BLEEDING
WORKERS PUT DIRT
IN THE WOUND.

Top: *Obsidian tongue*, 2009. Graphite on cotton paper. 28 ½ × 36 ⅝ in. (72.5 × 93 cm) (framed).
Bottom left: *Obsidian is so sharp that when you are cut, Mexico*, 2009. Pencil and incisions on cotton paper. 32 × 24 in. (81.5 × 61 cm).
Bottom right: *Obsidiana mexican, homenaje a Fontana, Mexico*, 2009. Incisions on cotton paper. 32 × 24 in. (81.5 × 61 cm).

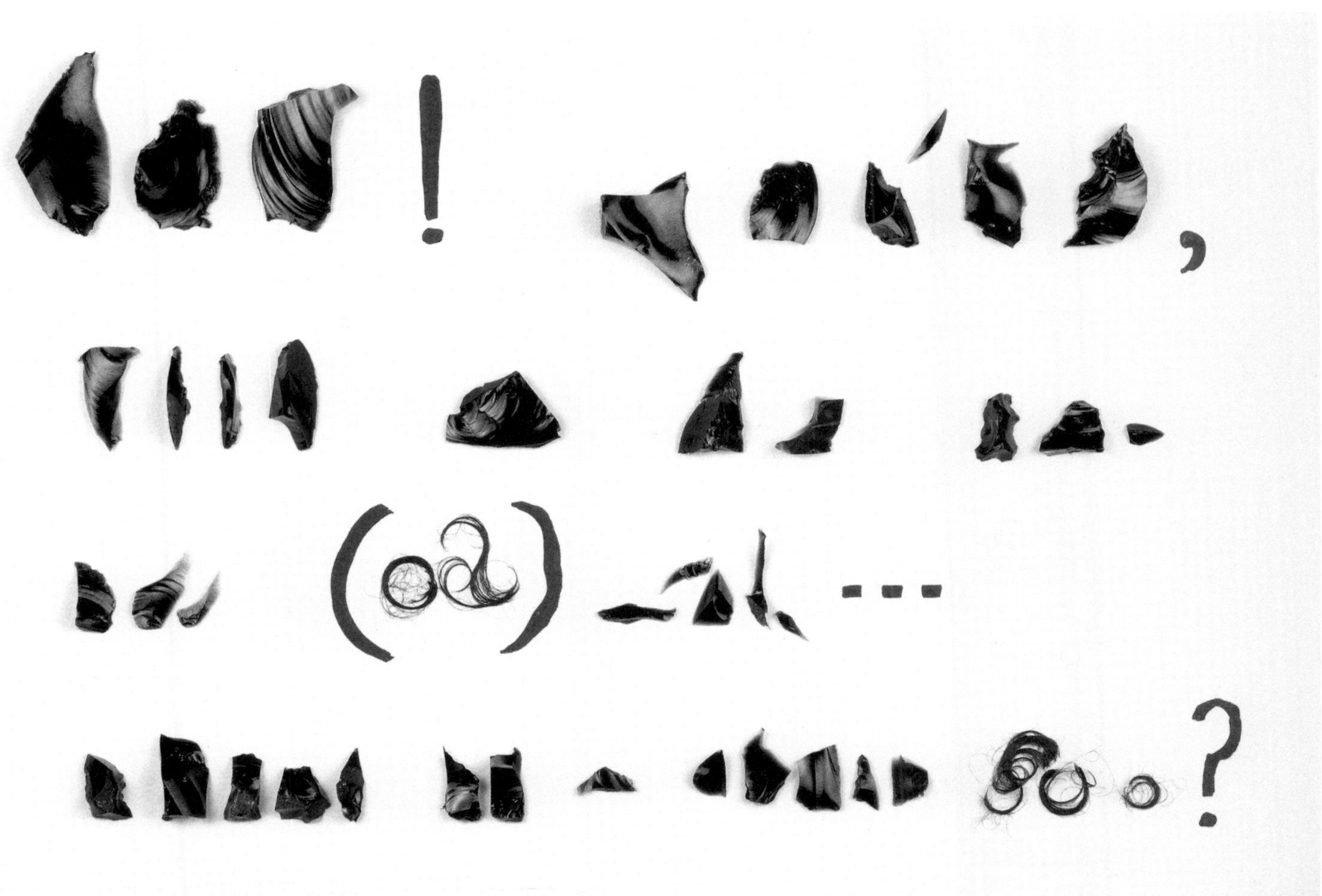

 Obsidian arabesque, 2009. Obsidian, human hair, acrylic paint on wood panel. 24 × 31 × ¾ in. (61 × 79 × 1.7 cm).

(1)

A Scottish Conspiracy

In the late 1600's Scotsmen began to live amoung the Cherokees, Creeks, and Choctaws of the Southeast of the U.S. They were accepted into communities and married local women.

This soon became a situation of internal colonization. The Scottish Indians had African slaves and were quite rich.

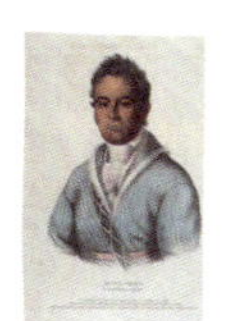

DAVID VANN, A CHEROKEE CHIEF IN 1830. HIS GRANDFATHER WAS A SCOT

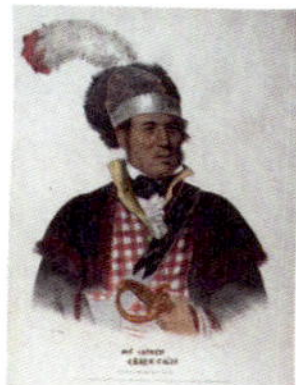

McINTOSH, A CREEK CHIEF

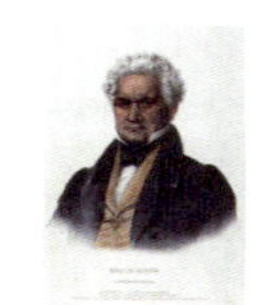

MAJOR RIDGE, A CHEROKEE CHIEF

PADDY BARR, A CREEK CHIEF →

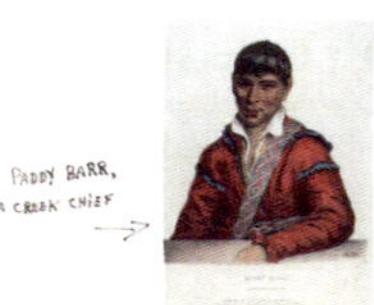

(2)

In the 1830's the U.S. forced American Indians from the Southeast of the country into Oklahoma.

At that time the principal chief of the Cherokees was John Ross. His mother was a McDonald and his first wife was Quatie Brown.

The U.S. commissioner of Indian Affairs was Joseph McMinn. The chief of the U.S. Army was Winfield Scott and the army officer dealing with Cherokees was McGinn. The Supreme Court judge was John McLean.

Except for a bunch of dead Indians it was like Scots fighting Scots.

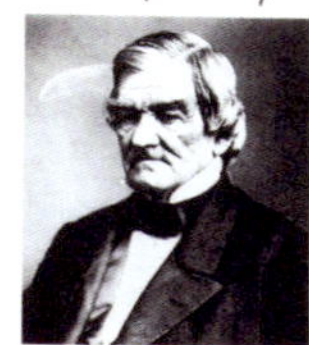

JOHN ROSS, PRINCIPAL CHIEF OF THE CHEROKEES FROM 1828–1866

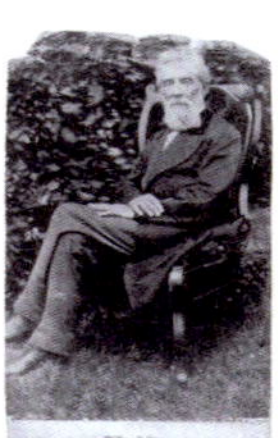

HIS NEPHEW BILL, PRINCIPAL CHIEF IN THE 1870'S

A Scottish Conspiracy, 2010. Pencil and collage on paper. 30 × 23 in. (76 × 58 cm) each of 2.

I Want You To Hear These Words About Jo Ann Yellowbird
(Ars Poetica)

From what kind of yellow bird comes the name Yellowbird?
It must mean Kunh gwo, the sacred Yellowhammer.

Ka (But now), no more dreaming or explaining;
Jo Ann Yellowbird took rat poison and died.

A chorus was provided a year before in
A pamphlet concerning related events:
"STOP THE GENOCIDE OF INDIAN PEOPLE"
"Jo Ann Yellowbird, an activist in
the American Indian Movement, was seven months
pregnant when she was kicked in the stomach
by a police officer. Two weeks later her
baby Zintkalazi was born dead. Jo Ann
has filed suit against the officer who kicked her
and the authorities who refused her medical treatment."

And to show that I am a sophisticated poet and
Not a pamphleteer, I quote from the Vocabulary
Of a Lakota Primer printed to educate those children
Of the Pine Ridge who have not been kicked to death:

"Billy Boy said	Billy eya
I like the sheriff	canakaa wustuca lake
Overtake by night	a han he ju
starve	aki ran
pneumonia	caru na pere
wash your face	ete glu ja ja
your face is dirty	ete nu sapa
comb your hair	glak ca yo
wash your clothes	ha klu ja ja pi
Supervisor	Igmu wa pa se
always take a bath	ye han nu wan po
be silent!	inila yanka yo
My eye hurts	ista mayazan
Commissioner of Indian Affairs	Ta kal Tunkashile ya pi
earth	maka
plow	maka iyublic
160 acres	maka i yu ta pi sope la
shovel	ma ki pap te
allotment	makove owapi
My chest hurts	maku mayazan
I have none	manice
Heaven	Marpiya
the Pope	Oyublaye
Church	Owacekiye
Your ears are dirty	nure ni sape
my ears ache	nure opa mayazan
wrong proceedure	ogna sni
cut your hair	pehin gla sla yo

Lord Byron's normal name
was George Gordon.
He was the cousin of the
artist Douglas Gordon.

BUT THIS DISPLAY IS ABOUT
THE GLENFIDDICH WHISKEY DISTILLERY,
WHICH, WE HAVE BEEN INFORMED, IS
OWNED BY THE GORDON FAMILY.

I INCLUDE A POEM I
WROTE ABOUT JO ANN YELLOWBIRD
BECAUSE SHE LIVED IN
GORDON, NEBRASKA

GORDON, NEBRASKA

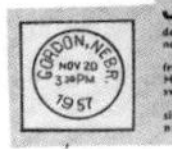

JOHN GORDON of Sioux City would have remained unknown if a lieutenant in charge of a detachment of U.S. cavalry had not acted unwisely.

Gordon set out with a train of freight wagons to reach the Black Hills at a time when the area swarmed with hostile Indians.

About five miles from the present site of the city that now bears his name, in Sheridan County, Nebraska, near a branch of the Niobrara River, Gordon's wagon train was overtaken by a unit of U.S. Cavalry whose officer demanded they should halt and return.

Gordon refused, whereupon the cavalry lieutenant ordered that the oxen be turned loose and the wagons and freight burned. For this offence the officer was later severely disciplined. But the event lived on in local legend and today a thriving city, incorporated in 1921, bears the name of this otherwise long-forgotten wagon master.

'Chinese' Gordon

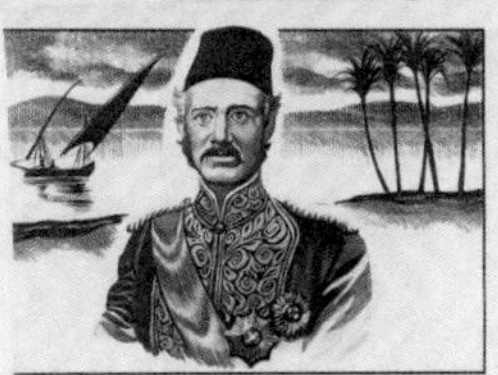

GENERAL CHARLES GORDON (1833-85) was one of the great heroes of the Victorians, who particularly admired him for his bravery and firm religious beliefs. His career was so extraordinary and his character so fascinating that people are still arguing about his life and tragic death.

He joined the Royal Engineers and became world famous in the 1860s when he led a force of Chinese guerillas, known as the Ever Victorious Army, which crushed a rebellion in China, winning battle after battle against fantastic odds. Gordon was armed with a light cane, which became known as Gordon's Wand of Victory, and he himself became known as "Chinese" Gordon.

He next amazed the world by incredible feats of government and engineering in the Sudan; then, after serving in South Africa, Ireland, Mauritius and India, he was sent back to the Sudan in 1884 by the British Government. A religious leader known as the Mahdi had declared a Holy War. Gordon's rather vague orders were to evacuate the garrisons in rebel territory and report on the situation. He reached Khartoum, the capital of the Sudan, in February. A month later the city was under siege.

Gordon had a few thousand Egyptians to ward off many more thousands of fanatical Arab tribesmen, known as Dervishes. Without his inspiring leadership they could never have held out for ten grim months. The British Government delayed sending a relief expedition, not believing that Gordon was in any real danger. Finally, an army started up the Nile in September. It proceeded too slowly and, meanwhile, Gordon's situation was growing desperate.

Lord Byron's Poem, 2010. Pencil and collage on paper. Two sheets, typed sheet: 23 ⅜ × 16 ¾ in. (59.3 × 42.5 cm); written sheet: 30 ⅛ × 22 ⅝ in. (76.5 × 57.5 cm).

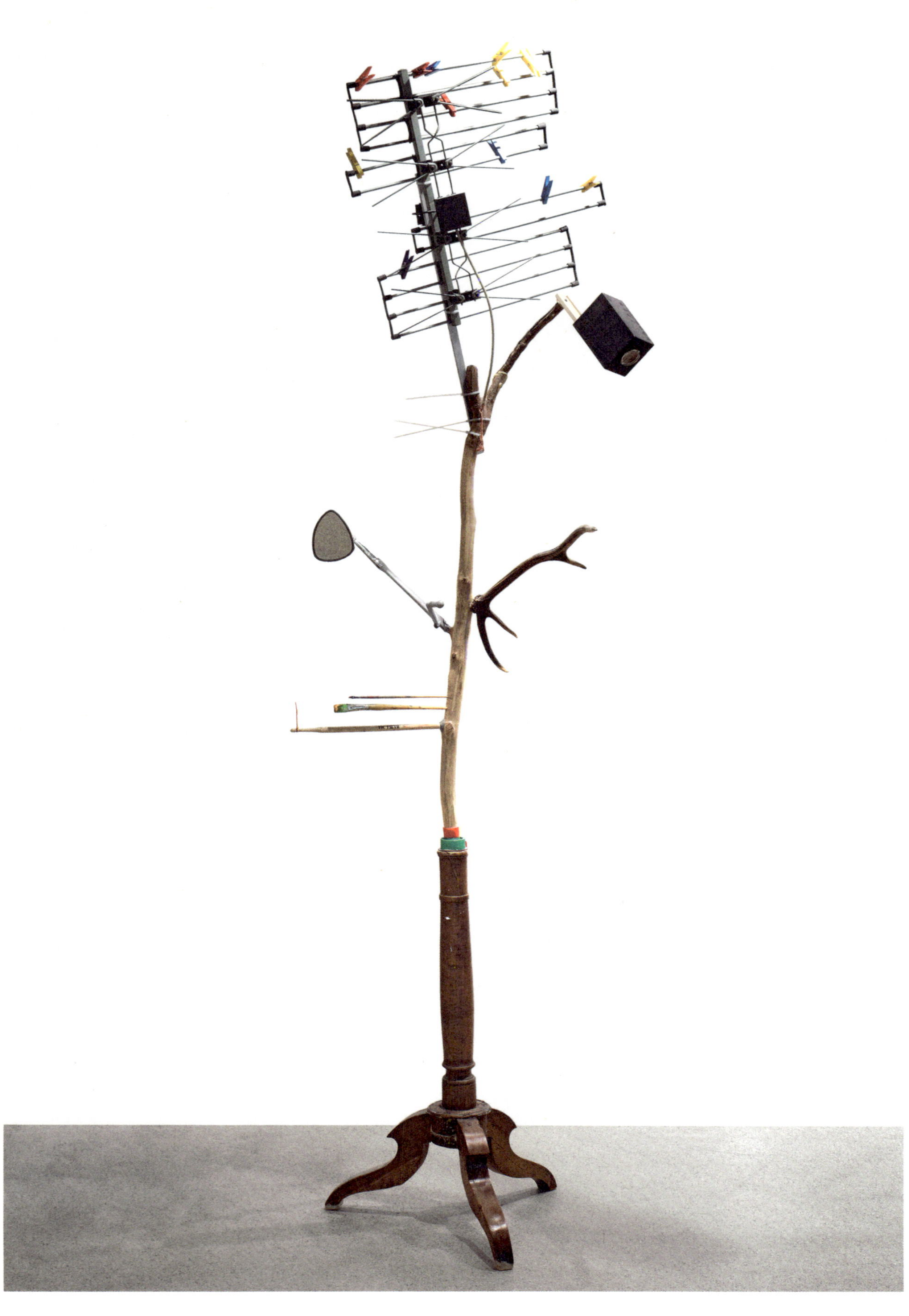

The Bluebird of Happiness and the Miner's Canary (Classic Rock), 2008. Handmade hat rack base (American black walnut), plywood, rearview mirror, deer antler, television antenna, drumstick, two paintbrushes with dried acrylic paint, clothespins, oak sapling, glass bottle, acrylic paint, electrical wire, plastic, zip ties. 118 ⅛ × 31 ½ × 35 7/16 in. (300 × 80 × 90 cm).

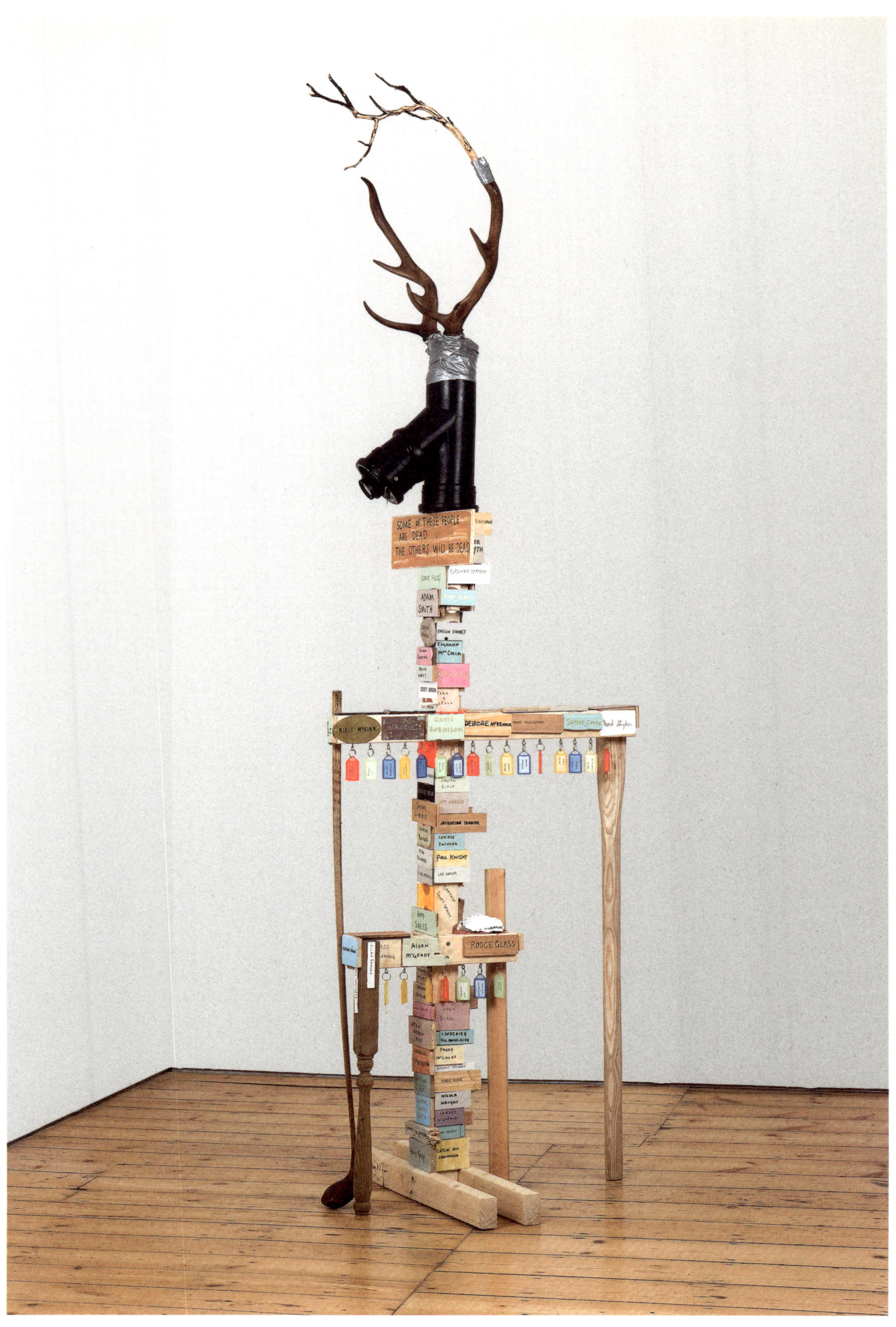

Some of These People Are Dead, 2010. PVC, duct tape, deer antler, elm branch, golf club, found furniture parts, plastic key chains, acrylic paint, ink, wood.
98 ½ × 27 ½ × 29 ½ in. (250 × 70 × 75 cm).

A CERTAIN LACK OF COHERENCE

JIMMIE DURHAM

1988

I want all of our history. I need every name, every artefact, every effort. I need to know the minute specific of our history because I need to be part of it. But I am part of it, and could not choose otherwise, the way a Jew is part of the Holocaust. In the Cherokee language the word for the world and the word for history are the same. Our history is, however, too closely tied to yours for the past three hundred and fifty years. It has become strange, untenable, unbearable and, in unbearable ways, untrue. Our history has become lies within your history. The lies have caused me great suffering from the day I was born, but at least I may (must) react to that suffering. You also suffer from the terrible unreality of a false story badly told, but must live within it, and like the torturer or his family in the evening at supper after a day's work, must do your best to continue to pretend that all is normal. I must return to the idea of torturer later, with great reluctance, (but now that it has been written, its themes lock in with one of the bases of what I'm about to consider).

From our position . . . so much is lost, and being lost, we do not recognize the loss. In one twenty-five-year period we lost half our people, not once, but twice. Those who remained were in a state of continuous warfare against you, a war aimed at our destruction. Again we lost half our people, and of the remaining, a death here, an early death there, a desperation of flight, which required of us every moment of energy and thought. Only imagine, half our doctors, our scientists, our philosophers, our historians (our children). Then again. Again. Again. And in such a war (such a *long* war!) that to laugh or dance or to make something was an incredibly arrogant act of resistance.

Here is something we have kept: an absolutely true and scientific account of our origins. The other animals held a council to see about creating humans (Cherokee). They couldn't agree because each wanted humanity to be like himself. Arguing, they fell asleep at nightfall. The coyote then took a bite from each, swallowed it all and regurgitated a Cherokee . . . with attributes of all the animals, but most like the coyote in the love of singing and acting crazy. We have, of course, kept much more, perhaps because we had no books or libraries to rely on or to be burned.

My question must always be, does what we know matter? Does it *matter if* I interrupt your authoritative history with a correction or a footnote? I mean, to the ongoing human discourse in which your declamations must surely be short-lived? Or to you collectively and personally?

As Crazy Horse was being murdered by Indians in U.S. uniforms, he said, after the first few bayonet stabs, "Let me go my friends, you have hurt me enough." His concern was for them as much as for himself. He understood the relentless confusion that had made them don the uniforms, and wanted to give them a chance to turn back in their hearts at some future moment. (But that made them so afraid they became frenzied, and bayoneted him into their own complete oblivion.)

From now back to the beginnings of our mutual encounter we have tried to protect you in such ways. In honour of that human bravery, I must not take comfort or make profit from the situation. As a victim, I cannot have the luxury of being the victim; nor would it be a kindness (although a great entertainment!) to you.

Neither can you allow yourselves the luxury of curious detachment (and I know, if you have the least bit of intelligence, you must feel detached). The England that you know is made from our deaths. Both the ships and the great machinery, even the cogwheels and gears which crushed little children's hands in the textile mills of the industrial revolution, were made from American wood. They were made from the timber of trees from places called 'Virginia', 'Carolina', and 'Georgia'. Great fortunes, dynasties, were made first from the exploitation of sassafras, then tobacco, then sugar, (three medicines which cause cancer if misused); and always the sale of the skins of the animals who in council had decided that we were a good idea.

As Europeans you must surely hate and fear the monstrosity of the U.S., the banality of Canada, and the cheerful mindlessness of Australia. But I want you to see them as your best efforts, as the most logical extension of your culture. Your permanent settler colonies are your standard, your proper measure, not an aberration which you can disclaim.

You cannot disclaim them and maintain a necessary intelligence: intelligence demands integrity. Without that integrity there is only gangsterish cunning.

The torturer: Franz Fanon wrote that Frenchmen torturing Algerians suffered nightmares and bad nerves. The U.S. torturer in El Salvador feels proud and excited. He is a more perfect Frenchman, a more perfect British colonel. The U.S. is not simply a giant cancerous part of England: it is the perfect England.

Oh. Jesus! How am I ever going to sell any artwork here, talking like that? Well, of course I know that *you* personally are as gentle and lost as I am, so that we can discuss matters calmly and irrationally.

When I began researching the lives and myths of Pocahontas and Attakulakula in London I found such a morass of lies and of important truths untold, I realized that there was no way I could present a counter-narrative, even on the most elemental level. There are many interesting facts, however, which I've uncovered in preparation for this work, all the more interesting because of the method and substance with which they have been covered. Some of them may help guide you through the four-point space of dreams and tricks which I've prepared.

The story of Pocahontas as written by her husband John Rolfe was taken whole-cloth from a book by Richard Hakluyt, published in London in 1603. Hakluyt's book, however, told the story with a heroic crusader captain and a beautiful Arab princess as the two characters. Hakluyt himself moved to Virginia later on, and Rolfe may have known him there. The story in both books is about an English captain whose life is saved by the princess, but in Rolfe's version the captain was John Smith. The myth of Pocahontas and John Smith became an important operant in the construction of America, and had its counterparts all over the hemisphere. In Brazil the story is told about a woman named Iragema; in Mexico, Malinche.

But John Rolfe determined to make it real, to participate personally in the myth. He brought Pocahontas to London, had her re-named 'Lady Rebecca', and had a child by her (John Rolfe Jr). The name by which she was known back home was 'Metoaka', so we may suppose that the change from 'Pocahontas' to 'Rebecca' was of no great concern to her, (the dialect of the Cherokee language that she spoke had no 'l's, so she would have said, "Mi nahmi issi Rahdy Ribbeccah").

She died on the Thames, on her way home, but anyway, the river by which she had played as a child had already been re-named the 'James', in that 'Virgin Forest' called 'Virginia'.

Let the Little Carpenter be your spiritual guide, as he is the guardian of these trashy dime-novel treasures I've laid out. In his language he is known as Attakulakula, but his nick-name was 'The Fixer'. He was a guy who attempted to bring together society's disparate elements, disputing factions and potentially profitable trade undertakings. His nick-name was mis-translated as the 'Little Carpenter', but as one of our official delegates to the Royal Court in 1730, he is listed on the Treaty as 'Colonna', which was his military title (corresponding to 'Captain').

He was a very personal man, and his unbending loyalty to friends ultimately brought him isolation in the desperate times of war. Even when fighting the British he protected the lives of his British friends. What did he think of London in 1730? Where did he go, and what museums did he visit? Did he see any plays— *The Tempest*, perhaps? He called London the 'Pigeon Place', (we did our own re-naming).

The Treaty of 1730 between England and the Cherokee Nation was of constant importance to us. We fought with England against the colonists, which brought us grief. In the Second World War young Cherokee men went to fight with England in honour of that treaty, and there is still told around campfires the prophecy that some day men in red coats will come from across the sea to help us.

"PROBABLY THIS WILL NOT WORK"

JIMMIE DURHAM

1994

People ask me in the U.S., where I was born and I have to give a Cherokee-answer, that begins with the beginning of the universe and goes through the creation of Cherokee people up to my birth. Partly, because that's the way we like to see things, in a whole situation, and partly, because where I was born is a political situation called the U.S., not in a so-called 'state' of the U.S. You might say I was born under the state of Arkansas, because my people were there long before the State of Arkansas. The state of Arkansas is against us, we're not a part of it, nor the state of Oklahoma nor Arizona or any other of these states. But to say that I was born under the state of Arkansas makes it as though I am already dead! I've written three new pages to read, after which I'm probably going to ramble incoherently!

We seem so often now to be on the brink of some absurd world war, wherein the enemy is not clearly seen. When we look at the globe we must think, maybe the war has actually begun. And what strange and drastic changes have occurred just in the past ten or twelve years.

But we would have a great unease even without the stupid chaos of these recent times, because so many phenomena are reaching crises points simply through mathematical statistics. I've read, for example, that the world population might stabilize in the next twenty to fifty years, either at ten billion people or twenty billion people. We'll have ten billion very soon. And how are we to think of that? How can we think of art, literature, or, really, any human project with this almost obscene figure, ten billion people? Where, even, is any human knowledge at that level?

And then our places are changing before our eyes, even as we defend old, practically imaginary places. Immigrants from south-east Asia are changing demographic and cultural politics, not only in the western U.S., but also in Ireland, unnoticed, while Catholics and Protestants try to solve their old dilemma.

In Mexico the government kills Indians. The fact is not known much in the world, not even in Mexico City. But it is not especially newsworthy. The scale is not on that of Rwanda, and the world has troubles enough to consider. But 1994 began with an armed Indian uprising, in southern Mexico, that soon spread to other Indian communities around the country.

In late January I wrote to a friend in Europe about my frustrations. I said the obvious, that art has no possibility of functioning, of influencing, of making even the most subtle or timid intervention in a crisis. Art needs a longer time, a quieter time, a complex, indirect approach. It doesn't function well in the short run. In Mexico I have been confronted with a crisis that demands immediate action. And my work cannot find a place. Just a few months ago we had been struggling to maintain some serious discourse about art itself in Mexico, against bourgeois colonial attitudes and cultural gangsterism. In June I was in Belgium, showing with a group of young Mexican artists. The dialogue I'd intended fell apart in front of the new Mexican Indian war.

But, even though we, and certainly I, cannot be coherent about our expectations for art, as part of some vague humanizing project, we *do* have those expectations. We think art must be doing something . . . that artists must be more than crafts people or iconoclasts, more than entertainers.

I do not like most art and why should I? No one expects to like most writing, that is, most of the books published each year. It seems to me that artists agree to be stupid in the name of sophistication. Someone has told us that art really is separate from other human endeavours. The implication of such a nonsensical proposition is stunning. If art is just art, or if any human endeavour is a separate singularity without reference to all others, then it would have to be what used to be called bestial, but bestial to some other beast than the human beast, since part of our species' program is the integration of systems and the creation of meaning.

But the art I do not like comes from artists who *know* so much. They're so sure of things, I imagine they have been hypnotized. And so, the work is complacent; it pretends. Then we find ourselves pretending along with the pretense, pretending to ourselves that we don't notice it, something destructive, something at variance with our human project is thereby produced.

This complacency that I see artists having, I think probably it comes from fear and from fear of facing fear. And if that's the case, then we are in danger of becoming something really monstrous. It's more than just whistling in the dark. I think we as artists and as an art system, as an art discourse with critics, galleries, collectors, magazines and so on, I think we can generate inhumanity. I think it's easy for us to generate inhumanity, when we're not generating humanity, when we're not deliberately doing something with the human project, when we're just having fun or doing something frivolous, which is different from funny or silly, I think.

We join the war on the side of the enemy. We generate inhumanity, that's what I think. I recently read an interview with V. S. Naipaul, the British Indian writer, that I like very much, because he's a curmudgeonly complainer. And I have a soft spot for those kinds of people. He said he doesn't like most writing. But he especially doesn't like books that have plots, because if a book has a plot, a beginning, a middle and an end, then the writer is pretending that the world is known, and telling the reader that the world is known, that the universe is known, when In fact it is not known. And we're not a known development.

What we can most see in this century is not that we made automobiles and computers but that we saw gaps in our knowledge: about biology, about psychology, about our humanism, indeed about the world, the universe. We learnt our lack of knowledge in this century. We learnt uncertainty against the certainty that we had before. When we look at the history of this century we learnt that we truly are perverse.

Let me say something about chimpanzees. We said for the first half of this century that chimpanzees were just animals, and that was it. And then we said, no they're like us, they're very kind and they're very social. And then we kept studying over just the past fifteen, twenty years and we said, yes they're just like us. They're murdering bastards. And they're cute and sweet. We come from a perverse group of animals, the primates are a ridiculous crowd. And among the primates we seem to be the most ridiculous, but very primate-like all the same, very much like everyone else. In this century we began to learn biological uncertainty, we learnt of our incompleteness. And we learnt that we're not good, that we're not bad. There's not already a known factor about us, everything is to be discovered. And it's probably not going to work, because we probably won't have time. Why do you want to know something about twenty billion crazy monkeys getting in each other's face? There's nothing very interesting there, except the consequent suffering and the squalor. At least, we now are frightened by the various problems. We're probably not going to work them out. We're probably not going to amount to anything.

There's a literary device, that science fiction writers use, that's called in the U.S. "if this continues, if this goes on". And it's a mechanism that a science fiction writer can use. He says, or she says: "All right there are five billion people and then there will be ten billion people. And if this goes on then there will be hundreds of billions of people. And I can write a story about these hundreds of billions of people." So, it's easy to write a book that way. But it's back to what Naipaul is complaining about, as though the universe was known. Because it pretends that the future will be similar to the present, only more. The writer pretends to prophecy, so we can see what it would be like. It would be like now, only more, instead of a few seats filled, every place would be filled.

It looks like the complacency of fear. But it is a complacency of fear that makes us stupid and we continue. And our main project, which is to be stupid, to be more stupid, to be more inhuman, to forget that there might be something that we can call the: human project. That's a continuing secondary project, that Homo sapiens have, that probably will take us over, as I can see.

Let's look at the future! When I stack up my evidence about it, I don't see one, or I rather don't see one that I might like. But that's the same, if I saw one that I did like, it would be the same, I think. And it's what Gertrude Stein said just after the First World War. She explained how the generals of Europe, the military leaders, knew that the First World War was going to be different from the wars of the century before. And they knew that they had to prepare for a different kind of war. And that's what they all tried to do. And what they did instead was to prepare for the wars of the century before, because they didn't know how to prepare for something unknown. They knew something unknown would happen. But you can't prepare for something unknown. You can only prepare for what is known, which is preparing for the past. And then you get something completely unsatisfactory.

So, if there are artists who say, usually very sentimentally: "My work is for the future", or "I work for the future", it's a pretty arrogant statement, isn't it? It's a strange kind of arrogance.

Then there's the arrogance of working for the present, even if the artist doesn't say: "I'm working for the present". The artist might say something New York flip: "I don't care about these philosophical ramblings" or "I don't care about all this confusion and angst about art. I do my work now, I have my shows, blah, blah, blah." You heard the Rev. That's not something that we can easily tolerate as artists, from ourselves. We can't easily tolerate that kind of monstrosity. That's the only thing I can call it, this cute, cheerful monstrosity.

When I'm interviewed for articles and newspapers or something, there's usually the question: "Why did I take up art?" If the interviewer knows that I'm a political activist and that I have been a political activist full-time, the question is: "Why did I take up art?" This is a little subtle and it may seem that if I make something of nothing, I think I'm not. If I were, if I were European, if I were some normal artist, if I were a normal American, the opposite question might well be asked instead: "Why did you take up politics?" You see the difference. And this is for me the more correct question, the question why did I take up politics, as a full-time activist, since I was already an artist, since making art was my primary goal. I don't know what project, what employment, my role in life may be.

I started doing political work full-time in the early seventies, because there wasn't a choice at first. The U.S. put American Indians in a situation, where we had to respond. And we just had to respond, whether we liked it or not. We had been in that situation at other times in our history with the U.S. When you are forced to respond, you must. But second, besides being a clear responsibility that I couldn't ignore, I thought we would win. I thought we would win our political goals, perhaps by the mid-eighties. It looked like we could win. This was a time when so much of Africa had just gotten out from under European colonialism, so much of Africa was just about to. And the most horrible aspects of neocolonialism and decolonialism hadn't happened fully yet. We thought we might get somewhere. Instead we lost more than we started with. We went backwards in time and history. By the time Reagan came in, in the eighties, we lost more than I can imagine. We can never return to this point.

The question, why did I take up art, implies that, since I'm from an oppressed people, a colonized people, politics is my proper job. And therefore I do art, because we lost politically. In other words, that the first level of fighting for me is, and should be, politics, and the second level might be literature, or writing, or art, or music, or something. But that's only an assumption made about third world people. The opposite assumption is not made for Europeans, for white folks, in general. So it's a subtle difference. But it's an important difference, isn't it? I think art is my primary thing. It's not a way of doing politics. It's not a way of fighting the whites. There aren't any clear political goals to my artwork. But it would be a little silly to say, here I would do this art and over here is politics. And to say you can't mix art and politics, that's a very silly thing. Someone has told us to say: You can't mix this with that. You can't mix this category with that category. And the people who made the categories have told us that you can't mix them. And these are not just some people sitting up somewhere. It's the 'states'. You know what I mean by the people?

I want all art to be political. My art has to be political, but it doesn't have to be political. It's just, the point is to integrate instead of to separate. The point is to make some coherency instead of contributing to this inhumanity that I was talking about earlier.

I wonder now, especially these days, how I can make art. And I wonder how any of us can make art. I'm working on two big shows now in Europe. And I don't have a clue about what I'm doing and how to do it. I think, not because I'm an Indian artist, but rather because I'm not. Not because I don't know how to make art that will reach people. But we're in a situation, that we don't even know what art might be for us. The framework is there. You can't interrupt the framework. We recently tried that in a group show in Marseille, to do artwork that hadn't a sign of art to it, except that it was in a commercial gallery. Well, that word 'except' has implications. Because people came to the commercial gallery knowing they would see art, that didn't look like art. Art that has a sign "not art" is a kind of art now isn't it? We all know that sign, "this is not art art".

If I make some art that really has no art sign and I put it in a place that has no art sign, no one could see it. I can't make magic art. No one can make magic art.

There is a set of art discourses, as we all know. And we all know that now they aren't serving us well. They are not working. And we live in a time where nothing is probably going to work. If, as an artist, I interrupt the discourse and say: "No, no I don't want to talk about that. I don't want to talk about this, that I just made." It's only an interruption. And I think we have to be responsible and take ourselves seriously enough as artists to do something more than interruption, because it can't be heard and an interruption is just an interruption. If we can, instead, steer the conversation over to some other place and then, if someone picks up that approach, then we can see how we might work. In other words, we can see ways out of our art crisis, only in social situations, in art discourses, not in the private arrogance contained in our own brains. For each of us to think of answers and bring the answers to the body. Then there is not a possibility for the artist to do anything except make gesture after gesture after gesture. And we all get bored, but we all pretend we're not bored. And we all pretend we're interested, because it is art. And that is what we all wished we loved.

I have a friend in Ghent who says that I'm always explaining things as though the situation was colonial and as though that mattered. And he tells other people, "Jimmie always throws in the word *colonial*, and it doesn't really matter. It's just a word he likes." Well, he's my friend. So I won't hit him, until I can find a way to hit him properly. The colonial reality is the only reality we have. All of our thoughts are a consequence of colonial structure, the universe we live in, to the extent that it is known, is known through this colonial mentality.

When you watch television, you watch a colonial situation. I watched a simple little show a few days ago on CNN, and some American white man, about my age, was talking to three so-called 'third world' television journalists, much younger. And he was being very nice to them, very understanding and very gentle, just like a colonial father. And they were taking it in, they were believing him. And when you see it there, I think people who are watching the show didn't say, "Jesus, look at this colonial set-up I'm seeing. It's intolerable." I think people said, "Hmm, they're saying some stupid things, it's television. It's neutral television. It's nothing to do with colonialism."

I can't make art that says: colonialism is bad, but we can, we can make an art system that takes into account that we are trapped in this stupidity that's not good for us. That tells us how to see the world and it's not the way that the world will be. When I think of how I might make good art, if I could make good art, I think of writers more than I think of artists. Because I don't like most art.

But having started the process of moving to Dublin I've been re-reading James Joyce's book of short stories called *Dubliners*, which I enjoyed thirty years ago. But reading it now, I'm really struck by how perfect and how sharp his hatred of Dublin is. And how his hatred of his fellow Dubliners makes him write such brilliant stories, that contribute something to the life of Ireland through his hatred of their intolerable stupidity. There's not one story that's cute. There's not one story that gives anyone a break in Dublin. There's not one story that celebrates the Irish people. He wrote these before or during the First World War, when Ireland was in serious trouble with England, when people were suffering. He didn't give them a break. He wasn't interested in explaining to them, or to the world, or to himself any sentimentality, or any hope. He only wanted to say: "I hate this stupidity and I have to write this hatred. I have to attack this stupidity. I hate my people this way, and this way, and this way and this way." And he lays it all out in *Dubliners*. If I could be that sharp, and if I could somehow start a discourse in the art world, where that might be seen as a possibility, not on such a literal level, because we are not talking about writing. We are talking about something, we don't even know yet, something that we don't know how to do, as visual art.

I'm going to end with the not knowing how. I'm going to end with the lack of hope. Because I'm from the U.S., I have a more sharp problem with hope. The U.S. is famous for calling itself a nation, and a government built on law, not on men. For us this is a special, acute problem, because American Indians have law on our side. We have treaties with the U.S. And the supreme court over the years has upheld the fact of the treaties, and the nature of the treaties, that these are treaties between governments, between countries, between the Cherokee nation and the U.S. nation for example. And the law is not upheld. And all of this century we have been imagining that if we got sharp enough lawyers or a sympathetic enough jury, the law will be upheld and it never has been. So, after having gone through centuries of military defeat and death by every imaginable kind of genocide, then we have to come to the point.

How might we do something in the U.S.? The U.S. is against the law. The law won't work for us, no matter what. We can't convince the public of our just cause. And we can't take up guns and drive them back over here. And people say: "Do you think the Cherokee language can maintain itself and develop itself?"

And I say: I don't see how and I don't think so. Because it's not taught in schools. It's not spoken at home. And there is television. Electricity now means television and television means American shows, American languages, and it's not in the Cherokee languages and it's not our television. And then people say: "Well, do you think you can maintain yourselves culturally as Cherokees?" And I say: No, I don't think so, for the very same reasons. We are more and more dispersed. We are more and more intermarried. We are more and more this, that and the other. And I can't imagine a place where we can be, even in the next generation, in the next twenty-five years, but certainly not in the next hundred years. I don't see any Cherokees in the future in the next hundred years, or Apaches, or Sioux, or Comanches.

In other words, I'm in the same position that my great-grandfather was in. And here I'm saying that. There however is a way in which he didn't quite lose his battle, even though it would seem in every way that you can look at, he lost.

What we see now with law is that it's not working, because criminality has become the new plague of the world. And the law can't take care of it anymore. It doesn't matter if genocide is against the law, it never has. It doesn't matter if serial murdering is against the law. It doesn't matter if rape is against the law.

All these crimes are growing. All these crimes are multiplying. But the law is based on an older system. The law is based on torture, medieval torture in Europe. The law is based on that. Act the way the state tells you to, or the state will burn you, or cut off your hand, or whip you, or something bad. That's where the law comes from. It's breaking down now. And whilst I don't have any hope, we don't know what's going to happen.

If we make art as though we know what's going to happen, whether it is hopeful or cynical, we're not working on an art project—we're working against an art project! Only with a great uncertainty and with a great deal of dialogue about that uncertainty can some very small achievements be made for some future that we cannot see or imagine. We have to work in strange ways and hopeless ways but not cynical ways. Not the naivety of cynicalness, which puts us in the same boat, which puts us all in the colonial boat. All in a boat where we can say: "Well, we'll go for that swim and we're probably going to drown. It's probably not going to work!"

The text is a transcript from a speech given at the International Association of Art Critics Congress, Copenhagen, 1994.

SILLY CRIMES OF THE ACADEMI-CIANS

JIMMIE DURHAM

2014, Napoli

In 1992 or '93 I was in NYC working on a gallery show. Gabriel Orozco had just moved to New York and was helping me put things together. He brought over a young white woman who had that kind of naïve arrogance that seems to pass for sophistication in NYC. She said that the time of 'identity art' was over. I had not heard the phrase before and had to think for several days about what it might mean.

It seems clear to me now that so much art reflects the art system itself. That is a particularly detrimental phenomenon that can be called 'identity art' - - - re-enforcing a hermetic system. I know that American crime novel writers constantly reference the system of crime novels but when I look for a book to read I am looking for actual writing about thoughts; I am not looking for that kind of 'bookism' that would hush my brain. It is actual writing of thoughts that I want; not 'books'. For me it is the same with art. Not about style, talent, material or content - - - something more that I often call 'intellectual', by which I mean the same things I mean when choosing a book to read or music to hear or a film to watch.

In Europe the history of art is the history of strengthening personal identity through the identity of the state. I often refer to the marble carving of a giant white man made by Michelangelo to represent a Jewish shepherd. More pervasive are the thousands of paintings in Europe purporting to be of biblical scenes only set in Europe with European costumes. Much more important to European identity are the paintings of Jesus. He is always portrayed with fair skin and hair, blue or hazel eyes. So much so that the world 'knows' that is how he looked. Identity art to a very high degree.

In NYC I divided the gallery into left and right. As one entered 'art' works hung on the left side. Pieces typical of things I was making at the time, similar to works I'd made for Exit Art a couple of years earlier. These works have no 'message', political or otherwise. They do, however, have a political edge, in the form of texts that are part of the work, or juxtapositions of kinds of material or in different ways.

On the right-hand side of the gallery all of the works were 'anti-art', and purported to be made by a fictitious character from English literature, Caliban.

I still try to see what about this show brings forth the clearly accusatory label 'identity art'. The 'art' side was works in which I attempted to break out of the hermeticism of known art ways. The Caliban side was more overtly political but there still was no message. I tried to show the stupidity of British colonialism and racism but at no time did I make statements, condemnatory or explanatory. Caliban, a fictional character, tried to see his face, unsuccessfully.

The following decade witnessed the explosion of art by artists who were not white and not following the accepted ways of art. Often they, like the Europeans, however, would include imagery or other references to specific places or family.

It is certainly true that very many Native American artists have been making paintings of Native Americans. Similar, I suppose to paintings of guys like those by Chuck Close, Elizabeth Peyton, David Salle, David Hockney and others, but these artists are exempt from the charge of identity art.

I have written about a statement by the actor Ian McKellen. He said that often straight people complain that gay people tend to 'go on' too much about gay life. Straight people, he said, never cease talking about their dates, spouses, honeymoons. A constant barrage of chatter about their straightness that seems only natural to them, not to be interrupted by 'others' talk.

So many artists who were not white and not doing the art that the white guys were doing. It must surely have been quite tiring to the white world. By about 2005 many different curators had come to describe my work as dealing with my identity. No matter how much I protested and tried to explain they cheerfully kept the label. Only curators, though. I have never heard another artist, critic, or even gallerist or collector use the phrase.

That says to me that it came from and spread among curatorial departments and programs.

It seems clear that they mean art by non-white artists, because it is used exclusively against us.

About two years ago the American art historian Jessica Horton and I were talking about the phenomenon of art by non-white artists being labeled 'identity art'. Horton said it is a nonsense phrase that is not used by art historians. We agreed that it is against clarity and knowledge.

The reasons why it now becomes so popular are really more than stupidity, even though that is an important factor in why so many curators will take up a phrase to be seen as 'in-the-know'. Racism is the primary reason.

As I write, in 2014, the Museum of Contemporary Art in Antwerp has a large group show called *"Don't You Know Who I Am?" Art after Identity Politics*.

The director and curator are both friends whom I respect. Without having seen the show I find it perverse.

The show includes many non-white artists, so that we can see that the museum does not mean anything covertly racist, as is so often the case. Among these are Haegue Yang and Oscar Murillo, whose works seem in many ways to rely on their backgrounds and identities. I do not mean that pejoratively. I also do not want to make the show central to my argument. Reading the statement about it, though, one can see that the inclusion of the phrase 'Identity Politics' in the title means art of a particular political or polemical nature. (Leaving aside for the moment the fact that what all of the art people normally mean when they use the phrase 'identity art' is art that is political and is made by artists who are not white.)

There certainly is much bad art out there these days, and as Jone Kvie says, that is a main criterion for commercial success. The main reason there is so much bad art, though, is that there is so much art.

A publisher friend in NYC thirty-five years ago was lamenting that good books could not be published because all the publishing houses were run by accountants who looked only at volume sales. Now we see thousands of bad books on sale in every airport, train station, supermarket. Difficult to find a good book, and therefore writers' seriousness of intent unconsciously goes small.

The art system is similar.

What is most energizing now is that anything goes. Art now really can be anything if a serious artist makes it seriously. (I tend to like the seriousness of truly humorous art, so don't think I mean portentousness.) Because of minority artists, ok yes, as well as Marcel Duchamp, Guy Debord and Bas Jan Ader, but not beginning with them; because of minority artists art is now free of all bourgeois frames.

If we want or need to be tired of something let it be lying art and bad art. These two kinds go through all the fake and misleading categories the academicians can dream up.

BEKKAH AND SON, AND ELPIDIO

JIMMIE DURHAM

2014, Napoli

I knew Son and Bekkah in San Francisco.

He had a place called 'Sonny's Pima Pizza and Poetry'. It was mostly a permanent stage where he could recite his poetry and sometimes his rap monologs which were only sometimes poems. Every few months he would have an evening of reading from his favorite poets, T. S. Eliot, Walt Whitman, E. E. Cummings; writers I have always intensely disliked. He did not invite anyone else to read, though, and had a mile-a-minute overly-energetic way of talking that allowed no interruption nor discussion.

The restaurant was not exactly in the Mission District, but close by. He said that he called it 'Sonny's' because the name Son had no poetry. Son's mother was Pima, from the Mexican side of that strange border originally, but came to the U.S. as a child. Son was her first born and hence given the name. She had no other children but perhaps intended to have.

Son did not know his father although he always said he was Apache. No, not always, now that I remember. Sometimes he said his father was Yaqui.

Bekkah was a wolf. A mountain lion. What we call a Beloved Woman, if only we had our sense back. She was Cherokee from Oklahoma, except that she was Black. From that community that are descendants of Africans who were slaves 'belonging to' some Cherokee families.

Oklahoma is really racist and Oklahoma Cherokees can be mortifyingly stupid.

Bekkah was a warrior. A Spirit. She had those incredible green-violet eyes you often see in Black Cherokees from the Carolinas. Take your breath away.

Probably not yet twenty when she came out to San Francisco. A lot of people were suspicious of her, even if no one would say what exactly they were suspicious of. Many Oklahoma Cherokees went out to California over the years, though, and a blond-haired Cherokee woman at the Community House introduced Bekkah to Son to see if she could get a job. It's Bekkah who told me this.

She was a good waiter and popular with everyone, helping Son's business more than he knew.

Son often hung out with movie star-types, or maybe they just sort of tolerated him. At least that's the way I always saw it. Kind of like a pet Indian but movie stars don't really seem to be so loyal to pets.

But there was a guy from Mexico, more an actor than a movie star, and he started hanging out at the restaurant.

One time this guy brought another Mexican; guy named Elpidio.

You know what happened next. He and Bekkah started hanging out together. Easy to see why --- Elpidio was good-looking in a way that was really rough, but children cottoned to him right away, and different kinds of older working women who can often act dangerous and bad. I never could figure out how he charmed them without even trying. And he was a good guy. Not funny, but he loved other people's humor.

So you can also see what happened next. Son got jealous. He didn't make a show-down or nothing. Started being bad to Bekkah.

Once they had a fight. He said, 'You even speak Cherokee?'

Bekkah is a warrior. She went cold, as they say. 'You speak Pima?' 'You need my license?' 'My certificate?' 'I told you about us.' 'I do not speak trash like you do.'

It gets worse. Ugly. Son had to go to Los Angeles for a couple of weeks.

Bekkah and a couple of others were taking care of the Pima Pizza parlour. Elpidio was there. About ten-thirty on that Friday night in late September two government agents came in and arrested him.

No one ever saw him again.

From what Bekkah could find out Elpidio was not legally in the U.S. She told me later in Boston that Elpidio is Purepecha. 'Legal in any part of the Americas', she said.

When I saw her in Boston those years later we spent a week or so together, or maybe a decade, it was so strong.

She told me she did everything she could but could not find Elpidio. Stayed completely cold to Son. Finally just left. Went east. She'd been reading Louise Erdrich and went east.

I heard from a Penobscot guy that she lived with Darrell Cannuk in Canada for awhile.

She learned French, moved to Paris.

I guess Son is still in California, haven't heard anything.

This is a piece of fiction, written for the occasion of an art show by Lawrence Paul Yuxweluptun at the Museum of Anthropology in Vancouver.
Special note to Canadians: the word 'canuck' is a fairly common surname among First Nations people in Quebec and Ontario. j d

CHAPTER TWO

BEKKAH IN EUROPE

JIMMIE DURHAM

2014, Napoli

So Bekkah landed up in Paris.

She knew it was not going to work out with Darrell Cannuk in Montreal; she said he was always acting about himself.

But she didn't just wash up in Paris like James Baldwin had done so many years earlier. She knew Hombart Lyle back in Tulsa and he is the brother of Maryanne Wolf who had been in Paris for more than thirty years. Maryanne had been famous earlier, and she was not only a folk singer but she also sang opera and she used to brag that she never sang Carmen. So Hombart gave her Maryanne's address and told Maryanne that she was coming.

Back in San Francisco Bekkah was really a knock-out but now she was beautiful in ways that are not describable. It was like her beauty had found her and she wasn't even expecting anything. She had let her hair grow to shoulder length. It was afro hair but at the same time it was Cherokee afro hair. So much of her hair had turned deep, deep red, blackish red and was more than curly but still not typically African hair. Sometimes her skin seemed to be even darker than it had been and sometimes her eyes seemed to be even more violet than they had been. Ok, sorry, it's just that I was quite often in Paris in those days from being in Strasbourg so much.

Maryanne Wolf you might say had become French. I think she forgot everything about Oklahoma and the life there and I think she was really gracefully proud of the forgetting. She had lived with a composer-guy for a long, long time but then married another guy also French but I don't know what he did in the music business. She had one son who in turn had two sons and a daughter. These three young French people were very proud to be Creek even though none of them had ever been to the US much less Oklahoma. But here now: one of the boys, Pascal, fell more or less in love with Bekkah. I mean, pretty much as soon as she got to Paris she fell in with a crazy bunch and was in a strange way part of a very strange part of Paris life. The artistic music life. She was always happy to be with Pascal but she said later that their cheerful apolitical attitudes began to drive her nuts. At the same time she began to meet other, more interesting guys. So that for the next year she was in what we might call a constant whirlwind of love affairs, political actions and even tried some singing herself.

She had a lot of fights and she was able to; not just because of Maryanne's introduction, but because everyone could see how she was. And over that first year her Canadian French got better and better real French. She got a reputation very quickly for not taking any nonsense. People would say, "How is it that you are Black?" And with a fierceness that was almost physical, she would say, "How is it that you are Pink?" People would say, "Do you speak Cherokee?" And she would rattle off some insulting phrase in a way that they had to know that they were being put down.

But there was this one time, there was a bunch of us at Maryanne's house, including a couple of Indian artists from the West Coast. Some woman who was kind of French but maybe Algerian, said to Bekkah, "But do you mean that you and your family are not recognized as Cherokees because you are Black? I have been to Oklahoma several times and I have seen that most Cherokees around Tahlequah look English or Irish! Just because your family were slaves, you are not Cherokee? That's like American Blacks not being American because their ancestors were slaves!" Bekkah looked at her but she didn't say anything and stayed pretty much quiet the rest of that evening.

Not so many people know that the truth about Paris is its suburbs. It is a city of giant and invisible unacknowledged suburbs. Bekkah met a guy and lived out there somewhere. He was kind of like one of those guys who could do anything. He had no money. He had no nothing but he was always up. He was from the Gha tribe in Ghana and once when I was visiting he explained to a bunch of us that although the Gha were not the most populous of the various tribes in Ghana or the most powerful, they were the people who could get things done between all of the other people. He said he was a born diplomat. He was trying to be an artist in a system where there are few artists and a bunch of pretenders. This is the kind of art he was making. He had a big handled ax and a short hatchet. He could take abandoned cars apart with these tools and he tried to make, or maybe I should say, unmake, things with the parts of cars that he could not resell as regular car parts. Now, as strong as this guy was, maybe still is for all I know, he had a mother, Georgina. His mother was even stronger and took to Bekkah naturally right away. Bekkah did not treat her like a mother but like a close friend which she was.

I don't know how to say about what they did but here is what they did: they started an organization and they got many other women involved. First from that neighborhood and then from other neighborhoods. It was as though people were ready for some sort of planned action; kind of spread like wildfire, you might say. Nothing to do with the guy but with just Bekkah and her friend: they went to Ghana. They went to Senegal. They came back and spent a lot of time in Geneva and in Strasbourg. They spent a lot of time in Brussels. Bekkah told me that she saw more racism in Brussels than she had ever seen in eastern Oklahoma. Their organization grew and it never stopped working. Never stopped being right-on. And of course, maybe that was the problem. Another woman in the organization, she wasn't even from Ghana, accused Georgina of trying to have sex with her. Georgina did not deny or affirm it. She just tried to ignore it but then it wasn't more than a couple of weeks later that some woman in the French government said that they might have been embezzling money. Bekkah started spending more time in Geneva and Brussels. Georgina went back to Ghana and before the year was out she was dead.

More than a month passed before I saw Bekkah again. She came to Strasbourg where I was staying practically dead herself. It was as though she was dead. I don't know how long she stayed but just a day or two. After that she disappeared. I don't know why but I never asked around for her. I guess I was afraid to. I was in Paris quite often and I would go around to where she often used to be but I never asked anybody anything. Two years later I moved back to the US and lived in New York City and never saw anybody who knew her and I still never asked anybody about her.

It was more than twenty years later maybe almost twenty-five, I was in Mexico City and I saw someone from San Francisco from the old days. She was in the city for a conference, she came running up to me. "Did you see Bekkah?" she said. "What do you mean?" I said, "Where?" "Here, she's been here for at least a week." "Where? Do you know where she is staying?" I called the hotel but she had checked out that morning. Then I looked up the woman who had told me about her to see what all she knew. Bekkah had been living in Venezuela. She didn't know how long but a long time.

Bekkah was part of an animal rights group who were doing things with wild animals in northwestern Venezuela.

I guess I never stopped being in love with her but I never said that to her and I was never very forceful one way or another. I thought about going to Venezuela but I never did. Then even more years passed by and I heard from somebody that Bekkah was back in Brussels. I was almost never in Europe anymore and pretty much was never in the US either by that time.

THE KING OF SARDINIA

JIMMIE DURHAM

ca. 2015

"Don't you love your country?", they ask.

"Why don't you go back where you came from?" someone in the U.S. asked me during a demonstration in the '70s. (My family has lived there for about fifteen thousand years - - -.)

It seems a hard irony that most Europeans these days do not see themselves as nationalistic. They feel no need for loyalty to an abstract state; but more a continued frustration with the politics and leaders of whatever nation-state they find themselves in. Ironic because it is here where the concept of nation-states coagulated into its first solidity and then infected the entire world.

Look how they fought each other, and slaughtered their own and each other's citizens all those years! Only to finally shrug it all off. (This new sophistication has not yet reached Serbia and a few other Eastern countries far from the centers of Paris, Rome or Berlin.)

(Not very far away by the standards of Africa or the Americas, of course.) And France and England must remain chauvinistically nationalist as part of their traditional strategies against each other.

Certainly we do not want too many Africans and Arabs moving in and making our lives uncomfortable. Mostly, though, we are all happily European, and are mentally free to live in several countries.

Still, there is the tendency, common to much of humanity, to imagine that what is has practically always been and will probably always be."There will always be an England," the English say. Every European country has its heroes of the nation-state having been born; its Garibaldi or Jan Czynski, but this has pretty much become the stuff of old stories.

We think Italy has always been Italy and also that it has little reality. In the days of kingdoms (England, the Netherlands, Belgium, Sweden and Norway still have kings and queens) Sardinia included the country of Savoy, which lay between Switzerland and France. The king of Sardinia had Savoy as part of his realm. Not long ago!

One may safely prophesy, then, the end of England in the not-too-distant future.

Therefore, also Brazil and the U.S., but such heresy can hardly be safely uttered; lest it seem that the utterer is advocating this demise.

The newest nation-state is South Sudan. Sudan was the invention of the slave trade and colonization. Its current president was once in the Egyptian army. Here is a case, most typical of Africa, wherein the super-patriotism we find in so many of the American countries would seem absurd. More to our point, what is South Sudan now supposed to do? And how?

The people wanted freedom from oppression. In our present condition that desire necessitated nationhood.

Can we truly imagine that anyone there might have the kind of quasi-religious patriotism and 'love of country' that we have all been taught is the only morally correct stance?

What is a nation-state good for anyway? To protect us from other nation-states. What goes on inside, as China is now so vehemently pontificating in the case of Syria, is sacrosanct against outside interference. In my own lifetime I think the European countries would not have blinked an eye when the German government decided to kill all Jewish and Roma people if Germany had not attacked Poland—another nation-state.

In short, nation-states are thuggery. They attack each other. Sure, I know humans attack each other individually and in small family groups, but that is not at the level of Brazil's attack on Paraguay or Japan's attack on China. To be successful a people, or an area of people we must now say, needs a strong army to protect the national borders against the other nations. Then this area of people must have strategic allies within various organized groups of thugs. This area of people might, for example, send a representative to some league of states and ask for a vote of censure against one of the league's members because of its aggression. A word of warning: do not send your representative to petition the gang of gangs unless you have made the necessary alliances beforehand! Your area of people will lose the vote and be more vulnerable than before.

What I mean is: we take this completely absurd situation as normal. We take it as the only reality. We speak blithely about 'international co-operation' as though no other form of co-operation could exist. Could be imagined.

Things were much simpler in the old days, weren't they? When the existing nation-states were all in Europe. Even the ridiculous concept of race was more simple in its complexity. In 1912 there was the Polish 'race' living in Poland. Race and Nation were the same stupid concept. "Have you no love for your mother—the Polish land?" one Pole writes to another who has moved to Chicago.

Coming from the Americas I am always impressed at how Europeans love their actual countries—how they love the land; and how they do not despoil it. Olive trees thousands of years old. Country-side farms right up to the edge of the city, itself filled with parks.

We know well the details of this evolution: in the first place the king and his close cousins owned all the land. Part of Sardinia was Mont Blanc and other famous alps. The king did not strip-mine them nor turn the mine into hell, like Potosi in Bolivia. It is the several second places that are more interesting: The Polish worker did move to Chicago and São Paulo.

I am writing this in Molise, a beautiful hilly province of south-east Italy. It has very few people because they all emigrated. Some were still leaving for Paris on foot, with no papers, in the late 1950s. Many still return in the summer because more than from other parts of Italy, perhaps, the emigrants keep a memory of love of the land.

Before they all left, however, they had, over generations, almost completely denuded the hills and valleys of trees. Wood for cooking, for winter heat. Too many people for the land to support. As they began to leave the land began to heal. The same was true for the Polish peasants and for all of Europe.

What an ecological boon to Europe has been the move to Australia, South Africa, New Zealand, South America, North America! What an ecological disaster for those places!

Would anyone write, "Have you no love for your stepmother—the Illinois land?" No American patriot has ever loved the astounding Great Plains of which the State of Illinois is part. When the songwriter sings, "O, beautiful, for spacious skies, for amber waves of grain!" he sings not of prairie grasses; he counts bread instead. Bread made from a non-indigenous grain which is detrimental to the natural environment.

The grandchildren of our Polish auto-worker have never seen the land in which they were born. Their best 'experience' of the land of the U.S. will be to go white-water rafting down a river on the other side of the Great Plains—to view the land as a recreational rollercoaster ride. Land as amusement park. If the worker ended up in São Paulo instead of Chicago his grandchildren will probably 'experience' nature by taking a cruise on the Amazon.

Concomitant to immigration has been colonization. These days of international cooperation need not so much direct colonization: just recently the British ambassador to Brazil sought a meeting with President Dilma to help solve an economic problem Great Britain is having. If I read the newspaper article correctly, England's credit rating might be degraded if its mining industry cannot improve profits. This in turn hinges upon a new mine opening in Brazil. Due to more stringent ecological regulations in Brazil the English mine there has not been able to open, so the ambassador seeks a special favor. (For which, we assume, he might promise a return-favor in the near future.)

There are developing countries, we say. Zambia is one of them; developing along quite well in the early nineteen seventies on the strength of the sale of raw copper once it freed itself from British colonization in the sixties. This poor country has few other natural resources, few other ways to make money. Following the example of developed, civilized countries, it can send about half of its work force to Paris and Manchester. It can simultaneously establish a colony in the north of England, reaping huge profits from the various goods there. A second colony in Spain would not hurt.

Wait, though. Let us leave poor Zambia to dig its own grave. It is now against 'international' law for it to establish colonies, so it must compete on the international market with whatever it can scrounge and offer for sale. We must ask, is colonialism really over? Do we really live in post-colonial times?

Recently, several economists have begun to call the new super-capitalist system we now live under an 'international

Ponzi scheme'. A chain-letter idea in which every participant will become wealthy. We know the truth of this suspicion when we stop and notice that more poor Zambians are getting poorer.

This system results from and invents the international world of nation-hood. Which are the nations outside of Europe? In the Americas, Australia and New Zealand; a substantial and powerful portion of our system, the nations are run by the settlers. The nations are the European settlers. In every instance their mentality is colonial European. The U.S. is still today commercially cutting what is left of its Sequoia Redwood forests, almost all of which are privately owned by lumber companies. Every country in North and South America is an ongoing, accelerating ecological disaster, exploited for money.

This exploitation seems perfectly natural to the Europeans who call themselves Mexican, Argentinean, and so forth. They have no other relationship to the land. The American nations are colonial constructions against the land. Otherwise, wouldn't it be curious that every single politician in those two continents who is known to be 'conservative' is so against the protection and safe-guarding of the actual land? Why do they not want to conserve? Their 'conservativism' is always radically for more colonial-style raping.

The world's nations must compete with each other. To do this, to survive, let's say, they must own land and 'natural resources' within the land. So that these resources can be extracted and sold. The nation then becomes strong and takes its place among the other strong nations. (In the English language of the U.S. mining companies, land is referred to as 'overburden'.) It could not possibly be that the nation was the land; the nation must be removed from that part of the world, must be abstract. Because it would not be able to compete, otherwise, and would die.

There is a strong condemnation now of the behaviour of 'multi-national' corporations—especially the oil and pharmaceutical ones. This is certainly correct even if it appears to be ineffective on the whole. Maybe we do not usually notice how dependent these companies are upon the various nations. They must operate exactly 'inter-nationally'.

We can hardly help but imagine a near future in which these ghostly monsters have increasingly more power over our lives and over the natural world.

In that case I will rather imagine a more distant future with no nations. It is not really miraculous that this utopia of my imagination is not run by a world government called Shellmonsantoastrozeneca: I imagine it is not, because this is the far future after many ecological and economic collapses. The multi-nationals have also collapsed.

Would not the wine maker in Burgundy still take pleasure in making good wine without the existence of France? The cheese-maker still make the cheese he can be proud of? I, as a member of those peoples made homeless, who live at the sufferance of those nations established specifically against us and the land upon which we live, I can well imagine a world without nations. It would need a large police force for many years, run by a world government, of course. But I can imagine it.

What I cannot imagine in this distant future is how they operate without money.

But that is another story.

THIS IS AN EVICTION PLAN

(NEW YORK IN THE 1980s)

JIMMIE DURHAM

2016

I first went to New York City in 1974, to find lawyers and others to attend our first treaty conference. Harry Belafonte hosted a meeting at his apartment about the possibilities of an expanded American Indian Community House in the city, which was to be funded by the federal government.

The government was planning such centers in many major cities, and the word was being spread that much money was available because in the recent census many people had said that they were Native Americans because they were born in the United States. Others, it was claimed, wrote that they were American Indians because their families were from India.

Harry already had strong contacts with AIM and liked to be at the front of things.

I knew no one at the meeting except him, but I met Suzan Shown, who had run a radio program about Indian affairs and was there with artist Frank Harjo; Oren Lyons, who knew the city because he had been a sports illustrator; and a few other people. There was a woman who said she was Cherokee, whose name I've forgotten. She had very thin, long braids and blue eyes (I know there are many Cherokees with blue eyes). She explained to us that Chinese travelers long before Columbus described seeing blue-eyed Indians, and she showed us an eagle feather she kept in a wooden box, explaining that she was the only woman ever given an eagle feather by the Cherokees. (Why she needed to bring it to the meeting was not explained.) There was another woman who said she was a professional opera singer. I never saw either of these two women again and left NYC after a week.

By strange accident I passed by a small gallery owned by Tuscarora artist Lloyd Oxendine and was attracted to it by a horse skull painted blue that was on display. Years later Oxendine became the director of the gallery of the American Indian Community House.

When I returned in 1975 to open the International Indian Treaty Council office, I at first had no contact with any of that crowd, except Harry Belafonte, of course. But I soon met an artist who was married to a lawyer we knew. She was part of a group of artists who met to make an "anti-catalogue" against a bicentennial art show planned by the Whitney Museum of American Art.[1] They had invited Benny Andrews, a black artist just returned from Documenta, and wanted an "Indian" artist. It was a good gang of people and I was glad to be part of it. Their meetings were held in people's lofts, which I had never seen before.

The day of my first loft visit I had spent several hours in Andy Warhol's studio with Russ Means. Warhol was taking photos of him for a portrait. When I got to the loft I told the first person I saw that I'd spent the day at Warhol's studio. He said his name was Joseph Kosuth and that Warhol had done his portrait too.

After the anti-catalogue came out I had no more contact with art stuff in New York, and little with the American Indian Community House, though the director there was a constant friend and a supporter of our work at the United Nations.

Before moving to New York I had not been on the East Coast of the United States at all. Living in Geneva, I knew Paris and London well, so New York did not seem impressive. In those Treaty Council days I traveled constantly to Geneva, Latin America, and various communities in the western United States, was seldom "at home." Hardly noticed New York.

Maria Thereza Alves, a Brazilian whose parents had moved the family to the United States to escape the dictatorship in Brazil, came to volunteer at the Treaty Council in 1978 because she wanted to learn how Brazilian Indians might form a national organization with international support. In 1979 she presented a paper she had prepared about Brazilian abuses of human rights to the United Nations Human Rights Commission in Geneva. She and I and Ted Means had flown over for its annual meeting.

More than a year later I quit my job because of disagreements with Russ Means, and Maria Thereza left home. When we began living together she knew vaguely that I was an artist and I began to make collage-paintings in my spare time. Since we had no money we both took whatever jobs we could find. Maria Thereza said once that she had always wanted to make art, so we decided that she should go to art school. After a semester or two at Parsons (during which I got many free canvases from their garbage), she enrolled at Cooper Union, which was small and free.

Puerto Rican painter Juan Sánchez was the admissions officer and they became friends. At Maria Thereza's suggestion Juan put a couple of my pieces in a show he curated in 1982 at the Henry Street Settlement in the Lower East Side (*Beyond Aesthetics: Art of Necessity by Artists of Conscience*).

That was the beginning of a very busy few years for both of us, participating in many group shows, always with other minority artists.

In those days artists who were not white curated group shows in whatever spaces were available in Harlem, the Lower East Side, Brooklyn, and the Bronx, all before gentrification . . . at the time when buildings were being burnt down for insurance scams, with no real thought of commerce. That gave us all freedom to experiment and to try to make pertinent works with a political edge.

It is not that we did not want financial reward, it was just not a criterion for making or showing art. Very much against the current that was running over the city.

It was a time of large disco clubs, expensive restaurants, and celebratory rudeness. I remember too well the strange phenomenon of people waiting in long lines to enter a club to be insulted by bouncers and waiters as though it were a privilege or some sort of initiation rite.

All over the city, apartment buildings were going co-op, and tenants who had the money could buy their apartment. Those without sufficient funds were evicted. The most common legal document for a building intending to go co-op had the heading in bold letters, "This Is an Eviction Plan."

Close to our place near Columbia University an open garbage Dumpster on the street was filled one morning with the worldly goods of a woman who had been an exotic dancer in the 1950s. There were scrapbooks, which had clippings of the singer Carlos Gardel and Tongolele (the Mexican dancer so famous they named a beer after her), and clothes of all sorts. Three young affluent white people, probably students at the university, were standing in the Dumpster laughing, shouting, and throwing things about. It is from that debris that I found a dance costume made of a pair of underwear covered with red feathers and beads. Sewn onto the back was a coconut-fiber flap, a small skirt, which had more feathers and three tropical bird heads. I made *Pocahontas' Underwear* (1985) from the front part and another work from the back.

Homeless people were seen more and more, as were flamboyantly dressed young businessmen who delighted in publicly lecturing them.

A kind of meanness was so strong in the air that everyone was infected. As though normally nice people turned hard and could not cooperate. I remember younger artists coming to parties at our place only to leave before entering, seeing no one famous enough to spend time with.

It was during this time that I took the job of running the Foundation for the Community of Artists (FCA). I had been doing construction labor jobs, which were too hard on my back. The FCA was an organization set up by a group of artists to offer services such as insurance, health hazard information, and similar activities—functioning kind of like a union for artists. When I started they had no money at all, so the urgent task was to raise enough to pay me a modest salary, keep the monthly newspaper going, and straighten out the insurance program. After a few months of begging, I had a base safe enough to bring in Paul Chaat Smith, who fixed up many problems quickly.

The work brought me into contact with much of the art scene in NYC. Just a couple of years earlier Maria Thereza and I were constantly encouraged by the funny work inside subway stations by Keith Haring. In the early 1980s he became famous and a generous supporter of the FCA.

Many people were. James Rosenquist, Sol LeWitt, Carl Andre, Claes Oldenburg, and Coosje van Bruggen; no one refused to help. Even so, except for Leon Golub and Nancy Spero, no one in the established art circles really saw any of us minority artists on the Lower East Side. The board of directors of the FCA were a different lot; mostly teachers, they were not successful artists even though they were good. Larry Rosing was the head of the art department at Rutgers University, until he was fired for being too far left. Elliot Barowitz, a great painter who also guided our newspaper and got unknown young writers like Adam Gopnik to contribute to it for free, planned to approach a gallery year after year but had no taste for actually showing his paintings to one.

But quite a few of our bunch who showed together in alternative spaces later made well-known contributions to the art system: Juan Sánchez, David Hammons, Faith Ringgold, Catalina Parra, Fred Wilson, Ana Mendieta. Never part of any histories of New York City art of the time.

Maria Thereza and I remained very poor, and I relied on a constant variety of excellent garbage from the streets: human bones discarded by Columbia Medical School, a stuffed moose head, an antique handmade American flag, every sort of contraption and printed matter. This rich lode became necessary as art material.

The first criterion for choices of art material has always been for me the cost. Free material is best. Luckily, it is also usually the most interesting, even though my love of any material is practically religious.

Neither of us had wanted to stay in New York, but we had no money to leave. In 1987 we scraped together enough to move, with our stray cat, to Mexico. It was never part of any agenda to relocate to a place conducive to furthering "art careers," which neither of us had. I had known Cuernavaca in the early 1970s as a center for leftish intellectuality, so we headed there.

Almost impossible changes were taking place from the 1970s to the 1980s in NYC. As an AIM representative I worked closely with the Puerto Rican Socialist Party (PSP) and many organizations pushing for social change.

People working on gay rights issues were numerous and very active. By the time the decade changed, the PSP had practically disappeared. Gay rights were almost a given, however, and fancy club "baths" were springing up everywhere. A few doors away from our place a group of gay black men had bought an empty building and fixed it up for themselves. A good bunch of guys, they all had federal or municipal jobs. By 1987, when we left, the building was empty. AIDS had blown them all away.

AIDS hit like a bomb. For a couple of years it was believed to attack only gay men, which seemed too sinister to credit or deny. The bath clubs closed and everyone who could went home and closed the doors.

Still, NYC is tough. Many artists began to do special projects in solidarity with Latin American situations. That created or strengthened friendships. Maybe it made some better, some pertinent art. For my part, everything I did for specific reasons in those times was not good enough. I still do not know why, but I just could not make good work that way.

Maybe it was a question of too much planning in ways exterior to my private feelings. But at the same time I could make interesting work at someone's request. Corrine Jennings and Joe Overstreet asked me to be part of a self-portrait show at Kenkeleba Gallery. I said I did not do self-portraits and then made one the same afternoon. What I mean is, I have no idea what's going on.

Notes

1. Artists Meeting for Cultural Change (AMCC) was a loose coalition created in reaction to the Whitney Museum's presentation of *American Art: An Exhibition of the Collection of Mr. and Mrs. John D. Rockefeller III*. The AMCC's publication *An Anti-Catalog* included Durham's 1976 essay "Mr. Catlin and Mr. Rockefeller Tame the Wilderness." —Ed.

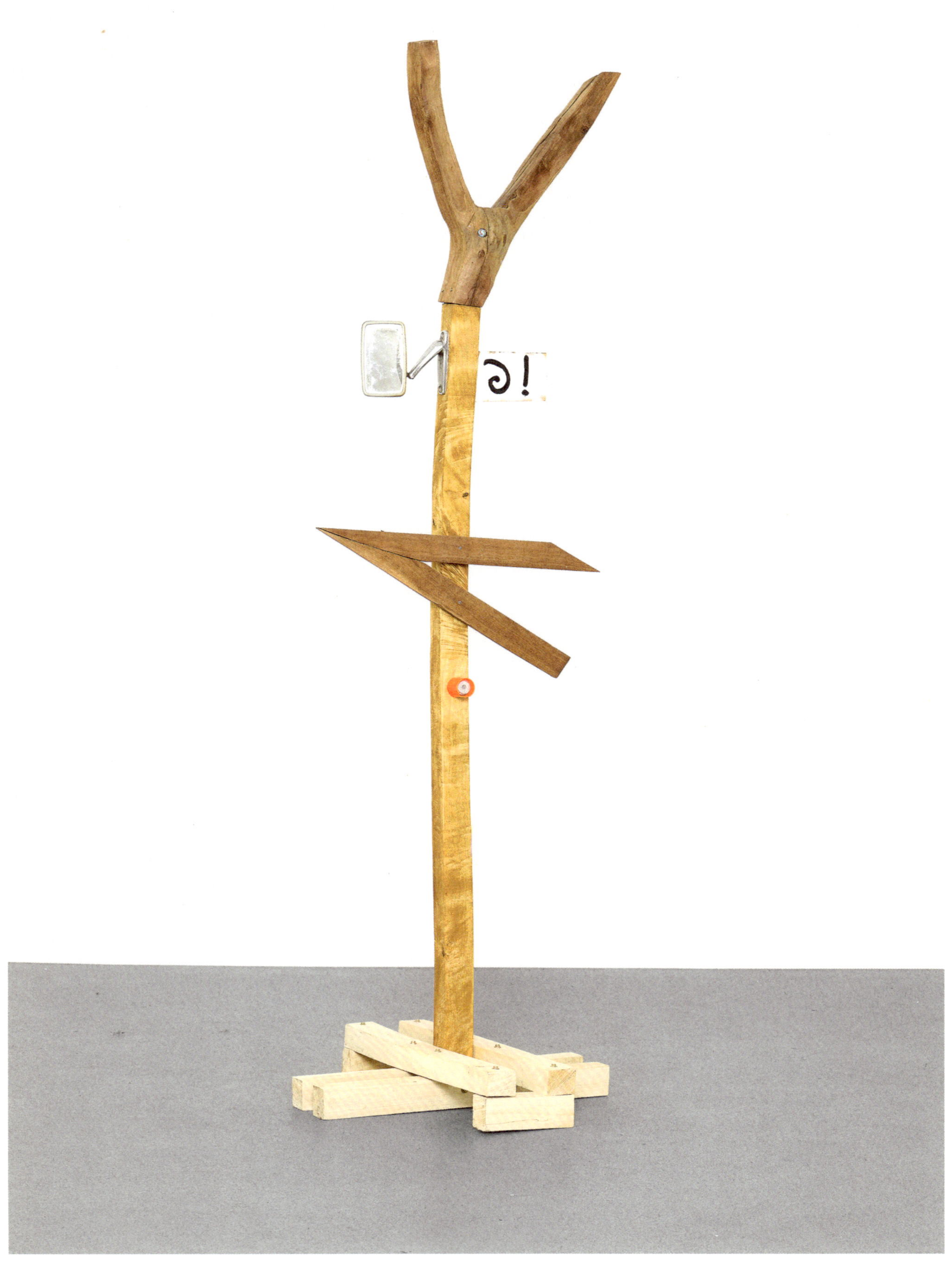

Ka, 2007. Pine, tree branch, rearview mirror, reflector, glass marble, acrylic paint on board. 79 $^{15}/_{16}$ × 23 $^{5}/_{8}$ × 23 $^{5}/_{8}$ in. (203 × 60 × 60 cm).

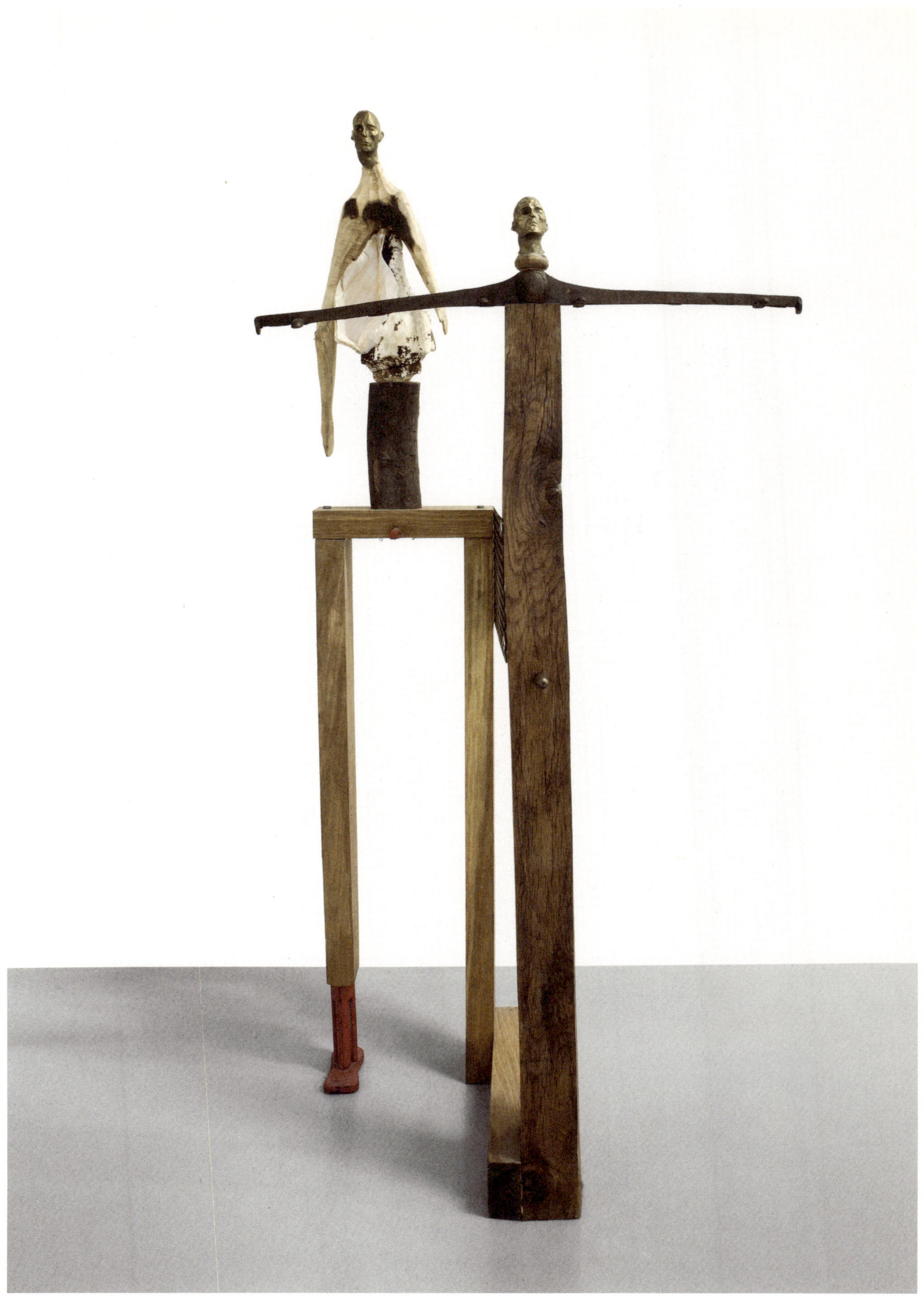

Red Foot, 2007. Oak, pine, seashell, cast brass, metal, acrylic paint. 55 × 25 × 12 in. (140 × 64 × 30 cm).

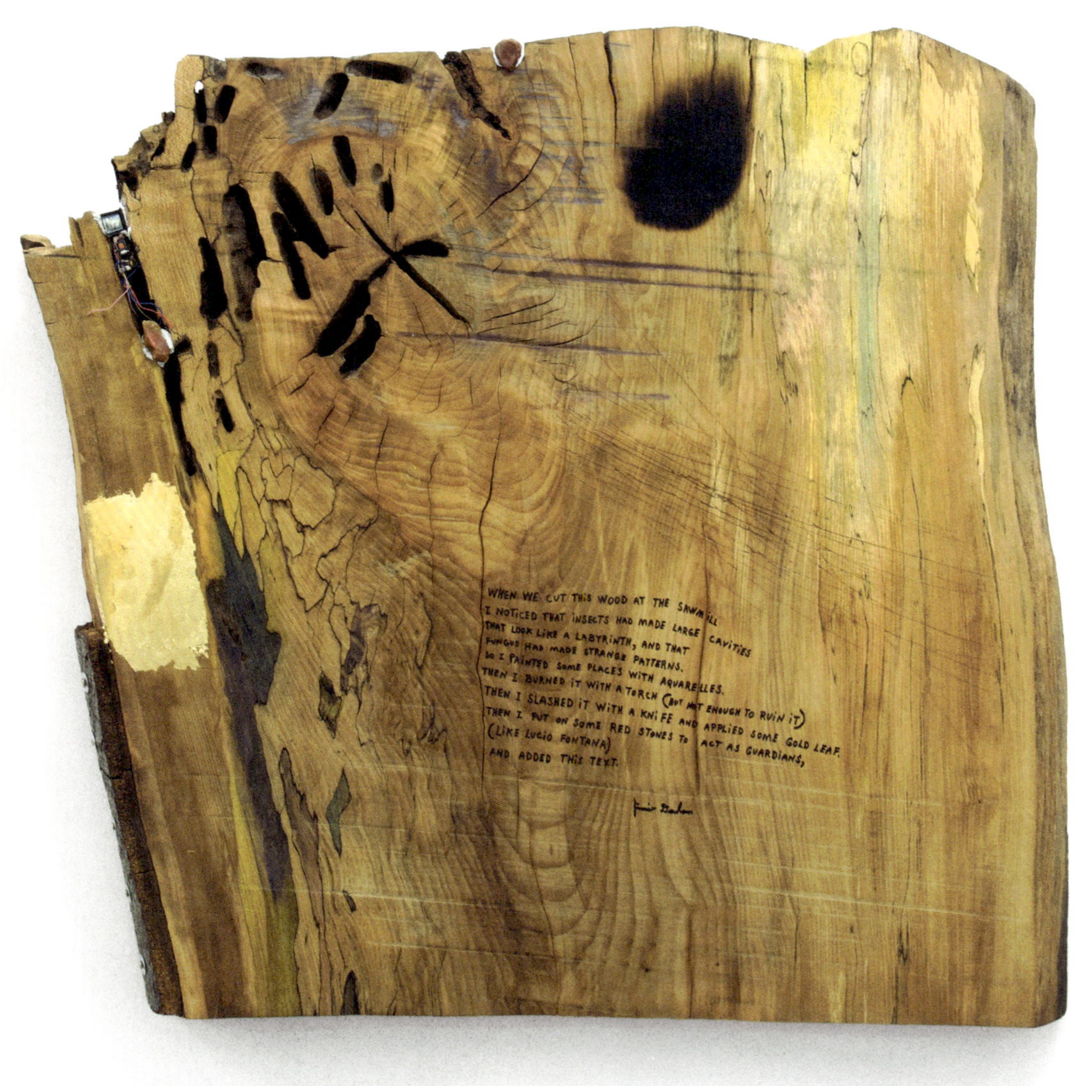

Slash and Burn, 2007. Beech, red stones, gold leaf, electronic parts, watercolor, ink. 36 × 36 × 2 ½ in. (92 × 86 × 6.5 cm).

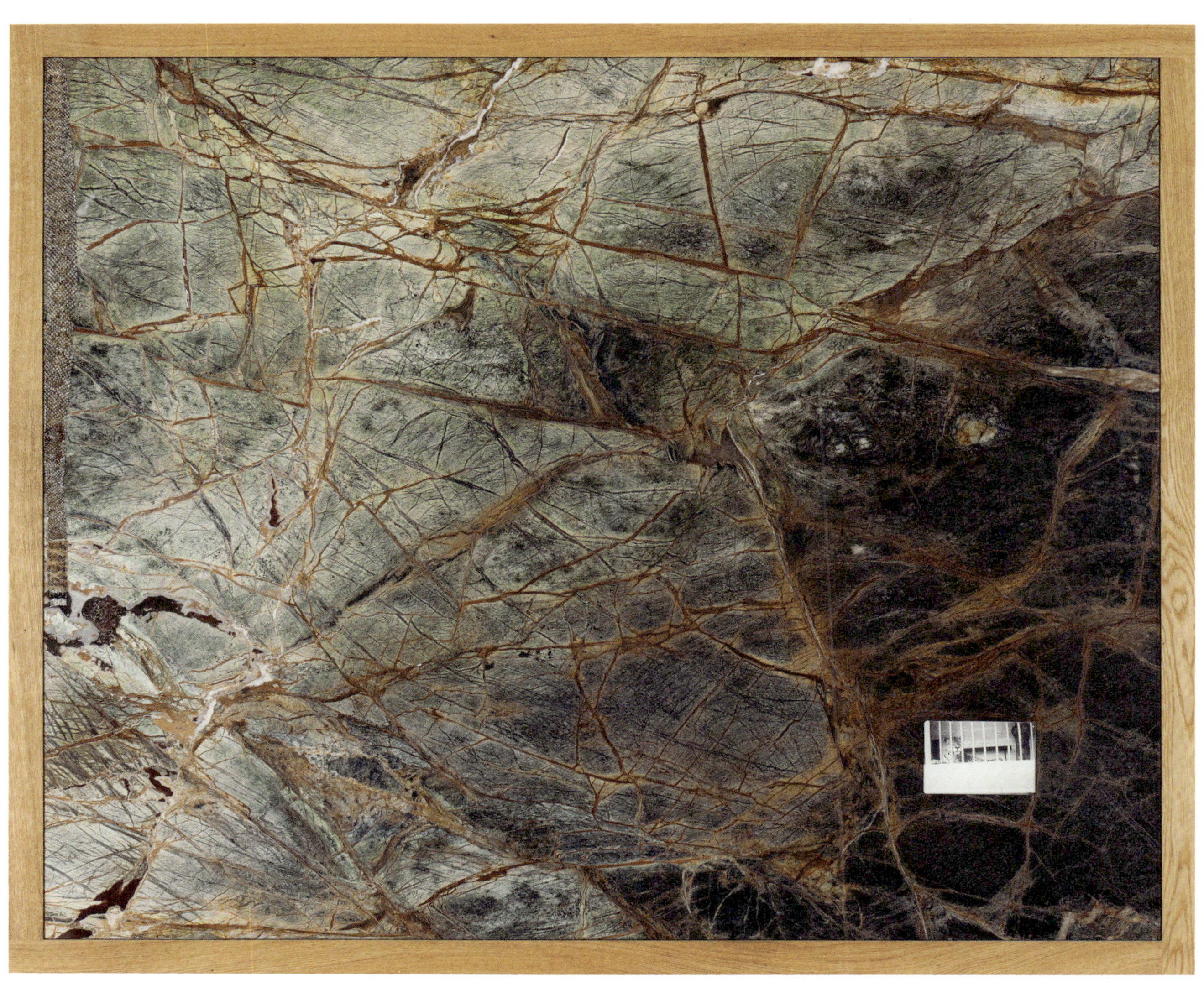

Belo Horizonte, 2013. Serpentine stone, snakeskin, porcelain tile, oak frame. 51 ½ × 63 × 2 ⅜ in. (131 × 160 × 6 cm).

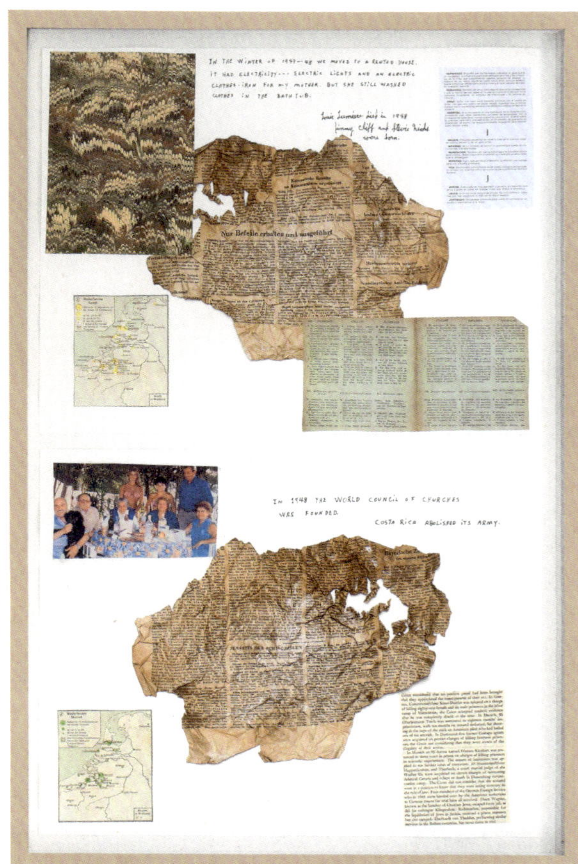

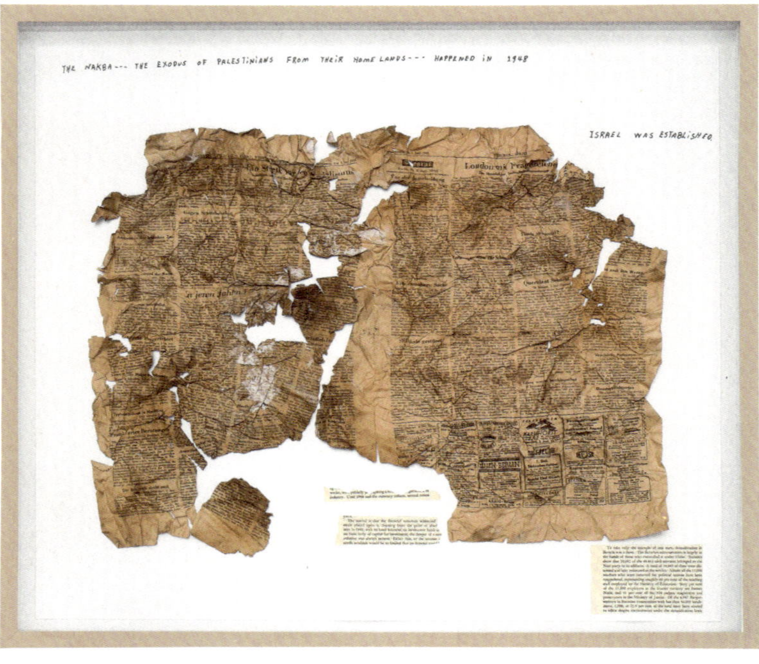

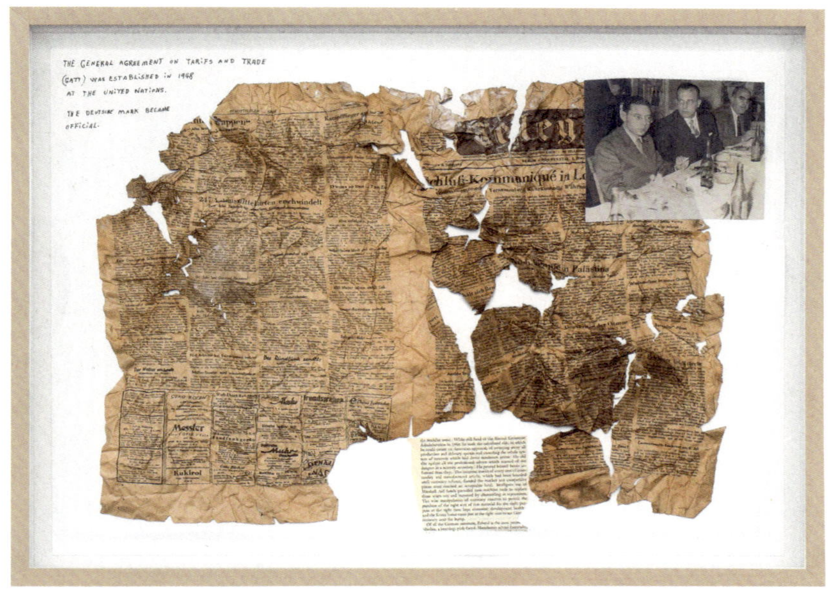

1948, 2012. Newspaper, ink, collage on paper. Series of eight works in five frames, frame 1: 34 ⅝ × 22 ¼ in. (88 × 56.5 cm); frame 2: 26 ¼ × 30 in. (66.5 × 76.5 cm); frame 3: 22 ⅜ × 30 in. (56.8 × 76.5 cm); frame 4: 26 ¼ × 42 ¾ in. (66.5 × 108.5 cm); frame 5: 26 ¼ × 42 ¾ in. (66.5 cm × 108 cm).

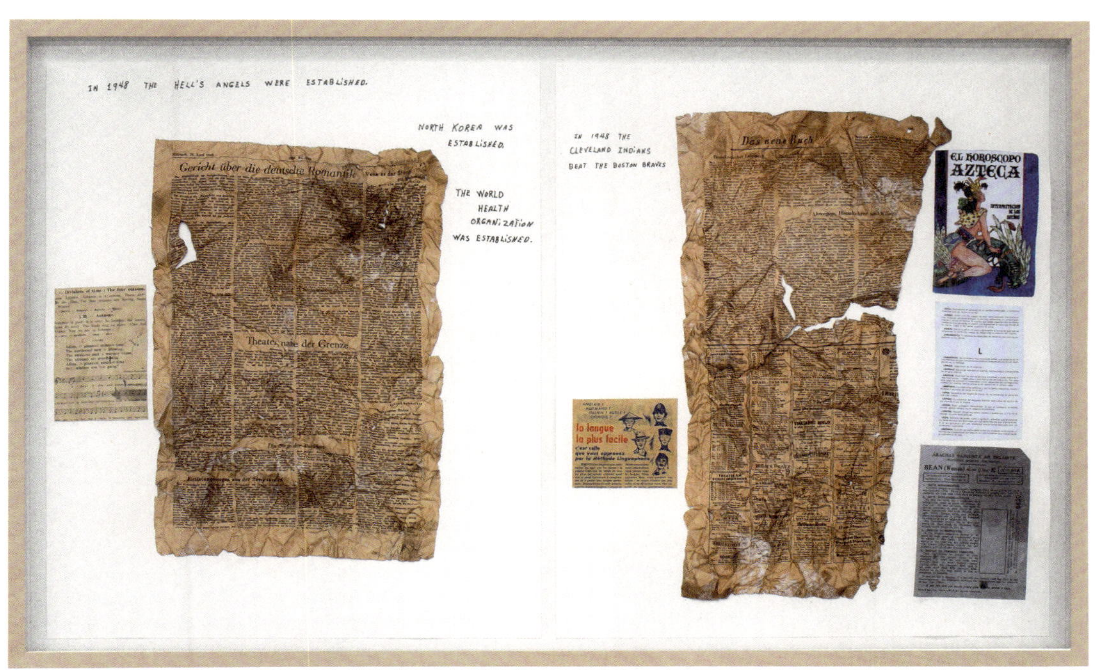
IN 1948 THE HELL'S ANGELS WERE ESTABLISHED.
NORTH KOREA WAS ESTABLISHED.
THE WORLD HEALTH ORGANIZATION WAS ESTABLISHED.
IN 1948 THE CLEVELAND INDIANS BEAT THE BOSTON BRAVES
Gericht über die deutsche Romantik
Theater nahe der Grenze
la langue la plus facile
Das neue Buch
EL HOROSCOPO AZTECA

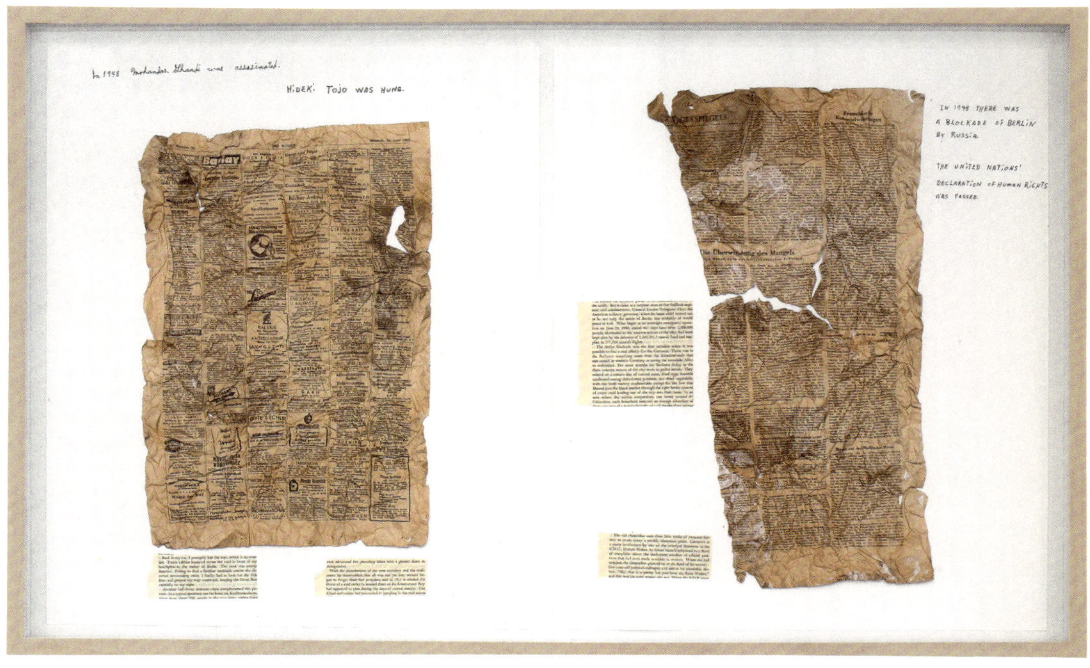
In 1948 Mohandas Ghandi was assasinated.
HIDEKI TOJO WAS HUNG.
IN 1948 THERE WAS A BLOCKADE OF BERLIN BY RUSSIA.
THE UNITED NATIONS' DECLARATION OF HUMAN RIGHTS WAS PASSED.

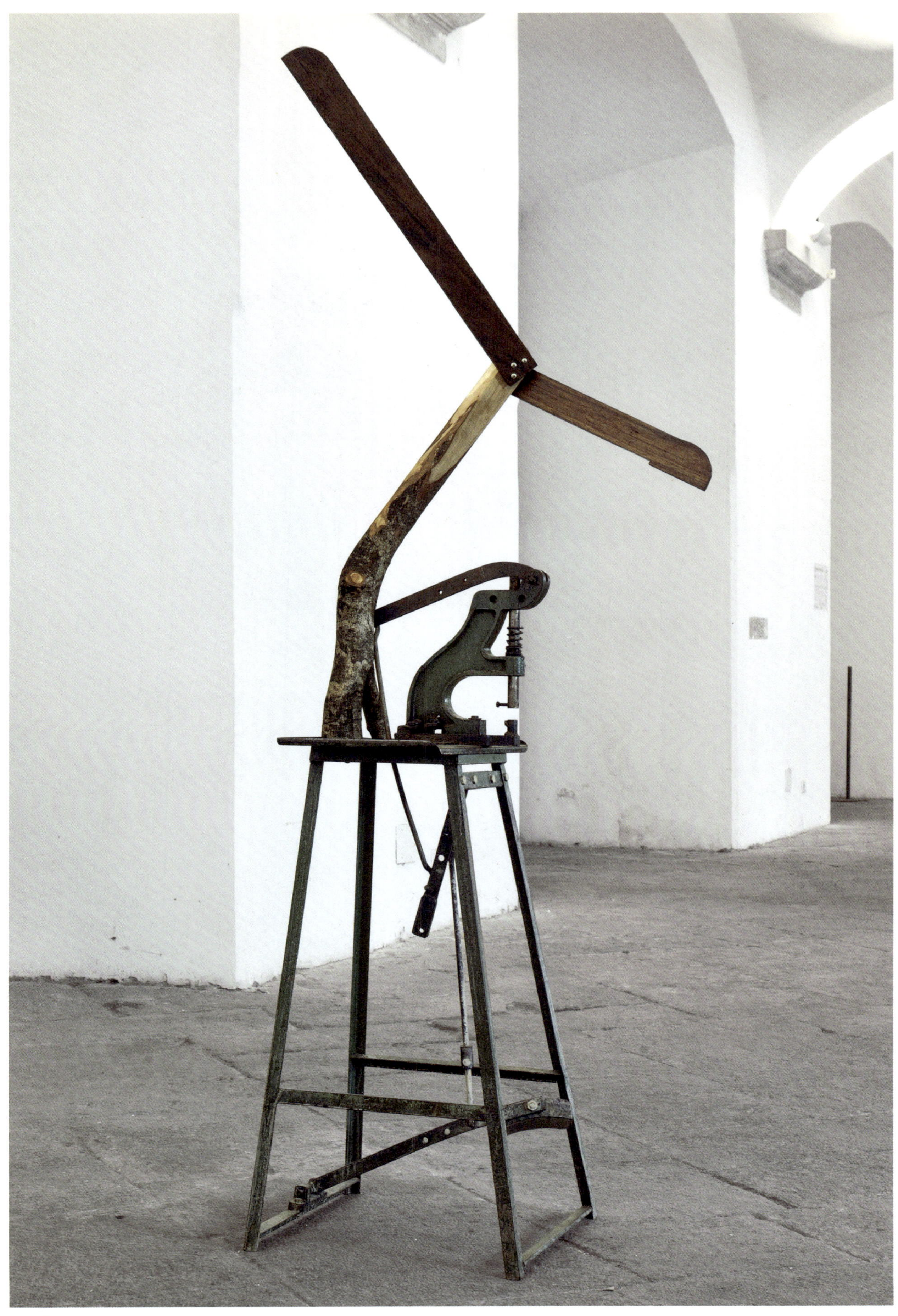

This should explain, 2012. Olive branch, found walnut, metal from industrial machine. 82 ¾ × 25 ½ × 27 ½ in. (210 × 65 × 70 cm).

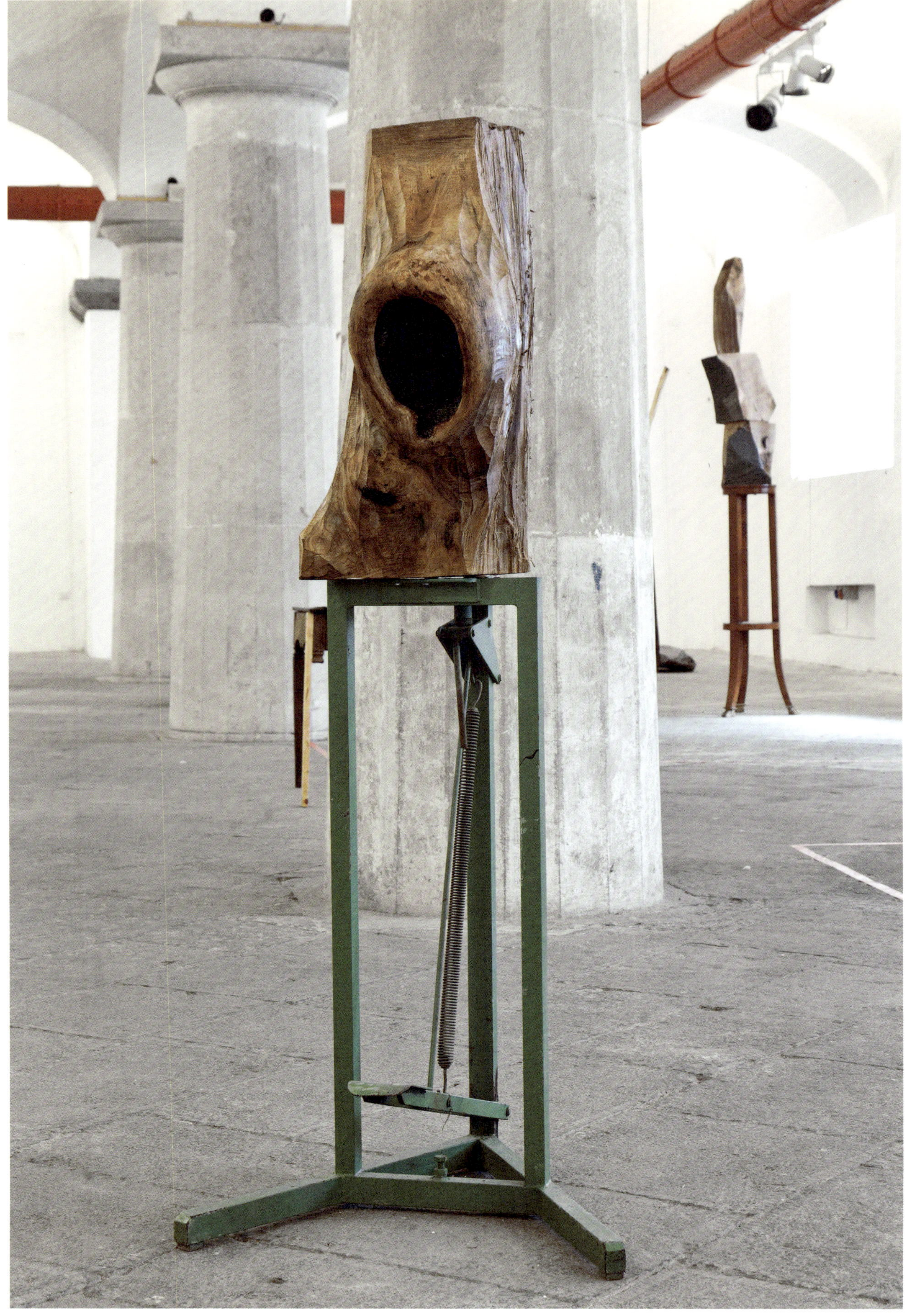

It should work, 2012. Olive trunk, metal from industrial machine. 65 × 29 ½ × 27 ½ in. (165 × 75 × 70 cm).

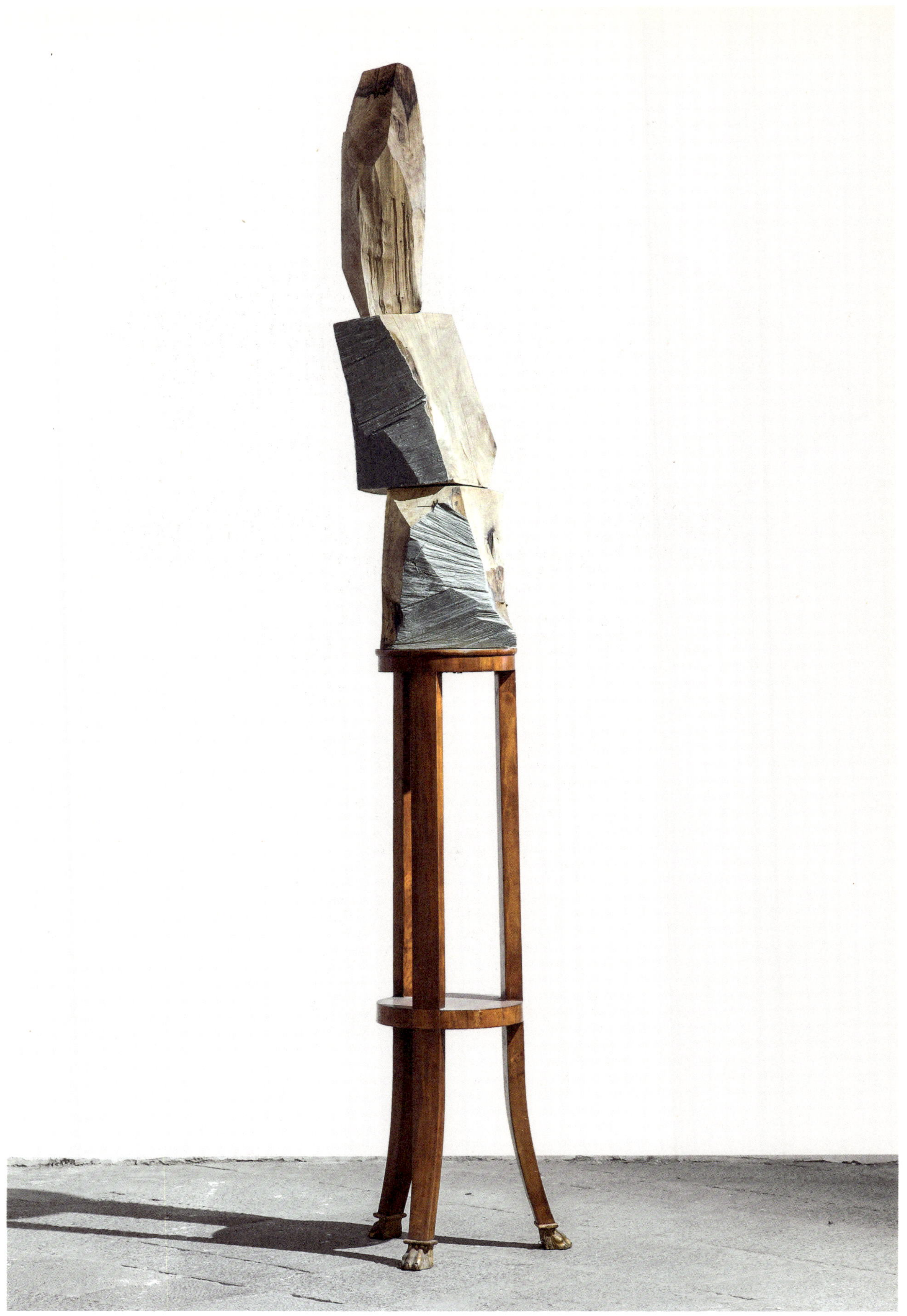

The Forest and Brancusi, 2012. Three pieces of carved walnut, acrylic paint, found wood and brass table. 110 ¼ × 19 ¾ × 15 ¾ in. (280 × 50 × 40 cm).

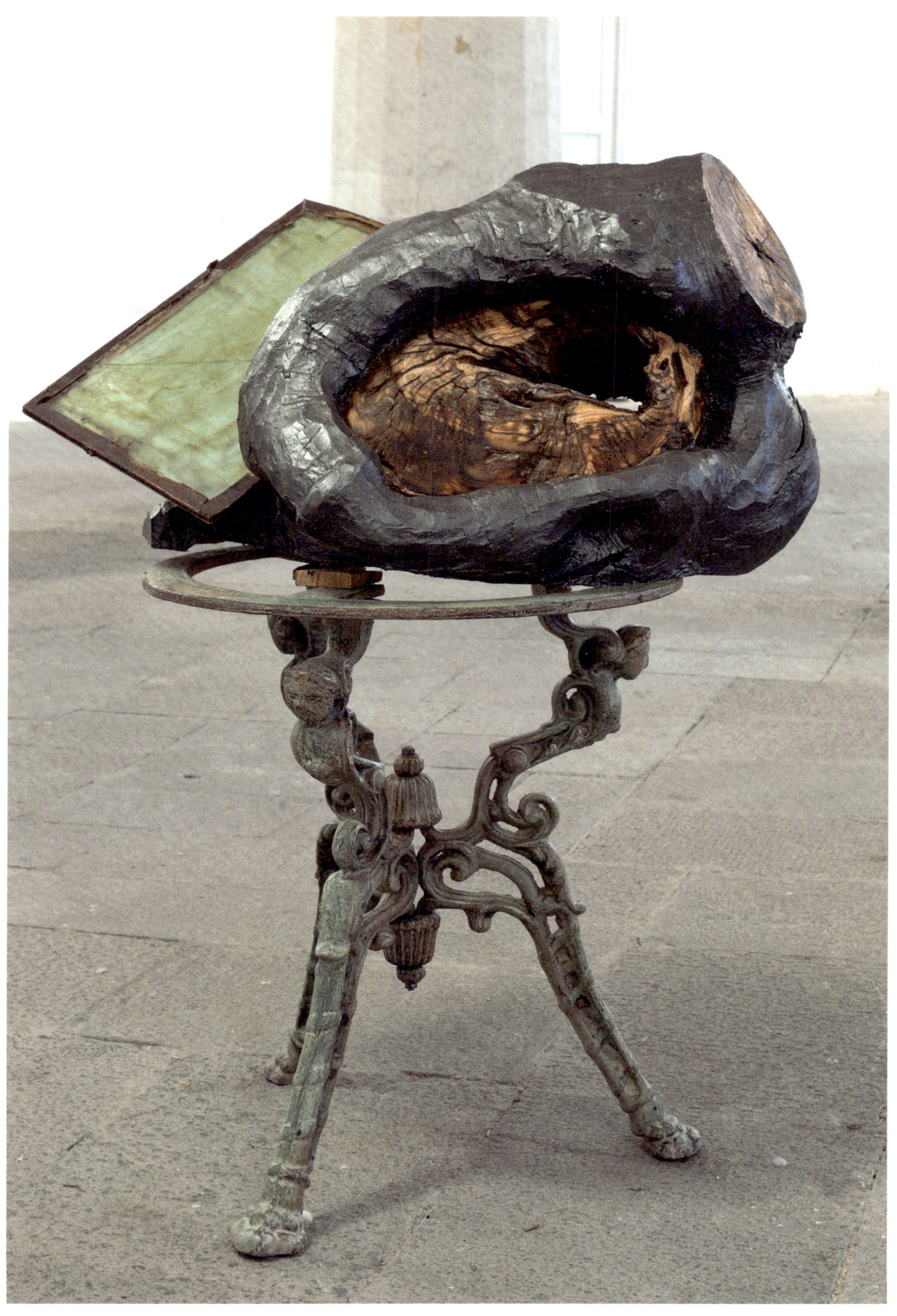

Elephant Skull Study #2, 2013. Olive trunk, acrylic paint, glass, iron. 47 ¼ × 35 ½ × 31 ½ in. (120 × 90 × 80 cm).

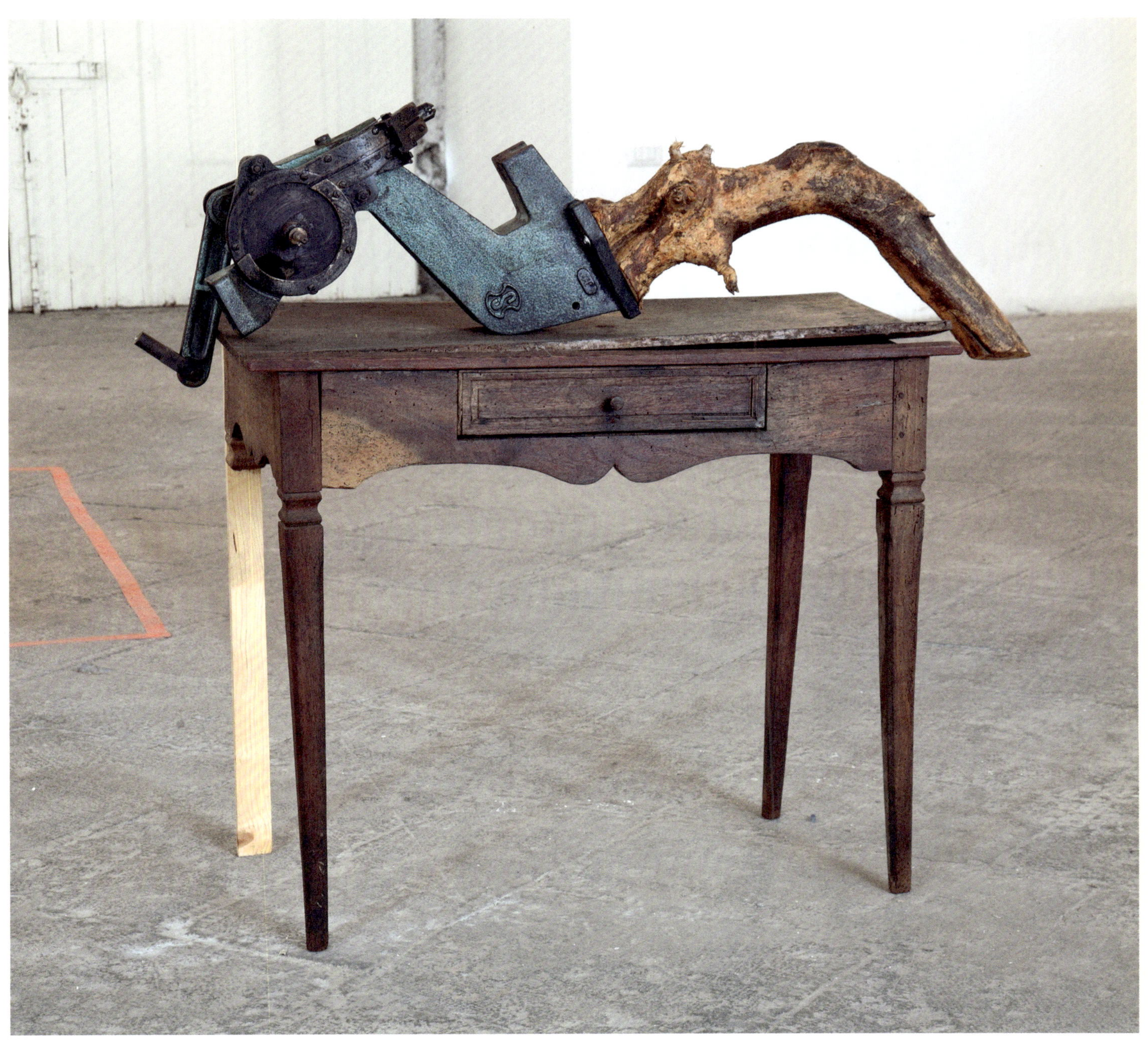

In the interest of science, 2013. Wood table, metal industrial machine, olive branch. 45 ¼ × 51 × 19 ½ in. (115 × 130 × 50 cm).

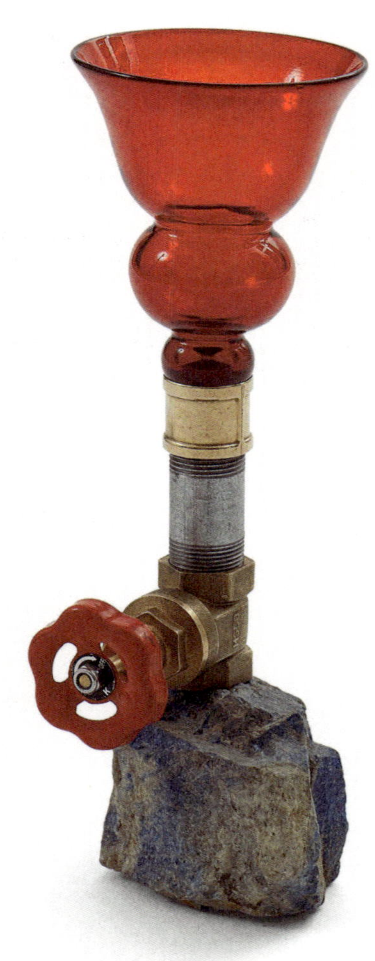

Lapis Lazuli with Venetian Red Glass, a Valve, Et Cetera, 2015. Lapis lazuli stone, glass, steel, brass. 12 × 5 ¼ × 5 ¼ in. (30.5 × 13.3 × 13.3 cm).

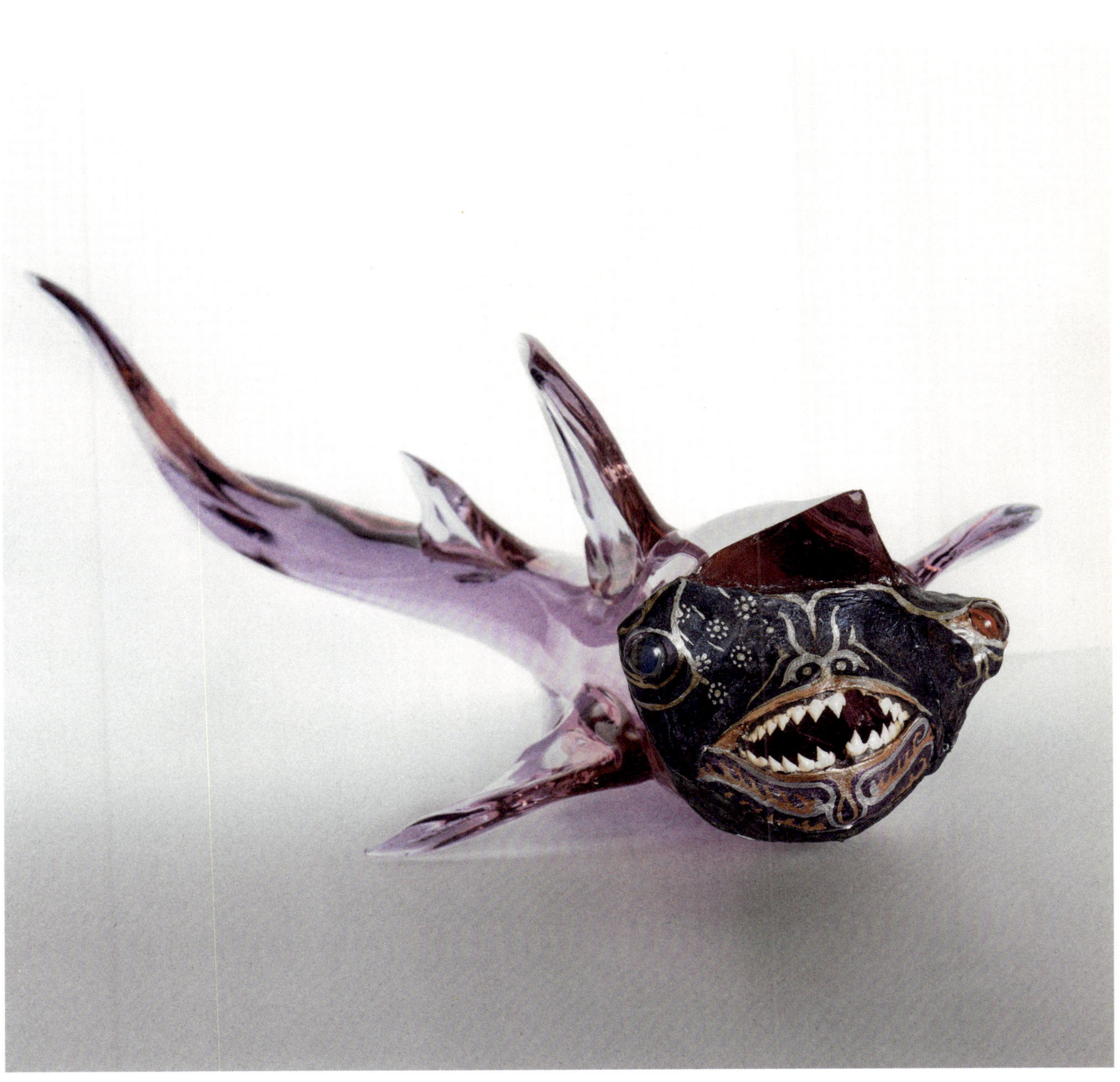

Carnivalesque Shark in Venice, 2015. Glass, goat leather, piranha teeth, papier-mâché, acrylic paint. 12 × 13 × 28 in. (30 × 33.5 × 71 cm).

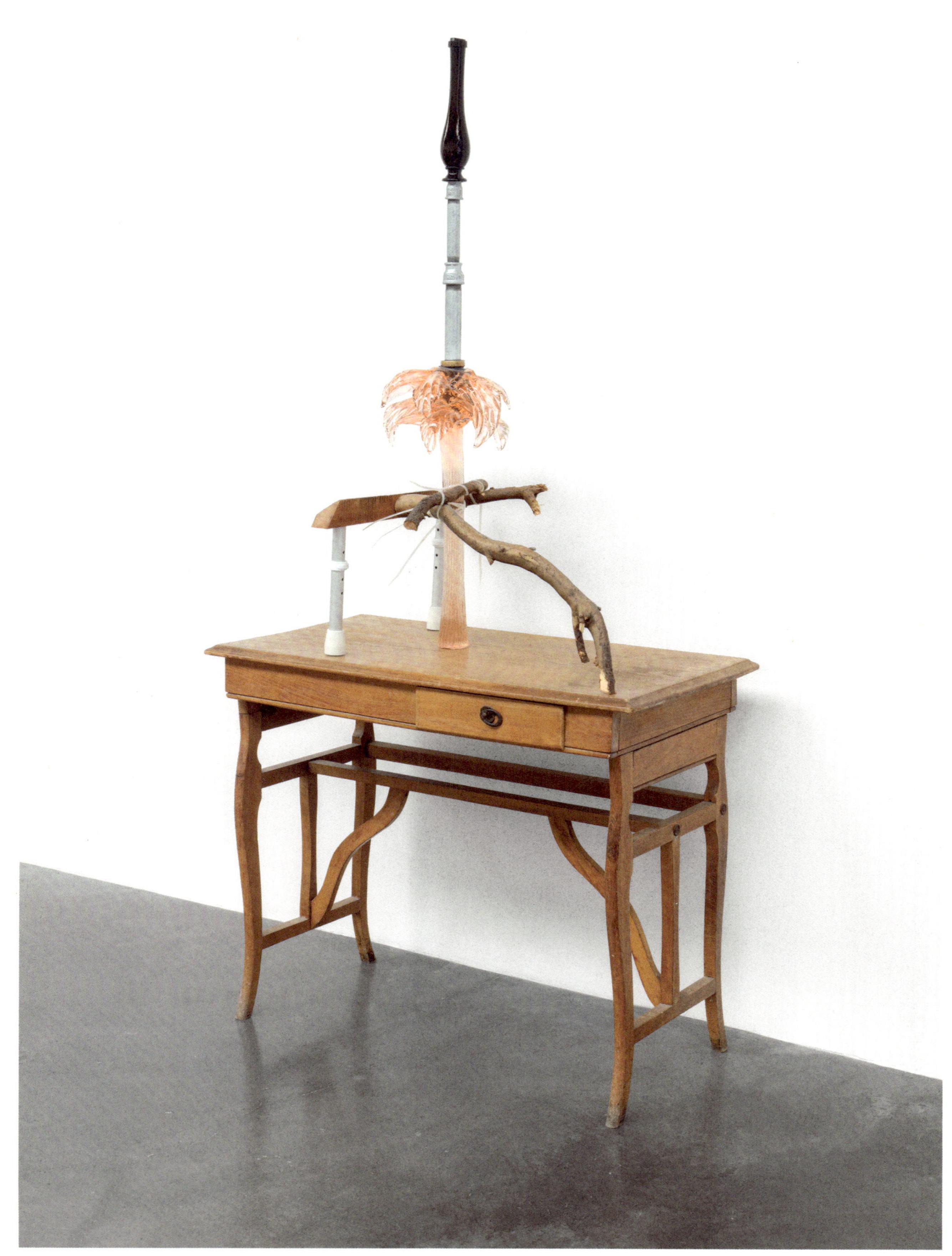

Pink Palm-Tree-Like Glass Construction with Various Decorative Elements, 2015. Glass, steel, hawthorn branch, aluminum, plastic, found chestnut table.
65 ½ × 35 ½ × 19 ¾ in. (166.3 × 90.1 × 50.1 cm).

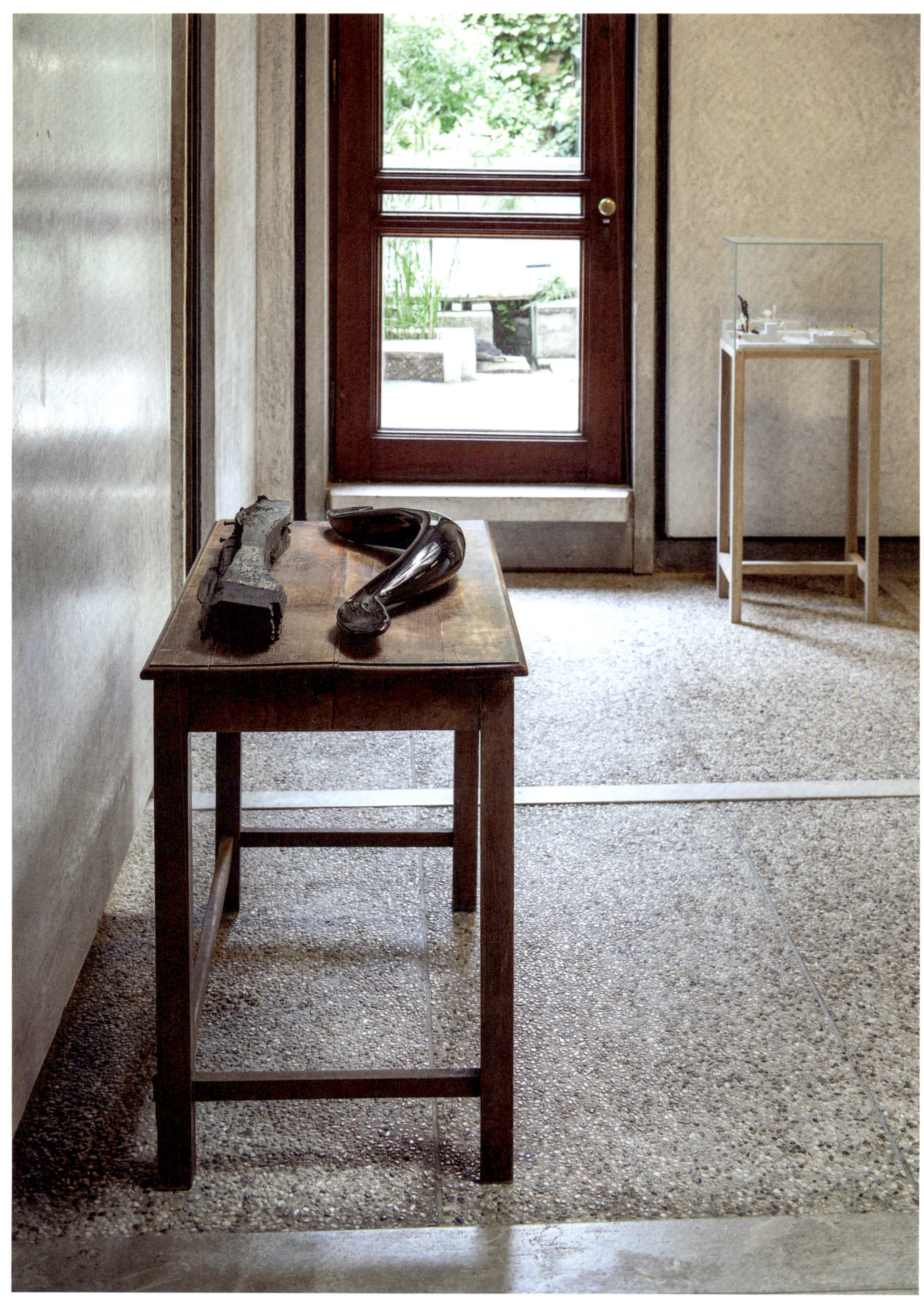

Different Ways of Organizing Matter in Venice, 2015. Wood, glass, iron on wood table. Wood: 30 ⅜ × 5 ⅛ × 2 ½ in. (77 × 13 × 6.5 cm); glass: 30 ⅜ × 7 ⅞ × 4 in. (77 × 20 × 10 cm); table: 27 ½ × 34 ¼ × 19 ¼ in. (70 × 87 × 48.9 cm).

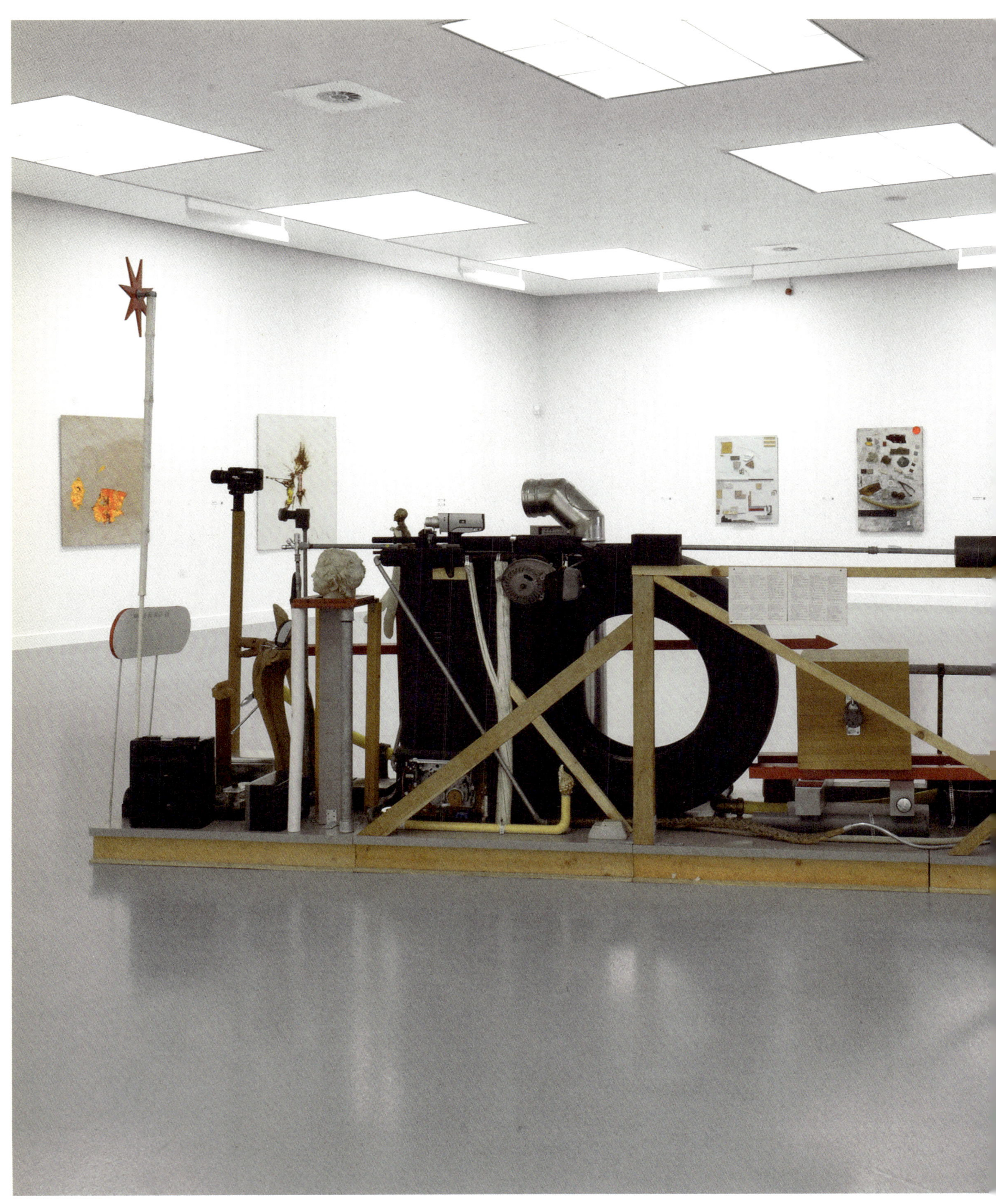

Something . . . Perhaps a Fugue or an Elegy, 2005. Cameras, television, VHS player, amplifier, tripod, steel pipes, hardware, PVC, plastic, rope, acrylic paint, pine, seashell, brass heads, cast marble-dust head, oak box, glass bottle, wood furniture parts, tree branches, tire, mirrors, metal lock, metal chains, lights, wires, plywood pallets, armadillo shell, cow skull and bones, ink on paper. 71 × 275 ½ × 63 in. (180 × 700 × 160 cm). Installation view, *A Matter of Life and Death and Singing*, Museum van Hedendaagse Kunst, Antwerp, 2012.

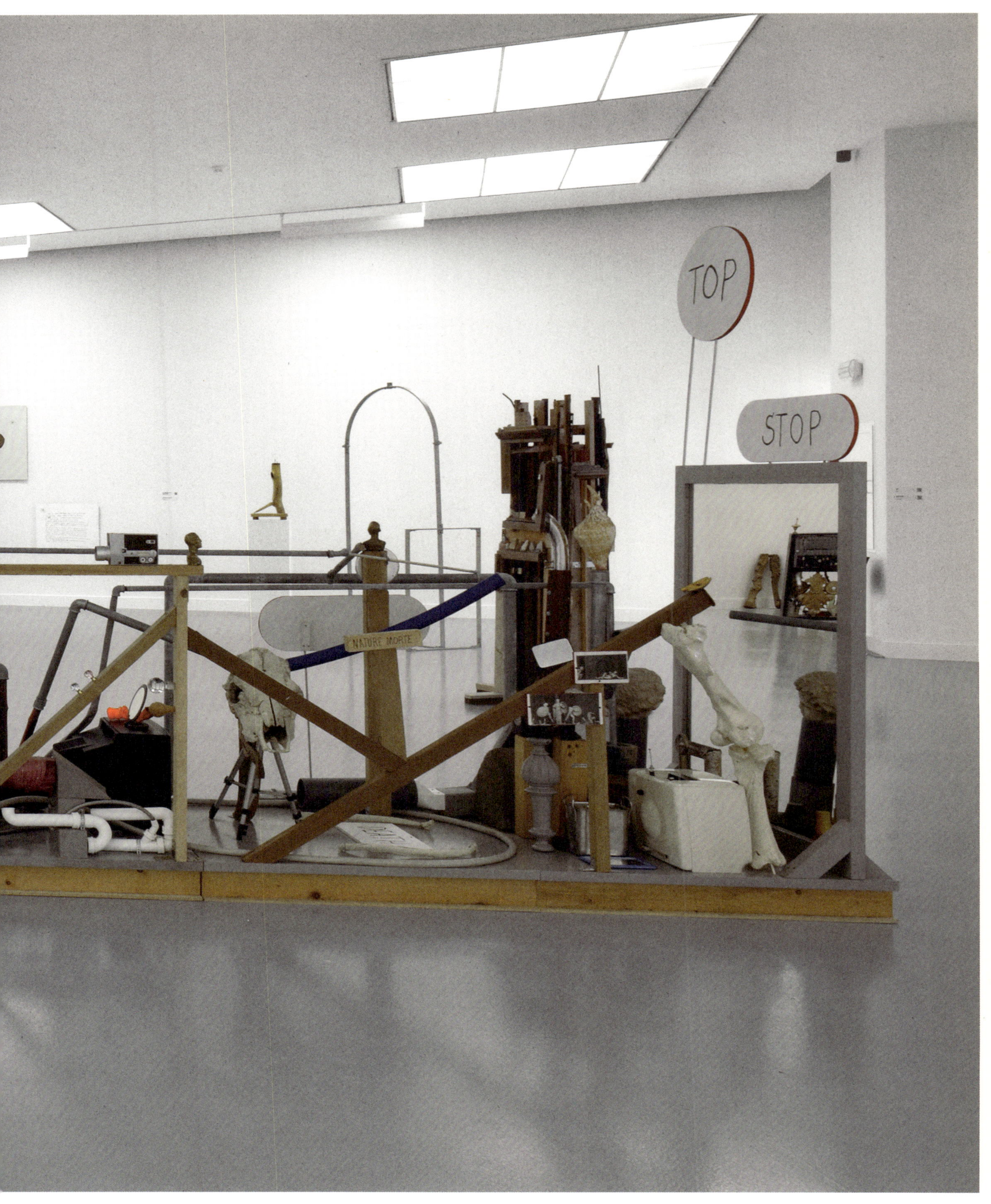
TOP
STOP
NATURE MORTE

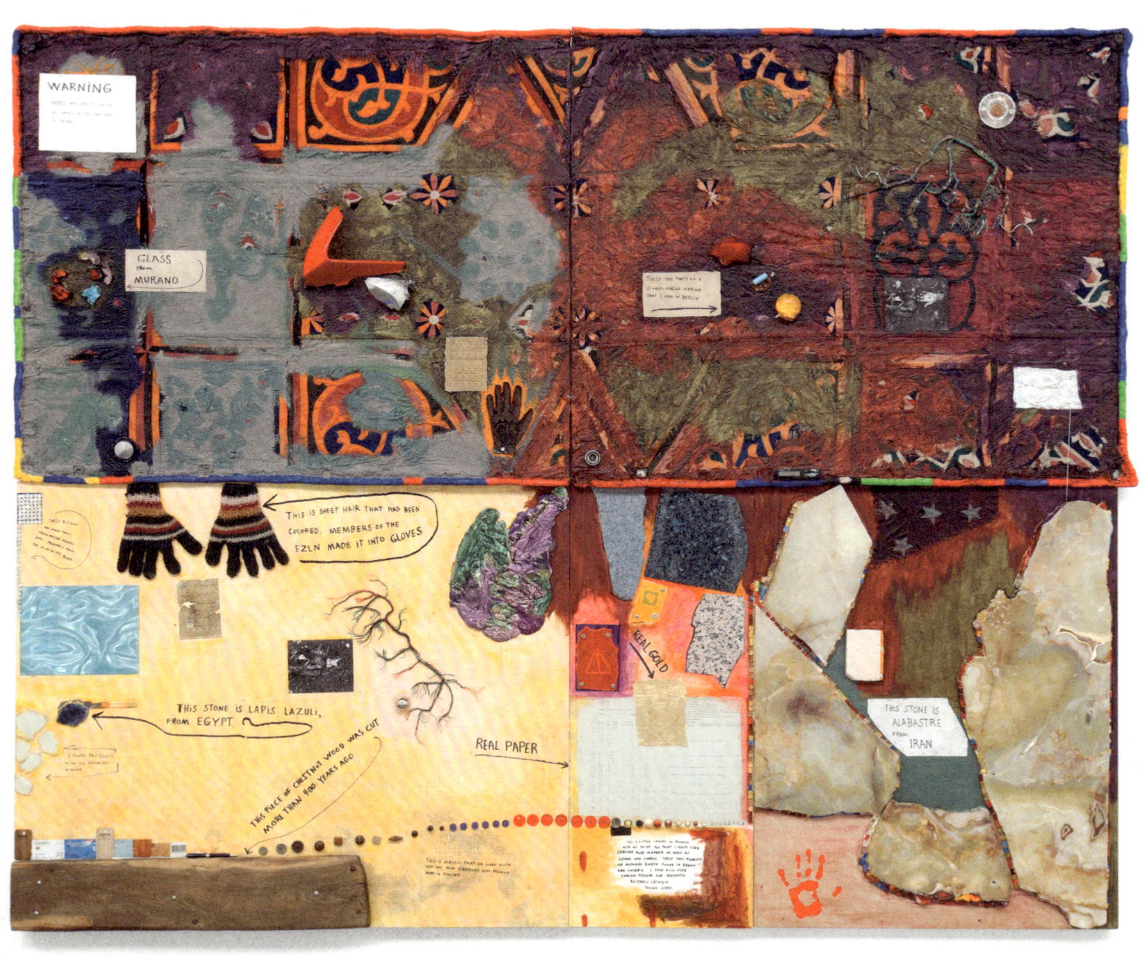

Various Elements from the Actual World, 2009. Acrylic and oil paint, Formica, gold leaf, wool gloves, leather glove, various stones, paper, Egyptian wedding canopy, buttons made of mussels, shards of glass, airplane parts, plywood, chestnut, black-and-white photographs, ink. 93 ½ × 118 ⅛ in. (250 × 300 cm).

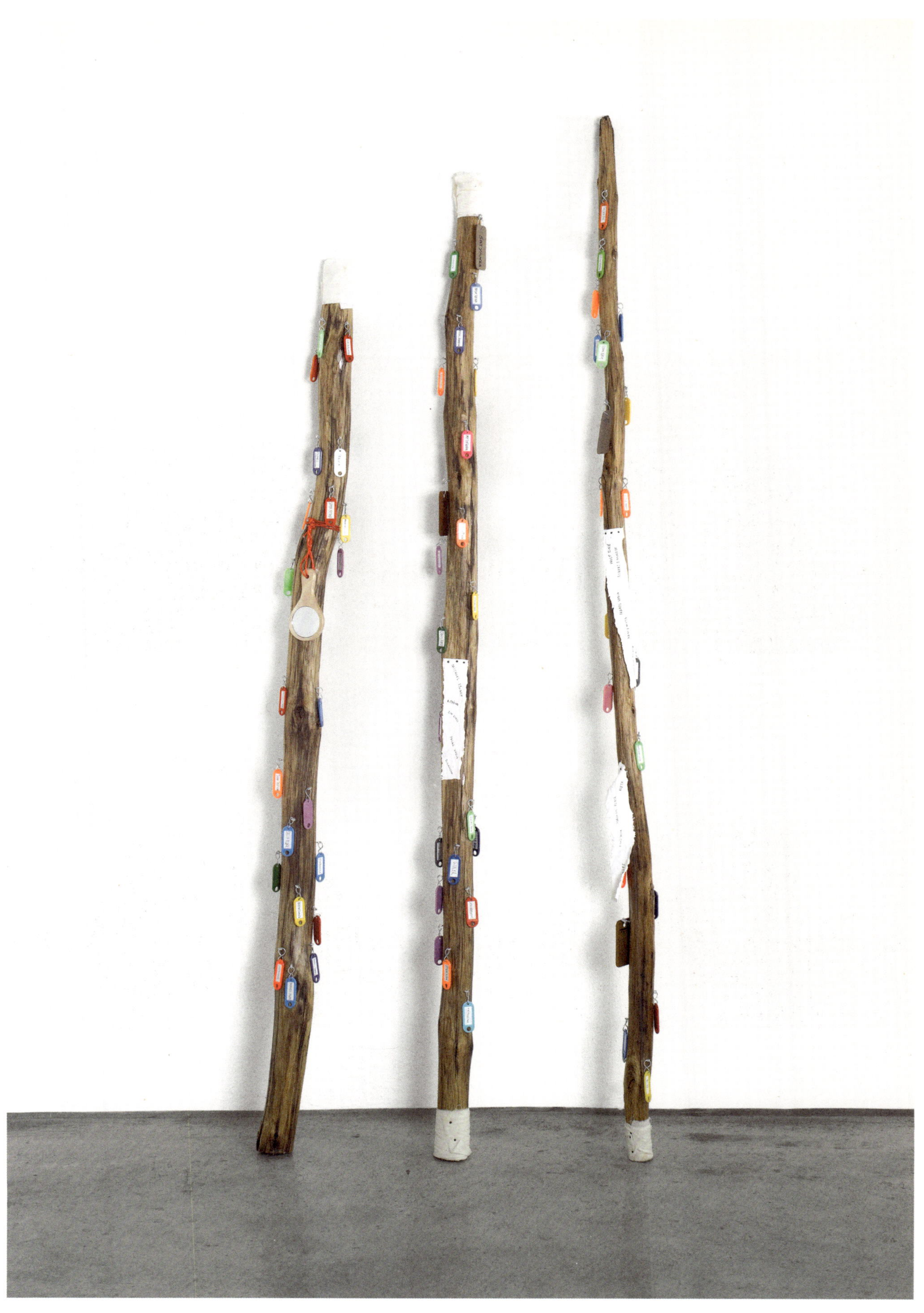

A Staff to Mark the Center of the World, Gwangju Biennale, 2004. Hawthorn, plastic and metal key rings, mirror, cotton, ink on paper.
Three parts, 77 ¼ × 3 in. (196.2 × 7.6 cm); 71 × 3 in. (180.3 × 7.62 cm); 66 ½ × 3 in. (168.9 × 7.6 cm).

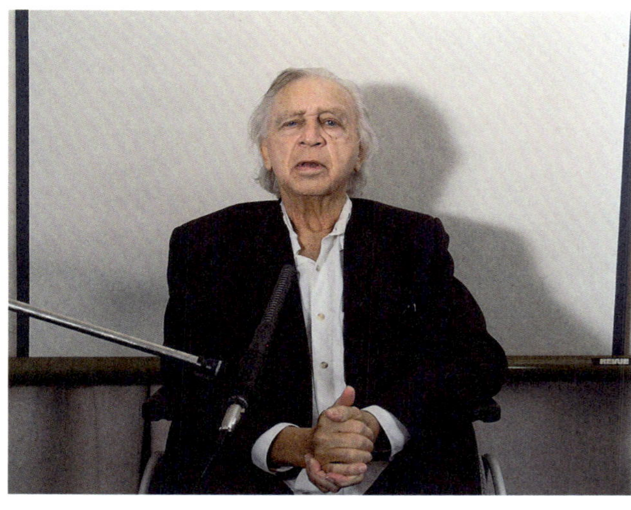
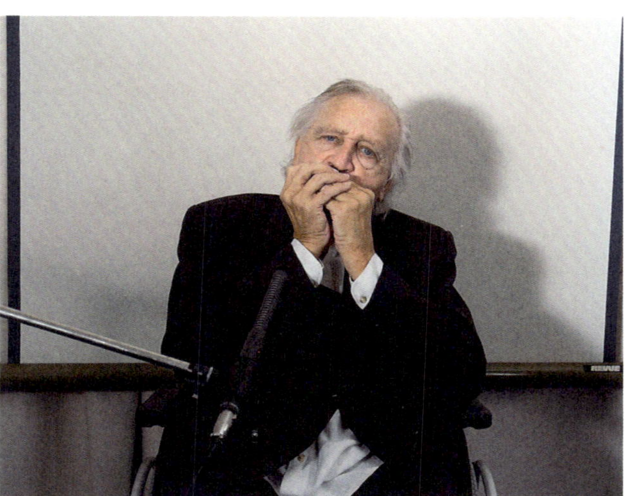
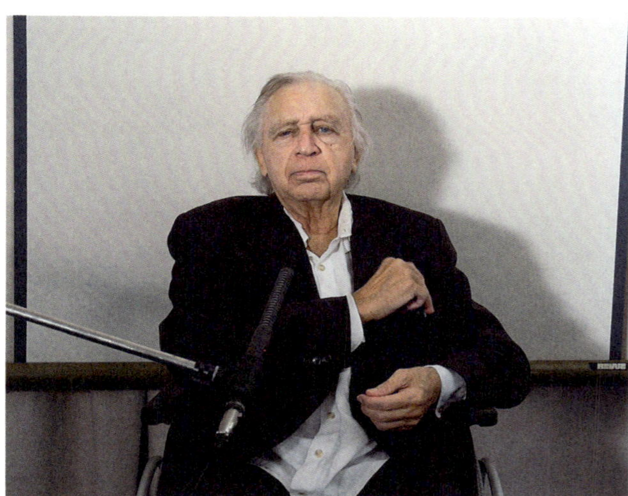
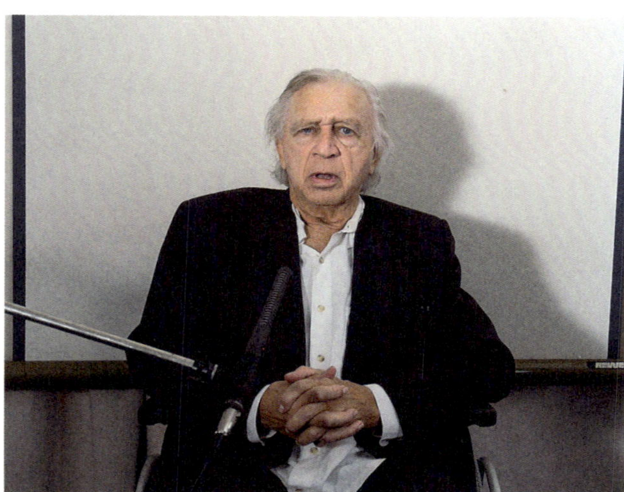

Songs of my Childhood. Part One: Songs to Get Rid Of; Part Two: Songs to Keep, 2014. Two-channel video installation, color, sound. 11:51 min. each of 2

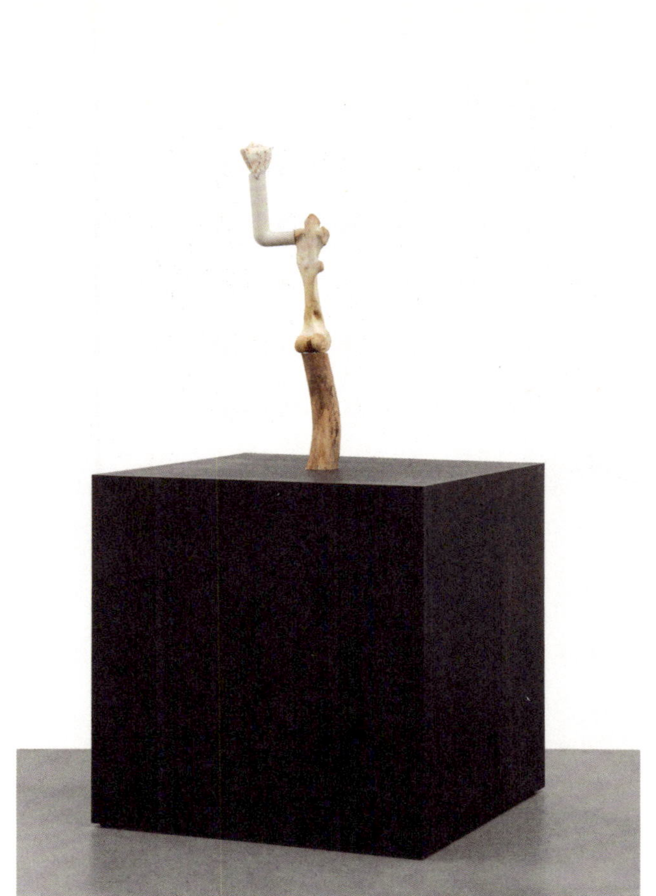

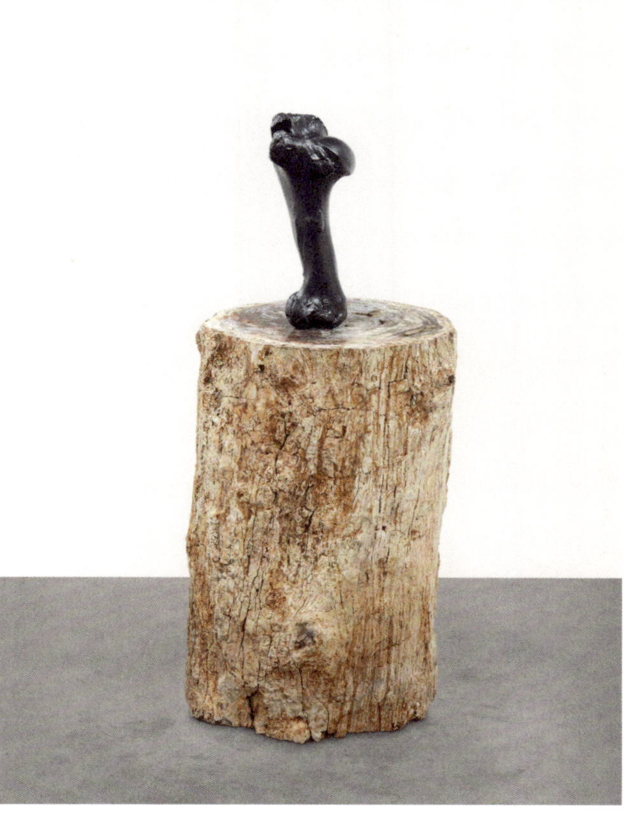

Left: *Inexplicable*, 2016. Wood, bone, PVC, seashell, stain. 78 × 39 ¼ × 39 ¼ in. (198 × 100 × 100 cm).
Right: *Much Has Already Happened*, 2016. Petrified wood, bone, metal, paint. 45 × 13 ¾ × 15 ¾ in. (114 × 35 × 40 cm).

SELECTED CHRONOLOGY

MACKENZIE STEVENS

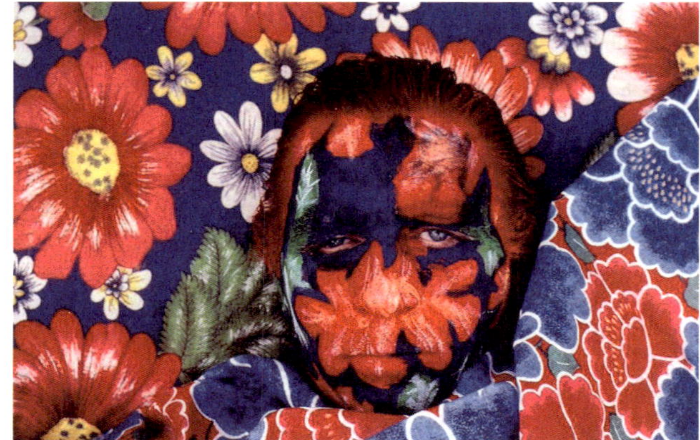

Portrait of Jimmie Durham, 1984. Photo by Maria Thereza Alves.

1940
Jimmie Durham is born July 10 in Washington, Arkansas.

1956
Leaves home at the age of sixteen and travels around the country working a variety of jobs, from rancher to construction supply store clerk.

1959
Enlists in the US Navy and spends the first year in Las Vegas. In the summer of 1960, he applies for ship duty in the Pacific and is assigned to two different vessels. He travels to Japan, Vietnam, Hong Kong, and the Philippines. While serving, he learns machine diesel mechanics.

1963
Is discharged from the navy in March and moves to Houston, Texas.

Becomes close friends with American poet Vivian Ayers Allen and contributes to her magazine ***Adept***, also doing editorial work for the magazine on occasion. A year later, he begins to contribute poems and drawings to ***The Fly's Eye***, a publication founded by students at the University of Houston in 1964, featuring poems and short stories written by students from various colleges and universities. Durham befriends Jon Conlon, who will serve as associate editor of ***The Fly's Eye*** in 1966.

1964
Family moves to Houston. Durham's first performance, ***My Land***, takes place at the Alley Theater in Houston. He performs alongside Muhammad Ali, who recites his own poetry, and Ayers Allen, who reads from a poetic play titled ***The Hawk***. Durham's poem "Song of Myself" (1984) includes an homage to Ali's performance.

> I started my art life in theater. My hero was Augusto Boal. People in my group were mostly black, and we worked very closely with Teatro Campesino, who were Chicanos. Our primary idea was politically organizing the community, educating people about their rights with the idea of liberating ourselves at the same time. ("Jimmie Durham Interviewed by Manuel Cirauqui," ***Bomb***, no. 118 [Winter 2012]: 82)

1965
Moves from Houston to Austin, where he has his first solo exhibition at A Clean Well Lighted Space gallery, featuring paintings of fictional animals on wood panels. He begins making jewelry and creates his first commissioned artwork, a carved-wood bull sculpture with iron legs, as a birthday present for his friend Jose Rubi at the request of Rubi's wife.

1967
Exhibits collages, assemblages, and sculptures at the University of Texas at Austin. Installs an exhibition at the gallery of ***Adept*** magazine, which is located in Ayers Allen's Houston apartment. The show includes objects installed on the wall, among them a leather lizard with a long tail.

1968
In July the American Indian Movement (AIM) is formed in Minneapolis, Minnesota, by American Indian activists Dennis Banks, Clyde and Vernon Bellecourt, and George Mitchell, among others. Issues of concern include police brutality, discrimination, poverty, unemployment, housing, and sovereignty over American Indian reservations.

1969
Durham relocates to Geneva, Switzerland, at the suggestion of Maurice Grober, a Swiss seminary student Durham had befriended in Austin and who had recently moved to Geneva. Durham soon begins studying at the École des Beaux-Arts, Université de Genève (having returned to the United States, he will graduate in 1974 in absentia with a diploma stating "completed four years"). Durham studies with Lithuanian artist Gabriel Stanulis. Durham and three other sculptors in his program—Roque Carmona, Danielle Fiard, and Gonzalo Torres—form Draga, a group conceived to explore the role of art in society and whose members often worked publicly, organizing street performances and installations, and engaging in forms of civil protest. Durham's performances include sculptures dragged through the city or lowered into the Rhône and allowed to float away. The group performs together four or fives times over the course of one year.

AIM occupies the abandoned federal penitentiary on Alcatraz Island, off the coast of San Francisco, from November 20, 1969, to June 11, 1971. This act of civil disobedience attracts much media attention and brings greater visibility to AIM's causes.

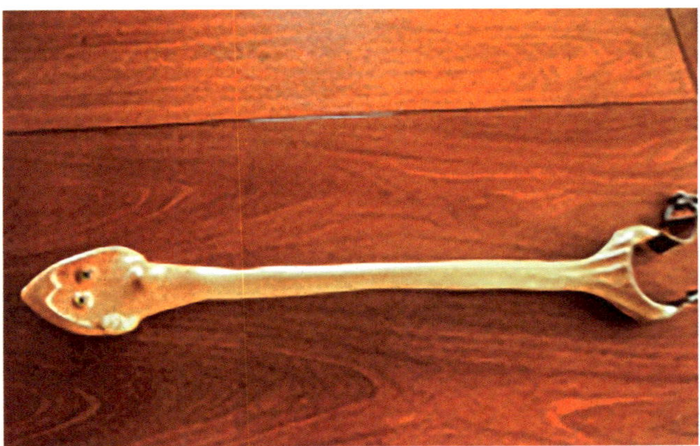

Untitled, 1971. Object used in Draga street performance. Beech, glass eyes, leather, metal. 51 × 4 in. (130 × 10 cm). Current location unknown.

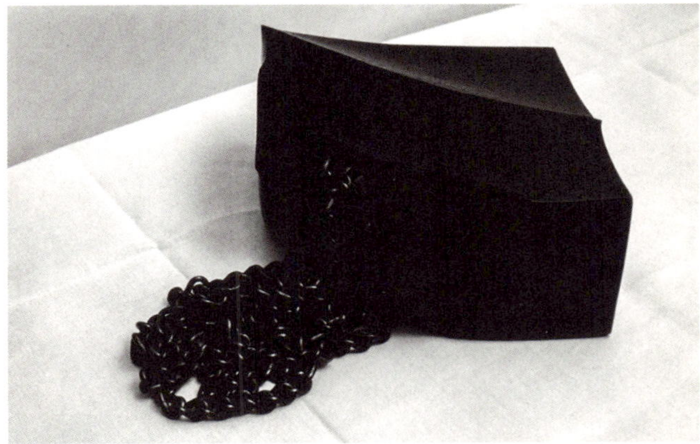

Untitled, 1971. Black granite, iron chain. 6 × 18 × 8 in. (15.2 × 45.7 × 20.3 cm). No longer extant.

1970
In Geneva Durham initiates an organization called Incomindios—together with a Mapuche Indian from Chile named Enrique Manzo and an Aymara Indian from Bolivia named Tomas Conde—to enlist international support for Indians of the Americas. The name ***incomindios*** refers to places in Latin America that are similar to American Indian reservations. The group would become active in fund-raising in Europe for AIM, especially after the uprising at Wounded Knee in South Dakota in 1973; at that time, knowing that he would be returning to the United States to take part in AIM activities there, Durham establishes Incomindios chapters in various European cities to help raise funds for the cause.

The First Convocation of American Indian Scholars takes place at Princeton University, where a plan is drafted to develop Native American Studies as an academic discipline.

1971
Durham has a solo show at Circa Gallery in Geneva titled ***Little Black Things***, for which he produces a large number of small black objects that are sold for "minus one centime" each, so when a visitor made a purchase, Durham would give him or her one cent back. Nothing sold.

Exhibits a variety of abstract sculptures at Centre des Rencontres outside Geneva, including a work with a black spray-painted chain attached to a carved piece of black granite, and a number of large carved-wood sculptures, several of which were later given to Ayers Allen.

1972
AIM, along with other Indian rights organizations from the United States and Canada, organizes the "Trail of Broken Treaties" caravan from Seattle to Washington, DC, to present President Richard M. Nixon with a twenty-point sovereignty proposal written by AIM. The caravan, constituting the largest group of American Indians ever gathered in the capital, arrives in Washington in early November, just prior to the national election. After Nixon refuses to meet with them, they occupy for approximately one week the Department of the Interior building that houses the Bureau of Indian Affairs national offices.

Durham has another solo show at Circa Gallery in Geneva as well as an exhibition at the École des Beaux-Arts.

1973
On February 27, the occupation of Wounded Knee begins with the participation of more than two hundred activists. Wounded Knee, on the Pine Ridge Indian Reservation in South Dakota, was chosen by Russell Means and Dennis Banks as the site for the protest because of the massacre of more than 150 Lakota at the hands of the US military in 1890. The occupation, which lasted seventy-one days, centered on AIM's demands that the US government reopen treaty negotiations that had not been honored and address the poor living conditions on reservations.

Having closely followed the occupation of Wounded Knee, Durham decides he must return to the United States to participate in the civil rights struggles of American Indians. He arrives in November, first stopping in Houston, then moving to the Pine Ridge Indian Reservation in early 1974, where he becomes a full-time organizer for AIM.

1974
Completes his undergraduate thesis in absentia for the École des Beaux-Arts, focusing on Swiss masks and the effect of tourism on Swiss "folk" culture. Much of his research was obtained by traveling around the country visiting carnivals and museums and listening to traditional music. Photographs from this trip along with appropriated images from a 1930s book on Swiss culture would later be used in his work ***Maquette for a Museum of Switzerland*** (2012), which addresses the history of Swiss culture through the lens of finance, clock making, and traditional masks.

Begins working at Pine Ridge as a fund-raiser for AIM and becomes part of the Wounded Knee Legal Defense/Offense Committee, which raises money to provide legal representation for those arrested and going to trial. Durham spends time in Sioux Falls, South Dakota, where the legal office is headquartered, and also travels regularly to Minneapolis and Saint Paul (where the trials of Russell Means and Dennis Banks were taking place); Sioux Falls and Rapid City, South Dakota; and Lincoln, Nebraska. He becomes good friends with Bill Kunstler, the attorney defending Means and Banks, and raises money for the members' legal needs, as well as for basic necessities for the families at Pine Ridge. Durham also teaches periodically at "We Will Remember" survival schools in Sioux Falls and Saint Paul and at Pine Ridge during 1974 and 1975.

The International Indian Treaty Council (IITC) is established at an AIM conference in Standing Rock, a reservation north of Pine Ridge. The purpose of the IITC is to bring Indians from the United States, Latin America, Canada, and Mexico together to push for international recognition within the United Nations and for their sovereignty and treaty rights. AIM representatives decide to establish an office in New York, near the United Nations, and choose Durham as director.

Later in the year, AIM establishes a Central Council of the primary members, which consisted of Larry Anderson; Pat Ballinger; Dennis Banks; Clyde and Vernon Bellecourt; Jimmie Durham; Bill, Ted, and Russell Means; Madonna Thunderhawk; and John Trudell.

1975
Durham relocates to New York to take up his post as executive director of the IITC; he will serve in this position until 1979. In his role there, he becomes the representative for Indians of North and South America to the United Nations, and is the first official representative from a minority group within the organization.

Beginning this year, Durham will travel to Geneva approximately every six months to present papers at the meetings of the UN's Human Rights Commission (later the Human Rights Council) and the Subcommittee on Decolonization. The goal of the IITC is to pass a resolution that would allow AIM to address the General Assembly of the UN on behalf of Indians of North and South America. From 1975 to 1980 Durham serves as coeditor, with Paul Chaat Smith, of the ***Treaty Council News***, the IITC's monthly newspaper.

Leonard Peltier, whom Durham met at Pine Ridge, is taken into custody for the alleged killing of two FBI officers on the reservation. Peltier is later convicted of first-degree murder and sentenced in 1977 to two consecutive life terms in prison. He remains incarcerated.

1977
The paper "Indigenous Populations and International Forums" is submitted on behalf of the IITC at the International NGO (Non-Governmental Organization) Conference on Discrimination against Indigenous Populations in the Americas sponsored by the UN and held in Geneva on September 20–23. Although Durham had originally proposed the conference, he did not attend. More than 250 people representing some sixty indigenous nations participated, and it marks the first time that indigenous delegates were able to speak for themselves at a UN conference. The conference produced the first draft of what became, in 2007, the UN Declaration on the Rights of Indigenous Peoples and resolved "to observe October 12, the day of so-called 'discovery' of America, as an International Day of Solidarity with the Indigenous Peoples of the Americas." Of this resolution, Durham wrote at the time, "Why is that so important? . . . It means that we have made a very large part of the world recognize who we are and even to stand with us in solidarity in our long fight. From now on, children all over the world will learn the true story of American Indians on Columbus Day instead of a pack of lies about three European ships" (Archives of Indigenous Peoples Day, http://ipdpowwow.org/Archives_1.html).

1978
Durham meets Brazilian activist and artist Maria Thereza Alves, who works as a volunteer for the IITC. In 1983 he would write of his partner, "Maria Thereza has given me my life. . . . She has also been my energy and support in a time that has been in other ways the lowest point in my life. Her anger and courage, and her love, have been my support" ("History, Too Close for Comfort," in ***Columbus Day*** [Albuquerque: West End Press, 1983], 2).

From February to July, AIM's action "The Longest Walk" takes place, in which people walked from Alcatraz Island to the Washington Monument on the National Mall to protest eleven bills coming before Congress that would have limited rights guaranteed to American Indians through existing treaties with the US government. None of the bills passed. Durham had argued against the action, believing that AIM's focus should be on changes to international law and not on negotiating with the federal government, and thus did not participate in the march, though he did go to Washington when the marchers arrived to help organize. For the following week, thousands of participants took part in rallies, demonstrations, tribal ceremonies, and workshops.

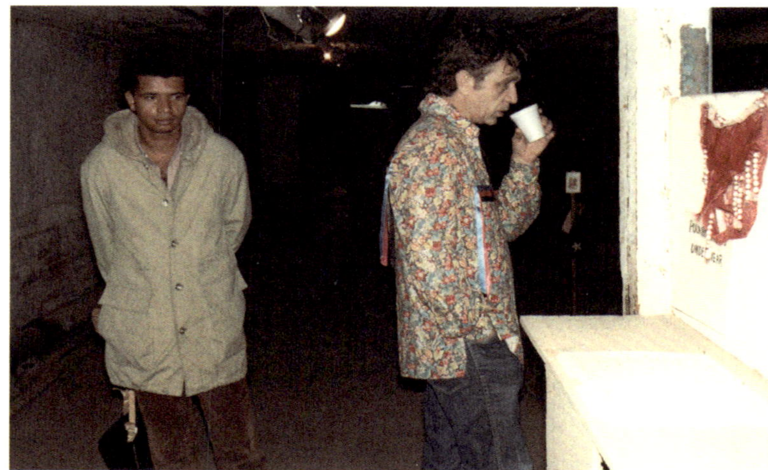

Jimmie Durham (right) and Ricardo Brey at the opening reception for *Bedia's First Basement*, 22 Wooster Gallery, New York, 1985.

1979
On February 15, the IITC makes a presentation to the UN's Human Rights Commission in Geneva, arguing that protections granted by the US Constitution and by treaties between the government and Indian nations, and upheld by the Supreme Court, were continually being violated, denying Indians their rights to self-determination, stealing their natural resources, and leaving them in abject poverty.

In the summer, Durham resigns from the IITC; in December of 1980 he will write, with Paul Chaat Smith, "An Open Letter on Recent Developments in the American Indian Movement/International Indian Treaty Council," explaining their reasons for leaving the movement, including a loss of faith in the group's leadership, while still declaring their commitment to the "ongoing struggle" ("An Open Letter," in ***A Certain Lack of Coherence: Writings on Art and Cultural Politics***, ed. Jean Fisher [London: Kala Press, 1993], 56).

1980
Alves and Durham move to Hoboken, New Jersey, and Alves begins studying art at Cooper Union in New York City, where artist Juan Sánchez is the admissions officer. Alves and Durham befriend Sánchez.

1981
From 1981 to 1983, Durham is the director of the artists advocacy organization Foundation for the Community of Artists (FCA), which provides artists with health care, among other services. He coedits the organization's newspaper, ***Art and Artists***, which provides a platform for artists and young writers, including Adam Gopnik and Paul Chaat Smith.

1982
In May, Durham participates in his first group exhibition in New York, ***Beyond Aesthetics: Art of Necessity by Artists of Conscience***, curated by Sánchez, at the Henry Street Settlement. He shows several mixed-media collages depicting the hardships of American Indians living on the reservation. The works incorporate details of photographs by Richard Erdoes, an Austrian photographer and writer Durham met in New York and at the Pine Ridge and Standing Rock reservations during Wounded Knee. On June 4, Durham reads poetry alongside

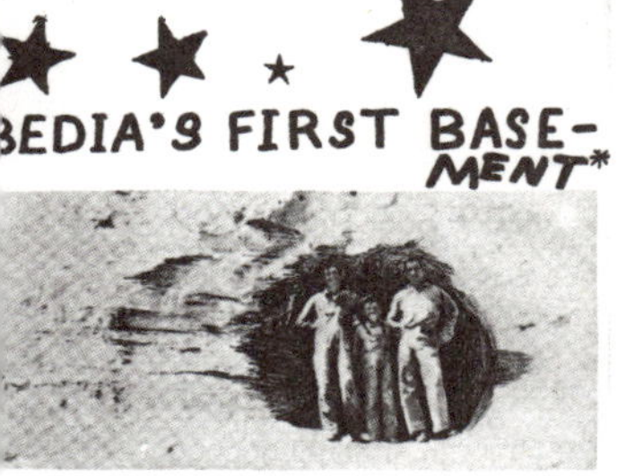

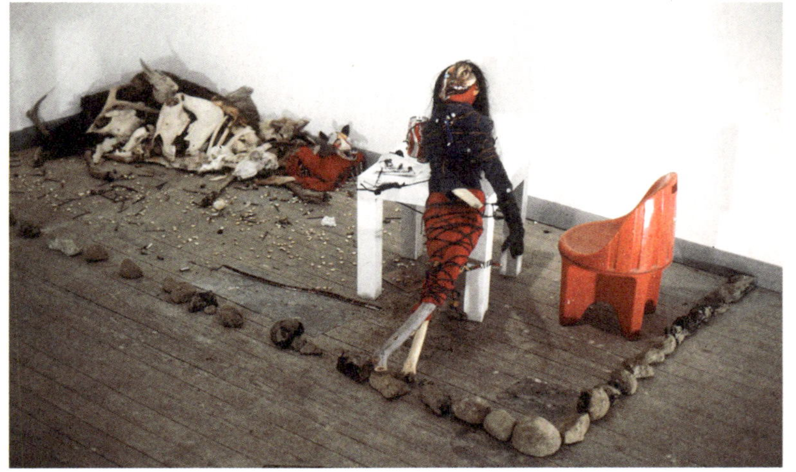

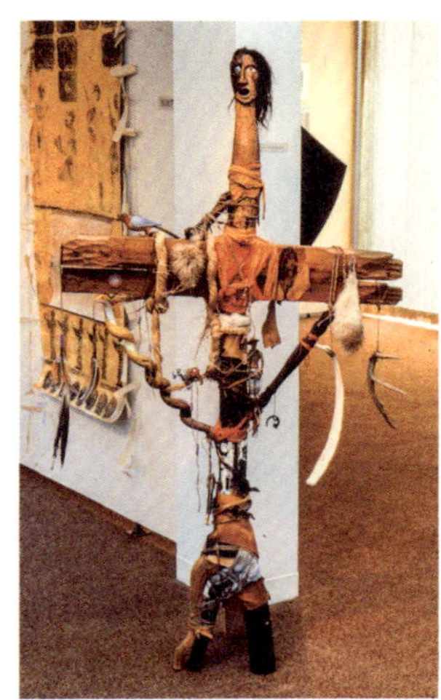

Left: Poster for *Bedia's First Basement*, 1985.
Middle: Set for Durham's performance *The History of Indians including the Death of Paul Smith*, Minor Injury Gallery, Brooklyn, 1985.
Right: *Los Americos*, 1986. Wood, leather, fur of different types, feathers, string, plastic, glass, hair, cloth, printing ink, photo, mule deer antler, bone. No longer extant.

Amiri Baraka, Fay Chiang, Sandra María Esteves, and Alma Villegas as part of "Words of Necessity: A Poetry Reading," organized in conjunction with the exhibition.

Ritual and Rhythm: Visual Forces for Survival, a group exhibition also curated by Sánchez, opens at Kenkeleba Gallery in the East Village on October 17. Kenkeleba's mission is to support artists of color, and Durham's ***Manhattan Festival of the Dead*** is exhibited alongside the works of Papo Colo, David Hammons, Ana Mendieta, Faith Ringgold, and others.

1983
Thanksgiving is performed with Corrine Jennings, one of the founders of Kenkeleba Gallery, and Robbie McCauley at PS122 in New York City. The choreography for Durham's dance, in which he held a coyote skull, was based on a performance he saw in Panama, in which the dancer wore an animal skull and mimicked the movements of that animal.

Columbus Day, Durham's first book of poems, is published by West End Press.

1984
Durham participates in ***ARTISTS CALL against U.S. Intervention in Central America***, which consists of exhibitions, actions, and performances at commercial galleries and alternative spaces throughout New York City. He is one of the artists to sign a letter soliciting the support and participation of other artists for ***ARTISTS CALL*** in the summer of 1983. His work is included in an ***ARTISTS CALL*** exhibition in the sanctuary of Judson Memorial Church, which opens on January 21. The exhibition travels to the Museo Universitario del Chopo, Mexico City, and then to the Centro de Arte Contemporáneo Wifredo Lam, Havana, where it is titled ***Por encima el bloqueo*** [***Against the Blockade***]; Durham's work was lost in Mexico.

Participates in other group exhibitions, including ***Call and Response: Art on Central America*** at Colby College, Waterville, Maine, curated by Lucy R. Lippard, and ***Racist America*** at Dramatis Personae, New York. He performs ***A Trick*** at AAA Gallery, New York, about the history of American Indians and stereotypes of them, with Richard Hoover, who pretends to be a member of the audience and heckles Durham as he sings and dances. Hoover then joins him on the stage and reads a statement written by Durham about the harsh realities of American Indian life in the United States.

Durham's first solo show in New York, ***A Matter of Life and Death and Singing***, organized by chief curator Geno Rodriguez, opens at the Alternative Museum on December 19. He creates a new body of sculptures that integrate animal skulls that were either collected in New York City or given to him by family members and friends. Of this work, he wrote:

> In the work I am doing now, using the skulls and bones of animals (including human), like any artist I start with a private and subjective motivation. In this case I try to understand what each particular animal (I mean the individual not the generic) feels about being dead, and then I try to interpret that feeling through a variety of media such as color and paint, stones, symbolic objects. In making each piece I try to become, or at least to dance with, a specific dead animal, which is a kind of insanity. Then I bring the dead animal to you and we are all reclaimed; death is not lost. (***A Matter of Life and Death and Singing*** press release, 1984)

1985
Makes several works inspired by the drawings of José Bedia, whose art was introduced to him by Cuban artist Nelson Dominguez in 1982. ***Bedia's Stirring Wheel*** is included in the group show ***Start Again*** at Ground Zero Gallery, New York, in January, and ***Bedia's Muffler*** is shown in ***Forecast: Images of the Future***, which opens in February at Kenkeleba Gallery. The muffler and the steering wheel, along with the tire that would be used in ***Bedia's Stirring Wheel***, had been found on the street the year prior. Durham described both works as "artifacts of the future" in the press release for a subsequent exhibition, ***Bedia's First Basement***, and in a documentary film made in 1992 titled ***War against the Indians*** (dir. Harry Rasky). ***Bedia's First Basement*** opens on March 2 in the basement of 22 Wooster Gallery, New York. Like the "artifact" works, the installation is inspired by Bedia's portrayals of fake Indian ruins and archaeological sites and the use of a made-up language; the objects in ***Bedia's First Basement*** are attributed to Bedia himself, whom Durham describes as "the famous Cuban explorer/archaeologist" in the press release. The installation purports to be the first basement built on Manhattanas, a prison for the last living American Indian, discovered by Bedia in the third millennium. Although he had never met Durham, Bedia, along with other Cuban artists, including Ricardo Brey, attends the opening; Durham and Alves befriend Bedia, Brey, and other Cuban artists, some of whom would later live with them in New York City.

Durham performs ***Manhattan Give-away*** at Franklin Furnace, New York, for PAD/D (Political Art Documentation/Distribution), curated by Lucy R. Lippard, in which he gives away small objects he made, such as wooden carvings, to members of the audience. After all the small objects have been dispersed, Durham then gives away his bracelet and shirt. The performance begins with a cleansing ceremony in which smoke from burning cedar wood is fanned throughout the space; it ends when Durham announces that it is over and walks to the side of the room. His multipart installation ***On Loan from the Museum of the American Indian***—presenting personal effects alongside found objects, appropriated images, and fake artifacts in a quasi-museological display—is included in the group show ***Dimensions in Dissent*** at Kenkeleba Gallery.

Performs ***The History of Indians including the Death of Paul Smith*** at the opening reception for his exhibition of the same name at the Minor Injury Gallery in Brooklyn.

Reads poems from ***Columbus Day*** at the American Indian Community House, New York, on November 14. The reading is in conjunction with ***Not Quite Dead in Manhattan***, an exhibition of Durham's work organized by Lloyd Oxendine.

1986
His solo exhibition ***Jimmie Durham: Paintings and Multi-Media Constructions*** opens at John Jay College's Wall Gallery in New York on January 13.

Ni' Go Tlunh a Doh Ka (We are always turning around on purpose), a group exhibition of works by American Indian artists, opens on April 8 at the Amelie A. Wallace Gallery at the State University of New York at Old Westbury, subsequently traveling to Massachusetts College of Art, Boston, and Central State University in Edmond, Oklahoma. The exhibition—organized by Durham and British art historian and curator Jean Fisher, who was introduced to Durham by artist Luis Camnitzer, her supervisor at SUNY—includes the work of Edgar Heap of Birds, G. Peter Jemison, Jean LaMarr, Richard Ray, Jolene Rickard, and Richard Ray Whitman. Although Durham was generally opposed to the idea of ethnically specific shows and skeptical of the tendency to group artists together based on race, gender, or sexuality, he was impressed with Fisher's intelligence and commitment, and swayed by her argument that because American Indian artists were so overlooked, it was important to provide visibility for them.

For the group exhibition ***Self-Portrait***, at Kenkeleba Gallery, Durham creates ***Self-portrait***, which becomes one of his best-known works: a life-size painted construction of his body with texts humorously detailing various aspects of his physique, interests, and personality.

1987
Durham and Alves move to Cuernavaca, Mexico. Although they did have one friend there—Cedric Belfrage, an Englishman Durham met in New York who had started a leftist magazine in 1948 called the ***National Guardian***—most of the major figures who had settled in Cuernavaca, such as Austrian philosopher and priest Ivan Illich, Mexican bishop and human rights activist Sergio Méndez Arceo, and German-born artist and architect Mathias Goeritz, were no longer there. Nonetheless, the city was still a vital center for leftist activity, intellectuals, and artists. Because of his visa, Durham has to return to the United States every few months, and continues to exhibit regularly in New York.

On March 29, Durham performs ***I Want to Say Something (Bilingual Education)*** at La MaMa Theater in New York as part of a festival about American Indian performance; wearing a coyote pelt, he performs a dance and reads a short piece written in French.

Durham and Fisher organize ***We the People***, a group show of contemporary American Indian artists that opens on November 12 at Artists Space in New York. It includes a modified version of Durham's ***On Loan from the Museum of the American Indian*** as well as ***She Rose from Her Warm Bed***, which consists of small wooden dolls carved and painted by Durham and a group of boys he befriended and employed in Cuernavaca. The catalogue contains Durham's essay "Savage Attacks on White Women, As Usual."

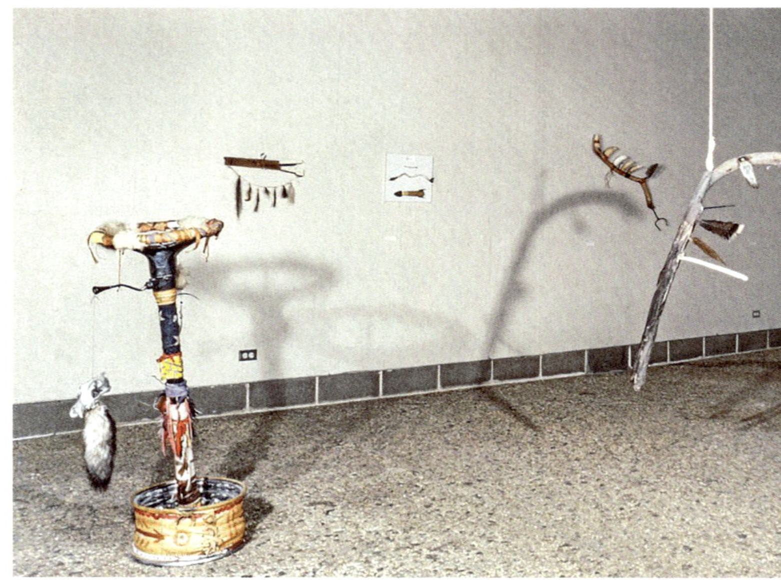

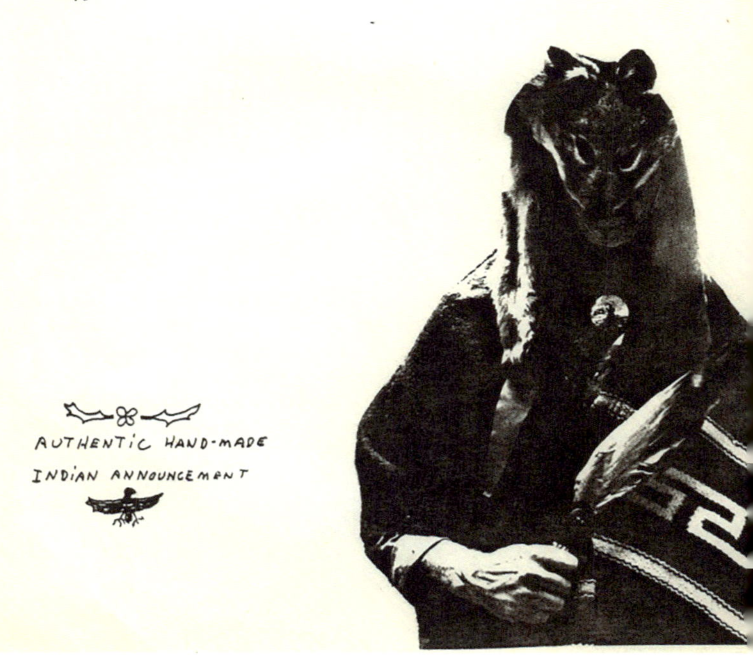

Top: *Ni' Go Tlunh a Doh Ka (We are always turning around on purpose)*, installation view, Amelie A. Wallace Gallery, State University of New York at Old Westbury, 1986.
Bottom: Announcement for *I Want to Say Something (Bilingual Education)*, La MaMa Theater, New York, 1987.

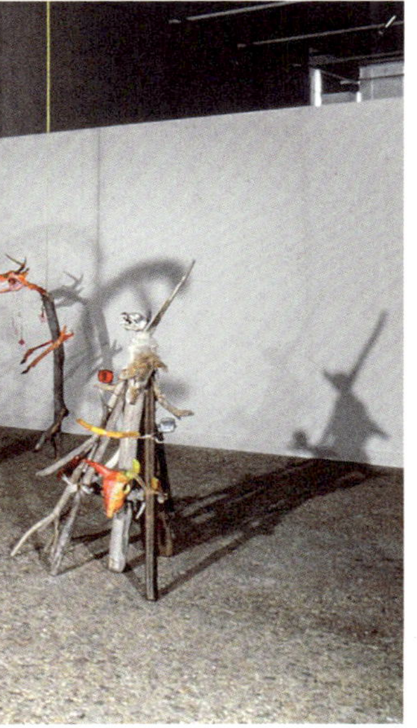

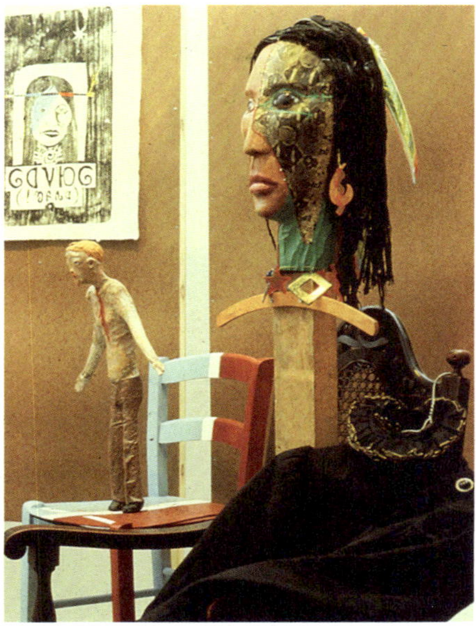

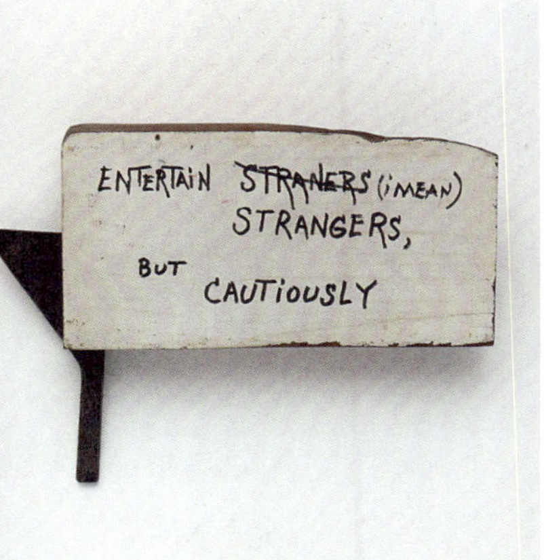

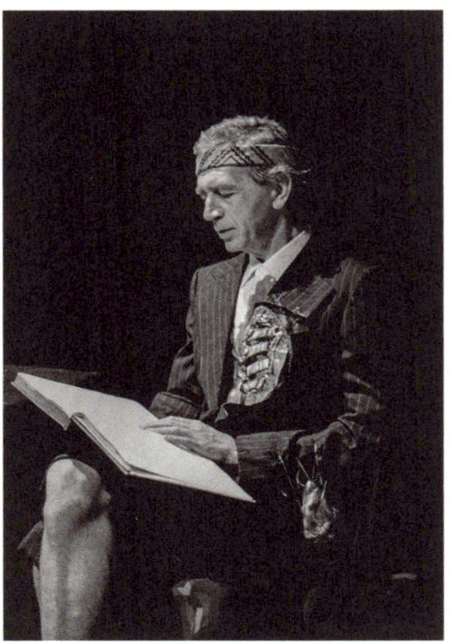

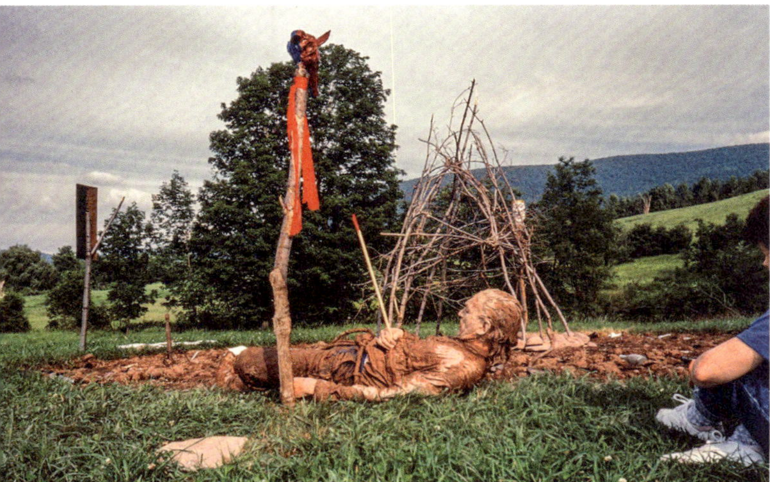

Top: *Mataoka Ake Attakulakula Anel Guledisgo Hnihi (Pocahontas and the Little Carpenter in London)*, installation view, Matt's Gallery, London, 1988.
Middle left: *Give-away* from *Savagism and You* performance, 1990. Wood, acrylic paint, ink, metal. 6 ⅛ × 8 ¼ × 1 ¾ in. (15.6 × 21 × 4.4 cm).
Middle right: *Crazy for Life* performance, Bessie Schonberg Theatre, New York, June 10, 1990.
Bottom: *Catskills Give-away* performance, Art Awareness, Lexington, New York, 1990.

1988

Four of Durham's poems are included in ***Harper's Anthology of Twentieth Century Native American Poetry***: "Columbus Day," "Justiniano Lame Has Been Killed," "Middle," and "A Woman Gave Me a Red Star to Wear on My Headband."

Begins to show his work in Europe. ***Mataoka Ake Attakulakula Anel Guledisgo Hnihi (Pocahontas and the Little Carpenter in London)***, organized by Jean Fisher, opens at Matt's Gallery in London on October 10. The catalogue includes Durham's essay "A Certain Lack of Coherence," which becomes the title of a volume of essays, poems, and other texts by Durham published in 1993. His show "***. . . very much like the Wild Irish": Notes on a Process which has no end in Sight*** is organized by Deelan McGonangle for Orchard Gallery in Derry, Northern Ireland, and includes the outdoor performance ***Four Scenes for the British Army***. During the performance, Durham erects a sculpture of what he calls a "savage video camera," which faces the army's cameras at the city gate (Durham to Jeanette Ingberman and Papo Colo, November 27, 1988, Exit Art Archive, MSS 343, Series I, box 21, folder 19, Fales Library and Special Collections, New York University Libraries).

1989

Durham's solo exhibition ***The Bishop's Moose and the Pinkerton Men***, curated by Jeanette Ingberman, opens at Exit Art in New York on November 1 and then travels to Western Washington University's Western Gallery in Bellingham, Washington, and to the Museum of Civilization (now the Canadian Museum of History), in Hull, Quebec. The exhibition includes works made between 1985 and 1989, featuring sculptures, works on paper, and canvases that examine the history of Manhattan, as well as "texts which critically explore issues of identity and culture" (exhibition press release, Exit Art Archive, MSS 343, Series I, box 21, folder 18, Fales Library and Special Collections, New York University Libraries). Durham presents ***Hermeneutical Considerations of the Bishop's Moose*** at the opening in New York City, in which he performs as an Alistair Cooke–like television-show host alongside Verna Hampton, Robbie McCauley, Abi Sheperd, and Vincent Terrell. In the script, written by Durham, his opening lines are: "Perhaps you are unaware that I am a savage—Oh, yes; to the manner born, as they say. My family has been fiercely savage since the great upheaval of 1492, when savagism first came into its own." The catalogue features essays by artist Luis Camnitzer and art historian Lucy R. Lippard, as well as an interview of the artist by Ingberman.

1990

Durham is included in the performance program of ***The Decade Show: Frameworks of Identity in the 1980s***, a large exhibition in New York co-organized by the New Museum of Contemporary Art, the Museum of Contemporary Hispanic Art, and the Studio Museum in Harlem. He performs ***Crazy for Life***, with artist and filmmaker Shu Lea Cheang, at the Dance Theater Workshop's Bessie Schonberg Theatre in New York on June 10; in it Durham reads from his writings, including a fictional and highly satirical memoir in the voice of Crazy Horse, and from texts he wrote in several European languages. He also contributes an essay, "A Central Margin," to the catalogue.

Is included in ***Savoir-vivre, Savoir-faire, Savoir-être*** at the Centre International d'Art Contemporain de Montréal, Quebec. Among the works on view are ***Pocahontas' Underwear*** (1985), ***Not Lothar Baumgarten's Cherokee*** (1990), and ***Not Joseph Beuys' Coyote*** (1990, now lost).

Catskills Give-away is performed at Art Awareness in Lexington, New York. During the performance, Durham hands out bloodied money and objects to the audience. ***Savagism and You*** is performed at the Whitney Museum Downtown branch, and ***The Savage Hour*** at Exit Art.

On November 29, the Indian Arts and Crafts Act is signed into law by President George H. W. Bush. The law states that a person who exhibits Native American art for sale must be able to prove that the maker is American Indian, defined under the act as "a member of an Indian tribe, or . . . certified as an Indian artisan by an Indian tribe." For first-time violations, an individual could be fined up to $250,000 and/or face up to five years in jail; an exhibiting space could be fined up to $1 million.

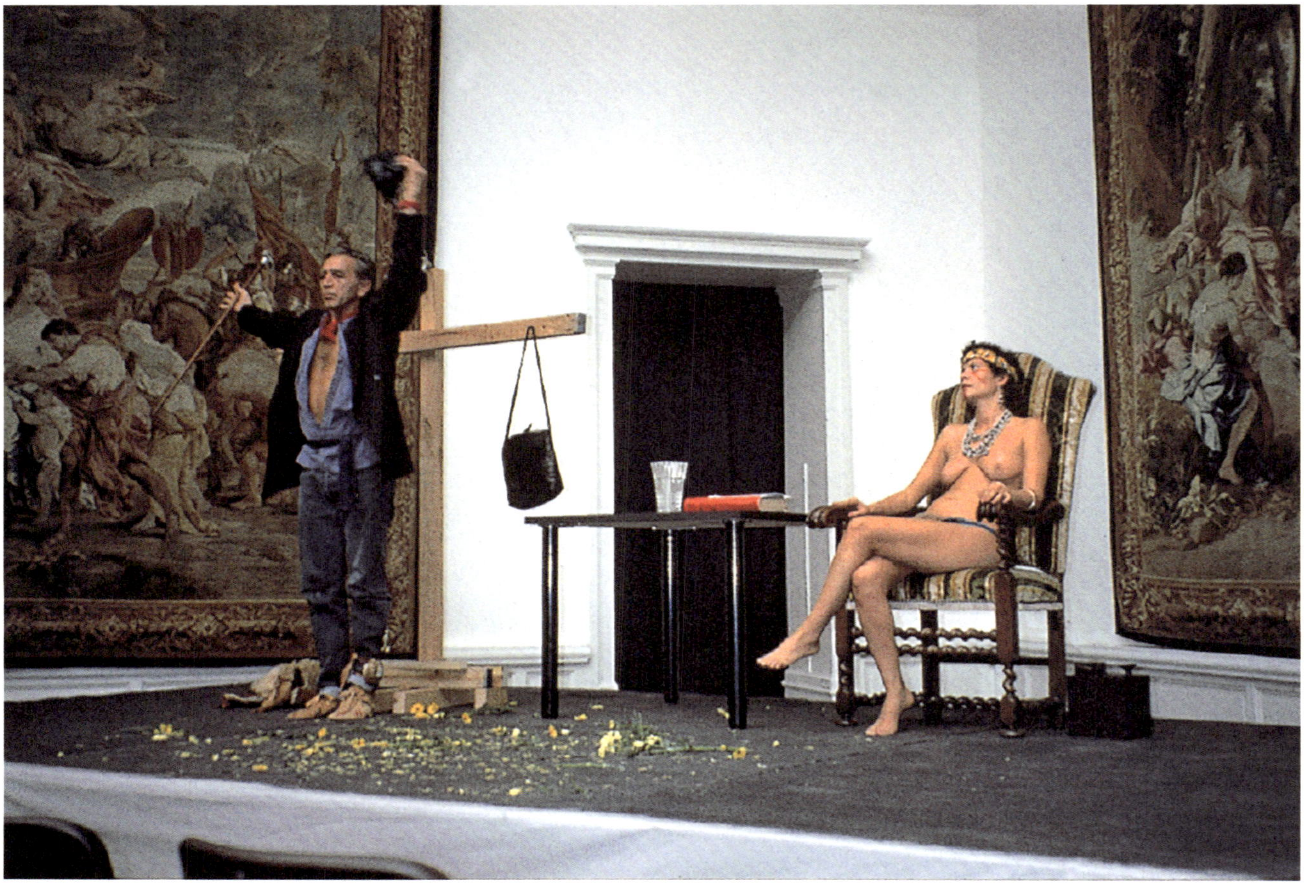

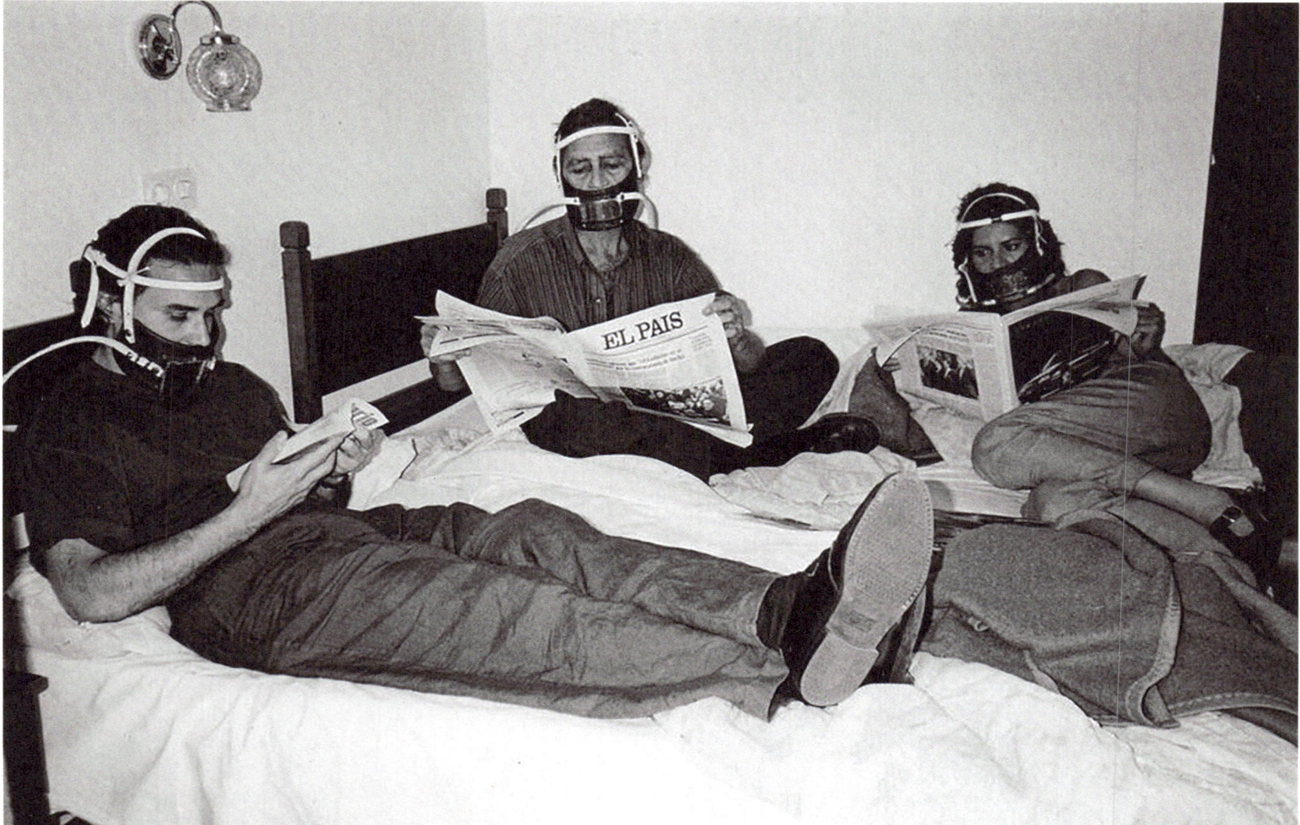

Top: *Savage* performance, Time Festival, Stedelijk Museum voor Actuele Kunst, Ghent, 1991, with Maria Thereza Alves.
Bottom: *Virginia/Veracruz* performance, Edge '92 Festival, Madrid, 1992, with Maria Thereza Alves and Alan Michelson.

1991
At the invitation of Jan Hoet, Alves and Durham perform ***Savage*** at the Time Festival, organized by the Museum van Hedendaagse Kunst (now Stedelijk Museum voor Actuele Kunst), Ghent, on May 24.

On June 4, Robert B. Gaylor, director of the Center for Contemporary Arts of Santa Fe, officially cancels ***The Bishop's Moose and the Pinkerton Men*** under pressure from certain members of the American Indian community on the grounds that, because Durham is not registered as Cherokee with the US government, he is not protected under the Indian Arts and Crafts Act. Although Gaylor had hoped to postpone the exhibition until this issue was "cleared up," it never took place at the museum, nor did it travel to venues in Boulder and Santa Barbara as originally planned. In a letter to Durham, Gaylor wrote: "I realize that the issue of personal and tribal identity continue to be both complex and unfair . . . there are thousands of people who are clearly 'Indians,' but don't want to submit to the humiliation of certain processes [meaning registering with the federal government] . . . this is all much more complex than I imagined" (Robert B. Gaylor to Jimmie Durham, June 4, 1991, Exit Art Archive, MSS 343, Series I, box 21, folder 21, Fales Library and Special Collections, New York University Libraries). For similar reasons, and with Durham's support, the exhibition ***John Rollin Ridge, Zorro and The Joad Family Players*** is moved from the American Indian House in San Francisco to the Luggage Store over fears that government funding will be withdrawn from the originating venue.

In September, Durham is included in the New Museum's exhibition ***The Interrupted Life***, organized by France Morin, exploring the various ways different cultures contend with the subject of death. He also contributes an essay titled "The Immortal State" to the catalogue.

1992
Virginia/Veracruz—a performance with Durham, Alves, and Alan Michelson—takes place at the Edge '92 Festival in Madrid and London in May, curated by Olivier Debroise.

Documenta IX, curated by Jan Hoet, opens in Kassel, Germany, on June 13, and Durham contributes several new works, including ***Jesus (Es geht um die Wurst)***, ***Treff***, and the two-part outdoor sculpture ***This Stone Is from the Mountain/This Stone Is from the Red Palace***, made of two pieces of sandstone found in the city center of Kassel and meant as a commentary on exhibition culture; it remained on view in Kassel until 2015. The catalogue includes Durham's essay "Approach in Love and Fear" about the presence of those two emotions in humans and animals and how they are interrelated.

Will/Power opens at the Wexner Center for the Arts in Columbus, Ohio, on September 26, and includes a large-scale sculptural installation by Durham titled ***The Banks of the Ohio*** (no longer extant), as well as works by Papo Colo, David Hammons, Edgar Heap of Birds, Adrian Piper, and Aminah Brenda Lynn Robinson.

Durham begins to be represented by Nicole Klagsbrun Gallery in New York and exhibits new work in a solo exhibition titled ***Janus and His Double***, which opens on November 7. The installation divides the gallery into two parts, one containing "art" and the other "anti-art." As in ***Bedia's First Basement***, Durham adopted a persona, in this case the Shakespearean character Caliban from ***The Tempest***, whose identity was "mediated" through Durham by way of drawings, paintings, and sculptures.

1993
Is included in the Whitney Biennial curated by Elisabeth Sussman, with Lisa Phillips, John G. Hanhardt, and Thelma Golden. His installation comprises several small sculptural reliefs depicting guns and cameras and three floor sculptures, some made in New York and others in Cuernavaca, all of which include short texts in a variety of languages borrowed from major works of the Western canon. In her review for the ***New York Times***—"At the Whitney: A Biennial with a Social Conscience"—Roberta Smith identifies the political underpinnings of the exhibition, deeming the show "pious and often arid" but also "a watershed" even if it "illuminates the pitfalls of politically inclined art far more than its triumphs" (***New York Times***, March 5, 1993).

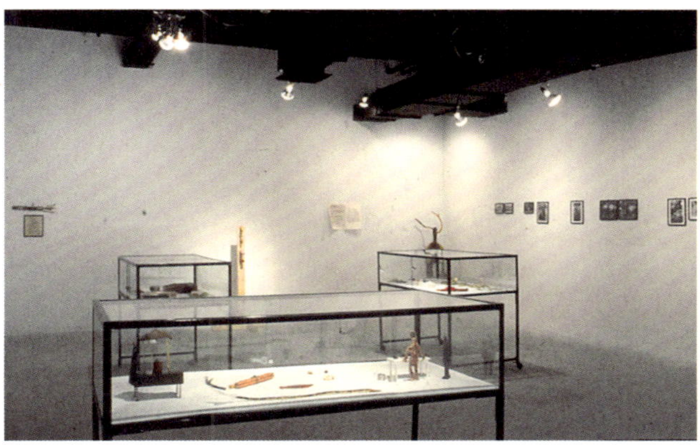

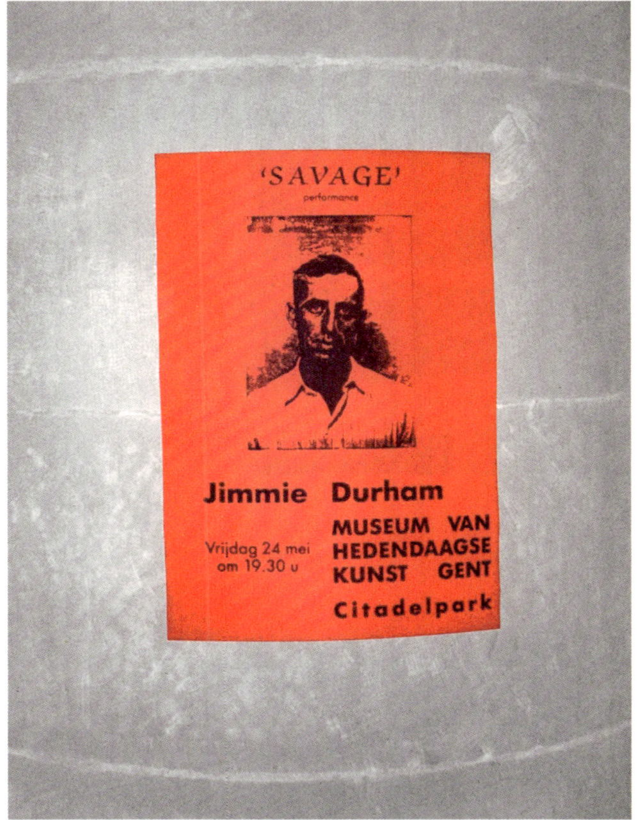

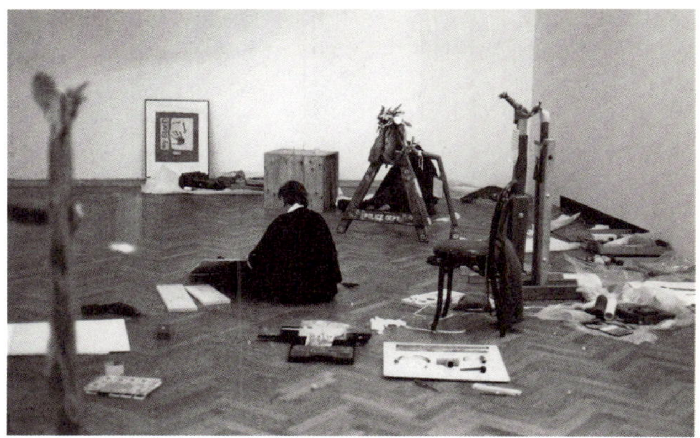

Top: *Savoir-vivre, Savoir-faire, Savoir-être*, installation view, Centre International d'Art Contemporain de Montréal, Quebec, 1990.
Middle: Announcement for *Savage* performance, Time Festival, Museum van Hedendaagse Kunst, Ghent, May 24, 1991.
Bottom: Durham installing *A Certain Lack of Coherence*, Palais des Beaux-Arts, Brussels, 1993.

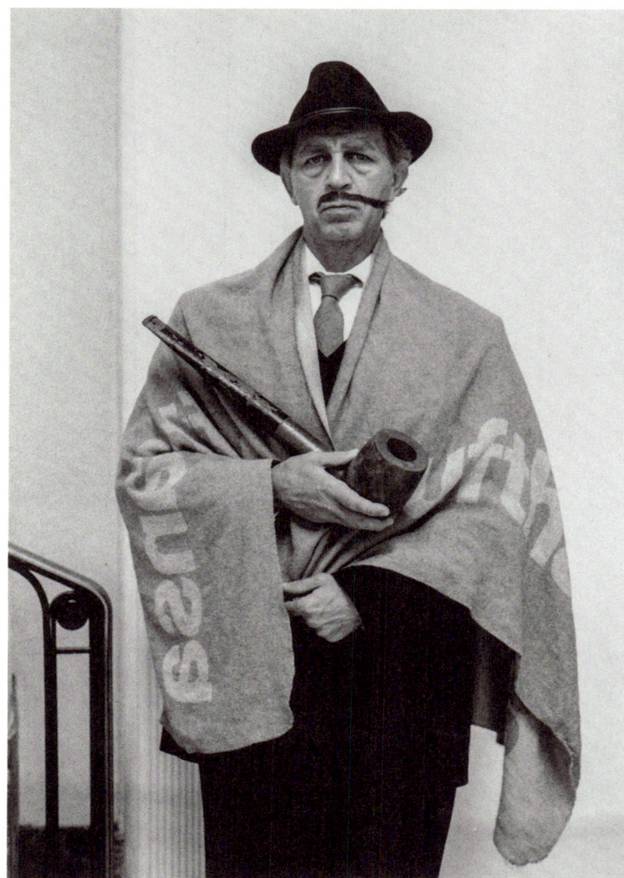

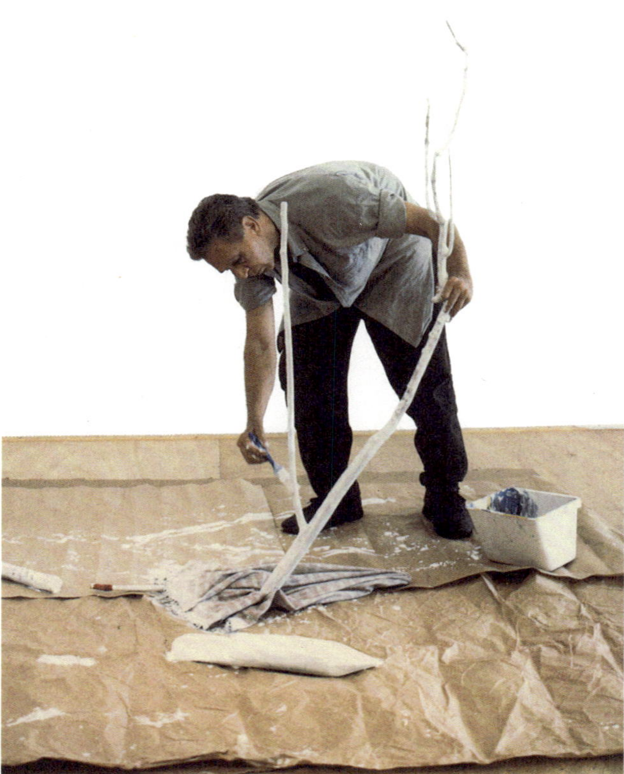

Top: Front cover photograph of Durham for the exhibition invitation for *A Certain Lack of Coherence*, Palais des Beaux-Arts, Brussels, 1993.
Bottom: Durham preparing work for *Economies*, Galerie Roger Pailhas, Marseille, 1994.

Durham's traveling solo exhibition ***A Certain Lack of Coherence***, organized by Dirk Snauwaert and Pete Coussens, opens at the Palais des Beaux-Arts, Brussels, on September 30. Renamed ***Original Re-Runs***, it travels throughout 1994 to the Institute of Contemporary Arts (ICA), London; Douglas Hyde Gallery, Dublin; and Kunstverein, Hamburg. ICA Book Works in London publishes ***My Book, The East London Coelacanth, Sometimes Called, Troubled Waters: The Story of British Sea-Power*** in conjunction with the exhibition.

An anthology of Durham's writings, ***A Certain Lack of Coherence: Writings on Art and Cultural Politics***, edited by Jean Fisher, is published by Kala Press, London.

1994
Durham is invited by Fram Kitagawa to participate in ***Faret Tachikawa***, a public art project realized on the site of a decommissioned air base in Tokyo. His contribution is a granite boulder with a stainless-steel cable connecting the boulder to the ground.

Durham and Alves then move to Europe, where they have lived ever since. Following a three-week residency at the Museum of Modern Art in Dublin, they relocate to Brussels and stay in Belgium for two years.

Roger Pailhas, who became friends with Durham and Alves after visiting them in Cuernavaca, includes Durham in the group show ***Economies*** at Galerie Roger Pailhas in Marseille later this year. He is also included in the group exhibition ***Raw and Cooked (Cocido y crudo)***, curated by Dan Cameron, at the Museo Nacional Centro de Arte Reina Sofía, Madrid, along with artists such as Mark Dion, Marlene Dumas, Bodys Isek Kingelez, and Doris Salcedo.

1995
Durham's exhibition ***Ropa Vieja (Spring Collection)*** opens at Nicole Klagsbrun Gallery in New York on April 29.

Lex Ter Braak invites Durham to Middelburg, the Netherlands, to realize the exhibition ***The Center of the World at Middelburg***, which includes the first ***Pole to Mark the Center of the World*** and is installed at De Vleeshal on October 28. As part of the exhibition, Durham reads his poem "Center of the World," written in New York in the 1980s with actor Natasha Drootin's husband, Puerto Rican singer Roy Brown.

Durham and Alves travel to Lille for a residency at the MAJT (Young Worker House) and collaborate on a series of videos, including ***13, Rue Fenelon***, ***Enough!***, ***A Heavy Stone***, and ***Un Projet à Lille***, which is cumulatively titled ***Collected Stones*** (1995–2002). In several, Durham uses stones to smash objects or to animate a static object.

Durham travels to Plasy in the Czech Republic for a weeklong residency with other international artists in a twelfth-century monastery. Perhaps commenting on the ownership of the monastery—by the noble Metternich family—Durham makes a ***Pole to Mark the Center of the World*** out of a linden sapling he cut down nearby and places it in a large field outside the monastery. Within a day, the pole is vandalized, and a few days later it is stolen. He will later make poles in Brussels, Yakutsk, Reims, and several other locations.

1996
In early spring Durham and Alves move to Marseille. Durham has two solo shows in France. For ***La porte de l'Europe (Les bourgeois de Calais)*** at Le Channel, Galerie de l'Ancienne Poste in Calais, he creates the first ***Arc de Triomphe for Personal Use***, made of pieces of wood painted red, yellow, and blue. An antidote to the monumentality of architecture, his arcs for personal use are human-scale and portable pieces of architecture that can be folded up and easily transported. Another version, made of iron and painted in bright colors, and with wheels to make it even more mobile, is included in the Istanbul Biennial curated by Rosa Martínez in 1997.

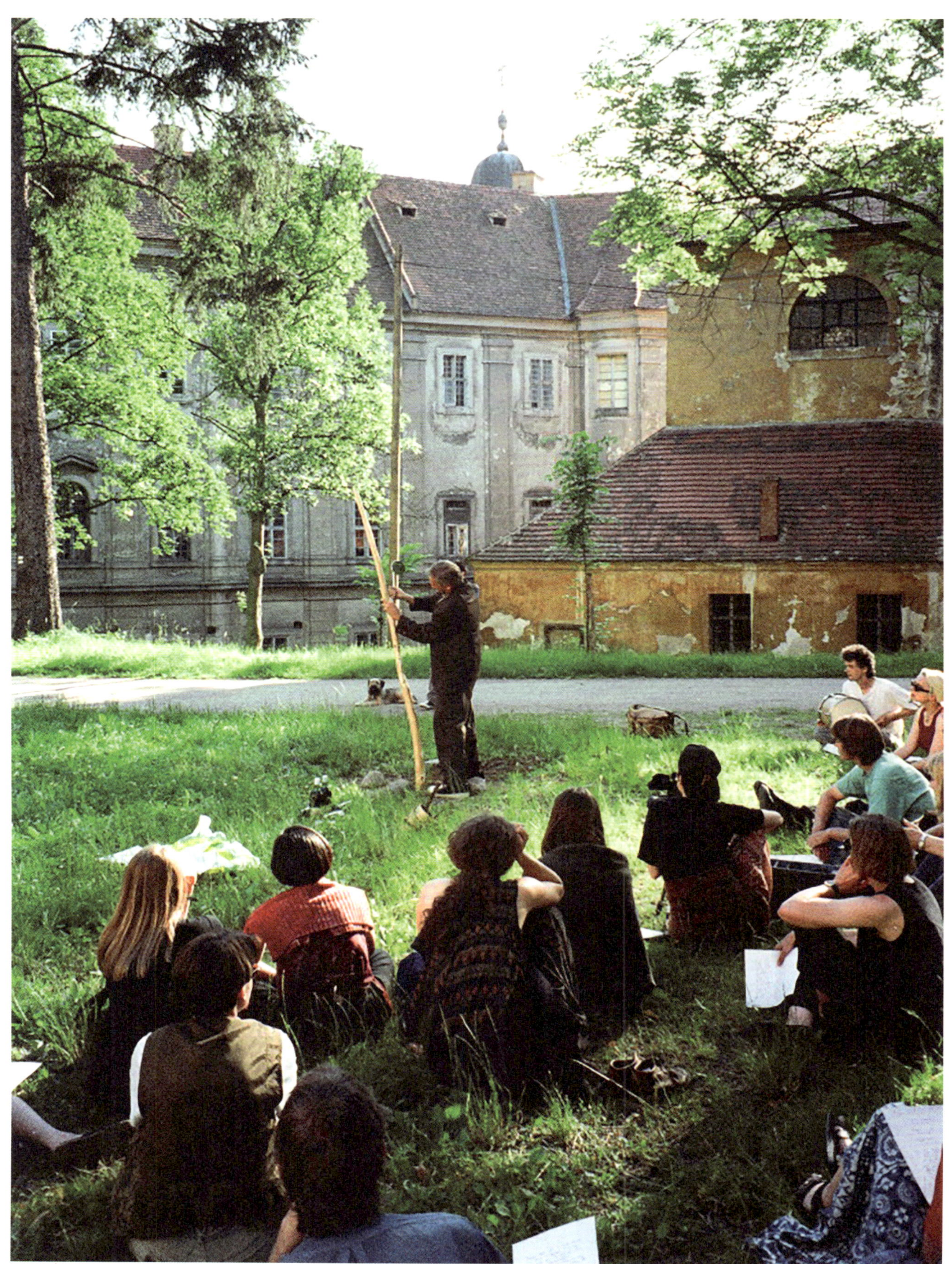

Durham installing *Pole to Mark the Center of the World*, Plasy, Czech Republic, 1995.

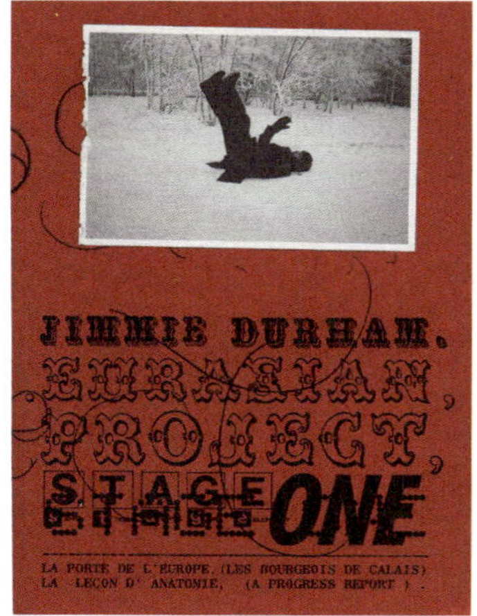

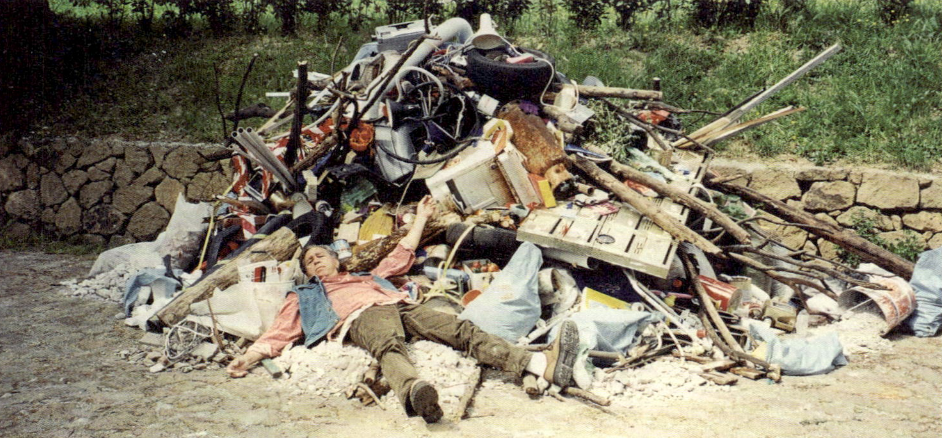

Left: Cover of *The Eurasian Project [Stage One]: La porte de l'Europe (Les bourgeois de Calais); La leçon de l'anatomie (A Progress Report)* (Reims: Le Collège Éditions, FRAC Champagne-Ardenne, 1996).
Right: *Public Monument for the Birthday of Rome*, site-specific installation for *Città Natura*, Rome, 1997.

La leçon de l'anatomie (A Progress Report) opens on April 5 at Collège/FRAC Champagne-Ardenne in Reims, the traditional city for the crowning of French kings. The objects in the exhibition are meant to disrupt narratives of power. For example, ***Shrouds and Swaddling Clothes of Ex-Saints***—white clothing soiled with mud—was inspired by the decommissioning of saints by popes, and ***St. Frigo*** involved a performative activity wherein the artist threw cobblestones at an old refrigerator every morning for several days to alter its shape:

> It took nine or ten days. Every morning I threw stones at the refrigerator. It was as if I were just going to work. You leave home early in the morning and throw cobblestones at the fridge, until you've changed its shape. . . . Instead of carving a sculpture out of the stone with tools, I wanted to use the stone itself as a tool. Not to create a new form, but to change an already existing object. (Interview with the artist in Naples, April 14, 2016)

The Eurasian Project [Stage One] is published in conjunction with the exhibitions in Calais and Reims.

The Libertine and the Stone Guest opens on March 22 at Wittgenstein Haus, Vienna. This solo exhibition continues Durham's "attack" of sorts on architecture and monumentality. Publishes ***Der Verführer und der steinerne Gast*** (in German only) as part of the project.

Durham resides in Venice for six months to teach at the Istituto Universitario di Architettura.

1997
Begins teaching at the Malmö Art Academy in Sweden, where he will teach off and on as an adjunct professor until 2006 for two to three weeks at a time. In Rome, Durham participates in ***Città Natura***, an exhibition curated by Carloyn Christov-Bakargiev marking the city's third millennium, with a site-specific work, ***Public Monument for the Birthday of Rome***. A large pile of local trash situated outside with a view of Saint Peter's Basilica, the work has to be protected by security guards to keep viewers from taking individual pieces away. This is not Durham's first installation with trash. Several installations in the 1980s—including ***Haymarket/Prairie Grasses*** at Tweed Gallery in Plainfield, New Jersey (1984), ***Bedia's First Basement***, and ***The Death of Paul Smith*** (1985)—featured trash heaped on the floor.

A residency in Stockholm allows Durham to create more videos with Alves. While there he begins experimenting with what he calls "lithographs," meaning he makes graphs using a stone. As with prior stone actions, the stones "perform" the work.

The Center of the World at Chalma, organized by Marketta Seppälä, opens on September 5 at the Pori Art Museum in Finland. Durham covers the floor of the gallery, the museum's offices, bathrooms, and gift shop with small stones and also dumps stones around the perimeter of the building. A handwritten text on the wall tells the story of an ahuehuete tree in Chalma, Mexico, that is a pilgrimage site. The text is an allegory, describing how those who don't complete the journey are turned to stone and, therefore, one should kick a small stone on their journey, to bring the others along. A map placed next to the text shows how one could potentially walk from Pori to Chalma.

Jimmie Durham opens at Galerie Micheline Szwajcer in Antwerp on December 11, including ***A Fountain in Case Your Roof Leaks*** and ***Triptych as Sandwich in White Marble and Sheep Hair*** as well as other sculptures, wall pieces, and videos.

1998
Participates in a residency at DAAD in Berlin; at DAAD's gallery he shows a large group of drawings—portraits of people and animals—produced during the residency. ***Between the Furniture and the Building (Between a Rock and a Hard Place)*** opens at Kunstverein, Munich, on November 13. The exhibition includes, among other works, ***St. Frigo*** (1996); ***Imbissstammtisch*** (1998), a sculpture composed of a truck wheel, a tree trunk, a marble, a paper coffee cup, and a paper plate with trash scattered on the floor around it; and ***Eleven Stone Parts*** (1998), a mixed-media installation in a vitrine. ***Arch of Peace***, a project described by Durham in the essay from which the exhibition title was derived, was never realized but would have been made of nine large pieces of carved granite sourced from the west coast of Sweden. ***Arch of Peace*** was actually meant to be a feature-length film wherein the granite—once intended to be source material for Adolf Hitler and Albert Speer's "Arch of Peace" for postwar Berlin—would be freed from its history. Durham's plan was to put the granite on a barge and sink it in the middle of the Baltic Sea:

> The film will not be a documentary, although it will kind of "document" itself. . . . We'll get one of those barges that have no engine, and after taking the stones by truck through the forests to the harbour, load the stones onto the barge and tow them across the Baltic . . . then we'll sink them, barge and all, in the Baltic Sea . . . the stones will be free—and light . . . but they'll be eternal, too, as carved granite cannot be, because they will be art, and art is eternal, people say. (Jimmie Durham, ***Between the Furniture and the Building (Between a Rock and a Hard Place)*** [Munich: Kunstverein München, 1998], 93)

1999
Is included in the 48th Venice Biennale, ***dAPERTuttO*** (meaning "everywhere" in Italian), curated by Harald Szeemann, exhibiting ***St. Frigo***, both the refrigerator itself with its numerous indentations and the video of the refrigerator being stoned in 1996. His solo exhibition ***Jimmie Durham: Interruptions*** opens on May 7 at the Museu do Chiado in Lisbon. The installation occupies the entire ground floor of the museum and includes an old boat painted red, piles of stones painted shades of blue and green, and painted yellow sticks alongside a small table and three texts adhered to the wall. The exhibition is accompanied by a catalogue of the same name that includes essays by the exhibition's curator, Pedro Lapa, Italo Calvino, and Durham.

2000
Is invited by Fram Kitagawa to participate in the 1st Echigo-Tsumari Art Triennale in Japan, which opens on July 20 and includes more than one hundred and fifty artists from thirty-two countries. Durham's contribution is a large pile of debris set in the forest outside of Matsunoyama and a ***Pole to Mark the Center of the World at Matsunoyama***. That fall, ***Stoneheart*** is made during a residency at the Center for Contemporary Art (CCA), Kitakyushu; the work is on view October 30–November 17. A limited-edition book about the project is published by the CCA in 2001.

2001
Durham participates in the 49th Venice Biennale, ***Plateau of Humankind***, in a project called the ***Markers Project*** for which he and Mexican artist Cisco Jiménez create a banner that is installed outside on Via Garibaldi, alongside other artists' banners.

For the Yokohama Triennale, curated by Shinji Kohmoto, Akira Tatchata, Nobuo Nakamura, and Fumio Nanjo, Durham creates ***The Petrified Forest***, consisting of office furniture, computers, and copy machines covered in layers of caked-on cement, with an audio track in the adjacent darkened room playing the sounds of shoveling. This ambitious work is destroyed at the end of the show. Another version of ***The Petrified Forest*** will be installed at the Galerie im Taxispalais in Innsbruck, Austria, in 2004, in the group exhibition ***Movables***.

2002
Durham's ***The Pursuit of Happiness: A Screenplay*** is published by Double Lucy Books. His essay "The Right to Dismiss" is published in ***October***'s spring issue, which focuses on the theme of obsolescence; in it Durham circles around that theme, locating it first in language, then in television, film, and architecture, and finally landing on the obsolescence of art in a culture completely consumed by capitalism.

2003
Is included in the 50th Venice Biennale, in the exhibition ***The Everyday Altered***, staged in the Arsenale and organized by artist Gabriel Orozco. Durham's contribution is ***Hommage à Filliou (A Piece of Wood Sculpted by a Dog, Painted by a Human. A Piece of Wood Sculpted by a Machine, Painted by a Human)*** (2003), consisting of a tree branch chewed by a dog and a piece of machine-cut wood, both painted gold; it was made in honor of French Fluxus artist Robert Filliou, who died in 1987. A second piece—a PVC pipe covered in bird droppings—was made in situ in response to Orozco's encouragement to be spontaneous and was added just before the exhibition opening. Titled ***Hommage à Filliou 2***, it was installed on the floor and disappeared soon after the exhibition opened. Of this work, Durham stated, "I found a piece of grey PVC pipe that had so much pigeon dung on it that it looked like a stalagmite formation. I then placed it along with the sign, . . . 'Please do not shit on this piece,' next to a work by another artist which had the warning, 'Please do not sit on this piece'" (http://ensembles.mhka.be/items/3697?locale=en). Durham also contributes a poster to the Utopia Station Poster Project, curated by Molly Nesbit, Hans Ulrich Obrist, and Rirkrit Tiravanija.

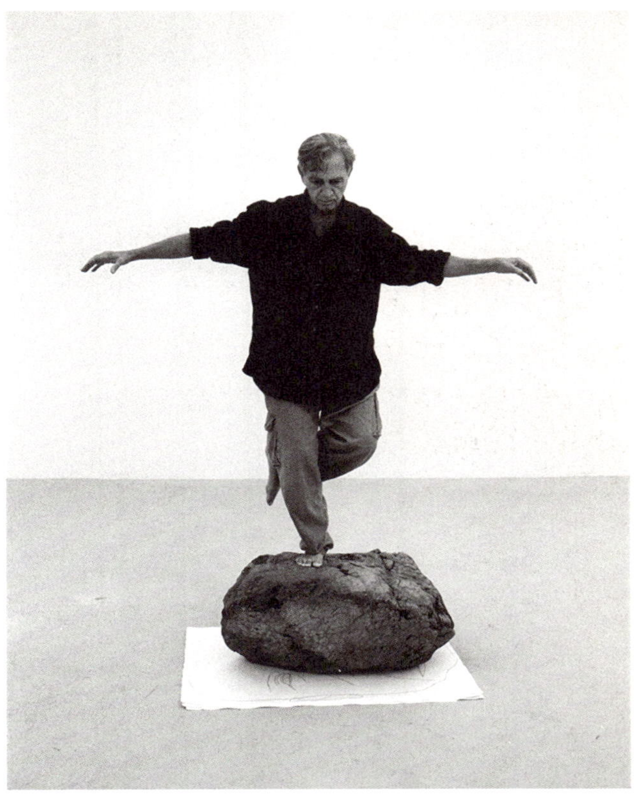

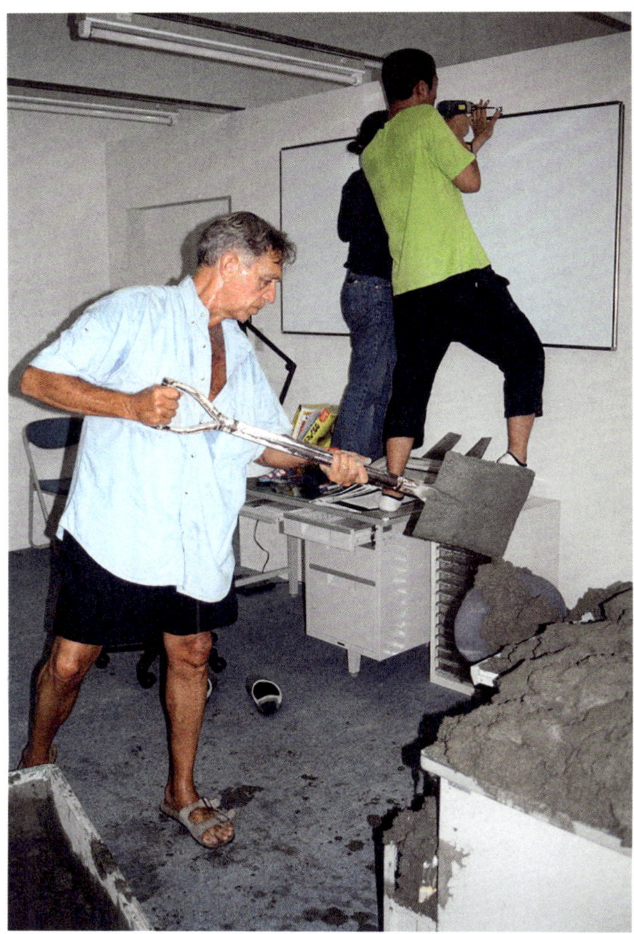

Top: Durham installing *Stoneheart* at the Center for Contemporary Art, Kitakyushu, 2000.
Bottom: Durham installing *The Petrified Forest* at the Yokohama Triennale, 2001.

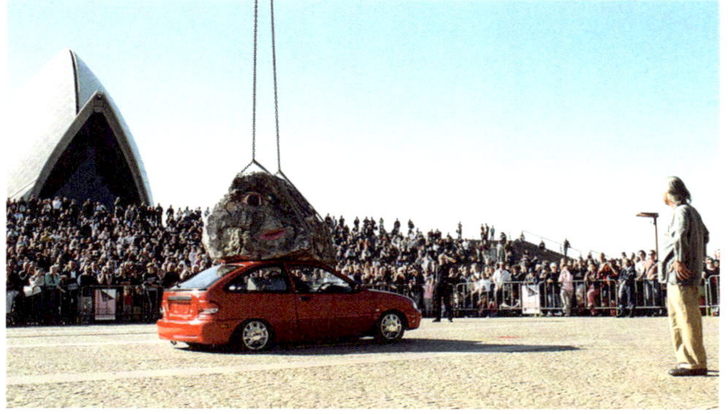

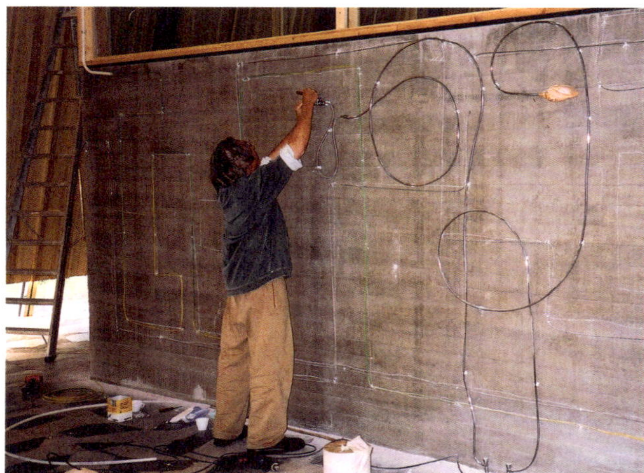

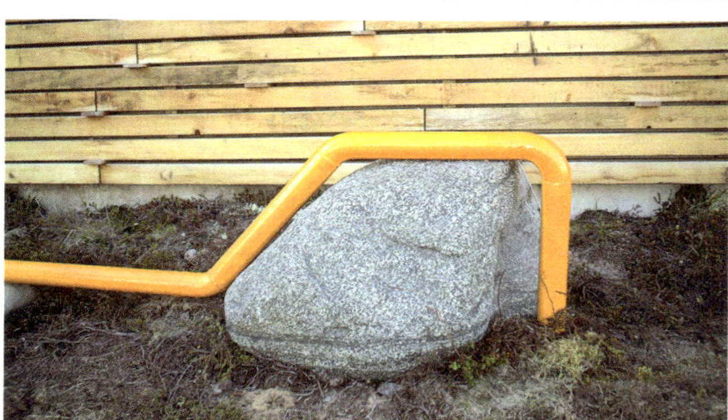

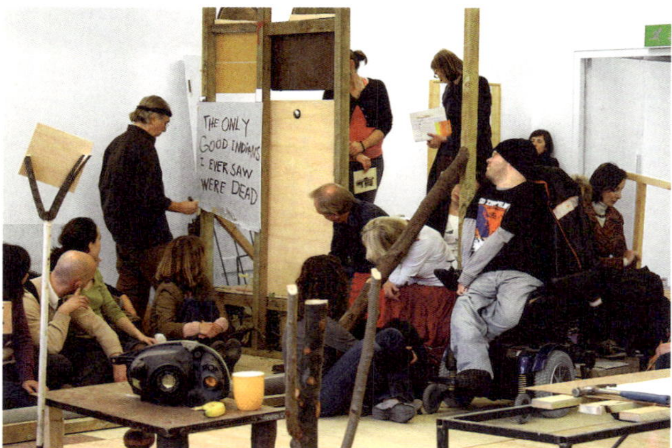

From top:
Still Life with Stone and Car, 2004, installation view, 14th Biennale of Sydney, *On Reason and Emotion*, 2004.
Durham installing *The Seven Directions*, Sami courthouse, Tana, Norway, 2004.
The Seven Directions, 2004 (detail), Sami courthouse, Tana, Norway.
Durham (at left, standing) during the public installation of *Building a Nation*, Matt's Gallery, London, 2006.

2004

Still Life with Stone and Car—a large boulder on top of a red Ford Festiva, placed in front of the Sydney Opera House—is Durham's contribution to the 14th Biennale of Sydney, ***On Reason and Emotion***, curated by Isabel Carlos. He oversaw the smashing of the car and then painted a face on the boulder. He also installs another outdoor work consisting of red PVC pipe running through a stream and ***One Thousand Beautiful Things***—a large wooden crate filled with found objects, including a plaster cast of a goanna lizard—under the stairwell in the Museum of Contemporary Art in Sydney. Carlos had invited Durham to participate, and he did so, in part, because he considered it an important opportunity to respond to the unequal treatment that Aboriginal Australians faced in Australian society. Durham contributes an essay for the catalogue titled "A New World."

Stones Rejected by the Builder opens at the Fondazione Antonio Ratti in Como, Italy, on July 22, and ***A Staff to Mark the Center of the World in Gwangju*** is included in the 5th Gwangju Biennale, ***A Grain of Dust, A Drop of Water***, in Korea, curated by Youngwoo Lee with Kerry Brougher and Sukwon Chang. The latter work is a commemoration of Vietnamese boat people who drowned in the Pacific Ocean while trying to escape the country after the Vietnam War had ended. Durham includes their names on tags attached to the staffs, all of which have mirrors added to them, which are meant to reflect away all bad thoughts and bad spirits.

Artists John Baldessari and Meg Cranston include Durham in the group exhibition ***100 Artists See God***; it opens at the Laguna Art Museum, Laguna Beach, California, on August 1 and travels to other venues throughout the United States and to the ICA, London. Durham includes a painting on wood panel entitled ***My New God*** (2004).

Creates a site-specific permanent installation for the first Sami (indigenous people of the far north of Europe) courthouse in Tana, Norway. ***The Seven Directions*** consists of objects Durham brought to the site, including a seashell, a spent bullet, and an arrowhead, as well as objects he found locally. A series of pipes and PVC tubing meanders inside the courthouse and outside the building.

2005

Something . . . Perhaps a Fugue or an Elegy is included in Rosa Martínez's section of the 51st Venice Biennale, ***Always a Little Further***, located in the Arsenale. The sculpture is a combination of numerous assembled objects such as cameras, steel pipe, brass heads, a seashell, mirrors, a cow skull and bones, and an armadillo shell. It is meant to function as an endless flow of analogies, inviting multiple interpretations from the viewer.

Hans Zender's opera ***Chief Joseph***, featuring Durham's set designs, opens at the Berlin State Opera on June 23.

Durham and art historian and curator Richard William Hill co-organize the large group exhibition ***The American West***, which opens at Compton Verney, England, on June 25. The exhibition explores the American myths of "cowboys and Indians" and includes the work of Maria Thereza Alves, Abraham Cruzvillegas, Cisco Jiménez, James Luna, Alan Michelson, and others. The accompanying catalogue contains essays by Jen Budney, Durham, Jean Fisher, Bonnie Fultz, Hill, and Simon Ortiz.

2006

Building a Nation opens at Matt's Gallery in London on November 1. Durham builds the large-scale sculptural installation over the course of the exhibition's two-week run. It includes quotes from American writers, politicians, and public figures—such as Mark Twain, Theodore Roosevelt, and John Wayne—that reveal their racist attitudes and attempts to justify the genocide of American Indians, handwritten or typed by the artist and then applied to the structure. Every Saturday, Durham is present to talk to the public about the progress of the structure and to share his ideas.

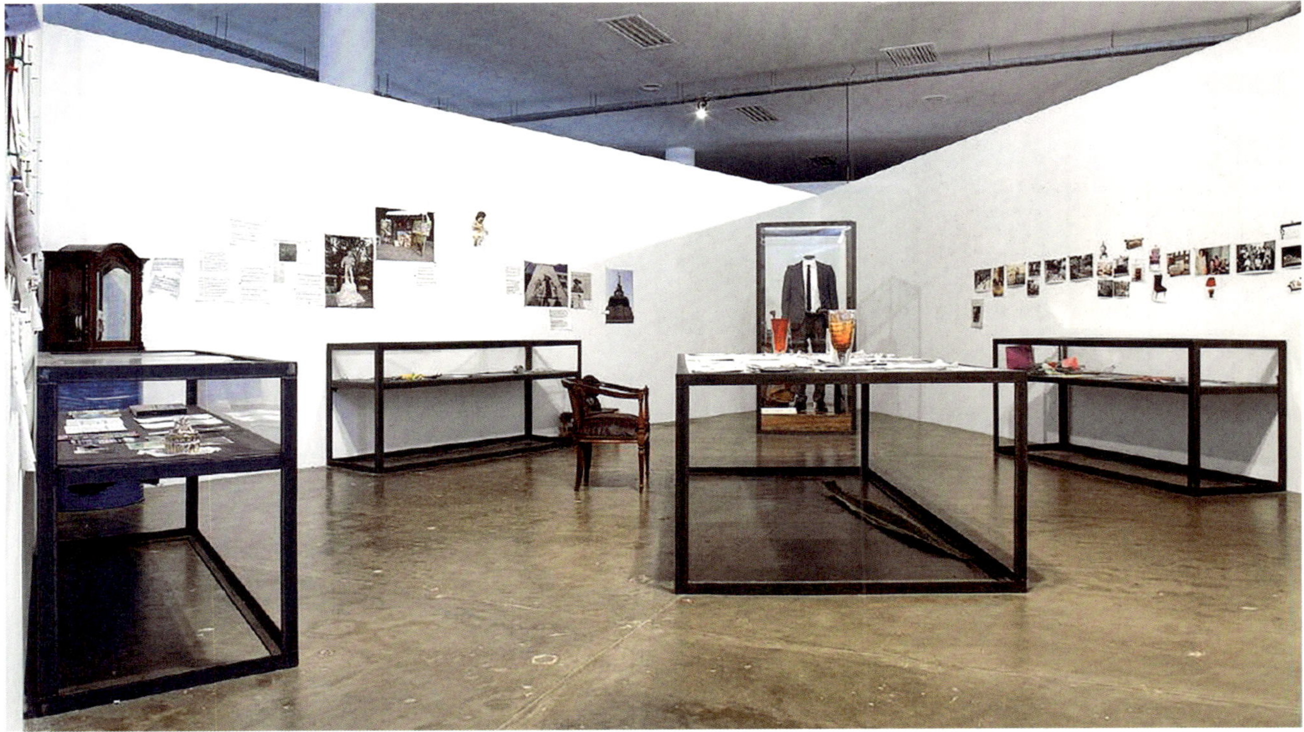

The Bureau for Research into Brazilian Normality, installation view, 29th Bienal de São Paulo, 2010.

Durham's video ***La Poursuite du Bonheur*** (The pursuit of happiness) (2003) is included in the Whitney Biennial, ***Day for Night***, cocurated by Philippe Vergne and Chrissie Iles, and is a rare instance of the artist agreeing to exhibit in the United States.

2007
Durham and Alves move to Rome, where they live part-time until 2012. ***Labyrinth (part 1)*** opens at the Château d'Oiron, France, on June 23. Most of the objects in the exhibition are made from a beech tree Durham found in a field in Strasbourg that had been blown down during a recent storm and in which he discovered bullet holes dating back to WWI and WWII. While in residence at the Atelier Alexander Calder, in Saché, France, and inspired by Calder's ***Circus***, Durham uses scraps from the Strasbourg beech tree and from oak and acacia trees he found in and around Saché to carve several small figurines for a two-day exhibition at the Atelier titled ***Labyrinth (part 2)***, June 2–3. ***Labyrinth (part 3)***, consisting of another group of sculptures made from the beech tree, opens on May 24 at Michel Rein in Paris.

2008
The Museum of European Normality is installed at Manifesta 7, curated by Anselm Franke, Hila Peleg, Adam Budak, and Raqs Media Collective, in Trento, Italy, from July 19 to November 2, and is a collaboration with Alves and Michael Taussig. Essentially a small "museum" installed in an old post office near Bolzano, it includes a map of migration patterns within Europe from the fifth to the ninth centuries. The "Migration Period" was marked by a mass influx of different ethnic groups throughout the continent who, according to Durham, "left few monuments but created the ethnic make-up of so-called European 'normality'" (interview with the author, Naples, April 14, 2016).

Jimmie Durham opens at the Museo d'Arte Contemporanea Donnaregina in Naples, which is organized by Mario Codognato in collaboration with Franco Soffiantino Contemporary Art Productions and includes the large-scale sculptures ***Something . . . Perhaps a Fugue or an Elegy*** (2005) and ***The Petrified Forest*** (2004), as well as several other works.

2009
Pierres rejetées (Rejected Stones), organized by Laurence Bossé and Julia Garimorth, opens at the Musée d'Art Moderne de la Ville de Paris on January 30. A survey of work beginning in 1994, when Durham and Alves moved to Europe, it includes several large-scale works such as ***Encore tranquillité*** (2008), a sculpture consisting of a Cessna airplane that has been smashed, and permanently grounded, by a large stone in the cockpit.

The 10th Biennale de Lyon, ***The Spectacle of the Everyday***, curated by Hou Hanru, opens on September 16. Durham's installation, ***Regarde/ Look***, is in La Sucrière, an old sugar factory turned warehouse turned Biennale site, and consists of scaffolding and CCTV cameras—a response, perhaps, to surveillance culture in Europe.

Has his first solo exhibition after joining kurimanzutto gallery in Mexico City, titled ***Obsidiana***. It consists of several sculptures that pair large obsidian stones sourced from the region with "twin" forms cast in German silver (a combination of copper, zinc, and nickel), placed on customized steel tables, along with drawings, a video, and other works.

2010
Is included in a number of group exhibitions, including the 29th Bienal de São Paulo, Brazil, curated by Moacir dos Anjos and Agnaldo Farias, for which he creates, in collaboration with Alves, ***The Bureau for Research into Brazilian Normality***—a take on ***The Museum of European Normality*** realized in 2008 for Manifesta 7. One of the objects is based on a heroic statue of an Indian bounty hunter Durham saw while visiting São Paulo: a mannequin, dressed in a fake Gucci suit and equipped with toy guns and golf clubs, standing among a series of tables lined with Brazilian fashion and TV magazines, books, food, trinkets, and trash. The work is vandalized and the Rolex watch stolen off the mannequin's wrist. While in Rio de Janeiro, Durham collects local wood and scrap lumber from demolished houses in Santo Christo and makes objects that are featured in a solo exhibition at Progetti gallery titled ***Provas Circunstanciais do Brasil***. As is typical of Durham's practice, he makes

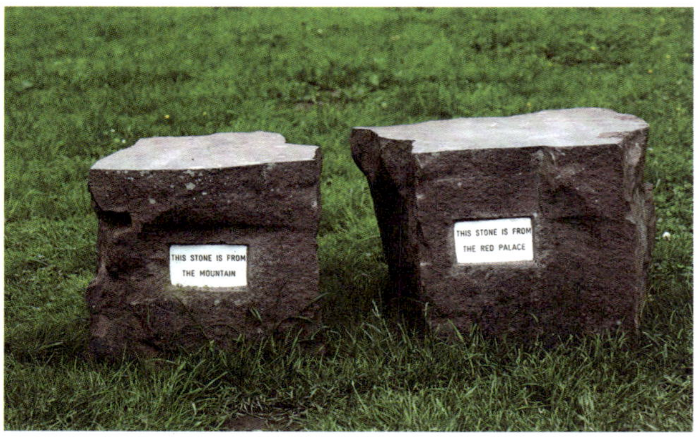

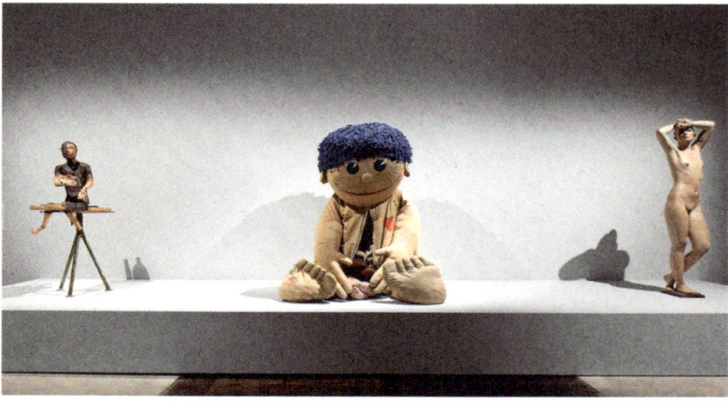

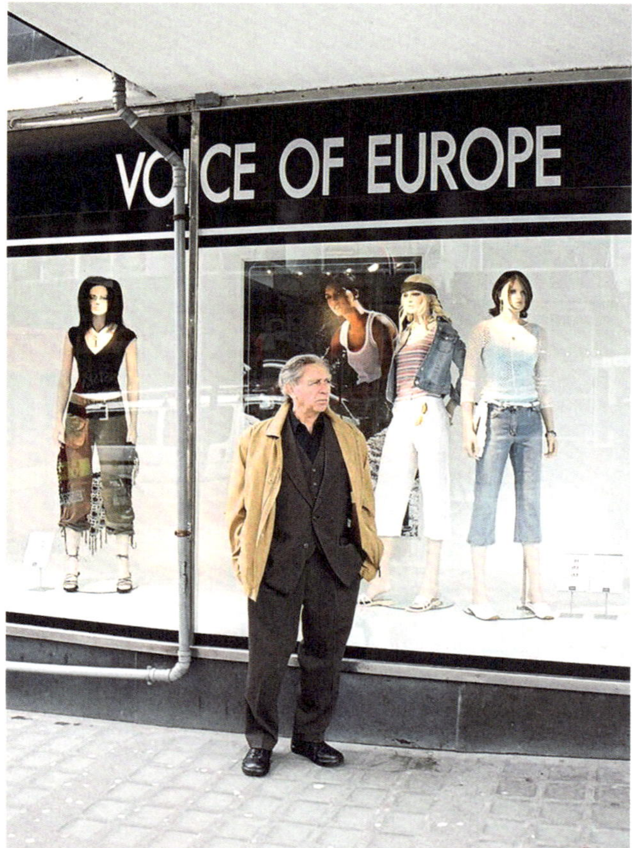

Top: *This Stone Is from the Mountain/This Stone Is from the Red Palace*, 1992. Sandstone. 16 ½ × 15 ¾ × 19 in. (42 × 40 × 48 cm) each of 2. Installation view, Documenta IX, 1992.
Middle: *Jesus (Es geht um die Wurst)* (left), with Paul McCarthy, *Children's Anatomical Educational Figure* (center), and John DeAndrea, *Ariel II* (right), installation view, 55th Venice Biennale, 2013.
Bottom: Self-portrait from Durham's book *In Europe* (Berlin: Neuer Berliner Kunstverein, 2015).

all of the works while in Rio, and the installation includes sculptures of wood, stone, and found objects, many of which include texts containing details about the materials (sometimes in the voice of that material) and narratives related to local histories.

Works produced while in residence for three months at the Sculpture Studios in Glasgow are included in ***Jimmie Durham: Universal Miniature Golf (The Promised Land)***, which opens there on April 16. True to form, the works combine Durham's wit and humor with his interest in history. ***A Scottish Conspiracy***—a collage incorporating text and image—recounts the complicated, intertwined histories of Scottish settlers in the Midwest and of American Indians.

2011
A Pole to Mark the Center of the World (at Winnipeg) is installed in Plug In Institute for Contemporary Art's exhibition ***Close Encounters: The Next 500 Years***, curated by Candice Hopkins, Steve Loft, Lee-Ann Martin, and Jenny Western, which opens in Winnipeg on January 22.

Makes a large outdoor sculpture for the Cologne Sculpture Park, located in the city center on the banks of the Rhine. ***Pagliaccio non son*** consists of a huge African mahogany tree trunk from the Congo that was originally destined to be cut up for wood veneer; the trunk is still part of the sculpture park.

Jimmie Durham opens at the Artist's Institute in New York on August 24 and begins with thirteen short videos created between 1995 and 2002 titled ***Collected Stones***, which are recorded performances of Durham dropping, throwing, or placing stones on top of a telephone, a model boat, and a refrigerator, among other things, to alter the object. In addition to works by Durham, archival materials pertaining to ***Beyond Aesthetics: Art of Necessity*** and ***Ritual and Rhythm: Visual Forces for Survival***—both curated by Juan Sánchez—are included in the exhibition; Durham also does a series of performances and talks.

2012
Maquette for a Museum of Switzerland opens at the Swiss Institute in New York on March 7 (exhibited the previous year at Art Basel with Opdahl Gallery, Stavanger/Berlin). The installation includes photographs of traditional Swiss masks that Durham originally encountered while living in that country in the late 1960s and early 1970s. Like the ***Bureau for Research into Brazilian Normality*** (2010), this installation includes texts and images displayed in vitrines alongside objects meant to be indicators of local culture—in this case, Swiss watches, sausage links, and ski hats, among others.

Borrowing its title from Durham's first solo exhibition in New York at the Alternative Museum in 1984, ***A Matter of Life and Death and Singing***, a retrospective exhibition organized by Bart De Baere and Anders Kreuger, opens at the Museum van Hedendaagse Kunst in Antwerp on May 24.

Participates in Documenta XIII, curated by Carolyn Christov-Bakargiev, which opens in June, and the Taipei Biennial, curated by Anselm Franke, which opens in September. The small Korbinian apple tree that Durham and Christov-Bakargiev plant for the artist's contribution to Documenta is vandalized in July 2015. Durham also contributes work to ***In the Holocene***, organized by João Ribas for the MIT List Visual Arts Center in Cambridge, Massachusetts, and has a solo exhibition titled ***Streets of Rome and Other Stories*** at the Museo d'Arte Contemporanea in Rome featuring works made during the years he lived there. ***Wood, Stone and Friends*** opens at the Palazzo Reale—Sala Dorica, Fondazione Morra Greco, Naples, on December 12.

A book of Durham's poetry from the mid-1960s through 2012, ***Poems That Do Not Go Together***, is published by Wiens Verlag in Berlin.

2013
Durham's 1992 sculpture ***Jesus (Es geht um die Wurst)*** is included in the 55th Venice Biennale. It is installed on a large plinth alongside Paul McCarthy's ***Children's Anatomical Educational Figure*** (ca. 1990) and John DeAndrea's ***Ariel II*** (2011) in a gallery curated by Cindy Sherman.

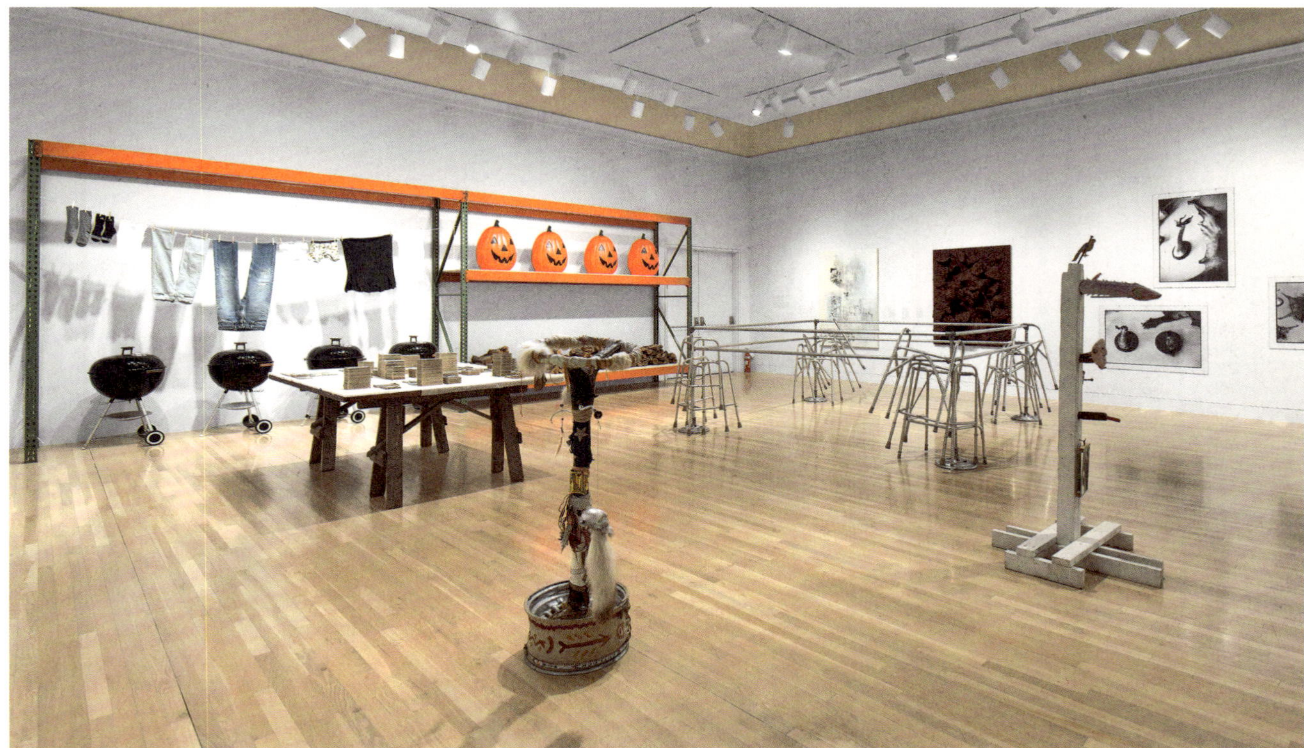

Above: *Take It or Leave It: Institution, Image, Ideology*, installation view, Hammer Museum, Los Angeles, 2014.
Following spread: *Venice: Objects, Work and Tourism*, site-specific intervention, Fondazione Querini Stampalia, Venice, 2015.

2014
Choose Any Three (1989) is included in the Whitney Biennial in New York, in the section curated by Anthony Elms. The solo exhibition ***Jimmie Durham: Traces and Shiny Evidence*** opens at Parasol Unit in London on June 12. The installation is spread across two floors of the building: the ground floor includes painted oil barrels and PVC piping, and the second floor contains graphite frottage works on paper and the video ***Smashing*** (2004), in which Durham, dressed in a suit and sitting at a desk, smashes objects brought to him by students at the Fondazione Antonio Ratti over the course of twenty-two days.

Bedia's Stirring Wheel (1985) and an untitled sculpture from his 1991 show at the Luggage Store in San Francisco are included in ***Take It or Leave It: Institution, Image, Ideology*** at the Hammer Museum in Los Angeles. Curated by Johanna Burton and Anne Ellegood, the exhibition explores the overlapping strategies of institutional critique and appropriation in American art beginning in the 1970s.

2015
Durham's solo exhibition ***Here at the Center*** opens at the Neuer Berliner Kunstverein in Berlin on June 6, and includes videos, drawings, and sculptures created between 1995 and 2015. ***In Europe***—a publication that includes a series of humorous self-portraits Durham made at different locations in Europe in which the word "Euro" is visibly associated with an array of products and businesses—is published in conjunction with the exhibition. Another solo exhibition, ***Venice: Objects, Work and Tourism***, opens on May 6 at the Fondazione Querini Stampalia Carlo Scarpa Gallery, Venice, curated by Chiara Bertoli. Durham creates a body of new works exploring tourism and labor after spending time with a number of Venetian locals who work in a variety of professions—boat builders, glass blowers, goldbeaters, woodcarvers, restaurant employees, and so forth. He incorporates such materials as broken pieces of Murano glass and 300-year-old Venetian bricks into his own assemblages and also as interventions in the museum's period rooms. ***Jimmie Durham: Various Items and Complaints*** opens at the Serpentine Gallery in London on October 1, curated by Hans Ulrich Obrist.

2016
In January, it is announced that Durham is the recipient of the prestigious Goslar Kaiserring Prize, which is awarded to the artist on October 8 in conjunction with an exhibition of new work exploring the history of Goslar and the surrounding Harz mountain range, which is installed at the Mönchehaus Museum Goslar in Germany.

On February 5, ***Jimmie Durham: Sound and Silliness*** opens at MAXXI Museo Nazionale delle Arti del XXI Secolo, Rome, curated by Hou Hanru and Giulia Ferracci. Two sound pieces, ***Swifts Door Capuana*** (2013) and ***Domestic Glass*** (2006), are shown alongside two video works—***A Proposal for a New International Genuflexion in Promotion of World Peace*** (2007) and ***Fleur de Pas Mal*** (2005).

In December Durham presents a work at Museo d'Arte Contemporanea Donnaregina in Naples, where he is the second recipient of the Matronata alla Carriera prize.

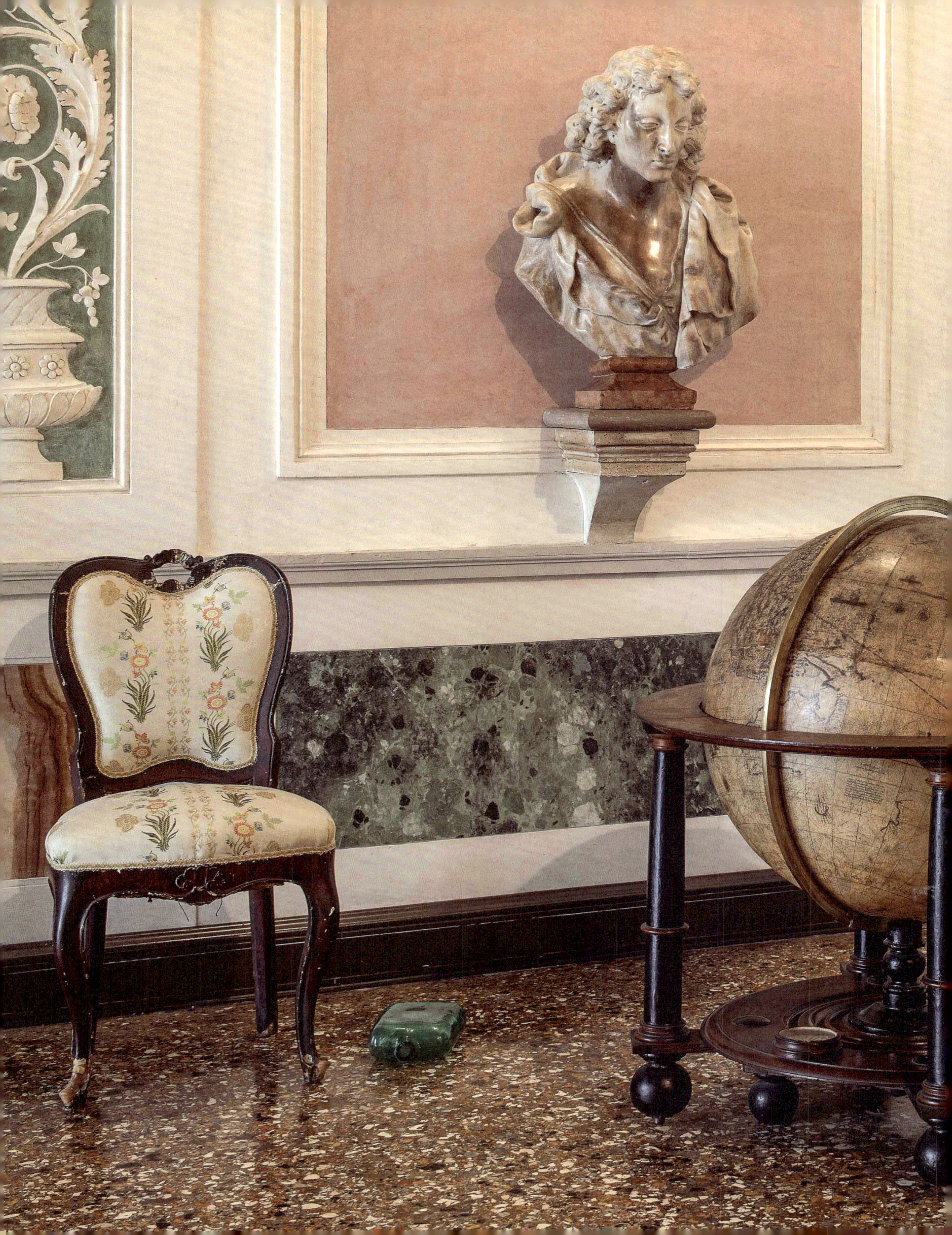

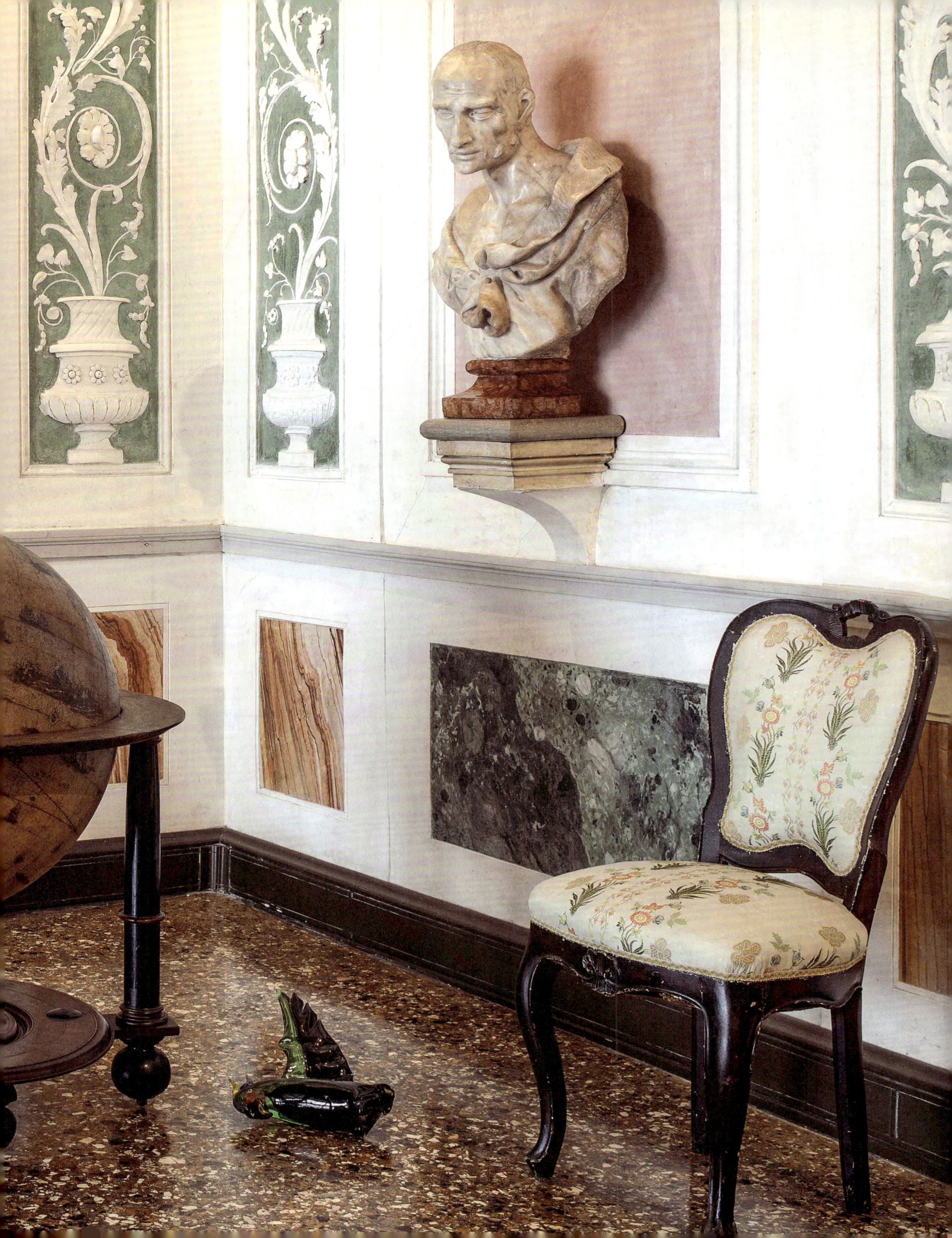

Supporting Statements by Other Artists

The following statements were made to Mr. Durham during personal interviews or telephone conversations, and while, as Durham points out, this book was not always discussed specifically, the quotations are ver batim.

James Rosenquist: "I'm not sure I understand what your want from me."

Sol Le Witt: "Sure, I'd be glad to."

Keith Haring: "Who do I make the check out to?"

Claes Oldenburg: "It's nice to meet you."

Mary Beth Edelson: "No, I'm sorry, I just don't do that."

Mel Edwards: "I've never heard of Livingston, Texas."

Juan Sanchez: "Hi, is Maria Thereza there?"

Leon Golub: "It's nice to meet you."

Rudolf Baranik: "Hello Jim, is Gerardo there?"

Nancy Spero: "Nice to meet you."

May Stevens: "Nice to meet you."

Andy Warhol: "It's nice to meet you."

Pablo Picasso: "How about Thursday next week, at your place? I'll bring some wine. Will Maria Thereza be there?"

Pages from Durham's unpublished artist book *The Mystery of the Two Islands: The true story of how Cuban Communists gained control of Trump Tower*, 1987.

OFFICIAL DEED AND TITLE

For: Trump Tower
725 Fifth Avenue
Manhattan Island

Now wherefore Jimmie Durham, the sole owner of all of the materials used to build, construct and operate said Trump Tower, by virtue of the fact that he (Durham) is the exclusive representative of all of the Native American Red Indigenous Indians in the land, both living and dead, does hereby agree to sell said materials to Jose Bedia for one string of Santeria beads and 98¢ U.S. currency, with the stipulation that said materials will only be used for artistic purposes by Mr. Bedia or other Cuban artists as may be designated by said Jose Bedia. Therefore this Deed and Title does supercede, nullify and cancel any and all previous or existing claims to said materials.

Sworn before me this seventh day of the month of March in the Year of Our Lord 19 and 85, on the Island of Manhattan.

(PETER STUYVESANT)

EXHIBITION CHECKLIST

Height precedes width precedes depth.

Unless otherwise noted, all works are courtesy of the artist and kurimanzutto, Mexico City.

I will try to explain, 1970–2012
Plywood with redwood veneer, copper, Swiss cat fur and leather, goatskin with ink
Two parts, wood board: 31 ¼ × 48 × 1 in. (79.4 × 122 × 2.5 cm); leather: 28 ¼ × 27 ¼ in. (71.8 × 69.2 cm); 53 ⅛ × 48 × 1 in. (135 × 122 × 2.5 cm) overall
Private collection, courtesy of kurimanzutto, Mexico City
Page 38

Red Granite and Grey Cristalina Granite, 1971
Red and gray granite
Two parts, 3 ½ × 10 × 5 ⅛ in. (9 × 25.5 × 13 cm); 3 ⅛ × 9 ⅞ × 6 in. (8 × 25 × 15 cm)
Private collection, courtesy of kurimanzutto, Mexico City
Page 39

Karankawa, 1982
Human skull, cedar, seashells, abalone shell, alabaster, beads, button, turquoise, cow leather, fish bone, parrot feathers, woodpecker feather, two deer teeth, white and black ink
19 × 9 × 9 in. (48.3 × 22.9 × 22.9 cm)
Collection of Robert Cantor and Margo Levine, New York
Page 41

Untitled, 1982
Baby buffalo skull, beads, goat leather, hawk feather, shells, acrylic paint
16 ½ × 13 ¼ × 7 in. (41.9 × 33.7 × 17.8 cm)
Collection of Joe Overstreet and Corrine Jennings, New York
Not illustrated

Wahya, 1984
Bear skull, tree branch, carved wood, beads, shells, stones, mother of pearl, leather, horse fur, paint
53 × 24 × 36 in. (134.6 × 61 × 91.4 cm)
Collection of Luis H. Francia and Midori Yamamura
Page 43

New York Gitli, 1984
Dog skull, plastic, acrylic paint, seashells, leather
47 ¼ × 27 ½ × 11 ½ in. (120 × 70 × 29 cm)
Collection of Ines and Philippe Kempeneers, Belgium
Page 42

Tlunh Datsi, 1984
Puma skull, shells, turquoise, turkey feathers, metal, sheep and deer fur, pine, acrylic paint
40 ½ × 35 ¾ × 31 ¾ in. (103 × 91 × 81 cm)
Private collection, Belgium
Page 45

Bedia's Muffler, 1985
Metal muffler, acrylic paint on cotton stars from American flag, leather
34 × 61 ⅞ × 4 ¾ in. (86.4 × 157 × 12 cm)
Collection of Roel Arkesteijn
Page 47

Bedia's Stirring Wheel, 1985
Car steering wheel with shifter, metal car wheel, cotton American flag, cow leather, fur, sheepskin, pigeon feather, dog skull, beads, plastic doll, acrylic paint
42 ¼ × 18 in. diam. (107.3 × 45.7 cm diam.)
Collection of Karen and Andy Stillpass
Page 46

The Indian's Family, 1985
Photographs with collage on paper
10 × 10 ½ in. (25.4 × 26.7 cm) each of 5
Page 50

Pocahontas' Underwear, 1985
Dyed chicken feathers, shells, beads
13 ¼ × 13 ¼ in. (33.6 × 33.6 cm)
Private collection
Page 49

Whale Tooth Stick, 1985
Whale teeth, bodark wood, leather, metal, twine
46 × 12 × 4 in. (116.8 × 30.5 × 10.2 cm)
Collection of Papo Colo, New York City
Page 53

Whose Hair Is It?, 1985
Pine, string, metal screws, ivory piano keys, human, dog, and synthetic hair
11 ½ × 20 × 2 ¾ in. (27.9 × 50.8 × 7.2 cm)
Collection of Papo Colo, New York City
Page 52

Types of Arrows, 1985/86
Oak, flint arrowheads, cow leather, turkey feathers, canvas over board, ink on paper
11 ¼ × 11 ¼ × 2 ⅛ in. (28.8 × 28.8 × 5.4 cm)
Collection of Coleen Fitzgibbon and Tom Otterness
Page 51

My Blood, 1985/1991
Acrylic paint, artist's blood, and ink on paper
22 ½ × 18 ½ in. (57.2 × 47 cm)
Collection of John Morace and Tom Kennedy, Los Angeles
Page 48

Self-portrait, 1986
Canvas, cedar, acrylic paint, metal, synthetic hair, scrap fur, dyed chicken feathers, human rib bones, sheep bones, seashell, thread
78 × 30 × 9 in. (198.1 × 76.2 × 22.9 cm)
Whitney Museum of American Art, New York; purchase, with funds from the Contemporary Painting and Sculpture Committee
Page 56

The Two Johns, 1988
Carved ash from Cuernavaca, synthetic hair, acrylic paint, cotton cloth, found painted stool
Figure: 24 × 21 ¼ × 2 ¼ in. (61 × 54 × 6 cm); stool: 23 ⅝ × 15 ¾ × 15 in. (60.5 × 40 × 38 cm)
Collection of Robin Klassnik, Matt's Gallery, London
Page 145

Malinche, 1988–92
Guava, pine branches, oak, snakeskin, polyester bra soaked in acrylic resin and painted gold, watercolor, cactus leaf, canvas, cotton cloth, metal, rope, feathers, plastic jewelry, glass eye
70 × 23 ⅝ × 35 in. (177 × 60 × 89 cm)
Stedelijk Museum voor Actuele Kunst (SMAK), Ghent, Belgium
Page 143

The Arrogant Little Peasant, 1989
Carved ash, elm branch, acrylic paint, pigeon feathers, jute string, metal, ink on paper
13 ¾ × 46 × 4 in. (35 × 117 × 10 cm)
Collection of Magali Lara, Cuernavaca, Mexico
Pages 116–17

Articles 2 and 3 from the 1986 Pinkerton's Agency Manual, 1989
Mahogany, polyester resin with red dye 2, ink on wood panel
Sculpture: 56 × 5 ½ in. (142 × 14 cm); text: 9 ¾ × 9 ¾ in. (25 × 25 cm)
Page 86

The Cathedral of St. John the Divine in Manhattan is the World's Largest Gothic Cathedral. Except, of course, that it is a fake; first by the simple fact of being built in Manhattan, at the turn of the century. But the stone work is also re-inforced with steel which is expanding with rust. Someday it will destroy the stone. The Cathedral is in Morningside Heights over-looking a panoramic view of Harlem which is separated by a high fence., 1989
Moose skull with antler, metal pipes, construction lumber, acrylic paint, seashell, sunglasses lens, metal hardware
96 × 60 × 54 in. (243.8 × 152.4 × 137.2 cm)
The Museum of Modern Art, New York; Committee on Painting and Sculpture Funds, 2013
Page 97

Choose Any Three, 1989
Carved ash, magnolia, pine, metal, glass, acrylic paint
99 ¼ × 49 ¼ × 48 in. (252 × 125 × 122 cm)
Hammer Museum, Los Angeles. Purchased with partial funds provided by Susan Bay Nimoy and Leonard Nimoy
Page 85

An Electron Beam Generater, 1989
Pine, cow vertebrae, plastic telephone part and cord, acrylic paint
59 ¾ × 6 ¾ × 20 ½ in. (151.5 × 17 × 52 cm)
Page 87

Footnote, 1989
Bronze, metal chain, acrylic paint on wood, ink on paper
4 × 12 ¼ × 2 ¾ in. (10 × 31 × 7 cm)
Marc Embo, St. Martens Latem, Belgium
Page 89

New Clear Family, 1989
Tree branches, carved wood, cotton cloth, leather, twine, string, beads, acrylic paint, metal
17 ¾ × 4 in. (45 × 10 cm) each of 19
Collection of Roel Arkesteijn
Page 90

Over the River and Through the Woods, 1989
Plum tree branches, pine, stones, acrylic paint, beads, pigskin leather over carved pine, upholstery tacks, twine
25 × 9 × 9 in. (63.5 × 22.9 × 22.9 cm)
Courtesy of Nicole Klagsbrun Gallery, New York
Page 91

Raccoon (Skunk), 1989
Skunk skull, pine, acrylic paint, leather, seashells, rearview mirror, car bumper part, black-and-white photograph
67 × 24 ½ × 20 ½ in. (170 × 62 × 52 cm)
Private collection, Antwerp
Page 67

Six Authentic Things, 1989
Acrylic paint, enamel spray paint, ink, and pencil on paper, with turquoise, gold, emeralds, obsidian, flint
29 × 23 11/16 in. (73.7 × 60.1 cm) each of 6 (framed)
Private collection, Topanga, California
Pages 92–93

The Testament According to John, 1989
Acrylic paint and graphite on canvas
36 ¾ × 67 ¾ in. (93.5 × 172 cm)
Private collection, courtesy of kurimanzutto, Mexico City
Page 94

Tradition, 1989
Deerskin, acrylic paint, ink
34 × 34 × 1 in. (86.4 × 86.4 × 2.4 cm)
Collection of Stuart Anthony & Will Rogers, New York City
Page 88

Zeke Proctor's Letter, 1989
Acrylic paint, ink, and enamel spray paint on paper
32 ⅛ × 22 in. (81.6 × 55.9 cm) each of 4
Hammer Museum, Los Angeles. Promised gift of Beth Rudin DeWoody
Page 95

Give-away, 1990
Wood, acrylic paint, ink, metal, paper
6 ⅛ × 8 ¼ × 1 ¾ in. (15.6 × 21 × 4.4 cm)
Anonymous lender
Page 293 middle left

Not Lothar Baumgarten's Cherokee, 1990
Charcoal and paper collage on paper
16 × 21 in. (40.6 × 53.3 cm)
Whitney Museum of American Art, New York; purchase, with funds from the Drawing Committee
Page 70

Science I, 1990
Dry pastels and pencil on paper
20 × 16 in. (50.8 × 40.6 cm)
Page 166

Science II, 1990
Dry pastels and pencil on paper
20 × 16 in. (50.8 × 40.6 cm)
Page 167

Ahead, 1991
Pine, black walnut, metal, cotton shirt, tie, fiberglass, resin
65 × 23 ¾ × 25 ½ in. (165 × 60 × 65 cm)
Private collection, courtesy of kurimanzutto, Mexico City
Page 62

Half Off, 1991
Pine, acacia, acrylic paint, human hair, ink, paper, cardboard
59 ¼ × 24 ¼ × 24 ¼ in. (50.5 × 61.5 × 61.5 cm)
Page 63

I Would like the Smithsonian . . . , 1991
Acrylic paint on paper with collage
20 × 16 ½ in. (50.8 × 41.9 cm)
Hammer Museum, Los Angeles. Promised gift of Rosette V. Delug
Page 55

Modern Art with Dead Bird, 1991
Iguana head, beads, acrylic paint, oak, pine, walnut, metal brake drum part, plastic, color photograph
55 ¾ × 25 ½ × 20 ¾ in. (141.5 × 65 × 53 cm)
Private collection, Mexico City
Page 69

Untitled, 1991
Construction lumber, walnut, palm tree, oak, catfish head, catfish tail, papier-mâché, acrylic paint, plastic, black-and-white photograph
64 ¼ × 30 ¾ × 28 ¼ in. (163.2 × 78.1 × 72 cm)
Collection of Karen and Andy Stillpass
Page 68

Untitled, 1991
Arkansas plum, ironwood branches, cottonwood, construction lumber, oil on canvas, paint, shells
59 × 27 ½ × 27 ½ in. (150 × 70 × 70 cm)
Museum of Contemporary Art Antwerp (M HKA), Antwerp, Belgium
Page 64

Untitled (Armadillo), 1991
Armadillo skull, oak, acrylic paint, beads, black-and-white photograph
51 ⅛ × 9 7/16 × 24 ⅜ in. (130 × 24 × 62 cm)
Museum of Contemporary Art Antwerp (M HKA), Antwerp, Belgium
Page 66

Would and Cotton, 1991
Carved black walnut, oak, cottonwood, pine, cotton pant leg, abalone shell, linseed oil
72 ¼ × 21 ⅝ × 22 in. (184 × 55 × 56 cm)
Page 65

Cortez, 1991–92
Fiberglass and resin, PVC, metal car parts, leather, glass, acrylic paint, rebar, sheet metal, pulleys, handles
88 ½ × 57 × 20 ½ in. (225 × 145 × 52 cm)
Stedelijk Museum voor Actuele Kunst (SMAK), Ghent, Belgium
Page 142

Anti Flag, 1992
Acrylic on unstretched canvas
21 × 14 in. (53.3 × 35.6 cm)
Page 72

Caliban Codex, 1992
Pencil on paper
Twelve sheets: 21 × 15 in. (53.3 × 38 cm); two sheets, 22 ¼ × 15 in. (56.5 × 38 cm)
Daled Collection, Brussels
Pages 124–25

Gezondheid, 1992
Silkscreen and graphite on paper
Edition 3/45
25 ¼ × 19 in. (64 × 48 cm)
Page 222

The Guardian (free tickets), 1992
Construction lumber, found wood box, PVC, acrylic paint, duct tape, paper tickets, ink on paper mounted to wood
76 ¾ × 40 ¼ × 34 in. (195 × 102 × 86 cm)
Collection of Lonti Ebers, New York City
Page 119

I Forgot What I Was Going to Say, 1992
Metal gun parts, carved yew tree from Ireland, wood dowel, bone, acrylic on canvas
24 ½ × 26 ½ × 2 ½ in. (62.4 × 67.2 × 6 cm)
Collection of Dieter & Birgit Broska
Page 128

Jesus (Es geht um die Wurst) [Jesus (It's all about the sausage)], 1992
Ash, acacia, guava, duct tape, dirt mixed with blood and white glue, acrylic paint, color photograph, cardboard, magnetite stones, metal
58 ¾ × 15 ¾ × 43 ¼ in. (152 × 40 × 113 cm)
Museum of Contemporary Art Antwerp (M HKA), Antwerp, Belgium
Page 139

Language is a tool for communication, like a city, or a brain, 1992
Lithograph
Edition of 200
22 ¼ × 29 ¾ in. (56.5 × 75.5 cm)
Page 71

Not Caliban's Nose, 1992
Acrylic paint and ink on paper
17 ¾ × 19 ¼ in. (45 × 48.7 cm)
Private collection, courtesy of kurimanzutto, Mexico City
Page 120 bottom

Poppies, 1992
Acrylic paint, ink, and burn on paper
19 ¼ × 13 ¼ in. (48.9 × 33.6 cm)
Page 120 top right

Small action painting, 1992
Acrylic paint and ink on paper
20 ½ × 20 ¼ in. (52.1 × 51.4 cm)
Private collection, courtesy of kurimanzutto, Mexico City
Page 120 top left

Some noses, 1992
Cast brass, acrylic paint, wood
37 × 3 × 2 ¾ in. (94 × 7.5 × 7 cm)
Page 122

Treff [Encounter], 1992
Guava, Mexican cedar, palm trunk, iron, hubcap, black-and-white photograph, acrylic paint, ink on paper
84 ¾ × 80 ¾ × 42 in. (215 × 205 × 107 cm)
Museum of Contemporary Art Antwerp (M HKA), Antwerp, Belgium
Page 140

Untitled (Caliban's Mask), 1992
Mud, glue, glass, button, PVC
9 ½ × 6 ¼ × 2 in. (24 × 16 × 5 cm)
Private collection, Topanga, California
Page 123

Untitled (It's Got Mr. Durham's Teeth), 1992
Oak, beech, leather glove, acrylic paint, Jimmie Durham's teeth, seashell buttons, epoxy resin, ink on canvas
44 ¼ × 13 ¼ × 26 in. (108 × 31.2 × 62.4 cm)
Denver Art Museum; Funds from Modern and Contemporary Collectors and Native Arts Accession Fund
Page 121

Wahlverwandtschaften [Elective affinities], 1992
Wood, nails, fabric doily, dried plant, tooth, brass plaque, acrylic paint, and paper-pulp collage on board
18 ¼ × 10 ¾ × 2 ⅝ in. (46.3 × 27.3 × 6.7 cm)
Collection of Peter, Annie, and Connor Remes, Minneapolis
Page 141

Another Chance, 1993
Black walnut and acrylic paint
64 ¼ × 24 × 20 in. (153 × 57.6 × 48 cm)
The Eileen Harris Norton Collection
Page 133

Behold my hands and my feet, that it is myself: Handle me and see; for a spirit hath not flesh and bones – as ye see me have., 1993
From Luke 24:39
Painted wood box, cow eyebrow ridge bone, glass lens, bullet shell from 45-caliber pistol, ink on paper
4 × 6 × 10 in. (10.2 × 15.2 × 25.4 cm)
Page 126

The East London Coelacanth, 1993
Video, color, sound
10:20 min.
Filmed in Xochicalco, Morelos, Mexico
Courtesy of the artist and Cisco Jiménez
Page 146 top

False Orthografie, Broken English, 1993
Guava branch, rifle part, goat bone, coyote rib bone, spent bullet casing, acrylic paint, metal, canvas, tape
69 × 25 × 4 ½ in. (175.3 × 63.5 × 11.4 cm)
Private collection, Topanga, California
Page 131 top

Forbidden Things, 1993
Oak, raw canvas, polyester resin, acrylic on untanned deerskin, plastic bowl
89 × 56 ¾ × 32 ⅜ in. (226.1 × 114.1 × 82.2 cm)
Museum of Contemporary Art San Diego; Museum purchase, Elizabeth W. Russell Foundation Fund
Page 134

He bid his Angels turn askance the poles of Earth twice ten degrees and more from the sun's axle; they with labor pushed oblique the centric globe:, 1993
From John Milton's *Paradise Lost*, 1667
Wood doorknob, metal, oil can part, ink on paper
Sculpture: 9 ½ × 1 ½ × 5 ¾ in. (24 × 3.7 × 15 cm); text: 3 ¼ × 7 × 2 in. (8.5 × 18 × 5 cm)
Page 127 bottom

In flaming fire take vengeance upon them that know not God and that obey not the gospel of our Lord Jesus Christ., 1993
From 2 Thessalonians 1:8
Metal ice-cream scoop, plum wood, ink on paper
Sculpture: 10 ¾ × 3 ½ × 8 in. (27 × 9 × 20.3 cm); text: 2 ¼ × 1 ¾ in. (5.5 × 4.7 cm)
Page 127 top

Mishap in the jungle. The rest of them were mostly Indians: tough young fellows with wiry strength and impassive faces. The whitest, 1993
Plywood, plastic handle, paint, ink on paper
6 ¼ × 31 × 1 ⅛ in. (16 × 79 × 3 cm)
Page 130 bottom

Sequence of Events, 1993
Acrylic paint and collage on wood panel
36 ¼ × 36 ¼ in. (92 × 92 cm)
Page 200

So saß sie, wenn sie nicht liegen musste, in Gesellschaft der Rätin Spatz, verhielt sich still und hing, eine Handarbeit im Schoße, an der sie nicht arbeitete, diesem oder jenem Gedanken nach. [So, even when she was not required to lie down, she would sit, disregarded needlework in her lap, in the company of Mrs. Spatz, keeping still and pursuing this or that line of thought.], 1993
From Thomas Mann's *Tristan*, 1903
Plastic tube, plastic handle, wood, cord, tape, metal, ink on paper
15 × 28 × 4 in. (38.1 × 71.1 × 10.2 cm)
Page 131 bottom

Tu ne cede malis, sed contra audentior ito. [Yield not to misfortunes, but advance all the more boldly against them.], 1993
From Virgil's *Aeneid*, ca. 29–19 BCE
Carved guava branch, glass, metal, ink on paper
Sculpture: 9 × 17 × 2 ½ in. (22.9 × 43.2 × 6.4 cm); text: 3 ⅜ × 7 1/16 in. (8.5 × 18 cm)
Page 129

Types of Murder Weapons by Maigret, 1993
Metal, copper, plastic, wood, ink on wood board
24 × 24 × 2 in. (61 × 61 × 5 cm)
Collection of Dirk Snauwaert, Brussels
Page 168

Types of Pipes by Magritte, 1993
Metal, copper, plastic, wood, ink on wood board
24 × 24 × 2 in. (61 × 61 × 5 cm)
Collection of Dirk Snauwaert, Brussels
Page 169

ελθων δ΄ εξ ορεος μεΥας αιετος αΥκυλοχειλης πασι κατ΄ αυχενας ηξε και εκτανεν [A great eagle came swooping down from a mountain and dug his curved beak into the neck of each of them until he had killed them all.], 1993
From Homer's *Odyssey*, 800 BCE
Wood axe handle, wood dowel, metal, ink on paper on canvas
19 × 12 ¾ × 1 ½ in. (48.5 × 32.5 × 4 cm)
Page 130 top right

Весь этот и следующий день друзья и товарищи Ро́стова замечали, что он не скучен, не сердит, но молчалив, задумчив и сосредоточен. Он неохотно пил, старался оставаться один и о чем-то все думал [All that day and the next his friends and comrades noticed that Rostov, without being dull or angry, was silent, thoughtful, and preoccupied. He drank reluctantly, tried to remain alone, and kept turning something over in his mind.], 1993
From Leo Tolstoy's *War and Peace*, 1869
Fire hose, Coke bottle coated in leather, wood, acrylic paint, ink on paper
59 5/8 × 17 × 9 5/8 in. (150 × 43.2 × 23 cm)
Page 132

Sonderbar kam es mir vor, daß sie diese Übung an einer alten Stadtmauer ohne die mindeste Bequemlichkeit für die Zuschauer vornehmen; warum sie es nicht im Amphitheater tun, wo so schöner Raum wäre! [It seemed strange to me that they carry on this exercise by an old lime wall, without the slightest convenience for spectators; why is it not done in the amphitheater, where there would be such ample room?], 1993–2012
From Johann Wolfgang von Goethe's *Italian Journey*, 1816
Maple, pine, glass and metal headlamp, leather, slide viewer, metal wire, ink on paper
39 × 15 × 15 in. (99 × 38 × 38 cm)
Page 130 top left

Graphite on Paper, 1994
Paint and graphite on paper
20 3/4 × 20 in. (52.5 × 51 cm)
Page 223 top

Graphite on Paper #1, 1994
Graphite on paper
17 × 22 1/4 in. (43.2 × 56.5 cm)
Page 225

Graphite on Paper #2, 1994
Graphite on paper
22 1/4 × 30 in. (56.5 × 76 cm)
Private collection, courtesy of kurimanzutto, Mexico City
Page 223 bottom

The Man Who Had a Beautiful House, 1994
Video transferred to DVD, color, sound
Edition of 7
7:27 min.
Filmed in Xochicalco, Morelos, Mexico
Page 146 bottom

Self-Portrait pretending to be Rosa Levy, 1994
Color photograph
32 × 24 in. (81.2 × 60.9 cm)
Collection of fluid archives, Karlsruhe. Courtesy of ZKM Center for Art and Media, Karlsruhe
Page 206

Untitled (Grafite, Soil), 1994
Dirt, hair, white glue, graphite on canvas over plywood
17 × 22 in. (43.2 × 55.9 cm)
Page 224

Dirt, Human Hair and Cotton in Steel Bucket #2, 1995
Dirt, human hair, cotton in stainless-steel bucket
9 1/2 × 11 1/4 × 10 1/2 in. (24.5 × 29 × 27 cm)
Private collection, courtesy of kurimanzutto, Mexico City
Page 149

Dirt, Human Hair and Cotton in Steel Bucket #3, 1995
Dirt, human hair, cotton in stainless-steel bucket
10 × 11 3/4 × 10 1/2 in. (25.8 × 30 × 26.7 cm)
Page 152 top

Dirt, Human Hair and Cotton in Steel Bucket #4, 1995
Dirt, human hair, cotton in stainless-steel bucket
10 1/4 × 12 × 10 1/2 in. (26 × 30.5 × 27 cm)
Private collection, courtesy of kurimanzutto, Mexico City
Page 148

Dirt, Human Hair and Vegetable Fiber in Steel Bucket #2, 1995
Dirt, human hair, vegetable fiber in stainless-steel bucket
4 × 9 1/4 × 8 1/4 in. (10.5 × 23.5 × 21.2 cm)
Page 150

Dirt, Human Hair and Vegetable Fiber in Steel Bucket #3, 1995
Dirt, human hair, vegetable fiber in stainless-steel bucket
3 × 8 1/4 × 8 1/4 in. (8 × 21 × 21 cm)
Page 151

Dirt, Human Hair and Vegetable Fiber in Steel Washtub, 1995
Dirt, human hair, vegetable fiber in stainless-steel washtub
11 1/2 × 24 1/2 × 24 1/2 in. (29 × 62 × 62 cm)
Page 153

Dirt, Human Hair, Squirrel Hair and Cotton in Steel Bucket, 1995
Dirt, human hair, squirrel hair, cotton in stainless-steel bucket
10 1/2 × 12 3/4 × 11 1/2 in. (26.5 × 32.5 × 29.3 cm)
Private collection, courtesy of kurimanzutto, Mexico City
Page 152 bottom

Resurrection, 1995
TV (plastic, glass, wire), flagstone
Editions 9/21, 17/21, 20/21
Approx. 17 3/4 × 26 × 17 3/4 in.
(45 × 66 × 45 cm) each of 3
Courtesy of the artist and Galerie Barbara Wien, Berlin
Page 155

Une étude des étoiles [A study of stars], 1995
Acrylic paint, ink, sweet gum leaf, bottle caps, plastic, metal, computer key, and cotton stars from American flag on wood
33 1/2 × 20 1/2 in. (85 × 52 cm)
Hervé Lebrun Collection, Marseille, France
Page 73

Collected Stones: 13 short videos (Incident at Middelburg, 1996; A Stone from Metternich's House in Bohemia, 1996; 13 Rue Fenelon, 1996; Enough!, 1995; A Heavy Stone, 1996; HTV, 1996; Pink Granite at Work, 1997; Un Projet à Lille, 1996; Nature Morte, 2000; Towards Light, 1999–2002; A Stone at Home in Bed Asleep, 2000; Stoning the Refrigerator, 1996; Brazilian Bloodstone, 1997), 1995–2002
Single-channel video, color, sound
21:39 min.
Page 147

Self-Portrait Pretending to Be Maria Thereza Alves, 1995–2006
Color photograph
Edition of 1 + 1 AP
32 × 24 in. (81.2 × 60.9 cm)
Collection of fluid archives, Karlsruhe. Courtesy of ZKM Center for Art and Media, Karlsruhe
Page 207

Arc de Triomphe for Personal Use, 1996
Pine, acrylic paint, metal hardware, padlocks, keys
78 3/4 × 31 1/2 × 31 1/2 in. (200 × 80 × 80 cm)
Collection of Maria and Alexandre Bosoni, Paris
Page 187

A Fountain in Case Your Roof Leaks, 1996
Pine, broken glass, stainless-steel salad bowl, metal skillet, plastic tubing
48 1/2 × 19 5/8 × 19 5/8 in. (123 × 50 × 50 cm)
Private collection
Page 186

Le lesson d'anatomie no. 4 [Anatomy lesson no. 4], 1996
Reims cotton shirt, artist's hair, dirt
29 1/2 × 26 3/8 × 1 3/16 in. (74.9 × 70.1 × 3 cm)
Hammer Museum, Los Angeles. Purchase
Page 154

St. Frigo, 1996
Metal refrigerator
52 × 23 1/2 × 23 1/2 in. (132 × 60 × 60 cm)
Collection of Ministry of Culture, Lisbon, Portugal
Page 157

Stoning the Refrigerator, 1996
Video, black and white, sound
3:27 min.
Page 156

Brazilian Bloodstone, 1997
Brazilian bloodstone, orange, graphite, acrylic paint on wood panel
32 5/8 × 47 1/4 × 2 3/4 in. (83 × 110 × 7 cm)
Private collection, Nottingham
Page 198

Homage to David Hammons, 1997
Porcelain, stone, PVC
Dimensions variable
Collection of Dr. Karel and Martine Hooft, Belgium
Page 204

Drawn Lines and Faces, 1998
Graphite on paper
Six sheets (irregular), 21 1/4 × 74 1/2 in.
(54 × 189 cm) overall (framed)
Berliner Künstlerprogramm/DAAD, Berlin
Pages 228–29 top

Gerhard Schröder, 1998
Graphite and pastel on paper
16 1/8 × 11 5/8 in. (41 × 29.5 cm)
Berliner Künstlerprogramm/DAAD, Berlin
Page 231 right

Kaspar König, 1998
Graphite on paper
16 1/8 × 11 5/8 in. (41 × 29.5 cm)
Berliner Künstlerprogramm/DAAD, Berlin
Page 231 left

Pinochet, 1998
Graphite on paper
16 1/8 × 11 5/8 in. (41 × 29.5 cm)
Berliner Künstlerprogramm/DAAD, Berlin
Page 230

Someone Stole my Diamond, 1998
Rose quartz, acrylic paint, graphite, ink on wood panel
32 1/4 × 49 1/4 × 2 3/4 in. (82 × 125 × 7 cm)
Private collection, Nottingham
Page 199

Three Faces, 1998
Graphite on paper
Six sheets (irregular), 21 1/4 × 74 1/2 in. (54 × 189 cm) overall (framed)
Berliner Künstlerprogramm/DAAD, Berlin
Pages 228–29 bottom

Untitled, 1998–99
Black chalk on paper
42 15/16 × 31 5/16 in. (109 × 79.5 cm)
UCLA Grunwald Center for the Graphic Arts, Hammer Museum, Los Angeles. Purchased with funds provided by the Helga K. and Walter Oppenheimer Acquisition Fund
Page 227 left

The Dangers of Petrification II, 1998–2007
Wood and glass vitrines with objects: stones, two knives, spoon, four ceramic plates, ceramic bowl, three wood chopping boards, ink on paper
39 1/4 × 51 × 29 1/2 in. (100 × 129.5 × 75 cm) each of 2
Private collection, Dallas
Pages 170–71

Mäßige Materialfehler [Moderate material defects], 2000
Suite of nine etchings on paper and colophon sheet with text
Edition 4/6
16 1/2 × 12 1/2 in. (41.9 × 31.7 cm) each of 10
UCLA Grunwald Center for the Graphic Arts, Hammer Museum, Los Angeles. Purchased with funds provided by the Helga K. and Walter Oppenheimer Acquisition Fund
Page 184

Gray granite (removed) on Dr. Best's, 2001
Acrylic paint and toothpaste on wood board
43 1/4 × 33 1/2 in. (110 × 85 cm)
Collection of Joanne Gold and Andrew Stern
Page 236

No Men Clature in Paris, 2002
Felt hat, cobblestone, acrylic paint on wood panel
43 1/2 × 33 5/8 × 5 1/2 in. (110.5 × 85.5 × 14 cm)
Page 237

Stone (Removed) on Glass and Ink on Paper, 2002
Ink on paper
40 × 31 in. (101.6 × 78.7 cm)
Collection of Zach Feuer and Alison Fox
Page 226

Hommage à Filliou (A Piece of Wood Sculpted by a Dog, Painted by a Human. A Piece of Wood Sculpted by a Machine, Painted by a Human), 2003
Pine, purpurin dye, acrylic paint, ink
39 3/4 × 29 1/2 × 13 in. (100 × 75 × 33 cm)
Private collection, Mexico City
Page 201

La Poursuite du Bonheur [The pursuit of happiness], 2003
35mm film transferred to DVD, color, sound
13:00 min.
Page 190

The names of the team of scientists who published an article on human chromosome 14 in Nature magazine, 2003
Plywood, oak, acrylic paint, ink, metal, electrical wire, sardine can
51 × 39 1/4 in. (130 × 100 cm)
Collection of H.L.T.M. Hunting, Eindhoven
Page 180

Suggested Proposal for a New Architecture n°3, 2003
Carved walnut, stone, ink on paper
10 1/2 × 34 1/2 × 4 in. (27 × 88 × 10 cm)
Collection of Roberto Pinto, Milan
Page 188 top

A Pole to Mark the Center of the World in Berlin, 2004
Hawthorn, mirror, cable
71 1/2 × 4 in. (182 × 10 cm)
Private collection
Page 75

Prehistoric Stone Tool, 2004
Acrylic paint and ink on wood panel and flint stone
Wood panel: 35 1/2 × 25 5/8 in. (90 × 65 cm); shelf: 7 7/8 × 7 7/8 in. (20 × 20 cm)
Courtesy of Franco Soffiantino Contemporary Art Productions, Milan, Italy
Page 234

Smashing, 2004
Digital video, color, sound
Edition of 7 + 1AP
1:31:54 min.
Page 210 bottom

A Staff to Mark the Center of the World, Gwangju Biennale, 2004
Hawthorn, plastic and metal key rings, mirror, cotton, ink on paper
Three parts, 77 1/4 × 3 in. (196.2 × 7.6 cm); 71 × 3 in. (180.3 × 7.62 cm); 66 1/2 × 3 in. (168.9 × 7.6 cm).
Private collection
Page 285

Suggested Proposal for a New Architecture n°2, 2004
Carved walnut, stones, metal wire
14 1/2 × 23 1/2 × 6 in. (37 × 60 × 15 cm)
Courtesy of Franco Soffiantino Contemporary Art Productions, Milan, Italy
Page 188 bottom

Untitled 4 ("Stoning" series), 2004
Graphite on paper
27 1/2 × 19 1/2 in. (70 × 49.5 cm)
Collection of Marc J. Lee, Los Angeles
Page 227 right

Anti-Brancusi, 2005
Cardboard, wood, serpentine stone, rope, ink on paper
48 × 17 × 31 1/8 in. (122 × 43 × 79 cm)
Collection of Michel Rein, Paris
Page 202 right

Fleur de Pas Mal, 2005
Digital video, color, sound
Edition of 2 + 1 AP
00:28 min. (loop)
Page 210 top

Something . . . Perhaps a Fugue or an Elegy, 2005
Cameras, television, VHS player, amplifier, tripod, steel pipes, hardware, PVC, plastic, rope, acrylic paint, pine, seashell, brass heads, cast marble-dust head, oak box, glass bottle, wood furniture parts, tree branches, tire, mirrors, metal lock, metal chains, lights, wires, plywood pallets, armadillo shell, cow skull and bones, ink on paper
71 × 275 1/2 × 63 in. (180 × 700 × 160 cm)
Fondazione Morra Greco, Naples, Italy
Pages 282–83

Confessional, 2006
Hair and dirt on canvas, acrylic paint, agate, animal taxidermy glass eye, ink on wood
73 × 35 1/2 × 6 in. (185 × 90 × 15 cm)
Collection of H.L.T.M. Hunting, Eindhoven
Page 158

With Maria Thereza Alves
Grunewald, 2006
Digital video transferred to DVD, color, sound
Edition of 7
13:35 min.
Page 191

Head, 2006
Wood, papier-mâché, hair, seashells, turquoise, armadillo shell, human dentures, metal tray
10 × 16 × 16 in. (25 × 40 × 40 cm)
Fondazione Morra Greco, Naples, Italy
Page 159

A Mushroom from the Grunewald Forest, 2006
Dried mushroom, acrylic paint, ink on two wood boards
Two parts, 33 1/2 × 26 1/4 × 4 in. (85 × 67 × 10 cm); 21 × 26 1/4 × 4 in. (53 × 67 × 10 cm)
Page 235

Self-Portrait Pretending to Be a Stone Statue of Myself, 2006
Color photograph
Edition of 1 + 1 AP
31 ¾ × 24 in. (80.7 × 60.9 cm)
Collection of fluid archives, Karlsruhe. Courtesy of ZKM Center for Art and Media, Karlsruhe
Page 205

Self-Portrait with Black Eye and Bruises, 2006
Color photograph enlarged from photomaton print
38 × 23 ½ in. (79 × 60 cm)
Collection of Sabrina Recoules, London
Page 208

Snake Eyes!, 2006
Objects from the artist's studio on canvas with graphite and primer over wood panel: stone, plastic, bone, metal, aluminum, seashells, deerskin, hair, ceramic shards
49 ½ × 32 in. (125 × 81 cm)
Mima and César Reyes Collection, Puerto Rico
Page 173

A Stone Rejected by the Builder (1), 2006
Stone, wood, acrylic paint
Stone: 34 × 41 × 20 in.
(86.3 × 104.1 × 50.8 cm); table: 55 × 48 × 35 in.
(139.7 × 121.9 × 88.9 cm)
Collection of Lois Plehn, New York
Page 185

The Telephone Call, 2006
Digital video, color, sound
Edition of 7
2:35 min.
Page 211 top

Untitled (Damaged face drawings), 2006
Graphite on paper
39 ½ × 27 ½ in. (100 × 70 cm) each of 3
Collection of Beth Rudin DeWoody
Page 232–33 bottom

You Cannot Book a Judge Under Cover, 2006
Carved walnut furniture parts, PVC, branch, glass bottle, plastic bottle, ice-cream scoop, clothespins, hair dryer, painted tin box, wire bedspring, cords, screwdriver, metal hardware, plastic and metal tubing in a found sound mixer
47 ¼ × 31 ½ × 31 ½ in. (120 × 80 × 80 cm)
Fondazione Morra Greco, Naples, Italy
Page 189

Homage to Constantin Brancusi #1, 2007
Poplar, acrylic paint, bedspring from Alexander Calder's studio
47 ¼ × 19 ⅝ × 19 ⅝ in. (120 × 50 × 50 cm)
Collection of Maria and Alexandre Bosoni, Paris
Page 202 left

Homage to Alexander Calder, 2007
Wood, aluminum chair (with back removed), aluminum labels, acrylic paint, wire from Alexander Calder's studio
84 ⅝ × 33 × 13 ¾ in. (215 × 84 × 35 cm)
Collection of Peter and Mari Shaw, Philadelphia
Page 203

Ka, 2007
Pine, tree branch, rearview mirror, reflector, glass marble, acrylic paint on board
79 15/16 × 23 ⅝ × 23 ⅝ in. (203 × 60 × 60 cm)
Collection of Andrée Sfeir-Semler, Hamburg
Page 266

L'Essence, 2007
Oil barrels, linen canvas, wood boat, PVC, acrylic paint, polyester and metal fasteners
138 × 118 × 45 ¼ in. (350 × 300 × 115 cm)
Deichtorhallen Hamburg/Falckenberg Collection
Page 212

Painted Self-Portrait, 2007
Acrylic paint and marker on color photograph
Unique
27 ½ × 23 in. (70 × 58 cm)
Courtesy of Christine König Galerie, Vienna
Page 209

A Proposal for a New International Genuflexion in Promotion of World Peace, 2007
Video SD, color, sound
00:26 min. (loop)
Page 211 bottom

Red Foot, 2007
Oak, pine, seashell, cast brass, metal, acrylic paint
55 × 25 × 12 in. (140 × 64 × 30 cm)
Collection of Michel Rein, Paris
Page 267

Slash and Burn, 2007
Beech, red stones, gold leaf, electronic parts, watercolor, ink
36 × 36 × 2 ½ in. (92 × 86 × 6.5 cm)
Mima and César Reyes Collection, Puerto Rico
Page 268

Untitled (The Penis Mightier), 2007
Graphite on acid-free cotton paper
30 ¼ × 23 in. (77 × 58 cm) each of 3
Collection of Raul Zorrilla/Alberto Bremermann, Mexico
Pages 232–33 top

The Bluebird of Happiness and the Miner's Canary (Classic Rock), 2008
Handmade hat rack base (American black walnut), plywood, rearview mirror, deer antler, television antenna, drumstick, two paint-brushes with dried acrylic paint, clothespins, oak sapling, glass bottle, acrylic paint, electrical wire, plastic, zip ties
118 ⅛ × 31 ½ × 35 7/16 in. (300 × 80 × 90 cm)
Collection of H.L.T.M. Hunting, Eindhoven
Page 246

THERE'S PLENTY MORE WHERE THESE CAME FROM, 2008
Objects from the artist's studio, acrylic paint, and ink on wood panel
40 × 27 ½ in. (101.5 × 70 cm)
Private collection, Mexico City
Page 172

The Doorman, 2009
Steel, gold, Murano glass, olive oil can, acrylic paint, obsidian, seashell, wood, bike lock, surveillance cameras, electrical wires, duct tape
64 × 32 × 27 ½ in. (162 × 81 × 70 cm)
Mima and César Reyes Collection, Puerto Rico
Page 238

Obsidian arabesque, 2009
Obsidian, human hair, acrylic paint on wood panel
24 × 31 × ¾ in. (61 × 79 × 1.7 cm)
Private collection, Mexico City
Page 243

Obsidian is so sharp that when you are cut, Mexico, 2009
Pencil and incisions on cotton paper
32 × 24 in. (81.5 × 61 cm)
Collection of Moisés Cosío Espinosa, Mexico City
Page 242 bottom left

Obsidian tongue, 2009
Graphite on cotton paper
28 ½ × 36 ⅝ in. (72.5 × 93 cm) (framed)
Page 242 top

Obsidiana, 2009
Single-channel video transferred to DVD, color, sound
Edition of 3 + 1 AP
5:43 min. (loop)
Page 239

Obsidiana mexican, homenaje a Fontana, Mexico, 2009
Incisions on cotton paper
32 × 24 in. (81.5 × 61 cm)
Collection of Moisés Cosío Espinosa, Mexico City
Page 242 bottom right

Upon reflection, I was no longer sure of my position, 2009
Obsidian, German silver (copper, zinc, and nickel), steel table, obsidian mirror with colored tin frame
Mirror: 13 ½ × 10 × ¾ in. (34 × 25 × 2 cm); table: 39 ½ × 197 × 23 ½ in.
(100 × 500 × 60 cm); obsidian: 18 ½ in. (47 cm) diameter; German silver: 17 ¾ in. (45 cm) diameter
Hammer Museum, Los Angeles. Purchase
Pages 240–41

Various Elements from the Actual World, 2009
Acrylic and oil paint, Formica, gold leaf, wool gloves, leather glove, various stones, paper, Egyptian wedding canopy, buttons made of mussels, shards of glass, airplane parts, plywood, chestnut, black-and-white photographs, ink
93 ½ × 118 ⅛ in. (250 × 300 cm)
Collection of Lonti Ebers, New York City
Page 284

Lord Byron's Poem, 2010
Pencil and collage on paper
Two sheets, typed sheet: 23 ⅜ × 16 ¾ in.
(59.3 × 42.5 cm); written sheet:
30 ⅛ × 22 ⅝ in. (76.5 × 57.5 cm)
Courtesy of the artist and Sprovieri, London
Page 245

A Scottish Conspiracy, 2010
Pencil and collage on paper
30 × 23 in. (76 × 58 cm) each of 2
Courtesy of the artist and Sprovieri, London
Page 244

Some of These People Are Dead, 2010
PVC, duct tape, deer antler, elm branch, golf club, found furniture parts, plastic key chains, acrylic paint, ink, wood
98 ½ × 27 ½ × 29 ½ in. (250 × 70 × 75 cm)
Courtesy of the artist and Sprovieri, London
Page 247

The Forest and Brancusi, 2012
Three pieces of carved walnut, acrylic paint, found wood and brass table
110 ¼ × 19 ¾ × 15 ¾ in. (280 × 50 × 40 cm)
Private collection, Nottingham
Page 275

It should work, 2012
Olive trunk, metal from industrial machine
65 × 29 ½ × 27 ½ in. (165 × 75 × 70 cm)
Private collection, Nottingham
Page 273

1948, 2012
Newspaper, ink, collage on paper
Series of eight works in five frames, frame 1: 34 ⅝ × 22 ¼ in. (88 × 56.5 cm); frame 2: 26 ¼ × 30 in. (66.5 × 76.5 cm); frame 3: 22 ⅜ × 30 in. (56.8 × 76.5 cm); frame 4: 26 ¼ × 42 ¾ in. (66.5 × 108.5 cm); frame 5: 26 ¼ × 42 ¾ in. (66.5 cm × 108 cm)
Courtesy of the artist and Christine König Galerie, Vienna
Pages 270–71

This should explain, 2012
Olive branch, found walnut, metal from industrial machine
82 ¾ × 25 ½ × 27 ½ in. (210 × 65 × 70 cm)
Page 272

Untitled (provisional auxilliary horizon), 2012
Ink on cotton paper
12 ½ × 9 ½ in. (31.8 × 24.1 cm)
Collection of Martha Reta and Ricardo Mendoza, Mexico City
Back endsheet

Untitled (sections), 2012
Ink on cotton paper
12 ½ × 9 ½ in. (31.8 × 24.1 cm)
Collection of Gabriel Kuri and Frances Horn, Brussels
Front endsheet

Belo Horizonte, 2013
Serpentine stone, snakeskin, porcelain tile, oak frame
51 ½ × 63 × 2 ⅜ in. (131 × 160 × 6 cm)
Defares Collection, Amsterdam, the Netherlands
Page 269

Elephant Skull Study #2, 2013
Olive trunk, acrylic paint, glass, iron
47 ¼ × 35 ½ × 31 ½ in. (120 × 90 × 80 cm)
Fondazione Morra Greco, Naples, Italy
Page 276

Hertz Receiving Apparatus, 2013
Satellite dish, steel pipe, mahogany, carob tree branch, plywood, acrylic paint, chameleon paint
80 ¾ × 21 ¼ × 19 ¼ in. (205 × 54 × 49 cm)
Collection of Michel Rein, Paris
Page 176

In the interest of science, 2013
Wood table, metal industrial machine, olive branch
45 ¼ × 51 × 19 ½ in. (115 × 130 × 50 cm)
Fondazione Morra Greco, Naples, Italy
Page 277

Untitled (On a Scale of One through Ten, Recalcitrant Trends, Ill Wind, Seven Lines Indicating Various Colors and Trends, The Turquoise Line Is Probably Indicative, Red and Blue Meeting, Water, Lightning and Anger, Clearly, Not Everything Functions, Indications of the Frequent Escape Mechanisms of Clarity, from Normality . . . , More a Process Than a Beginning and an End), 2013
Suite of eleven drawings; graphite and pencil on paper
Two sheets, 11 ½ × 16 ½ in. (29.5 × 42 cm); two sheets, 16 ½ × 23 ¼ in. (42 × 59 cm); seven sheets, 20 × 28 ¾ in. (51 × 73 cm)
Pages 174–75

Yellow Higgs Transmitting Apparatus, 2013
PVC, metal, wood, acrylic paint
34 ¼ × 37 × 11 ¼ in. (87 × 94 × 29 cm)
Hoche Partners, Luxembourg
Page 177

The Effect of Gamma Rays on Certain European Plants—Volume III, 2014
Bronze, acrylic paint, wood
52 ¼ × 17 ¾ × 17 ¾ in. (130 × 45 × 45 cm)
Collection of Ellen and Bill Taubman, New York City
Page 179

Songs of my Childhood. Part One: Songs to Get Rid Of; Part Two: Songs to Keep, 2014
Two-channel video installation, color, sound
Edition of 12 + 5 AP
11:51 min. each of 2
Page 286

Carnivalesque Shark in Venice, 2015
Glass, goat leather, piranha teeth, papier-mâché, acrylic paint
12 × 13 × 28 in. (30 × 33.5 × 71 cm)
Collection of Eleanor Heyman Propp, New York
Page 279

Different Ways of Organizing Matter in Venice, 2015
Wood, glass, iron on wood table
Wood: 30 ⅜ × 5 ⅛ × 2 ½ in. (77 × 13 × 6.5 cm); glass: 30 ⅜ × 7 ⅞ × 4 in. (77 × 20 × 10 cm); table: 27 ½ × 34 ¼ × 19 ¼ in. (70 × 87 × 48.9 cm).
Private collection
Page 281

Lapis Lazuli with Venetian Red Glass, a Valve, Et Cetera, 2015
Lapis lazuli stone, glass, steel, brass
12 × 5 ¼ × 5 ¼ in. (30.5 × 13.3 × 13.3 cm)
Collection of Maria and Alexandre Bosoni, Paris
Page 278

Pink Palm-Tree-Like Glass Construction with Various Decorative Elements, 2015
Glass, steel, hawthorn branch, aluminum, plastic, found chestnut table
65 ½ × 35 ½ × 19 ¾ in. (166.3 × 90.1 × 50.1 cm)
Page 280

Inexplicable, 2016
Wood, bone, PVC, seashell, stain
78 × 39 ¼ × 39 ¼ in. (198 × 100 × 100 cm)
Page 287 left

Much Has Already Happened, 2016
Petrified wood, bone, metal, paint
45 × 13 ¾ × 15 ¾ in. (114 × 35 × 40 cm)
Page 287 right

SELECTED BIBLIOGRAPHY

ARTIST'S WRITINGS AND ARTIST BOOKS

Columbus Day: Poems, Drawings and Stories about American Indian Life and Death in the Nineteen-Seventies. Albuquerque: West End Press, 1983.

A Matter of Life and Death and Singing. New York: Alternative Museum, 1984. Exhibition brochure.

Columbus Day: A Play, with Natasha Drootin. Unpublished screenplay, 1985.

Ni' Go Tlunh a Doh Ka (We are always turning around on purpose). Old Westbury: Amelie A. Wallace Gallery, State University of New York, Old Westbury, 1986. Exhibition brochure.

The Mystery of the Two Islands: The true story of how Cuban Communists gained control of Trump Tower, with José Bedia et al., 1987. Unpublished artist book included in the exhibition *Jimmie Durham: The Bishop's Moose and the Pinkerton Men*, Exit Art, New York, 1989.

"Savage Attacks on White Women, As Usual." In *We the People*, n.p. New York: Artists Space, 1987. Exhibition catalogue.

"A Certain Lack of Coherence." In *Mataoka Ake Attakulakula Anel Guledisgo Hnihi (Pocahontas and the Little Carpenter in London)*, n.p. London: Matt's Gallery, 1988. Exhibition brochure.

"Four Poems." In *Harper's Anthology of 20th Century Native American Poetry*, edited by Duane Niatum, 129–34. New York: Harper Collins, 1988.

"The Ground Has Been Covered," with Jean Fisher. *Artforum* 26, no. 10 (Summer 1988): 99–105.

"Here at the Centre of the World." *Third Text*, no. 5 (Winter 1988): 21–32.

"Shoot Three Hands: A Screenplay," 1988 (unpublished).

"Those Dead Guys for 100 Years." In *I Tell You Now: Autobiographical Essays by Native American Writers*, edited by Brian Swann and Arnold Krupat, 156–66. Lincoln: University of Nebraska Press, 1989.

"A Central Margin." In *The Decade Show: Frameworks of Identity in the 1980s*, 163–75. New York: Museum of Contemporary Hispanic Art; New Museum of Contemporary Art; Studio Museum in Harlem, 1990. Exhibition catalogue.

"Cowboy S-M." *New Observations*, no. 80 (November–December 1990): n.p.

"Troubleshooting: Jimmie Durham on Collecting." *Artforum* 29, no. 9 (May 1991): 20.

"Approach in Love and Fear." In *Documenta IX*, vol. 2, n.p. Stuttgart: Edition Cantz, 1992. Exhibition catalogue.

"Geronimo!" In *Partial Recall: Photos of Native North Americans*, edited by Lucy R. Lippard, 55–58. New York: The New Press, 1992.

A Certain Lack of Coherence: Writings on Art and Cultural Politics. Edited by Jean Fisher. London: Kala Press, 1993.

"Gilgamesh and Me: The True Story of the Wall." In *On taking a normal situation and retranslating it into overlapping and multiple readings of conditions past and present*, n.p. Antwerp: Museum van Hedendaagse Kunst, 1993. Exhibition brochure.

"A Friend of Mine Said That Art Is a European Invention." In *Global Visions: Towards a New Internationalism in the Visual Arts*, edited by Jean Fisher, 113–19. London: Kala Press, 1994.

"Nothing Works Out Right (except sometimes almost)," with Maria Thereza Alves. *Whitewalls: A Journal of Language and Art*, nos. 33–34 (1994): n.p.

"Probably This Will Not Work." In *Strategies for Survival—NOW!: A Global Perspective on Ethnicity, Body and Breakdown of Artistic Systems*, edited by Christian Chambert, 222–35. Lund: Swedish Art Critics Association Press, 1995.

What Is This? What Is That?, with Maria Thereza Alves. Unpublished audio play, 1995.

"The Gheorghe Mihoc Memorial Letter," with Maria Thereza Alves. In *Around Us, Inside Us*, 23–27. Borås, Sweden: Borås Konstmuseum, 1997. Exhibition catalogue.

Between the Furniture and the Building (Between a Rock and a Hard Place). Munich: Kunstverein München; Berlin: Berliner Künstlerprogramm/DAAD; Cologne: Walther König, 1998.

Nature in the City: A Diary. Berlin: BüroFriedrich, 2001.

"Personal Triumphs of the Fourth Kind." In *Unfolding Perspectives*, 68–69. Helsinki: Museum of Contemporary Art, Kiasma, 2001. Exhibition catalogue.

"Belief in Europe." In *Unpacking Europe: Towards a Critical Reading*, edited by Salah Hassan and Iftikhar Dadi, 290–93. Rotterdam: NAi Publishers, 2002.

"On Contact." In *Plug In*, n.p. Prague: Futura, 2004. Exhibition catalogue.

"Stones Rejected by the Builder" and "Second Thoughts." In *Jimmie Durham*, edited by Anna Daneri, Giacinto Di Pietrantonio, and Roberto Pinto, 21–25, 117–30. Milan: Charta; Como: Fondazione Antonio Ratti, Advanced Course in Visual Arts Publications, 2004.

The Second Particle Wave Theory: As Performed on the Banks of the River Wear, a Stone's Throw from S'underland and the Durham Cathedral. Introduction by Robert Blackson and Candice Hopkins. Banff: Walter Phillips Gallery Editions, 2005. Exhibition catalogue.

"An Essay with No Internal Structure." In *Less: Alternative Living Strategies*, 143–53. Milan: Padiglione d'Arte Contemporanea, 2006. Exhibition catalogue.

"Polemic: Boycott São Paulo Biennale." *Art Monthly*, no. 294 (March 2006): 8.

"Popocatepétl and Its Environs." In *Quauhnahuac: Die Gerade ist eine Utopie (Cuernavaca: The Straight Is a Utopia)*, n.p. Basel: Kunsthalle Basel, 2006. Exhibition catalogue.

"1,000 Words: Jimmie Durham Talks about His Survey This Month at the Musée d'Art Moderne de la Ville de Paris/ARC." *Artforum* 47, no. 5 (January 2009): 186–89. Introduction by Anne Ellegood.

"A New World Order." In *17th Biennale of Sydney: The Beauty of Distance, Songs of Survival in a Precarious Age*, edited by David Elliott, 100–103. Sydney: Biennale of Sydney and Thames & Hudson, 2010. Exhibition catalogue.

"Bureau for Research into Brazilian Normalcy." *29th Bienal de São Paulo*, edited by Agnaldo Farias and Moacir dos Anjos, 392–95. São Paulo: Fundação Bienal de São Paulo, 2010. Exhibition catalogue.

"A Gift to the Future." *Peep-Hole Sheet*, no. 10 (Fall 2011): 3–6.

Amoxohtli: A Road Book. Cologne: Walther König, 2011.

Jimmie Durham: Material. 100 Notes, 100 Thoughts. Documenta 13, no. 049. Ostfildern, Germany: Hatje Cantz, 2012.

Poems That Do Not Go Together. Edited by Barbara Wien and Wilma Lukatsch. Berlin: Wiens Verlag, 2012.

The Usual Song & Dance Routine with a Few Minor Interruptions. Edited by Barbara Wien and Wilma Lukatsch. Berlin: Wiens Verlag, 2012. Transcript of a lecture given in Glasgow in 2010.

"Against Internationalism." *Third Text* 27, no. 1 (January 2013): 29–32.

"Building a Nomadic Library." In *Life between Borders: The Nomadic Life of Curators and Artists*, edited by Steven Rand and Heather Felty, 39–44. New York: Apex Art, 2013.

"Celebrating Europe." Paper delivered at the European Commission's "New Narrative for Europe" symposium, June 12, 2013. Republished in *Jimmie Durham: Various Items and Complaints*. London: Serpentine Gallery, 2016. Exhibition catalogue.

Waiting to Be Interrupted: Selected Writings, 1993–2012. Edited and with a foreword by Jean Fisher. Milan: Mousse Publishing; Antwerp: Museum van Hedendaagse Kunst, 2014.

In Europe. Berlin: Neuer Berliner Kunstverein, 2015. Published on the occasion of the exhibition *Jimmie Durham: Here at the Center*, Neuer Berliner Kunstverein, 2015.

"Is This Interesting?" *Mousse Contemporary Art Magazine*, no. 42 (2015): 194–95.

Venice, Work and Tourism. Milan: Mousse Publishing, 2015. Published on the occasion of the exhibition *Venice: Objects, Work and Tourism*, Fondazione Querini Stampalia, Venice.

EXHIBITION CATALOGUES, BROCHURES, MONOGRAPHS, AND BOOKS

Animism: Modernity through the Looking Glass. Cologne: Walther König, 2012. Texts by Jimmie Durham, Sabine Folie, Anselm Franke, and Maurizio Lazzarato.

Der Verführer und der steinerne Gast (The Libertine and the Stone Guest). Vienna: Wittgenstein Haus & Springer, 1996. Texts by Jimmie Durham and Ulli Lindmayr.

Durham: The Center of the World. Middelburg: De Vleeshal, 1995.

Fisher, Jean, ed. *The American West*. Warwickshire, England: Compton Verney, 2005. Exhibition curated by Jimmie Durham and Richard William Hill. Texts by Mark Diaper, Jimmie Durham, Jean Fisher, Richard William Hill, John Leslie, and Kent Monkman.

Fisher, Jean. Introduction and "What cheer, Englishmen, what cheer, what do you come for?" In *Mataoka Ake Attakulakula Anel Guledisgo Hnihi (Pocahontas and the Little Carpenter in London)*, n.p. London: Matt's Gallery, 1988. Exhibition brochure.

Hill, Richard. "Building and Unbuilding." In *Building a Nation*, n.p. London: Matt's Gallery, 2006. Exhibition brochure.

Huberman, Anthony. *Today we should be thinking about*. New York: Artist's Institute and Koenig Books, 2015.

The Hybrid State. New York: Exit Art, 1991. Texts by Luis Camnitzer, Papo Colo, Joshua Dector, Jimmie Durham, Guillermo Gomez-Peña, Celeste Olaquiaga, Cecilia Vicuña, Krzysztof Wodiczko, and Warren Niesluchowski.

The Interrupted Life. New York: New Museum of Contemporary Art, 1991. Texts by France Morin, Sylvère Lotringer, bell hooks, Peter Greenaway, Gerald Vizenor, Anthony Vidler, Charles Merewether et al.

Jimmie Durham. London: Phaidon Press, 1995. Interview with Dirk Snauwaert and contributions by Jimmie Durham, Mark Alice Durant, and Laura Mulvey.

Jimmie Durham: A Matter of Life and Death and Singing. Antwerp: Museum van Hedendaagse Kunst & JRP|Ringier, 2012. Introduction by Bart De Baere and Anders Kreuger; texts by Guy Brett, Jimmie Durham, and Richard William Hill.

Jimmie Durham: Essence. Zurich: de Pury & Luxembourg, 2007. Text by Anselm Franke.

Jimmie Durham: Labyrinth. Oiron, France: Château d'Oiron; Sache: L'Atelier Calder, 2007. Texts by Jimmie Durham and Paul-Hervé Parsy.

Jimmie Durham: La ragioni della leggerezza. Turin: Franco Soffiantino Arte Contemporanea, 2004. Text by Roberto Pinto.

Jimmie Durham: Pierres rejetées (Rejected stones). Paris: Musée d'Art Moderne de la Ville de Paris/ARC, 2009. Foreword by Fabrice Hergott; interview with Laurence Bossé and Julia Garimorth; texts by Adel Abdessemed, Pascal Beausse, Mircea Cantor, Sandra Cattini, Anselm Franke, David Hammons, Friedrich Meschede, and Anri Sala.

Jimmie Durham: The Bishop's Moose and the Pinkerton Men. New York: Exit Art, 1990. Texts by Luis Camnitzer, Papo Colo, Jean Fisher, Jeanette Ingberman, and Lucy R. Lippard.

Jimmie Durham: Various Items and Complaints. London: Serpentine Gallery, 2016. Foreword by Julia Petron-Jones and Hans Ulrich Obrist; texts by Jimmie Durham, Jean Fisher, and Kate Nesin.

Jimmie Durham: Workshop. Jolster, Norway: Eikaas Galleriet & Galleri Sølvberget, 2003.

Land, Spirit, Power: First Nations at the National Gallery of Canada. Ottawa: National Gallery of Canada, 1992. Texts by Robert Houle, Diana Nemiroff, and Charlotte Townsend-Gault.

Lippard, Lucy R. *Mixed Blessings: New Art in a Multicultural America*. New York: Pantheon Books, 1990, 48, 97, 199, 204, 208–11.

Mistaken Identities. Santa Barbara: University Art Museum, 1992. Text by Abigail Solomon-Godeau.

My Book, The East London Coelacanth, Sometimes Called, Troubled Waters: The Story of British Sea-Power. London: ICA Book Works, 1993. Texts by Dan Cameron and Jimmie Durham. Published on the occasion of the exhibition *Original Re-Runs* at ICA, London.

Ni' Go Tlunh a Doh Ka (We are always turning around on purpose). Old Westbury: Amelia A. Wallace Gallery, State University of New York, Old Westbury, 1986.

1993 Whitney Biennial. New York: Whitney Museum of American Art, 1993. Texts by Thelma Golden, John Hanhardt, Lisa Phillips, and Elisabeth Sussman.

Revisions. Banff: Walter Phillips Gallery, Banff Centre for the Arts, 1992. Texts by Deborah Doxtater, Jean Fisher, and Rick Hill.

Sakahàn: International Indigenous Art. Edited by Greg Hill, Candice Hopkins, and Christine Lalonde. Ottawa: National Gallery of Canada, 2013.

Sánchez, Juan. *Ritual & Rhythm: Visual Forces for Survival*. New York: Kenkeleba House Gallery, 1982.

Smith, Paul Chaat. *Everything You Know about Indians Is Wrong*. Minneapolis: University of Minnesota Press, 2009.

Some Collide Some Escape. Berlin: 7Hours Haus 19, Series #2, 2005. Published on the occasion of the exhibition of the same name at Humboldt-Universität, Berlin.

Stoneheart. Kitakyushu, Japan: Center for Contemporary Art, 2001.

Taussig, Michael. "Jimmie Durham." In *On Reason and Emotion: Biennale of Sydney 2004*, 82–85. Sydney: Biennale of Sydney, 2004.

We the People. New York: Artists Space, 1987. Texts by Jimmie Durham, Jean Fisher, and Paul Chaat Smith.

will/power. Columbus: Wexner Center for the Arts, Ohio State University, 1992. Texts by Claire Aguilar, Ann Bremner, Bart De Baere, Jane Farver, Coco Fusco, Joseph Nevaquaya, and Sarah Rogers; interview by Larry Abbott with Edgar Heap of Birds.

ARTICLES AND REVIEWS

Alcalde, Maxence. "Jimmie Durham: Distant Drums." *Art 21*, no. 21 (February–March, 2009): 12–19.

Appleford, Robert. "Jimmie Durham and the Carpentry of Ambivalence." *Social Text 105* 28, no. 4 (Winter 2010): 91–111.

Barker, Joanne. "Indian U.S.A." *Wicazo Sa Review* 18, no. 1 (Spring 2003): 25–79.

Bhabha, Homi K. "Beyond the Pale: Art in the Age of Multicultural Translation." *Kunst & Museum Journal* 5, no. 4 (1994): 15–23.

Canning, Susan. "Jimmie Durham." *New Art Examiner* 23, no. 2 (October 1995): 33–35.

Cembalest, Robin. "What's in a Name?" *Art News* 90, no. 7 (September 1991): 36.

Chinnery, Colin. "Jimmie Durham's 'Arts, Media, and Sports' at Sprovieri, London." *Art Agenda*, December 4, 2010, n.p.

Fiduccia, Joanna. "Jimmie Durham: Musée d'Art Moderne de la Ville de Paris/ARC." *Artforum* 47, no. 9 (May 2009): 248–49.

Fisher, Jean. "In Search of the 'Inauthentic': Disturbing Signs in Contemporary Native American Art." *Art Journal* 51, no. 3, Recent Native American Art (Autumn 1992): 44–50.

Fisher, Jean. "Jimmie Durham: Holding Up a Mirror to Humanity." In *Jimmie Durham: Various Items and Complaints*, 8–11. London: Serpentine Gallery, 2016.

Foster, Hal. "The Artist as Ethnographer." In *The Return of the Real: Critical Models in Art and Theory Since 1960*, 171–203. Cambridge, MA: MIT Press, 1996.

Foster, Hal. "The Politics of the Signifier: A Conversation on the Whitney Biennial." *October* 66 (Autumn 1993): 3–27, with Benjamin Buchloh, Silvia Kolbowski, Rosalind Krauss, and Miwon Kwon.

Franke, Anselm. "The Negation of Negation." *Parkett*, no. 92 (2013): 36–41.

Haq, Nav. "Jimmie Durham's 'Works of Science and Yellowness.'" *Art Agenda*, November 6, 2013, n.p.

Henry, Max. "Ricardo Brey/Jimmie Durham's 'looking at my own work (and his).'" *Art Agenda*, April 19, 2012, n.p.

Hess, Elizabeth. "Who Is Jimmie Durham?" *Village Voice*, December 1989, 127.

Hooks, Bell. "Book Review: Certain Lack of Coherence." *Bookforum* 32 (Summer 1994): 28–29.
Hopkins, Candice. "Making Things Our Own: The Indigenous Aesthetic in Digital Storytelling." *Leonardo* 39, no. 4 (2006): 341–44.
Horton, Jessica. "Study It Lightly." *Parkett*, no. 92 (2013): 48–53.
Horton, Jessica, and Cherise Smith. "The Particulars of Postidentity." *American Art* 28, no. 1 (Spring 2014): 2–8.
Horton, Jessica, and Janet Catherine Berlo. "Beyond the Mirror." *Third Text* 27, no. 1 (January 2013): 17–28.
Huberman, Anthony. "Jimmie Durham: For the Price of a Magazine." *Afterall: A Journal of Art, Context and Enquiry*, no. 30 (Summer 2012): 28–37.
Irvine, Jaki. "Jimmie Durham: Original Re-Runs." *Third Text* 8, nos. 28–29 (Autumn/Winter 1994): 179–84.
Jones, Amelia G. "Jimmie Durham: Exit Art." *Artscribe* 80 (March–April 1990): 78–79.
Kandel, Susan. "Durham's Works Explore the Edge of Absurdity." *Los Angeles Times*, September 2, 1993.
Kreuger, Anders. "Stone as Stone: An Essay about Jimmie Durham." *Afterall: A Journal of Art, Context and Enquiry*, no. 30 (Summer 2012): 14–27.
Kunitz, Daniel. "Jimmie Durham Brings His Sculptures Made from Storied Objects to Belgium's M HKA." *Modern Painters*, October 2012, 96.
Kwon, Miwon. "Postmortem Strategies." *Documents* 1, no. 3 (Summer 1993): 123–31.
Lippard, Lucy R. "Jimmie Durham: Postmodernist 'Savage.'" *Art in America* 81, no. 2 (February 1993): 62.
McEvilley, Thomas. "Jimmie Durham: Nicole Klagsbrun." *Artforum* 30, no. 6 (May 1993): 106.
McKenna, Kristine. "Art: Money Can't Buy This Guy's Love: Why does artist Jimmie Durham short-circuit his own fame and fortune? It's simply a matter of his own personal politics." *Los Angeles Times*, August 22, 1993.
Mosquera, Gerardo. "Stealing from the Global Pie: Globalization, Difference, and Cultural Appropriation." *Art Papers* 21, no. 2 (March–April 1997): 12–15.
O'Neill-Butler, Lauren. "Rocky Picture Show." *Artforum* 54, no. 5 (January 2016): 103.
Pagel, David. "Jimmie Durham at LA Louver." *Art Issues*, no. 4 (November–December 1993): 46.
Philippi, Desa. "Jimmie Durham: Matt's Gallery." *Artscribe*, no. 74 (March–April 1989): 73–74.
Prince, Mark. "Jimmie Durham: London, at Sprovieri." *Art in America.com*, March 31, 2014.
Purdom, Judy. "Who Is Jimmie Durham?" *Third Text* 8, nos. 28–29 (Autumn/Winter 1994): 173–78.
Reid, Calvin. "Jimmie Durham at Exit Art." *Art in America* 78, no. 5 (May 1990): 238–39.
Rickard, Jolene. "Sovereignty: A Line in the Sand." *Art and Design* 10, nos. 7–8 (1994): 19–25.
Rush, Michael. "Whitney Museum of American Art/New York: The 1993 Biennial Exhibition." *Art New England* (June–July 1993): 61.
Rushing, W. Jackson. "Another Look at Contemporary Native American Art." *New Art Examiner* 17, no. 6 (February 1990): 35–37.
Rushing, W. Jackson. "Critical Issues in Recent Native American Art." *Art Journal* 51, no. 3 (Autumn 1992): 6–14.
Rushing, W. Jackson. "Jimmie Durham, Trickster as Intervention." *Artspace* 16 (January–April 1992): 62–65.
Schjeldahl, Peter. "1993 Biennial." *Village Voice*, March 9, 1993, 10, 74.
Schwabsky, Barry. "The Stone Dies Away Also." *The Nation*, September 10, 2012, 32–34.
Shiff, Richard. "The Necessity of Jimmy Durham's Jokes." *Art Journal* 51, no. 3 (Fall 1992): 74–80.
Smith, Roberta. "At the Whitney: A Biennial with a Social Conscience." *New York Times*, March 1993, sec. C, 1, 27.
Snauwaert, Dirk. "The Great Stoneface." *Parkett*, no. 92 (2013): 22–27.
Turney, Laura. "Ceci n'est pas Jimmie Durham." *Critique of Anthropology* 19, no. 4 (December 1999): 423–42.
WalkingStick, Kay. "Democracy, Inc.: Kay WalkingStick on Indian Law." *Artforum* 30, no. 3 (November 1991): 20–21.
WalkingStick, Kay. "Native American Art in the Postmodern Era." *Art Journal* 51 (Fall 1992): 15–17.
Watson, Mark. "Jimmie Durham's *Building a Nation*: Across Post-Indian, Post-American Modernities." *American Art: Smithsonian American Art Museum* 28, no. 1 (Spring 2014): 16–24.

INTERVIEWS

Bell, Kristy. "Various Elements." *Frieze*, no. 150 (October 2012): 180–87.
Canning, Susan. "Jimmie Durham." *Art Papers* 14, no. 4 (July–August 1990): 31–35.
Cirauqui, Manuel. "Jimmie Durham." *Bomb*, no. 118 (Winter 2012): 76–83.
"Covert Operations: A Discussion between Jimmie Durham and Michael Taussig with Miwon Kwon and Helen Molesworth." *Documents* 1, no. 3 (Summer 1993): 110–22.
Fisher, Jean. "Jimmie Durham: Attending to the Words and Bones: An Interview with Jean Fisher." In *Art and Design* 10, nos. 7–8 (1995): 47–55.
Gisbourne, Mark. "Interviewed at the ICA." *Art Monthly* 173 (February 1994): 7–9.
Hill, Richard William, and Beverly Koski. "The Centre of the World Is Several Places (Part I)." *Fuse Magazine* 21, no. 3 (1998): 24–33; and "The Centre of the World Is Several Places (Part II)," *Fuse Magazine* 21, no. 4 (1998): 46–53.
Ingberman, Jeanette. "Conversation between Jimmie Durham and Jeanette Ingberman." In *Jimmie Durham: The Bishop's Moose and the Pinkerton Men*, 30–33. New York: Exit Art, 1990.
Papastergiadis, Nikos. "A Thousand Beautiful Things: Nikos Papastergiadis, Jimmie Durham, and Maria Thereza Alves." In *Criticism, Engagement, and Thought: 2004 Biennale of Sydney*, 42–51. Woolloomooloo, Australia: Artspace Visual Arts Center, 2004.
Papastergiadis, Nikos, and Laura Turney. *On Becoming Authentic: Interview with Jimmie Durham*. Cambridge, UK: Prickly Pear Press, 1996.
Snauwaert, Dirk. "Interview: Dirk Snauwaert in Conversation with Jimmie Durham." In *Jimmie Durham*, edited by Laura Mulvey, Dirk Snauwaert, and Mark Alice Durant, 7–29. London: Phaidon Press, 1995.

Anne Ellegood is senior curator at the Hammer Museum. In addition to organizing exhibitions and building the collection, she oversees the Hammer Projects series and the Public Engagement program. Prior to joining the Hammer in 2009, she was curator of contemporary art at the Hirshhorn Museum and Sculpture Garden in Washington, DC, and previous to that, associate curator at the New Museum of Contemporary Art, New York. Recent exhibitions include *Take It or Leave It: Institution, Image, Ideology* (2014); *Made in L.A. 2012*, the Hammer's inaugural biennial of Los Angeles–based artists; and *All of this and nothing* (2011). She has also organized numerous solo projects, including those with Shannon Ebner, Latifa Echakhch, Charles Gaines, My Barbarian, Kelly Nipper, John Outterbridge, Pedro Reyes, Francis Upritchard, Sara VanDerBeek, and Lily van der Stokker. Ellegood was selected by the Australian Council for the Arts to curate Sydney-based artist Hany Armanious's exhibition for the Australian Pavilion at the Venice Biennale in 2011.

Jennifer A. González is professor of history of art and visual culture at the University of California, Santa Cruz. She also is an instructor in the Whitney Museum Independent Study Program, New York. She is the author of *Pepón Osorio* (University of Minnesota Press, 2013) and *Subject to Display: Reframing Race in Contemporary Installation Art* (MIT Press, 2008), which was a finalist for the Charles Rufus Morey Book Award from the College Art Association. She has written for numerous periodicals, including *Frieze*, *Bomb*, *Camera Obscura*, and *Art Journal*. She recently coedited "Visual Activism," a special issue of the *Journal of Visual Culture* (2016). She has received fellowships from a number of organizations, including the Ford Foundation, the American Association of University Women, and the American Council of Learned Societies.

Jessica L. Horton is assistant professor of modern and contemporary art at the University of Delaware, specializing in Native American art and political histories in a global context. She is the author of *Art for an Undivided Earth: The American Indian Movement Generation* (Duke University Press, 2017), which examines the work of Jimmie Durham, James Luna, Kay WalkingStick, and others. Her essays on globalization, ecology, new materialisms, and indigenous spatial politics have appeared in journals such as *Art History*, *American Art*, *Journal of Transnational American Studies*, and *Third Text*, as well as in books such as *A Companion to American Art* (2015) and *Shapeshifting: Transformations in Native American Art* (2012). Her research has received support from the Getty Research Institute, the Smithsonian Institution, the Center for Advanced Study in the Visual Arts, the Terra Foundation for American Art, and the Social Science Research Foundation, among other organizations.

Fred Moten is the author of *In the Break: The Aesthetics of the Black Radical Tradition* (University of Minnesota Press, 2003) and coauthor, with Stefano Harney, of *The Undercommons: Fugitive Planning and Black Study* (Minor Compositions/Autonomedia, 2013). His books of poetry include *The Service Porch* (Letter Machine Editions, 2016), *The Little Edges* (Wesleyan University Press, 2015), *The Feel Trio* (Letter Machine Editions, 2014), *B. Jenkins* (Duke University Press, 2010), and *Hughson's Tavern* (Leon Works, 2008). He lives in Los Angeles and teaches at the University of California, Riverside.

Paul Chaat Smith is a Comanche author, essayist, and curator. His books and exhibitions focus on the contemporary landscape of American Indian politics and culture. He is the author of *Everything You Know about Indians Is Wrong* (University of Minnesota Press, 2009), and coauthor, with Robert Allen Warrior, of *Like a Hurricane: The Indian Movement from Alcatraz to Wounded Knee* (New Press, 1996), a standard text in Native studies and American history courses. Smith joined the Smithsonian Institution's National Museum of the American Indian (NMAI) in 2001, where he serves as associate curator. His projects there include the permanent history exhibition at NMAI's National Mall museum (2004), *Brian Jungen: Strange Comfort* (2009), and *Fritz Scholder: Indian/Not Indian* (2008). He curated performance artist James Luna's *Emendatio* at the 2005 Venice Biennale. His middle name has no hyphen and rhymes with hot. Like Kobe Bryant and LeBron James, he turned pro right after high school and has no college or university degrees.

MacKenzie Stevens is a curatorial assistant at the Hammer Museum, where she has supported Hammer Projects with Marwa Arsanios, Maria Hassabi, Pedro Reyes, Avery Singer, Francis Upritchard, and Lily van der Stokker, as well as *Made in L.A. 2016: a, the, though, only*. Prior to joining the Hammer, she was part of the curatorial team for *Naked Hollywood: Weegee in Los Angeles* at the Museum of Contemporary Art, Los Angeles (2011).

Elisabeth Sussman joined the Whitney Museum of American Art as curator in 1991 and was named Sondra Gilman Curator of Photography in 2004. She has curated or cocurated numerous major exhibitions, including *Collected by Thea Westreich Wagner and Ethan Wagner* (2015); the 2012 Whitney Biennial (with Jay Sanders); *Paul Thek: Diver, A Retrospective* (2010, with Lynn Zelevansky); *William Eggleston: Democratic Camera, Photographs and Video, 1961–2008* (2008, with Thomas Weski); *Gordon Matta-Clark: "You Are the Measure"* (2007); and the 1993 Whitney Biennial. She cocurated, with Catherine de Zegher, *Eva Hesse Drawing* at the Drawing Center, New York, and *Eva Hesse: Sculpture* at the Jewish Museum, New York (2006). For the San Francisco Museum of Modern Art, she co-organized, with Renate Petzinger, a retrospective exhibition of the work of Eva Hesse (2002), and, with Sandra Phillips, the retrospective *Diane Arbus: Revelation* (2003). She was a fellow at the Getty Research Institute (2003) and at the Rockefeller Study and Conference Center in Bellagio (1999). She served as interim director (1991) and deputy director for programs (1989–91) at the Institute of Contemporary Art, Boston, following stints as chief curator (1982–89) and curator (1976–82). She won the Bard Award for Curatorial Excellence in 2013.

Jessica Berlanga Taylor is a curator and art critic. Currently she is chief curator at Fundación Alumnos47, an organization in Mexico City dedicated to the exchange of knowledge and the exploration of present-day issues through contemporary art and its relationship with other disciplines. She coordinates the transdisciplinary, collaborative research-action projects Liminal Zones, which explores art as social action, and Proyecto Líquido, in which artists investigate themes such as *Fear* (2012) and *Desire* (2016). She holds an MA in art history with a special focus on contemporary art and gender studies. Her articles, essays, and reviews have appeared in numerous books, catalogues, and journals, including *Frieze*, *Artforum*, and *Milenio*. She was editor of the online magazine *re-d: arte, cultura visual y género* for the Instituto de Investigaciones Estéticas (Institute for Aesthetic Research) and the Universidad Nacional Autónoma de México (National Autonomous University of Mexico) Gender Studies Program (PUEG).

LENDERS TO THE EXHIBITION

Stuart Anthony & Will Rogers, New York
Roel Arkesteijn
Berliner Künstlerprogramm/DAAD, Berlin
Maria and Alexandre Bosoni, Paris
Dieter & Birgit Broska
Robert Cantor and Margo Levine, New York
Christine König Galerie, Vienna
Papo Colo, New York
Daled Collection, Brussels
Defares Collection, Amsterdam
Deichtorhallen Hamburg/Falckenberg Collection
Rosette V. Delug
Denver Art Museum
Beth Rudin DeWoody
Lonti Ebers, New York
Marc Embo, St. Martens Latem, Belgium
Moisés Cosío Espinosa, Mexico City
Zach Feuer and Alison Fox
Coleen Fitzgibbon and Tom Otterness
fluid archives, Karlsruhe
Fondazione Morra Greco, Naples
Luis H. Francia and Midori Yamamura
Franco Soffiantino Contemporary Art Productions, Milan
Galerie Barbara Wien, Berlin
Joanne Gold and Andrew Stern
Hammer Museum, Los Angeles
Hervé Lebrun Collection, Marseille
Hoche Partners, Luxembourg
Dr. Karel and Martine Hooft, Belgium
H.L.T.M. Hunting, Eindhoven
Cisco Jiménez, Cuernavaca, Mexico
Ines and Philippe Kempeneers, Belgium
Robin Klassnik, Matt's Gallery, London
Gabriel Kuri and Frances Horn, Brussels
kurimanzutto, Mexico City
Magali Lara, Cuernavaca, Mexico
Marc J. Lee, Los Angeles
Ministry of Culture, Lisbon, Portugal
John Morace and Tom Kennedy, Los Angeles
Museum of Contemporary Art Antwerp (M HKA), Belgium
Museum of Contemporary Art San Diego
The Museum of Modern Art, New York
Nicole Klagsbrun Gallery, New York
The Eileen Harris Norton Collection
Joe Overstreet and Corrine Jennings, New York
Roberto Pinto, Milan
Lois Plehn, New York
Eleanor Heyman Propp, New York
Sabrina Recoules, London
Michel Rein, Paris
Peter, Annie, and Connor Remes, Minneapolis
Martha Reta and Ricardo Mendoza, Mexico City
Mima and César Reyes Collection, Puerto Rico
Andrée Sfeir-Semler, Hamburg
Peter and Mari Shaw, Philadelphia
Dirk Snauwaert, Brussels
Sprovieri, London
Stedelijk Museum voor Actuele Kunst (SMAK), Ghent
Karen and Andy Stillpass
Ellen and Bill Taubman, New York
UCLA Grunwald Center for the Graphic Arts, Hammer Museum, Los Angeles
Whitney Museum of American Art, New York
Raul Zorrilla/Alberto Bremermann, Mexico
and private collections

Published on the occasion of the exhibition *Jimmie Durham: At the Center of the World*
Organized by the Hammer Museum, Los Angeles

The exhibition is organized by Anne Ellegood, senior curator, with MacKenzie Stevens, curatorial assistant.

Exhibition Itinerary
Hammer Museum, Los Angeles, January 29–May 7, 2017
Walker Art Center, Minneapolis, June 22–October 8, 2017
Whitney Museum of American Art, New York, November 3, 2017–January 28, 2018
Remai Modern, Saskatoon, April–July, 2018

Jimmie Durham: At the Center of the World is presented by

Taubman

Lead support for the exhibition is provided by the Henry Luce Foundation and The Andy Warhol Foundation for the Visual Arts.

Generous support is provided by Maggie Kayne and the National Endowment for the Arts. Additional funding is provided by Lonti Ebers, The Ampersand Foundation / Jack Kirkland, and Adam Lindemann.

Major support for the catalogue is provided by kurimanzutto.

Hammer Museum
10899 Wilshire Boulevard
Los Angeles, CA 90024-4201
310-443-7000
www.hammer.ucla.edu

The Hammer Museum is operated and partially funded by the University of California, Los Angeles.

Occidental Petroleum Corporation built the museum's building and established its endowment.

DelMonico Books, an imprint of Prestel, a member of Verlagsgruppe Random House GmbH

Prestel Verlag
Neumarkter Strasse 28
81673 Munich

Prestel Publishing Ltd.
14-17 Wells Street
London W1T 3PD

Prestel Publishing
900 Broadway, Suite 603
New York, NY 10003

www.prestel.com

Published in 2017 by the Hammer Museum and DelMonico Books • Prestel

ISBN: 978-3-7913-5568-9

Library of Congress Cataloging-in-Publication Data

Names: Ellegood, Anne. | Durham, Jimmie. Works. Selections. | Hammer Museum, organizer, host institution.
Title: Jimmie Durham : at the center of the world / Anne Ellegood.
Description: Los Angeles : Hammer Museum and DelMonico Books/Prestel, 2017. | Includes bibliographical references.
Identifiers: LCCN 2016046596 | ISBN 9783791355689 (hardback)
Subjects: LCSH: Durham, Jimmie--Exhibitions. | BISAC: ART / Individual Artists / Monographs. | ART / Native American.
Classification: LCC N6537.D875 A4 2017 | DDC 709.2--dc23 LC record available at https://lccn.loc.gov/2016046596

A CIP catalogue record for this book is available from the British Library.

Designer: Purtill Family Business
Editor: Michelle Piranio
Proofreader: Dianne Woo
Director of publication management: Melanie Crader
Project manager: Courtney Smith
Color separations: Echelon, Santa Monica, California
Printer: Conti Tipocolor, S.p.A, Florence, Italy

Cover: *Malinche*, 1988–92 (detail). Guava, pine branches, oak, snakeskin, polyester bra soaked in acrylic resin and painted gold, watercolor, cactus leaf, canvas, cotton cloth, metal, rope, feathers, plastic jewelry, glass eye. 70 × 23 ⅝ × 35 in. (177 × 60 × 89 cm). Stedelijk Museum voor Actuele Kunst (SMAK), Ghent, Belgium.
Front endsheet: *Untitled (sections)*, 2012. Ink on cotton paper. 12 ½ × 9 ½ in. (31.8 × 24.1 cm). Collection of Gabriel Kuri and Frances Horn, Brussels.
Pages 4–5: *Public Monument for the Birthday of Rome*, site-specific installation for *Città Natura*, Rome, 1997.
Back endsheet: *Untitled (provisional auxilliary horizon)*, 2012. Ink on cotton paper. 12 ½ × 9 ½ in. (31.8 × 24.1 cm). Collection of Martha Reta and Ricardo Mendoza, Mexico City.

REPRODUCTION CREDITS

All works by Jimmie Durham are © the artist; all images appear courtesy of the artist and the lenders or owners of the materials depicted. The following list applies to those for which additional acknowledgments are due.

Photo by Leo van Kampen: 15; Photo by Geoffrey Clements: 16, 195 (bottom); Courtesy of kurimanzutto, Mexico City: 18, 19 (right), 22, 29, 30, 76, 77 (bottom), 80, 81 (bottom), 85, 95, 119, 124, 125, 128, 154, 159, 164, 170, 171, 179, 180, 186, 187, 193, 194 (top left), 195 (top), 198, 201, 202 (left), 212, 232, 233, 237, 238, 240–41, 242, 246, 268, 269, 273, 275, 278, 279, 284, 285, 289, 291 (left), 292–93 (top), 293 (middle right, and bottom), 295 (middle), 296 (top); Courtesy of Kenkeleba Gallery: 19 (left), 40; Courtesy of James Luna: 23; © Andrea Fraser, courtesy of Andrea Fraser and Galerie Nagel Draxler, Berlin/Cologne: 24 (left); Courtesy of the Maryland Historical Society, MTM004: 24 (right); Courtesy of Charles Gaines and Paula Cooper Gallery, New York: 27; Courtesy of Matt's Gallery, London: 31, 34, 300 (bottom); Photo © Museum Associates/LACMA: 33; Courtesy of the Library of Congress: 37; Photo by Adam Reich: 41, 43, 52, 53, 88, 91; Courtesy of Museum of Contemporary Art Antwerp (M HKA), Belgium: 42, 45, 49, 67, 89, 130, 157, 158, 188, 209, 267, 282–83; Courtesy of Andy Stillpass, photo by Tony Walsh: 46, 68; Photo by Vincent Everarts: 47, 90, 176, 177; Photo by Elon Schoenholz: 48, 133, 227 (right); Photo by Seth Lamberton: 51; Photo by Jeff McLane: 55, 92, 93, 131 (top); Digital image © Whitney Museum, New York: 56, 58–60, 70; Photo by David Giancatarina: 73; Courtesy of Musée d'Art Moderne de la Ville de Paris, photos by Thierry Langro: 77 (top), 81 (top), 185, 234; Photo © Roman März: 77 (middle); Associated Press: 78; Courtesy of Pori Art Museum, Finland, photos by Erkki Valli-Jaakola: 79; Photo by Xander: 82; Digital Image © The Museum of Modern Art/Licensed by SCALA/Art Resource, NY: 97; Image © Denver Art Museum: 121; © Jimmie Durham 1993: 134; Photo by Gene Pittman: 141; © S.M.A.K./Dirk Pauwels: 142, 143; Photos by Marcus Leith: 145, 208, 244, 245; Photos by Nick Ash: 155, 228–31; Courtesy of Jessica Berlanga Taylor: 161, 162 (top); Photos by Philippe De Gobert: 168, 169; Courtesy of Paul van Esch & Partners, photo by Gert Jan van Rooij: 172; Courtesy of Barbara Wien, Berlin, photo by Roman März, Berlin: 173; Photo by Camillo Ripaldi: 189; Art © Jasper Johns/Licensed by VAGA, New York: 194 (top right); © 2016 Bruce Nauman/Artists Rights Society (ARS), New York: 194 (bottom left); © Kiki Smith, courtesy of Pace Gallery: 194 (bottom right); Photos courtesy the Oldenburg van Bruggen Studio. © 1977 Claes Oldenburg: 196 (both top); © Tate, London 2016: 196 (bottom); Photo by Matthew Hollow: 199; Photo by Marc Domage: 202 (right); Photo by Pete Mauney: 226; Courtesy of Barbara Wien, Berlin, photo by Sebastiano Pellion di Persano: 235; Courtesy of Barbara Wien, Berlin, photo by Akiyasu Shimizu: 236; Photo by Volker Renner: 266; Photo © Danilo Donzelli: 276, 277; Courtesy of Christine König Galerie: 291 (middle); Courtesy of The Fales Library and Special Collections/New York University: 293 (top right), 295 (top); Photo by Brian Forrest: 293 (middle left); Courtesy of Pierre Huyghe: 296 (bottom); La Biennale di Venezia—Archivio Storico delle Arti contemporanea, photo by Giorgio Zucchiatti: 302 (middle); Courtesy of Hammer Museum, Los Angeles, photo by Brian Forrest: 303; Courtesy of Fondazione Querini Stampalia, photo by Francesco Allegretto: 304–5